# Professional Chef

## Level 2 Diploma

*Also available in this series:*

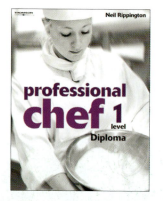

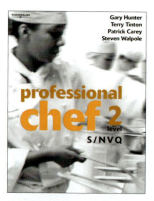

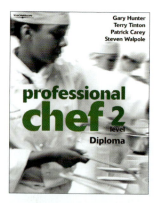

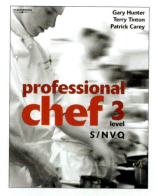

**Title:** Professional Chef
Level 1 Diploma
**ISBN:** 9781844805303

Professional Chef
Level 2 S/NVQ
9781844805051

Professional Chef
Level 2 Diploma
9781844807062

Professional Chef
Level 3 S/NVQ
9781844805310

# Virtual Kitchen www.virtualkitchen.co.uk

Dedicated online resource for students and lecturers of food preparation and cookery at levels 1–3
including:

- 400 video demonstrations
- theory content
- assessment questions
- image bank

**Title:** Virtual Kitchen Level 1
**ISBN:** 9781844807383

Virtual Kitchen Level 2
9781844807390

Virtual Kitchen Level 3
9781844807406

## Contact your Thomson Representative for bespoke pricing options

*Also coming, new titles in:*

- Food service
- Hospitality supervision
- Level 3 Professional Cookery Diploma

*To place your order or for more information, please contact our* College Sales Executive at +44 (0) 20 7067 2500 or collegesales@thomson.com or mail to:
**College Sales Executive**
Thomson Learning, High Holborn House, 50–51 Bedford Row
London WC1R 4LR, United Kingdom

GARY HUNTER, TERRY TINTON,
PATRICK CAREY and STEVEN WALPOLE

# Professional Chef

## Level 2 Diploma

THOMSON ™

Australia • Canada • Mexico • Singapore • Spain • United Kingdom • United States

**THOMSON**
™

*The Professional Chef: Level 2 Diploma*
Gary Hunter, Terry Tinton, Patrick Carey and Steven Walpole

| | | |
|---|---|---|
| **Publishing Director**<br>John Yates | **Publisher**<br>Lib Wight | **Development Editor**<br>Lizzie Catford |
| **Content Project Editor**<br>Lucy Mills | **Manufacturing Manager**<br>Helen Mason | **Marketing Manager**<br>Jason Bennett |
| **Typesetter**<br>Book Now Ltd, London, UK | **Production Controller**<br>Maeve Healy | **Cover Design**<br>HarrisCookTurner |
| **Text Design**<br>Design Deluxe Ltd, Bath, UK | **Printer**<br>Seng Lee Press, Singapore | |

# Brief contents

# CONTENTS

## 14 Unit 214 Bakery products 470

## 15 Unit 213 Desserts and puddings 524

# About the authors

### GARY HUNTER

Head of Culinary Arts at Westminster Kingsway College, Gary has 14 years' experience of teaching within further, higher and vocational education. He has travelled the world as a consultant for Barry Callebaut giving seminars on chocolate and cuisine. He is also an experienced international culinary competition judge. As a leading Chef Patissier in the UK, he has won numerous awards and competition medals and has worked with and trained many of today's successful chefs. Gary has recently helped to write the diploma in professional cookery qualification at levels 1, 2 and 3.

### TERRY TINTON

A Chef Lecturer and Professional Chef Diploma Course Coordinator in Culinary Arts at Westminster Kingsway College, Terry is a strong and confident chef with many awards spanning a hugely successful career. He has held a senior chef position at the House of Commons and worked extensively across Switzerland and Germany. He holds the Advanced Hygiene Award and is the driving force for developing first-year students at the college.

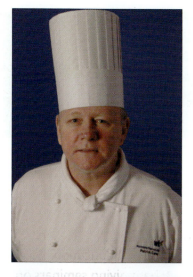

## PATRICK CAREY

Senior Lecturer and Course Coordinator at Westminster Kingsway College, Patrick is a qualified lecturer with 12 years' experience in vocational education. An exceptionally experienced international chef with a vast knowledge of classical and present day cookery techniques, he is currently running the Foundation Degree in Culinary Arts. He was the winner of the Senior Toque d'Or Competition, gaining distinctions across the board in the 706/3 examination.

## STEVEN WALPOLE

Steven is a lecturer with six years' experience from levels 1–4 within further and vocational education. He specialises in health and safety issues, nutrition and modern styles of cookery. He has appeared on regular TV cookery shows for both terrestrial and cable, and was the winner of the Annual Awards of Excellence 2000, from the Academy of Culinary Arts.

# Acknowledgements

## Personal Acknowledgements

| | | | |
|---|---|---|---|
| Sarah-Jane Hunter | Charlotte Hunter | Estelle Hunter | Hilary Hunter |
| Phillip Hunter | Paul Hunter | Patricia Long | John Long |

Dom Healy, Jimmy Mair and Martin Jermy for their inspiration

| | | | |
|---|---|---|---|
| Margaret Tinton | Lewis Tinton | Sharon Carey | Aoife Carey |
| Yvonne Hall | Terence Tinton | Kate Tinton | Liam Lane |
| Rosaleen Lane | Andy Tinton | Paul Lane | |

Neil Rippington, the author of the Level 1 book in this series, for all his contributions throughout the project

## College Acknowledgements

| | | | |
|---|---|---|---|
| Andy Wilson | Geoff Booth | Ian Wild | Allan Drummond |
| Jose Souto | Simon Stocker | Bob Brown | Javier Mercado |
| Chris Loder | Barry Jones | Alexandra Roberts | Vince Cottam |

## Students

| | | | |
|---|---|---|---|
| Kyle Mcgrady | Tony Hayes | Heather Gil-Abillera | Samantha Doorgachurn |
| Luke Fouracre | Maxium Shearer | Lucien Bintcliffe | Andrew Giles |
| Robert Hall | Robert Boer | Luca Boccia | Luke Monaghan |
| Kirstie McIntyre | Leon Coultress | Selin Kiazin | Ben Arnold |

## Reviewers

| | | |
|---|---|---|
| Steve Thorpe of City College, Norwich | Tony Taylor of Bournemouth and Poole College | Keyth Richardson of Gloucestershire College of Arts and Technology (GLOSCAT) |

## Sponsors

| | | | |
|---|---|---|---|
| Russums Catering Suppliers | Furi Knives | Barry Callebaut Chocolate | Steelite Catering Crockery |

## Chef Contributors

| | | | |
|---|---|---|---|
| Richard Hughes | Matthew Owens | Nick Vadis | Cyrus Todiwala |
| Steve Munkley | Martin Blunos | David Mulcahy | Andrew Turner |
| Andrew Pern | Nigel Haworth | Andrew Bennett | Steve Love |
| Mark Allison | Paul Gregory | Julie Sharp | Terry Shoesmith |

## Photography and Resources

William 'Bill' Hull Professional Photography

| | | | |
|---|---|---|---|
| Billingsgate Fish Market | Smithfield's Meat Market | New Covent Garden | Compass UK |
| Westminster Kingsway College | Barchester Healthcare | Russums | Electrolux |
| The Ritz Hotel | Think Vegetables | Eureka | Havering Catering Services |
| | Tom Aikens | | |

Quality Meat Scotland (QMS) represents the Scottish red meat industry and promotes Scotch Beef, Scotch Lamb and Specially Selected Pork to a national and international audience. Our activities range from helping the industry improve their methods of production and quality of products to increasing customer awareness and preference for Scotch product. QMS also helps in the development of new markets in the UK and around the world. For additional information: www.qmsscotland.co.uk and www.chefsguidetoscotchbeef.org.

# Foreword

PHOTO DAVID LOFTUS

I loved my time at Westminster College, there wasn't a day that went by without me being totally inspired by something or other.

If you're planning on becoming a professional chef, this book, along with the rest in the series, is going to become your best friend! You won't want to be without it. You'll find it an essential learning tool, whether you're just starting out or whether you're already working in a restaurant kitchen and need a catch-up.

The chefs who have given their time and expertise in support of it are all superbly qualified and they've put together a concise, step-by-step guide to pretty much anything food-wise that you'll come across in most restaurant kitchens.

Becoming a chef is bloody hard work and it requires dedication, stamina and a hell of a lot of passion. But if you want to become a half-decent chef, you also need to learn the core skills to start you off on a great career journey for life. You've taken the first steps. This book will now help to provide you with a strong platform for learning how to become a talented chef.

Good luck, all the best!

*Jamie Oliver*

# A quick reference guide to the qualification

The philosophy behind the diploma is the principle that a chef needs to have a sound foundation of high quality skills and to be able to apply these skills across a range of techniques and using a broad variety of commodities.

The qualification has been designed for delivery in a College environment or similar learning resource. It does not replace the NVQ/SVQ but intends to provide learners with a breadth of skills and knowledge and to make them better prepared to meet the modern needs of industry. There is also more emphasis on teaching and learning in comparison to the assessment model presented by the NVQ.

All candidates enrolled on a Diploma in Professional Cookery will follow a specific learning programme, completing a range of theoretical and practical tasks and activities.

Individuals will also receive a final grade for each unit to highlight areas of high achievement.

# A quick reference guide to the qualification

## The Level 2 Diploma units

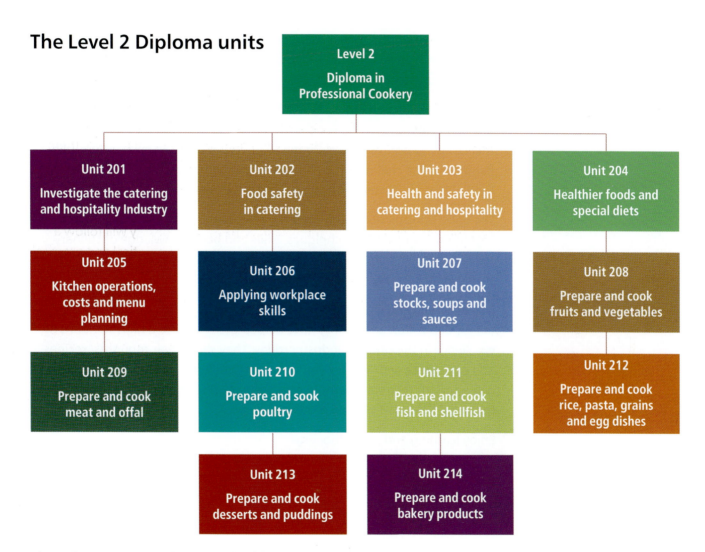

The units are structured in a standard format and comprise of the following:

*Unit reference number and title* – e.g. Unit 208 Prepare and cook fruits and vegetables

*Rationale* – explaining the aims and purpose of the unit

*Connections with other qualifications* – e.g. NVQs and Key Skills

*Assessment details* – detailing the requirements for the assessment of practical skills and underpinning knowledge

*Learning outcomes* – specifying the practical skills and/or the underpinning knowledge to be covered

*Range* – providing detail as to the content of each learning outcome

*Guidance* – for delivery and best practice

# Introduction

The intention of this book is to guide you to the skills and introduce the foundation knowledge required to become a chef in the hospitality and catering industry.

Cooking, serving and eating food has become a major communication practice across the world. Food is prepared as a gift, as a medicine, to create friendship, to nourish, to celebrate, to generate business and to stimulate happiness. The chef now has the capacity to communicate through their food, initiate fulfilment and joy and conceive relationships.

The basic principles of being a worthy professional chef are to combine good ingredients with sound techniques, skills and basic knowledge of culinary science with attention to detail. Only then will you have the basis to show your culinary artistry and creative talents.

This book will also illustrate some of the top chefs in this country whose talent, dedication and energy have helped them achieve a high standard of excellence in the catering industry today. They share their thoughts, recipes and experience with you for you to learn from. It will also provide you with an important reference point to attain the professional skills and knowledge for today's classically based modern cuisine.

Enjoy learning and enjoy cooking!

*Gary Hunter*

# About the book

**1**
**Health and safety in catering and hospitality**

**UNIT 203**
1. Explain the importance of health and safety in the catering and hospitality industry
2. Identify hazards in the catering and hospitality workplace
3. Control hazards in the workplace
4. Maintain a healthy and safe workplace

**LEARNING OBJECTIVES**

The aim of this chapter is to provide the candidate with an understanding of the requirements and benefits of health and safety legislation. A basic level of understanding will help to develop proficiency and put into practice knowledge of the health, and safety practices within the work place. It discusses the health and safety requirements and policies that you will need to know about if you are to work safely and responsibly in the kitchen. This will also include information on the resources at the disposal of the chef to implement any Government and sector guidelines and legislation.

At the end of this chapter you will be able to:

■ Identify the correct attire for the chef in the workplace
■ Understand the implications and responsibility in the workplace for personal health and hygiene

**Mapped to the qualification**
Each chapter addresses a specific unit of the Level 2 Professional Cookery Diploma qualification.

**Learning objectives** at the start of each chapter explain the skills and knowledge you need to be proficient in and understand by the end of the chapter.

**Step-by-step preparation of chicken for roasting**

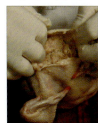

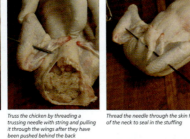

*Remove the wishbone and add the stuffing if required*

*Truss the chicken by threading a trussing needle with string and pulling it through the wings after they have been pushed behind the back*

*Thread the needle through the skin flap of the neck to seal in the stuffing*

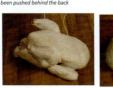

*Push the legs back in towards the breast*

*Push the needle through the legs*

*Tie off with a firm knot*

**Step-by-step sequences** illustrate each process and provide an easy-to-follow guide.

## Assessment of knowledge and understanding

You have now learned about the use of the different types of stocks and sauces and how to produce a variety of them utilising an array of commodities and cooking techniques.

To test your level of knowledge and understanding, answer the following short questions. These will help to prepare you for your summative (final) assessment.

1 Identify the three main categories of roux.
   i) _____ ii) _____
   iii) _____

2 Explain how to store freshly made stock correctly.
   _____
   _____

3 Describe three ways of removing fat from a stock.
   i) _____ ii) _____
   iii) _____

4 Explain the reason for using good quality ingredients when making a stock or sauce.
   _____
   _____

**Assessment of knowledge and understanding** at the end of each chapter contains questions, so you can test your learning.

### PURCHASING SPECIFICATION

■ Cauliflowers should have tight and firm flower heads that are white in colour.
■ Other brassicas should also have tight heads and bright colouring.
■ They should not feel limp and the stems should be strong.

**Purchasing Specification** provide helpful advice for buying commodities.

## Recipes
Modern and traditional recipes for each commodity.

## Poached halibut with a cherry tomato confit and vegetable julienne crisps

| INGREDIENTS | 4 PORTIONS | 10 PORTIONS |
|---|---|---|
| Halibut suprêmes | 4 × 120g | 10 × 120g |
| Vine-ripened cherry tomatoes | 200g | 500g |
| Olive oil | 100ml | 250ml |
| White pepper | To taste | To taste |
| Sea salt | 2tsp | 5tsp |
| Chopped fresh garlic | 1 clove | 3 cloves |
| Dry white wine | 50ml | 125ml |
| Fresh bay leaves | 1 | 2 |
| Julienne of carrot | 100g | 250g |
| Julienne of leek | 100g | 250g |
| Finely sliced onion | 2 small onions | 5 small onions |
| Butter | 50g | 125g |
| Fish stock | 200ml | 500ml |

**CHEF'S TIP**

When poaching or boiling whole fish do not allow the liquid to boil as it will cause the fish to break.

**CHEF'S TIP**

Poach fish for approximately 5–7 minutes for a thickness of 2.5cm starting in hot liquid (or until the core temperature of the fish is 63°C). Reserving the poaching liquid and turning it into a sauce to accompany the halibut will add another element to this dish.

### Method of work
1. Preheat a deep fat fryer to 160°C and an oven to 170°C.
2. Cut the carrot and leek into julienne. Place onto a sheet of silicone paper and dry in an oven at 110°C or under heat lamps for 30 minutes.
3. Carefully deep fry the julienne carrot and leek separately, moving constantly in the hot fat to maintain an even cooking of the vegetables. Remove from the fat and dry on absorbent paper.
4. Place back under the heat lamps or the oven again and dry for a further 30 minutes.
5. Prepare a dish to poach the halibut in by brushing the base with butter and set the onion on the bottom.
6. Place the halibut on top, season well and drizzle the dry white wine over. Add the bay leaf and warm fish stock. Cover with tin foil and poach for approximately 15 minutes in the oven, until tender and just cooked.

### CHEF'S PROFILE

**Name:** ANDREW PERN
**Position:** Chef/Owner
**Establishment:** The Star Inn, Harome, Helmsley, North Yorkshire
**Current job role and main responsibilities:** As Chef Patron I have many responsibilities – menus, cooking, recruiting, publicity – the whole running of the business involved with the Star Inn. Our butchers, café and accommodation are all part of our 'little industry'. We buy direct from a farmer who supplies our butchers, who then supplies us – giving a complete field to fork experience.
**When did you realise that you wanted to pursue a career in the catering and hospitality industry?** From a young age! I cooked at home from when I was about 8 years old, as my mother has MS. We were a very sociable family, with dinner parties and Sunday lunch always playing a part. This led me to catering college eventually, having worked at local pubs washing up and helping with the food. My story is of a 'local lad' from Whitby, who has done well on his own doorstep.
**Training:** I spent 3 years at Scarborough Technical College (now Yorkshire Coast College), gaining 207,1,2,3, Pastry, Bakery and Food Beverage Exams. I gained invaluable experience by going to France on placements, where I had access to Rungis market and by taking a two-month summer job working for HM Forces, cooking and washing up for 600 squaddies a day.
**Experience:** After leaving college I worked at two small country inns before buying the Star Inn at the age of 26 years. Buying our own place, we worked for 20 months, seven days a week from 7.30 am to 2.30 am! This ordeal built the foundations to the success we have today.
**What do you find rewarding about your job?** I always say it is a hobby to me and a lifestyle. All four of our children have been born whilst we have been at The Star, so it is more of a home to us than a business, where we welcome guests into our own little world. We have been well rewarded with the many awards and accolades we have gained, which has allowed us to carry on doing various projects to a very high level. Offering hospitality and allowing our guests to enjoy themselves is the main aim of the game.
**What do you find the most challenging about the job?** Keeping our high standards day in, day out. If you do your best every time then hopefully the customer will benefit. If you don't, you are letting the customer and yourself down.
**What advice would you give to students just beginning their career?** Be prepared! The more you give to the job, the more you will get back. Also enjoy what you do and do it to the best of your ability!
**Who is your mentor or main inspiration?** In my early twenties I did the Roux Scholarship and Albert and Michael Roux had a big influence in my college days. Marco Pierre White published *White Heat* when I was at college, which opened my eyes to new ways of presenting the old classics. Then people like Paul Heathcote, Terry Laybowne and the late Denis Watkins from the Angel Inn have inspired my northern food ethos.
**Secrets of a successful chef:**
1. Have an open mind about everything that people offer to teach you.
2. Stamina.
3. Eye for presentation.
4. Be a good team member.
5. Don't be lazy!
**A brief personal profile:** My family are all from a farming background, so I am the odd one out! However, this has set me up for my style of cookery, which is very seasonal and very local, using produce from the North Sea, game from the moor and meat from our own butchers. I have had a Michelin star for five years. We have won 3 Cateys, 'the Oscars of the catering industry', and many other awards such as Gastro Pub of the Year. We now own The Star Inn, The Star at Scampston (a café in a 4½ acre walled garden), Cross House Lodge (private dinning and accommodation), Black Eagle Cottage (three self-catering suites), The Farmhouse (where a chalet style chef cooks in a part-thatched farm house for families/groups), Pern's of Helmsley (butcher/deli) and the Corner Shop (deli/crockery shop).
**Can you give one essential kitchen tip or technique that you use as a chef:** Communication, be it with suppliers, chefs, Front of House, customers or guests. It is always good to communicate.

## Chef's Profile
provide advice from leading industry figures and an insight into what motivated them during their training.

### HEALTH & SAFETY
Wash your hands with a liquid gel from a sealed dispenser. Soap should be discouraged because bar soap can accumulate germs when passed from hand to hand.

## Health and safety boxes
draw your attention to important health and safety information.

## Scrambled eggs

| INGREDIENTS | 4 PORTIONS | 10 PORTIONS |
|---|---|---|
| Medium eggs | 4–8 | 10–20 |
| Butter | 80g | 200g |
| Cream | 40–80ml | 100–200ml |
| Good-quality salt and pepper | To taste | To taste |

### HEALTH & SAFETY
Use unsalted butter and low sodium salt.

**VIDEO CLIP**
Scrambling eggs

### Method of work
1. Melt the butter in a thick-bottomed sauté pan.
2. Beat the eggs in a basin and season.
3. Add to the pan and cook very gently.
4. When they begin to set, add the cream, remove from the heat and continue to stir until lightly set (baveuse).
5. Serve immediately.

## Video Clip
If your college adopts the virtual kitchen at this level (www.virtualkitchen/level2.co.uk) you will be able to view a video demonstration online.

### CHEF'S TIP
Ensure the clams are very fresh for the best results. The clams can be substituted for oysters; additionally the white wine vinegar can be replaced with sherry vinegar or champagne vinegar.

## Chef's tip boxes
share the authors' experiences of the catering industry, with helpful suggestions for how you can improve your skills.

### QUALITY POINTS
- Cock birds have a tendency to be drier and tougher than hens
- Bronze birds can have residual dark feather stubs; these can be removed with duck tweezers
- The flesh should be dry to the touch without excess blemishes
- If the windpipe is still intact, it should be pliable and not rigid
- The breast should be plump in domesticated birds an slightly leaner in the rarer wild variety

## Quality Points
provide information to help you assess the freshness of products.

# 1

# Health and safety in catering and hospitality

## LEARNING OBJECTIVES

The aim of this chapter is to provide the candidate with an understanding of the requirements and benefits of health and safety legislation. A basic level of understanding will help to develop proficiency and put into practice knowledge of the health, and safety practices within the work place. It discusses the health and safety requirements and policies that you will need to know about if you are to work safely and responsibly in the kitchen. This will also include information on the resources at the disposal of the chef to implement any Government and sector guidelines and legislation.

At the end of this chapter you will be able to:

■ Identify the correct attire for the chef in the workplace
■ Understand the implications and responsibility in the workplace for personal health and hygiene

- Be able to report illnesses and minor accidents
- Recognise the importance of security in the workplace and how to enforce emergency procedures
- Indicate potential hazards in the workplace and how to effectively deal with them
- Identify the legislation and action enabling the reduction of hazards and risks at work

# INTRODUCTION TO SAFETY

Whatever function you have in the hospitality industry, everyone is required to behave safely and professionally. Reasonable care must be taken to safeguard the health and safety of yourself and others who may be affected by what you do. You must always be responsible for your own behaviour and ensure that your actions do not cause a health and safety risk to yourself, others that you work with or customers. This includes co-operation with your employer, owner or manager to ensure that health and safety procedures are followed. All employers, employees, managers, indirect employees (such as suppliers or self employed maintenance engineers), local authorities and health and safety inspectors have a wide ranging responsibility to ensure that current legislation is maintained.

*Chefs working in a clean and tidy kitchen*

# PERSONAL HEALTH

The safeguarding of personal health is important to prevent the introduction of germs and bacteria into food preparation areas. To maintain physical fitness sufficient rest, good exercise and a nutritious diet are essential.

## HEALTH & SAFETY

When handling or preparing food, blue plasters should be used so that they are easily identifiable when lost. These dressings can feature an internal metal strip that allows them to be detected by electromagnetic equipment and metal detectors in large food production units.

## First Aid

Employers must have appropriate and adequate first aid arrangements in the event of an accident or illness occurring. All employees should be informed of the first aid procedures including:

- Where to locate the first aid box
- Who is responsible for the maintenance of the first-aid box
- Which member of staff should be informed in the event of an accident or illness occurring
- The staff member to inform in the event of an accident or an emergency.

The **Health and Safety (First Aid) Regulations 1981** state that workplaces must have first aid provision. The Health and Safety Executive (HSE) have recommended a minimum standard of first aid kits for use in food production areas. This should contain a minimum level of first aid equipment as set out in the table on the following page, although this is by no means a restricted list.

*A first aid kit*

**CONTENTS OF A FIRST AID BOX FOR A KITCHEN**

| NUMBER OF EMPLOYEES | 1–10 | 11–50 |
|---|---|---|
| First aid guidance notes | 1 | 1 |
| Triangular bandage | 4 | 8 |
| Sterile eye pad | 2 | 6 |
| Sterile dressings – large | 3 | 5 |
| Sterile dressings – medium | 5 | 11 |
| Blue detectable plasters | 20 | 60 |
| Blue fingerstalls | 2 | 12 |
| Blue detectable tape | 1 | 1 |
| Blue disposable polythene gloves | 1 pair | 3 pairs |
| Moist wipes | 6 | 20 |
| Safety pins | 6 | 12 |
| Burn gel sachets | 3 | 3 |

# Cuts

All cuts should be covered with a waterproof dressing after the cut has been cleaned and dried. When there is substantial bleeding it should be slowed as much as possible before transferring the person to professional medical care. The bleeding may be reduced by applying direct pressure, or by the use of a firm bandage attached to the wound.

# Burns and Scalds

Types of burns:

■ Dry – caused by flames, hot metal and friction

■ Scalds – caused by steam, hot water and hot fat

■ Electrical – caused by domestic current, high voltage and lightning

■ Cold – caused by freezing metal or liquid nitrogen

■ Chemical – caused by industrial and domestic chemicals

■ Radiation – caused by exposure to the sun or extreme heat in an oven.

As soon as possible place the injury under slowly running cold water or place an ice pack on top of it for a minimum of ten minutes. If the burn or scald is serious the wound should be dressed with a sterile dressing and professional medical help sought immediately. It is important that adhesive dressings, lotions or kitchen cloths do not come into contact with the injury.

Sometimes the person may go into a state of shock due to the significance of the burn or scald. The signs are clammy skin with a pale face, faintness, lethargic characteristics and sometimes vomiting. The person in shock should be treated by keeping them comfortable at all times, lay them down in the recovery position and keep them warm with a light blanket.

**HEALTH & SAFETY**

- First aid should only be given by a qualified first-aider.
- A first aid certificate is only valid for three years. After this period, it must be renewed with additional first aid training.
- Know what action you can take within your responsibility in the event of an accident occurring.

For electric shock, switch off the current immediately if possible. Any burns should be dealt with as above and professional medical advice should be sought once the person is comfortable.

## Reporting of Injuries, Diseases and Dangerous Occurrences Regulations (RIDDOR) (1995)

All injuries must be reported to the member of staff responsible for health and safety: this includes injuries involving guests, visitors and staff. The kitchen accident book must be completed with basic personal details of the person or persons involved, together with a detailed description of the incident. Each accident report book should comply with the recent Data Protection Act 2003.

The Act's key message is that you must report:

- Any fatal accidents
- Work-related diseases
- Major injuries sustained whilst at work
- Any potentially dangerous event that takes place at work
- Accidents causing more than three days' absence from work.

# LEGAL RESPONSIBILITIES

If you cause harm to a customer, or place them at risk, you will personally be held responsible and could be liable to criminal prosecution. There are many legislative directives relating to health and safety and the details are widely available. It is your duty to become aware of your own accountability and responsibilities towards this.

## The Health and Safety at Work Act (1974)

The Health and Safety at Work Act (1974) covers employees, employers, the self-employed, customers and visitors. It describes the minimum standards of health, safety and welfare required in each area of the workplace. The Act's key message is that when working in a kitchen you must maintain a safe and healthy working environment at all times.

## Health and Safety (Information for Employees) Regulations (1989)

These regulations require the employer to provide employees with health and safety information in the form of posters, notices and leaflets. The Health and Safety Executive provides relevant publications.

Regular health and safety checks should be made to ensure that safe practices are being used. Employees must co-operate with their employer to provide a safe and healthy workplace. As soon as any hazard is observed, it must be reported to the designated authority or line manager so that the problem can be rectified. Hazards can include:

- Obstructions to corridors, stairways and fire exits
- Spillages and breakages
- Faulty electrical machinery.

## The Workplace (Health, Safety and Welfare) Regulations (1992)

This Act provides a set of benchmarks to cover the legal requirements necessary in a working environment such as ventilation, indoor temperature, lighting and staff facilities. The Act's key message is that when working in the hospitality industry you must maintain a safe and healthy working environment. Another issue covered is the maintenance of the workplace and equipment, cleanliness and the handling of waste materials.

## The Control of Substances Hazardous to Health (COSHH) Regulations (1999)

COSHH is a workplace policy that is relevant to everyday working practices. Toxic chemicals such as detergents are hazardous and present a high risk. They must be stored, handled, used and disposed of correctly in accordance with COSHH.

Hazardous substances are usually identified through the use of identified symbols, examples of which are shown to the right.

Any substance in the workplace that is hazardous to health must be identified on the packaging and stored and handled correctly.

Hazardous substances can enter the body via:

- The skin
- The eyes
- The mouth (ingestion)
- The nose (inhalation).

The COSHH regulations were recently consolidated in 2002 and employers are held responsible for assessing the risks from hazardous substances and for controlling exposure to them to prevent ill health. Any hazardous substances identified should be formally recorded in writing and given a risk rating.

## Electricity at Work Regulations (1989)

With the often heavy use of electrical equipment in kitchens this Act is particularly important. These regulations state that every item of electrical equipment in the workplace must be tested every twelve months by a qualified electrician.

*Hazard symbols*

In addition to this annual testing, a trained member of staff or qualified electrician should regularly check all electrical equipment for safety. This is recommended every three months but generally most employers undertake this annually. A quick visual inspection by the chef before using an electrical item on a daily basis is a good method of reducing potential accidents or breakdowns. Records must be kept of the check and will include:

- Electrician's name/contact details
- Itemised list of electrical equipment complete with serial number for identification purposes
- Date or purchase or disposal
- Date of last inspection.

General checks should be undertaken and reported for potential hazards, such as exposed wires in flexes, cracked plugs or broken sockets, worn cables and overloaded sockets.

Any electrical equipment that appears faulty must be immediately checked and repaired before use. It should also be labelled or have the plug removed to ensure that it is not used by accident before repairing.

**VIDEO CLIP**
Moving heavy objects

**HEALTH & SAFETY**

When unpacking a delivery, always ensure the product packaging is undamaged to help avoid possible personal injury from broken goods.

| Stand with your feet apart | Your weight should be evenly spread over both feet | Bend your knees slowly keeping your back straight | Stand with your feet apart | Tuck your chin in towards your chest |

    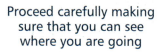 

| Get a good grip on the base of the box | Bring the box to your waist height keeping the lift as smooth as possible | Keep the box close to your body | Proceed carefully making sure that you can see where you are going | Lower the box, reversing the lifting procedure |

## The Manual Handling Operations Regulations (1992)

These apply where manual lifting occurs. The employer is required to carry out a risk assessment of all activities undertaken which involve manual lifting. The Act provides guidelines on how to protect oneself when lifting heavy objects.

# HAZARDS AND RISKS

The Health and Safety Act covers all full-time and part-time employees and unpaid workers (such as students in work placements). Everyone needs to be aware of their legal duties for health and safety in the workplace as required by the Health and Safety at Work Act 1974.

The Health and Safety Executive (HSE) is the body appointed to support and enforce health and safety in the workplace. They have defined the two concepts for hazards and risk:

1  A *hazard* is something with the potential to cause harm
2  A *risk* is the likelihood of the hazard's potential being realised.

A hazard has the potential to cause harm and everyone must identify working practices within the kitchen environment which could harm people. All staff are required to make sure that the kitchen equipment and the workplace in general is well maintained and safe to use.

Two examples of this are:

1  A light bulb that requires replacing is a hazard. If it is one out of several it presents a very small risk, but if it is the only light within a 'walk-in' refrigerator, it poses a high risk.
2  A pot of boiling hot oil on a trolley top is a potential hazard that can fall off, causing spillage onto clothes, causing burns and creating a slippery floor surface unless cleared away immediately. Therefore it is high in risk.

**HEALTH & SAFETY**

All hazardous substances must be identified when completing the risk assessment. This includes cleaning agents and some preservatives. Where possible high-risk products should be replaced with lower-risk products. COSHH assessment should be reviewed on a regular basis and updated with the inclusion of any new products.

## Warning Signs in the Kitchen

Safety signs are used in the kitchen and surrounding areas to help identify hazards, obligatory actions and prohibited actions for all staff, customers and visitors. Usually these signs are clearly displayed and should be made in laminated plastic. All signage should comply with the relevant health and safety regulations and different colours signify different actions.

■ Yellow – warning signs to alert people to various dangers such as slippery floors and hot water.

■ Blue – mandatory signs to inform everyone what they must do in order to progress safely through a certain area. Usually this would indicate the need to wear protective clothing.

■ Red – prohibition signs are designed to stop persons from certain tasks in a hazardous area, such as no smoking or no access.

■ Green – escape route signs, designed to show fire and emergency exits to staff, visitors and customers.

The local authority Environmental Health Department enforces the Health and Safety at Work Act, and an environmental health officer will visit and inspect local business premises on a regular basis.

The inspector identifies any area of danger and will issue an improvement notice. It is the responsibility of the employee to remove this danger within a designated period of time. Failure to comply with the notice will lead to prosecution. The inspector also has the authority to close a business until they are satisfied that all danger to employees and the public has been removed.

# FIRE

The **Fire Precautions Act 1971** declares that all staff must be aware of and trained in fire and emergency evacuation procedures for their workplace. The emergency exit route will be the easiest route by which all staff, customers and visitors can leave the building safely. Fire action plans should be prominently displayed to show the emergency exit route.

The fire evacuation procedure should be carried out at least once a year and should be reviewed regularly to account for personnel changes or physical changes to the building in which you work.

A fire certificate is a compulsory requirement of the Act if there are more than 20 employees, or more than 10 employees are on different floors at any one time.

## The Fire Precautions (Workplace) Regulations 1997

This requires that every employer must carry out a risk assessment for the premises under the Management of Health and Safety Regulations 1999.

■ Any obstacles that may hinder fire evacuation should be identified as a hazard and be dealt with.

■ Suitable fire detection equipment should be in place.

■ All escape routes should be clearly marked and free from obstacles.

■ Fire alarm systems should be tested on a weekly basis to ensure it is in full operational condition.

Firefighting equipment should be easily accessed in a specified area of every kitchen. This should only be used when the cause of the fire has been identified: the use of a wrong fire extinguisher can make the fire worse. Only use firefighting equipment when correctly trained to do so.

Fire extinguishers are available to tackle different types of fire. It is important that these are checked and maintained as required.

### CAUSE OF FIRE AND CHOICE OF EXTINGUISHER

| CAUSE | EXTINGUISHER | LABEL COLOUR |
|---|---|---|
| Electrical fire | Carbon dioxide ($CO_2$) | Black |
| Flammable liquids | Foam | Cream/yellow |
| Solid material fire | Water | Red |
| Vaporising liquids | Dry powder | Green |
| | | Blue |

Fire blankets are used to smother a small, localised fire such as a hot fat fire or burning caramel.

Fire can only occur when three factors are present:

1 Fuel

2 Air (oxygen)

3 Heat.

Should any one of these factors be removed, ignition cannot take place, therefore it is essential that flammable materials are stored safely and securely in a locked fireproof cupboard. Gas canisters are kept stored away from direct sunlight and any other direct heat source.

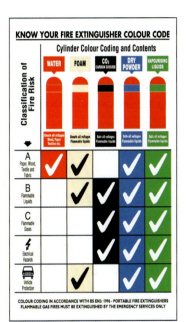

*Firefighting equipment*

**ACTIVITY**

Think of several potential causes of fire in the kitchen. How could each of these be prevented?

In the event of a fire it is essential that no-one is placed at risk and that the emergency alarm is operated as soon as possible to alert others. The emergency services should also be contacted immediately. Fires can spread quickly and easily – so it is important to leave the building at once, closing doors to prevent the spread of fire, and report at the identified fire assembly point.

## SECURITY AND OTHER EMERGENCIES

The security of the workplace is associated with:

- Protection of personal and customer property
- Correct locked storage of flammable materials
- Workplace security procedures.

The workplace should have a clearly defined set of security procedures for every employee, visitor and customer to follow. It is essential that employees are fully aware of these measures in order to help identify potential breaches of security.

Usually there is a set of useful telephone numbers in the kitchen office or by the kitchen phone such as local plumbers, gas engineers, electricians, emergency services and local maintenance persons.

In the event of possible threats to security, such as a bomb alert, all employees must be trained in the appropriate emergency procedures.

This will involve the recognition of a suspect package, how to deal with a bomb threat, evacuation of staff and customers and contacting the emergency services. Your local Crime Prevention Officer can advise on bomb security and the security of the premises in general.

Security concerns should be taken into consideration to prevent loss of stock through theft.

1 The restaurant/service/public area should be designed to be in full view of employees and with a security camera placed for additional security if needed.

2 Stock should be kept in a secure area, accessed only by those with authority to do so.

If there is suspicion that a customer has stolen from the premises, and that there is sufficient evidence, the employer has the right to make a citizen's arrest under the Police and Criminal Evidence Act 1984. It is critical that the employer's policy on theft is totally understood.

Other possible emergencies that could occur relate to fumes and flooding. Employees should learn where the water and gas stopcocks are located and in the event of a leakage, the stopcocks should be switched off and the appropriate emergency service contacted.

The wellbeing of employees should be a foremost concern to employers. A variety of welfare facilities should also be provided for employees in catering and hospitality operations. The basic requirements are as follows:

- Toilets
- Washing facilities
- Changing areas
- PPE (Personal Protective Equipment) storage facilities
- Drinking water
- Rest facilities

## Assessment of knowledge and understanding

You have now learned about the health and safety responsibilities for everyone in the workplace. This will enable you to ensure your own actions reduce risks to health and safety.

To test your level of knowledge and understanding, answer the following short questions. These will help to prepare you for your summative (final) assessment.

1 State the main responsibilities under the Health and Safety at Work Act 1974.

2 Explain the word *risk*.

3 Explain the word *hazard*.

4 State the procedure for dealing with an accident in the workplace.

## Research Task A

Evidence is important when creating your portfolio within your own work role. Provide some detailed examples on how you have taken steps to reduce those health and safety risks which you may come into contact within the kitchen.

## Research Task B

Carry out a COSHH assessment on the following products. Consider the hazard, the risk, who is at risk, the degree of the risk and the action to be taken to reduce the risk.

(a) Heavy duty oven cleaner

(b) Washing detergent

# 2

# Applying workplace skills

## LEARNING OBJECTIVES

The aim of this chapter is to enable the candidate to develop competence in putting into practice the effective organisation of their own work and the contribution that can be made to working effectively with colleagues in a team. It discusses the importance of communication, working relationships and behaviour issues. This will also include information on how to improve yourself, preparing a job application and developing your own skills and knowledge.

At the end of this chapter you will be able to:

- Maintain a professional personal appearance
- Follow recipes and instructions
- Keep your work organised and organise your workspace as efficiently and cleanly as possible
- Understand the importance of providing work on time and to the exact specifications

- Identify your responsibility as a team member
- Maintain good working relationships
- Deliver clear and effective communication within the team
- Deal with feedback in a positive manner
- Plan a Curriculum Vitae
- Create an efficient learning plan to develop your skills

# INTRODUCTION TO APPLYING WORKPLACE SKILLS

Working within a team environment involves many process skills, interpersonal skills and personal qualities which are important to the effectiveness of the team when undertaking various projects, for example preparing for a large buffet. This includes co-operation with your employer, owner or manager to ensure that health and safety procedures are always followed.

*A chef's team planning meeting*

One of the most vital skills an employer will be looking for is your ability to become a valued member of a team. The skills listed below are an essential contribution to the effectiveness of a team and its overall performance.

## Process Skills

- Target setting
- Planning
- Reviewing the work
- Organising
- Obtaining resources
- Clarifying roles and responsibilities.

**VIDEO CLIP**
Working effectively in a professional kitchen

**VIDEO CLIP**
A professional kitchen during service

## Interpersonal Skills

- Teamwork and supporting co-workers
- Communicating ideas and needs
- Listening to others
- Showing assertiveness
- Negotiating support
- Asking for help and feedback
- Handling disagreement and conflict.

## Personal Qualities

- Reliable
- Confident
- Empathetic
- Self-aware
- Open to feedback
- Willing to learn from experience
- Persistent.

CHEF'S TIP

**CHEF'S TIP**

When working in a kitchen, regardless whether it is a large company chain or small indepenant restaurant, you are an important member of the team. You will be working with other people that you do not know, and yet will have to develop an instant working relationship. As an integral part of the team you will need to quickly establish who the other members of the team are, who is responsible for different things and to whom you need to go to for any help and guidance.

Effective teamwork is an essential ingredient in all successful organisations. The traditional kitchen brigade has always been a strong team that is usually made up from smaller groups with specific tasks and roles. Nowadays these traditional hierarchies have given way to flatter structures and chefs are more multiskilled. Some teams can be relatively permanent, and repetitive tasks

IMAGES COURTESY OF RUSSUMS.CO.UK

and familiar work mean that each team member has a fixed role. Experience shows that teamworking increases creativity, makes the most of a range of skills and knowledge, improves understanding, communication and a sense of shared purpose and overall it will improve efficiency.

*Changes in working methods and technology have had a profound effect on work. People who work well in groups, are well organised and can solve their problems are the people who get on best at work and get promoted.*

*Employment Policy Institute*

## Personal Health, Hygiene and Appearance

The appearance of a chef or food handler should promote a high standard of cleanliness and professionalism. Employees in the workplace should always reflect the desired image of the profession that they work in.

A chef's uniform is both traditional and functional. From a traditional viewpoint, it is a compelling symbol of all that a chef stands for. Originated on a whim of Napoleon, who wanted his favourite cooks in a military-style uniform, it has evolved into a functional outfit.

## Jacket

This is designed to protect the food from the chef and the chef from the physical dangers of the kitchen. Originally made of cotton and linen, the materials have evolved into modern, lightweight textiles. It is double-breasted to protect the chest and stomach from the heat from ovens and stoves, burns and scalds. It acts as a barrier and gives a few vital extra seconds to protect its wearer if there is a spillage of hot liquid onto the upper body. The sleeves should be worn to the wrist to give the arms protection from burns. It has become fashionable to wear short-sleeved jackets because of the hot temperatures in the kitchen. This practice should be discouraged for students in hot kitchens to reduce the risk of burns.

## Trousers

These are generally made of lightweight cotton or mixed material and Teflon-coated fabric. They should not be worn tight-fitting to the leg as this creates a hazard if a spillage occurs and will also be uncomfortable during work in a kitchen.

## Necktie

The original use of the necktie was to mop the brow – due to the lack of ventilation and the heat generated by solid fuel stoves. In the modern kitchen the necktie is largely traditional, but in larger organisations such as the armed forces, contract caterers, hotels and most catering colleges, a system of coloured neckties allows for recognition of department or seniority within the workplace.

## Chef's hats (toques)

The tall hat has always epitomised the stature of the chef. Traditionally an apprentice cook would wear a skull cap and graduate to a toque when they reached a position of Chef de Partie. Nowadays even some head chefs prefer the skull cap. The main function of the hat is to stop loose hair falling into the food and help absorb perspiration on the forehead. However, when the hair is worn beyond collar length it cannot be contained in a hat. In this case a hairnet should be worn.

*A toque*

## Footwear

Shoes should be of a sturdy design with non-slip soles and steel toecaps. It is important that the footwear worn is comfortable and will give support to the chef, who will be on their feet for many hours.

The wearing of trainers and non-specialist shoes should be prohibited. They give no protection to the feet, the soles are invariably not non-slip which is dangerous, and they will not give sufficient protection from spillages.

## Aprons

This item is probably the only article of chef's clothing that has remained unchanged over the years. It is one of the most important items of protection and must be worn at full length to protect the legs (always to below the knee). If a spillage of hot liquid occurs it is the first line of protection. It should be tied at the front to allow for quick release. Aprons are sometimes different in colour depending on the work the chef is engaged in.

Uniforms must be changed on a shift-by-shift basis. It is good practice to change uniforms when a spillage takes place, although this cannot always be achieved. The clothing should be of an easily washable material. Generally all chef's attire is white in colour so that it shows when clothing has been soiled and thus when it needs to be changed.

No jewellery should be worn whilst preparing food with the exception of plain wedding bands (even this can lead to danger when operating machinery and can harbour germs and bacteria). All outward and visible jewellery must be removed, and this includes ears, eyebrows, lips, cheeks, tongues, etc. Body piercing can attract dirt and bacteria, which can lead to contamination. Additionally jewellery can fall off into the food being prepared, unknown to the wearer! Watches should not be worn because particles of food may be caught under the strap and bacteria could multiply there until transferred to the food. Cosmetics, if used by chefs, should be used in moderation, but ideally their use should be discouraged.

 **HEALTH & SAFETY**

It is wise to have relevant inoculations, including those against tetanus and hepatitis, to protect against ill health.

**HEALTH & SAFETY**

Cuts and abrasions on hands should be covered with a clean, waterproof, blue-coloured dressing to minimise the risk of secondary infection. Disposable gloves may be worn for additional protection.

*A chef washing her hands using a nail brush*

**HEALTH & SAFETY**

Wash your hands with a liquid gel from a sealed dispenser. Soap should be discouraged because bar soap can accumulate germs when passed from hand to hand.

# MAINTAINING PERSONAL HYGIENE

It is vital that the chef maintains a high standard of personal hygiene. Bodily cleanliness is achieved through daily showering or bathing. An anti-perspirant or deodorant may be applied to the underarm area to reduce perspiration and thus the smell of sweat. Clean underwear should be worn each day.

## Hands

Hands and everything that has been touched are covered with bacteria, and although most of these are harmless, some can cause ill health. Hands must be washed regularly and frequently, particularly after visiting a toilet, before commencing the preparation of food and during the handling of food. They should be washed using hot water with the aid of a nailbrush and an antibacterial gel or liquid. The frequent use of sanitising wipes to disinfect hands is convenient for the killing of a wide range of bacteria and is efficient on a day-to-day basis.

To ensure good health and safety practice some employers insist on the use of plastic disposable gloves when preparing food items. When wearing these, remember that the gloves should be changed with every task to prevent cross-contamination.

Fingernails should always be kept clean and short. Nails should be cleaned with a nailbrush and nail varnish should not be worn. Dirt can easily accumulate under the nails and will then be introduced into food.

## Hair

Hair should be clean, washed regularly and kept tidy. It should be cut and maintained on a frequent basis. If hair is worn long it should be covered within a hairnet and tied back. The hair should never be scratched or touched whilst preparing food as bacteria can be transferred to the food.

## Feet

Feet should be kept fresh and healthy by washing them daily and drying thoroughly. Deodorising foot powder can be applied and toenails should be short and clean.

## Mouth and Teeth

There are many germs within and around the area of the mouth, and it is essential that the mouth does not come into contact with utensils or hands that will come into contact with food. Cooking utensils and fingers should *not* be used for tasting food as bacteria will be transferred to food quickly. A clean disposable spoon should be used for tasting and thrown away afterwards. Coughing over foods and working areas is to be avoided at all costs to prevent the spreading of bacteria from illness.

## Smoking

Smoking must never take place near food preparation areas: when a cigarette is taken from the mouth using the fingers, bacteria from the mouth can be transferred onto the fingers and therefore onto food. Any ash found on food is unacceptable and it is an offence to smoke whilst preparation of food is taking place.

# ORGANISING YOUR OWN WORK

Planning is a crucial part of work in a kitchen and in the workplace generally. In order to complete a task effectively and on time planning is always involved. Larger tasks will need to be broken down into smaller-sized, more manageable tasks, with 'milestones' along the way. Planning needs to be undertaken to:

- Identify what needs to be done, when and by whom.
- Help to foresee any potential problems so plans can be developed to tackle them.
- Provide a method for monitoring and controlling work, helping to ensure that things are done to the correct standard and on time.

Action plans will vary in detail depending on the level of task that needs to be completed. At every level, the first stage is to identify the steps that need to be taken to get the task done. It is often helpful to begin by brainstorming a list of tasks and then sketching a rough diagram, using boxes and arrows, rather than just trying to list the steps in order from the start. Sometimes this is referred to as a workflow diagram.

It can be difficult to estimate how much time is required to carry out a task. It is always helpful to check recipes and cooking times in order to have a reasonable idea of how long a task will take. Other activities will also need to be thought about, such as assembling the ingredients and tools, preparing pans and baking sheets, preheating ovens and ensuring that all tools and equipment are clean and hygienic. These activities are essential to the successful completion of a specific task and are collectively referred to as mise-en-place, a French term which means 'getting everything ready and in its place'. There are six basic organisational skills needed before actual preparation and cooking can take place. The flowchart illustrates these skills and how a flowchart of work can be produced.

> **CHEF'S TIP**
>
> A 'milestone' is a significant point where you can stop to review what has been achieved on your way to the overall completion of the actual task.

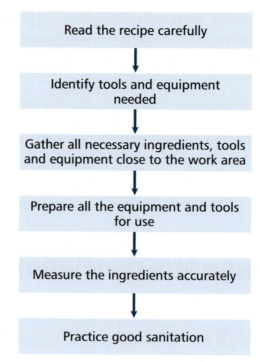

```
┌─────────────────────────────┐
│    Read the recipe carefully │
└─────────────────────────────┘
              │
              ▼
┌─────────────────────────────┐
│  Identify tools and equipment│
│           needed             │
└─────────────────────────────┘
              │
              ▼
┌─────────────────────────────┐
│ Gather all necessary         │
│ ingredients, tools           │
│ and equipment close to the   │
│ work area                    │
└─────────────────────────────┘
              │
              ▼
┌─────────────────────────────┐
│ Prepare all the equipment    │
│ and tools for use            │
└─────────────────────────────┘
              │
              ▼
┌─────────────────────────────┐
│ Measure the ingredients      │
│ accurately                   │
└─────────────────────────────┘
              │
              ▼
┌─────────────────────────────┐
│   Practice good sanitation   │
└─────────────────────────────┘
```

*A chef reading a recipe*

# Reading the recipe carefully

Reading the recipe carefully is the first skill of a successful chef. As tedious as this may seem, many people scan the recipe too quickly and miss the specific information, methods, ingredients or tools required to complete the task. If it is read unsystematically, the recipe may not turn out as expected because the chef did not have the necessary ingredients, tools or skills to prepare it. Recipes are specific ingredients in exact quantities: some professional pastry chefs refer to these as formulas.

# Identifying the tools and equipment needed

*A selection of tools and equipment on a rack*

As a recipe is studied, the chef should be making a note of which tools and equipment will be needed. If a specific tool is not available, can another be substituted without jeopardising the recipe? For example if a chicken mousseline recipe is being prepared and a food blender is needed but unavailable, what could be used instead? Some chefs try to make substitutions that do not work. For example, if a sponge cake recipe that relies on the aeration of eggs says fold the egg whites into a batter with a spatula but a whisk is used instead, what is the end result? The sponge may not rise because air was lost when the egg was folded in too roughly with an inappropriate tool and technique.

# Gathering the necessary ingredients, tools and equipment close to the work area

Once the chef is ready to commence, all the ingredients, tools and equipment must be gathered and brought close to the work area. If these items are not gathered beforehand, too much time will be spent running around the kitchen looking for the ingredients and tools, wasting valuable time and energy. One piece of equipment that *must* be prepared if being used is the oven. Preheating the oven should be done at least 10–15 minutes before it will be used.

## Preparing the equipment and tools for use

Before the actual preparation of food begins, all equipment and tools need to be checked to ensure that they are clean and in good repair. Certain equipment such as baking sheets will need to be prepared, this could include greasing, lining with baking parchment, or greasing and flouring.

## Measuring the ingredients accurately

Measuring ingredients properly is the foundation of success. Recipes in cookbooks have already been tested with specific amounts of ingredients. It is important to measure each ingredient *accurately* so that the recipe works consistently every time it is used. Digital scales are easier to use, faster and more accurate than many of their predecessors. There are different ways to measure ingredients; by volume (litres and millilitres) and by weight (kilograms and grams).

## Practising good sanitation

It is critical for any person preparing food in a kitchen to keep ingredients sanitary and to practise good hygiene. Sanitation refers to the various practices used to reduce the number of micro-organisms that can lead to food contamination and food-borne illnesses. Avoid cross-contamination or spreading bacteria from one surface to another by washing your hands, tools and work surfaces before starting each new task.

# WORKING TO DEADLINES

Working to realistic deadlines is an important factor for a chef, especially during a busy luncheon or dinner service. Doing this effectively depends on the prior skills of estimating how long the task is and being able to prioritise individual jobs. Once that is achieved, it may be helpful to set intermediate deadlines related to relatively short and defined cookery or food preparation-based tasks.

Time management is an important skill for chefs working in the hospitality industry. In order to manage your time more effectively, you must have a realistic assessment of all the tasks required (as mentioned earlier in the chapter) and then plan the workload accordingly.

The ability to set shared targets and make plans is essential for successful

*A selection of tools to prepare a dish*

*A chef preparing a baking sheet with melted butter*

*Measuring flour using digital kitchen scales*

*Sanitizing a work station and knife*

teamwork. If chefs do not know what they are aiming to achieve, they cannot determine what has been achieved. If there is no real planning, progression cannot be properly monitored to review how well things are going and to be able to learn from the experience. It is during these stages that team members can support each other and provide help where necessary to achieve the end result.

# SUPPORT THE WORK OF YOUR TEAM

Teams often have to agree targets and plans when preparing a luncheon, special function or dinner. The most effective plans have SMART targets that clearly set out what needs to be done to achieve the targets.

**SMART AND SMARTER**

| SMART TARGETS | |
|---|---|
| Specific | Specific targets outline exactly what the group aims to do, rather than expressing vague general aims. |
| Measurable | Outlining how the group will know it has met the targets and what evidence will show this. |
| Achievable | Challenging for the group, but not too difficult. |
| Realistic | The opportunities and resources should be available. |
| Time-bound | There should be both interim and final deadlines. |
| Targets can be even SMARTER. They can be: | |
| Enjoyable | |
| Rewarding | |

It is important that during this early stage job roles are clearly defined and given to specific employees. Each job role should be considered strategically so that it meets the requirements of the organisation and contributes successfully to the effectiveness of the team.

# COMMUNICATION SKILLS

To become an effective communicator – speaking *and* listening – you should have an understanding of non-verbal communication (NVC), or body language.

NVC can take many forms:

1 Touch: greetings, agreements, apologies, goodbyes

2 Posture: sitting or standing straight, leaning forward or back

3 Proximity: distance between people, personal territory

4 Dress: clothes, hair, appearance

5 Eye contact: indicates interest and attention or the opposite

**CHEF'S TIP**

It is important to be aware of cultural and gender variations in the meaning of some gestures, posture and facial expressions.

**6** Hand gestures: agreement, disagreement, impatience, welcome

**7** Facial expression: shows emotions and provides feedback.

Asking questions or making a point during discussions is an essential element of effective communication. Many people will want to ask questions but some will not do so because they lack the confidence to put their thoughts across at the right moment. It is a key sign of support if you can ask questions in a positive manner.

■ Briefly express your appreciation of the speaker, e.g. That was a really interesting point.

■ Briefly summarise the point made by the speaker, e.g. I was particularly interested in what you said about…

■ Ask your question. If you need to, write it down and read it out: try to make it clear, concise, relevant and informed, and do not be aggressive.

Listening skills are essential for effective communication and teamwork. They ensure that we obtain the right information from the right people, help us understand what information or support other people need and help us to work more effectively as a group.

Always remember that a good listener aims to get a thorough understanding of what the other person is saying before starting to form an opinion about it.

Other forms of communication are the telephone and written formats (e.g. email, memorandum, fax or letter). The telephone is a fast and effective way of communicating specific requirements or orders to a supplier or to communicate events from another location that may affect the overall outcome of a specific task. Remember that when you are using the telephone your face cannot be seen, so it is important to consider your tone of voice and to speak clearly.

With the advent of information technology and email it is now easier than ever to record conversations and attach relevant documents. Suppliers can now usually accept orders electronically via an email system which makes it easier to see potential mistakes in the order and gives greater clarity. Staff training in areas of communication, especially IT awareness, is imperative if the organisation is to develop and succeed.

 **CHEF'S TIP**

How to be a good listener:

■ Clear your mind of other things
■ Spend a few minutes thinking about the topic before the meeting or discussion
■ Avoid distractions
■ Recognise how you are feeling (interested? bored? tired? cross?)
■ Remember you are there to learn what the other person has to say, not the other way round
■ Focus on the speaker – look at them, nod, encourage, use NVC to acknowledge what is being said
■ Show interest, even if you disagree
■ Let the speaker finish what they are saying before you agree, disagree or ask for clarification
■ Ask questions to increase your understanding.

Confirm your understanding by expressing what was said in your own words, or by summarising.

*Suppliers can now usually accept orders electronically via email*

**CHEF'S TIP**

Always make sure that your written records are accurate. Incorrect or incomplete information could result in potential accidents or misunderstanding.

# PREPARING FOR A JOB APPLICATION

## The Curriculum Vitae

Curriculum vitae (CV) is a Latin term meaning 'the story of your life'. It should be a maximum length of two sides of A4 paper. This requires a selective approach. Do not list things in too much detail; include the highlights of your education, experience and career.

Your CV is a marketing document, and it should include *everything* that reflects you in the most positive light for a specific position with a particular company. One of the main purposes of the CV is to obtain an interview, so it needs to persuade the recruiter that they want to meet you in person to discuss your qualities.

Before beginning to write a CV, the first task is to try brainstorming all you have to offer an employer on to a piece of paper. Focus on getting all your details on paper.

It is essential that you do your research before applying for a position. Find out as much as you can about the company, the industry sector and the specific position. It is more productive to spend time undertaking a lot of preparation and applying for fewer posts that you have researched thoroughly, than to send out lots of CV's across the board.

When focusing on the positions and companies that you are interested in, it is important to consider the following:

- What are the company's needs?
- How and what can you contribute to this organisation?
- What are the main requirements for the post?
- Are there any general or specific skills that are required?
- What are the specific qualifications needed?

It is important to try to match your details in your brainstormed paper to the requirements of the job. Rather than just listing your skills, think of an example as evidence of how you have gained, developed or used a specific skill. On your brainstorm paper write this evidence beside each item.

## Appearance and Style

First impressions really do count. Research has shown that recruiters initially spend only 30 seconds scanning a CV to see if the qualifications match and if the potential applicant has qualities that are needed by the company. This means that appearance and presentation of the CV are very important. When writing a CV, you do not have to use sentences. Short, concise phrases that get straight to the point, with positive words to describe any roles you have performed are fine. Use bullet points to help emphasise this impression.

Always keep a copy for your records to take with you to the interview. Use an A4 envelope to avoid folding your CV.

The following points should be considered when producing the CV:

- Use bold fonts where necessary, apply the font size and lower/upper case to make the section headings and key points stand out.
- Be consistent and logical in the use of bold and plain fonts, underline and font size.
- Centre it on the page with top and bottom margins of equal size, as well as left and right margins.
- Use good white or cream paper only.
- Print on one side only using a printer which gives a good quality printout.
- Get someone to proof-read, check spelling, grammar and punctuation.
- Size 12 and Times New Roman or Arial font are usually acceptable because they tend to be easier on the reader's eye.

There may be some aspects of your life that are difficult to tackle on a CV, for example a disability or gaps in your education and employment due to ill health. How you choose to approach this will be a personal evaluation that you may feel strongly about. However, there are methods of disclosing information positively so that it does not look too negative in the CV. Alternatively you can choose not to disclose this information at all. There are no easy answers to this dilemma and the decision is ultimately a personal choice, but you may find it beneficial to discuss this with a Careers Adviser.

## The Content of a CV

While there is no standard format to a CV, there are some general expectations of what it should contain. The key areas are the following:

### Personal details

Always include your name, address, telephone number, mobile telephone number and email address at the beginning.

Use your name as an overall heading rather than the words 'Curriculum Vitae'.

It is not necessary to include your nationality, sex or marital status. If you are a mature graduate and you fear ageism, you may wish to exclude your date of birth or state it at the end. It may be advantageous to put 'no work permit needed' or 'permanent UK resident', but only if there is anything on your CV to suggest otherwise.

### Education and qualifications

These should be listed in reverse order, starting with the most recent. State your qualifications, schools, colleges and university with the appropriate dates.

It is not necessary to give the full address of your college, university or school and it is not necessary to go further back than secondary school.

If you have studied overseas, list each qualification and state its equivalence to UK qualifications. It may be helpful to provide further information, but do not include grades that an employer may not understand. You do not have to list any examinations you may have failed. Only emphasise your successes.

## Work history

Once again, this needs to be listed in reverse order, starting with the most recent and working in reverse. You can include details of full and part-time paid work. You should also include work experience or placements.

State the job title first, then the name and location of the organisation, the dates and a brief description of responsibilities and duties of the position. It is not necessary to give the full address of every employer.

Explain the overall purpose of the job in its context, rather than simply listing all the tasks. Describe the most demanding or responsible aspects of the job and highlight any special achievements obtained during this time.

Highlight the skills that you developed which are relevant to the post you are applying for.

If you have a long work history, you may need to make some firm decisions about what to include or leave out. Do not leave any gaps which cannot be accounted for – most recruiters expect you to account for your time. If there are long periods of time unaccounted for, they may imagine the worst.

## Interests or achievements

In this section you might include sports, voluntary work, travel, membership of clubs and societies, positions of responsibility and competition work which have developed teamworking skills or other important personal qualities.

Quality is more important than quantity. One or two interests that you have developed to a high level, or shown long-term commitment to, are better than a long list. Culinary competition work, in which you have performed well or undertake regularly, look better than a long list of sports events of which you are just a spectator or have not played since school.

## References

Include at least two references, preferably an academic reference and one from a recent employer.

State the name, address, telephone number and occupation of the referee and how they know you. Always ask referees first if they are happy to be used.

Keep them informed about the type of position you are looking for and the result of the applications. Give them a copy of your CV and always thank them - especially when you are successful! If there is a particular reason why you do not wish to give details of references at this stage, then you can state 'references available on request'.

In addition to the above sections, there are a number of others which might be included. You will need to decide on these, according to what works best for you. Start by listing everything you wish to include, and then decide how to organise it.

### Key skills

Under this heading you can list the skills that are most relevant to the post, for example, communication, teamwork, attention to detail and problem-solving. Always offer an example of something you have done as evidence that you possess the skills you are claiming.

### Exhibitions, awards, prizes, achievements

For chefs this may be one of the most important aspects of the CV.

### Personal profile

This can provide a useful summary at the top of the CV which draws together your career goals with the highlights of your CV.

### Languages

List languages spoken, or written and level of fluency. For example German (fluent), French (read and understand), Spanish (basic).

# COVERING LETTERS

A CV should always be accompanied by a covering letter. It should explain why you are sending your CV and it must grab the attention and lead the reader into wanting to look at your CV.

The covering letter is where you can make your case for being the right person for that post in that particular organisation. The letter should be well presented, with perfect spelling and grammar that demonstrates your ability to express yourself correctly in good business English. This is the case even if you are applying for a post where writing skills are not critical.

The style should be positive, convincing and convey enthusiasm. 'I would welcome' is better than 'I am willing to'. 'I am especially enthusiastic about . . .' is more positive than 'I am quite interested in'.

This must not sound like a standard letter and it should be tailored to the individual position and to the organisation you are addressing. If possible, address it to a named person. The letter should be no longer than one side of A4, and set out as a formal business letter. Always be concise and to the point. It would normally be word-processed; however some employers do ask for hand-written letters.

# THE INTERVIEW

Your application form, CV and covering letter were successful and you have been invited to interview. Interviewing is an expensive process for any employer, so you must have met most, if not all, of the requirements of the job for the employer to want to meet you. Having got so far, how can you ensure that you excel at the interview?

You should always consult all the materials listed in libraries and practice answering questions out loud. While you should not learn your answers off by heart, practicing with friends or family will help develop your confidence and mean you will be equipped for the most general questions.

Although many employers use sophisticated recruitment methods, especially for senior positions, the interview still forms a vital part of the process.

The employer will want to quiz you on certain aspects of your application form/CV, make a judgement as to how well you will do the job and assess how you will cope in different situations. They will be asking, 'Will your skills and personality complement those of others in the team? Will you get on with other people? Will you identify with the aims of the organisation?'

On your side the interview gives you the chance to meet future colleagues, ask any questions you may have about the post or the company, try to get a feeling for the culture of the organisation and possibly see where you will be working. You will be asking yourself, 'Can I see myself working here? Will I be successful? Is the job likely to give me what I am looking for?'

Sometimes an employer may ask you to do a work trial for a limited time so that they can see you in their environment. This is also a good tool for you to understand the background to the organisation and meet your potential team members.

Many factors are outside your control, such as the format of the interview, the personalities of the interviewer(s) and the quality of the other candidates. However, many factors that contribute to a successful interview are within your control.

The key area for this is preparation.

## Making a good impression

If the company has a brochure or web page, look to see what people are wearing in any photos - that can often give you a indication of the company philosophy.

If you feel you ought to buy something new to wear to the interview, make sure it feels comfortable. If in doubt wear a suit and tie, or smart skirt/ trousers and a jacket. Do not wear jeans or too much jewellery or scent. Always look clean and tidy. Rightly or wrongly, interviewers will always draw conclusions about you from your appearance.

Plan your route, double-checking train or bus times and parking arrangements if driving. Aim to arrive 15 minutes early. It is better to sit and reread your application than to arrive in a panic. If possible, do a 'dummy run' to the place of interview the day before.

Read the brochure and web site again, together with any job description, person specification, copies of menus and restaurant reviews. Read the Annual Report (if available) and any other information you can find about the employer.

Check that you know:

■ Something of the company background

■ Its products, services, menus and accolades

■ The approximate number of employees

■ The mission statement of the company

It is very important to consider and list questions you want to ask about the post and the organisation.

## Current Issues

In the days and weeks before your interview, read the business sections of the quality press and specialist hospitality and catering journals to find out everything you can about the organisation, its rivals and the marketplace in which it operates. Use the internet to gather information. You will be expected to show at the interview that you are aware of current issues affecting the organisation and your specific job.

Dealing with questions can be the most daunting part of the interview process. It helps to understand the nature of questioning, what different types of questions are commonly used and how to respond effectively.

# TYPES OF QUESTIONS USED IN INTERVIEWS

■ Open – 'Tell me about your qualifications'. This question is often used at the start of an interview to allow you to relax and talk freely.

■ Technical – 'What types of menu are you familiar with?' Used to find out how much you know and assess your level of competence in relation to the job description.

■ Hypothetical – 'What would you do if . . .?' This is used to test your ability to think on your feet and to check your skills in problem-solving and prioritising.

■ Leading – 'I see you changed your course, couldn't you cope?' This is a more insinuating way of challenging you and making you justify a decision or action.

■ Reflective – 'Am I right in thinking from what you say that . . .?' By repeating what you have said to encourage you to expand your thoughts.

## GOLDEN RULES WHEN ANSWERING QUESTIONS IN INTERVIEWS

■ Look the interviewer in the eye.

■ If it is a panel interview, look at other members of the panel from time to time to 'include' them in the conversation.

■ Speak clearly and confidently. Try not to speak too fast or too quietly.

■ If you don't understand the question ask for it to be repeated or clarified.

■ There is not always a right or wrong answer. The interviewer is sometimes more interested in how you respond to the question or hypothetical situation.

## WHAT EMPLOYERS LIKE TO SEE AT THE INTERVIEW

■ Genuine interest in the post and organisation.

■ Saying what they want to hear - demonstrate that you have what they are looking for.

■ An open and frank approach.

■ A willing attitude.

■ An interest in developing yourself and being trained.

■ Motivation towards the job rather than money.

■ Appearance and attitude matching the organisation's image.

## WHAT EMPLOYERS DO NOT LIKE TO SEE

■ Lack of openness.

■ Blaming other people for any problems you have had.

■ Little effort made to find out about the organisation or post.

■ Inappropriate dress and appearance.

■ Too many questions about pay, pensions and holidays.

■ Arrogance or a negative attitude.

■ Being over familiar, e.g. using the interviewer's first name.

■ Smoking, chewing gum, eating or drinking (unless offered refreshments).

# EVALUATING THE INTERVIEW

If you do not achieve the result you wanted and do not get the post, it is important to evaluate and try to work out what, if anything, went wrong. Consider asking the company to give you feedback. Many will do this and it could help you to be successful at your next interview.

REMEMBER: there might have been nothing wrong with you or the way you performed. It could simply be that on the day there was a stronger candidate. Try not to think of it as a failure, but as a learning experience that can be used to perform even better at the next interview.

If you continue to get interviews but they do not result in job offers, do not get despondent. Arrange to talk it over with a careers adviser to see how you can improve your interview technique.

# CONTRIBUTE TO YOUR OWN DEVELOPMENT OF SKILLS

Appraisal or progress reviews, where one member of staff looks at the way another employee/member of staff is performing in their job role, are an important method of communication. It is usual for an employee to receive an appraisal from their line manager.

Appraisals provide an opportunity to review individuals' performance against the targets set. Each team member has their own strengths and weaknesses, and it is important to utilise these in a plan of action to build on and improve weaknesses with appropriate personal goals.

Performance appraisal will identify:

■ Results achieved against preset targets

■ Any additional accomplishments and contributions.

This may seem overwhelming, but it is an important and useful process. It can also be used to your advantage:

■ Identify with your line manager the tasks you see that need to be accomplished, and how these will be met

■ Identify training needs: this will provide you with a greater range of skills and expertise, which will ultimately improve your opportunities for promotion, giving you increased responsibilities

> **CHEF'S TIP**
>
> Continuing Professional Development (CPD) is the term used by professionals to describe constantly updating their skills. Every opportunity to continue to update and learn new skills, techniques and knowledge should be explored.

■ Identify obstructions which are affecting your progress

■ Identify what additional responsibilities you would like

■ Identify and focus on your achievements to date against the targets set

■ Update your action plan, which will help you achieve your targets.

In order to develop personally and to improve your skills professionally, it is important to have personal targets against which you can measure your achievement. If these are confidential, the workplace policy on confidentiality should be observed. As mentioned earlier in the chapter, all targets set should be SMART.

It is important to your employer that you are consistent. You must always perform your skills to the highest standard and present and promote a positive image of the industry and the business you represent.

Entering culinary competitions where you will have the chance to meet and compete against other chefs will give you the opportunity to see new techniques, exchange ideas and develop your skills. This is an immense learning strategy and will also create a positive reputation for you and your place of work. There are many different competitions both on a local and national basis with categories for junior and senior chefs.

Chefs can also learn and develop through the membership of professional associations. Developing a network of associates, friends and peers is very important for business and learning. Chefs, employers, suppliers, training providers and managers are able to exchange ideas and to discuss ways to help meet industry targets such as training, profitability and links to other industries across the world.

The continuation of learning is essential to succeed in this industry, and the prospect of continuing to acquire knowledge and further develop skills to advance ones' career is a great incentive. Colleges have diverse courses of study to help match your development plan: they also assess the skills that the industry will require in the future in order for your job to be carried out effectively and for you to progress in your profession.

Your individual learning plan can be based on the following chart. It is imperative that you can revisit the chart on a regular basis to review your progress and match your aims and objectives against this.

## CHEF'S TIP

In quieter periods observe colleagues who have more advanced qualifications and experience.

Practise your skills at every opportunity! The more you practise the more skilled and efficient you will become.

## CHEF'S TIP

Find out which tasks take priority over others. Some jobs are more important or urgent than others and will need to be done first. Remember, that if you have to leave a task halfway through, make sure that you get back to complete it at the earliest convenient moment.

## Meeting Personal Development Targets

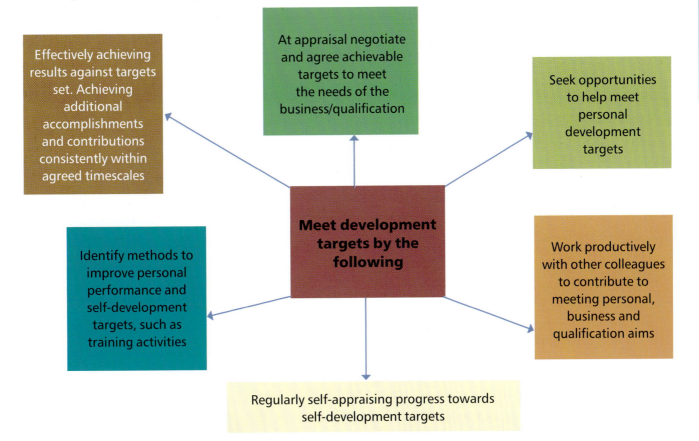

## Assessment of knowledge and understanding

You have now learned about your responsibility to work effectively as a team member and the importance of communication and improving yourself. This will enable you to ensure your own positive actions and contribute effectively towards the whole team.

To test your level of knowledge and understanding, answer the following short questions. These will help to prepare you for your summative (final) assessment.

**1** State two important aspects of effective teamwork.

i) _____ ii) _____

**2** Explain the French term 'mise en place'.

_____

**3** Identify the significance of being able to communicate effectively.

_____

**4** List three examples of effective teamwork.

i) _____ ii) _____

iii) _____

**5** State the purpose of an appraisal or performance review.

_____

_____

**6** Explain the importance of improving on your own knowledge and skills to help the work of your team.

_____

_____

**7** State the importance in reviewing your learning plan on a regular basis.

_____

_____

## Research Task A

Evidence is important when creating your portfolio within your own work role. List five learning aims that you would like to achieve in the next six months and make them into SMART targets.

i) _____

ii) _____

iii) _____

iv) _____

v) _____

# 3
# Food safety in catering

**UNIT 202**
1. **Behave as responsible individuals within food safety procedures**
2. **Keep him/herself clean and hygienic**
3. **Keep the working area clean and hygienic**
4. **Receive and store food safely**

## LEARNING OBJECTIVES

The aim of this chapter is to enable the candidate to acquire expertise and put into practice their knowledge of the health and hygienic practices within the workplace. It discusses the health and hygiene requirements and policies that you will need to know about if you are to work safely and hygienically in the kitchen. This will also include information on the resources at the disposal of the chef to implement regulations to prepare, cook and hold food safely.

At the end of this chapter you will be able to:

- Identify the correct attire for the chef in the workplace
- Be aware of your responsibility for personal cleanliness during food preparation and cooking in the workplace and for unsafe behaviour
- Maintain clean and hygienic work surfaces and equipment

- Check food into the premises and identify specific labels
- Understand the correct use of storage control, the stock rotation system and keeping records
- Know how to safely defrost food and thoroughly wash food
- Know the regulations for the safe cooking, the safe holding and the safe reheating of food
- Chill and freeze cooked food that is not for immediate consumption
- Identify food bacteria and other organisms and food hazards in the workplace

# INTRODUCTION

The chef must be particularly conscious of the need for hygiene: many commodities have to be handled and prepared for the customer without any type of heat treatment. High standards of hygiene are essential to prevent food poisoning, food spoilage, loss of productivity, pest infestation and potential criminal prosecution for malpractice.

Food hygiene implies more than just the sanitation of work areas. It includes all practices, precautions and legal responsibilities involved in the following:

1 Protecting food from risk of contamination
2 Preventing organisms from multiplying to an extent which would pose a health risk to customers and employees
3 Destroying any harmful bacteria in food by thorough heat treatment or other techniques.

# PERSONAL HYGIENE

It is a requirement that good hygiene systems are followed by all food handlers. Chapter 1 covers personal hygiene in depth, but some points need to be highlighted in this chapter in relation to the subject matter.

Regular hand washing is a requirement of the chef, and in all aspects of a chef's working day. The following procedures should apply:

1 An approved hand washing detergent should be provided by the employer, preferably in liquid form and from a dispenser.
2 Hot water and an approved drying system should be in place.
3 The application of an alcohol-based hand disinfectant allows for maximum disinfection.

Hand washing must be undertaken:

- Before commencing work (to wash away general bacteria)
- After using the toilet or in contact with faeces

*Two students fully dressed in chef's uniform. Personal hygiene is important for chefs.*

■ After breaks

■ Between touching raw food and cooked food

■ Before handling raw food

■ After disposing of waste

■ After cleaning the workspace

■ After any first aid or dressing changes

■ After touching the face, nose, mouth or blowing your nose

■ Hand washing and sanitation should take place at every possible opportunity.

## Tasting Food Whilst Cooking

Whilst it is good practice for a chef to constantly taste food during cooking, you must use a spoon that is washed between tastings. It is best pactice to use a disposable plastic spoon that is discarded after tasting.

## Hair

This should be washed regularly and kept covered. If shoulder length it should be tied up and placed inside a hairnet. To maintain food hygiene standards there are now many types of hat available from suppliers, most of which are disposable. They also present a professional image in serving and kitchen areas that are visible to the public and customers.

## Cuts, Boils and Septic Wounds

Food handlers should always cover cuts, grazes, boils and septic wounds with the appropriate dressing or with brightly coloured blue waterproof plasters. Cuts on fingers may need extra protection with waterproof fingerstalls or latex disposable gloves.

## Smoking

This is prohibited where food is being prepared because of:

■ The danger of contaminating food by *Staphylococci* on the fingers which may touch the lips and from saliva from the cigarette end.

■ It also encourages coughing.

## Jewellery and Cosmetics

Food handlers and chefs should not wear earrings, watches, rings or other piercing because they can harbour dirt and bacteria. Plain wedding bands are permitted, but these can still harbour significant levels of bacteria. Strong-smelling perfume may cause food to be tainted and make-up should be used minimally.

## Protective Clothing

Every person handling food must wear protective clothing which should be lightweight, washable and strong. White clothing has the advantage of

*A chef tasting food with a clean spoon*

*Hair tied back with a hairnet and hat*

*A skullcap*

showing up dirt more easily. However, it is important that chefs wear the following protective garments in the kitchen environment:

1 Chef hat or skullcap

2 Chef jacket – double breasted

3 Apron – long and made from heavy cotton

4 Non-slip safety shoes

5 Trousers – comfortable fit and preferably cotton

6 Chef neckerchief – coloured appropriately (if required).

# A CLEAN AND HYGIENIC WORK AREA

The use of premises which are clean and can be correctly maintained is essential for the preparation, cooking and service of food. Cross-contamination risks should be minimised by the provision of separate preparation areas for the various raw and cooked foods. The table describes the various fittings and fixtures that need to be considered in a kitchen before the main equipment is planned:

| FIXTURES AND FITTINGS | RECOMMENDATIONS |
|---|---|
| Ceilings | White in colour to reflect the light. Smooth-textured, without cracks or peeled paint/plaster. Usually panelled to hide the ventilation system. |
| Floors | Should have a durable, non-slip and non-permeable material. They can be tiled but polyurethane screeds are now used extensively in food processing areas. This type of screed is fast to install, offers good levels of chemical resistance even to the most aggressive acids and fats, and can be installed to withstand steam cleaning. It is a slip-resistant surface (equally important), designed to give a textured finish. |
| Lighting | Good lighting is essential to avoid eye strain. Natural light is best but where artificial lighting is used some thought should be given to the type used. |
| Ventilation | The requirements of a high-performance kitchen ventilation system for the modern kitchen. The extracted air should be free from grease and odours, and be discharged up single or multiple chimney stacks. A canopy system should be built around the existing structure of the kitchen to cover at least all cookery areas. The incorporation of a balancing system to ensure equal extract along the whole cook line is very important. Replacement air is introduced into the kitchen through low-velocity diffusers mounted in the front face of the canopy and spot cooling nozzles can also provide a cooler air temperature in the kitchen. These are a potential source of dirt, grease and dust and should be cleaned on a very regular basis. |
| Walls | Ceramic wall tiles were considered the best surface for areas where liquids splash a wall surface, potentially overcoming a damp or hygiene problem. Many such areas still exist in industrial and commercial hygiene-sensitive areas. Their durability, long-term appearance and cost of maintenance can be questionable and today there is a viable alternative to consider. Modern alternatives to ceramic wall tiles include PVC wall cladding systems, resin wall coatings and screed mortars. They offer a hygienic finish capable of withstanding heavy-impact use. |

# EQUIPMENT

Work surfaces and equipment for the preparation, cooking and service of food should be impervious (non-absorbent) and easy to clean. Equipment should be constructed from materials which are non-toxic, corrosion resistant, smooth and free from cracks. Apparatus such as a **bain-marie** should be able to store hot food for up to two hours at an ambient temperature of 63°C and regular temperature checks should be taken. The surfaces should be easy to clean even when hot and should allow the food to be presented in an attractive manner.

## Worktops and chopping boards

It is very important to keep all worktops and chopping boards clean because they touch the food your customers are going to eat. If they are not properly clean, bacteria could spread to food and make your customers ill.

■ Always wash worktops before you start preparing food.

■ Wipe up any spilt food straight away.

■ Always wash worktops thoroughly after they have been touched by raw meat, including poultry, or raw eggs.

■ Never put ready-to-eat food, such as tomatoes or fruit, on a worktop or chopping board that has been touched by raw meat, unless you have washed it thoroughly first.

**VIDEO CLIP**
Colour coded chopping boards

If you have a dishwasher, this is a very effective way to clean plastic chopping boards. Dishwashers can wash at a very high temperature, which kills bacteria. Otherwise, wash chopping boards thoroughly with hot water and washing-up liquid.

Ideally, it is standard practice to have separate chopping boards for raw meat and for other foods. A standardised system of coloured boards and knife handles which help to minimise cross-contamination are widely available. They should be as follows:

■ Red      – raw meat and poultry

■ Yellow   – cooked meat and poultry

■ Blue     – raw fish (in this book, white and wooden backgrounds may be used for photographic purposes)

■ Brown    – vegetables

■ Green    – fruit and salads

■ White    – dairy and pastry items.

These boards must be cleaned between use, ideally with sanitiser and clean cotton, non-woven fabric or specialised paper cleaning cloths. They should be soaked over night in a sterilising solution on a regular basis. The boards are stored in racks and should not be touching each other.

*Colour codes for high-density chopping boards*

If boards become damaged they should be discarded. Bacteria can multiply in cracks and blemishes, and be the cause of contamination.

## Kitchen Cloths

Dirty, damp cloths are the perfect breeding ground for bacteria. It is very important to wash kitchen cloths and other cleaning cloths, sponges and abrasive materials regularly and leave them to dry before using them again.

Ideally, try to keep different cloths for different jobs. For example, use one cloth to wipe worktops and another to wash dishes. This helps to stop bacteria spreading.

The safest option is the use of disposable kitchen towels to wipe worktops and chopping boards. This is because you throw the kitchen towel away after using it once, so it is less likely to spread bacteria than cloths you use again.

Tea towels can also spread bacteria, so it's important to wash them regularly and be careful how you use them. Remember, if you wipe your hands on a tea towel after you have touched raw meat, this will spread bacteria to the towel. Then, if you use the tea towel to dry a plate, the bacteria will spread to the plate.

## Knives, Spoons and Other Utensils

It is important to keep knives, wooden spoons, spatulas, tongs and other utensils clean to help stop bacteria spreading to food. It is especially important to wash them thoroughly after using them with raw meat, otherwise they can spread bacteria to other food.

Once again, a dishwasher is a very effective way to clean knives and other utensils because dishwashers can wash at a very high temperature, which kills bacteria. Otherwise, wash them thoroughly with hot water and washing-up liquid.

# HAZARD ANALYSIS CRITICAL CONTROL POINTS

Hazard Analysis Critical Control Points (HACCP) are an internationally recognised and recommended system of food safety management. They focus on identifying the critical points in a process where food safety problems (or hazards) could arise and putting steps in place to prevent things going wrong. This is sometimes referred to as controlling hazards. Keeping records is also an important part of HACCP systems.

## HEALTH & SAFETY

As a result of changes in European food hygiene regulations on 1 January 2006, the Food Standards Agency has issued new guidance on temperature control legislation in England, Wales and Northern Ireland. The guidance contains advice on the types of foods that are required to be held under temperature control and on the circumstances in which some flexibility from the temperature control requirements is allowed. The guidance is intended to complement best practices in the food industry, which might involve, for example, keeping foods at chill temperatures below the legal maximum and thereby providing additional assurances of food safety.

HACCP involves the following seven steps:

1 identify what could go wrong (the hazards)
2 identify the most important points where things can go wrong (the critical control points – CCPs)
3 set critical limits at each CCP (e.g. cooking temperature/time)
4 set up checks at CCPs to prevent problems occurring (monitoring)
5 decide what to do if something goes wrong (corrective action)
6 prove that your HACCP plan is working (verification)
7 keep records of all of the above (documentation).

Your HACCP plan must be kept up to date and you will need to review it from time to time, especially whenever something in your food operation changes. You may also wish to ask your local Environmental Health Officer for advice. Remember that even with a HACCP plan in place, you must comply with all of the requirements of current food safety legislation.

**The Food Hygiene (England) Regulations 2006** provide the framework for the EU legislation to be enforced in England. There are similar regulations in Wales, Scotland and Northern Ireland. The Food Safety (General Food Hygiene) Regulations 1995 and the Food Safety (Temperature Control) Regulations 1995 no longer apply. Many of the requirements of these regulations are included in the new EU legislation, so what businesses need to do from day to day has not changed very much. The main new requirement is to have 'food safety management procedures' and keep up to date records of these.

Disposal of waste is another HACCP matter, as bacteria and pathogens can multiply at an alarming rate in waste disposal areas. In ideal circumstances the areas for cleaning crockery and pots should be separate from each other and from the food preparation area.

Waste bins in the kitchen should be emptied at regular and short intervals and be kept clean. Food waste can be safely disposed of in a waste disposal unit. Oil can only be disposed of by a specialist oil disposal company and must not be placed in a sink or waste disposal unit.

# THE REPORTING OF MAINTENANCE ISSUES

The preparation of food for cookery must take place on surfaces that are hygienic and suitable for use. Work surfaces, walls and floors can become damaged, and they too can be a source of contamination and danger to customers and staff alike. This should be reported to your line manager. A maintenance reporting system can easily be designed to suit each establishment and each section in that kitchen. Areas for attention are:

**HEALTH & SAFETY**

Food handlers must receive appropriate supervision, and be instructed and/or trained in food hygiene, to enable them to handle food safely. Those responsible for developing and maintaining the business's food safety procedures, based on HACCP principles, must have received adequate training. There is no legal requirement to attend a formal training course or get a qualification, although many businesses may want their staff to do so. The necessary skills may also be obtained in other ways, such as through on-the-job training, self-study or relevant prior experience. The operator of the food business is responsible for ensuring this happens.

- Cracks in walls
- Damage to tables and workbenches
- Cooking equipment such as pots, pans and utensils
- Windows, sanitary systems and lights
- Flooring an any other structural issues
- Electrical equipment relating to that particular operation.

**VIDEO CLIP**
Receiving, washing, storing, preparing and cooking foodstuffs

**VIDEO CLIP**
A goods receiving area in a large hotel

# SAFE FOOD STORAGE

A HACCP food management system will also examine the point of food storage. It should cover the receiving of goods where the core temperatures and condition of the delivery is thoroughly checked. Fresh meat that has been delivered should have a core temperature of a maximum of 8˚C. All fresh produce should be delivered in unbroken, clean packaging and in clean delivery vehicles that are refrigerated. If you suspect a delivery has not met the requirements of your HACCP it should be refused and returned immediately to the supplier. A goods inwards sheet showing the company, invoice number, core temperature, any problems and how they were dealt with allows received goods to be monitored.

An example of a Goods Received Checklist.

Chef's name _____

Production area _____

## Goods Received Checklist

| Date | Time | Supplier | Order correct | Delivery note/ Invoice number | Fault (Identify product) | Action | Temperature reading | Signature |
|------|------|----------|---------------|-------------------------------|--------------------------|--------|---------------------|-----------|
|  |  |  |  |  |  |  |  |  |
|  |  |  |  |  |  |  |  |  |
|  |  |  |  |  |  |  |  |  |
|  |  |  |  |  |  |  |  |  |
|  |  |  |  |  |  |  |  |  |
|  |  |  |  |  |  |  |  |  |
|  |  |  |  |  |  |  |  |  |
|  |  |  |  |  |  |  |  |  |
|  |  |  |  |  |  |  |  |  |
|  |  |  |  |  |  |  |  |  |
|  |  |  |  |  |  |  |  |  |
|  |  |  |  |  |  |  |  |  |

After the commodity has been received it needs to be correctly stored. Raw meat and fish should be stored, covered, in separate refrigerators at 4°C. If there is not enough capacity for two separate refrigeration systems, *cooked products must be stored above fresh meat*. Fish should be stored as low in the refrigerator as possible. This is the coldest part of the refrigerator and a layer of crushed ice will help to keep the temperature down. This method eliminates cross-contamination from storage and optimises quality. All foods should be labelled with the date of delivery/production, a description of the contents and the recommended use by date.

*A well laid-out store room*

# TYPES OF BACTERIA THAT CAUSE FOOD POISONING

**VIDEO CLIP**
Effective stocking of a walk-in fridge and freezer

## *Salmonella*

There are approximately over 2000 types of Salmonella; the commonest varieties are *Salmonella enteriditis* and *Salmonella typhimurium*. These organisms survive in the intestine and can cause food poisoning by releasing a toxin on the death of the cell. The primary source of salmonella is the intestinal tract of animals and poultry. It will therefore be found in:

- Human and animal excreta
- Excreta from rats, mice, flies and cockroaches
- Raw meat and poultry
- Some animal feed.

## *Staphylococcus Aureus*

About 40–50 per cent of adults carry this organism in their nose, mouth, throat, ears and hands. If present in food, *Staphylococcus aureus* will produce a toxin which may survive boiling for 30 minutes or more. The majority of outbreaks are caused by poor hygiene practices which result in direct contamination of the food from sneezing or uncovered septic cuts and abrasions. Frequently, the cooked food has been handled whilst still slightly warm, and these storage conditions have encouraged the organism to produce its toxin.

## *Clostridium perfringens*

This is commonly found in human and animal faeces and is present in raw meat and poultry. This organism forms spores which may survive boiling temperatures for several hours. Outbreaks can involve stews and large joints of meat which have been allowed to cool down slowly in a warm kitchen and either eaten cold or inadequately reheated the following day.

## *Bacillus cereus*

This is a spore-forming organism. The spores survive normal cooking and rapid growth will occur if the food has not cooled quickly and refrigerated. This bacteria will induce nausea and vomiting within five hours of ingestion.

## Food storage and temperatures

Raw meat, poultry and game and charcuterie – 4°C or below. Store away from cooked meat and cooked meat products to avoid any risk of cross-contamination.

Cooked meat – 4°C or below. Keep away from raw meat and meat products.

Uncooked fish – 4°C or below. Keep in separate compartments or in plastic fish trays with lids if possible, and away from other foods which may become tainted.

Frozen food – –18°C or below. Thaw only immediately prior to using the commodity.

Fish (smoked or cured) – 8°C. Keep in chilled storage away from other foods, which may become tainted.

Fruit (fresh and dried). Store in a cool, dry, well-ventilated area, away from other food, at least 15cm from the ground. Discard at the first sign of mould growth. Do not overstock.

Pasta, rice and cereals – Store in self-closing tightly lidded containers in dry cool storeroom or cupboard.

Eggs – Refrigerate at 8°C or below. Use strictly in rotation and ensure the shells are clean.

Fats, butter, dairy and non-dairy spreads – 8°C or below. Keep covered and away from highly flavoured food, which may taint.

Milk and cream – 8°C or below. In a separate dairy refrigerator that is used for no other purpose and in strict rotation.

Canned and bottled goods – Cool, dry, well-ventilated storage area. Blown, rusty or split tins must not be used.

Root vegetables – Store in sacks or nets as delivered in cool, well-ventilated area.

Leaf and green vegetables – 8°C. Use on day of delivery.

*Glass fronted fridge*

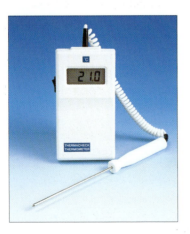

*Digital food thermometer*

Freezers, whether upright or chest freezers, should be maintained at a maximum temperature of –18°C. All food should be covered to prevent freezer burn and labelled with the date of production and a use by date.

Ambient stores should be clean and well ventilated, with mesh over windows and doors to help with pest control. All foodstuffs must be stored away from the floor and be rotated on a first in and first out basis.

# PREPARING, COOKING AND STORING FOOD SAFELY

Frozen food should be defrosted in a refrigerator and treated as fresh food with the same use by date. All root vegetables must be washed prior to peeling and then rewashed after peeling. Leaf vegetables such as cabbage and spinach should be washed in several changes of cold water to allow soil and grit to go to the bottom of the sink. Ideally a separate preparation area should be facilitated to help prevent cross-contamination.

Chilling food not for immediate use should ideally be achieved in blast chillers where the core temperature is brought down from 70°C to 4°C in 90 minutes or less. With these temperature ranges both pathogenic and bacterial growth is inhibited although not completely stopped.

If food that has been cooked is not for immediate consumption, or is to be frozen, it should be well covered with cling film or ideally vacuum packed to create an airtight barrier and prevent freezer burn. Storage should be within manufacturer's guidelines and the foods must be clearly labelled as previously mentioned.

### CHEF'S TIP

The correct measurement of temperature should be monitored by the use of an accurate digital food thermometer. The probe is inserted into the centre of meat joints or placed onto the surface of other ingredients to give a temperature reading within a few seconds. Alcohol-based sanitiser wipes should be used to clean the stainless steel probe after every use to prevent cross-contamination.

# AREAS WHERE HAZARDS MIGHT OCCUR

| STEP | HAZARD | CONTROL |
| --- | --- | --- |
| Receipt of goods | ■ Contaminated high-risk foods<br>■ Damaged or decomposed goods<br>■ Incorrect specifications<br>■ Growth of pathogens between the time of receipt and storage | ■ All deliveries inspected and checked by a staff member<br>■ Appropriate labelling<br>■ Prompt and correct storage |
| Storage | ■ Contamination of high-risk foods<br>■ Contamination through poor handling<br>■ Contamination by pests<br>■ Spoilage of food by decomposition | ■ Correct usage of refrigeration regimes<br>■ Foods must be suitably stored in the correct packaging or receptacles<br>■ Materials that are in direct contact with food must be of food-grade quality<br>■ A contract for a pest control service must be in place<br>■ Correct stock rotation<br>■ Out of date and unfit food stuffs must be segregated from other foods and removed from the premises |
| Preparation | ■ Contamination of high-risk foods<br>■ Contamination through poor handling<br>■ Growth of pathogens and toxins | ■ Keep raw and cooked foods separate<br>■ Use pasteurised eggs for raw and lightly cooked egg dishes<br>■ All food contact surfaces must be fit for purpose<br>■ Food handlers must be trained in hygienic food handling techniques<br>■ Keep the exposure of fresh foods at ambient temperatures to a minimum<br>■ Label all food that is to be used more than one day in advance of production with its description and use by date |
| Cooking | ■ Survival of pathogens and spores | ■ Cook all foods to the minimum recommended temperature |
| Chilling | ■ Growth of pathogens, spores = toxin production<br>■ Contamination | ■ Cool foods as quickly as possible, to 8°C in 90 minutes<br>■ Keep food that is chilling loosely covered<br>■ Use only clean equipment |

| STEP | HAZARD | CONTROL |
|---|---|---|
| Hot hold | ■ Growth of pathogens and toxin production<br>■ Contamination by staff and customers, especially in self-service operations | ■ Maintain food at 63°C and discard after 2 hours<br>■ Keep containers covered when not in service<br>■ Use sneeze screens<br>■ Supervise self-service |
| Cold hold | ■ Growth of pathogens and toxin production<br>■ Contamination by staff and customers especially in self-service operations | ■ Keep food at 5°C and discard after 4 hours<br>■ Keep containers covered when not in service<br>■ Use sneeze screens<br>■ Supervise self-service |

## Assessment of knowledge and understanding

You have now learned about the health and hygiene responsibilities for everyone in the workplace. This will enable you to ensure your own work areas, food preparation, cookery and service actions reduce risks in health.

To test your level of knowledge and understanding, answer the following short questions. These will help to prepare you for your summative (final) assessment.

1 State the food safety hazards that wearing jewellery can cause.

_____

2 Identify who health hazards are reported to.

_____

3 Identify the importance of reporting illnesses quickly and the significance of stomach illnesses.

_____

4 State three reasons why work surfaces and chopping boards should be clean and hygienic.

i) _____  ii) _____

iii) _____

5 Explain the reason for regular maintenance checks.

_____

6 Explain the importance of storing food at the correct temperature.

_____

7 Describe the term 'stock rotation'.

_____

## Research Task A

Carry out a HACCP assessment on the following products. Consider the hazard, the critical control point and the action to be taken.

(a)  Fresh raw poultry _____

(b)  Fresh fruit and vegetables _____

# 4

# Investigate the catering and hospitality industry

**UNIT 201**

1. **Demonstrate knowledge of the hospitality and catering sector**
2. **Demonstrate knowledge of national and international employment opportunities in the catering industry**

## LEARNING OBJECTIVES

At the end of this chapter you will be able to:

■ Understand the terms 'hospitality' and 'catering'

■ Compare the sectors and different types of operations in the industry

■ Describe the main features of establishments within the different sectors

■ Identify staffing structures and job roles in different establishments

■ Identify training opportunities, related qualifications and employment rights and responsibilities

■ List some of the associations related to professional cookery

# HOSPITALITY AND CATERING

**CHEF'S TIP**

The hospitality sector as a whole currently employs in the region of 1.9 million people across the UK.

The hospitality and catering, leisure, travel and tourism sector covers the following 14 industries:

| | | | |
|---|---|---|---|
| 1 | Hotels | 8 | Events |
| 2 | Restaurants | 9 | Gambling |
| 3 | Pubs | 10 | Travel services |
| 4 | Bars and nightclubs | 11 | Tourist services |
| 5 | Contract food service providers | 12 | Visitor attractions |
| 6 | Hospitality services | 13 | Hostels |
| 7 | Membership clubs | 14 | Holiday centres and self catering accommodation. |

Each operation is unique, but each has in common the provision of food and drink and/or accommodation. A large number of people are employed in core hospitality occupations such as chefs, kitchen assistants, reception staff, food service and bar staff. The main industries employing the majority of these people are as follows:

- Travel
- Retail
- Business
- Education
- Healthcare
- Corporate and executive dining
- Government and local authority provision
- Leisure venues and events (concerts, sporting events, parties)
- Restaurants
- Hotels.

*The dining area of a cruise ship*

## The sectors and different types of operations within the industry

The scope for employment in this industry is huge with many career pathways available. As leisure time continues to increase so have the many venues people can visit to enjoy their free time. Theme parks, family friendly pubs, coffee shops, restaurants, major sporting events and hotels have been established to accommodate this growing trend.

The industry is broken down into two main sectors, described as the commercial sector and the catering services sector. Organisations can be categorised into the two sectors according to the main purpose and aim of the business.

*The commercial sector* – in this case, the provision of hospitality and catering is the main purpose of the organisation which aims to make a profit in return for the supply of their products and services. Examples include restaurants and hotels.

*The catering services sector* – in this case, the provision of hospitality and catering is a secondary purpose of the organisation, although the organisation may still aim to make a profit in return for the supply of their products and services. Examples include the catering supplied to employees working in a large bank or factory. In these examples, banking and production are the main purposes of the organisations and catering is supplied as a secondary feature, a 'service' to the staff employed in either of these organisations.

For example, an employer has 20 staff. The caterers quote a price of £3.50 to supply lunch for each member of staff (Total – 20 × £3.50 = £70.00). As a perk (benefit) to the staff, the employer contributes £30.00 to the caterer, reducing the total cost to £40.00. Each member staff now has a reduced (subsidised) cost to purchase their lunch (£40.00 ÷ 20 = £2.00). Each time a lunch is sold, the employee spends £2.00, the employer has contributed £1.50 and the caterer receives the £3.50 originally quoted.

# THE MAIN FEATURES OF ESTABLISHMENTS WITHIN THE DIFFERENT SECTORS

## Contract food service

Contract food service providers support a number of wider industries from hotels and restaurants to schools and airlines. Traditionally the sector has provided food and drink service but it is increasingly developing into other areas such as retail opportunities, facilities management, fine dining restaurants, vending, healthcare, school meals provision and prison catering.

An overview of the sectors within the hospitality and catering industry

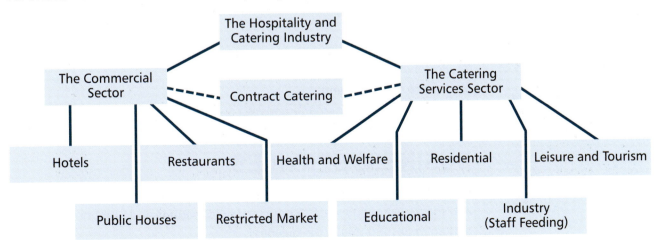

**CHEF'S TIP**

Some catering services may be subsidised by the company. A 'subsidy' is a payment by the company to keep the selling price at a low rate to individual employees

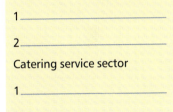

**TASK**

Identify the scope of the local industry by finding two organisations that would fall into the commercial sector and two that would fall into the catering service sector.

Commercial sector

1_____

2_____

Catering service sector

1_____

2_____

**CHEF'S TIP**

Hospital catering is sometimes classified as 'welfare catering'. The object is to assist the medical staff to get a patient back to health as soon as possible.

## Healthcare and hospitals

Healthcare homes provide accommodation, meals and personal care, but also have professional registered nurses and experienced care assistants in constant attendance. The focus is to provide a balanced nutritious diet using fresh, quality ingredients and to maintain high standards of food production and presentation. The dishes prepared can be designed to include the requests of residents. The residents may also choose to eat a meal in the home's dining room or, if they prefer, in the comfort of their own room.

In many hospitals the patients are provided with a daily menu choice of breakfast, lunch and supper. This is usually ordered a day in advance. Dieticians are employed to liaise with the head chef or catering manager to help plan each menu, to design specialised diets for individual patients and to help introduce diet conscious recipes and advice to patients.

Dining area at the Ritz hotel

# HOTELS

It is estimated that there are over 12,000 individual hotels in the UK. With the addition of smaller hotels and guest houses the total is probably nearer 30,000. The structure of hotels is defined into the following categories:

- Budget hotels
- Bed and breakfast accommodation (guest houses)
- One star
- Two star
- Three star
- Four star
- Five star (luxury).

Large hotel chains generally have the market share of business and comprise the majority of hotels found across the world today. Aside from food and drink service where chefs, kitchen assistants and service staff are required, hotels will also employ staff in other specialised areas to cater for the accommodation and leisure facilities. For instance in areas such as:

- Reception
- Housekeeping
- Front office management
- Porter service
- Leisure management
- Events and banquet management.

# BUSINESS SERVICES

Because hotels are residential they will provide breakfast, lunch, tea, dinner and snacks (sometimes for 24 hours a day). Banquets and functions will also play an important role in the business.

# RESTAURANTS

The restaurant sector is the largest area in the hospitality and catering industry. This has had a steady increase of turnover and it is estimated that there are over 65,000 restaurants in the UK.

Restaurants can be classified by their origin of cuisine; European, North American, Asian, Oriental, Central and South American. The restaurant industry is broken down into four different segments:

- Fast food establishments
- Cafes and coffee shops
- Mainstream restaurants
- Fine dining restaurants

# PUBLIC HOUSES, BARS AND CLUBS

A high proportion of the industry's workforce is employed on a part-time basis. In this sector custom tends to be concentrated into a short number of hours (evenings and weekends) so the amount of staff needed in peak hours is considerably higher than at quieter times. A relatively high proportion of this workforce describe their employment as casual, many of whom may be working in the industry while studying.

Public houses and bars provide alcoholic and non-alcoholic beverages. They are increasingly also providing snacks or food through a restaurant service. There are many similarities between a bar and a public house, but the most obvious factor is the style and ambience. One way to segment the sector has been to look at ownership:

- **Managed houses** – include those which are owned by a brewery and employ salaried staff who manage and work in the outlet.
- **Tenanted or leased pubs** – are owned by a brewery but are occupied by licensees who pay rent to the brewery and agree to take their supply of beer and alcohol from them.
- **Freehouses** – are owned and managed by the licensee and deal with a number of different suppliers and brewers.

Nightclubs are establishments where the primary offer is that of dancing to music and where drink and food are offered as a secondary service (or where there is a legal requirement to do so).

Bars can obviously be found in other sectors, such as hotels and restaurants and other areas, such as sports grounds.

*Food signs at a theme park*

# VISITOR ATTRACTIONS

The visitor attraction industry is small in terms of establishments, employment and turnover. However, popular visitor attractions that attract high numbers of visitors are vital to local economies.

- Theme parks and gardens
- Sporting locations (e.g. football stadium)
- Museums
- Other attractions – including theatres.

Usually there will be some form of food and drink provision from vending facilities to restaurants, some of which may be sub-contracted out to the catering services industry.

# QUALIFICATIONS, TRAINING AND EXPERIENCE WITHIN THE INDUSTRY

## Staffing structures and job roles

Organisations, regardless of their size will have a staffing structure, with members of staff performing different job roles that contribute to the overall aims of the organisation.

Organisations range from individuals working by themselves to very large companies with thousands of employees.

Staffing structures can be divided into three main categories. These are as follows:

*Operational staff* – Operational staff are the employees who perform the everyday practical operations. They are the staff who cook the food and serve the customers, clean the bedrooms and public areas and generally provide the services that customers expect from the organisation.

*Supervisory staff* – Supervisory staff are generally more experienced than operational staff. They will oversee the work and performance of operational staff and deal with any day-to-day issues as they arise. Supervisory staff should also provide a first point of call for operational staff if they have a problem that they need help with.

*Management staff* – Managers have responsibility for ensuring that the organisation is performing well, that suitably trained staff are employed and customers receive the products and services they expect. Managers have many other responsibilities including planning for the future, managing finance and ensuring health and safety policies and employment laws are followed.

CHEF'S TIP

In the case of the smaller organisations, it is likely that individuals will have to perform a wide variety of roles as all operational (and management) requirements have to be completed by a few people. In larger organisations, job roles are likely to be more specific as many people are working towards the aims of the organisation and the breakdown of roles can be more detailed.

CHEF'S TIP

Depending on the size of the organisation, managers often perform supervisory and operational roles. As organisations become larger that managers perform these tasks on a less frequent basis, or perhaps never at all.

Examples of staff in a medium to large kitchen operation would be:

*Manager* – Head Chef (In larger organisations, sometimes referred to as the executive head chef).

*Supervisor/s* – Sous chef (second chef); Chef de partie (Section chefs).

*Operational* – Commis chefs; Apprentices.

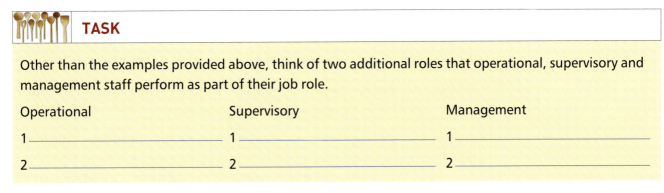

**TASK**

Other than the examples provided above, think of two additional roles that operational, supervisory and management staff perform as part of their job role.

| Operational | Supervisory | Management |
|---|---|---|
| 1 _____ | 1 _____ | 1 _____ |
| 2 _____ | 2 _____ | 2 _____ |

Staffing structures of a large city centre hotel

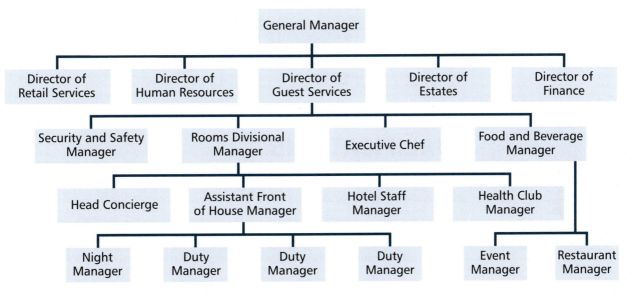

# Training opportunities, related qualifications and employment rights and responsibilities

Working in the hospitality industry and particularly as a chef is a never ending learning opportunity. There is always more to learn with constant innovation from very talented chefs from around the world. The innovative ways in which to work with new commodities and applying different approaches and techniques can make working in the industry an interesting and personally rewarding experience.

As someone entering the industry without any, or very much, experience, the training opportunities are vast and varied. The following describes some of the ways in which training is provided:

*On the job* – this refers to bite size, regular chunks, of training that is provided while at work. Occasionally, short courses (e.g. one or two days) may be provided to learn about specific aspects of the job – health and safety and food hygiene, for example.

*College based* – most colleges in the UK offer courses and qualifications in hospitality and catering. This provides the opportunity for students to learn about the industry and develop skills in an educational environment. There are also opportunities to learn other subjects and improve other skills such as the use of language, number and IT.

*Training providers* – work in conjunction with employers and perform the assessment of skills for apprentices in the workplace.

*E-learning* – although it may be considered more difficult to learn skills through IT based resources, modern materials are being produced with a very interactive and personalised approach. The streaming of video-based material also makes it possible for learners to review material at their own pace.

*Work placement* – a placement provides a controlled period of time when there is a great opportunity to observe the way in which an organisation operates and performs tasks.

# QUALIFICATIONS

There are many qualifications designed for people working or aspiring to work in the catering and hospitality industry. For trainee chefs, there are vocational (career based) qualifications that are designed to meet the current needs of the industry. The two main routes, although there are others, are the NVQ (National Vocational Qualification) and the Diploma qualification.

NVQs are designed as an assessment based qualification in which candidates prove their competence (capability and knowledge) against a range of tasks. For example, it will take a period of time before a developing chef will be able to fillet a fish correctly and accurately. However, after a period of practising, his or her skills and confidence will improve to a point where an assessment of the skill can take place. Successful assessments build up until sufficient skills and knowledge have been gained for the student to be awarded the overall qualification.

Diplomas have been designed as a college-based qualification. There is much more emphasis on teaching and learning in comparison to the assessment based NVQ. All candidates enrolled on a Diploma in Professional Cookery will follow the same programme, completing the same theoretical and practical tasks. Individuals will also receive a final grade for each unit to highlight areas of high achievement.

Attached to college-based qualifications and the apprenticeship framework are key skills. Key skills are seen as an important addition to vocational qualifications as they are intended to improve the functional skills of individuals. The main key skills are in the areas of communication (written, spoken, body language, etc.), the application of number (use of number in vocational contexts) and IT. These additional skills are seen as vital additional attributes to individuals at work, making them more employable and increasing potential promotion opportunities in the future.

As well as main qualification aims, as described above, there are many short courses that people working in the industry may take to increase their knowledge in specific areas. Examples include short courses in health and safety, food safety, communication and the certificate for personal licence holders.

Qualifications are also written at different levels to enable individuals to build on their existing skills and knowledge.

NVQs and VRQs in Food Preparation and Cooking/Professional Cookery are written at levels 1, 2 and 3. This intends to develop skills and knowledge from a broad and sound base to a refinement of skills as candidates move from one level to the next.

There are also academic (more scholarly/less practical) qualifications written for the hospitality and catering industry. Such qualifications usually take a broader view of the industry from a more business oriented perspective. Qualifications and courses along this route range from level 1 through to Foundation, Bachelors and Masters Degrees.

# EMPLOYMENT RIGHTS AND RESPONSIBILITIES

Employers and employees have certain rights and responsibilities.

Employers must supply a job description and contract of employment, detailing the following:

- Contracted working hours, and
- Holiday entitlement.

They must also provide a healthy and safe working environment.

Employees must:

- Work to the conditions as described in their job description and contract of employment, and
- Follow organisational policies.

They must also follow health and safety working practices, including food safety.

## Some of the associations related to professional cookery

- The Academy of Culinary Arts
- The Association Culinaire Française
- The Craft Guild of Chefs
- Euro Toques
- Craft Guild of Chefs and Master Craftsmen of Great Britain
- PACE (Professional Association of Catering Education)
- HCIMA (Hotel, Catering, International Management Association).

## Assessment of knowledge and understanding

You have now learned about the different sectors of the industry. The hospitality, leisure, travel and tourism sector is an important sector across the whole of the United Kingdom, in terms of employment and economic output. In most cases it is seen as a priority sector.

To test your level of knowledge and understanding, answer the following short questions.

## Hospitality and catering

1  Describe the term 'hospitality'.
2  Describe the term 'catering'.
3  Explain the difference between 'commercial' and 'service' sectors.

## Hospitality and catering establishments

Explain the difference in menus between the following catering/hospitality operations:

- Healthcare home
- Guest house
- Restaurant
- Large city bank.

## Research task

Explain the types of qualifications that may be required for the following job roles:

- Head chef
- Commis chef
- Waiter
- Bar manager.

# 5
# Kitchen operations, costs and menu planning

## LEARNING OBJECTIVES

The aim of this chapter is to enable the candidate to acquire basic knowledge relating to kitchen organisation and the principles of menu planning. It discusses the awareness of costing dishes, the elements of cost control within the kitchen and calculating selling prices.

At the end of this chapter you will be able to:

- Illustrate the kitchen organisation
- Plan menus and dishes for a variety of catering operations
- Understand about the related associated costs within the catering industry
- Apply basic calculations used in the costing of dishes and menus

# THE IMPORTANCE OF THE DESIGN OF THE KITCHEN

The primary area of a kitchen will include the storage section where raw foods and products are stored and cold rooms and freezers are positioned. Part of this area is also the positioning of a separate entrance for the arrival and checking of supplies. This department has to be spacious and equipped with a control office, a waste goods zone and an area for employees.

The equipment used in this department will vary according to the size of the establishment and the type of products used. There should always be a large and small set of accurate scales, loading trolleys, stainless steel tables for the temporary placing of supplies and close access to refrigeration and freezer space.

It is in the primary area that the first and most important check of purchased ingredients and supplies is made. This activity should be a thorough and methodical approach to checking the quality, quantity, temperature, packaging and freshness of the supplies being delivered. Ideally, an area required for unpacking is required to remove packaging and dispose of it in an environmentally acceptable manner.

The stores area should be attached to this department with enough space to allow for the correct storage of non-perishable goods. The space has to be divided sensibly in the following manner:

■ General store

■ Drinks store (with refrigeration available)

■ Chemical and cleaning store.

Separate but in an adjacent area perishable foods such as fruit, vegetables, dairy, fish, meat and poultry products should be stored.

Shelving systems should be well divided, easily cleaned and fixed properly to avoid collapsing. Other issues to consider for the safe storage are:

1 Store all products away from direct sunlight to prevent condensation from building up, or loss of colour in certain products.
2 All products should be stored away from outside walls to avoid problems with contamination and humidity.
3 Tinned foods should be stored in a dry place to avoid the formation of rust.
4 All products should be maintained at an even temperature and sudden changes in temperature should be avoided.

The areas dedicated to employees are an important factor. It is advisable to have a separate entrance to the kitchen or the food delivery zone because of possible contamination threats. It is also advisable to have separate toilets and changing areas for females and males to avoid employees using the facilities for customers.

The secondary area is the preparation zone. In an ideal design, this would be situated immediately adjacent to the primary sector and is the most important area because this is where the preparation of several prime ingredient categories such as meat, poultry, vegetables, fish, dairy products and fruits takes place. Sometimes, with large catering outlets such as hospitals, airport terminals and canteens, the space given to this area is large and all preparation zones can be installed in a line to help with the work flow.

To adhere to current regulations separate working areas are required for different ingredients such as meat, fish and vegetables. Therefore within one area certain blocks of preparation tables and equipment should be divided for single use.

CHEF'S TIP

Keep all raw meat areas separate and include separate equipment and refrigeration zones to deter cross contamination.

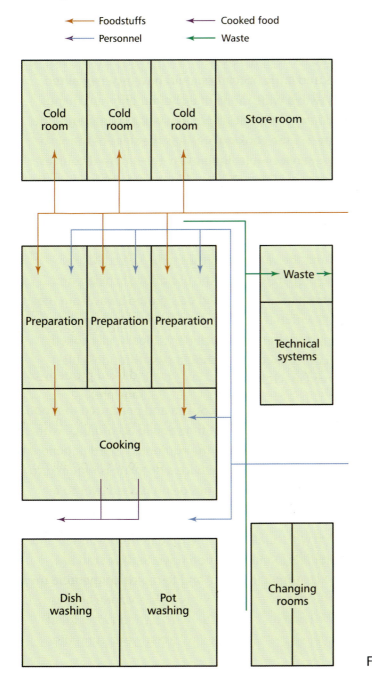

Figure 5.1

The importance of separating the preparation areas cannot be under estimated. If there is a separate bakery or pastry kitchen it should be located in an area furthest away from the cooking zone, as the preparation of bakery and pastry products is always delicate and it is necessary to take into account the ambient heat, odours from the cooking area and the likelihood of cross contamination.

The waste zone needs to be accessible from all the preparation zones, as well as from the cooking and dishwashing areas. It is important that it is positioned in a place whose access is not via the cooking area or the kitchen office.

The ideal position for the cooking area is immediately after the preparation section. Access to this area must be simple, without obstacles or additional sections placed in between the preparation area and the cooking area. The equipment for this zone, and its design, rely heavily on the type of service to be carried out. Restaurants and large hotels generally have a personalised service for their customers with a wide range of dishes on different menus. There may also be a banqueting service available that will also influence the design of this area. In Figure 5.1 the cooking area has the sides of the cooking block vertical to the service table. In this way the different courses can be divided into separate cooking sections within the area. A functional cooking range (stove) is required to meet the needs of the chef, the brigade and the speed of service. Particular attention should be given to the type of cooking ranges required, and the right choice at this stage will greatly enhance the final product and the variety of dishes to be served. Closely linked to the cooking of the prepared food is the use of blast chillers and possibly vacuum-packing machines. This should be situated away from the main cooking range but still within the cooking area to facilitate workflow and the usage of these important items of machinery.  Ideally, all cooked foods, blanched foods and precooked foods should pass through a blast chiller before being conserved in a refrigerator.

Another key area is the service counter. Once cooked and presented the food has to be taken to the customer in the briefest time and in accordance with hygiene standards. The delivery methods and the equipment used depend on the type and style of food service. For waiter service a hotplate is required to help maintain the core temperature of hot dishes being passed over to a service team to serve to customers.

A self-service counter system will usually have the food items portioned and presented in hot display cabinets in multi-portion trays. Service staff are typically on hand to aid the customer in choice and to replenish the food on a regular basis.

*A hotplate in a kitchen for a restaurant service*

*A hotplate in a self service area*

# CATERING OPERATIONS

There are different catering operations that serve food and drink to customers in a number of diverse ways. Dependant on the needs and requirements of the customer or guest the facility of service is always determined. Each operation has its own workflow organisation but there are certain elements that should remain constant throughout the different operations:

- Effective communication between departments
- Increased efficiency
- Accident prevention
- Promotion of good health, safety and food safety practice
- The provision of an effective service to the customer
- High-quality end product.

## Hospitals and Healthcare Homes

Hospital catering is usually classified as welfare catering. The service of food is of great importance to hospital patients and residents of healthcare homes. Good-quality food can help to increase health, and certainly creates a sense of well-being.

Carefully prepared, cooked and presented food can be served directly to the patient or within a restaurant area. The workflow element of this particular service is sometimes problematic because wards can be spread over a wide area in large hospitals and long distances are required for the food to travel.

Dietary constraints must be particularly adhered to and clear information about the type of food or meal to be served to individuals should be communicated effectively.

## Hotels

Hotels will generally provide breakfast, luncheon, afternoon teas, dinners, room service, banquets and bar snacks. In large hotels there may be satellite kitchens to help prepare and serve food quickly and efficiently for banquets and room service. The careful preparation of food is essential for a busy service so that orders can be executed quickly and efficiently. With the wealth of different services required for a hotel operation, the planning of work and mise-en-place needs to be accurate and clearly communicated to the different teams as the requirements of the day ahead.

## Restaurants

There are many different types of restaurants that can be privately owned, part of a larger company (such as a hotel) or part of a chain. Therefore they

### CHEF'S TIP

In many hospitals a qualified dietitian is responsible for designing and supervising special diets and instruction of the preparation of special dishes. They may even assist in the training of chefs and cooks with regard to food nutrition and specialist dietary products.

will vary with the style of food that is served and often serve luncheon and dinner, although some restaurants will open for breakfast and afternoon tea. The introduction of electronic booking, ordering and cash register systems are designed to mimic the workflow of a typical sit-down restaurant operation. This helps the restaurant plan the next service according to set timings so that the chefs will know when the busy period of service will be.

## Contract Catering Services

The provision of staff dining rooms and corporate dining is a large part of the catering and hospitality industry. There are diverse systems of service employed to ensure the clients and customers are satisfied and therefore more productive within their own aspect of work. Staff restaurants serving breakfast, luncheon and sometimes a dinner service are required together with retail facilities, coffee shops, vending operations, banquets and conference dining. Once again the kitchen workflow system needs to be flexible enough to cope with the diversity of operations that are provided throughout the day.

## School Meals

Schools have traditionally provided a lunchtime meal for children up to and including the secondary school age, and this has been a statutory requirement of local education authorities since the early 1940s. Due to various economic changes some local education authorities have contracted out of this provision and have introduced contract catering companies to provide a food and lunchtime service to schools.

Many schools now offer a multi-choice menu with an emphasis recently placed on healthy eating and health conscious choices. Other schools now offer a healthy breakfast service in addition to their luncheon service. Generally, the service style is counter service with school cooks and kitchen assistants serving the food to the students and school staff. Due to the timetabled constraints of an educational establishment a quick and efficient service is required so that the school can return to teaching and learning at a set time.

# TRADITIONAL KITCHEN HIERARCHY

Many kitchens have different organisational kitchen teams with varying structures afforded them. Mainly this is due to the complexity of the menu, style of the food presented on the menu and the system which is used to prepare, cook and present the menu dishes.

Establishments that provide a limited menu are able to organise a small team to serve a large number of customers. The required standard can be produced because limited skills may be required to produce dishes on the menu; however an organised and systematic workflow is important to the success of these businesses to ensure speed of service.

Auguste Escoffier (1846–1935) was a French chef, restaurateur and culinary writer who fashioned and updated traditional French classical cookery methods. He is a legendary figure among chefs and gourmets, and was one of the most important leaders in the development of modern French cuisine. Much of Escoffier's technique was based on that of Antoine Carême (1784–1833), the founder of French *haute cuisine*. Escoffier's achievement was to simplify and modernise Carême's elaborate style. Alongside the recipes he recorded and invented, another of Escoffier's contributions to cooking was to elevate it to the status of a respected profession, and to introduce discipline and structure to a kitchen brigade. He organised his kitchens using the brigade system, with each section run by a chef de partie. He also replaced the practice of service à la française (serving all dishes at once) with service à la russe (serving each dish in the order printed on the menu).

An example of a traditional kitchen brigade based on Escoffier's design is seen in the diagram below.

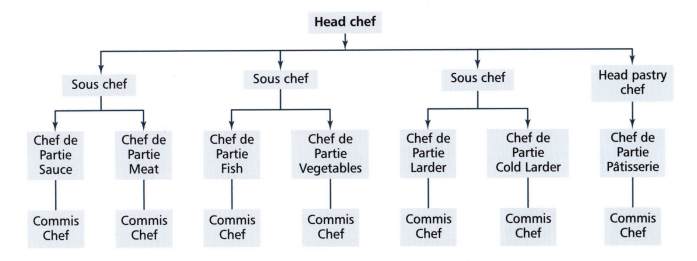

# Head Chef *(Chef de Cuisine)*

The role of the Head Chef has grown in recent years in an administrative context. Sometimes known as an Executive Chef, the role of the Head Chef is extensive and can incorporate more duties than those listed below:

- Kitchen organisation, staff work rota
- Menu writing
- Food and resource ordering
- Cost and budget control
- Training (in liaison with the HR Department)
- Kitchen supervision

- Implementation of food hygiene and health and safety policies
- Equipment purchase and maintenance
- Team management
- Effective communication with guests, clients, kitchen brigade and other departments.

## Second Chef *(Sous Chef)*

The Sous Chef relieves the Head Chef as and when required. The primary function of this role is to supervise the work in the kitchen team that is attributed to each Sous Chef. In large kitchen brigades there will be Sous Chefs with specific responsibility for separate services such as banquets and room service. The supervision of all health and safety and food hygiene aspects, in conjunction with quality control and line managing a team of chefs, is an integral part of the Sous Chef's role.

## Head Pastry Chef *(Chef Pâtissier)*

The position of the Head Pastry Chef is equivalent to that of the Sous Chef, although because of the delicate and specialised nature of this department they often operate with a diverse team of specialists such as a baker *(boulanger)*, ice cream chef *(glacier)* and a decorative chef *(chef décor)* who specialises in chocolate, ice carving and sugar display work.

## Chef de Partie

The Chefs de Partie are in charge of their own sections within the kitchen. These can comprise:
- Sauce section *(saucier)*
- Meat section *(rôtisseur)*
- Fish section *(poissonier)*
- Vegetable section *(l'entremettier)*
- Cold larder section *(garde-manger)*
- Larder/butchery section *(boucher)*
- Pastry section *(pâtissier)*
- Relief chef *(chef tournant)*.

*A busy kitchen*

## Commis Chef

These are the first chefs of the kitchen brigade. They are responsible for the set day-to-day tasks in accordance with standard operating procedures as determined by the Head Chef. Sometimes in large establishments there will be different levels of Commis Chef ranging from First Commis, Second Commis, Commis and Apprentice Chef.

## Other Kitchen-Based Positions

There are many other important positions that have a significant role to play in the kitchen team. These can be as follows:

- Staff cook *(chef communard)*
- Breakfast Chef *(chef de petit déjeuner)*
- Kitchen clerk *(l'aboyeur)*
- Kitchen porters *(garçons de cuisine or plongeur)*
- Stores *(l'economat).*

It is essential that good communication and relationships are formed within the kitchen brigade to help the efficiency of the operation. It will also create a pleasant environment in which to work, which will in turn benefit the customer service and improve the productivity of staff.

# PLANNING A MENU

The word 'menu' as it relates to food is first found in print in 1718 in French. The *Oxford English Dictionary* (2nd edition) confirms the English word menu was borrowed from the French. However menu can be traced to the Latin word *minutus* which means a detailed list.

From the early 1770s, the use of a printed menu in restaurants that allowed each customer to choose his or her own dish marked another innovation in food service. Before the emergence of the restaurant, a menu had always been a list of all those foods to be served during a particular meal, such as a banquet. Until this point all the food served on a *table d'hôte* (table of the day) had no menu and all of the food arrived together at the same time. The restaurant's role as a place for the service of food and drink, however, necessitated a new sense of the menu: the creation of a list of available items from which each customer made personal choices in sequence at the most convenient moment.

When forming a restaurant menu, the chef has produced a highly individualistic set of dishes, differentiating themselves from the other restaurants nearby. By the mere presence of a menu, the restaurant's style of service demanded a degree of self-definition. Restaurants had printed menus because they offered their customers a choice of unseen dishes. However, another concept was that the printed menu allowed restaurateurs to calculate costs of individual dishes and set fixed prices and dish descriptions to customers.

Today's menu is an important communication method from the caterer to the customer. It is a legal requirement for restaurants to display menus that clearly inform customers about the price and other inclusions, such as the addition of VAT (Value Added Tax) and any service charges that are applied.

**LUNCH MENU**
Wednesday
6th September 2006

**CÊP**
Roasted cêps with cauliflower cassonade,
cêp ravioli and cauliflower purée

Or

**COCO BEAN**
Chilled coco bean soup with poached chicken
and coco bean mousse

**SEA BASS**
Roasted fillet of sea bass, celeriac fondant
puy lentils, bacon and langoustine emulsion

Or

**PORK**
Roasted loin of pork with black pudding,
glazed pork belly and rosemary sauce

**APPLE**
Poached apple with vanilla tapioca
and apple granité

Or

**CHEESE**
From our lunch selection of French cheeses

**COFFEE AND PETIT FOURS**
A selection of tea, coffee and tisanes

**LUNCH MENU**          £29.00 inclusive of VAT

Optional 12.5% service charge will be added to your bill

*A table d'hôte lunch menu*

# Types of menus

There are various types of menus that are used in restaurants, hotels, hospitals, schools and contract food service outlets.

1 À la carte. This is a menu with individually priced dishes so that the customer can select a series of particular dishes to compile their own menu of choice. In the true sense of the term a dish from the à la carte menu should be cooked to order, although with new technology and skilled chefs in today's kitchen most menus will be cooked to order.

2 Table d'hôte. This is a set menu with a set price. There may be a choice of dishes available for each course but it is not compulsory. Usually there are two, three or four different courses to this type of menu.

## LES SPECIALITES

Smoked Scottish Salmon £12.50    Melon £9.75    Dressed Crab £13.50

Omelette "Arnold Bennett" £9.75    Oeuf Poché Bénédictine £8.50
Oeufs en Cocotte aux deux Caviars £9.50    Pea and Ham Soup £6.50

## LES PLATS DU JOUR

### . . . AT DINNER . . .

MONDAY
Pot Roasted Veal "Bonne Femme" £17.75

TUESDAY
Fillet of Beef "Wellington" £17.00

WEDNESDAY
Honey Baked Ham with Creamed Spinach £15.95

THURSDAY
Roast Sirloin of Beef "Marchand de Vin" £18.50

FRIDAY
Roast Norfolk Duck cooked with
Almond and Apples £15.50

SATURDAY
Roast Sirloin of Beef and Vegetable Casserole £18.50

The above "plats du jour" include Chef's choice of vegetables

## LES GRILLADES

Sirloin Steak £17.50    Fillet Steak £18.50    Mixed Grill £17.50

Lamb Kidneys with Bacon £14.50

Lamb Cutlets £16.50    Châteaubriand (2 cvts.) £39.50

## LES LEGUMES À LA CARTE

Les Pommes £3.50
Dauphinoise, Nouvelles au Cumin, Sautées, Berny

Les Légumes £3.75
Haricots Verts, Mange Tout, Carottes Glacées
Epinards Palace, Brocoli Milanaise, Céleris Braisés

## HORS D'ŒUVRE

Chicken Liver Pâté with Tomato Chutney £8.75

La Salade de Langoustines aux Epices £14.85
*(Salad of rocket leaves, Dublin Bay prawns and Chiriso sausage with a spiced dressing)*

La Salade de Bresaola et Pecorino £9.50
*(Salad of bresaola dried salt beef, with rocket leaves, Pecorino cheese and truffle oil)*

## LES POTAGES

Le Consommé de Volaille aux Truffes et Céleri Rave £6.50
*(Chicken consommé with truffle, celery and pistache dumplings)*

## LES POISSONS

La Sole Meunière ou Grillée £18.95    Les Goujons de Sole aux Fruits de Bois £18.25
*(Butter-fried or grilled Dover sole)*    *(Sautéed fillets of sole with wild mushrooms)*

## LES ENTREES

Le Sauté d'Agneau "Niçoise" £16.25    Les Ris de Veau poêlés "Marquise" £14.25
*(Pan-fried loin of lamb on Provence style vegetables)*    *(Braised sweetbreads with Savoy cabbage and onions)*

Le Tournedos de Boeuf Rossini £18.20    L'Escalope de Veau Holstein £16.90
*(Pan-fried beef fillet topped with foie gras)*    *(Pan-fried breaded escalope with a fried egg and anchovies)*

## LES DESSERTS ET FROMAGES

La Sélection de Notre Chef Pâtissier £5.90
Les Fromages Variés £5.90

*An à la carte menu*

*Consommé Solange*

\*\*\*

*Grilled Split Herring Ecossaise*
*(coated in butter and oatmeal, with mustard sauce and lemon)*

\*\*\*

*Omelette Tonkinoise*
*(with creamed crabmeat and chopped spring onion)*

\*\*\*

**Canton Chicken Curry**
*(chicken leg in a hot ginger curry sauce with saffron rice, condiments, poppadums and Bombay duck)*

\*\*\*

*Grilled Lamb Loin Chops*
*(with mushrooms and grilled tomato)*

\*\*\*

*Garden Peas*          *Frittered Egg Plant*

*French Fried and Boiled New Potatoes*

\*\*\*

**Blackcurrant Sponge Pudding with Custard Sauce**

\*\*\*

*Tutti Frutti Semolina Milk Pudding*

*A hospital menu*

3 Hospital menus. These usually consist of a limited choice written onto a card that is filled in by the patient indicating their choice on the day prior to receiving the ordered dishes. Usually the menu choice consists of two or three different courses with dietary options available. Hospitals will usually cater for special dietary requirements on the grounds of religion, vegetarianism and allergies.

### Daily Sample Menu

#### Breakfast
Fruit Juice, Grapefruit Segments, Prunes
Selection of fresh fruit, Yoghurts, Cereals
Porridge with Maple Syrup

*Or*

Full English Breakfast

Toast and Preserves
Tea or Coffee
***

#### Morning Coffee
Triple Chocolate and Hazelnut Cookies
***

#### Lunch
Pea and Sweet Basil Chowder

*Or*

Florida Cocktail

Coq Au Vin

*Or*

Devilled Mackerel with Mint and Tomato Salsa

*Or*

Tempura of Vegetables Shezuan

Sauté Potatoes
Cheddar Crushed Potatoes
Panache of Seasonal Fresh Vegetables
***

#### Afternoon Tea
Selection of Home Made cakes
***

#### Supper
Cinnamon Chicken and Apricot Cous Cous

*Or*

Wensleydale Caramelised Onion Bagel

Fresh Fruit Salad and Ice Cream

*Or*

Blackcurrant Sponge Pudding and Guinness Laced Custard

*A healthcare menu*

4 Healthcare menus. With residential healthcare homes, the dining experience has to be a pleasant, social experience to look forward to and be enjoyed by all. Menus are generally comprised of fresh and seasonal foods which are nutritious, flavoursome and balanced. The dishes need to reflect the likes and requests of residents and include a varied choice.

# Menu 1

## Autumn/Winter 2006/2007

Weeks Commencing 4th Sept, 25th Sept, 16th Oct, 13th Nov, 4th Dec, 8th Jan, 29th Jan, 26th Feb, 19th Mar.

| Monday | Tuesday | Wednesday | Thursday | Friday |
|---|---|---|---|---|
| Crumb Coated Haddock Grill | Home-made Red Onion & Cheddar Quiche | Home-made Neopolitan Pasta | Roasted Chicken Fillet | Home-made Cheese & Tomato Pizza |
| Cheesy Wrap Stacks | Pork Sausages | Home-made Chicken Nuggets | Home-made Sweet Potato & Lentil Korma | BBQ Chicken Drumstick |
| Shepherds Pie | Home-made Chicken & Tomato Pasta | Home-made Meat Pie | Home-made Moussaka | Home-made Salmon & Broccoli Pasta |
| Potato Smiles | Home-made Potato Wedges | Potato Lyonnaise | Baked Potatoes | Tri-Coloured Pasta |
| Mashed Potato | New Potatoes | Mashed Potato | Rice | New Potatoes |
| Baked Beans | Fresh Broccoli | Peas | Sweetcorn | Baby Carrots |
| Sweetcorn | Fresh Cauliflower | Fresh White Cabbage | Fresh Curly Kale | Green Beans |
| Chocolate & Orange Sponge & Custard | Sultana Cake & Custard | Fruit Ice Smoothies | Cherry Slice & Custard | Apple & Date Flapjack & Custard |

Each day a meal consists of one item from each row, i.e. a main course, potato, rice or pasta, vegetable or salad and a dessert. Fresh Salad, Fresh Yoghurt, Fresh Fruit, Cheese & Breadsticks/Biscuits are also available daily. Wholemeal bread with spread is available in addition to these items are for those children with larger appetites. This meal aims to give the balance of nutrients required by your child but due to the nature of the items written in red the potato row may be substituted with additional vegetables or salad if your child wishes.

*A Junior school menu*

5 School menus. Recently the emphasis on healthy eating has been firmly placed onto the school menu agenda. All menus written have to be nutritionally balanced and offer suitably sized portions to give each student a healthy and nutritious lunch every day. Choices are offered and catering for vegetarianism and religious diets are commonplace. Investing in good-quality food and a balanced diet is a primary function for school caterers so that school children will benefit from the social experience of eating with others, developing a taste for different foods, and gaining confidence to make the right food choices.

| Week 1 | Monday | |
|---|---|---|
| Around the World | Kerala Style Bhuna Beef with Boiled Rice *H* | 🟠 |
| Traditional | Herb Crusted Lamb Chop with Rosemary Jus | 🟠 |
| Theatre | Shaved Breast of Turkey with Crusty Bread & Cranberry Sauce | 🟣 |
| Carvery | | |
| Dish of the Day | Three Cheese & Spring Onion Puffs *V* | 🟠 |
| Balanced Choice | Fish of the Day | 🟣 |
| Pizza – Meat/Fish | Pepperoni | |
| Pizza – Vegetarian | Vegetable *V* | |
| Pasta – Meat | Ham & Parmesan | |
| Pasta – Vegetarian | Classic Tomato *V* | |
| Potatoes | Parmentier & New | |
| Vegetables | Green Beans & Cauliflower | |
| Hot Sweet 1 | Apple Upside Down Cake | |
| Hot Sweet 2 | Plum & Apricot Pie | |

*A contract catering menu*

Key:

🟣 Low Fat      *H* Halal

🟢 Medium Fat      *V* Vegetarian

🟠 High Fat

6 Contract catering menus. Generally these are menus that are served to people at their place of work and sometimes at a subsidised price to the customer. Providing quality food for employees is an essential part of keeping them happy and motivated. Contract catering companies strive to provide innovative and high-quality solutions, developing and delivering original food and service in the workplace, schools, colleges, hospitals, leisure centres and stadia, airlines or in remote environments for specialist functions. Clients are increasingly seeking more specialised answers to their needs, and operating in different regions and cultural environments means that menus have to be adapted to suit the locality. Executive dining menus are also catered for with the finest possible executive dining facilities for boardrooms, hospitality suites and at major social events.

# Planning the menu

When providing menu choices to customers, whether in a school, restaurant, hotel or hospital, it is important to plan menus adequately. This planning will not only ensure that they are attractive and acceptable to target customers but also that other aspects receive due consideration. Effective planning and control will result in accurate and timely purchasing, the reduction of waste, a more productive operation, and better customer satisfaction through consistent quality and better service.

A series of factors need to be considered before writing a menu, including the following:

- Type of customer. Writing menus to a certain style will attract different customers but may deter others from becoming a new customer. Customer demand must be considered and traditional dishes and modern food trends need to be taken into account.
- Type of establishment. As mentioned earlier, there are a significant variety of different menus available for distinct establishments. This requires careful consideration alongside other issues such as the location of the premises.
- Pricing policy. Pricing needs to be seen as fair or considered good value if repeat custom is developed.
- Availability of commodities. If the restaurant will be aimed at a specialist market, certain commodities will need to be available throughout the year and be of a high quality. Storage may also be a factor and this will have a direct effect on the pricing of the menu.
- Equipment and space available. The correct kitchen resources should be available to be able to prepare and cook the menu effectively. The chef should be aware of potential equipment deficiencies or lack of space that may make certain dishes difficult to produce.
- Staffing. Training is important to establish a good team of kitchen and front of house staff to deliver the requirements of the menu skilfully and efficiently.
- Competition from competitors. It is important to be aware of the locality and what is offered by the competition, which should include monitoring their price and quality.
- Seasonality. Local foods in season will usually be in good supply and reasonable in price. The temperature and time of year should also be considered: dishes suitable for cold weather will prove unpopular during the summer. Special dishes for different festivals can be considered such as St Valentines Day, Christmas and Shrove Tuesday.
- Balanced menu. Avoid repetition of ingredients, flavours, colours and textures. Create a menu with variety.

# BASIC COST CONTROL

It is essential to understand the exact cost of every dish produced. To undertake this, a reliable system of cost analysis and cost information is required. The advantages of an efficient costing system will include:

■ The effective calculation of net profit made by each dish, department and the business. Preparation and cooking losses can be calculated alongside wastage percentages.

■ The disclosure of potential savings or economic measures that can result in greater cost-effectiveness.

■ Information necessary to form a sound pricing policy.

■ Facilitates the head chef to maintain budget control.

■ Maintenance of costing records for future reference or to supply quotations for special events.

■ The effective monitoring of commodity prices and potential fluctuation.

The calculation of the total cost of a specific dish involves identifying the total cost of all items that combine to make up the dish.

1 Food or material cost. These are known as variable costs because the actual cost will vary according to the volume of business, quality of food purchased, control of wastage and accurate weighing, measuring and portion control.

2 Labour. All labour costs are divided into direct and indirect costs. Direct labour costs are attributed to the wages paid to chefs, waiters, bar staff and kitchen assistants where the cost can be directly related to the income from food and drink sales. Indirect labour costs are credited to the wages paid to managers, office staff and maintenance personnel who work for all departments and therefore their costs are spread over the number of departments that have a direct income.

3 Overheads (gas, electricity, rates, servicing, advertising, rent and equipment). It is important to factor the costs of overheads into every dish because these are the 'unseen' aspects of the serving of an individual dish. An area that is sometimes overlooked is cleaning materials. It is important to understand and recognise the costs of these and to ensure that an allowance is made for them in this section.

## Gross and Net Profit

To enable the caterer to control the element of profits it is usual to express this in terms of a percentage of the selling price of a dish. There are two terms of profit that must be distinguished.

1 **Gross profit** is the difference between the cost of the food to prepare the dish and the selling price of the dish.

Selling price – Food cost = Gross profit

**2 Net profit** is the difference between the selling price of the dish and the total cost of the dish (labour, overheads and cost of food).

*Selling price – Total cost = Net profit*

The table below uses crème caramel as an example of the dish in question and how it relates to costing and profit analysis.

| | |
|---|---|
| Selling price for a crème caramel | £4.50 |
| Food cost for a crème caramel | £1.00 |
| Addition of labour and overheads | £1.50 |
| Total cost of the crème caramel | £2.50 |
| Gross profit | £3.50 |
| Net profit | £2.00 |

To determine the percentage gross profit of the crème caramel the following calculation needs to be used:

$$\frac{\textbf{Gross profit (£)}}{\textbf{Total sales (£)}} \times 100 =$$

(or)

3.50 (gross profit) × 100 ÷ 4.50 (selling price) = 77% (percentage gross profit).

To determine the percentage net profit of the crème caramel the following calculation needs to be used:

$$\frac{\textbf{Net profit (£)}}{\textbf{Total sales (£)}} \times 100 =$$

(or)

2.00 (net profit) × 100 ÷ 4.50 (selling price) = 44% (percentage net profit)

A rule that can be applied to effectively calculate the food cost price of a dish is to let the food cost of the dish equal 35 per cent and fix the selling price at 100 per cent.

For example:

**Cost of the crème caramel = 100p = 35%**

$$\textbf{Selling price} = \frac{100(p) \times 100}{35} = 285p = £2.85$$

Selling the crème caramel at £2.85 makes 65 per cent gross profit above the 35 per cent cost price.

# Six Elements to Control Food Cost

1 Ensure that you are charging the correct price for everything on your menu.
   (A) Remember to include a 40 or 50 per cent dish cost when calculating the dish cost. Calculating the cost of sauces, accompaniments such as salt, pepper, bread and butter it is surprising what these items will add up to.
   (B) The cost for commodities will rise by approximately 3–5per cent per year. If the menu is not updated every 6–12 months, this increase in cost will shorten the profit margin.

2 Complete a weekly stock take and food cost calculation.
   (A) A weekly food cost calculation should be completed. An example of this is the stock take, which should be divided into a number of different categories (dairy, meat, vegetables, fruit, dry commodities). This will be helpful if a problem arises and the food cost is too high, because the chef can quickly determine the area of the stock that was increased.
   (B) Keep in mind that when the weekly food cost total is received from the accountant, it usually does not take into account the stock take and will be based solely on food purchases.

3 Eliminate theft.
   (A) The back door is still a major area where food can disappear. There should be an alarm on this door and no employee should be allowed to exit through this door without a manager present to turn off the alarm.
   (B) Employee purses, bags and coats should be kept out of the kitchen area. This will lessen the chances of food or other products being taken.

4 Control waste
   (A) Complete rubbish bin inspections on a regular basis. At the end of a service, taking a few minutes to check through discarded food from the kitchen.

5 Portion control
   (A) Constantly check portion sizes during service. Set specifications for each dish and ensure the team knows what they are.

6 Do not purchase cheap commodities, purchase good products at a fair price.
   (A) There is always a reason why something is cheaper! Purchase named brand products whenever possible. The consistency of the product will generally be better. Purchase fresh ingredients and maintain the purchase of local, seasonal products wherever possible to ensure freshness and that travelling distance has been kept to a minimum.

## Assessment of knowledge and understanding

You have now learned about the planning of menus, kitchen operations and cost control. This will enable you to effectively cost dishes and menus and write appealing menus to be sold to customers.

To test your level of knowledge and understanding, answer the following short questions. These will help to prepare you for your summative (final) assessment.

## Kitchen Organisation

1 Explain the **importance** of a good workflow in a kitchen.

2 Describe the **traditional kitchen hierarchy** using a diagram. Use a separate piece of paper.

3 Describe how the role of a Head Chef might differ in the running of a kitchen in a hospital to that of a Head Chef in a Restaurant.

## Planning Menus

1 Explain the importance of a menu, stating the **three** main aspects a menu should communicate to a customer.

i) _____ ii) _____

iii) _____

2 State what a **table d'hôte** menu is.

## Basic Calculations

1 Describe **two** factors which must be monitored to control food costs.

i) _____ ii) _____

2 Describe **one** factor which must be monitored to control net profit.

i) _____

3 Explain the term net profit and gross profit.

## Research Task A

Design a balanced menu of **six** dishes covering **three** courses to include starters, main course and dessert. Two of the dishes should take into consideration a customer who is a vegetarian.

## Research Task B

Select **one** dish from **each** course and calculate the selling price per portion, based on a food cost of 40 per cent and achieving a gross profit of 60 per cent.

# 6

# Cold starters, salads and canapés

**UNIT 207/208/209/210/211**
**Preparing and presenting cold food**

## LEARNING OBJECTIVES

The aim of this unit is to enable the candidate to develop skills and apply knowledge in the principles of producing a range of cold larder items that include salads, cold starters, **buffet** items, cold sauces and ââdressings. The chapter will also introduce the use of relevant materials, ingredients and equipment.

At the end of this chapter you will be able to:

- Identify each type of salad and how they are composed
- Understand the use of relative ingredients and their quality points
- Understand how to prepare basic cold sauces and dressings
- Understand the quality points in the presentation of cooked, cured and prepared foods
- Identify the storage and holding procedures of cold salads, starters and buffet items
- Identify the correct tools and equipment to utilise during the production and presentation of cooked, cured and prepared foods
- Recognise the healthy eating options when preparing and presenting cold foods for presentation

# HORS D'OEUVRES, APPETISERS AND STARTERS

Although they are a relatively minor element in a full menu, the set of first courses is significant. Great care and attention needs to be taken because their quality will give an indication of the menu to follow. The service of canapés is similar because they too represent the tone of a meal and tempt the palette before a meal commences. The first rule is to keep canapés and starters simple in their composition: they should not be overpowering in taste or have too many contrasting flavours. Dishes are usually chosen for the menu in order to compliment and balance the main course. However, the starter selection should be balanced to cover all dietary requirements, for example **vegetarian** or religious restrictions and various allergies.

There are generally two main kinds of hors d'oeuvre.

**Hors d'oeuvres** varieties can be classed as a starter, main course or extended further into a buffet selection. There will be a good choice of salads, eggs, vegetables, fruits, meats, fish, game and poultry items to select from. These dishes should always be presented in small portions, replenished frequently and should be **diced** or cut into small strips or pieces for ease of service.

Single hors d'oeuvres, as the name implies, usually consist of a single item, but can also consist of two or more compatible items. Classically, the service of hors d'oeuvres was on a hors d'oeuvre trolley. Similar to a **canapé** tray or cheeseboard, there would be a selection of different items on the trolley. A restaurant service team would bring the trolley to the table, suggest a selection and serve to the guest, or let the customer choose for themselves.

# COMMODITIES USED AND QUALITY POINTS

## Caviar

This is the roe of the Sturgeon fish which has been removed, salted and packed into tins. The best known types are *Beluga* (a large grain with a light colour), *Sevruga* (a small grain with a darker colour) and *Oscetra* (a small grain and darker colour).

Caviar should be stored at 1–2°C and should always have a bright, almost shiny appearance. The best quality caviar is usually served direct from the tin, which sits on an ice socle or crushed ice, and is served with blinis.

*Caviar served on a quail egg*

## Oysters – Huîtres

English oysters are in season from September to April each year. During the remaining summer months they are breeding and should not be eaten.

British oysters are termed as 'natives', with the best known being from Colchester, Whitstable, Poole and Shannon. The most recognised imported varieties are Belon from France, these are purchased in graded sizes: number 1 is the largest and number 4 is the smallest.

It is important that oysters are alive, which can easily be established as their shells should be tightly closed. Furthermore it is imperative that they are stored in a cool damp room and kept in the wooden containers that they were delivered in.

*Fresh oysters*

## Charcuterie

Charcuterie consists of a wide range of cured meats and sausages such as bratwurst, mortadella, salamis and Parma ham, which should be cut into thin slices or carved in front of the guest.

*Mortadella, salamis and Parma ham*

## Fruits

Citrus fruits are popular for turning into cocktails, with oranges and grapefruit being the most used. They can be mixed with other fruits such as pineapple, grapes, nectarines, melons and mangoes. The natural sharpness of these fruits is an ideal balance within a selection of hors d'oeuvres or as a starter.

## Vegetables

Before preparation, all vegetables should be thoroughly washed and dried. The natural colours of fresh vegetables greatly enhance any starter or hors d'oeuvre display: they should be carefully cut in their raw state and never overcooked if cooking is required.

Crudités are raw vegetables that have been cut into bite-sized shapes and presented on a serving plate with a selection of dressings and sauces. Other vegetable preparations include pickled onions, cucumber, celery or red cabbage.

A range of cooked vegetable hors d'oeuvres are presented within the technique named à la grecque and à la portugaise.

When checking for the quality points of fresh vegetables it is important to ensure that they are ripe, not bruised, have a good colour and aroma and that they have no infestation by insects.

*Citrus fruits are popular for turning into cocktails*

**CHEF'S TIP**

Ensure that all fruits are fresh without bruising or blemishes and are not over-ripe.

## Herbs

The use of fresh herbs within cooking will always add aroma, colour and flavour to any presented dish. Some aromatic herbs such as tarragon, fennel

*A selection of herbs*

**CHEF'S TIP**

Keep herbs fresh for a few days by wrapping in damp kitchen paper and placing into a plastic bag before storing in a refrigerator.

*Terrine mould*

**CHEF'S TIP**

Gelatine is widely used in the setting of terrines. As gelatine is made from boiled beef bones, remember to replace it with agar agar, which is made from seaweed, when creating vegetarian dishes.

**HEALTH & SAFETY**

When you are using a knife, do not cut towards you or your fingers. Pay particular attention to where the edge of your sharp blade is pointing and make sure it cannot harm you or others if you slip.

and basil are excellent to infuse in oils and vinaigrettes. Others, such as dill, chervil, chives, mint and parsley, add colour and flavour to salads.

It is best to purchase fresh herbs in smaller quantities as and when required. Prior to use it is important to remove any bruised or damaged leaves.

## Terrines

These are named after the mould they are made in. Terrines are produced in different sizes and can be made from meat, game, fish and vegetables.

There are many varieties of terrine, all of which will provide the chef with the opportunity to use different colours, textures and flavours in a creative fashion.

Terrines can be cooked or cold set mousses, coarse pâtés, fine smooth parfaits, meat jellies or cooked layered ingredients that have been cold pressed. The terrine mould is usually lined with either bacon, seaweed, vegetables or fat because this helps to hold the terrine together for presentation and cutting.

## Pâtés and Parfaits

Generally made of offal, meat, fish, vegetable or game products, pâtés are usually served coarse while parfaits are fine, smooth pastes that are rich in flavour and have a consistency of whipped cream or butter.

## Mousses

Similar to both parfaits and terrines, these can be either raw or cooked. Mousses tend to be of a lighter texture because they have the addition of cream but are not as rich in flavour as pâtés or terrines and therefore a little more versatile to use.

# PREPARATION OF SANDWICHES

## Open or Scandinavian Sandwiches

These are ideal buffet and reception items. An open sandwich is one layer of any variety of bread with a filling decorated on top and garnished in an attractive way to display the sandwich and its contents. This type of sandwich is considered more appealing to guests than a closed sandwich.

However, the time required to prepare open sandwiches is usually longer due to the decorative sequence and preparation. It is thought that the open sandwich originates from Russia where they were used as an item of food for drinks receptions and parties. Various breads can be used including French, Vienna, rye, wholemeal, pumpernickel and small bread rolls. The principle of a sandwich menu is that it should be balanced, consisting of a selection of meat, fish, vegetarian, dairy and egg fillings.

## Closed Sandwiches

These varieties are also sometimes referred to as tea sandwiches, buffet sandwiches, conventional sandwiches and reception sandwiches. Closed sandwiches are more sophisticated and far easier to prepare, present and eat because the filling is enclosed. Furthermore, they will keep slightly longer if prepared in advance and stored, covered by plastic film, in a refrigerator.

The fourth Earl of Sandwich was reputed to have invented the sandwich because he required something to eat whilst spending his time (and money) gambling. Perhaps this was the forerunner to the 'fast food' fashion of today. The afternoon tea sandwich is a light and delicate presentation and is usually cut into finger shapes or smaller triangles. Currently, club sandwiches, modern wraps or tortillas are popular as they can be easily cut and are visually effective.

# THE DIFFERENT TYPES OF BUFFET

## Full Cold Buffet

When producing different sections for a full cold buffet it is essential that you present food that is eye-catching and easily served. The buffet should always be well presented, even after the 150th guest has been served. Usually a team of service staff are on hand to help the flow of service and to clearly communicate and explain the broad range of food on show.

A full cold buffet is usually produced for weddings, state or official banquets and celebration ceremonies; therefore a full table service is maintained with the exception that guests are required to be served at the buffet table. To help select the dishes and presentation of the food certain criteria must be followed to ensure a successful service:

1 Refrigeration should be used to display food where possible. If this is not available, food should only be presented to guests at the last possible moment directly from a storage refrigerator.

2 Ensure that all accompaniments, dressings, sauces and **garnishes** are served next to the appropriate buffet item.

3 Make certain that serving equipment is always available for service staff and guests to use.

4 Create a centrepiece (usually an ice carving, fat carving, or the most superior dish available) and build the other items around this.

5 When planning the display, ensure that guests have a natural route to negotiate access to the whole buffet table in as quick a time as possible.

6 Make use of different styles of presentation such as small dishes, shot glasses, soup spoons, different-shaped platters and ornate butler's trays.

**HEALTH & SAFETY**

Always use appropriately coloured chopping boards for preparation of ingredients to minimise the risk of food contamination, which could lead to food poisoning.

**HEALTH & SAFETY**

When you are working with a knife and you lay it down, do not lay it down with the blade pointing up. Ensure it is away from the edge of the work surface so that it cannot fall off or catch anyone passing by.

**HEALTH & SAFETY**

Always remember that steam will rise out of a boiling pot of water when you take off the cover. Remove the cover far side first so that the steam does not scald your hand.

**HEALTH & SAFETY**

Chopping boards, equipment, containers and hands should be washed before and immediately after use.

**HEALTH & SAFETY**

Store food correctly. Never store raw meats or fish above cooked. All items should be labelled and dated correctly.

**HEALTH & SAFETY**

Refrigerator and freezer temperatures should be recorded regularly to comply with health and safety regulations.

**HEALTH & SAFETY**

Refuse should be kept away from working areas and removed entirely from the kitchen regularly.

*Buffet*

**HEALTH & SAFETY**

Always use a sanitiser after the surface has been cleaned with soapy water. It will remove any grease before disinfecting.

**HEALTH & SAFETY**

Spillages should be cleaned immediately and an appropriate sign put in place to make other staff aware and help prevent accidents.

# Fork Buffet

This type of buffet should be served to guests where there is limited space to sit down and eat.

Normally guests will stand and eat from the buffet table; this is a style of service most suited for large business functions and luncheons where conversation and interaction between guests is of equal importance to the food. The items of food on display must therefore be small and easy to serve. Some hot food selections may also be provided.

# Finger Buffet

This is the least formal of all buffets and will usually be at a reception where the main aspect of the assembly is to meet in a social capacity or as a business function. This is not regarded as a full meal and there is no cutlery used to consume the food, hence its name. The food should be bite-sized and not difficult to eat but still well presented and flavoured.

# Breakfast Buffet

The breakfast buffet should have a varied display of foods. Consequently, a choice of hot and cold food items should be available, for example cured meats, kippers, vegetarian options, cereals and bakery items. A fresh selection of fruit juices, smoothies, fruit and yoghurts should also be provided.

# Speciality Buffets

These can vary from buffets with certain religious requirements to modern and trendy ways of serving foods. It is becoming increasingly popular and necessary in hospitality to be aware of every type of eating trend, habit and allergy. Focus is now far more customer-oriented and the whole experience should be a memorable one.

In this style the chef and the service team can be more extravagant in the presentation and service of the food and follow themes and directions in connection with the customer's wishes (e.g. product launches or sporting themes).

Utilising individual, open, food presentation tables around a room with each serving a different style of food or course is a good way of organising a buffet. Guests can move freely between different sections as they desire, making the event more relaxed and sociable. Another benefit is that it can distribute the workload evenly around the sections, as guests will not all follow the same service route.

# SALADS

Salads are a presentation of raw, cooked, cold or warm food items that are usually dressed and seasoned. Their purpose is to offer an alternative within the menu or as an accompaniment to another dish. They are a lighter and usually healthier option.

The range of different styles of salads has grown over the past twenty years, as the ease of long distance travel has exposed more people to different styles of cuisine. Below are some varieties of salad items.

## Simple Salads

A **simple salad** consists of one basic ingredient served with a dressing or sauce: sometimes a garnish can be added for decoration. Examples include cucumber salad, tomato salad and beetroot salad.

## Compound Salads

**Compound salads** are composed of more than two ingredients and dressed appropriately. They can be a mixture of leaves, vegetables, fruit, meats or fish. Examples include Florida salad, mimosa salad, Waldorf salad and Russian salad.

## American Salads

American salads usually accompany a roast dish such as turkey or duck. In North America during a banquet or function the sauce would also be served with a salad rather than vegetables. For example, orange salad with duck.

## Salades Tiède

Tiède means warm. This type of salad is usually made from ordinary salad vegetables but dressed with a hot dressing in place of the usual cold ones. In many instances this salad uses a small item of hot meat such as foie gras or chicken livers, where the fat and juices of the pan are used to make the hot dressing. **Salad tiède** is utilised for starters or main courses rather than a side accompaniment. It has to be prepared quickly and served immediately so the hot elements do not wilt the cold ingredients such as lettuce. An example would be salades tiède bergère.

## Cooked Served Cold Salads

These originated during the time when there was no form of refrigeration to preserve food and therefore these salads would have a longer shelf life as they were pickled, lightly cooked or placed in a sauce. À la grecque is a classic example because in translation it means 'to be cooked in a Greek style'; this process is cooking in a vinegar and oil solution with aromatic spice. These salads can be meat- and fish-based but are generally vegetable.

**HEALTH & SAFETY**

High-risk foods such as raw meat, fish and eggs should be stored and cooked as quickly as possible to reduce the risk of food poisoning.

# COLD SAUCES

The word sauce comes from the Latin word *salus* which means 'salted', as salt has always been a condiment served with food.

The function of a sauce is to add flavour, moisture and additional texture to a particular dish and compliment the combined ingredients. Classical sauces have names derived from regions, countries and cities and they generally denote a speciality of the area or a certain technique. Sauces Cambridge, Albert and Cumberland are all traditional English sauces, whereas sauce L'italienne is an Italian-based sauce. Other sauces often allude to their content within the name, such as à la diable, which translated means 'a devil' sauce: it is a highly spiced. Other sauces and garnishes are attributed to its creator or to a person's influence, such as sauce Vincent and sauce Mornay.

Modern trends have redefined the classic French names and methods of cookery. An example of this is *sauce tartare*, which is commonly thought of as mayonnaise with chopped parsley, capers, gherkin and onion. However, classically it should be chopped spring onion, chopped chives and chopped chervil with mayonnaise. The sauce recipes below form the base for cold sauces generally.

## Mayonnaise

This is suitable for serving with hors d'oeuvre and cold meats and is a major base component in many salads and dressings.

The ingredients are:

- 3 egg yolks
- 10g white wine vinegar
- ½ tsp mustard powder
- Salt and white pepper to **season**
- 400ml olive or vegetable oil

**Whisk** together the egg yolks, vinegar, mustard and seasoning.

Whilst whisking continuously, slowly add the oil in a slow and steady stream. An emulsion should take place between the egg yolks and oil. Adjust seasoning and consistency with a little hot water if necessary.

## Sauce Rémoulade

This originates from the Picardy word meaning black radish. The finished sauce tastes and looks similar to that of black radish. The ingredients are:

- 900g mayonnaise
- 25g chopped capers
- 50g chopped gherkin
- 10g chopped fresh parsley, chervil and tarragon
- 2tbs anchovy essence.

All ingredients are carefully combined. This sauce is suitable for fried fish.

# Aïoli

A Provençale mayonnaise-based sauce. Its name comes from the word *ail* which means garlic and *oli* which means oil. The ingredients are:

- 30g chopped fresh garlic
- 3 egg yolks
- 450ml olive oil
- 2tbs lemon juice
- ½ tbs warm water.

Pound the chopped garlic with a pinch of salt until it resembles a **purée**. Mix together with the egg yolks and slowly drizzle in the oil (as for mayonnaise). Finish with the lemon juice and warm water to adjust the consistency. Season before serving.

# Sauce gribiche

This is a classic French sauce named after Napoleon's favourite general in his army. As a debt of gratitude, Napoleon's chef was asked to create a sauce in his honour. Sauce gribiche is served with cold fish and meats. The ingredients are:

- 1tsp French mustard
- 200ml white wine vinegar
- 650ml vegetable oil
- 50g chopped gherkins
- 50g chopped capers
- 25g chopped fresh herbs
- 3 sieved hard-boiled eggs.

Mix the mustard, sieved egg yolks and vinegar together, slowly adding the oil. Mix well and add the remaining ingredients, season with salt and pepper.

# Vinaigrette

This is a non-protein-based emulsion. It was made as an accompaniment for cured fish, salads or cold meats to aid digestion. Another widely used name for this dressing is *sauce ravigote*. The ingredients are:

- 100ml white wine vinegar
- 350ml olive oil
- 30g finely chopped shallot
- 20g finely chopped capers
- 10g finely chopped aromatic herbs.

Whisk the oil and vinegar together and add the shallot, capers and herbs. Season with salt and pepper and serve.

# Raw Tomato Coulis

Various fresh herbs can be added to the recipe to add a further flavour dimension. The base ingredients are:

- 400g tomato **concassé**
- ½ tsp lemon juice
- 2tbs olive oil
- Seasoning.

Place all of the ingredients into a food blender and then **pass** through a sieve. **Correct** the seasoning before serving.

# Pesto

**Pesto** is an Italian sauce which is quite coarse in texture but highly flavoured. The ingredients are:

- 100g pine nuts
- 100ml olive oil
- 30g Parmesan cheese
- 1 clove of garlic
- ¼ bunch of basil or required flavour.

Toast the pine nuts under a grill or in an oven until golden brown. Pick basil leaves and **blanch** in boiling water then refresh in ice-cold water and squeeze to remove excess liquid. Place all the ingredients into a blender and blitz to the required texture.

# Flavoured and Scented Oils

Within a larder section these can be very useful, not only for colour but also when used in recipes to add a different dimension.

- 100ml vegetable oil
- 100g of picked herbs (variety of your choice)

  or
- 50–60g garlic cloves or root ginger

  or
- 5g saffron.

Warm the oil in a saucepan but do not allow it to boil, then remove from the heat and leave to stand. Add the ingredient or ingredients of your choice and leave to infuse for 20–30 minutes.

Now place in a liquidiser and **blend** for a few seconds. Again leave to stand before passing through a fine chinois and allowing to cool. If not for immediate use, oils can be stored with the ingredients in airtight jars or vacuum packed in sealed bags.

## SAUCE DERIVATIVES

| BASE INGREDIENTS | ADDITIONS | NEW SAUCE |
|---|---|---|
| Mayonnaise | Tomato ketchup, sherry, diced red pepper | Thousand Island or Andalusian |
| Mayonnaise | Chopped capers, gherkins, parsley, lemon juice | Modern tartare sauce |
| Mayonnaise | Chervil, chives, spinach, tarragon – all blanched then blended with the mayonnaise | Sauce vert or green sauce |

| BASE INGREDIENTS | ADDITIONS | NEW SAUCE |
|---|---|---|
| Vinaigrette | Tomato juice, concassé of tomato | Tomato vinaigrette |
| Vinaigrette | Wholegrain mustard, honey | Honey and mustard dressing |
| Vinaigrette | Chillies, chopped coriander, chopped ginger | Thai vinaigrette |
| Pesto | Sun-dried tomatoes or peppers | Red pesto |
| Pesto | Rocket | Rocket pesto |
| Pesto | Cashew nuts, coriander | Satay pesto |
| Flavoured vegetable or sunflower oil | Thyme or rosemary | Thyme or rosemary scented oil |
| Flavoured vegetable or sunflower oil | Chorizo sausage | Chorizo sausage-scented oil |
| Flavoured vegetable or sunflower oil | Wild garlic | Wild garlic-scented oil |

# TOOLS AND EQUIPMENT

The main items of tools and equipment are listed below and are essential for the preparation and final decorative work required to prepare and present cold food. This is a basic selection of the equipment and tools needed.

- Canelle knife
- Turning knife
- Tomato knife
- Small and medium-sized palette knives
- Parisienne cutters; large and small
- Serrated and scalloped carving knives
- Selection of piping bags and different size tubes
- Stainless steel bowls
- Wire balloon whisks
- Stainless steel or plastic tongs and spoons
- Electric food mixer
- Food processor and a food blender
- Colour-coded chopping boards.

*Preserving jars*

**HEALTH & SAFETY**

It is important that the selection of equipment used is thoroughly cleaned before and after each use. The potential for cross-contamination is high with the type and styles of preparation in this chapter so excellent standards of hygiene must be observed at all times.

**CHEF'S TIP**

When freezing items, the flatter and thinner things are, the quicker they will freeze and likewise the quicker they will defrost. Sliced items should be wrapped individually so they can be separated better.

# STORAGE PROCEDURES

The use of refrigeration and freezing facilities is essential and these must be maintained at the appropriate temperature zone at all times. Any rise in temperature must be reported immediately and suitable action taken.

Freezer organisation must at all times ensure that food which is to be frozen is correctly sealed in a moisture-free material such as vacuum packing, if at all possible. Frozen food, once defrosted, should never be re-frozen under any circumstances.

All foods that are to be refrigerated must be appropriately wrapped or sealed and labelled with the date, name of the product, quantity of the product and preferably the name of the person who is storing the item.

Stock rotation is essential in the reduction of wastage and the 'first-in, first-out' method of usage must be applied at all times. Any deterioration of stored foods should be immediately reported and constant monitoring of 'shelf life' dates on packaging is standard practice.

Before service, even if the buffet item, cold starter or hors d'oeuvre is refrigerated correctly, it should be remembered that the incubation time of 20 minutes for bacterial growth still applies.

Buffets should have a 'rolling service' where the food is replaced in small amounts to cut down on wastage and to make sure no items are left out for too long. Low-risk items should be incorporated into the menus to lessen the pressure of maintaining the high-risk elements of the buffet.

# RECIPES
## Asparagus spears, poached egg and Roquefort dressing

| INGREDIENTS | 4 PORTIONS | 10 PORTIONS |
|---|---|---|
| Asparagus | 20 spears | 50 spears |
| Eggs | 4 | 10 |
| Salad leaves | 200g | 900g |
| Roquefort cheese | 100g | 200g |
| Honey | 1tsp | 2tsp |
| White wine | 30ml | 50ml |
| Olive oil | 50ml | 100ml |
| Good-quality salt and pepper | To taste | To taste |

### Method of work

1 Peel and take off the woody root of the asparagus spears to fit the plate and in a saucepan of boiling salted water simmer until tender and **refresh** immediately in iced cold water.

2 In a liquidizer blend together the Roquefort, honey and white wine, and when a smooth paste is formed add slowly the olive oil.

3 Poach the hen eggs in a deep saucepan of boiling water with a little vinegar in until the eggs are just set.

4 To present, arrange the asparagus and crumbled Roquefort cheese around the plate and in the centre place a small bunch of mixed salad leaves, put a hot **poached** egg, **drizzle** around with the dressing and sprinkle with chopped chives.

## Caesar salad

| INGREDIENTS | 4 PORTIONS | 10 PORTIONS |
|---|---|---|
| Cos lettuce | 1 | 2 |
| Croutons | 25g | 50g |
| Parmesan | 50g | 100g |
| Olive oil | 100ml | 200ml |
| Garlic cloves | 1½ | 3 |
| Baby gem lettuce | 1 | 2 |
| Anchovy fillets | ½ tin | 1 tin |
| Egg yolks | 2 | 4 |
| Lemons | 1 | 2 |
| Good-quality salt and pepper | To taste | To taste |

### Method of work

1 Wash and pick the leaves off the lettuces.

2 **Grate** a quarter of the Parmesan and shave the remaining using a potato peeler.

3 Make the dressing by placing the garlic, half the anchovies, the zest and juice of the lemon and the egg yolks into a blender and blending to a paste, then incorporating the oil slowly to form an emulsion. Season and stir in the Parmesan.

4 Toss the salad leaves with anchovy fillets, croûtons, shaved Parmesan and the dressing. Serve.

# Celeriac and apple salad

| INGREDIENTS | 4 PORTIONS | 10 PORTIONS |
|---|---|---|
| Celeriac | 1 | 2 |
| Granny Smith apples | 2½ | 5 |
| Mixed leaves | 50g | 100g |
| Red dessert apples | 2½ | 5 |
| Greek yoghurt | 100ml | 200ml |
| Lemon juice and zest | 1 | 2 |

## Method of work

1 Peel and finely **slice** the celeriac, cutting into **julienne** or a **brunoise**.

2 Peel and finely slice the red dessert apples and cut into julienne or a brunoise.

3 Peel and finely slice the Granny Smith apples and cut into julienne or a brunoise.

4 Mix the celeriac and the apples together before adding the yoghurt, lemon juice and zest and seasoning.

5 To serve, place the salad in a ring and decorate the top with dressed curly endive leaves.

*Cutting brunoise of apples and celeriac*

# Chicken liver parfait with Cumberland sauce

| INGREDIENTS | 4 PORTIONS | 10 PORTIONS |
|---|---|---|
| Shallots | 60g | 150g |
| Duck livers (cleaned and trimmed) | 200g | 500g |
| Butter (melted) | 40g | 80g |
| Garlic cloves | 2 | 3–4 |
| Brandy | 20ml | 50ml |
| Double cream | 160ml | 300ml |
| Orange juice | 100ml | 200ml |
| Orange zest | 1 | 2–3 |
| Redcurrant jelly | 125g | 250g |
| Loaf of onion bread | ½ | 1 |
| Good-quality salt and pepper | To taste | To taste |

## Method of work

1 Melt the butter and fry off the shallots and garlic in butter.

2 In a hot pan **sear** the duck livers and **flambé** with the brandy.

3 In a food processor blend the shallots and the duck livers before adding the melted butter and cream.

*Slicing parfait with a hot knife*

4  Line a terrine mould with cling film and pour the parfait mixture in before folding the cling film over. Chill and press lightly.

5  To make the Cumberland sauce, place orange juice in a saucepan and bring to the boil, then add the redcurrant jelly and reduce. Meanwhile blanch the orange zest in boiling water first then refresh in iced water and drain. Now add to the orange sauce. Once reduced by one-third, remove from the heat and chill.

6  To serve, place a slice of parfait on the plate and garnish with a dressed pluche of salad, a cordon of the sauce and some toasted onion bread.

# Chicken Niçoise salad

| INGREDIENTS | 4 PORTIONS | 10 PORTIONS |
|---|---|---|
| Chicken breast | 2 | 4 |
| Tinned red peppers or fresh skinned | 1 tin or 2 fresh | 2 tins or 4 fresh |
| Pitted black olives | 120g | 250g |
| Basil leaves | 1 bunch | 1½–2 bunches |
| French beans | 120–150g | 300g |
| Potatoes | 400g | 1kg |
| Baby plum tomatoes | 8 | 20 |
| Balsamic vinegar | 50ml | 100ml |
| Dijon mustard | 1tsp | 2tsp |
| Olive oil | 100ml | 200ml |
| Honey | 1tsp | 2tsp |
| Good-quality salt and pepper | To taste | To taste |

*Blanching tomatoes*

## Method of work

1  Place the chicken breast onto a chopping board between a vac pac bag then bat it out with a meat bat or rolling pin until it forms a fairly even square shape.

2  Season the breast, then place a layer of red pepper, basil leaves and olives in the centre.

3  Roll up tight with double-wrapped cling film and steam in a steamer for about 17 minutes. Once steamed, place in a glass and chill until cold.

4  Cut the beans into small lengths and cook, refresh in iced cold water.

5  Cut the potatoes into a small dice and cook in a little butter, making sure they are kept firm.

6  Blanch, peel and deseed the tomatoes before cutting into macedoine-size shapes.

7  For the dressing combine the vinegar, mustard and a little honey together, whisk in the oil and season.

8  Combine all the salad items and dress with the dressing. Place a ring onto the plate and press in some of the salad. Slice the chicken and arrange around the salad. Lift off the ring and dress with the dressing around the outside.

*Mixing the niçoise salad together*

 **VIDEO CLIP** Making Niçoise salad

# Fennel à la grecque

*Cooking fennel in the liquor*

| INGREDIENTS | 4 PORTIONS | 10 PORTIONS |
|---|---|---|
| Fennel | 3 | 6 |
| Olive oil | ¼ litre | ½ litre |
| Peppercorns | 2 | 4–5 |
| Parsley stalks | 10g | 25g |
| Bay leaf | ½ | 1 |
| Salad leaves | 40g | 100g |
| White wine vinegar | 1/8 litre | ½ litre |
| Lemon juice | 1 lemon | 3 lemons |
| Coriander seeds | 2 | 4–5 |
| Thyme | 1 sprig | 3 sprigs |
| Garlic | 1 clove | 2 cloves |
| Good-quality salt and pepper | To taste | To taste |

## Method of work

1 Cut the fennel into quarters or eighths depending on the size.
2 Mix all the remaining ingredients together in a pan and bring to the boil.
3 Add the fennel and cook for 20 minutes or until the fennel has softened.
4 Remove the pan from the heat and allow the mixture to cool naturally to infuse the spices into the fennel.

### CHEF'S TIP

Try cooking other vegetables using this method, for example mushrooms, celery and carrots.

# Florida salad

| INGREDIENTS | 4 PORTIONS | 10 PORTIONS |
|---|---|---|
| Pink grapefruit | 2 | 4 |
| Oranges | 2½ | 5 |
| Mixed leaves | 50g | 100g |
| White grapefruit | 2 | 4 |
| Pineapple | ½ | 1 |
| Passion fruit | 2 | 4 |
| Malibu or coconut liquor | 15ml | 30ml |
| Caster sugar | 50g | 100g |
| Mint or Thai basil | ¼ bunch | ½ bunch |

## Method of work

1 Segment all the citrus fruits then cut into a **paysanne** ensuring that all the juices are retained.

2 Skin and de-core the pineapple before cutting into quarters, remove the stalk and then dice into **macedoine**.

3 Cut the passion fruit in half and remove the seeds before mixing with the grapefruit juice and the coconut liquor to make a dressing.

4 Mix the pineapple with the segments then bind with the dressing, reserving some for the decoration.

5 Take a cocktail glass and dip the rim into the remaining dressing to **coat** the edge, and then dip into the sugar to form a coated edge. Carefully spoon in the salad and drizzle over some dressing

6 Decorate with basil or mint leaves before serving.

*Segmenting citrus fruit*

# French bean, shallots and garlic mayonnaise salad

| INGREDIENTS | 4 PORTIONS | 10 PORTIONS |
|---|---|---|
| French beans | 500g | 1kg |
| Garlic | ½ head | 1 head |
| Radicchio | 75g | 150g |
| Shallots | 100g | 200g |
| Mayonnaise | 125ml | 250ml |
| Good-quality salt and pepper | To taste | To taste |

## Method of work

1 Top and tail the French beans before placing them into a large saucepan of boiling salted water and cook until the French beans are soft but still retain their vibrant green colour. Refresh immediately in iced cold water and drain.

2 Finely chop the shallots and garlic and fry in a little butter until softened, season and remove from the pan to chill.

3 Mix the drained beans with the shallots and garlic, then bind with the mayonnaise.

4 Decorate with the radicchio leaves that have been cut into a **chiffonade**.

*Mixing all the ingredients together*

**CHEF'S TIP**

Try using other beans to create a mixture of flavours, shapes and textures such as sugar snap pea, mange tout, broad beans and peas.

# Game pie with plum compote

| INGREDIENTS | 4 PORTIONS | 10 PORTIONS |
|---|---|---|
| Game pie | 4 slices, 100g each | 10 slices, 100g each |
| Shallots diced | 200g | 500g |
| Mixed leaves | 100g | 220g |
| Plums | 900g | 1.8kg |
| Red wine | 250ml | 500ml |
| Cinnamon | 15g | 28g |
| Nutmeg | 15g | 28g |
| Cloves | 15g | 28g |
| Sumac | 15g | 28g |
| Orange zest | 1 orange | 2 oranges |
| Sugar | 800g | 1.8kg |
| Good-quality salt and pepper | To taste | To taste |

*Cooking plums in liquor*

## Method of work

1 Halve the plums, remove the stones and place into a saucepan, then add the shallots, wine and the spices and orange zest in a muslin bag.

2 Cook gently for 15–20 minutes or until the skins become soft. Remove the spice bag and add the sugar.

3 Stir until dissolved and bring the mixture to the boil. Boil rapidly for approximately 10 minutes or until the mixture reaches setting point (105°C).

4 Remove from the heat and allow to cool. Once cool place in a sterilised jar, seal and label.

5 Place slices of the game pie on a plate, putting a small amount of the compôte into a ramekin. Add a pluche of the dressed mixed leaves.

*Adding sugar and boiling the syrup*

# Goat's cheese and red pepper tartlet, with split balsamic dressing

| INGREDIENTS | 4 PORTIONS | 10 PORTIONS |
|---|---|---|
| Goat's cheese | 150g | 300g |
| Eggs | 2 | 4 |
| Pastry cases | 4 | 10 |
| Olive oil | 75ml | 150ml |
| Red peppers | 2 | 4 |
| Double cream | 250ml | 500ml |
| Balsamic syrup | 15ml | 25ml |
| Good-quality salt and pepper | To taste | To taste |

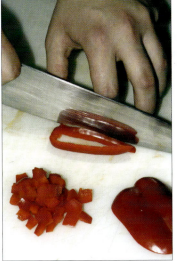

## Method of work

1 Prepare the red peppers by dicing into **gros brunoise**.

2 Cut the goat's cheese into 1cm dice.

3 Make the quiche mix by beating the eggs and cream together. Season.

4 Put the diced red pepper in the pastry case followed by some cheese on top and then pour over the quiche mix. Bake at 180°C until egg mixture is almost set.

5 Make the dressing by mixing the balsamic syrup with the oil.

6 To serve, place the tartlet on the plate, garnish with a pluche of salad (if required) and the dressing.

*Preparing the peppers*

# Melon with exotic fruit and a champagne dressing

| INGREDIENTS | 4 PORTIONS | 10 PORTIONS |
| --- | --- | --- |
| Ogen, Galia or Charentais melon | ½ | 1 |
| Star fruit | 1 | 2 |
| Kiwi fruit | 1 | 3 |
| Mango | 1 | 2 |
| Papaya | 1 | 2 |
| Lychee | 4 | 10 |
| Physallis | 4 | 10 |
| Passion fruit | 2 | 5 |
| Strawberry | 4 | 10 |
| Raspberry | 12 | 30 |
| Champagne | 120ml | 300ml |

## Method of work

1 Top and tail the melon, peeling off the outer skin. Cut in half length ways and scoop out the seeds.

2 Next thinly cut across the melon so that you achieve half-moon-shaped slices.

3 Cut all the other fruit up, trying to retain some of the original shape, i.e. don't cut up the berries, slice the kiwi and because the pineapple is large dice it small.

4 Now place the slices of melon into a rose shape, overlapping slices to look like petals ensuring a hole is left in the centre for the fruit.

5 Arrange all of the cut fruit inside the centre of the melon.

6 A splash of champagne now will give a bubbly effect and is visually appealing.

 **CHEF'S TIP**

Keep any left over pieces of the fruits which can be frozen and used later for a fruit soup, smoothies or coulis.

# Mimosa salad

*Halving and shredding the baby gems*

| INGREDIENTS | 4 PORTIONS | 10 PORTIONS |
|---|---|---|
| Orange | 2½ | 5 |
| Black grapes | 200g | 400g |
| Baby gem hearts | 3 | 6 |
| Mixed leaves | 150g | 350g |
| White grapes | 200g | 400g |
| Banana | 3 | 6–7 |
| Acidulated cream | 150ml | 300ml |

## Method of work

1 Segment the oranges.
2 Cut the grapes in half.
3 Peel and slice the banana.
4 Halve the gem hearts and **shred** finely.
5 Mix the grapes, orange segments, bananas, gem hearts and acidulated cream together.
6 Serve in a bowl, garnished with the leaves.

# Potato and chive salad

| INGREDIENTS | 4 PORTIONS | 10 PORTIONS |
|---|---|---|
| New potatoes (Jersey's when in season) | 400g | 1kg |
| Chives | ½ bunch | 1 bunch |
| White wine vinegar | 40ml | 100ml |
| Spring onion bunches | 1 | 2 |
| Lemon juice | 12ml | 25ml |
| Olive oil | 100ml | 200ml |
| Wholegrain mustard | 1tsp | 2tsp |
| Garlic leaves (when in season) | 20g | 40g |
| Onion cress | 20g | 40g |
| Good-quality salt and pepper | To taste | To taste |

## Method of work

1 Wash and scrub the potatoes then place into cold salted water bring up to the boil and **simmer** until tender before draining and chilling.
2 Cut the cooked potatoes into an even dice. (The skin can be removed or left on according to preference and personal taste.)
3 Finely slice the spring onions and finely chop the chives.
4 Whisk the mustard and the vinegar together until combined then slowly add the oil until an emulsion is formed.
5 Combine the potatoes, spring onions, chives and vinaigrette together. Add the lemon juice and season.
6 Serve garnished with garlic leaves cut into a chiffonade and a small pluche of onion cress.

# Moroccan salad

| INGREDIENTS | 4 PORTIONS | 10 PORTIONS |
|---|---|---|
| Cous cous | ½ box | 1 box |
| Dried apricots | 25g | 50g |
| Chillies (red) | 1 | 2 |
| Coriander | ¼ bunch | ½ bunch |
| Honey | 25ml | 50ml |
| Ground coriander | 12g | 25g |
| Ground cumin | 12g | 25g |
| Mixed peppers | 1 of each | 3 of each |
| Sultanas | 25g | 50g |
| Garlic | 1 clove | 2 cloves |
| Mint | ¼ bunch | ½ bunch |
| Turmeric | 12g | 25g |
| Olive oil | 50ml | 100ml |
| Mixed leaves | 50g | 100g |
| Good-quality salt and pepper | To taste | To taste |

## Method of work

1 Cut the peppers into macedoine.

2 Crush the garlic and finely chop the chillies.

3 **Sweat** off the peppers, garlic and chillies in the olive oil before adding the dried spices and cooking out.

4 Dice the dried apricots and add to the sultanas.

5 Place the cous cous into a bowl and bring the water to the boil before pouring over the cous cous. Cover in cling film and allow to steam for a few minutes before mixing the previous ingredients and spices with a fork and refrigerating.

6 Mix in the chopped mint and coriander. Add the honey and season.

7 Serve in a bowl and garnish with leaves.

*Cooking the peppers, garlic and chillies*

### CHEF'S TIP

Instead of using water to make up the cous cous, try using a reduction of stock for more flavour.

# Pork satay

*Skewering the sliced pork and marinating*

| INGREDIENTS | 4 PORTIONS | 10 PORTIONS |
|---|---|---|
| Loin of pork trimmed and boned | 500g | 1kg |
| Vegetable oil | 240ml | 500ml |
| Red chillies | 1 | 2 |
| Peanut oil | 75ml | 150ml |
| Coriander | ¼ bunch | ½ bunch |
| Garlic | 1 clove | 3 cloves |
| Ginger | 40g | 100g |
| Soy sauce | 10ml | 30ml |
| Peanut butter | 300g | 600g |
| Shallot | 100g | 200g |
| Ground cumin | 5g | 10g |
| Ground coriander | 5g | 10g |
| Ground turmeric | 5g | 10g |
| Cream | 100ml | 200ml |
| Good-quality salt and pepper | To taste | To taste |

## Method of work

1  Cut the pork loin into strips and place onto skewers, with three pieces per portion.

2  Mix together both oils, chopped chilli, garlic, coriander, ginger and soy sauce and place skewers into this marinade, leaving for 24 hours.

3  Warm peanut butter so it will easily come out of the jar.

4  Dice shallots and sweat in a pan with some of the peanut oil then add the dried spices followed by the peanut butter. Once this has infused add the cream to thin it down. The sauce should be kept warm for service.

5  Skewers should be sealed off in a pan with a small amount of the marinade oil.

6  To serve, place the sauce into a ramekin and serve with some mixed leaves and a few skewers.

**VIDEO CLIP**
Making potted shrimps

# Prawn and white crab salad, with mango and chilli salsa

| INGREDIENTS | 4 PORTIONS | 10 PORTIONS |
|---|---|---|
| Crevettes | 60 | 150 |
| Mixed leaves | 200g | 500g |
| Garlic cloves | 2–3 | 7–8 |
| Mango | 2 | 5 |
| Sugar | 50g | 125g |
| Crab meat (white) | 1kg | 2.5kg |
| Butter | 100g | 250g |
| Parsley | ½ bunch | 1¼ bunches |
| Chilli | 2 | 5 |
| White wine vinegar | 50ml | 125ml |
| Good-quality salt and pepper | To taste | To taste |

## Method of work

1 Steam the crabs for 14 minutes, then blast chill until cold.

2 Remove the claws and the shell, retaining all the meat and keeping all white meat separate. **Flake** the meat to make sure all shell or cartilage has been removed.

3 Peel the crevettes, leaving the head and tip of the tail on.

4 Peel and mince the garlic then mix with the butter, finely chop the parsley and wash and pick the leaves.

5 To make the salsa, dice the mango, finely chop the chilli, and then heat in a pan. Add the sugar and vinegar, cook down and chill.

6 Melt some of the garlic butter in a pan, cook the crevettes until done and add the crab meat to heat through.

7 To serve, place the crevettes and flaked crab meat on the salad and garnish with the salsa.

# Salad bonne femme

| INGREDIENTS | 4 PORTIONS | 10 PORTIONS |
|---|---|---|
| Button mushrooms | 400g | 1kg |
| Lardons of bacon | 150g | 300g |
| Vinaigrette | 25ml | 50ml |
| Leeks | 2 | 4 |
| Parsley | ¼ bunch | ½ bunch |
| Mixed leaves | 50g | 100g |
| Good-quality salt and pepper | To taste | To taste |

## Method of work

1 Wash and quarter the mushrooms then in a large saucepan sweat down the mushrooms with some seasoning until cooked. Remove the pan from the heat and chill.

2 Cut the leeks into paysanne, wash and drain. Then in a saucepan sweat down in some butter until cooked, remove the pan from the heat and chill.

3 Blanch the lardons in boiling water first to remove some of the excess fat then refresh in cold iced water and drain. Now in a **sauté** pan fry the lardons until crisp before removing from the pan, draining and allowing to cool.

4 Mix the mushrooms, bacon and leeks together. Add the vinaigrette and chopped parsley. Season.

5 Serve in a bowl garnished with the leaves.

*Blanching the lardons*

# Spanish rice salad

| INGREDIENTS | 4 PORTIONS | 10 PORTIONS |
|---|---|---|
| Long grain rice | 300g | 600g |
| Plum tomatoes | 3 | 6 |
| Vegetable oil | 30ml | 70ml |
| Red onions | ½ | 1 |
| Chorizo sausage | 1½ | 3 |
| Olive oil | 75ml | 150ml |
| Frozen garden peas | 75ml | 150g |
| Mixed peppers | ½ of each | 1 of each |
| Garlic | 1 clove | 2 cloves |
| Red and green chillies | 1 of each | 3 of each |
| Sherry vinegar | 20ml | 50ml |
| Good-quality salt and pepper | To taste | To taste |

## Method of work

1  Wash the rice, then cook in boiling salted water until cooked. Refresh under a running tap.

2  Finely chop the red onions, peppers, chillies and garlic and in a thick-bottomed saucepan season and sweat off without colour.

3  Dice the chorizo into macedoine and add this to the onions and garlic mixture and sweat off until cooked, remove from the pan and chill.

4  Blanch, refresh, peel and concassé the tomatoes. Blanch the peas in boiling salted water and refresh quickly in iced water.

5  Mix the rice with the chorizo, peppers and concassé. Add the peas, vinegar and olive oil. Season as required.

CHEF'S TIP

By refreshing the rice you are removing any excess starch which will stop the rice from sticking together.

# Tomato, red onion and basil salad

| INGREDIENTS | 4 PORTIONS | 10 PORTIONS |
|---|---|---|
| Red cherry tomatoes | 200g | 500g |
| Basil | ½ bunch | 1 bunch |
| Salad leaves | 40g | 100g |
| Sun-dried tomatoes | 40g | 100g |
| Honey | 20ml | 50ml |
| Red onion | 2 | 5 |
| Plum tomatoes | 4 | 10 |
| Balsamic vinegar | 25ml | 50ml |
| Yellow cherry tomatoes | 200g | 500g |
| Purple basil | ½ bunch | 1 bunch |
| Beefsteak tomatoes | 2 | 5 |
| Extra virgin olive oil | 20ml | 50ml |
| Good-quality salt and pepper | To taste | To taste |

## Method of work

1 Blanch the plum and beefsteak tomatoes and refresh in iced cold water before peeling, deseeding and cutting into large macedoine.
2 Wash the cherry tomatoes then halve.
3 Peel and finely slice the red onions.
4 Dice the sun-dried tomatoes.
5 Combine all the tomatoes with the onions.
6 Tear the basil and add to the onion and tomato mix.
7 Add the balsamic vinegar, honey, seasoning and oil to the salad.

# Smoked salmon with traditional garnish

| INGREDIENTS | 4 PORTIONS | 10 PORTIONS |
|---|---|---|
| Sliced smoked salmon (pack) | 400g | 1kg |
| Lemons | 2 | 3 |
| Horseradish | 10g | 20g |
| Capers | 40g | 100g |
| Shallots | 40g | 100g |
| Cream | 120ml | 250ml |
| Selection of leaves | To garnish | To garnish |
| Good-quality salt and black pepper | To taste | To taste |

## Method of work

1 Finely chop the shallots and capers.
2 Grate the horseradish, semi-whip the cream and mix together.
3 Cut the lemons into wedges.
4 Place the slices of smoked salmon on the plate to fill the circle.
5 To serve, garnish the plate with a pluche of salad, a sprinkle of shallots, capers, a lemon wedge, and a rosette of horseradish cream. Season to taste.

# Waldorf salad

| INGREDIENTS | 4 PORTIONS | 10 PORTIONS |
|---|---|---|
| Celeriac | ½ | 1 |
| Red apples | 5 | 10 |
| Soured cream | 100ml | 200ml |
| Mixed leaves | 50g | 100g |
| Celery | ½ head | 1 head |
| Mayonnaise | 70g | 150g |
| Lemon juice | ½ lemon | 1 lemon |
| Walnuts | 100g | 200g |
| Good-quality salt and pepper | To taste | To taste |

## Method of work

1 Blanch and peel the walnuts and wash all fruit and vegetables.
2 Peel the celeriac and cut into macedoine.
3 Peel the celery and cut into macedoine.
4 Cut the apples into macedoine.
5 Combine the apple, celery, celeriac and walnut.
6 Add the mayonnaise and soured cream.
7 Season with salt, pepper and lemon juice. Garnish with mixed leaves if required.

*Blanching the walnuts*

# Assessment of knowledge and understanding

You have now learned about cold larder work and the range it can cover utilising an array of commodities and cooking techniques.

To test your level of knowledge and understanding, answer the following short questions. These will help to prepare you for your summative (final) assessment.

1  Explain the purpose of canapés within a dinner menu.

_____

_____

2  When creating a cold starter menu, important factors need to be taken into consideration. Explain the factors that you would address and how they are of importance.

_____

_____

3  It is important to use the correct tools and equipment when creating complex cold products. List five key pieces of equipment and explain each individual item's use(s).

i) _____      ii) _____

iii) _____     iv) _____

v) _____

4  Explain the importance of following the correct preparation, cooking and finishing of products when compiling a complex cold dish.

_____

_____

5  Give five examples of healthy options or alternatives that could be used when preparing basic cold dishes or salads.

i) _____      ii) _____

iii) _____     iv) _____

v) _____

6  Cold items must be stored correctly and appropriately prior to use. Give three examples of how this can be done.

i) _____      ii) _____

iii) _____

# CHEF'S PROFILE

**Name: ANDREW TURNER**

**Position:** Executive Chef

**Establishment:** '1880' at the Bentley Kempinski Hotel

**Experience:** Andrew started his training in France after leaving catering college at the age of 18. He returned to England as an accomplished chef and went on to work with some of the world's most well known and talked about chefs, including Albert Roux and Anton Edelmann. Coming from Browns Hotel in Mayfair and having held positions such as Executive Chef at The Berkeley and Executive Sous Chef at Hanbury Manor, Andrew has amazing knowledge and experience within the industry.

**What do you find rewarding about your job?** Having learnt from the masters, Andrew has created his own style which he has mastered and made his own, 'the grazing concept':

*There are many choices available on the à la carte and sometimes it is difficult to choose. That is why I have created a unique dining experience inviting you to graze through, in miniature, the a la carte selection.*

*Every now and then, a dish comes along that totally changes the way you look at food. It does not have to be particularly fancy or complicated, but in its own way, it can provide you with a fascinating insight into the marvellous alchemy that is cooking. All of these menus, complemented by a large selection of wines by the glass, reflect my experiences with flavours.*

**Who is your mentor or main inspiration?** A protégé of Albert Roux, with whom he first worked at Hanbury Manor, Andrew acknowledges Roux's influence both in the culinary and restaurant management fields.

**A brief personal Profile:** Throughout his career Andrew has consistently employed his culinary skills to raise funds for charity and also for friends or colleagues struck by tragedy. In 2000 Andrew was responsible for arranging a meal for 190 people at The Berkeley Hotel working with 19 chefs including Pierre Koffman, Philip Howard, Mark Edwards, Pascal Aussignac, Albert Roux and Giorgio Locatelli, raising funds for the Leukaemia unit at Hammersmith Hospital. This has now become an annual event.

# Seared foie gras, coulis of green apple and confit neck

| INGREDIENTS | 10 PORTIONS |
|---|---|
| 1st quality foie gras | 2.5 lobes – 140g a/c – 70g tasting menu |
| Pomme purée | 500g |
| Fresh apple purée | 100g |
| Green apples (golden delicious) | 10 |
| Apple crisps | 20 |
| Perigourdine sauce | 500ml |
| Confit duck necks | 20 |

## Method of work

1 Cut the foie gras in the normal fashion and cook from cold and not at room temperature (always make sure that the foie gras is seasoned well).

2 Mix the pomme purée, apple purée and confit duck neck – follow the same procedure as for confit leg.

3 Adjust the seasoning where necessary, nappe the sauce around.

4 Place the foie gras on top of the purée and serve with a cloche.

### Garnish

Peel the skin of the apple and put it through the juicer. Serve immediately in a shot glass with an apple granite. Place 1 apple crisp on top of the glass with a neat line of apple sherbet across it.

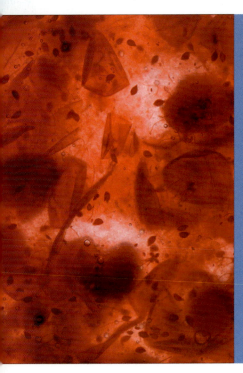

# 7

# Stocks, soups and sauces

## LEARNING OBJECTIVES

The aim of this unit is to enable the candidate to develop skills and implement knowledge in the preparation and cookery principles of stocks, soups and sauces. This will also include materials, ingredients and equipment.

At the end of this chapter you will be able to:

- Identify a variety of stocks, soups and sauces
- Understand the use of relative ingredients in stocks, soups and sauce cookery
- State the quality points of soups and of various stocks and sauces commodities and their uses in a selection of dishes
- Identify the storage procedures of stocks, soups and sauces
- Be competent at preparing and cooking a range of stocks, soups and sauces
- Identify the correct tools and equipment to utilise during the production of soups
- Recognise alternative healthy eating options in different soup recipes

# Stocks and sauces

## BASIC STOCKS

Stocks are the foundation of many soups, sauces, and jus. They are an essential part of the modern day professional kitchen and if made correctly will enhance any dish.

They are created by extracting the flavour (essence) from a base ingredient/ingredients and transforming them into a liquid. Stocks are obtained by gentle simmering of bones/carcasses with vegetables and aromatics (bouquet garni).

All stocks, whether white or brown, should be clear and grease free.

The process of making stocks goes through numerous stages and ensures a good quality is achieved.

### Deglazing

This is the process of allowing the caramelised pan or tray juices and sediment to be released into the liquid with the use of water, stock and wine when making a brown stock. The second stage is to pour off any excess fat, then add the bones to a pan and add liquid.

### Skimming

This process is one of the most important a chef must master. A well-skimmed stock will have clarity and clear flavour which will be ruined if left unattended. The use of a perforated spoon or small ladle to remove the scum and foam will prevent the stock from becoming cloudy and bitter.

Any excess oil can be removed by dragging dish papers across the top of the liquid until it is crystal clear. A brown stock can be chilled and the solidified fat can be removed before it is finished on the stove.

### Straining and Passing

Pouring the liquid through a conical strainer, chinois or muslin will ensure the finished stock will be sediment free. Removing the fat can be done in a number of ways: spooning off the excess from the surface or removing the fat once it has set having been chilled.

### Reducing

By reducing the liquid over a fierce heat a more intensified flavour is achieved; however, the volume is reduced and this must be taken into account when preparing a dish.

| CHEF'S TIP |
| --- |
| When deglazing a pan ensure the majority of fat has been removed. This will prevent a cloudy stock being formed. |

| CHEF'S TIP |
| --- |
| Skim a stock regularly to help prevent the stock turning cloudy and becoming bitter. |

*It is important to skim stock*

*Straining stock through a chinois*

This is the general process used for brown stocks, the cooking times vary according to the bones used. As a guide:

- Brown beef/veal – stock 6–8 hours
- Brown chicken – stock 3–4 hours
- Brown game – stock 4–6 hours (depending on the bone size and finished strength required).

A white stock (except fish) is prepared by bringing the bones to the **boil** then removing them from the liquid and thoroughly washing them. This will remove all the scum and help the finished stock stay **clarified**.

Fish stock does not require the bones to be washed due to the short cooking time which would result in a loss of flavour.

The general rule is:

- White beef/veal – stock 6–8 hours
- White chicken – stock 3–4 hours
- Fish – stock 20 minutes.

Due to the nature of the stock-making process it is imperative that the bones/carcasses and vegetables be of the highest quality. Old, stale or mouldy commodities will taint the colour and flavour of the stock.

Once stock has been cooked it should be strained and chilled/reduced otherwise it will become sour.

Stocks in general are protein-based and as such require careful temperature control and hygienic practices at all times.

Stocks can be reduced to form a **glaze**; this process requires the stock to evaporate until a sticky consistency is achieved.

These bases can be chilled and added to stocks/sauces which lack flavour.

Pre-prepared stocks are manufactured products created by boiling the stock until it is totally dry (powder) or mixed into a paste (**bouillon**). These bases are commonplace within the industry and are either used to make a stock or to improve the flavour of a homemade version.

Although the standard is improving year by year, the basic formula still contains colouring and a relatively high salt content so caution must be used if these bases are to be worked with.

# PREPARE, COOK AND FINISH BASIC HOT SAUCES

## Sauce

A sauce is most accurately described as a flavoured liquid which in essence is a base that has been thickened in one way or another. Sauces are normally classified according to their preparation method as follows:

**CHEF'S TIP**

Glazes can be stored in the freezer and diluted as required, saving time and money.

**VIDEO CLIP**
Convenience stocks

- Roux sauces
- Starch-thickened sauces
- Egg-based sauces
- Meat, vegetable and poultry roasting gravies.

# THICKENED

## Roux

The most well-known of all thickening agents in the kitchen, the basic **roux** is a combination of equal quantities of melted butter and flour mixed over the heat until the mix comes away from the sides of the saucepan.

There are three types of roux. A white roux (as described above) is generally used with milk to achieve a béchamel. A blond roux is achieved by cooking the mix for slightly longer until a light sandy colour develops. White stock is then added to create a **velouté**. The last is a brown roux which uses flour browned in the oven and then made with dripping or oil, brown stock (estouffade) is added which makes a brown sauce (**espagnole**).

When cooking a roux, keep it moving in the pan to ensure even cooking. It must be cooled slightly before adding the hot liquid to prevent lumps from forming in the pan.

The liquid must be slowly added to ensure the sauce becomes smooth and glossy; if the sauce is not cooked out correctly it will lose its shine.

The sauce will thicken due to the starch molecules exploding when cooked; this needs to be cooked further or the sauce will taste of flour.

Never use an aluminium pan when making the sauces as it will taint the colour and give a metallic taste to the finished sauce.

## Beurre Manié

**Beurre manié** is a combination of equal quantities of flour and butter which makes a paste, this cold uncooked mix is whisked into hot liquid and cooked out until the desired thickness is achieved.

## Breadcrumbs/Rice

These are used in a raw state and added to a hot sauce. The cooking process makes the starch in the products explode which creates a natural thickening agent.

**CHEF'S TIP**

A roux must be cooled slightly before the warm liquid is added to prevent lumps.

**CHEF'S TIP**

If a roux-made sauce is kept on the heat for too long it will become too thin due to chemical changes in the flour (dextrinisation).

**CHEF'S TIP**

Allow the beurre manie to be used at room temperature; it emulsifies within the sauce more easily and prevents lumps forming.

## Butter

Whisking or hand-blending small cubes of chilled unsalted butter into a hot sauce will give a glossy rich texture; however, the sauce must not be reboiled as the butter will split.

## Powdered Starch Thickening Agents

These come in numerous forms such as cornflour, arrowroot and fecule. To use these products a little powder should be mixed with cold liquid until a paste is formed, this mix is added to hot liquid which will instantly thicken. The paste must be smooth and added gradually because otherwise lumps will form in the sauce.

Arrowroot becomes transparent once added to sauce and is therefore used when thickening coulis, fruit sauces etc. when clarity is required.

## Egg Yolks and Cream (liaison)

This mixture is achieved by whisking the yolks, cream and a little hot sauce which is then returned to the pan. The sauce must not boil again as it will curdle. This sauce thickening agent is classically used when using velouté sauces.

**CHEF'S TIP**

Ensure the liaison is not poured directly into the sauce; it will split instantly and render the sauce useless.

| BASIC SAUCES AND THEIR DERIVATIVES | |
|---|---|
| **Béchamel** | |
| Anchovy (anchovy essence) | sauce anchois |
| Egg (diced hard-boiled egg) | sauce aux oeufs |
| Cheese (grated cheese and egg yolk) | sauce Mornay |
| Onion (sweated chopped onion) | sauce aux oignons |
| Soubise (passed onion sauce) | sauce Soubise |
| Parsley (chopped parsley) | sauce persil |
| Cream (cream, milk or yoghurt) | sauce crème |
| Mustard (mustard) | sauce moutarde |
| **Velouté** | |
| Caper sauce (capers) | sauce aux capres |
| Suprême sauce (mushroom trimmings, cream, egg yolk, lemon juice) | sauce suprême |
| Aurore sauce (supreme and tomato purée) | sauce aurore |
| Mushroom sauce (suprême, sliced mushroom, cream, egg yolk) | sauce aux champignons |
| Ivory sauce (suprême sauce, meat glaze) | sauce ivoire |

## BASIC SAUCES AND THEIR DERIVATIVES

| | |
|---|---|
| **Demi glace** – equal quantities espagnole (brown sauce) and estouffade (brown stock) reduced by half | |
| **Demi glace** (espagnole-based) | |
| Bordelaise sauce (red wine, shallots, bone marrow) | sauce bordelaise |
| Chasseur sauce (tarragon, white wine) | sauce chasseur |
| Devilled sauce (cayenne pepper) | sauce diable |
| Pepper sauce (crushed peppercorns) | sauce poivrade |
| Italian sauce (mushrooms, tomato, ham) | sauce italienne |
| Brown onion sauce (sliced onions, white wine) | sauce lyonnaise |
| Madeira sauce (madeira wine) | sauce madère |
| Sherry sauce (sherry) | sauce xérès |
| Port wine sauce (port wine) | sauce Porto |
| Piquant sauce (gherkins, capers, herbs) | sauce piquante |
| Robert sauce (white wine, mustard) | sauce Robert |
| Charcutiere sauce (gherkin, white wine) | sauce Charcutière |
| Reform sauce (ham, tongue, beetroot, truffle) | sauce réforme |
| Curry sauce (curry spices) | sauce kari |
| Roast gravy | jus roti |
| Thickened gravy | jus-lie |
| **Purée-based** | |
| Apple sauce | sauce aux pommes |
| Tomato sauce | sauce tomate |
| Smitaine sauce | sauce Smitaine |

Purée-thickened sauces use the natural commodity where possible to thicken, e.g. roasted peppers liquidised to give body to the sauce.

When using green leaves to colour a sauce they should be added at the last minute or the sauce will generally turn brown.

# RECIPES

## Vegetable stock

*Pass the stock through muslin*

| INGREDIENTS | 10 PORTIONS |
| --- | --- |
| Onion | 1 |
| Garlic | 1 clove |
| Fennel | ½ |
| Leek | 1 |
| White mushroom trimmings | 30g |
| Unsalted butter | 25g |
| Vegetable oil | 25ml |
| Tarragon | 2 sprigs |
| Coriander | 2 sprigs |
| Good-quality salt and white pepper | To taste |

### Method of work

1 Wash all the vegetables well, then drain.
2 Finely chop all vegetables and sweat in butter and oil for 2–3 minutes in a saucepan without letting the vegetables colour.
3 Add 500ml of water, bring to the boil then simmer for 15 minutes.
4 Add chopped herbs and cook for a further 5 minutes.
5 Pass, season, chill and use as required.

## Fish stock

**CHEF'S TIP**

Remove all gills, scales and unwanted parts of the fish before making the stock as it will taint the flavour and cause cloudiness.

*Skim the stock*

| INGREDIENTS | 10 PORTIONS |
| --- | --- |
| White fish bones | 500g |
| White mirepoix | 25g |
| Mushroom trimmings | 15g |
| Butter | 10g |
| White wine | 50ml |
| water | 500ml |
| Good-quality salt and white pepper | To taste |

### Method of work

1 Wash the vegetables well, and then drain.
2 Sweat off the mirepoix and mushroom trimmings in butter until softened, without letting them colour.
3 Add the prepared fish bones, white wine and water.
4 Simmer for 20 minutes skimming occasionally.
5 Pass the stock through muslin.
6 Season, chill or reduce as required.

**VIDEO CLIP**
Making a fish stock

# White chicken stock

*Reduce the wine with the carcass*

| INGREDIENTS | 10 PORTIONS |
|---|---|
| Chicken carcass | 500g |
| Shallots | 1 |
| Leek | 1 |
| Celery | 1 stick |
| Garlic | 1 clove |
| White wine | 50ml |
| Water | 1 litre |
| Bouquet garni | 1 |
| Onions | 1 |
| Cloves | 1 |
| Good-quality salt and white pepper | To taste |

## Method of work

1 Wash all the vegetables well and then drain.
2 Place the bones into a saucepan with the vegetables then add the wine and reduce until the wine has evaporated.
3 Add the water then bring to the boil.
4 **Skim** well then add the bouquet garni.
5 Reduce the heat; then allow simmering slowly for 3 hours, skimming occasionally.
6 Season, pass, chill and use as required.

**CHEF'S TIP**

A boiling fowl can be used to enhance the chicken flavour.

**VIDEO CLIP**
Making a chicken stock

# Brown chicken stock

**CHEF'S TIP**

Chicken can be fatty so ensure any fat is poured away once roasted and before making the stock.

| INGREDIENTS | 10 PORTIONS |
|---|---|
| Chicken carcass | 500g |
| Mushrooms | 50g |
| Carrots | 50g |
| Shallots | 1 |
| Leek | 1 |
| Celery | 1 stick |
| Garlic | 1 clove |
| White wine | 50ml |
| Water | 1 litre |
| Bouquet garni | 1 |
| Onions | 1 |
| Cloves | 1 |
| Good-quality salt and white pepper | To taste |

*Roast the bones until brown*

## Method of work

1 Wash the vegetables well and then drain.
2 **Roast** the bones until brown, drain any fat, and then place the bones into a saucepan with the vegetables.
3 Add the wine and reduce until it has evaporated.
4 Add the water, bouquet garni, onion and cloves then bring to the boil.
5 Simmer slowly over a low heat for 3 hours, skimming occasionally.
6 Season, pass, chill and use as required.

# Brown veal/beef/lamb/game stock

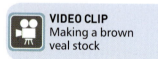

**CHEF'S TIP**

As game is a strong flavour, use a sharp piquant flavour when making the sauce to balance the dish.

**VIDEO CLIP**
Making a brown veal stock

| INGREDIENTS | 10 PORTIONS |
|---|---|
| Veal/beef/lamb/game bones | 500g |
| Mirepoix | 125g |
| Tomato purée | 50g |
| Water | 1 litre |
| Bouquet garni (onion, celery, bay, thyme, rosemary, peppercorns) (juniper for game) | 1 |
| Good-quality salt and white pepper | To taste |

## Method of work

1 Wash all the vegetables well and then drain.
2 Chop the bones and brown well on all sides with the vegetables and purée in a hot oven, drain off any fat and place in a stockpot.
3 **Deglaze** the pan with half the water and add to the bones.
4 Add the remaining water and bring to the boil.
5 Simmer for 6–8 hours, skimming occasionally.
6 Season, pass and chill or reduce as required.

# White veal/beef/lamb stock

**CHEF'S TIP**

Ensure a good colour is achieved during roasting as this will determine the end result.

| INGREDIENTS | 10 PORTIONS |
|---|---|
| Veal/beef or lamb bones. | 500g |
| Large white mirepoix of vegetables | 125g |
| Water | 1 litre |
| Bouquet garni (onion, celery, bay, thyme, rosemary, peppercorns) | 1 |
| Good-quality salt and white pepper | To taste |

*Wash the bones to remove scum*

## Method of work

1 Wash all the vegetables well and then drain.
2 Place the bones in water and bring to the boil.
3 Remove the bones and wash thoroughly to remove all the scum.
4 Discard the liquid and return the bones to the washed pot.
5 Add the vegetables, bouquet garni and water.
6 Bring to the boil and skim.
7 Reduce the heat and simmer for 6–8 hours, skimming occasionally.
8 Season, pass and chill or reduce as required.

# Béchamel

| INGREDIENTS | 4 PORTIONS | 10 PORTIONS |
|---|---|---|
| Butter | 20g | 50g |
| Flour | 20g | 50g |
| Milk | 200ml | 500ml |
| Clouté (onion studded with cloves) | ½ | 1 |
| Good-quality salt and white pepper | To taste | To taste |

**CHEF'S TIP**

To make a healthier sauce margarine can substituted for butter; however, the flavour can be slightly distorted.

**VIDEO CLIP**
Making béchamel sauce

## Method of work

1 Melt the butter in a saucepan (stainless steel if possible).
2 Add the flour and mix well.
3 Cook the mixture gently without colouring.
4 Remove from the heat and allow the roux to cool slightly.
5 Meanwhile heat the milk with the clouté then slowly add to the roux, stirring continuously until the mix is smooth.
6 Simmer gently for at least 20 minutes.
7 Pass the sauce through a conical strainer.
8 Season and use as required.

*Simmering the milk with the clouté*

*Cover the béchamel with the cartouche*

*Twist the muslin in opposite directions*

# Mornay sauce

**CHEF'S TIP**

Add a small amount of hot sauce to cream before returning to the main pan to prevent splitting.

| INGREDIENTS | 4 PORTIONS | 10 PORTIONS |
| --- | --- | --- |
| Béchamel sauce | 200ml | 500ml |
| Grated cheese | 40g | 100g |
| Egg yolks | 1 | 2 |
| Good-quality salt and white pepper | To taste | To taste |

## Method of work

1 Just before service whisk the cheese and egg yolk into the simmering béchamel.
2 Do not allow this sauce to reboil.

Note: this sauce is classically used to coat fish, meat and vegetables and is usually gratinated.

# Parsley sauce

**CHEF'S TIP**

Add the chopped parsley at the last minute to ensure the sauce stays green.

| INGREDIENTS | 4 PORTIONS | 10 PORTIONS |
| --- | --- | --- |
| Béchamel sauce | 200ml | 500ml |
| Chopped parsley | ½tbsp | 1tbsp |
| Good-quality salt and white pepper | To taste | To taste |

## Method of work

1 Just before service add the chopped parsley to the béchamel.
2 Re-season and use as required.

Note: this sauce is classically served with fish and vegetables.

# Anchovy sauce

**CHEF'S TIP**

Using finely chopped fresh anchovies in oil gives a more Mediterranean flavour.

| INGREDIENTS | 4 PORTIONS | 10 PORTIONS |
| --- | --- | --- |
| Béchamel sauce | 200ml | 500ml |
| Anchovy essence | ½tbsp | 1tbsp |
| Good-quality salt and white pepper | To taste | To taste |

## Method of work

1 Just before service whisk the anchovy essence into the béchamel sauce.

Note: this sauce is classically served with fish.

# Onion sauce *sauce Soubise*

| INGREDIENTS | 4 PORTIONS | 10 PORTIONS |
|---|---|---|
| Béchamel sauce | 200ml | 500ml |
| Finely diced onion | 40g | 100g |
| butter | 20g | 50g |
| Good-quality salt and white pepper | To taste | To taste |

### CHEF'S TIP

Small onions give a sweeter flavour to the sauce.

## Method of work

1 Melt the butter in a saucepan then add the onions and sweat without allowing them to colour.
2 Add the mixture to the béchamel, re-season and use as required.
3 For Soubise sauce pass through a chinois and serve.

Note: this sauce is classically served with mutton.

# Egg sauce

| INGREDIENTS | 4 PORTIONS | 10 PORTIONS |
|---|---|---|
| Béchamel sauce | 200ml | 500ml |
| Hard-boiled eggs, small diced | 1 | 2 |
| Good-quality salt and white pepper | To taste | To taste |

### CHEF'S TIP

Carefully stir in the egg to avoid the pieces becoming smashed and destroying the appearance required.

## Method of work

1 Just before service stir the diced egg into the béchamel sauce carefully to prevent them from breaking up too much.

Note: this sauce is classically served with fish.

# Cream sauce

| INGREDIENTS | 4 PORTIONS | 10 PORTIONS |
|---|---|---|
| Béchamel sauce | 200ml | 500ml |
| Cream or yoghurt (healthier option) | 50ml | 125ml |
| Good-quality salt and white pepper | To taste | To taste |

### CHEF'S TIP

Use a low-fat yoghurt to create a low-fat version of this sauce.

## Method of work

1 Just before service add the cream and the sauce, bring back to the boil.
2 Simmer, re-season and use as required.

Note: this sauce is classically served with fish and vegetables.

# Mustard sauce

 **CHEF'S TIP**

The predominant flavour in this sauce is mustard so use a high-quality one such as Pommery grain mustard.

| INGREDIENTS | 4 PORTIONS | 10 PORTIONS |
|---|---|---|
| Béchamel sauce | 200ml | 500ml |
| English mustard (grain mustard can also be used for appearance) | To taste | To taste |
| Good-quality salt and white pepper | To taste | To taste |

## Method of work

1 Just before service add the mustard.
2 Simmer, re-season and use as required.
3 The sauce should have enough mustard to give a hot taste.

Note: this sauce is classically served with grilled fish, especially herring.

# Velouté

**CHEF'S TIP**

Sauces are high-risk foods so must be stored at below 5°C in the refrigerator and −18°C in the freezer.

**VIDEO CLIP**
Making chicken velouté

| INGREDIENTS | 4 PORTIONS | 10 PORTIONS |
|---|---|---|
| Butter | 20g | 50g |
| Flour | 20g | 50g |
| White stock (fish, chicken, veal, beef) | 200ml | 500ml |
| Double cream | 20ml | 50ml |
| Egg yolks | 1 | 2 |
| Good-quality salt and white pepper | To taste | To taste |

## Method of work

1 Melt the butter in a saucepan (stainless steel if possible).
2 Add the flour and mix well.
3 Cook the roux gently until a very light golden colour is achieved (blond roux).
4 Remove from the heat and cool slightly.
5 Meanwhile bring the stock to the boil.
6 Slowly add the stock to the roux, mixing continuously until smooth.
7 Simmer gently for at least 50 minutes.
8 Season and pass through a conical strainer.

Note: the sauce can be enriched with the cream and yolk but should not be reboiled.

Make the blond roux

Stir in the stock

Pass through a conical strainer

# Caper sauce

| INGREDIENTS | 4 PORTIONS | 10 PORTIONS |
|---|---|---|
| Velouté sauce (mutton, lamb) | 200ml | 500ml |
| Capers | 1tbsp | 2tbsp |
| Good-quality salt and white pepper | To taste | To taste |

**CHEF'S TIP**

Thoroughly wash the capers before use as they are very salty and will ruin the sauce.

## Method of work

1   Just before service add the capers to the simmering velouté.

Note: the sauce is classically served with mutton.

# Suprême sauce

| INGREDIENTS | 4 PORTIONS | 10 PORTIONS |
|---|---|---|
| Velouté sauce (chicken) | 200ml | 500ml |
| Button mushroom trimmings | 20g | 50g |
| Double cream | 40ml | 100ml |
| Egg yolks | 1 | 2 |
| Lemon juice | ¼ lemon | ½ lemon |
| Good-quality salt and white pepper | To taste | To taste |

**CHEF'S TIP**

Thoroughly wash the mushroom trimmings or the dirt and grit will discolour and flavour the sauce.

## Method of work

1   Simmer the velouté and add the mushroom trimmings which should be well washed.
2   Pass the sauce through a chinois.
3   Make a liaison by whisking the egg yolks with the cream.
4   Add a little hot sauce to this mix then return it to the velouté.
5   Do not reboil the sauce again.
6   Add the lemon juice to taste and re-season.

Note: the sauce is classically served with chicken.

*Make a liaison with egg yolks and cream*

# Aurore sauce

**CHEF'S TIP**

Hot sauces should be kept in a bain marie during service to prevent over-reducing.

| INGREDIENTS | 4 PORTIONS | 10 PORTIONS |
|---|---|---|
| Velouté sauce (chicken) | 200ml | 500ml |
| Button mushroom trimmings | 20g | 50g |
| Double cream | 40ml | 100ml |
| Egg yolks | 1 | 2 |
| Lemon juice | ¼ lemon | ½ lemon |
| Tomato purée (fresh tomato sauce if possible) | To taste and colour | To taste and colour |
| Good-quality salt and white pepper | To taste | To taste |

## Method of work

1 Simmer the velouté and add the mushroom trimmings which have been well washed.
2 Pass the sauce through a chinois.
3 Make a liaison by whisking the egg yolks with the cream.
4 Add a little hot sauce to this mix then return it to the velouté.
5 Do not reboil the sauce again.
6 Add the lemon juice to taste and the tomato purée then re-season.
7 The sauce should be pale red in colour.

Note: the sauce is classically served with chicken and chaud-froid sauce.

# Ivory sauce

**CHEF'S TIP**

Using a pre-made glaze will speed up the preparation of this sauce.

| INGREDIENTS | 4 PORTIONS | 10 PORTIONS |
|---|---|---|
| Velouté sauce (veal) | 200ml | 500ml |
| Button mushroom trimmings | 20g | 50g |
| Double cream | 40ml | 100ml |
| Egg yolks | 1 | 2 |
| Lemon juice | ¼ lemon | ½ lemon |
| Reduced brown chicken stock (glaze) | To taste and to give an ivory colour | To taste and to give an ivory colour |
| Good-quality salt and white pepper | To taste | To taste |

## Method of work

1 Simmer the velouté and add the mushroom trimmings which have been well washed.
2 Pass the sauce through a chinois.
3 Make a liaison by whisking the egg yolks with the cream.
4 Add a little hot sauce to this mix then return it to the velouté.
5 Do not reboil the sauce again.
6 Add the lemon juice to taste and then re-season.
7 Add the meat glaze to achieve an ivory colour.

Note: this sauce is classically used with a blanquette of veal.

# Mushroom sauce

| INGREDIENTS | 4 PORTIONS | 10 PORTIONS |
|---|---|---|
| Velouté sauce (chicken) | 200ml | 500ml |
| Button mushroom trimmings | 20g | 50g |
| Double cream | 40ml | 100ml |
| Egg yolks | 1 | 2 |
| Lemon juice | ¼ lemon | ½ lemon |
| Sliced button mushrooms | 40g | 100g |
| Butter | 20g | 50g |

**CHEF'S TIP**

Use only the freshest mushrooms available as they are not only visible but are the main flavouring.

## Method of work

1 Simmer the velouté and add the mushroom trimmings which have been well washed.
2 Pass the sauce through a chinois.
3 Make a liaison by whisking the egg yolks with the cream.
4 Add a little hot sauce to this mix then return it to the velouté.
5 Do not reboil the sauce again.
6 Add the lemon juice to taste and then re-season.
7 In a separate pan melt the butter and sweat the sliced mushrooms without letting them colour then add to the sauce.

Note: the sauce is classically served with chicken.

# Brown sauce *sauce espagnole*

*Make the brown roux*

| INGREDIENTS | 4 PORTIONS | 10 PORTIONS |
|---|---|---|
| Dripping or oil | 10g | 25g |
| Flour | 15g | 30g |
| Tomato purée | 5g | 10g |
| Brown stock (estouffade) | 200ml | 500ml |
| Mirepoix | 80g | 200g |
| Good-quality salt and white pepper | To taste | To taste |

**CHEF'S TIP**

This sauce will enhance the flavour of the original stock; it is therefore important that the original stock is of the highest quality.

## Method of work

1 Heat the dripping/oil in a saucepan (stainless steel if possible).
2 Add the flour and mix well.
3 Cook the roux until a light brown colour is achieved (brown roux).
4 Cool slightly and add the tomato purée.
5 Meanwhile boil the stock then slowly add to the roux, stirring continuously until smooth.
6 Brown the vegetables in a frying pan or hot oven, drain any excess fat then add to the sauce.
7 Simmer the sauce for a minimum of 4 hours.
8 Regularly skim the sauce.
9 Pass through a conical strainer then re-season as required.

# Demi glace

| INGREDIENTS | 4 PORTIONS | 10 PORTIONS |
|---|---|---|
| **Brown stock** (estouffade) | 200ml | 500ml |
| **Brown sauce** (espagnole) | 200ml | 500ml |
| **Good-quality salt and white pepper** | To taste | To taste |

## Method of work

1. Simmer the two together in a saucepan (stainless steel if possible).
2. Reduce by half.
3. Skim regularly.
4. Pass through a chinois and re-season.

# Chasseur sauce

*Deglaze the pan with white wine*

| INGREDIENTS | 4 PORTIONS | 10 PORTIONS |
|---|---|---|
| **Butter** | 20g | 40g |
| **Finely diced shallots** | 10g | 20g |
| **Sliced button mushrooms** | 50g | 100g |
| **White wine** | 50ml | 100ml |
| **Tomato concassé** | 90g | 180g |
| **Demi glace** | 200ml | 500ml |
| **Chopped tarragon** | 1tbsp | 2tbsp |
| **Chopped parsley** | ½tbsp | 1tbsp |
| **Good-quality salt and white pepper** | To taste | To taste |

## Method of work

1. Melt the butter in a saucepan (stainless steel if possible).
2. Add the shallots and sweat without letting them colour.
3. Add the mushrooms and sweat without letting them colour, then deglaze with white wine.
4. Reduce by half then add the tomato concassé and **demi glace**.
5. Simmer, add herbs and correct seasoning.

# Devilled sauce

| INGREDIENTS | 4 PORTIONS | 10 PORTIONS |
|---|---|---|
| Finely diced shallots | 40g | 100g |
| Mignonette pepper | Pinch | Pinch |
| White wine | 5ml | 20ml |
| White wine vinegar | 5ml | 20ml |
| Cayenne pepper | To taste | To taste |
| Demi glace | 200ml | 500ml |
| Good-quality salt and white pepper | To taste | To taste |

### CHEF'S TIP

Cooking out spices before adding liquids prevents sauces from becoming bitter.

## Method of work

1 Make a reduction of shallots, pepper, wine, vinegar and cayenne.
2 Reduce by half.
3 Add the demi glace and simmer for 5 minutes.
4 Pass through a fine chinois and re-season with extra cayenne.

# Italian sauce

| INGREDIENTS | 4 PORTIONS | 10 PORTIONS |
|---|---|---|
| Butter | 20g | 50g |
| Finely diced shallots | 8g | 20g |
| Finely chopped button mushrooms | 30g | 80g |
| Demi glace | 200ml | 500ml |
| Finely chopped cooked ham | 15g | 40g |
| Tomato concassé | 70g | 180g |
| Chopped tarragon, parsley, chervil | 1tbsp | 2tbsp |
| Good-quality salt and white pepper | To taste | To taste |

### CHEF'S TIP

Avoid fatty ham as it is visible in the sauce.

## Method of work

1 Melt the butter and sweat the shallots without letting them colour then add the mushrooms and cook for a further 2 minutes.
2 Add the demi glace, tomatoes and ham, simmer for 5 minutes.
3 Re-season and add the herbs.

# Brown onion sauce

| INGREDIENTS | 4 PORTIONS | 10 PORTIONS |
|---|---|---|
| Butter | 20g | 50g |
| Finely sliced onions | 80g | 200g |
| Red wine vinegar | 2tbsp | 5tbsp |
| Demi glace | 200ml | 500ml |
| Good-quality salt and white pepper | To taste | To taste |

### CHEF'S TIP

If the sauce appears slightly bitter at the end add a little sugar; this will transform the end product.

## Method of work

1 Melt the butter and sweat the onions until very soft.
2 Add the vinegar and reduce.
3 Add the demi glace then simmer for 5 minutes.
4 Skim if required then re-season.

# Madeira/sherry/port wine/red wine sauce

| INGREDIENTS | 4 PORTIONS | 10 PORTIONS |
|---|---|---|
| Alcohol as above | 10ml | 25ml |
| Demi glace | 200ml | 500ml |
| Chilled diced butter | 20g | 50g |
| Good-quality salt and white pepper | To taste | To taste |

### CHEF'S TIP

When using alcohol in sauces it is important to reduce and/or burn it off first, otherwise the sauce will taste bitter.

## Method of work

1 Bring the demi glace to the boil then add the alcohol and reboil for 5 minutes.
2 Whisk the diced butter into the sauce, re-season and serve.

# Bread sauce

| INGREDIENTS | 4 PORTIONS | 10 PORTIONS |
|---|---|---|
| Fresh milk | 400ml | 1100ml |
| Onion studded with 2 cloves and half a bay leaf | ½ onion | 1 onion |
| White breadcrumbs | 30g | 70g |
| Good-quality salt and white pepper | To taste | To taste |
| Butter | 10g | 25g |

## Method of work

1 Bring the milk to the boil with the studded onion and simmer for 10 minutes.
2 Remove the onion and add the breadcrumbs, simmer for a further 3 minutes.
3 Season and add the butter on top to prevent a skin from forming. Stir well before serving.

# Robert sauce

| INGREDIENTS | 4 PORTIONS | 10 PORTIONS |
|---|---|---|
| Butter | 10g | 20g |
| Onions finely diced | 50g | 100g |
| Red wine vinegar | 50ml | 100ml |
| Demi glace | 200ml | 500ml |
| English mustard | 1tbsp | 2tbsp |
| Sugar | ¼tbsp | ½tbsp |
| Good-quality salt and white pepper | To taste | To taste |

**CHEF'S TIP**

Ensure the mustard is mixed with water before adding to the sauce; this will allow emulsification and prevent tiny mustard lumps forming.

## Method of work

1 Melt the butter and sweat the onions until transparent.
2 Add the vinegar and reduce completely.
3 Add the demi glace and simmer for 5 minutes.
4 Mix the sugar, mustard with a little warm water and add to the sauce.
5 Simmer for 5 minutes, re season.

Note: add gherkin julienne to the finished sauce and it becomes charcutière sauce.

# Reform sauce

| INGREDIENTS | 4 PORTIONS | 10 PORTIONS |
|---|---|---|
| Mirepoix small cut | 30g | 80g |
| Butter | 15g | 30g |
| Peppercorns | ½ tsp | 1tsp |
| Red wine vinegar | ½tbsp | 1tbsp |
| Redcurrant jelly | ½tbsp | 1tbsp |
| Demi glace | 200ml | 500ml |
| Julienne of cooked egg white, cooked beetroot, tongue, truffle, gherkin and mushroom | 50g | 120g |
| Good-quality salt and white pepper | To taste | To taste |

**CHEF'S TIP**

The julienne needs to be very neat as it is the main focal point.

## Method of work

1 Melt the butter and brown the mirepoix, drain the fat and add the peppercorns and vinegar.
2 Reduce by half.
3 Add the demi glace and simmer for 20 minutes.
4 Skim regularly.
5 Add the redcurrant jelly and simmer for a further 5 minutes.
6 Pass through a fine chinois and re-season.
7 Garnish the sauce with the julienne.

# Jus roti

| INGREDIENTS | 4 PORTIONS | 10 PORTIONS |
|---|---|---|
| **Bones** (chicken, beef, lamb, veal) | 200g | 500g |
| **Brown stock** | 200ml | 500ml |
| **Mirepoix** | 80g | 200g |
| **Good-quality salt and white pepper** | To taste | To taste |
| **Cornflour** (jus lie) | 1tbsp | 3tbsp |

> **CHEF'S TIP**
>
> The addition of garlic or ginger can improve a sauce's flavour as long as it suits the dish and is used correctly.

## Method of work

1 Brown the bones and mirepoix in a pan or a hot oven.
2 Drain any fat off.
3 Bring the bones, stock and mirepoix to the boil and skim.
4 Simmer for 2 hours and skim regularly.
5 Once the roast joint is cooked, remove from the tray and rest.
6 Strain off the fat.
7 Place the tray on the stove and deglaze with the stock.
8 Simmer for 5 minutes.
9 For the jus lie – mix the cornflour with a little water and add to the stock; stirring continuously.
10 Re-season and pass through muslin.

# Hollandaise sauce

| INGREDIENTS | 4 PORTIONS | 10 PORTIONS |
|---|---|---|
| **White wine vinegar** | 1tbsp | 2tbsp |
| **Water** | 1tbsp | 2tbsp |
| **Crushed peppercorns** | ½tsp | 1tsp |
| **Egg Yolks** | 2 | 4 |
| **Clarified butter** | 125g | 250g |
| **Lemon juice** | ¼ lemon | ½ lemon |
| **Good-quality salt and cayenne pepper** | To taste | To taste |

## Method of work

1 Place the vinegar, water and peppercorns in a saucepan and reduce by one third. Strain the liquid and allow to cool slightly.
2 Whisk the egg yolks with the reduced liquid and over a bain-marie until the ribbon stage is achieved.
3 Slowly drizzle the warm clarified butter into the egg mix, whisking constantly until the sauce is thick and glossy. Add the lemon juice and season well.
4 Keep warm until ready for service.

# Curry sauce

| INGREDIENTS | 4 PORTIONS | 10 PORTIONS |
|---|---|---|
| Finely diced onion | 40g | 100g |
| Chopped garlic | 2 cloves | 4 cloves |
| Butter | 10g | 20g |
| Flour | 10g | 20g |
| Ground curry spices (turmeric, cumin, coriander, garam masala) | 1½tbsp | 3tbsp |
| Tomato purée | 1 ½tbsp | 3tbsp |
| Vegetable stock | 200ml | 500ml |
| Grated ginger | 1tbsp | 2tbsp |
| Grated Cox's apple | 2 | 4 |
| Mango chutney | 1½tbsp | 3tbsp |
| Grated fresh coconut | ¼ | ½ |
| Coconut milk | ½ tin | 1 tin |
| Good-quality salt | To taste | To taste |

**CHEF'S TIP**

If possible grind the spices freshly; this will give a much cleaner, more fragrant and aromatic taste.

## Method of work

1  Melt the butter and sweat the onion and garlic without letting them colour.
2  Add the flour and curry spices then cook for a further 2 minutes.
3  Add the tomato purée then slightly cool the mix.
4  Meanwhile boil the stock and then slowly add to the roux.
5  Mix until the sauce is smooth.
6  Add the remaining ingredients and simmer for at least 20 minutes.
7  Regularly skim, and then blend until smooth, re-season.

# Roasted pepper sauce

| INGREDIENTS | 4 PORTIONS | 10 PORTIONS |
|---|---|---|
| Onions sliced | 1 | 2 |
| Garlic chopped | 1 clove | 3 cloves |
| Olive oil | 20ml | 50ml |
| Peppers, peeled and deseeded | 400g | 1kg |
| Red wine | 40ml | 100ml |
| Thyme | Sprigs | Sprigs |
| Good-quality salt and white pepper | To taste | To taste |

## Method of work

1 Sweat the onions and garlic in the oil for 10 minutes without letting them colour.

2 Roast the peppers with the thyme for 10 minutes.

3 Add to the onions.

4 Add the wine and reduce until almost evaporated.

5 Cover with a tight-fitting lid.

6 Cook on a very low heat for 15 minutes.

7 Liquidise, correct the seasoning and use as required.

# Plum tomato coulis

| INGREDIENTS | 4 PORTIONS | 10 PORTIONS |
|---|---|---|
| Onions sliced | 1 | 2 |
| Garlic chopped | 1 clove | 3 cloves |
| Olive oil | 20ml | 50ml |
| Plum tomatoes, peeled and quartered | 400g | 1kg |
| White wine | 60ml | 150ml |
| Basil | ½ bunch | 1 bunch |

## Method of work

1 Sweat the onions and garlic in the oil for 10 minutes without letting them colour.

2 Add the tomatoes and cook for a further 10 minutes .

3 Add the wine and reduce until almost evaporated.

4 Add the basil and cover with a tight-fitting lid.

5 Cook on a very low heat for 1 hour.

6 Liquidise, correct the seasoning and use as required.

**CHEF'S TIP**

Once liquidised this sauce should not be reboiled as it will split.

## Assessment of knowledge and understanding

You have now learned about the use of the different types of stocks and sauces and how to produce a variety of them utilising an array of commodities and cooking techniques.

To test your level of knowledge and understanding, answer the following short questions. These will help to prepare you for your summative (final) assessment.

1 Identify the three main categories of roux.

i) _____  ii) _____

iii) _____

2 Explain how to store freshly made stock correctly.

_____

_____

3 Describe three ways of removing fat from a stock.

i) _____  ii) _____

iii) _____

4 Explain the reason for using good quality ingredients when making a stock or sauce.

_____

_____

5 State the times used to cook fish stock.

_____

_____

6 Explain the problem that could occur if a liaison is added directly into a hot liquid.

_____

_____

7 Explain the correct storage conditions for cold stocks and sauces.

_____

_____

# CHEF'S PROFILE

**Name: NICK VADIS**

**Position:** Executive Head Chef, British Airways Heathrow

**Main responsibilities:** I am responsible for all staff feeding at Heathrow, overseeing terminals 4 and 1, first-class dining and from 2008, Terminal 5.

I am also responsible for all Chef development and training for 6 sites, which is approximately 52 staff.

**When did you realise you wanted to pursue a career in the catering and hospitality industry?** It was always there – my father was a chef and my mother was a teacher. However, I also wanted to travel and see the world, so I combined this by joining the Royal Navy as a chef.

**Training:** I started as a trainee chef in the Royal Navy at the Royal Navy Cookery School Chatham, Kent. I then did senior courses at the Army Catering School Aldershot, before attending Farnborough College of Technology and Portsmouth University.

**Experience:**

1. Royal Navy ships and establishments world wide (23 years)
2. Taught at St Omens barracks Aldershot, Level 2 NVQ
3. Head of kitchen larder, Royal Navy Cookery School
4. Senior naval verifier Royal Navy Cookery School
5. Head of Naval Cookery Training Cookery School Cornwall
6. Executive Head Chef Robinson College (Cambridge University)
7. Executive Head Chef Waterside British Airways
8. Group Executive Chef B.A. Contract

**What do you find rewarding about your job?** Being a chef means no two days are the same. It is a creative profession, and to me is rewarding and interesting job. I could never imagine doing anything else. Training and chef development are key to this industry and seeing chefs in your brigade(s) develop is as rewarding as anything can be.

**What do you find the most challenging about the job?** Some of the greatest challenges are usually brought about by yourself. Working with a 'can do' attitude, critically looking at all you do in order to make things better and constantly looking at ways to develop yourself and your brigade are self-set challenges, which make the job diverse and interesting.

**What advice would you give to students just beginning their career?** Work hard and listen; it is a tough profession and you will work long hours if you are to succeed. Be a sponge and soak up ideas and advice. The rewards are there but you will have to work for it.

Enjoy your journey, there is no better job for creativity and to show craft and skill.

**Your mentor or main inspiration:** My main inspiration must be my mother. She always stood by me at school and when I said I wanted to be a chef she supported me.

**Secrets of a successful chef:**

1. Creative, flair, artistic and flexible
2. Not afraid to work hard
3. Has a passion and belief in their own ability
4. Constantly revaluates their work, and looks at ways to make it better
5. Level headed and is clam during a crisis

**Can you give one essential kitchen tip or technique that you use as a chef?** Listen to your brigade and work with them. To earn respect you have to give respect. Never think you know everything.

# Ravioli of chicken on tomato and pancetta fondue leaf salad, white bean and foie gras cappuccino sauce

| INGREDIENTS | 8 PORTIONS |
|---|---|
| Fresh egg pasta | 1 batch |
| Chicken mousse | 150g |
| Pancetta small crisp lardons | 120g |
| Leaf spinach fresh picked | 100g |
| Rocket leaf fresh picked | 100g |
| White bean sauce | ½ pint |
| Foie gras | 50g |
| Tomato and mushroom fondue | 100g |
| Truffle oil | Small drizzle |
| Salt and pepper | |

### Pasta recipe

| INGREDIENTS | 8 PORTIONS |
|---|---|
| Eggs | 2 |
| Egg yolks | 3 |
| Flour | 0/0300g |
| Olive oil | 1tbs |

## Method of work

1 Place the flour into a robo coupe and pulse.
2 Add the oil and pulse then the egg yolks. It should be like cous cous.
3 Remove from the bowl and work on the bench by hand to form smooth dough.
4 Rest and use as required.

### White bean and foie gras cappuccino

| INGREDIENTS | 8 PORTIONS |
|---|---|
| Chicken stock | 16floz |
| Cooked white beans | 9oz |
| Double cream | ¼ pint |
| Truffle oil | 2tsp |
| Chilled cold butter | 1oz |
| Chilled Foie Gras | 1oz |

## Method of work

1 Boil the stock until reduced to about ½ pint.
2 Mean while puree the beans in a liquidizer, and then scrape into a clean bowl.
3 Using and hand blender, slowly whisk in the stock and cream and truffle oil.
4 Season to taste and pour the sauce into a saucepan.
5 Bring back to the boil and remove whisk in the foie gras.
6 To stabilize the sauce add the chilled butter.

## To assemble the dish

1 Place a portion of pancetta and warmed tomato in the centre of the bowl.
2 Place a small amount of wilted leaf on top of the tomato and pancetta.
3 Make sure that the pancetta is distributed through out the four portions.
4 Place one large ravioli on top of the leaf.
5 Spoon the frothed sauce over the ravioli.
6 Drizzle a little truffle oil around the plate or bowl and dust with powdered mushrooms and serve.

# Soups

## INTRODUCTION

Soup has long been the foundation of menus across the world and a general source of nutrition. From the hearty main course soup of minestrone served with focaccia bread, drizzled in olive oil to the most delicate of consommés accompanied by the lightest profiteroles; both the contemporary chef and the humblest of family cooks need a deep understanding of the preparation and finishing of soups.

It is widely thought that the first recorded soup recipe was of a barley soup from a Roman cook book. Originally in France the *soupe* was the slice of bread on which was poured the contents of a cooking pot (potage), the contents were usually gruel, boiled water with vegetables and grains. Later, the emergence of the stockpot came about, where cooks would add mutton, beef or other bones to a big cooking pot that would endlessly simmer away and be replenished when required, hence the term *pot-au-feu*.

Soups are easily digested and have been prescribed for invalids since ancient times. The modern restaurant industry is said to be based on soup. *Restoratifs* (where the word 'restaurant' originates) were some of the first items served in public restaurants in eighteenth-century Paris. Broth (*pot-au-feu*), **bouillon**, and **consommé** started at this point. French classic cuisine has produced many of the soups we recognise today.

Advancements in science enabled soups to take many forms, such as portable, canned, dehydrated and microwave-ready. 'Pocket soup' was carried by colonial travellers, as it could easily be reconstituted with a little hot water. Canned and dehydrated soups were available from the turn of the nineteenth century: these initially supplied the military and eventually the home pantry. Advances in science also permitted the adjustment of nutrients to fit specific dietary needs such as low in salt, high-fibre diets and gluten-free diets.

> **CHEF'S TIP**
>
> On the modern menu, a soup is usually served as a first course where its function is to stimulate the appetite. Soups should be a delicate flavour and a natural colour. Thick soups should not be too heavy in consistency.

## A BRIEF HISTORY OF CANNING

During the early Revolutionary Wars, the French government offered a cash award of 12,000 francs to any inventor who could invent a cheap and effective method of preserving great quantities of food. The massive armies of the time needed regular supplies of food, and so preservation became a necessity. In 1809, a French confectioner called Nicolas Appert developed a method of vacuum-sealing food inside glass jars. However, glass containers were unsuitable for transportation, and soon they had been replaced with steel cans. Soup was an ideal food used in these early preservation tests.

Based on Appert's methods of food preservation, the packaging of food in sealed airtight tin cans was first patented by an Englishman, Peter Durand, in 1810. Initially, the canning process was slow and labour-intensive, making the tinned food too expensive for ordinary people to buy.

A number of inventions and improvements followed, and by the 1860s, the time to process food in a can had reduced from six hours to 30 minutes. Urban populations in Victorian-era Britain demanded ever-increasing quantities of cheap, varied, good-quality food that they could keep on the shelves at home. Demand for tinned food increased hugely during the First World War, as military commanders searched for cheap, high-calorie food which could be transported safely and would survive trench warfare conditions.

# SOUP CLASSIFICATION

Soups can be categorised as follows:

- *Purée* – a soup named after or thickened by its main ingredient such as mushroom, potato and leek or tomato. Dried vegetables cooked with stock can also be used.

  **VIDEO CLIP**
  Making carrot purée soup

- *Cream* – a purée soup with the addition of cream, thin béchamel, crème fraîche or a liaison of egg yolks and cream. Cream of mushroom, cream of potato and leek, cream of tomato and cream of vegetable are all variations. It is essential that these soups have a smooth consistency and have been passed.

- *Velouté* – a cream soup to which a liaison of cream and egg yolk is added. These soups are prepared from a base roux with the addition of an appropriately flavoured stock. Mushroom velouté and velouté of potato and leek are examples.

  **VIDEO CLIP**
  Making chicken and sweet corn velouté

- *Broths* – a soup that is comprised of a strongly flavoured stock and accompanied by a named garnish such as mutton. This is a soup that is not passed and the vegetables are cut in varying shapes according to the recipe requirement. Examples are mutton broth and Scotch broth. Potages also come under this type of soup.

  **VIDEO CLIP**
  Making Scotch broth

- *Consommé* – clear soups that are prepared from stock flavoured with various meats and vegetables. They are clarified and should be clear when finished. Bouillons also come under this category but are not clarified to the same level. Examples can be consommé julienne (with julienne of vegetables), consommé madrilène (with pancake) and consommé royale (with egg custard).

- *Bisque* – taken from the French term 'Bi cuit' (biscuit), it is a soup made from crustaceans and is traditionally served with water biscuits. It is thickened with rice and the shell of the crustacean used and finished with cream. Examples are lobster and prawn bisque.

■ *Chowder* – this is generally a seafood soup, based upon molluscs, but it can have the addition of smoked white fish. It is usually associated with New England, the most popular of which is clam chowder. The term may also describe a buttery, hearty soup made with corn and chicken. The origins of the word 'chowder' may derive from the French word for a large cauldron, *chaudiere*, in which Breton fishermen threw their catch to make a communal fish stew. Examples can be clam, cockle or chicken and sweetcorn chowder.

■ *Foreign* – Also known as miscellaneous soups; these are all soups of a traditional, modern and national nature that do not fall into any other category, such as the simple Jewish chicken soup, and the gumbos made from okra, chicken, seafood or meat, of the American south. India has many types of lentil soups; Middle Eastern Muslims break their Ramadan fast with harira, made from lentils, chickpeas and lamb. Japan is famous for soups based on miso (fermented soybean paste).

Eastern Europe possesses goulash (a beef and paprika stew that started life as soup) and borsch (beetroot and meat soup). Spanish gazpacho is always in vogue; the Greek avgolemono is an egg and lemon soup and Italy has numerous bean and pasta soups, such as minestrone. Scotland is renowned for cullen skink (smoked haddock soup) and Scotch broth (mutton and barley soup).

The skills required to create an outstanding soup are the same as those needed to make a delicate sauce. The modern chef has a wider variety of ingredients at their disposal to meet the requirements of today's more perceptive customer. The balance of flavours, seasoning, consistency, texture and temperature needs to be understood to create a well-flavoured and satisfying soup.

## USE OF TOOLS AND EQUIPMENT

In the past, all chopping and blending was done by hand, making soup production at the upper end of the market very labour intensive. With the introduction of stick blenders and larger blending machines the making of fresh soups is almost as easy as using convenience soups.

The use of heavy-bottomed saucepans is recommended for soups that require a long simmering time. Their ability to consistently transfer even heat distribution to the soup reduces the risk of scalding or burning the contents of the pan.

The exact weighing and measuring of the ingredients is important to determine the correct consistency and flavour to each soup. Accurate measuring will also result in the right amount of portions produced for service and will result in less wastage.

*Weighing scales, blender, a stick blender, measuring jug, knives, chopping board, ladles, pots and muslin cloth*

When passing or straining a soup a conical strainer (chinois) is often used to great effect. It is used to strain out lumps and to create a smooth consistency to the soup. Alternatives are to use fine-graded sieves or muslin cloth to produce a velvety smooth or crystal clear finish to soups and consommés.

*Chinois*

## Checking the Quality of Vegetables

| | | |
|---|---|---|
| ■ Carrots | No apparent blemishes and crisp in texture | 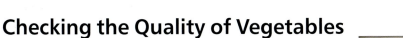 |
| ■ Onions | Firm to the touch, no mould and no brown flesh when cut in half |  |
| ■ Meat | Should be fat free and fresh with a pleasant smell and not sticky to the touch |  |
| ■ Celery | Light coloured, no blemishes and aromatic smell |  |
| ■ Herbs | Not wilted. Bright and aromatic when touched | |
| ■ Stocks | Freshly made, not greasy and not cloudy | |

*Sieve*

**CHEF'S TIP**

When passing soup through a chinois, use a sauce ladle and gently bounce it in the bottom of the strainer. This creates a vacuum effect and forces the soup through.

If you are in doubt about the quality and freshness of ingredients bring it to the attention of the chef or line manager who will identify your concerns and communicate them to the supplier.

# HEALTHY OPTIONS

There are always alternatives to take to make a soup healthier. The addition of yoghurt or single cream instead of double cream and the use of unsaturated oils instead of butter reduce fat and cholesterol intake. In general soups are a healthy part of our diet, especially lightly cooked broths that are nutritious and easily digested. During this chapter each recipe will have variations attached. The list is not restricted: it is only limited by the imagination and skills of the chef.

**QUALITY POINTS**

■ It is imperative to use unblemished, fresh ingredients when making soups.

■ Always check that the ingredients meet with the dish requirements by using correct mise en place methods and weighing each ingredient prior to preparation.

# GARNISHES AND ACCOMPANIMENTS

Most soups are accompanied by bread, usually in the form of bread rolls or sliced baguettes. However, croûtons, sippets and toasted flutes are served at the table. Today croûtons are sometimes more rustic, with larger pieces of bread drizzled with olive oil and baked in the oven until crisp.

Croûtons, sippets and croûtes de flûte

**VIDEO CLIP**
Solferino and croûton garnishes for soup

## Croûtons

Small cubes of white crustless bread (1 x 1cm) that are pan fried in **clarified butter**. Heat the butter in a pan and add the diced bread, constantly shaking the pan so that the croûtons colour evenly. Spoon out onto kitchen paper and pat dry.

## Sippets

Triangles of bread cut from the corners of pan loaves, thinly sliced and toasted in an oven. To add flavour garlic can be rubbed onto the bread before turning over to toast the other side.

## Croûtes de Flûte (Toasted Flutes)

Slices taken from a thin baguette. They can either be toasted on both sides or brushed with melted butter and crisped in the oven.

*Brunoise*

## Vegetable Garnishes

Used as a light garnish for consommés, broths or purée-based soups. Careful cutting into neat, even and standardised shapes is important to the finished result.

- *Brunoise* cut equal amounts of carrot, turnip, leek and celery into 2mm dice for consommés and slightly larger for broths.
- *Julienne* cut equal amounts of carrot, turnip, leek and celery into thin strips up to 35mm in length.
- *Paysanne* cut equal amounts of turnips, carrots, swede, potato, leek and celery into 1cm squares.

*Julienne*

*Paysanne*

## Consommé garnishes

Consommé is named on the menu after its garnishes. The following are a selection of the most frequently used.

- *Consommé brunoise* a fine brunoise of cooked carrot, onion celery and leek. Add to the soup at the last minute; use approximately 20g per portion.
- *Consommé julienne* fine julienne of cooked carrot, onion celery and leek. Add to the soup at the last minute using approximately 20g per portion.
- *Consommé Celestine* julienne of savoury pancake. Add at the last minute, approximately 10g per portion.
- *Consommé vermicelli:* cooked broken vermicelli pasta approximately 10g per portion.

# SERVING TEMPERATURES AND QUANTITIES

Hot soups should be served very hot and any accompanying garnishes should be added when serving. The Food Hygiene (England) Regulations 2005 state that hot food needs to be kept at or above 63°C in order to control the growth of pathogenic micro-organisms or the formation of toxins. The soup should not be kept for service or on display for sale for a period of more than two hours.

Cold soups should be served chilled at below 8°C and not at room temperature.

Calculate the required amount of a soup for a given number of portions, on the basis of the following points:

- Dependent on the size and style of the menu and the amount of courses that follow
- That the recipe is followed correctly
- That each ingredient is accurately measured for the recipe
- No more than between 200–250ml per portion should be served.

*Consommé Celestine*

*Consommé Julienne*

*Consommé Vermicelle*

*Consommé Brunoise*

# RECIPES

## Vegetable soup *Purée de légumes*

| INGREDIENTS | 4 PORTIONS | 10 PORTIONS |
|---|---|---|
| Carrots | 80g | 200g |
| Onion | 80g | 200g |
| Leeks | 80g | 200g |
| Celery | 80g | 200g |
| Turnip | 40g | 100g |
| White vegetable stock | 1 litre | 2½ litres |
| Good-quality salt | 5g | 10g |
| White pepper | To taste | To taste |
| Bouquet garni | 1 small | 1 medium |
| Butter | 40g | 100g |
| White or wholemeal flour | 40g | 100g |

## Method of work

1 Wash, peel and rewash the vegetables.
2 Roughly chop all the vegetables and sweat them in the butter until soft and translucent. Do not let them colour.
3 Add the flour to make a loose roux, again without colour being added during the cooking process, and allow to cool slightly.
4 Add the hot white vegetable stock and bring to the boil.
5 Add the bouquet garni and allow to simmer for 45 minutes, skim when necessary.
6 Remove the bouquet garni and using a stick blender, liquidise the soup until it is smooth.
7 Pass the soup through a fine chinois.
8 Return to a clean saucepan and bring back to the boil, adjust the seasoning and consistency.
9 Serve with croûtons.

### CHEF'S TIP

This soup can be enriched with cream or a liaison of cream and egg yolks to give a cream finish. Alternatively replace half the quantity of the white vegetable stock with a béchamel sauce.

*Ingredients for a bouquet garni*

*Using a stick blender*

*Passing the soup through a chinois*

# Mushroom soup *Purée de champignon*

| INGREDIENTS | 4 PORTIONS | 10 PORTIONS |
|---|---|---|
| White button mushrooms | 200g | 500g |
| Caps of chestnut mushrooms | 40g | 100g |
| Onion | 40g | 100g |
| White of leek | 40g | 100g |
| Butter | 40g | 100g |
| Good-quality salt | 5g | 10g |
| White pepper | To taste | To taste |
| White flour | 40g | 100g |
| White stock (vegetable or chicken) | 1 litre | 2½ litres |
| White wine | 40ml | 100ml |
| Bouquet garni | 1 small | 1 medium |

## Method of work

1. Wash the vegetables and carefully clean the mushrooms before cutting them into macedoine. Melt the butter in a saucepan.
2. Add the vegetables and mushrooms and sweat.
3. Add the white wine and reduce the quantity by half.
4. Add the flour to make a loose roux, again without colouring.
5. Remove from the heat to cool slightly before adding the hot stock, the bouquet garni and bringing to the boil.
6. Simmer for 45 minutes, skimming when required.
7. Remove the bouquet garni, liquidise and return to a clean pan, reboil.
8. Correct the seasoning and consistency.
9. Thinly slice the chestnut mushroom caps. Lightly cook in a little stock or clarified butter and serve as a garnish on top of the soup.

*Varieties of mushrooms that could be used: oyster, cep and morel*

# Potato soup *Purée Parmentier*

| INGREDIENTS | 4 PORTIONS | 10 PORTIONS |
|---|---|---|
| Potatoes | 400g | 1kg |
| Onion | 80g | 500g |
| White stock (vegetable or chicken) | 1 litre | 2½ litres |
| Butter | 40g | 100g |
| Bouquet garni | 1 small | 1 medium |
| Good-quality salt | 5g | 10g |
| White pepper | To taste | To taste |
| Chopped fresh flat leaf parsley | 15g | 30g |
| Croûtons | 25g | 60g |

## Method of work

1 Peel, wash and thinly slice the onions, melt the butter and sweat the onions in the butter until soft and translucent without letting them colour.

2 Wash, peel, re-wash and chop the potatoes into a 1cm dice.

3 Add the potatoes, hot stock and bouquet garni to the saucepan with the onions.

4 Lightly season and bring to the boil. Allow to simmer for approximately 45 minutes, skimming when necessary.

5 When the potato has completely amalgamated into the liquid remove the bouquet garni.

6 Liquidise the soup and pass through a fine sieve into a clean pan.

7 Bring back to the boil, correct the seasoning and consistency.

8 Serve with croûtons and the chopped flat leaf parsley.

### CHEF'S TIP

Gradual sweating of vegetables brings out their flavour. A floury potato such as Desiree, Maris Piper or Pentland Dell will give a smoother and creamier texture to this soup.

## Variations of Potato Soup

This basic soup has many variations with the simple addition of another ingredient.

| | | |
|---|---|---|
| Potato and leek soup | Add 50g of white of leek per portion and sweat with the onions. Garnish with julienne of leek |  |
| Potato and chive soup | Add 15g of chopped chives per portion of soup |  |
| Potato and bacon soup | Add 25g of cooked pancetta lardons |  |
| Sweet potato soup | Substitute sweet potato for potatoes in the basic recipe |  |
| Potato and watercress soup | Add 25g of blanched watercress to the soup 5 minutes before puréeing (note: less white pepper will be required in this recipe) | |
| Potato and chorizo soup | Use 25g of chorizo per portion. Gently fry small cubes of chorizo and use the oil to drizzle over the soup just before service | |

# Tomato and basil soup

*Making the gastrique*

| INGREDIENTS | 4 PORTIONS | 10 PORTIONS |
|---|---|---|
| Ripe plum tomatoes | 400g | 1kg |
| White stock (vegetable or chicken) | 1 litre | 2½ litres |
| Onion | 80g | 200g |
| Leeks | 80g | 200g |
| Celery | 80g | 200g |
| Good-quality salt | 5g | 10g |
| White pepper | To taste | To taste |
| Garlic | 1 clove | 3 cloves |
| Olive oil | 40ml | 100ml |
| Granulated sugar | 20g | 50g |
| Red wine vinegar | 20ml | 50ml |
| Smoked bacon rind | 40g | 50ml |
| Fresh basil leaves and stalks | 20g | 50g |

## Method of work

1  Wash, peel, re-wash and roughly chop the vegetables. Place into a saucepan with the olive oil and sweat with the lid firmly placed on the pan.

2  Add the granulated sugar and red wine vinegar, allow to reduce to a light syrup, forming a gastrique.

3  Wash and roughly chop the tomatoes. Add them with the basil stalks and allow to cook for 10 minutes before adding the hot white stock.

4  Bring to the boil whilst stirring occasionally. Add the bacon rind and allow the soup to simmer for 30 minutes, skimming when necessary.

5  Remove the bacon rind, liquidise the soup and pass through a fine chinois.

6  Return to the pan and reboil, add the chopped basil and correct the seasoning and consistency.

7  Serve garnished with a chiffonade of basil and croûtons.

### CHEF'S TIP

When making a gastrique for flavouring tomato soup you can tell if the vinegar has evaporated by waving a hand over the pan and smelling the vapour. Boiling vinegar has a rather acidic smell. The addition of this will sweeten and draw out the flavour of the tomato.

### CHEF'S TIP

Some of the chopped tomato flesh can be reserved and added after liquidising to make a more rustic soup. A focaccia croûte placed on the top of the soup and sprinkled with Parmesan makes a hearty lunchtime indulgence.

# Red lentil soup

| INGREDIENTS | 4 PORTIONS | 10 PORTIONS |
|---|---|---|
| Red lentils | 200g | 500g |
| Butter or sunflower oil | 40g | 100g |
| Carrot | 40g | 100g |
| Leek | 30g | 80g |
| Onion | 40g | 100g |
| Good-quality salt | 5g | 10g |
| White pepper | To taste | To taste |
| Dry cured bacon | 50g | 125g |
| White stock (vegetable) | 1½ litres | 3½ litres |
| Ripe tomatoes | 50g | 125g |
| Croûtons | 25g | 75g |
| Bouquet garni | 1 small | 1 medium |

 **CHEF'S TIP**

Red lentils are used a great deal in Indian cuisine; they are mildly spiced to accompany meat dishes. They are often called dhal, which is a general Hindi term for split lentils.

 **CHEF'S TIP**

This soup can be made from any dried lentil or pulse. For example; yellow split peas, Puy lentils, or green and brown lentils. Some of the pulses will need to be soaked prior to cooking.

## Method of work

1  Wash the lentils in several changes of cold water.

2  Place in a saucepan, cover with cold stock, bring to the boil and skim. At this stage refrain from adding any seasoning.

3  Wash, peel and chop the remainder of the ingredients but leave the bacon whole. Sweat them off with the butter or oil and then add to the lentils.

4  Add the remainder of the ingredients including the bouquet garni and simmer gently, continue to skim and allow to simmer until tender (approximately 45 minutes).

5  Remove the bacon and bouquet garni, liquidise and pass through a chinois.

6  Reboil, check the seasoning and adjust the consistency.

7  Serve with the croûtons.

*Soup being skimmed with a spoon*

# Green pea soup *Potage Saint Germain*

### 🗒 CHEF'S TIP

There are various derived potages made from this green pea soup:
- *Potage Lamballe* As for the green pea soup recipe and garnished with boiled Tapioca seed
- *Potage Longchamps* As for the green pea soup recipe and garnished with broken, cooked vermicelli, chopped sorrel and fresh chervil.

Other potages use haricot beans, lentils, red beans and yellow split peas as a replacement for the green split peas.

| INGREDIENTS | 4 PORTIONS | 10 PORTIONS |
|---|---|---|
| Green split peas | 200g | 500g |
| Butter or sunflower oil | 40g | 100g |
| Carrot (1 whole piece) | 40g | 100g |
| Leek | 30g | 80g |
| Onion | 40g | 100g |
| Good-quality salt | 5g | 10g |
| White pepper | To taste | To taste |
| Dry cured bacon (1 whole piece) | 50g | 125g |
| White stock (vegetable or chicken) | 1½ litres | 3½ litres |
| Bouquet garni | 1 small | 1 medium |
| Croûtons | 25g | 75g |

## Method of work

1. Wash the peas in several changes of cold water.
2. Place in a deep saucepan, cover with cold stock and bring to the boil. Skim when necessary.
3. Wash, peel and chop the onion and leek and place them into a pan with the fat to sweat them with the whole washed and peeled carrot.
4. Add all the ingredients to the peas, season and simmer gently. As scum forms, skim the surface as required. Allow to simmer until the peas are tender (approximately 1 hour).
5. Remove the bacon, carrot and the bouquet garni. Liquidise the soup and pass through a chinois.
6. Reboil in a clean pan, season, and correct the consistency of the soup.
7. Serve with croutons to accompany.

# Butternut squash and coriander soup

| INGREDIENTS | 4 PORTIONS | 10 PORTIONS |
|---|---|---|
| Butternut squash | 400g | 1kg |
| Onion | 40g | 100g |
| Celery | 40g | 100g |
| White of leek | 40g | 100g |
| Cumin powder | 10g | 20g |
| Good-quality salt | 5g | 10g |
| White pepper | To taste | To taste |
| Nutmeg | To taste | To taste |
| Butter | 40g | 100g |
| Fresh coriander | 50g | 120g |
| White vegetable stock | 1½ litres | 3¼ litres |
| Bouquet garni | 1 small | 1 medium |

*Cutting the squash into 2cm dice*

## Method of work

1 Wash and cut the butternut squash in half, peel and dice into 2cm cubes. Repeat the process with the onion, celery and leek.

2 Melt the butter in a large saucepan and add the cumin powder. Gently sweat for about 2 minutes to release the full flavour of the spice

3 Add all the chopped vegetables and sweat for 5 minutes or until they are translucent.

4 Add the white vegetable stock, bouquet garni, season well with the salt, pepper and a little grated nutmeg and simmer until all the vegetables are cooked: this may take approximately 45 minutes. Skim the surface as necessary.

5 Remove the bouquet garni. Liquidise the soup using a blender and correct the seasoning and consistency of the soup.

6 Wash and remove the coriander leaves from the stalks. Cut the coriander into a chiffonade and add to the soup after it has been brought back to the boil.

7 Cook for a further 2 minutes to infuse the coriander flavour and then serve immediately.

# Cream of chicken soup *Crème de Volaille*

*Cooking out the roux*

| INGREDIENTS | 4 PORTIONS | 10 PORTIONS |
|---|---|---|
| Butter | 50g | 125g |
| Flour | 50g | 125g |
| Onion | 40g | 100g |
| Celery | 40g | 100g |
| White of leek | 40g | 100g |
| Good-quality salt | 5g | 10g |
| White pepper | To taste | To taste |
| White chicken stock | 800ml | 2 litres |
| Cooked white chicken meat (garnish) | 45g | 110g |
| Single cream | 200ml | 550ml |
| Bouquet garni | 1 small | 1 medium |

## Method of work

1 Wash and chop the vegetables into a mirepoix. Sweat the chopped vegetables in melted butter in a large saucepan without letting them colour.

2 Add the flour, stirring and cooking over a moderate heat to make a roux without colour, then allow to cool slightly.

3 Gradually add the hot chicken stock, stir and bring to the boil.

4 Season well with the salt and pepper and add the bouquet garni.

5 Simmer for 45 minutes, skimming the surface of the soup when necessary.

6 Remove the bouquet garni and liquidise the soup with a blender. Pass through a fine strainer into a clean pan and reboil.

7 Add the single cream and correct the seasoning and the consistency.

8 Dice the cooked chicken meat and add to the soup. Serve immediately.

# Cream of spinach soup

| INGREDIENTS | 4 PORTIONS | 10 PORTIONS |
|---|---|---|
| Spinach | 300g | 750g |
| Butter | 40g | 100g |
| Onion | 40g | 100g |
| Potato | 80g | 200g |
| Leek | 40g | 100g |
| Good-quality salt | 5g | 10g |
| White pepper | To taste | To taste |
| White stock (chicken or vegetable) | 1 litre | 2½ litres |
| Grated nutmeg | To taste | To taste |
| Single cream | 200ml | 550ml |
| Bouquet garni | 1 small | 1 medium |

### CHEF'S TIP

If you blanch the spinach for a few seconds in boiling water and refreshing quickly in iced water a great deal of the colour of the spinach will be retained, which will benefit the overall colour of the soup.

### CHEF'S TIP

Add toasted pine nuts as a final garnish to create a variation of texture and flavour to the finished soup.

## Method of work

1 Wash, peel and finely dice the onion, leek and potatoes into brunoise. Wash the spinach well in several changes of water to remove any sand, grit and dirt pockets.

2 Melt the butter in a large heavy-based saucepan and add the brunoise of vegetables. Sweat gently for 10 minutes.

3 Prepare a large saucepan of boiling water and plunge the spinach into the water to blanch for a few seconds. Drain immediately in a colander and refresh the spinach in iced water whilst the remainder of the ingredients are sweating.

4 Add the hot white stock and bouquet garni to the vegetables and simmer for a further 15 minutes.

5 Next add the spinach and the grated nutmeg.

6 Simmer for another 5 minutes and remove from the heat.

7 Take out the bouquet garni and liquidise the soup until smooth.

8 Pass the soup through a chinois, reboil and add the cream. Correct the seasoning and consistency.

9 Serve garnished with a julienne of cooked spinach and a generous portion of croûtons.

# Chicken and sweetcorn chowder

| INGREDIENTS | 4 PORTIONS | 10 PORTIONS |
|---|---|---|
| Diced lean raw chicken | 80g | 200g |
| Onion | 60g | 150g |
| Celery | 40g | 100g |
| White of leek | 40g | 100g |
| Sweetcorn (fresh, frozen or tinned) | 80g | 200g |
| Potato | 100g | 250g |
| White chicken stock | 1 litre | 2½ litres |
| White wine | 40m | 100ml |
| Butter | 40g | 100g |
| Salted water biscuits | 20g | 50g |
| Good quality salt | 5g | 10g |
| White pepper | To taste | To taste |

## Method of work

1 Wash, peel, re-wash and chop all the vegetables and sweat in the butter for 5 minutes without letting them colour.

2 Add the pieces of chicken and continue to cook for a further 4–5 minutes.

3 Add the white wine, white chicken stock and sweetcorn. Bring to the boil.

4 Simmer for 30 minutes.

5 Using a stick blender, lightly purée the soup to allow for an uneven texture (with some chicken pieces and sweetcorn still remaining).

6 Correct the seasoning and consistency.

7 Serve with crushed salted water biscuits liberally strewn on top of the chowder, chopped parsley is optional.

Adding the diced chicken to the vegetables

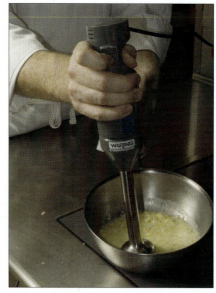

Lightly puréeing the chowder

Crushed salted water biscuits

# Clam chowder

| INGREDIENTS | 4 PORTIONS | 10 PORTIONS |
|---|---|---|
| Fresh clams | 400g | 1kg |
| Pancetta | 80g | 200g |
| Onion | 40g | 100g |
| Butter | 20g | 50g |
| Leek | 40g | 100g |
| Celery | 40g | 40g |
| Potato | 200g | 500g |
| Good-quality salt | 5g | 10g |
| White pepper | To taste | To taste |
| Fish stock | 1 litre | 2½ litres |
| Double cream | 100ml | 250ml |
| Bouquet garni | 1 small | 1 medium |

## Method of work

1 Wash the clams well in several water changes to purge all grit and sand.
2 Place the clams into a saucepan with the fish stock. With a lid over the pan cook the clams until their shells open.
3 Carefully remove the clams and remove them from their shells. Trim and chop the clams and retain to one side. Let the remaining fish stock stand for 10 minutes to let any grit and sand from the clams settle at the bottom. Strain very carefully and reserve for later use.
4 Remove the rind from the pancetta and cut into lardons. Melt the butter and cook the lardons slowly until a light golden brown colour has been achieved.
5 Add the washed and finely diced vegetables and sweat with the lardons.
6 Wash, peel and cut the potatoes into 4mm dice. And add to the vegetables in the pan, season lightly.
7 Add the stock and bouquet garni, bring to the boil and simmer for 30 minutes.
8 Add the clams and simmer for a further 5 minutes.
9 Finish by adding the cream and correcting the seasoning. Serve with crushed salted water biscuits, chopped parsley and a sprinkling of paprika if desired.

Cooking the clams

Removing the clams from the shells

# Scotch broth

| INGREDIENTS | 4 PORTIONS | 10 PORTIONS |
|---|---|---|
| Turnip | 40g | 100g |
| Carrot | 40g | 100g |
| Leek | 40g | 100g |
| Celery | 40g | 40g |
| Pearl barley | 20g | 50g |
| Good-quality salt | 5g | 10g |
| White pepper | To taste | To taste |
| White stock (vegetable or chicken) | 1¼ litres | 3¼ litres |
| Bouquet garni | 1 small | 1 medium |
| Fresh chopped parsley | For garnish | For garnish |

## Method of work

1 Wash the pearl barley and place in a large saucepan. Add the stock, bring to the boil and simmer for 1 hour, skimming occasionally.
2 Cut the vegetables into a 3mm brunoise and add to the broth, season and skim when necessary.
3 Simmer for approximately 30 minutes, once again skimming when necessary.
4 Adjust the seasoning and serve with chopped parsley.

# Mutton broth

| INGREDIENTS | 4 PORTIONS | 10 PORTIONS |
|---|---|---|
| Scrag end of mutton | 200g | 500g |
| Carrot | 50g | 125g |
| Onion | 50g | 125g |
| Turnip | 50g | 125g |
| Leek | 50g | 125g |
| Celery | 50g | 125g |
| Pearl barley | 20g | 50g |
| Good-quality salt | 5g | 10g |
| White pepper | To taste | To taste |
| White mutton or lamb stock | 1¼ litres | 3¼ litres |
| Bouquet garni | 1 small | 1 medium |
| Fresh chopped parsley | For garnish | For garnish |

## Method of work

1   Place the mutton into a saucepan and cover with cold water.
2   Bring to the boil and immediately remove from the heat and wash under running cold water.
3   Place the mutton into a clean pan, cover with the cold stock. Bring to the boil once again and skim as necessary.
4   Wash the pearl barley and add to the simmering mutton broth and continue to simmer for 1 hour.
5   Wash and dice the vegetables into a 2mm brunoise and add to the broth.
6   Add the bouquet garni and season well, allow to simmer for a further 20 minutes, skimming when necessary.
7   Remove the meat, cool and remove the fat. Cut the meat into a small dice, and return to the broth.
8   Correct the seasoning, add the washed and chopped parsley and serve.

*Adding the chopped and cooked mutton back to the broth*

# Chicken broth

| INGREDIENTS | 4 PORTIONS | 10 PORTIONS |
|---|---|---|
| Boiling fowl | 400g (¼) | 800g (½) |
| Carrot | 50g | 125g |
| Onion | 50g | 125g |
| Turnip | 50g | 125g |
| Leek | 50g | 125g |
| Celery | 50g | 125g |
| Long grain rice (Basmati) | 20g | 50g |
| Good-quality salt | 5g | 10g |
| White pepper | To taste | To taste |
| White chicken stock | 1¼ litres | 3¼ litres |
| Bouquet garni | 1 small | 1 medium |
| Fresh chopped parsley | For garnish | For garnish |

## Method of work

1   Ensure the boiling fowl is cleaned, then place into a saucepan and cover with the chicken stock. Simmer the boiling fowl and bouquet garni in the stock for approximately 1 hour until a rich, aromatic stock has been formed. Skim as required.
2   Wash, peel, re-wash and cut the vegetables into paysanne.
3   Remove the chicken and bouquet garni.
4   Add the vegetables and rice and simmer until cooked. This may take about 20 minutes.
5   Remove the meat from the chicken, cut into small dice and add to the broth.
6   Reboil and skim, season and add the chopped, washed parsley.
7   This can be served with sippets as a garnish.

*Adding the boiling fowl to the stock*

**CHEF'S TIP**

The use of a boiling fowl on the bone when cooking the stock will enhance the chicken flavour of this broth.

# Roasted Mediterranean vegetable soup

| INGREDIENTS | 4 PORTIONS | 10 PORTIONS |
|---|---|---|
| **Pepper** (red, yellow and green) | 1 whole | 5 whole |
| **Courgette** | 100g | 250g |
| **Red onion** | 100g | 250g |
| **Plum tomatoes** | 2 | 5 |
| **Aubergines** | 100g | 250g |
| Garlic | 1 clove | 3 cloves |
| Clear honey | 40g | 80g |
| Tomato juice | 200ml | 500ml |
| **Good-quality rock salt** | 5g | 10g |
| White pepper | To taste | To taste |
| **White vegetable stock** | 2 litres | 5 litres |
| Bouquet garni | 1 small | 1 medium |
| **Fresh basil** | 20g | 100g |
| Focaccia bread | 160g | 400g |
| **Olive oil** | 40ml | 100ml |
| **Pecorino cheese** | 40g | 100g |

## CHEF'S TIP

The variations of this soup are limited only to the chefs' imagination. For examples:
- Add toasted pine nuts to vary the flavour and texture.
- Add fennel to the roasted vegetables.
- Add seasonal squashes.
- Add a selection of cooked beans such as borlotti, Lima or broad beans.

## Method of work

1 Preheat an oven to 230°C.

2 Wash and chop the peppers, courgettes, aubergines, garlic and onions into a macedoine (neatly diced small cubes).

3 Mix with the honey and half of the washed and chopped basil. Pour over half the olive oil, season well with the salt and pepper, and place in the oven to roast for approximately 10 minutes or until all the ingredients are golden in colour.

4 Place the roasted vegetables in a large saucepan and add the stock and tomato juice.

5 Bring to the boil and simmer until all the vegetables are just cooked: this will take approximately 15 minutes.

6 Chop the remaining basil into a chiffonade and add to the soup.

7 Meanwhile, break the focaccia into chunky pieces of about 2cm, drizzle with olive oil, lightly season with the rock salt and pepper and bake in the oven until golden and crisp.

8 Serve the soup topped with shaved Pecorino cheese and the chunky croûtons or a julienne of peppers.

# Chicken noodle soup with spiced dumplings

*Adding the dumplings to the soup*

| INGREDIENTS | 4 PORTIONS | 10 PORTIONS |
|---|---|---|
| Grated fresh ginger | 20g | 50g |
| Finely sliced peppers | 1 | 2–3 |
| Good-quality salt | 5g | 10g |
| White pepper | To taste | To taste |
| Brown chicken stock | 1 litre | 2½ litres |
| Egg noodles | 80g | 200g |
| Finely sliced red chilli pepper | 1 | 2 |
| Dark soy sauce | 1tbsp | 2tbsp |
| Spiced dumpling ingredients | | |
| Minced chicken | 100g | 250g |
| Pork sausagemeat | 100g | 250g |
| Crushed garlic | 1 clove | 2–3 cloves |
| Szechuan pepper | Pinch | 2 pinches |
| Good-quality salt and pepper to taste | To taste | To taste |

## Method of work

1  Mix all the ingredients together to make the dumplings and season well. Form into small round dumplings of 10g each. Place on a tray and cover with plastic film before resting in the refrigerator for 1 hour to allow the spice to infuse with the chicken.

2  Bring a large pan of water to the boil. Take the pan off the heat and put the noodles into the hot water to soak for 15 minutes.

3  Wash and chop the ingredients for the soup mix them together in a saucepan, bring to the boil and simmer for 10 minutes, skimming occasionally.

4  Add the dumplings and simmer gently until they are cooked: this should take approximately 8 minutes.

5  Heat the noodles and place a portion in each soup bowl for service.

6  Pour over the soup making sure you distribute the dumplings evenly, and serve immediately.

### CHEF'S TIP

This clear soup can be thickened to give it more body. Arrowroot, cornflour or kuzu (which is of Japanese origin) can be used, but kuzu will thicken almost like gelatine, giving body to clear and hot soup.

# Minestrone soup

| INGREDIENTS | 4 PORTIONS | 10 PORTIONS |
| --- | --- | --- |
| Carrot | 40g | 100g |
| Leek | 40g | 100g |
| Onion | 40g | 100g |
| Celery | 40g | 100g |
| Savoy cabbage | 400g | 100g |
| Garlic | 2 cloves | 4 cloves |
| Olive oil | 20ml | 50ml |
| Tomato juice | 200ml | 500ml |
| Good-quality rock salt | 5g | 10g |
| White pepper | To taste | To taste |
| White vegetable stock | 1 litre | 2½ litres |
| Green beans | 20g | 50g |
| Potato | 40g | 100g |
| Bouquet garni | 1 small | 1 medium |
| Plum tomatoes | 2 | 5 |
| Spaghetti | 20g | 50g |
| Pancetta | 40g | 50g |
| Peas | 30g | 80g |
| Courgette | 40g | 100g |
| Tomato purée | 20g | 50g |
| Fresh chopped parsley | | |

## Method of work

1 Wash and peel the vegetables with half of the garlic and cut into paysanne.
2 Sweat the vegetables without letting them colour in the olive oil in a saucepan with a lid placed on top.
3 Add the white stock, bouquet garni, season well and simmer for approx 25 minutes, skimming occasionally.
4 Break the spaghetti into 2cm lengths, wash and peel and cut the potatoes into paysanne. Add to the soup.
5 Create a concassé with the plum tomatoes. Add to the soup and simmer gently until all the vegetables are almost cooked.
6 Add the tomato purée.
7 Add the washed green beans cut into diamonds, the washed courgette in paysanne and the peas and simmer for a further 8 minutes.
8 Meanwhile, mince the pancetta, parsley and the rest of the garlic and form into a paste.
9 Mould the paste into tablets the size of a marble and drop into the simmering soup.
10 Remove the bouquet garni and correct the seasoning.
11 Serve with shaved Parmesan and toasted flutes.

| *Laying the spaghetti in a kitchen cloth* | *Breaking the spaghetti* | *The broken spaghetti* |

# French onion soup  *Soupe à l'oignon*

| INGREDIENTS | 4 PORTIONS | 10 PORTIONS |
|---|---|---|
| Butter | 40g | 100g |
| Onion | 800g | 2kg |
| Garlic (optional) | 1 clove | 2 cloves |
| Good-quality salt | 5g | 10g |
| White pepper | To taste | To taste |
| Brown stock | 1 litre | 2½ litres |
| Gruyere cheese | 50g | 125g |
| Parmesan cheese | 40g | 100g |
| Bread flute | 1 small | 1 medium |

## Method of work

1   Peel, halve and finely slice the onions.
2   Melt the butter in a thick-based pan, add the sliced onions and cook over a gentle heat until soft and slightly caramelised.
3   Add the brown stock and bring to the boil, simmer for 10 minutes.
4   Slice and toast the flutes.
5   Finely grate and mix the two cheeses together.
6   Correct the seasoning of the soup and pour into ovenproof earthenware cups or marmites.
7   Layer the top with the toasted flutes. Sprinkle liberally with the cheese and gratinate under a **salamander** until bubbling and brown.
8   Serve immediately on a dish.

*Topping the soup with the cheese before placing under a salamander*

### CHEF'S TIP

Onions are rich in sulphur and vitamin C. The substance that makes the eyes water when cutting an onion is called allyl sulphide and it disappears on cooking. To peel onions in relative comfort, place them in a freezer ten minutes prior to peeling them.

# Consommé

| INGREDIENTS | 4 PORTIONS | 10 PORTIONS |
|---|---|---|
| Minced shin of beef | 200g | 2kg |
| Carrot | 40g | 100g |
| Onion | 40g | 100g |
| Celery | 40g | 100g |
| Leek | 40g | 100g |
| Bay leaf | 1 | 2 |
| Fresh thyme | 1 sprig | 2 sprigs |
| Good-quality salt | 5g | 10g |
| Black peppercorns | 4 | 4 |
| Cold brown beef stock | 200ml | 500ml |
| Egg whites | 2 | 5 |
| Hot brown beef stock | 1 litre | 2½ litres |

## Method of work

1  Wash, peel and chop all of the vegetables into macedoine.

2  Thoroughly mix all of the minced beef shin, vegetables, herbs, egg whites, cold stock and seasonings together (this is called the clarification) and place in a refrigerator for 30 minutes.

3  Place the hot stock in a large saucepan or preferably a stockpot with a tap at the base.

4  Mix the clarification well with the hot stock and bring to the boil as quickly as possible. Stir one more time whilst boiling and lower the heat so that the consommé is simmering gently. Avoid disturbing the clarification.

5  Allow to simmer gently for 2½ hours.

6  Strain through a dampened, folded muslin cloth. Remove all fat deposits using kitchen paper placed on the surface of the consommé to soak it up.

7  Adjust the seasoning with only salt and check the colour of the consommé. This is done by placing a small amount of the soup onto a clean, white plate. It should be a delicate amber colour without any traces of fat.

8  Degrease again if required. Reheat for service.

9  Serve in a warm consommé cup plain or with a named garnish.

*Making the clarification*

*Adding the cold stock*

*Straining the consommé using the muslin cloth*

# Cockie leekie

| INGREDIENTS | 4 PORTIONS | 10 PORTIONS |
|---|---|---|
| Boiling fowl | 400g (¼) | 800g (½) |
| White stock (chicken or veal) | 1¼ litres | 3¼ litres |
| Bouquet garni | 1 small | 1 medium |
| Onion | 50g | 100g |
| Butter | 40g | 100g |
| Leek | 150g | 400g |
| Good-quality salt | 5g | 10g |
| White pepper | 4 | 4 |
| Cooked and stoned prunes | 4 | 10 |

## Method of work

1  Simmer the boiling fowl and bouquet garni in the stock for 1 hour until a rich, aromatic stock has been formed. Skim when required.
2  Carefully remove the chicken and set aside to cool.
3  Cut the leek into a julienne and the onion into a fine dice and sweat in the butter.
4  Add the stock and simmer until the leek and onion are cooked and tender.
5  Remove the meat from the chicken and cut into julienne. Cut the prunes into a julienne and add both to the broth.
6  Reboil and skim, season and serve.

# Prawn bisque  *Bisque de crevettes*

| INGREDIENTS | 4 PORTIONS | 10 PORTIONS |
|---|---|---|
| Shell-on prawns (crevettes rose) | 300g | 750g |
| Butter | 40g | 250g |
| Carrot | 40g | 250g |
| Onion | 40g | 250g |
| Celery | 40g | 250g |
| Leek | 40g | 250g |
| Long grain rice | 50g | 125g |
| Tomato purée | 20g | 50g |
| Brandy | 50ml | 125ml |
| Fresh thyme | 1 sprig | 2 sprigs |
| Good-quality salt | 5g | 10g |
| White peppercorns | 4 | 4 |
| Fish stock | 1 litre | 2½ litres |
| Dry white wine | 80ml | 200ml |
| Bouquet garni | 1 small | 1 medium |
| Cayenne pepper | To taste | To taste |
| Unsalted butter | 80g | 200g |
| Double cream | 40ml | 100ml |

## Method of work

1 Peel, wash and dice the vegetables. Sweat in half of the unsalted butter in a large saucepan.
2 Add the prawns and cook at a slightly higher temperature.
3 Raise the heat and add the brandy. Shake the pan and flambé until the flames disappear.
4 Add the tomato purée and cayenne pepper.
5 Add the fish stock, rice, bouquet garni, fresh thyme and wine. Bring to the boil and simmer, skimming when necessary, for 45 minutes.
6 Remove the bouquet garni and liquidise the soup. Pass through a chinois into a clean pan. Adjust the seasoning and consistency.
7 Reboil and add the rest of the unsalted butter and double cream. Check the consistency.
8 Serve with crushed water biscuits.

# Thai chicken soup

| INGREDIENTS | 4 PORTIONS | 10 PORTIONS |
|---|---|---|
| Galangal | 200g | 500g |
| Lemongrass stalks | 4 | 9 |
| Lime leaves | 4 | 9 |
| Chicken leg | 1 whole | 3 whole |
| Cold water | 500ml | 1½ litres |
| Small red chillies | 2 | 5 |
| Coconut milk | 1 litre | 2600ml |
| Nam pla | 1tbsp | 4tbsp |
| Limes | 3 | 7 |
| Spring onions | 2 | 6 |
| Good-quality salt | 5g | 10g |
| White pepper | Pinch | Pinch |
| Fresh coriander | 20g | 55g |

## Method of work

1 Peel, wash and dice the galangal. Cut the lemongrass into 1cm lengths. Wash the lime leaves and finely chop the spring onions. Run the back of a heavy knife against the lime leaves and the lemongrass to help obtain a good infusion during cooking.
2 Place the galangal, lemongrass, lime leaves, chicken and water into a large saucepan and bring to the boil. Simmer for 30 minutes, skimming occasionally if required.
3 Once the chicken has cooked, remove it from the cooking liquor, cool and then cut the meat into small dice. Reserve to one side.
4 Add the chillies and then add the coconut milk. Heat slowly but do not let the soup reach boiling point. This will begin to infuse flavours and the heat should be maintained for 3–4 minutes.
5 Pass the soup into a clean pan, retain the chillies and cut into a fine julienne. Add the nam pla, juice from the limes, spring onions, chopped coriander and chicken.
6 Check the seasoning and consistency and serve with the chilli julienne as garnish.

Bruising the lime leaves and lemongrass with the back of a knife

Adding the galangal and ingredients to the water

Adding the coconut milk

# Gazpacho

| INGREDIENTS | 4 PORTIONS | 10 PORTIONS |
|---|---|---|
| Chives, fresh | 5g | 15g |
| Chervil, fresh | 5g | 15g |
| Parsley, fresh | 5g | 15g |
| Basil, fresh | 5g | 15g |
| Garlic clove | 2 | 4 |
| Red pepper | ½ | 1 |
| Green pepper | ½ | 1 |
| Bread crumbs | 40g | 100g |
| Plum tomato | 3 | 8 |
| Olive oil | 80ml | 200ml |
| Lemon | 1 | 2 ½ |
| Water or white vegetable stock | 500ml | 1 ¼ litres |
| Onion | 20g | 55g |
| Onion | 80g | 200g |
| Cucumber; diced | 80g | 200g |
| Sea salt, mill pepper | To taste | To taste |
| Garnish | | |
| Olives | 40g | 100g |
| Green peppers | 40g | 100g |
| Tomato concassé | 40g | 100g |
| Shallots | 40g | 100g |
| Croûtons | 40g | 100g |
| Red wine vinegar | 40ml | 100ml |

## Method of work

1 Wash and chop the herbs, then blend thoroughly with the garlic.
2 Peel and deseed the tomatoes and cut roughly, deseed and chop the peppers in the same way.
3 Liquidise the blended herbs, peppers and tomatoes in a food processor, adding the oil very slowly, and the lemon juice. Add the cold water or white vegetable stock.
4 Peel, wash and cut the onion as finely as possible. Peel, deseed and dice the cucumber and add to the soup.
5 Season and mix in the breadcrumbs. Chill for at least four hours before serving.
6 Serve accompanied by small bowls of chopped olives, shallots, green peppers, tomato concassé, croûtons and red wine vinegar.

## Assessment of knowledge and understanding

You have now learned about the use of the different varieties of soup and how to produce different soups applying an array of commodities and preparation techniques.

To test your level of knowledge and understanding, answer the following short questions. These will help to prepare you for your summative (final) assessment.

**1** List three examples of purée soup.

i) _____  ii) _____

iii) _____

**2** Give two examples of a broth.

i) _____  ii) _____

**3** Explain why a heavy-bottomed saucepan should be used when making large quantities of soup.

**4** Give two reasons why the weighing and measuring of ingredients is so important.

i) _____  ii) _____

**5** Explain the difference between liquidising and passing a soup.

_____

**6** Explain the reason for skimming a soup during the cooking process.

_____

**7** State two ways of finishing a cream soup.

i) _____  ii) _____

**8** State two healthy options when making soups.

i) _____  ii) _____

**9** State the correct temperature for holding a soup hot for service.

_____

## Research Task

Complete the following chart describing how to use, clean and maintain the following items of equipment and the safety considerations associated with them.

| | CLEANING | STERILISING | STORING | SAFETY PROCEDURES |
|---|---|---|---|---|
| Cooked meat chopping board | | | | |
| Stainless steel chinois | | | | |
| Electric stick blender | | | | |

# CHEF'S PROFILE

**Name: RICHARD HUGHES**

**Position:** Chef Proprietor

**Establishment:** The Lavender House

**Current job role and main responsibilities:** Owner and operator, responsible for all aspects of running the restaurant including:

- menu planning
- staffing and training
- marketing
- budgets
- purchasing.

I also still cook on service everyday!

**When did you realise that you wanted to pursue a career in the catering and hospitality industry?**
I decided on leaving school – the attraction of working and living in a busy hotel being the motivation!

**Training:** Apprenticeship at Imperial Hotel Great Yarmouth, which involved working four days a week and attending the local college one day. It took me four years to obtain the CGI1 706/1 and 706/11. I then transferred to Norwich Hotel School to complete Advanced Kitchen and Larder and then Advanced Pâtisserie.

**Experience:** Following my apprenticeship I moved to Rookery Hall Country House in Cheshire as a sous chef. I then held further positions at South Walsham Hall, Norfolk, and as a part-time lecturer at Norwich Hotel School, before opening my first restaurant in 1991: Number Twenty-four Wymondham, Norfolk. In 2002 I opened The Lavender House at Brundall Restaurant and Cookery School.

**What do you find rewarding about your job?** The job satisfaction I achieve from pleasing the customer. This in turn leads to a busy restaurant. There is nothing more satisfying than a full restaurant!

**What do you find the most challenging about the job?** Finding enough hours in the day! Being Chef Proprietor means you are responsible for VAT, tax, payroll, fridge temperatures, health and safety, marketing – you name it, it's your job! All this, and wanting to cook as well!

**What advice would you give to students just beginning their career?** Repetition is the key to consistency. Do not just do one task and think you know it all – you can learn in all situations. A good CV will reflect stability as well.

**Who is your mentor or main inspiration?** My first chef and employer, Roger Mobbs, shared my working practices. I am a great admirer of chef restaurateurs such as Rick Stein, Paul Heathcote and Germaine Schwab. They are all chefs who have risked much to establish their business. Raymond Blanc is a hero of mine – everything he does is about quality.

**Secrets of a successful chef:** Reliability and enthusiasm are the only traits you need. All the talent in the world is of no use if the chef is not totally committed.

**A brief personal profile:** I have published two books and write frequently for the press and local radio, as well as featuring on TV shows such as Rick Stein's Food Heroes.

**Can you give one essential kitchen tip or technique that you use as a chef:** Keep a note book in your knife roll and write down every recipe you find.

# Smoked haddock, saffron and potato chowder, poached egg

| INGREDIENTS | 4 PORTIONS |
|---|---|
| 1 fillet of undyed smoked haddock (skinned and boned) | 250g |
| Butter | 50g |
| Spring onion | 100g |
| Full fat milk | 1 litre |
| Potato, peeled | 200g |
| Good pinch of saffron | |
| Chopped chives | |
| Quail's eggs | 4 |

## Method of work

1  Wash the spring onions, finely slice.
2  Melt the butter, soften the spring onions in the butter.
3  Dice the potatoes into 5mm squares, add to the onions.
4  Pour on the milk, bring to the boil.
5  Add the pinch of saffron.
6  Cut the haddock into large pieces, place into the milk, turn down the heat and simmer until the potato is cooked. Stir gently to break up the fish.
7  Add plenty of finely chopped chive.
8  Poach the quails egg, place in the base of the cup.
9  Pour on the soup, ensuring the fish is equally distributed between the portions.

# 8

# Rice, pasta, grains and egg dishes

## LEARNING OBJECTIVES

The aim of this unit is to enable the candidate to develop skills and implement knowledge in the preparation and cookery principles of rice, pasta and grains. This will also include materials, ingredients and equipment.

Eggs are without doubt the most versatile of foods used by the chef. They feature on the menu from the hors d'oeuvres through to the dessert.

At the end of this chapter you will be able to:

- Identify each rice, pasta and grain variety and finished dish
- Understand the use of relative ingredients in rice, pasta and grain cookery
- State the quality points of various rice, pasta and grain commodities and dishes
- Prepare and cook each type of rice, pasta and grain variety

- Identify the storage procedures of rice, pasta and grain
- Be competent at preparing and cooking a range of rice, pasta and grain-based dishes
- Demonstrate techniques with the cooking, storage and quality points of eggs
- Demonstrate a range of cookery methods
- Be able to prepare omelettes, boiled, poached and scrambled egg dishes
- Identify and rectify problems when cooking and finishing egg dishes
- State the correct cooking and holding requirements for fresh egg dishes

# Rice

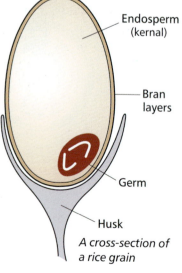

Endosperm (kernal)

Bran layers

Germ

Husk

*A cross-section of a rice grain*

## INTRODUCTION

### History

Rice descended from wild grasses, and is a staple food in South Asia. Historians believe that it was first produced and harvested in the area covering the foothills of the eastern Himalayas, and stretching through Burma, Thailand, Laos, Vietnam and southern China. Remains of early produced rice were found in the Yangtze valley dating to about 8500 BC. The commodity soon spread in all directions and was adapted by humans to create numerous varieties.

### What is Rice?

Rice is a type of short-living plant related to grass. The normal lifespan of a rice plant is 3–7 months depending on variety and climate. Rice is not a water plant but needs a large amount of irrigation for planting.

Rice is harvested from a field sometimes called a paddy field. Paddy is a complete seed of rice: one grain of paddy contains one rice kernel. Each paddy consists of many layers. The outermost layer of the rice shell is called a husk. A husk consists of two interlocked half-shells, each protecting one side of the paddy. The husk consists mostly of silica and cellulose.

The next layers are all called bran layers. Each is made up of very thin bran film. Bran is mainly fibre, vitamin B, protein and fat, the most nutritious part of rice.

At the base of each grain is the embryo which will grow and produce a new plant.

The central part is the rice kernel (endosperm), consisting mainly of two types of starch: amylose and amylopactin. Mixtures of these two starches determine the cooking texture of rice.

Rice is a very nutritious grain, especially brown rice. It has a high fibre content, vitamin B, carbohydrate and protein, but has no gluten, so is safe to eat for sufferers of coeliac disease and those with gluten allergies.

There are three main varieties of rice in the world, Indica (long grain), Japonica (round grain) and Javanica (medium grain).

Indica rice concentrates in a warm climate belt, from Indochina, Thailand, India, Pakistan, Brazil and the southern US. Japonica is grown in mostly cold climate countries, Japan, Korea, northern China and California. Javanica is grown only in Indonesia.

## Types of Rice

**VIDEO CLIP**
Different types of rice and associated products

There are more than 40,000 varieties of cultivated rice produced today, the exact figure is uncertain. Over 90,000 samples of cultivated rice and wild species are stored at the International Rice Gene Bank and are used by researchers all over the world.

The rice varieties can be divided into two basic groups, long grain/all purpose and speciality.

## Long Grain/All Purpose

All-purpose long grain rice is imported mainly from the US, Italy, Spain, Guyana and Thailand, and can be used for all styles of cooking. Long grain rice was once exported from India and was called Patna after the district in which it grew. Today most of the long grain rice is imported into the UK from America. Long grain rice is a slim grain which is 4–5 times as long as it is wide. When harvested it is known as 'rough' or 'paddy' rice. It undergoes different milling techniques to give different types of rice.

## Long Grain White Rice (Most Common)

One of the most popular types of rice because it has a subtle flavour which perfectly complements both rich and delicate sauces. Milled to remove the husk and bran layer, on cooking the grains separate to give an attractive fluffy effect. Extremely versatile, it is used extensively in Chinese cooking.

## Easy-Cook Long Grain White Rice (Parboiled/ Converted/Pre-fluffed)

This variety has a slightly rounded flavour. Unlike regular white rice which is milled direct from the field, it is steamed under pressure before milling. This process hardens the grain, reducing the possibility of over-cooking. It also helps to retain much of the natural vitamin and mineral content present in the milled layers.

*Long grain white rice*

*Indian Basmati Rice*

When raw the rice has a golden colour, but turns white upon cooking. This rice can be used in the same way as the common rice above. It works particularly well in salads.

# Brown Long Grain Rice (Wholegrain Rice)

This rice has a distinctly nutty flavour. Brown rice undergoes only minimal milling, which removes the husk but retains the bran layer. Because of this the rice retains more vitamins, minerals and fibre content than the common or easy-cook white rice. The grains remain separate when cooked, like long grain white, but take longer to soften. The cooked grains have a chewy texture, which many people enjoy. It is also available in easy-cook form.

# Speciality

These include the aromatics, risotto, glutinous and pudding rice which are particularly suited to ethnic cuisines. These are often grown, cooked and eaten in the same location. This is partly due to the climate in which the rice needs to grow.

Arborio rice is the classic risotto rice from the north Italian region of Piedmont; a medium to long grain rice, it absorbs a lot of cooking liquid yet still retains a good bite in texture, known as al dente.

# The Aromatics

The first class of speciality rice is aromatic rice. These contain a natural ingredient which is responsible for their fragrant taste and aroma. The fragrance quality of aromatic rice can differ from one year's harvest to the next, due to weather changes. The finest aromatic rice is aged to bring out a stronger aroma in the same way that wine is.

# Basmati Rice

This is a very long, slender-grained aromatic rice grown mainly around the Himalayas in India and Pakistan. Sometimes described as the Prince of Rice, it has a fragrant flavour and aroma and is used in Indian dishes. The grains are separate and fluffy when cooked. In Indian recipes it is often cooked with spices to enhance the grain's aromatic properties. Easy-cook basmati and brown rice basmati are also available. Brown basmati rice has higher fibre content and an even stronger aroma than white basmati. Aged basmati rice is a better quality, but is more expensive to buy.

# Jasmine Rice (Thai Fragrant Rice)

Another aromatic rice, although its flavour is slightly less pronounced than basmati. It originates from Thailand. The length and shape of the grains look as though they should remain separate on cooking but instead it has a soft and slightly sticky texture when cooked. Good with Chinese and South East Asian food.

## American Aromatics

The American rice industry has developed varieties of aromatic rice which are very similar to both basmati and jasmine rice. These varieties are not usually available in the UK except in specialist shops.

## Japonica Rice

Short and medium grain. Grown mainly in California, it comes in a variety of colours including red, brown and black. This type of rice is used in Japanese and Caribbean cookery due to its tacky, moist and firm nature when cooked.

## Wild Rice

This is not rice, but in fact an aquatic grass. Wild rice is extremely difficult to harvest. It is expensive but this is acceptable as the colour, a purplish black, and its subtly nutty flavour combine well with other dishes. It is a good colour enhancer for a special dish or rice salad and it can be mixed economically with other rice (but may need pre-cooking as it takes 45 to 50 minutes to cook, using one part grain to three parts of water).

*American wild rice*

## Ground Rice

This commodity is ground rice grains which are used for milk-based desserts.

## Rice Flour

This is rice finely milled to produce flour which is then used to thicken some soups.

## Rice Paper

This is paper made from milled rice and is mainly used in pastry kitchens.

## General Information

White rice has had the bran and germ removed which makes the end product more delicate and gives it a softer flavour. Brown rice is chewier and nuttier due to the bran being left on the rice kernel. It is also more nutritious.

## Other Products Made from Rice

### Liquid

Rice wines (also known as rice beer) because the fermentation process is undertaken with rice (beer-based) as opposed to fruit (grapes for wine).

Mirin is a sweet rice wine used to flavour sauces and cooked rice dishes (this particular wine is not usually drunk). Sake is the most famous of Japanese rice wines and is served warm. It does not keep well and unlike normal wine should be consumed within 1 year of bottling. Shaoxing wine is the Chinese variety of the Japanese sake.

 **CHEF'S TIP**

Rice wine is excellent for flavouring sushi; when the rice is cooked drizzle the rice wine into the hot rice and allow it to be absorbed.

**VIDEO CLIP**
Cooking using rice noodles

## Cooked products

Rice cakes are circular cooked cakes which have very little flavour and fat. Rice crackers are a Japanese snack now served in bars and restaurants.

## Noodles

Rice noodles are made with rice flour, are available dried and require **soaking** in hot water until transparent then used as required.

Laksa noodles are used to make the dish Laksa which is an Indonesian, Malaysian speciality. They resemble white spaghetti.

Rice flake noodles resemble tortilla chips and are dried. Soak in hot water and use as required.

Rice sticks – thin, medium or wide varieties are available. Thin are used in soups and salads, medium for the majority of dishes and wide for braised dishes or stir fry.

# THE PREPARATION AND COOKING OF RICE

**HEALTH SAFETY**

The bacteria commonly found in rice is *Bacillus Cereus*, which will multiply effectively if the rice is not kept above 75°C or below 4°C (best practice) in its cooked state.

The washing and soaking of rice removes any excess starch which when cooked could cloud the cooking medium and cause the rice to become 'gloopy'. By washing the rice any debris, dirt or impurities will be removed. It ensures the grains are clean and as such is recommended as good working practice.

When cooking rice the factors to be taken into account are the liquid used and the quantity, which varies depending on the dish being cooked and the variety of rice grain.

A general rule is:

- 1½ times liquid to rice for sushi
- 2 times liquid to rice for normal rice dishes
- 3 times liquid to rice for risotto
- 3 times liquid to rice for wild rice
- 4 times liquid to rice for paella.

These amounts are approximate and will of course vary depending on the grains used.

When cooking sushi, risotto and paella the idea is to allow the grains to burst and release starch which will act as a natural thickening agent. This process is caused by the size and shape of the grain.

Rice can be an extremely versatile commodity and is used extensively in international cooking for both sweet and savoury dishes.

Rice can be used as a starter, main course accompaniment and can be cost-effective as left over food can be reused or made into salads.
Rice lends itself well to a large selection of cooking methods:

- Boiling
- Braising
- Frying
- Steaming
- Stewing
- Microwaving.

The grains are porous and as such absorb large amounts of liquid. Flavours added before, during or after cooking will be taken on by the rice.

Most rice should be cooked al dente; this is an Italian phrase denoting the texture of rice as tender or soft on the outside but still firm to the bite within; its exact translation is 'to the tooth'.

If rice (boiled) is cooked in large quantities of liquid it will be necessary to drain the rice. This will dry the rice slightly and prevent the grains from over-cooking in the liquid.

Rice can be moulded when hot or cold; this practice does however require the rice to be perfectly cooked. Too little cooking and it will not stay in shape, too much and the rice will be stodgy and full of water. The best way to use a mould is by warming it slightly and brushing with melted butter to stop the rice sticking.

## Plain Boiled

The rice should be washed then poured into a large amount of boiling salted water. Stir regularly to prevent sticking to the bottom of the pan and burning. Once cooked al dente the rice should be drained and served or refreshed and refrigerated immediately.

## Braised

This method of cookery requires the rice to be cooked in the oven with a cartouche on top so the liquid is absorbed and the grains become light and fluffy.

## Stewing

This method is used for risotto and requires the rice to be cooked on the stove top. The rice absorbs all of the liquid causing the grains to swell.

## Stir Frying

This is a finishing method and the rice must be steamed or boiled in advance. The rice is tossed in hot fat with numerous flavours: this is a very quick method of reheating.

**CHEF'S TIP**

The liquid is a very important part of rice cookery; the rice will absorb any flavour added during cooking so quality, freshness and attention to detail are essential.

**VIDEO CLIP**
Braising rice

**VIDEO CLIP**
Stir frying rice

## Texture

The texture and flavour of cooked rice depends on the time, temperature and amount of liquid used. Undercooked rice is gritty, tasteless and hard whereas over-cooked rice is stodgy and unpleasant. Where possible use the guidelines of liquid to rice as this will help prevent poor cooking methods.

## Storage

Rice must be stored carefully once cooked as it can harbour the pathogenic bacteria *bacillus cereus* which can cause vomiting and diarrhoea. The risk can be minimised by storing the rice below 4°C in a covered container in a well-aerated refrigerator for no longer than 4 days and reheating to above 75°C. Dried rice can be stored in a sealed airtight container for as long as the use by date, usually approximately 6–9 months. The type of container is important as rice is porous and can be tainted by strong-smelling foods or moisture. Rice will deteriorate over time and signs of poor/out of date rice are:

1 Split grains
2 Dust
3 Musty smell.

**HEALTH SAFETY**

If possible only purchase the required amount of rice and ensure good stock rotation at all times.

# RECIPES

## 'Modern' kedgeree

| INGREDIENTS | 4 PORTIONS | 10 PORTIONS |
|---|---|---|
| Smoked haddock | 500g | 1.25kg |
| Butter | 50g | 125g |
| Red onions | 2 | 5 |
| Garlic | 3 cloves | 7 cloves |
| Boiled basmati rice | 250g | 625g |
| Eggs (hard boiled) | 2 | 5 |
| Crème fraîche | 100ml | 250ml |
| Finely sliced chillies | ½ | 1½ |
| Dill | Sprigs | Sprigs |
| Milk | 125ml | 300ml |
| Saffron | Pinch | Pinch |
| Good-quality salt and white pepper | To taste | To taste |

## Method of work

1 Poach the haddock in milk until it flakes into little pieces.
2 Sauté the onions, garlic and saffron in butter.
3 Add the fish and the cooked rice.
4 Add a little cooking liquor and cook gently until hot.
5 Add the seasoning, crème fraîche and chillies.
6 Peel and quarter the eggs.
7 Arrange the rice with wedges of egg and sprigs of dill.

**CHEF'S TIP**

Ensure you use natural smoked haddock and not the dyed variety; this will give a much gentler flavour and a more subtle appearance.

# Braised rice (pilaff)

| INGREDIENTS | 4 PORTIONS | 10 PORTIONS |
|---|---|---|
| Butter | 50g | 125g |
| Finely diced onion | 40g | 100g |
| Long grain rice | 125g | 300g |
| White chicken stock or vegetable stock | 250ml | 600ml |
| Good-quality salt and white pepper | To taste | To taste |

## Method of work

1 Preheat an oven to 200°C.
2 In a saucepan/sauteuse melt the butter and sweat the onions until they are translucent.
3 Add the pre-washed rice and cook for a further minute stirring until all the grains are coated.
4 Add the stock and bring to the boil.
5 Remove from the heat and cover with a cartouche.
6 Place in the oven to braise until tender for approximately 15 minutes.
7 Remove from the oven, discard the cartouche and season.

Note: the rice can be flavoured with cardamom, cinnamon, garlic or any aromatic required to give a distinct flavour and aroma.

> **CHEF'S TIP**
>
> This method of cookery involves the absorption of liquid into the rice, this is to maximise the flavour and delicacy. Adding cardamom pods, cinnamon sticks or star anise will add another dimension to the dish.

# Steamed basmati rice

| INGREDIENTS | 4 PORTIONS | 10 PORTIONS |
|---|---|---|
| Basmati rice | 125g | 300g |
| Optional flavours added after cooking | | |
| Lemon juice and zest | 1 | 2½ |
| Herbs | 1/8 bunch | ¼ bunch |
| Butter | 50g | 125g |
| Oils (basil, curry, chilli) | Drizzle | Drizzle |
| Cooked vegetables – peppers, carrots, onions, courgettes etc., cut into brunoise | 50g | 125g |
| Diced cooked fish, meat etc. | 50g | 125g |
| Good-quality salt and white pepper | To taste | To taste |

## Method of work

1 Wash the rice and drain well.
2 Place the rice into a gastronorm tray and just cover with cold water.
3 Place the gastronorm into the steamer for 25 minutes.
4 Remove, check the rice is cooked, season and stir gently to help the grains separate.
5 If required add the additional ingredients.
6 Mould, serve or chill as required.

# Risotto

| INGREDIENTS | 4 PORTIONS | 10 PORTIONS |
|---|---|---|
| Butter | 50g | 125g |
| Finely diced onions | 40g | 100g |
| Garlic chopped | 2 cloves | 5 cloves |
| White wine | 50ml | 125 ml |
| Arborio risotto rice | 125g | 300g |
| White chicken stock, vegetable stock | 200ml | 500ml |
| Grated and shaved Parmesan | 2tbsp of each | 5tbsp of each |
| Good-quality salt and white pepper | To taste | To taste |

 **CHEF'S TIP**

Arborio rice is ideal for making risotto as the grains contain enough starch to thicken the dish and are hard enough to prevent over-cooking. Using long grain rice or pudding rice will not give the correct consistency or appearance.

## Method of work

1 Melt half the butter and sweat the onions and garlic until translucent.

2 Add the rice and cook for 2 minutes stirring until all the grains are coated.

3 Add the wine and reduce until the mixture begins to dry out.

4 Gradually add the hot stock, stirring regularly until the liquid is absorbed and the rice is al dente.

5 At the last minute season the risotto and stir in the butter and grated Parmesan.

6 Finish with the Parmesan shavings.

Note: Do not allow the risotto to reboil once the cheese and butter have been added.

**VIDEO CLIP**
Making risotto

*Add the rice and cook until coated*

*Gradually add the stock, stirring regularly*

# Deep-fried rice and mozzarella balls

| INGREDIENTS | 4 PORTIONS | 10 PORTIONS |
|---|---|---|
| Toasted pine nuts | 25g | 75g |
| Cooked plain risotto (see recipe on p.168) | 500g | 1.25kg |
| Pasteurised eggs | 50ml | 125ml |
| Diced fried smoked bacon | 40g | 100g |
| Diced mozzarella | 75g | 225g |
| Breadcrumbs | 75g | 225g |
| Olive oil | 2tbsp | 5tbsp |
| Basil | ½ bunch | 1 bunch |
| Rocket | 50g | 125g |
| Shishu cress | ¼ punnet | ½ punnet |
| Good-quality salt and white pepper | To taste | To taste |

Form a hole in the rice for the bacon and mozzarella

## Method of work

1 Mix the rice, egg, chopped basil and chopped pine nuts together.
2 Shape into walnut-sized balls.
3 Make a hole in the centre of the rice and insert a piece of bacon and mozzarella then reshape the balls.
4 Roll in breadcrumbs and chill well.
5 **Deep fry** at 190°C constantly moving the balls for even colour.
6 Liquidise the basil with the oil and season.
7 Lightly dress the rocket leaves and place on the plate.
8 Finish with the balls.
9 Garnish with Shishu cress.

# Lemon and toasted mustard seed braised rice

| INGREDIENTS | 4 PORTIONS | 10 PORTIONS |
|---|---|---|
| Long grain rice | 200g | 500g |
| Finely diced onion | 50g | 125g |
| Butter | 50g | 125g |
| Vegetable stock | 350ml | 750ml |
| Lemon zest and juice | 1 | 2½ |
| Mustard seeds | 2tsp | 5tsp |
| Flat leaf parsley (chopped) | ¼ bunch | ½ bunch |
| Olive oil | 4tbsp | 10tbsp |
| Good-quality salt and white pepper | To taste | To taste |

### CHEF'S TIP

The lemon, oil and mustard seeds can be heated together and kept in a sealed container until required. This rice dish works especially well with chicken korma, as the acidity of the rice cuts through the creaminess of the curry.

*Mix in the lemon, parsley and oil*

## Method of work

1 Melt the butter in a saucepan and sweat the onions until translucent.
2 Add the rice and stir until all the grains are coated.
3 Add the stock and bring to the boil.
4 Remove from the heat, cover with a cartouche and place in the oven at 180°C.
5 Cook for approximately 15 minutes or until the liquid has evaporated and the rice is tender.
6 Take the pan out of the oven and leave to rest.
7 Toast the mustard seeds until they pop then mix into the rice.
8 Mix the lemon, oil and parsley into the rice, season well and serve.

# Paella with chicken, squid and prawns

*Add the peppers, onion, rice, tomato, mussel liquor and saffron to the pan*

| INGREDIENTS | 4 PORTIONS | 10 PORTIONS |
| --- | --- | --- |
| Squid cut into rings | 1 | 2 each |
| Live mussels | 400g | 1kg |
| Diced chicken breast | 200g | 500g |
| Uncooked tiger prawns (shelled) | 8 | 20 |
| Butter | 130g | 300g |
| Short grain rice (bomba or calasparra if possible) | 225g | 600g |
| Sliced onions | 1½ | 3 |
| Chopped garlic | 2 cloves | 6 cloves |
| Diced mixed peppers | 1 of each | 3 of each |
| Fresh tomato sauce | 80ml | 200ml |
| Saffron | Pinch | Pinch |
| Fish stock | 400ml | 1 litre |
| Good-quality salt and white pepper | To taste | To taste |

## Method of work

1 Heat a sauteuse and add the mussels. Add the white wine then remove once the shells have opened. Place the mussels in a bowl and save the liquid.
2 Quickly fry the squid and prawns in a large flat pan with the garlic.
3 Remove the squid and prawns from the pan and add the chicken. Fry the chicken until golden-coloured on all sides.
4 Add the peppers, onion, rice, tomato, mussel liquor and saffron.
5 Add the stock and simmer until the rice is cooked.
6 Season well then add the seafood, heat through and serve.

### 🍴 CHEF'S TIP

Bomba and calasparra rice are well known for their paella cooking qualities in Spain. The calasparra especially is used extensively in traditional Spanish restaurants, its grain composition requires extra liquid to cook but it can hold its shape and favour over a longer period. The use of round, short grain rice is acceptable but will never give the same qualities as bomba or calasparra.

# Chinese crab cakes with mango and lime salsa

*Fry the patties until golden brown*

| INGREDIENTS | 4 PORTIONS | 10 PORTIONS |
|---|---|---|
| Brown rice | 400g | 1kg |
| Chicken stock | 750ml | 2 litres |
| Spring onion | 1 bunch | 2½ bunches |
| Cooked white crab meat | 175g | 400g |
| Raw minced white fish | 175g | 400g |
| Ground rice | 25g | 65g |
| Eggs | 1 | 3 |
| Chinese five spice | 2tsp | 5tsp |
| Olive oil | 2tbsp | 5tbsp |
| Soy sauce | 1tbsp | 2½ tbsp |
| Mango | ½ | 1½ |
| Lime | 1 | 1½ |
| Coriander | ¼ bunch | ½ bunch |
| Red onion | ½ | 1½ |
| Good-quality salt and white pepper | To taste | To taste |

## Method of work

1. Place the rice in a pan with the boiling stock and simmer until tender.
2. Drain off any excess liquid and leave the rice to chill.
3. Roughly chop the spring onions.
4. Place the crab, fish, spring onion, ground rice, egg, soy and five spices in the food processor and pulse until the ingredients cohere.
5. Remove the ingredients from the food processor and mix with the rice; season well.
6. Divide the mixture into patties, three to a portion.
7. Take the patties and chill well.
8. Make the salsa by dicing the mango and red onion, then mix with lime juice and zest and chopped coriander.
9. Pan fry the cakes (finish in the oven if necessary) and serve with the cold salsa.

## CHEF'S TIP

The cakes can be made using brown crab meat for an earthier flavour or raw tiger prawns instead of the white fish. They can be coated in breadcrumbs and deep fried to give a crunchier flavour.

# Jambalaya

*Add the tomato, rice and stock to the pan*

| INGREDIENTS | 4 PORTIONS | 10 PORTIONS |
|---|---|---|
| Corn oil | 2tbsp | 5tbsp |
| Pork (shoulder or leg) cut into 2cm dice | 300g | 750g |
| Chicken cut into 2cm dice | 200g | 500g |
| Sliced onion | 1 | 3 |
| Chopped garlic | 3 cloves | 8 cloves |
| Diced green peppers | 1 | 3 |
| Green chillies diced | 2 | 5 |
| Chopped plum tomatoes | 400g | 1kg |
| Long grain rice | 300g | 750g |
| Chicken stock | 600ml | 1.5kg |
| Raw tiger prawns (shelled) | 8 | 20 |
| Sliced celery | 2 sticks | 5 sticks |
| Chopped flat leaf parsley | ¼ bunch | ½ bunch |
| Good-quality salt and white pepper | To taste | To taste |

## Method of work

1. In a frying pan sauté the chicken and pork until brown.
2. Remove the chicken and pork from the pan then add the celery, onion, garlic, peppers and chillies.
3. Add the tomato, rice and stock then simmer for 10 minutes.
4. Add the meat and prawns; cook for a further 5 minutes.
5. Season, serve and garnish with chopped parsley.

### CHEF'S TIP

This is a classic Louisiana dish full of varying ingredients with a strong meat element. The meat can be substituted with different fish and shellfish (try monkfish for the meatiness) and razor clams.

# Lemongrass risotto cakes with burnt chilli and crème fraîche

| INGREDIENTS | 4 PORTIONS | 10 PORTIONS |
|---|---|---|
| **Saffron risotto cooked with lemongrass** (use the base recipe on p. 168) | 600g | 1.5kg |
| **Polenta** | 50g | 125g |
| **Red chillies** | 4 | 10 |
| **Olive oil** | 4tbsp | 10tbsp |
| **Crème fraîche** | 4tbsp | 10tbsp |
| **Rocket leaves** | 40g | 100g |
| **Curly endive** | 40g | 100g |
| **Lime juice** | 1 lime | 3 limes |
| **Balsamic reduction** | 4tsp | 10tsp |
| **Good-quality salt and white pepper** | To taste | To taste |

## CHEF'S TIP

These cakes (made half the size) work well with pan-fried red mullet fillets as a fish course. For extra flavour use scotch bonnet chillies instead but be careful to balance the dish correctly.

## Method of work

1 Prepare a basic risotto adding saffron and 1 lemongrass stick when adding the liquid for every 4 people.
2 Pour the risotto into a tray and chill.
3 Then divide the risotto into cakes (two per person), roll in polenta and shape making criss-cross marks on top.
4 Take the chillies and hold over a flame until the skin starts bubbling and turning black.
5 Pan fry the cakes until golden.
6 Dress the curly endive and rocket with a little oil and lime juice then arrange on the plate.
7 Place the cakes on top.
8 Finish with the crème fraîche, balsamic and chilli.

*Divide the risotto and make it into cakes*

*Roll the risotto cakes in polenta*

*Make a pattern in the cakes with a knife*

# Teriyaki beef and wild rice filo parcels with pickled cucumber

*Make the beef parcels in stages*

| INGREDIENTS | 4 PORTIONS | 10 PORTIONS |
|---|---|---|
| Beef fillet cut into strips | 200g | 500g |
| Soy | 2tbsp | 5tbsp |
| Honey | 2tbsp | 5tbsp |
| Sesame seeds | ½ tbsp | 2tbsp |
| Filo pastry sheets | 8 × 5m squares | 20 × 5cm squares |
| Butter | 100g | 250g |
| Boiled wild rice | 40g | 100g |
| Boiled basmati rice | 120g | 300g |
| Cucumber julienne | 1½ | 3 |
| Red onion finely sliced | 1 | 2 |
| Coriander | ¼ bunch | ½ bunch |
| Sake rice wine | 2tbsp | 5tbsp |
| Rice wine vinegar | 3tbsp | 8tbsp |
| Good-quality salt and white pepper | To taste | To taste |

## Method of work

1. Marinate the beef for 1 hour in soy, honey and toasted sesame seeds.
2. Mix the cucumber with the red onion, chopped coriander (reserve some leaves for garnish), sake and rice wine vinegar and leave to marinate.
3. Quickly pan fry the beef then mix with the rice and season well.
4. Brush the filo with butter then divide the beef mix between each sheet.
5. Fold the corners in and turn over to form a parcel.
6. Lay the filo parcels on silicone paper and brush with butter.
7. Bake for 15 minutes 180°C until golden.
8. Arrange the parcels on the plate and finish with the cucumber mix and a few coriander leaves.

# Egg-fried rice with ham, prawns and vegetables

| INGREDIENTS | 4 PORTIONS | 10 PORTIONS |
|---|---|---|
| Sunflower oil | 100ml | 250ml |
| Boiled long grain rice | 400g | 1kg |
| Eggs | 2 | 5 |
| Diced peppers | 1 of each | 2 of each |
| Diced courgettes | 1 | 2 |
| Diced red onion | 1 | 2 |
| Blanched peas | 80g | 200g |
| Sliced button mushrooms | 160g | 400g |
| Diced honey roast ham | 160g | 400g |
| Cooked prawns | 120g | 300g |
| Lemon juice and zest | 1½ | 3 |
| Chopped parsley | ¼ bunch | ½ bunch |
| Good-quality salt and white pepper | To taste | To taste |

## Method of work

1 Take a wok and heat with a little oil then drizzle in the beaten egg, toss quickly and then remove.
2 Fry the vegetables and season well then remove and mix with the egg.
3 Fry the ham quickly then remove and add to the egg mix.
4 Fry the rice with the prawns until hot then add the egg mix, lemon and parsley.
5 Re-season and serve.

*Fry the egg in a hot wok*

*Fry the vegetables*

*Fry the rice and prawns*

# Lamb biryani

| INGREDIENTS | 4 PORTIONS | 10 PORTIONS |
| --- | --- | --- |
| Sunflower oil | 100ml | 250ml |
| Steamed basmati rice (see recipe on p. 167) | 200g | 600g |
| Diced leg of lamb | 300g | 800g |
| Finely diced onion | 80g | 200g |
| Chopped garlic | 3 cloves | 8 cloves |
| Grated ginger | 1tbsp | 3tbsp |
| Ground cumin | 1tbsp | 3tbsp |
| Ground coriander | 1tbsp | 3tbsp |
| Turmeric | 1tbsp | 3tbsp |
| Garam masala | 1tbsp | 3tbsp |
| Brown lamb stock | 400ml | 1 litre |
| Sliced red chillies | 1½ | 4 |
| Sliced lemons | 1½ | 4 |
| Sliced tomatoes | 3 | 8 |
| Chopped mint | ¼ bunch | ½ bunch |
| Chopped coriander | ¼ bunch | ½ bunch |
| Mustard seeds | 1tbsp | 3tbsp |
| Crème fraîche | 4 dessertspoons | 10 dessertspoons |
| Good-quality salt and white pepper | To taste | To taste |

CHEF'S TIP

This dish works well with normal long grain rice as the grains keep separate and absorb the curry flavours. The lamb can be substituted with chicken or beef.

## Method of work

1 Marinate the lamb with the onion, garlic, ginger and spices for 24 hours.

2 Fry the meat until golden brown then add the stock and simmer for 2 hours until tender.

3 Using a gastronorm tray place a 2cm layer of rice on the bottom, lay on some lemon, tomato, mustard seeds, chillies and chopped herbs.

4 Place a layer of lamb on top.

5 Continue the layering so there are three layers of rice mix and two layers of lamb.

6 Cover the trays with tin foil and bake in the oven for 40 minutes at 160°C.

7 Remove the tray from the oven, mix the biryani slightly and arrange in a bowl.

8 Finish with crème fraîche and mint.

# Tomato risotto with Gorgonzola and deep-fried basil

*Fold in the Gorgonzola and sun-dried tomatoes*

| INGREDIENTS | 4 PORTIONS | 10 PORTIONS |
|---|---|---|
| Arborio rice | 200g | 500g |
| Tomato juice | 400ml | 1 litre |
| Finely diced onion | 100g | 250g |
| Butter | 80g | 200g |
| Sun-dried tomato | 40g | 100g |
| Vegetable stock | 100ml | 250ml |
| Gorgonzola | 120g | 300g |
| Parmesan grated | 40g | 100g |
| Basil leaves | ½ bunch | 1 bunch |
| Good-quality salt and white pepper | To taste | To taste |

## Method of work

1 Sweat the onions with butter until translucent.
2 Add the rice and cook for 1 minute stirring to coat all the grains.
3 Add the tomato juice and vegetable stock until incorporated and the rice is cooked al dente.
4 Fold in the Gorgonzola and sun-dried tomatoes then season.
5 Deep fry the basil in a deep fat fryer at 180°C until crisp.
6 Arrange the risotto in a bowl and finish with the basil leaves.

### CHEF'S TIP

The Gorgonzola works best when ripe but deteriorates very quickly when added to the risotto so it must be used immediately. Tallegio can be substituted for Gorgonzola.

# Steamed courgette flowers stuffed with braised rice and oil-steeped cherry tomatoes

| INGREDIENTS | 4 PORTIONS | 10 PORTIONS |
|---|---|---|
| Courgette flowers | 8 each | 20 each |
| Braised rice | 8 tbsp | 20 tbsp |
| Diced aubergines | 2 tbsp | 5 tbsp |
| Diced red onion | 2 tbsp | 5 tbsp |
| Brunoise of red, green and yellow peppers | 2 tbsp | 5 tbsp |
| Cherry tomatoes on the vine (in threes) | 4 bunches | 10 bunches |
| Olive oil | 50ml | 125ml |
| Red wine vinegar | 15ml | 40ml |
| Garlic cloves | 2 | 5 |
| Good-quality sea salt and white pepper | To taste | To taste |

*Stuff the courgette flowers*

## Method of work

1 Fry the aubergines and red onions in oil until golden, then mix with the rice.

2 Open the courgette flowers and stuff with the rice.

3 Place the courgettes onto a plate and cling film tightly.

4 Warm the olive oil with the garlic and add the tomatoes, simmer for 20 seconds then leave at room temperature until needed.

5 Sweat the peppers until cooked then add the vinegar and enough oil to taste.

6 Steam the courgette flowers until the flesh is tender, remove from the film and place onto a warmed plate.

7 Drain the tomatoes, sprinkle with sea salt and place onto courgettes.

8 Spoon the pepper dressing around the finished dish.

### CHEF'S TIP

The steeped tomatoes can be made well in advance and chilled, they need only slightly warming again to be ready for reuse.

# Spiced basmati rice with sultanas and candied lime

### CHEF'S TIP

The limes can be substituted with lemons, clementines or oranges for a different effect; there is no need to change the ingredient quantities.

| INGREDIENTS | 4 PORTIONS | 10 PORTIONS |
|---|---|---|
| Steamed basmati rice | 400g | 1kg |
| Sultanas | 100g | 250g |
| Sea salt | Pinch | Pinch |
| Olive oil | 4tbsp | 10tbsp |
| Chilli flakes | Pinch | Pinch |
| Cox's apples, grated | 2 | 5 |
| Chopped coriander | ¼ bunch | ½ bunch |
| Lime juice | 2 | 5 |
| Lime sliced | 1 | 2½ |
| Caster sugar | 50g | 125g |
| Lemongrass | ¼ | ½ |
| Red chilli slices | ½ | 1 |
| Good-quality salt and white pepper | To taste | To taste |

## Method of work

1 Add the sugar and a little water to a saucepan and bring to the boil, add the lemongrass and simmer for a further 4 minutes or until the sugar solution begins to colour slightly.

2 Add the lime slices to the solution, remove from the heat and cool before storing in an airtight container in the refrigerator until required.

3 Steam the basmati until just cooked, remove from the steamer and add the sultanas, apple, chilli, coriander, lime juice, salt and oil.

4 Cover and leave to stand for 10 minutes.

5 Place the rice into a warm bowl, serve with the chilli slices and the candied lime.

*Add all of the remaining ingredients to the steamed rice*

# Tiger prawn and coconut rice

*Sauté the onion, garlic, chilli and spices*

| INGREDIENTS | 4 PORTIONS | 10 PORTIONS |
|---|---|---|
| Finely diced onion | ½ | 1½ |
| Chopped garlic | 1 clove | 3 cloves |
| Grated ginger | 1tbsp | 2½ tbsp |
| Chopped green chilli | 1 | 2½ |
| Ground cumin | ¼ tsp | ½ tsp |
| Ground coriander | ¼ tsp | ½ tsp |
| Coconut milk | 2tbsp | 5tbsp |
| Tiger prawns peeled and de-veined | 12 | 30 |
| Shredded chicory | 100g | 250g |
| Double cream | 200ml | 500ml |
| Lime juice | 2tbsp | 5tbsp |
| Grated coconut | 2tbsp | 5tbsp |
| Wild rice (boiled) | 100g | 250g |
| Basmati rice (boiled) | 300g | 750g |
| Picked coriander | Sprigs | Sprigs |
| Good-quality salt and white pepper | To taste | To taste |

## Method of work

1  Sauté the onion, garlic, ginger, chilli and spices.
2  Add the prawns, chicory and rice and cook for 3 minutes without letting them colour.
3  Add the coconut milk and cream then reduce by half.
4  Season well then serve in a warm bowl.
5  Finish with grated coconut, coriander and lime juice.

# Pesto rice with sun-dried tomatoes

| INGREDIENTS | 4 PORTIONS | 10 PORTIONS |
|---|---|---|
| Long grain rice (boiled) | 400g | 1kg |
| Basil | ½ bunch | 1 bunch |
| Pine nuts roasted | 100g | 250g |
| Garlic | 4 cloves | 10 cloves |
| Olive oil | 100ml | 250ml |
| Grated Parmesan | 8tbs | 20tbs |
| Sun-dried tomatoes julienne | 4tbs | 10tbs |
| Parmesan shavings | 50g | 125g |
| Good-quality salt and white pepper | To taste | To taste |

## Method of work

1  Blend half of the basil with the grated parmesan, garlic, pine nuts until smooth while drizzling in the oil.
2  Mix the pesto with the hot rice; season well and place into a warm bowl.
3  Garnish with Parmesan shavings, ripped basil, a few toasted pine nuts and sun-dried tomatoes.

# Chilli bean rice with crème fraîche

*Add the rice, beans, herbs and spices*

| INGREDIENTS | 4 PORTIONS | 10 PORTIONS |
|---|---|---|
| Boiled long grain rice | 300g | 750g |
| Olive oil | 4tbsp | 10tbsp |
| 1cm diced green peppers | 1 | 2½ |
| 1cm diced red peppers | 1 | 2½ |
| 1cm diced onion | 1 | 2½ |
| Red chilli | 1 | 2½ |
| Tomatoes roughly chopped | 2 | 5 |
| Cooked kidney beans | 125g | 325g |
| Basil | ¼ bunch | ½ bunch |
| Thyme | ¼ bunch | ½ bunch |
| Cajun spices | 1tsp | 2½ tsp |
| Crème fraîche | 4tbs | 10tbs |
| Good-quality salt and white pepper | To taste | To taste |

## Method of work

1 Sauté the peppers and onions until slightly softened.

2 Add the chillies and tomatoes then cook for a further 2 minutes.

3 Add rice, kidney beans, chopped herbs and Cajun spices. Cook until the dish begins to thicken naturally.

4 Serve in a warm bowl with a **quenelle** of crème fraîche and picked basil.

### CHEF'S TIP

Where possible use tinned kidney beans, wash them well and use as required. They require no soaking, extensive cooking and pose no potential threat unlike the dried version.

## Assessment of knowledge and understanding

You have now learned about the use of the different types of rice and how to produce a variety of rice dishes utilising an array of commodities and cooking techniques.

To test your level of knowledge and understanding, answer the following short questions. These will help to prepare you for your summative (final) assessment.

1  Identify the three main categories of rice.

   i) _____  ii) _____

   iii) _____

2  Identify three varieties of rice and offer a brief description of their qualities.

   i) _____  ii) _____

   iii) _____

3  State two ways in which wild rice can be used in a menu.

   i) _____

   ii) _____

4  State four different flavourings that can be used in rice dishes.

   i) _____  ii) _____

   iii) _____  iv) _____

5  State the liquid to rice ratio used for risotto, paella and braised rice dishes.

   _____

   _____

6  Specify the period of time that rice should be kept once cooked.

   _____

   _____

7  Identify the bacteria associated with rice.

   _____

   _____

## Research Task

Complete the following chart describing how to use, clean and maintain the following items of equipment and the safety considerations associated with them.

|  | CLEANING | STERILISING | STORING | SAFETY PROCEDURES |
|---|---|---|---|---|
| Stainless steel colander |  |  |  |  |
| Steamer tray |  |  |  |  |
| Paella pan |  |  |  |  |

## CHEF'S PROFILE

**Name: CYRUS TODIWALA** MBE

**Position:** Proprietor and Executive Chef of the Café Spice Namasté Group

**Background and training:** Cyrus was born and brought up in Bombay. Against his parents' original fears, Cyrus decided to pursue a career in catering, graduating in Hotel Administration and Food Technology from Bombay's Basant Kumar Somani Polytechnic and rising to become Corporate Executive Chef of the famous Taj Groups Taj Holiday Village, The Fort Aguada Beach Resort and the Aguada Hermitage in Goa. In 1989 he joined an old friend in restarting a famous restaurant in Poona. He left India for Australia in 1991, but upon the behest of one of his old friends came to London to run the Namasté restaurant in Alie Street where he developed his hallmark style of blending traditional Indian culinary techniques and flavours with more unexpected ingredients. Ever the keen environmentalist (he helped to establish two bird sanctuaries in Goa); Cyrus cooks with organic products and fully supports British produce wherever possible.

**Current Role:** Today, Cyrus runs two award-winning London restaurants and a new Cafe: the landmark Café Spice Namasté on the border of the City, The Parsee in Highgate and, Café 'T' in New Cavendish Street. The landmark Café Spice Namasté celebrated its 10th year with a special series of dishes dedicated to its loyal customers. The restaurant is a mainstay of all the stylish restaurant guides. Last year, Frommers London Guide named 'Café Spice' as their 'Favourite Indian Restaurant', while Tatler cited 'Café Spice' as one of the best restaurants in the capital serving Sub-continental cuisine. In 2006, Cyrus unveiled Café T, the coffee shop-cum-restaurant of Asia House, one of London's premier cultural centres, located on New Cavendish Street.

**Personal philosophy:** In addition to his dedication to bringing a fusion of flavours and cooking styles to our palettes, Cyrus is committed to investing in the development of skills and opportunities amongst his staff.

He is a valued ambassador for Investors in People and a great supporter of the 'Standard' – the tried and tested flexible framework initiative that helps organisations succeed and compete through improved people performance.

In 1998, Cyrus has also been a member of the National Advisory Counsel for Education and Training Targets. His role included working closely with the Government and key partners on a National Strategy for promoting the importance of learning throughout life and monitoring progress towards Learning Targets, advising Government and its partners at every level on the barriers to their attainment.

Cyrus is committed to the philosophy of lifelong learning and feels that training in his restaurants is 'almost a religion'. He is dedicated to his involvement in local and sector organisations and to support training initiatives.

# Gos No Pulao

There has always been an argument or a controversy about the difference between a Pulao with meat and a Biryani. I have myself often been grossly confused and sometimes such as in this recipe the answer cannot be given. For instance there are pulao's where the lamb or chicken is blended with the rice, both half cooked and then cooked in a sealed pot together until done. There is a biryani that uses a similar methodology and then the meat is blended in before service. By definition I think that a pulao is the one where both the meat and the rice are cooked together. A biryani on the other hand is where the meat and the rice are cooked in layers and then served up from the pot as they would come out straight onto the platter.

However forgetting all of this and leading onto our recipe below. Once again this is an old recipe redeveloped to suit modern day requirements and tastes but sticking to traditional means to give people an idea of how food was eaten and can be so today too albeit with a bit of caution in keeping our minds tuned towards high fat content etc.

## Method of work

1  Clean the lamb, wash and set aside.

2  Place in a pot and pour enough water to cover the lamb and cook until done and the water is almost dry. When done drain the water and set aside.

3  In another pot place two to two and a half litres of water, put a blob of ghee and bring to the boil.

4  Wash the rice and put it into the boiling water, along with 20gms of salt.

5  When rice is almost cooked (al denté is best) drain in a colander.

6  Take another pot and add 150gms of ghee and saute the sliced onions until brown. Remove some of the onions and set aside for garnish. Add the whole garam masala, nutmeg grated, mace and the shahi jeera. Both the last to be pounded in a mortar and pestle.

7  Blend the yoghurt into the boiled lamb.

8  Heat the saffron and add the juice of one lime. Sprinkle it over the boiled rice.

9  To the fried masala add the almonds sliced and the sultanas and fry for a while until golden. Blend the lamb and yoghurt with all of this and set aside.

10 Alternate the lamb and the rice in layers in the pot. Pour over any stock and place in a moderate oven for upto one hour.

11 Before serving sprinkle the brown onions on the top.

| INGREDIENTS | |
|---|---|
| **Basmati** | 1kg |
| **Lamb** | ½kg |
| **Salt** | 20gms |
| **Ghee** | 750gms |
| **Medium onion** (finely and evenly sliced) | 3 |
| **Chawal no masalo** (see rice masala) | 20gms |
| **Nutmeg** | ½ |
| **Javantri** | 5gms |
| **Shah jeera** (caraway seeds) | 2.5gms |
| **Dahi** | 500gms |
| **Kesar** | 1gm |
| **Lime** | 1 |
| **Almonds** | 125gms |
| **Sultanas** | 125gms |

# Pasta

### CHEF'S TIP

Durum wheat or semolina flour is best used for pasta as it has the highest gluten content of all flours. It is this gluten that holds the pasta together and gives it its springiness. If you cannot find either of these, try using a good bread flour as this will also have a relatively high gluten content.

## PASTA COMPOSITION

Pasta is a generic term used to describe many products made from semolina and/or flour which has been milled from the hardest of all wheat, durum wheat.

The secret to creating good pasta dough is to use the strongest, hardest flour which contains a high gluten content. Using softer wheat when making pasta paste gives a texture and colour which does not lend itself to the requirements of good paste. This gives the product a floury appearance when cooking in water and the end result is very soft and flavourless.

When making pasta dough you should ideally use only the best and freshest ingredients as this will ensure the end product will be of the highest quality both in appearance and flavour. Pasta dough, like most pastes, is affected by temperature both in the preparation and cooking stages.

The traditional way of making pasta dough is to prepare and create the mixture on a large unvarnished wooden table, which keeps the temperature and humidity constant.

This method, whereby you create a flour mound with a well in the centre for the eggs, oil and salt and then bring in the flour to form a dough slowly, then **knead**, is still used in classical training. The modern method now commonly implemented is to place all the ingredients into a food processor and blend for approximately 10 to 20 seconds until a loose ball is formed.

When using either method, the paste should feel just firm to the touch and not be sticky.

The finished paste should be wrapped in a plastic film and rested for a minimum of 30 minutes (overnight if possible), which will allow the gluten to relax and prevent shrinkage when rolling out the paste.

The dough can now be rolled out with a rolling pin or formed using a pasta machine, with the latter allowing large quantities to be rolled out to an exact thickness and with greater speed.

Once the pasta has been rolled out, numerous processes can be implemented, including cutting, shaping, filling, cooking or drying.

# EQUIPMENT NEEDED IN PASTA MAKING

This equipment is required for creating pasta at Level 2. It is quite straightforward as there is no real preparation required for this unit. General equipment is necessary and will include:

Spoons    Slotted spoons    Tongs    Conical strainer

Bowls    Metal spider    Fish slice

### CHEF'S TIP

As pasta is a paste it is very delicate. The best results are gained by resting after every movement of the product, i.e. after kneading, rolling or moulding.

### CHEF'S TIP

When making fresh long length pasta for service, it is always best to leave it to hang and dry slightly over a wooden handle or raised rolling pin. This will help the pasta not to stick when cooked as the strands will not tend to group together.

At a higher level, you will need further items:

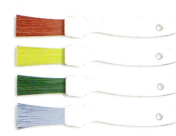

Pasta machine    Wooden chopping board for shaping    If required, small rolling pins and ravioli tray

Palette knives    Fluted cutter or roller

Pastry brushes

### CHEF'S TIP

Pastry brushes are essential both for wet jobs such as sealing and glazing and dry jobs such as removing excess flour, semolina and starch.

# Fresh or Dried Pasta

Many people assume dried pasta is just fresh pasta that has been set out to dry and, although this can be the case, dried pasta does have a recipe of its own.

Fresh pasta, which is traditionally made in northern and central Italy, is almost always made with eggs, which are highly perishable. Fresh pasta must be eaten within a few days of its preparation.

Dried pasta, a southern Italian trademark, almost never contains eggs. Its main ingredients are usually semolina flour, water and salt, meaning that dried pasta can last almost indefinitely without refrigeration.

Fresh pasta can be made with a wide variety of flours, including semolina flour (a derivative of durum wheat), chestnut flour and wheat flour. It is most often made with the more delicate bread flour, which is easier to roll and shape by hand. Dried pasta, on the other hand, almost exclusively relies on semolina flour.

**CHEF'S TIP**

If using a food processor to make pasta, the paste will need very little kneading when removed from the bowl as there is a risk of over-working it.

# Stuffed Pasta

This can be in the form of dried or fresh pasta and either open with a filling, such as cannelloni, or closed, such as ravioli. Pasta that is stuffed for items such as ravioli or tortellini has to be as thin as possible so that when the filling is added the product is not too hard to eat or cook.

The stuffing should be a pleasant marriage of flavours, neither too overpowering nor overpowered by the accompanying sauce or garnishes. The main difficulty and fault that occurs when stuffing pasta is poor sealing of the edges and failing to make them look neat. The same care has to be taken with pasta work as with pastry items.

**HEALTH & SAFETY**

All products not for immediate use should be stored correctly and be clearly labelled.

## QUALITY POINTS

- Dried pasta has come a long way in recent years and the quality of these products has greatly improved in both variety and taste.

- When choosing dried pasta, the box or container should not be opened or damaged. The pasta itself should not be broken or damaged: even though the product is dry, it will need to last for a long time. Furthermore a reasonable use by date should be applied to the packaging.

- Dry pasta should be completely dry and not damp in any way, and must be even in colour and not discoloured or speckled.

- With fresh pasta a lot more consideration has to be given to quality. Fresh pasta should be received at a temperature below 5°C and be evenly coloured, not mottled and not greying in colour.

- The pasta should not be ripped, torn, dried or damaged in any way.

- If stuffed, the pasta should not open at the seams or be uneven in shape.

- Ensure when receiving pasta that it has not stuck together which could mean that moisture has found its way into the packaging.

# PREPARATION AND COOKING METHODS

*Blanching* – this technique is used to speed up the cooking process and shorten service time. It can be utilised with both dried and fresh pasta using boiling salted water then ice cold water to refresh.

*Straining* – pasta is a delicate commodity, and a colander or spider should be used for straining. Pasta should be cooked and refreshed in more water than is necessary, thus ensuring that it has enough room to move, and that you are then able to remove it easily.

*Mixing* – for this method a larger container is required so that the items can be evenly mixed or bound together. Large spoons are best there, using large, gentle stirring movements which will help to prevent damage to the end product.

*Boiling* – a large deep saucepan with plenty of water is required for boiling pasta. Pasta is a starch-based product and has a tendency to absorb water: to help prevent it sticking together during the cooking process a large amount of boiling water is needed. Ensuring that there is more than enough liquid means the water is less likely to thicken and you will have plenty to actually cook the pasta.

When boiling batches of pasta for service the water needs to be changed at regular intervals so that the best end result can be achieved. Adding salt to the water can raise the temperature so that the water will maintain boiling or stay at a high temperature for longer. This also helps with the flavouring in general and will bring out the taste of the pasta.

*Baking* – this tends to be used for dishes that have already been made up or require no further preparation. Care must be taken so that the dish cooks evenly and has a nice all-over colour. Items that are baked should be cleaned up before and after cooking so that a more presentable dish can be achieved.

When baking, check at regular intervals to monitor quality. A probe should be used to check the core temperature so that when the product seems cooked and the correct colour is achieved you can ensure that it is also at a safe temperature for service.

*Combination cooking* – general boiling, poaching or deep frying will be the starting block for most pastas and sauces, closely followed by either baking or simmering.

A perfect example of this would be using fresh pasta. The pasta has to be blanched, the filling has to be cooked, and finally the dish has to be baked.

**CHEF'S TIP**

Filled pasta items should always be produced thinner than required as they will contract slightly on cooking and if they are too thick they will be heavy to eat.

**CHEF'S TIP**

When making stuffed pasta, work as quickly as possible to prevent the pasta dough from drying out and becoming too difficult to work with. This will also prevent problems occurring with the pasta sealing properly.

**CHEF'S TIP**

For best results with stuffed pasta, they should be blanched first in boiling salted water then placed onto a tray with a damp, clean cloth or paper towel to take off excess water.

*Olive oil flavoured with herbs and chillis*

# ISSUES WITH COOKING, HOLDING AND STORAGE

With the storage of dried pasta, the same rules apply to this that would with any dry or dried product, namely airtight containers that are clearly labelled, dated and stored in a cool dry place. Dried pasta can be stored for a few months in this way and generally tends to not lose its quality.

If the pasta is dried in flat form, i.e. pasta sheet, tagliatelle or noodles, then this should be stored in a large square container with greaseproof paper in between layers so that they do not stick.

When cooking and holding dried pasta for service, the pasta should be blanched, dried and then lightly coated in oil in order to prevent it from sticking. This rule applies to almost all shaped pasta but excludes sheets like lasagne or cannelloni which should be made dry and then baked in order to cook the pasta.

For service and holding, use only what is required as pasta can tend to over-cook very easily. As the pasta has been blanched its cooking time is greatly reduced and it should therefore only take minutes to reheat. The holding temperature should be maintained at about 65°C.

For fresh pasta the ruling is different. Fresh pasta is generally made with fresh or pasteurised eggs and so the shelf life is immediately reduced. When storing fresh pasta it should be wrapped tightly in plastic film with no holes or openings and placed into a refrigerator to avoid the paste from oxidising and turning grey. This should then be clearly labelled, including the date of production.

When pasta has been shaped it should be stored in a large container with semolina to prevent it from getting sticky and again, similar to dried flat pasta, in between layers of greaseproof paper in an airtight container.

Fresh pasta that as been stuffed or is in small shapes should be blanched, drained and frozen or chilled in small amounts so that it can be easily separated. The frozen pasta will keep for between one and three months.

For service, fresh pasta that is shaped can be cooked to order as the cooking time is short. Fresh pasta can be blanched but does not hold as well as dried pasta. The exception to this rule is stuffed fresh pastas such as ravioli or flat shapes such as lasagne which can be blanched and refreshed and will hold quite well.

In its raw form, fresh and blanched pasta should be stored in a fridge below 5°C. If it is for service then it should be held at 65°C.

# RECIPES

## Plain egg pasta dough

| INGREDIENTS | 4 PORTIONS | 10 PORTIONS |
|---|---|---|
| 00 grade flour | 72g | 180 |
| Eggs | 1 | 2 |
| Egg yolks | 1 | 3 |
| Olive oil | 5ml | 12ml |
| Good-quality salt and pepper | To taste | To taste |

Make a well in flour

Add eggs to flour

Incorporate into flour

Add oil to egg mix

Kneed to a smooth dough

Cover and rest

*Overlap so that pasta can be joined*

*Seal so that pasta becomes one looped piece*

*Adjust setting and feed pasta through continuously*

## Method of work

1 In a large bowl or on a clean work surface, sieve the flour and using your hands create a well by pushing the flour out to create a ring.

2 In a bowl beat the eggs, yolks and oil together.

3 Slowly add the egg mixture to the middle of the flour before gradually incorporating the two sets of ingredients to form a paste.

4 On the work surface, knead the dough until smooth.

5 Cover with plastic film and refrigerate for at least 15 minutes. Before rolling out using a little flour or semolina to dust the work surface so that it does not stick.

# Butternut squash ravioli with thyme, tomato and a red onion butter sauce

| INGREDIENTS | 4 PORTIONS | 10 PORTIONS |
|---|---|---|
| 00 grade flour | 72g | 180g |
| Eggs | 1 | 2 |
| Egg yolks | 1 | 3 |
| Olive oil | 5ml | 12ml |
| Filling | | |
| Butternut squash, peeled and deseeded | 1kg | 2.5kg |
| Fresh thyme (leaves only) | 1tbsp | 2tbsp |
| Red onion, finely chopped | 2 | 4 |
| Unsalted butter | 150g | 300g |
| Tomatoes, chopped | 3 | 6 |
| Garlic clove, finely chopped | 1 | 2 |
| Good-quality salt and pepper | To taste | To taste |

*Trim each square so that they are even in size*

*Place filling in the centre; do not over-fill*

*Crimp the edges with a fork*

**CHEF'S TIP**

Ensure that stuffed pasta is not overfilled as it becomes hard to seal and will break when blanched causing the filling to leak out into the water.

**VIDEO CLIP**
Filling pasta

**VIDEO CLIP**
Shaping ravioli and agnolotti

## Method of work

1. Make the pasta paste using the method in the recipe on p. 189.

2. Using one tablespoon of the butter, sweat the onion, garlic and thyme leaves for approximately 5 minutes or until all the ingredients have softened.

3. Add the tomatoes and continue to simmer for a further 5 minutes before removing from the heat and blast chilling.

4. Cut the butternut squash into large even pieces and in a saucepan cover them with vegetable stock. Bring the squash to the boil and simmer for approximately 15 minutes until tender. Place the squash onto a tray and allow the cooked squash to dry out in a moderate oven before gently mashing with a fork and seasoning.

5. Using a pasta machine, roll out the paste to a thickness at 'level 3' ensuring the pasta is kept covered and floured as much as possible.

6. Using an appropriately sized cutter, cut out pieces from the pasta sheets and set a spoonful of the butternut squash mixture into the centre. Use a little water around the edges of the pasta pieces before placing another piece of pasta over the top and sealing with your fingers or a fork. Leave the pasta to rest for 15 minutes.

7. Blanch the pasta in a large pan of boiling salted water.

8. Warm the tomato and red onion sauce until boiling. When the sauce is boiling, remove from the heat and whisk the rest of the cold butter into the sauce.

9. Add the drained pasta to the sauce, coat, garnish and serve.

# Cannelloni of chicken and red pepper with a sun-dried tomato cream sauce

| INGREDIENTS | 4 PORTIONS | 10 PORTIONS |
| --- | --- | --- |
| Dried lasagne sheets | 10 | 25 |
| Red pepper | 1 | 2 |
| Onion, finely chopped | 100g | 200g |
| Flat leaf parsley, finely chopped | 3tbsp | 6tbsp |
| Minced chicken | 300g | 750g |
| Egg yolks | 2 | 5 |
| Grated Parmesan cheese | 25g | 70g |
| Grated nutmeg | 5g | 12g |
| White breadcrumbs | 25g | 63g |
| Tomato sauce | 200ml | 500ml |
| Milk | 1 litre | 2.5 litres |
| Butter | 150g | 375g |
| Flour | 150g | 375g |
| Cream | 100ml | 250ml |
| Stock | 100ml | 250ml |
| Sun-dried tomatoes (chopped) | 50g | 125g |
| Béchamel sauce (see recipe on p. 113) | 250ml | 250ml |
| Good-quality salt and pepper | To taste | To taste |

*Pipe farce onto the lasagne sheets and roll into tubes*

Béchamel sauce (see recipe on p. 113)

## Method of work

1 Preheat an oven at 180°C. In a large saucepan of boiling salted water, blanch the lasagne sheets for the time stated on the packaging and refresh immediately in iced cold water.

2 Place the peppers into the preheated oven and roast until charred and black. Remove from the oven and cover the roasting tray with plastic film until cool. This will enable the skin of the pepper to be removed easily. Peel the peppers and cut into small squares.

3 To prepare the stuffing for the cannelloni, sweat the onion, nutmeg and fresh parsley gently in a little butter until softened. Allow to cool before adding to the minced chicken, egg yolks, cheese, roasted pepper and breadcrumbs. Stir in a tablespoon of the béchamel sauce to bind the ingredients together.

4 Drain the pasta sheets and lay them out flat. Using a piping bag, pipe the prepared mixture down one side of the sheets before rolling them up into tubes.

5 Place the prepared cannelloni into a suitable ovenproof baking dish, cover with the tomato sauce followed by the béchamel.

6 Sprinkle with the grated Parmesan before placing into a hot pre-heated oven at 190°C. Bake for approximately 30 minutes or until the cannelloni stuffing is cooked through and the topping is golden brown in colour.

### CHEF'S TIP

For speed, try placing the peppers onto a skewer or carving fork and roasting over an open gas flame, turning frequently to ensure an all-over blister. Once blistered either wrap in a container with plastic film or place into a sealable sandwich bag until cooled as the steam created by the retained cooking heat will allow the skin to separate from the pepper itself.

# Spaghetti bolognaise

*Add tomato purée to the mince and vegetables*

| INGREDIENTS | 4 PORTIONS | 10 PORTIONS |
|---|---|---|
| Spaghetti | 600g | 1kg |
| Oil | 1tbsp | 3tbsp |
| Bacon lardons | 50g | 125g |
| Onion, diced | 120g | 270g |
| Celery, diced | 75g | 180g |
| Carrot, diced | 100g | 200g |
| Minced Beef | 200g | 500g |
| Tomato purée | 50g | 125g |
| Beef stock | 400ml | 1 litre |
| Garlic, finely chopped | 3 cloves | 6 cloves |
| Marjoram leaves | 2tbsp | 5tbsp |
| Mushroom, sliced | 100g | 250g |
| Concassé of tomatoes | 200g | 450g |
| Good-quality salt and pepper | To taste | To taste |

## Method of work

1   If using spaghetti that requires pre-cooking, cook as per the packaging guidelines and refresh immediately in iced cold water.

2   In a large saucepan heat 1 tablespoon of the oil and fry the lardons for 3 minutes.

3   Add the prepared onion, carrot and celery to the lardons, place a lid onto the pan and sweat for a further 5 minutes until the vegetables have softened.

4   Remove the lid and add the mince. Over a high heat brown the mince stirring continuously.

5   Once the mince is completely browned, remove the pan from the heat and stir in the tomato purée, garlic and marjoram.

6   Return to the heat for two minutes to cook out the bitterness from the tomato purée before adding the stock and the tomato concassé. Bring the pan to the boil, season well and simmer for 15 minutes.

7   Mix in the prepared mushrooms and cook for a further 5 minutes before reheating the spaghetti and serving.

### CHEF'S TIP

Try enrichening the sauce with a tablespoon of balsamic vinegar or a dash of red wine and reduce to thicken.

# Tagliatelle campanola

*Add the broccoli and sausage mixture to the pasta*

| INGREDIENTS | 4 PORTIONS | 10 PORTIONS |
|---|---|---|
| Tagliatelle dried | 600g | 1.5kg |
| Italian sausage or salami, cut into slices | 250g | 650g |
| Red chilli, finely diced | 1 | 2 |
| Olive oil | 100ml | 250ml |
| Broccoli, small florets | 1 small head | 2½ small heads |
| Red pepper | 1 | 2 |
| Fresh oregano | 1tbsp | 2tbsp |
| Red onion, diced | 75g | 200g |
| Good-quality salt and pepper | To taste | To taste |

**CHEF'S TIP**

Fresh or dried pasta can be used in this dish. Try adding other Italian-derived ingredients such as olives or capers to add a different flavour.

## Method of work

1 Sprinkle the peppers with the oil and seasoning. Roast in a very hot oven until blistered and charred. Cover in cling film and allow to sweat whilst cooling down to release the skin before cutting into squares.

2 Blanch the tagliatelle in boiling salted water according to packaging instructions and refresh immediately in iced cold water.

3 Sweat the onion and chilli for 5 minutes in a little oil, add the **salami** and continue cooking until the sausage is fully cooked.

4 Add the broccoli florets and continue to cook in the pan until tender before adding the fresh oregano and correcting the seasoning. Serve.

# Linguine with crab and prawn, baby spinach and crème fraîche

| INGREDIENTS | 4 PORTIONS | 10 PORTIONS |
|---|---|---|
| Linguine | 800g | 1.6kg |
| Picked white crab meat | 50g | 250g |
| Prawns | 50g | 250g |
| Washed baby spinach leaves | 80g | 320g |
| Crème fraîche | 400ml | 900ml |
| Fresh coriander leaves, chopped | 1tbsp | 3tbsp |
| Olive oil | 1tbsp | 3tbsp |
| Good-quality salt and pepper | To taste | To taste |

## Method of work

1 Blanch the linguine in a large saucepan of boiling salted water for the time stated on the packaging.

2 Over a high heat, sauté the prawns in the olive oil before adding the cooked and drained linguine.

3 Fold in the crab meat and spinach leaves. Keep the pan on the heat for about 3 minutes to fully warm through the crab and gently wilt the spinach leaves. Season well.

4 Remove the pan from the heat and stir in the crème fraîche so that it does not split.

5 Stir in the coriander, check the seasoning and serve immediately.

**CHEF'S TIP**

Quickly sauté the prawns for no longer than 5 minutes or their muscles will toughen up making them tough to eat.

# Spinach cannelloni stuffed with ricotta and baked with a tomato and pine nut sauce

| INGREDIENTS | 4 PORTIONS | 10 PORTIONS |
|---|---|---|
| Dried spinach lasagne sheets | 12 sheets | 30 sheets |
| Ricotta cheese | 300g | 750g |
| Lemon zest and juice | 1 lemon | 2 lemons |
| Flat leaf parsley, finely chopped | 3tbsp | 6tbsp |
| Plum tomatoes | 200g | 500g |
| Basil | 2tbsp | 4tbsp |
| Shallots, chopped | 40g | 100g |
| Olive oil | 50ml | 125ml |
| Parmesan cheese, grated | 50g | 125g |
| Pine nuts | 20g | 50g |
| Sun-dried tomato, soaked and chopped (reserve liquor) | 20g | 50g |
| Good-quality salt and pepper | To taste | To taste |

*Pipe the ricotta mixture into lasagne sheets and roll them into tubes*

## CHEF'S TIP

Roast the pine nuts in an oven instead of under a grill as you will gain more of a roasted flavour to the sauce.

## Method of work

1. Preheat an oven to 190°C.
2. Cook the lasagne sheets in a large pan of boiling salted water for the stated time as shown on the packaging. Refresh immediately in iced cold water.
3. Beat the ricotta with a spoon until soft. Stir in the lemon zest and juice, chopped parsley and season well.
4. Using a piping bag, pipe the ricotta mixture down one side of each lasagne sheet and roll them up to form a cigar shape. Cover and chill in a refrigerator.
5. Roast the tomatoes, whole, in the oven for 30 minutes.
6. Gently sweat the shallots until softened, add the plum and sun-dried tomatoes and a little of the cooking liquor and simmer for 30 minutes before passing through a chinois.
7. Toast the pine nuts until golden and stir into the sauce before pouring the sauce over the prepared cannelloni.
8. Sprinkle with the cheese and bake at 190°C for 30 minutes or until golden and serve.

# Classic lasagne

*Make alternate layers of meat then pasta*

| INGREDIENTS | 4 PORTIONS | 10 PORTIONS |
|---|---|---|
| Lasagne | 200g | 500g |
| Olive oil | 1tbsp | 3tbsp |
| Lardons of bacon | 50g | 125g |
| Onion, diced | 170g | 350g |
| Celery, diced | 100g | 200g |
| Carrot, diced | 150g | 300g |
| Minced beef | 200g | 550g |
| Tomato purée | 50g | 125g |
| Beef stock | 400ml | 1 litre |
| Garlic, finely chopped | 3 cloves | 5 cloves |
| Fresh marjoram, leaves | 1tbsp | 2tbsp |
| Button mushrooms, sliced | 100g | 250g |
| Béchamel sauce | 250ml | 600ml |
| Cheddar cheese, grated | 50g | 150g |
| Butter for greasing | ½ tsp | 1tsp |
| Good-quality salt and pepper | To taste | To taste |

## Method of work

1 Preheat an oven to 190°C.

2 If using lasagne sheets that require pre-cooking, cook as per the packaging guidelines and refresh immediately in iced cold water.

3 In a large saucepan heat 1 tablespoon of the olive oil and fry the lardons for 3 minutes.

4 Add the prepared onion, carrot and celery to the lardons, place a lid on the pan and sweat for a further 5 minutes until the vegetables have softened.

5 Remove the lid and add the mince. Over a high heat brown the mince whilst continuously stirring.

6 Once the mince is completely browned remove the pan from the heat and stir in the tomato purée, garlic and marjoram.

7 Return to the heat for two minutes to cook out the bitterness from the tomato purée before adding the stock. Bring the pan to the boil, season and simmer for 15 minutes.

8 Mix in the prepared mushrooms and cook for a further 3 minutes.

9 Butter a suitable ovenproof dish before covering with a layer of the meat sauce followed by a layer of cooked lasagne sheets. Repeat this process two more times.

10 Cover the complete layers with béchamel sauce and top with the cheese before covering the dish with foil and baking for 20 minutes in the preheated oven. After this time, remove the foil and continue to bake for a further 15 minutes to gratinate the cheese.

**CHEF'S TIP**

For an even gratinated finish, place the lasagne under the grill for the last 3 minutes of cooking.

**CHEF'S TIP**

An alternative to this lasagne is to create a seafood lasagne using prawns, mussels, salmon, squid poached in fish stock and bound in the white sauce.

# Macaroni with blue cheese and leek bake

| INGREDIENTS | 4 PORTIONS | 10 PORTIONS |
|---|---|---|
| Macaroni | 200g | 1kg |
| Fresh milk | 1 litre | 2.5 litres |
| Butter | 150g | 375g |
| Flour | 150g | 375g |
| Blue cheese (Stilton) | 200g | 500g |
| Leek | 200g | 500g |
| Freshly chopped parsley | 1tsp | 3tsp |
| Unsalted butter | 1tsp | 3tsp |
| Good-quality salt and pepper | To taste | To taste |

## Method of work

1 Preheat an oven to 190°C.

2 Cook the macaroni in a large pan of boiling salted water for the time stated on the packaging. Refresh immediately in iced cold water.

3 In a medium-sized saucepan melt the butter and stir in the flour. Cook out the rawness of the flour over a medium heat for 1 minute before slowly starting to add the milk, one ladle at a time.

4 Continue adding a ladle of the milk at intervals, but only when the previous ladle has been mixed in, absorbed, the sauce is boiling and there are no lumps present within the sauce.

5 Continue to cook the flour out of the sauce by allowing the sauce to gently simmer over a very low heat for approximately 45 minutes. Season well.

6 In the butter, gently sweat the leek for 5 minutes.

7 Add the cooked leek and half the cheese to the béchamel, ensuring the cheese has completely melted. Add the cooked macaroni.

8 Pour into a suitable ovenproof dish and sprinkle with the remaining cheese before baking for about 20 minutes or until golden brown on top. Sprinkle with parsley and serve.

### CHEF'S TIP

Ensure you stir the béchamel frequently whilst cooking out the flour or a skin will form on the top and cause a lumpy sauce once stirred.

# Fusilli arrabiata

| INGREDIENTS | 4 PORTIONS | 10 PORTIONS |
|---|---|---|
| Fusilli pasta | 600g | 1.5kg |
| Olive oil | 2tbsp | 5tbsp |
| Garlic, finely chopped | 3 cloves | 5 cloves |
| Onion, finely chopped | 80g | 240g |
| Red chilli, brunoise | 1 | 3 |
| White wine | 200ml | 500ml |
| Concassé of plum tomatoes | 200g | 450g |
| Fresh oregano leaves | 1tbsp | 3tbsp |
| Good-quality salt and pepper | To taste | To taste |

*Add chopped tomatoes to the wine and onion mixture*

## Method of work

1 Cook the pasta in a large saucepan of boiling salted water following the guidelines on the packaging. Refresh immediately in iced cold water.

2 Gently heat the oil before adding the prepared onion, garlic, chilli and oregano. Sweat for 5 minutes or until softened.

3 Add the white wine and reduce until just a little liquid is left.

4 Add the concassé of plum tomatoes and leave to simmer for approximately 15 minutes or until all excess liquid has been evaporated.

5 Reheat the pasta and coat in the spicy tomato sauce. Serve immediately.

### CHEF'S TIP

When cutting brunoise use a very sharp knife to stop the ingredient bruising as this will effect the taste of the final product. Also, when cutting chilli ensure you use plastic gloves if you have sensitive skin or cuts and make sure you wash your hands thoroughly after preparing chillies.

# Farfalle with ham and mushroom

| INGREDIENTS | 4 PORTIONS | 10 PORTIONS |
|---|---|---|
| Farfalle pasta | 600g | 1.2kg |
| Ham, diced | 200g | 400g |
| Mushrooms, sliced | 320g | 650g |
| Double cream | 200ml | 400ml |
| Vegetable stock | 200ml | 400ml |
| Butter | ½ tbsp | 1 tbsp |
| Garlic, finely chopped | 1 clove | 2 cloves |
| Parsley, finely chopped | 1 tbsp | 3 tbsp |
| Good-quality salt and pepper | To taste | To taste |

## Method of work

1 Blanch the pasta in a large saucepan of boiling salted water. Refresh in iced water.

2 In a saucepan melt the butter and sweat the garlic and mushrooms for approximately 3 minutes until the mushrooms have softened.

3 Add the stock and reduce the mixture by half.

4 Add the cream and also reduce by half or until the sauce has reached a consistency capable of coating the back of a spoon. Season well and add the fresh chopped parsley, diced ham and the drained cooked pasta before serving.

### CHEF'S TIP

To ensure a better finish, use fresh stock instead of a stock cube as reducing stock made from a stock cube will give a salty taste to the finished sauce.

# Assessment of knowledge and understanding

You have now learned about the use of different types of pasta and how to produce a variety of pasta dishes utilising an array of commodities and cooking techniques.

To test your level of knowledge and understanding, answer the following short questions. These will help to prepare you for your summative (final) assessment.

1  Discuss the main difference between fresh and dried pasta products.

_____

_____

2  List four items of equipment that will be used for the blanching and draining of pasta, stating at which stage of the process each item will be used.

i) _____   ii) _____

iii) _____   iv) _____

3  Name the three main ingredients that are used in a pasta paste recipe.

i) _____   ii) _____

iii) _____

4  Name three varieties of dried pasta and give two examples of suitable dishes that each can be used in.

i) _____   ii) _____

iii) _____

5  List five ingredients you can add to pasta in order to improve the flavour and/or colour.

i) _____   ii) _____   iii) _____

iv) _____   v) _____

6  It is important to blanch dried pasta before service. Explain the blanching process and why this needs to be carried out.

_____

_____

7  Explain the term 'al dente'.

_____

_____

8  Explain the safety aspects when blanching large quantities of pasta in boiling water.

_____

_____

9  Describe the correct process for storage of both dried and fresh pasta once it has been cooked for service.

_____

_____

# Grains

## INTRODUCTION

Grains and cereals are among the oldest farmed products in the world. Cereal is a grass producing edible starchy seeds or grains. The cereals most commonly grown are wheat, rice, rye, oats, barley, corn (maize) and sorghum. The name cereal is christened after *Ceres*, the Roman goddess of grain, and grains were seen as so important that each type of grain was thought to be a gift from the gods.

Grains form a staple part of many diets across the globe because they are inexpensive and sustainable. Only in wealthy countries has meat and fish begun to replace cereals and grains as the primary food. Grains can be utilised in many different foods ranging from breads, salads, risottos and stews. It has also become a notable way for vegetarians to increase their variety in food products.

Whole grains are made of all three parts of a grain kernel: the bran, endosperm and germ.

Bran is the coarse, outer layer of the kernel that includes concentrated amounts of several nutrients, including:

- Fibre
- B vitamins (thiamine, riboflavin, niacin and folic acid)
- Minerals (zinc, copper, iron)
- Protein
- Phytochemicals (beneficial chemical compounds).

The endosperm is the middle layer and is the biggest section of the whole grain. It acts as the main energy supply for the living plant. It contains:

- Carbohydrates
- Protein
- Small amounts of B vitamins.

The Germ is the smallest part of the grain, but is crammed with nutrients. It develops into a new plant, so it will hold plentiful supplies of the following nutrients:

- Minerals
- B vitamins
- Vitamin E
- Phytochemicals (beneficial chemical compounds).

> **CHEF'S TIP**
>
> Grains are a very good way of improving the overall healthy eating aspect of dishes because of their nutritional value.

**Anatomy of a whole grain**

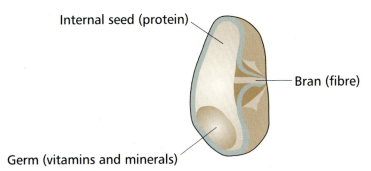

Internal seed (protein)

Bran (fibre)

Germ (vitamins and minerals)

Grain is a starch-based commodity so it is able to absorb a lot of water. This is why it is easier to boil or steam grains, as they will then become swollen and eventually softer in texture. Whole grains will take longer to cook than processed grains. Grains can be cooked dry without any pre-soaking, except for whole wheat, barley, rye and brown rice.

**CHEF'S TIP**

A processed grain has been broken down into flakes, nibs or ground into finer particles. Because it has been processed it will cook quicker than the hardened whole grain.

# THE CLASSIFICATION OF GRAINS

## Barley

Barley is available in two forms. Processed barley is known as pearled; unprocessed is known as unhulled and contains more vitamins, minerals and fibre. This is because it is unrefined and contains the germ and endosperm making it more nutritious to eat, although once cooked it tends to be quite chewy. Barley makes up approximately 7 per cent of the world's total grain production and has been used in cooking for thousands of years.

**VIDEO CLIP**
Preparing and cooking barley

## Buckwheat

Buckwheat is also available in different forms:

- Raw (whole)
- Roasted
- Cracked
- Hulled (processed).

The raw stage is a fruit seed which is reddish-brown in colour, is free from gluten and therefore is not classified as wheat. Once cooked it has a soft texture and can be combined with quinoa to create appealing salads. Roasted buckwheat is known as kasha and is stronger in flavour and drier than the raw form of buckwheat. Buckwheat is more commonly known and used in catering today as buckwheat flour, and is used for lightly textured

**CHEF'S TIP**

Barley and quinoa can be used as alternative thickening agents for soups or stews. Barley can also be used instead of rice for risotto.

Russian pancakes known as blinis. It is also found as an additional ingredient in bread, breakfast cereals and stuffing for poultry.

## Corn/maize

Corn is probably the most widely used grain and grows on a cob. It is also ground down into cornmeal which is then used to make breads and tortillas and used for animal feed. In the United States it is one of the largest crops grown.

It is more popularly known for polenta which can be substituted for rice and pasta and will accompany fish, meat and game dishes very well. Polenta is a classic dish from Italy, mainly from the northern regions. It is versatile and can be made into soft or firm pastes that can also be cut, shaped and grilled or baked. Polenta can also combine well with additional flavours such as fresh herbs, Parmesan cheese or garlic. Sometimes polenta can substitute flour in various pasta recipes.

## Oats

The history of oats dates back to Germany in 1000 BC, but its popularity did not extend across Europe quickly. This was due in part to the bland flavour and the commonly held view that it was a food more suited for animal feed. By the mid 1980s, the popularity of oats was boosted to health food status by some research suggesting that it helped to prevent heart disease. Oats are the edible seeds of a cereal grass which is available in two forms, raw (groats) and rolled (flaked). Oat flakes are used in porridge and other breakfast dishes such as muesli. Fine oatmeal can also be made into bannocks (Scottish griddle cakes).

## Millet

Millet is thought to be one of the first grains cultivated. The first recorded comments regarding millet date back to 5500 BC in China. Millet may have been domesticated in Africa hundreds or even thousands of years before, where it still grows wild. It was an extremely important grain whose popularity diminished somewhat with the arrival of maize and rice. The variety of this grain sold in Europe and North America for human consumption is called pearl millet. It is produced in grain form and in flakes which can be used like other grain flakes as a thickening agent for stews and soups.

## Wheat (bulgur, semolina, couscous)

The first evidence of wheat was discovered in an ancient civilization in what is now Iraq, dating back to at least 6700 BC. Wheat made its way to England

VIDEO CLIP
Preparing and cooking polenta

Grilled polenta

CHEF'S TIP

Never mix old and new grains together because the older grains can take longer to cook. The longer they are stored, even in correct conditions, the drier they will become.

around the twelfth century and is classified as either spring or winter wheat, depending on the time of year it was planted and grown. It is a plant which has many uses today such as bulgur wheat, couscous, durum wheat, cracked wheat and various flours including strong glutinous flours used for bread making or semolina.

*Bulgur wheat* is made by boiling wheat grains until they crack. As a result, this grain only has to be soaked or simmered in water. It is a staple commodity in the Middle East where it is combined with lamb to make kibbeh. It is also the main ingredient of the Lebanese salad called tabbouleh, which is usually served as a starter.

*Couscous* is a mixture of coarse grains of semolina that are mixed with finer grains of semolina until they coat each larger grain. Because traditional couscous takes a long time to cook the most commonly available is precooked so the cooking time is dramatically reduced. Read the labels carefully to check that the couscous is of the correct variety. Widely found in North Africa where it is cooked in a special tagine dish or a couscousière which allows it to be steamed in a pot above stewing vegetables.

*Couscous*

*Semolina* is the ground endosperm from the durum wheat. It is found as a fine powder or in a granular form that is primarily used to make fresh pasta. Semolina pasta is firmer than that made from other wheat-based flours and has a strong yellow colour. Semolina can be used to produce a dessert milk pudding, breads, cakes and gnocchi.

## Quinoa

Quinoa is actually a seed, rather than a grain, that has been grown for 5000 years in South America, in and around the Andes Mountains. The Incas called quinoa 'the Mother Grain' because eating this food tended to give long life. Quinoa contains 50 per cent more protein than wheat and is full of nutrition. It is a small disc-shaped seed with a very light flavour which can be prepared in dishes such as salads, stews and soups. Its cooking time is also very short. Not only is this grain healthy, due to its nutritional value, but it is also gluten free.

*Quinoa*

## Rye

This is a cereal grass similar to wheat. It has long been a staple grain in northern Europe and Russia. It is milled to produce rye flour and rye flakes to create rye bread (sometimes referred to as black bread). It produces a dark-coloured flour but it does have a lower gluten content than wheat-based flours. For this reason it is best to combine a strong flour with rye flour when making rye bread.

*Rye bread*

# THE PREPARATION OF GRAINS

The preparation of grains for cooking is quite simple. The focal detail for preparing them is the washing process, as they can have surface dust which may be harmless but should be removed under running cold water in a colander. Sometimes infestation may be present so it is important to identify any alien dark specs or insects within the grain before use. Although grain products are dried, very rarely do they need to be soaked. This is the same with oats and barley: soaking will speed up the cooking process. The majority of grains can be cooked from dry within a reasonable time limit.

As grains are starch-based the best method of cooking is boiling, stewing, steaming and braising because the apparent moisture in each cooking process will help the starch cells to swell and burst and they begin to cook at between 60–70°C, depending on the type of grain. These methods will ensure the grain will cook evenly. However, couscous, bulgur wheat and millet should have a boiling liquid poured over and be left to cool. As long as the mixture is stirred occasionally to stop the product sticking then the grain should never over-cook.

This method of cooking grains is ideal if no further cooking is required or the items are for salads. Another method to consider in the preparation and cooking grains is baking. Items like porridge oats, polenta and cornmeal can be soaked and flavoured or parcooked and then poured into a lined or greased baking tin and placed into the oven to bake. The dry heat from the oven will heat the grain mixture, the water mixed with the grain will cook the product and eventually the moisture will evaporate in the heat. Due to the way water is absorbed steaming is also another good and healthy way to cook grain either over water, stock or any flavoured and scented liquid.

> **CHEF'S TIP**
>
> If boiling or cooking grains in a saucepan; first line the pan with a touch of oil before heating, the grain will not stick against the sides of the pan and potentially burn.

# STORAGE

Grains in whole seed form will have the longest shelf-life span of any food group possible. When stored in a dry cool place within airtight plastic containers, grains retain their excellent nutritional and flavour characteristics over time unlike other food groups. This shelf life is greatly reduced the more refined the product becomes. Milled flours from grain will not last longer than a year if kept in the right storage condition compared to the numerous years in which whole grains can last. This is because the hard outer skin or husk that stops the oxidisation of the grain has been removed from flours, thus shortening their shelf life. When preparing to store grains the use of a vacuum pack machine is valuable. The vacuum bags are very strong and durable, and they prolong shelf life further because the air is removed during the sealing of the bags. The vacuum will also compact the grain into a smaller size so it is easier to store and will take up less room on the shelf.

> **CHEF'S TIP**
>
> Store grain in small amounts rather than in large batches so the quality will not deteriorate as quickly from opening one smaller batch to another.

**AVERAGE COOKING TIMES FOR GRAINS**

| GRAIN | LIQUID TO GRAIN RATIO | COOKING TIME (APPROXIMATE MINUTES) |
|---|---|---|
| Barley hulled/whole | 3 : 1 | 90 |
| Barley pearled | 3 : 1 | 45 |
| Millet | 2½ : 1 | 25 |
| Oats, whole | 3 : 1 | 60 |
| Oats, rolled | 2 : 1 | 15 |
| Buckwheat groats | 2 : 1 | 15 |
| Quinoa | 2 : 1 | 20 |
| Corn grits | 3 : 1 | 20 |
| Bulgur | 2 : 1 | 15 |
| Couscous | 2 : 1 | 1 |

# RECIPES

## Cornbread

*Pour the liquid into a well in the centre of the dry ingredients*

| INGREDIENTS | 4 PORTIONS | 10 PORTIONS |
|---|---|---|
| Soft white flour | 150g | 300g |
| Cornmeal | 150g | 300g |
| Baking powder | 4tsp | 8tsp |
| Granulated sugar | 30g | 60g |
| Fresh eggs | 2 | 4 |
| Full fat milk | 250ml | 500ml |
| Crème fraîche | 1tbsp | 2tbsp |
| Good-quality salt | 3g | 5g |
| Melted unsalted butter | 2tbsp | 4tbsp |

## Method of work

1 Preheat an oven to 190°C.
2 Mix the flour, cornmeal, baking powder, salt and sugar together in a bowl.
3 Pour in the beaten eggs, milk, crème fraîche and melted butter.
4 Mix well to create a smooth batter.
5 Pour the mixture in a greased and silicone paper lined square cake tin. Bake in the oven for approximately 30 minutes.
6 Leave to cool for five minutes in the cake tin before turning out onto a chopping board and cutting into square-shaped portions. Serve the bread warm.

# Sweetcorn and radish pearl barley 'risotto'

| INGREDIENTS | 4 PORTIONS | 10 PORTIONS |
|---|---|---|
| Washed pearl barley | 125g | 300g |
| Sweetcorn kernels | 50g | 125g |
| Finely chopped shallot | 70g | 140g |
| Finely chopped garlic | 1 clove | 2 cloves |
| Finely sliced red radishes with the leaves attached | 5 in number | 12 in number |
| Dry white wine | 50ml | 100ml |
| Vegetable stock | 200ml | 500ml |
| Double cream | 100ml | 250ml |
| Finely grated Parmesan cheese | 30g | 80g |
| Fresh parsley, chopped | 1tbsp | 2tbsp |
| Unsalted butter | 50g | 125g |
| Good-quality salt and white pepper | To taste | To taste |

*The consistency of the finished 'risotto'*

## Method of work

1 Wash the pearl barley under cold running water.

2 Melt the butter in a saucepan and add the chopped shallots and garlic. Sweat gently for 2 minutes until they have slightly softened.

3 Add the pearl barley and continue to sweat for another 2 minutes. Pour in the white wine and reduce by half.

4 Add half of the vegetable stock and bring to simmering point. Continue to add more stock as required, little by little, until the pearl barley is sufficiently cooked.

5 Add the double cream and cook until a creamy texture has been achieved.

6 Add the sweetcorn and radish and season well.

7 Serve with the Parmesan cheese and the chopped fresh parsley.

8 As a service option, remove the radish leaves and wash well in clean water. Dry and trim if necessary, liquidise with a little olive oil and seasoning. Use to dress the dish as required.

# Wholegrain blinis with shallow-fried salmon with a sorrel and dill yoghurt dressing

| INGREDIENTS | 4 PORTIONS | 10 PORTIONS |
|---|---|---|
| Cracked buckwheat | 50g | 125g |
| Buckwheat flour | 100g | 300g |
| Soft white flour | 100g | 300g |
| Fresh milk | 200ml | 600ml |
| Egg yolks | 2 | 6 |
| Egg whites | 2 | 6 |
| Baking powder | ½tsp | 1tsp |
| Butter | 50g | 120g |
| Prepared salmon suprêmes | 4 | 10 |
| Fresh watercress | 100g | 300g |
| Natural yoghurt | 100ml | 250ml |
| Fresh dill, chopped | 1tsp | 1tbsp |
| Crème fraîche | 50ml | 125ml |
| Good-quality salt and white pepper | To taste | To taste |
| Torn fresh sorrel leaves | 40g | 100g |

## Method of work

1 Wash the cracked buckwheat under cold water to wash off any dust.

2 Following the ratio 2 parts water to 1 part cracked buckwheat, bring the cracked buckwheat to the boil and simmer for approximately 15 minutes. Immediately refresh under cold running water and allow to cool down.

3 Sieve the two flours and the baking powder together. Combine the egg yolks and milk to a smooth paste. Season with salt and pepper.

4 Aerate the egg whites with a pinch of salt to stiff peaks and carefully fold into the batter, one-third at a time.

5 Melt the butter in a non-stick frying pan and add two tablespoons of the mixture separately, fry lightly until golden on each side.

6 Mix together the chopped dill, sorrel leaves, natural yoghurt and crème fraîche to form the dressing. Season with a little salt if necessary.

7 In a hot shallow pan, heat some vegetable oil and panfry the salmon (skin-side down first) until crispy. Turn over the fish, and continue to shallow fry until correctly cooked. Season well.

8 To serve, place the blinis onto the serving plate and then the salmon suprêmes. Lay a large plûche of fresh herbs and any remaining torn sorrel leaves on top.

9 Serve the dressing with the salmon.

*Carefully fold in the aerated egg whites, one third at a time*

### CHEF'S TIP

The addition of the cracked buckwheat will help to give the blinis texture, although this is not always necessary when making blinis.

# Eggs Florentine with millet cakes

| INGREDIENTS | 4 PORTIONS | 10 PORTIONS |
|---|---|---|
| Millet grain | 100g | 250g |
| Vegetable or chicken stock | 250ml | 625ml |
| Butter | 50g | 125g |
| Fresh eggs | 4 | 10 |
| Egg yolks | 2 | 4 |
| Spinach, washed and stalks removed | 250g | 600g |
| Cheese sauce (Mornay) | 350ml | 700ml |
| Grated Parmesan cheese | 20g | 50g |
| Soft white flour | 20g | 50g |
| Good-quality salt and white pepper | To taste | To taste |

## Method of work

1 Preheat an oven to 170°C.

2 Wash and drain the millet. Bring the stock to the boil in a saucepan.

3 Place the millet into a wide-based shallow pan and cover with the hot stock adding small pieces the butter. Soak for 2 minutes. Cover with a cartouche, and slowly bring to the boil.

4 Place in the oven and allow to bake for approximately 20 minutes until all the stock has been absorbed.

5 Using a fork stir the millet and then cover with clean, dry kitchen cloth and allow to cool down completely.

6 Poach the eggs gently in simmering water for 2–3 minutes until lightly set. Refresh immediately in iced water, trim each egg and retain in the iced water for service.

7 Season the millet and add the egg yolks to bind. Take the millet and mould into shallow round cakes approximately 5cm in diameter and 1cm thick, season again and coat lightly in flour.

8 Heat a little sunflower or vegetable oil in a shallow pan and add the millet cakes. Cook on both sides for about 2 minutes until golden in colour.

9 Heat a sauteuse pan until very hot and add a tablespoon of water which will create steam, add the prepared spinach, wilt quickly in the pan and season well.

10 To serve, place the millet cake on the serving plate followed by the spinach laid on top and reheat the poached egg by placing into simmering water for a few seconds.

11 Place the warmed poached egg on top and coat the hot cheese sauce over the egg and sprinkle with the Parmesan.

12 Glaze quickly under a hot salamander and serve immediately.

*Mixing the egg yolks and millet to the correct consistency*

# Grilled polenta with chestnut mushrooms

| INGREDIENTS | 4 PORTIONS | 10 PORTIONS |
|---|---|---|
| Water | 1.5 litres | 3 litres |
| Polenta | 300g | 600g |
| Butter | 50g | 100g |
| Chestnut mushrooms | 300g | 600g |
| Chopped shallots | 2 | 4 |
| Dry sherry or Madeira | 50ml | 100ml |
| Double cream | 250ml | 500ml |
| Good-quality salt and black pepper | To taste | To taste |
| Chopped fresh flat leaf parsley | 2tbsp | 4tbsp |

## Method of work

1  Pour the water and salt into a large heavy-based saucepan. Bring to the boil.

2  Gradually stir in the polenta, whisking continuously to ensure no lumps form. Reduce to a very low heat and cook for 35 minutes, or until thick and creamy in texture. Whisk occasionally to prevent a skin from forming and then stir in the butter.

3  Pour into an oiled baking tray and spread out evenly to a thickness of 1.5cm. Leave to cool and then set in a refrigerator.

4  Turn the sheet of set polenta out and cut into triangles. Brush with olive oil and then char grill for 3–4 minutes on each side.

5  Wash and cut the mushrooms into quarters. In a pan, heat a little oil and sweat the chopped shallots for 2 minutes before adding the mushrooms and the black pepper to season. Cook for a further 4 minutes.

6  Pour the sherry or Madeira into the pan and reduce by half before adding the double cream and reduce to a coating consistency. Season and add the chopped flat leaf parsley.

7  Place the grilled polenta onto a service plate and spoon some of the cooked chestnut mushrooms over it.

*Cutting the set polenta*

### CHEF'S TIP

A soft polenta can be produced and served with the chestnut mushrooms instead. Simply add 100g Parmesan cheese to the cooking polenta and serve it whilst still creamy and hot with the mushrooms laying on top.

# Tian of spiced quinoa with roasted peppers

| INGREDIENTS | 4 PORTIONS | 10 PORTIONS |
| --- | --- | --- |
| Quinoa | 150g | 375g |
| Garam masala | 2tbsp | 4tbsp |
| Vegetable stock | 300ml | 750ml |
| Chopped shallot | 1 | 2 |
| Butter | 50g | 125g |
| Green pepper | 1 | 3 |
| Yellow pepper | 1 | 3 |
| Red pepper | 2 | 5 |
| Olive oil | 100ml | 250ml |
| Garlic | 1 clove | 3 cloves |
| Fresh thyme | 3 sprigs | 6 sprigs |
| Good-quality salt and white pepper | To taste | To taste |
| Balsamic vinegar | To taste | To taste |

## Method of work

1 Preheat an oven to 190°C.

2 Wash the quinoa well in cold water and drain. Heat the butter in a saucepan and gently sweat the chopped shallot until it softens.

3 Add the garam masala powder and cook out for 2 minutes before adding the vegetable stock and simmering until all liquid has been absorbed. Cover the pan tightly with plastic film and set aside to keep warm.

4 Wash and cut the peppers in half.

5 Heat a roasting tray in the oven before adding a little olive oil, the peppers, thyme and crushed garlic. Gently roast for approximately 20 minutes until the pepper skins blister and start to peel away.

6 Remove the skin and seeds from the peppers. Cut a quarter of the red peppers into small pieces and place into a liquidiser to blend. Add a little of the flavoured oil left in the roasting pan to the puréed red pepper with a little balsamic vinegar and season to taste. Pass through a fine chinois and reserve to one side.

7 Season and stir the warm quinoa and pack into a round stainless steel mould before topping with slices of the different-coloured roasted peppers before spooning the red pepper coulis around the plate.

# Fruit couscous salad with feta cheese

| INGREDIENTS | 4 PORTIONS | 10 PORTIONS |
|---|---|---|
| Couscous | 150g | 450g |
| Vegetable stock | 300ml | 900ml |
| Dried cranberries | 10g | 25g |
| Dried apricots, diced | 10g | 25g |
| Sultanas | 10g | 25g |
| Mixed candied peel | 10g | 25g |
| Feta cheese, cut into small cubes | 40g | 100g |
| Fresh coriander, chopped | 2tbsp | 5tbsp |
| Good-quality salt and white pepper | To taste | To taste |

## Method of work

1  Bring the vegetable stock to the boil in a saucepan.
2  Place the couscous in a large bowl and pour the hot stock over it. Cover the bowl with plastic film and allow the couscous to absorb the stock for a few minutes until all the liquid has been taken in.
3  Allow the couscous to cool down and then mix in all the additional ingredients.
4  Season to taste.
5  Serve as an accompaniment to a lunch, buffet or eat as a salad.

Cover the couscous and hot stock with plastic film

> ### CHEF'S TIP
>
> Add 1tsp of saffron or ground coriander before adding the hot stock to give a different colour and flavour to the overall dish. A little olive oil may also be added if the couscous is a little too dry for service.

# Honey roasted oat-rolled cannon of lamb

| INGREDIENTS | 4 PORTIONS | 10 PORTIONS |
|---|---|---|
| Rolled oats | 100g | 225g |
| Clear honey | 50g | 125g |
| Prepared cannons of lamb | 2 | 5 |
| Butter | 50g | 125g |
| Finely chopped fresh rosemary | 10g | 25g |
| Good-quality salt and white pepper | To taste | To taste |
| Additional garnish | | |
| Fresh French beans and peas | 4 portions | 10 portions |
| Dauphinoise potatoes | 4 portions | 10 portions |

*Roll the cannons of lamb in the oat mixture*

## Method of work

1 Preheat an oven to 200°C.

2 Prepare the cannons of lamb and season well with the salt and pepper.

3 In a large frying pan melt the butter and add the oats. Mix together to coat all the oats with the butter. Add the honey continuing to stir for a few minutes until the honey begins to boil and coat the oats.

4 Remove from the heat and stir in the chopped rosemary.

5 While the mix is still warm take each lamb cannon and roll in the oat mixture until the cannons are completely covered.

6 Place a trivet in a roasting tray and place into the oven until the lamb has been cooked to medium pink colour in the centre. This will take approximately 20 minutes.

7 Serving suggestion: serve with some fresh French beans and peas and individual dauphinoise potatoes.

# Polenta gnocchi Romaine

| INGREDIENTS | 4 PORTIONS | 10 PORTIONS |
|---|---|---|
| Polenta | 150g | 400g |
| Water and milk | 300ml | 800ml |
| Fresh milk | 300ml | 800ml |
| Parmesan cheese | 130g | 300g |
| Egg yolk | 1 | 3 |
| Good-quality salt and white pepper | To taste | To taste |
| Grated nutmeg | To taste | To taste |
| Butter | 100g | 300g |
| Tomato sauce | 250g | 600g |

## Method of work

1 Bring the milk and water to the boil and add the polenta. Continuously stir with a whisk until it thickens, avoiding lumps. Season with salt, pepper and nutmeg.

2 Remove from the heat and add the most of the grated Parmesan – leaving approximately one quarter aside for later – and the egg yolk.

3 Mix well and then pour into a deep tray which has been lightly buttered. Spread to a thickness of approximately 1.5cm. Allow to cool and set.

4 Once cold, cut out discs with a 5cm round cutter and place into a buttered earthenware dish. Add any trimmings on the bottom to form a base for the discs to sit on.

5 Brush some melted butter on top of the polenta gnocchi discs and sprinkle generously with the remaining Parmesan cheese.

6 Gratinate under the salamander and serve accompanied by the tomato sauce.

# Bulgur wheat and courgette parcel with apricots and goat's cheese

| INGREDIENTS | 4 PORTIONS | 10 PORTIONS |
|---|---|---|
| Bulgur wheat | 100g | 225g |
| Courgettes | 1 | 3 |
| Semi-dried apricots, diced | 50g | 125g |
| Goat's cheese | 100g | 225g |
| Fresh mint, chopped | 1tbsp | 2tbsp |
| Vegetable stock | 200ml | 500ml |
| Crème fraîche | 100ml | 225ml |
| Good-quality salt and white pepper | To taste | To taste |

## Method of work

1 Wash the bulgur wheat well in a sieve or colander. Place into a bowl and add the boiling stock, season, and leave to soak for about 20 minutes. Drain well and pat with a dry cloth.

2 Thinly slice the courgettes on a mandoline and blanch in boiling salted water for a few seconds. Refresh immediately in iced water.

3 Using a dariole mould or ramekin dish, lightly oil the mould and line with plastic film. Lay the courgette strips inside the mould, overlapping each other until the base and side are completely covered.

4 Bring the double cream to the boil in a saucepan and whisk in the goat's cheese. Mix until a soft consistency has been obtained. Remove from the heat and add the apricots, chopped fresh mint and the drained bulgur wheat. Season well.

5 Spoon into each mould until it is half full. Place a further slice of courgette in the centre followed by more of the bulgur wheat mixture until three-quarters full. Fold over remaining courgette and cover the top with plastic film. Place in a refrigerator to chill for 1 hour.

6 To reheat the courgette parcel, place in a steamer for 5 minutes and turn out onto a serving plate accompanied by a freshly dressed mixed leaf salad.

*Wrapping the parcel*

# Assessment of knowledge and understanding

You have now learned about the use of the different types of grain and how to produce a variety of grain dishes utilising a range of commodities and cooking techniques.

To test your level of knowledge and understanding, answer the following short questions. These will help to prepare you for your summative (final) assessment.

1 Identify two grains that could be used as alternatives to rice in a risotto.

   i) _____    ii) _____

2 Identify the three main parts to a grain kernel.

   i) _____    ii) _____

   iii) _____

3 State two ways in which quinoa can be used in a menu.

   i) _____    ii) _____

4 Explain how to prepare couscous.

   _____

   _____

5 Explain the difference between serving a grilled polenta and a soft polenta.

   _____

   _____

6 Explain why adding oats to our everyday diet can enhance our health.

   _____

   _____

## Research Task

Complete the following chart describing how to use, clean and maintain the following items of equipment and the safety considerations associated with them.

| | CLEANING | STERILISING | STORING | SAFETY PROCEDURES |
|---|---|---|---|---|
| Plastic storage container | | | | |
| Bamboo steamer | | | | |
| Stainless steel colander | | | | |

# CHEF'S PROFILE

**Name: MARK ALLISON**

**Position:** Associate instructor

**Establishment:** Johnson & Wales University, College of Culinary Art, USA

**Current job role and main responsibilities:** Garde manger (main subject taught, which includes ice carving) and international cuisine.

Teaching second-year (sophomore) students on associate degree and bachelor degree courses.

International relations in education (e.g. setting up partnerships with the very best in best education and industry around the world for J&W).

Culinary team coach.

**When did you realise that you wanted to pursue a career in the catering and hospitality industry?** Like most chefs I was inspired by my mother's cooking: everything had been freshly made by my mother each day when we arrived home from school, and boy did it taste delicious. As a child, as far back as I can remember, I would help her make Sunday lunch and still do to this day when ever I'm back at home in the UK. I was also very fortunate to have a great home economics teacher who told me to pursue a career in hospitality instead of working in the ship yards at the time. She told me that I would never be out of work and could travel the world, and of course she was right.

**What do you find rewarding about your job?** I love the fact that I can make a difference in someone's life. Being able to advise and educate people is one of the greatest gifts anyone can do. I feel so privileged to be a teacher and a chef.

**What advice would you give to students just beginning their career?** Go to the best catering school you can go too, that way you will be getting the best instruction and the best advice, using the best possible produce, and leaving with a qualification that means something.

**Who is your mentor or main inspiration?**

*In education*: Robert Nograd, Dean Emeritus and former Corporate Executive Chef of Johnson & Wales University. You may not have heard of this great man in the UK but his life is an inspiration to all. He was a prisoner in a concentration camp in WW2 who vowed that if he survived, he would work to ensure that he would never know the pain of thirst and hunger again. Through his extraordinary journey after his liberation – evolving from cook to chef – he never lost his thirst for knowledge or his hunger to become a world-class master chef. Now well into his 70's he is still educating the young. If it were not for Robert I would not have had the opportunity of working at Johnson & Wales University, for which I am greatly indebted.

*In industry*: Anton Mosimann, a great craftsman and visionary, he changed the style of cooking in the 1970s and 1980s and in his 70s now is still travelling around the world today, doing what he loves most, cooking and entertaining.

**Secrets of a successful chef?** Look at the really great chefs we have in our industry, who have been around a long time and who have achieved their goal of being the best. Use them as mentors, follow in their footsteps, they all have one thing in common: 'they work hard'. If you do the same, work hard, the world really is your oyster in this game.

**Can you give one essential kitchen tip or technique that you use as a chef:** Buy the best quality knives you can afford, then keep them sharp; you'll be using them every day that you're in the kitchen. If you look after them they will last a lifetime.

# North Carolina beach rice

| INGREDIENTS | PORTION |
|---|---|
| Extra virgin olive oil | 25ml |
| Shallots, finely diced | 50g |
| Cloves garlic, finely chopped | 2 |
| Red pepper, small dice | 50g |
| Green pepper, small dice | 50g |
| Long grain rice | 200g |
| Warm chicken stock | 400ml |
| Bouquet garni | 1 |
| Sea salt and freshly ground black pepper | To taste |
| Sweetcorn | 25g |
| Small fresh clams or fresh mussels | 200g |
| King prawns | 100g |
| Lobster tails, cut in half lengthwise (optional) | 2 |
| Unsalted butter | 25g |
| Sprigs of chive | 4 |

## Method of work

1  Preheat the oven to 200°C.

2  In a medium-sized saucepan, heat the extra virgin olive oil, add the shallots, garlic and peppers, and cook for a few minutes without colour.

3  Add the rice and mix well, coating the grains with the oil. Add the warm stock. Stir to the boil.

4  Add the bouquet garni and seasoning. Cover with a greased cartouche and saucepan lid.

5  Braise in the oven for about 8 minutes, until the rice is half cooked. Using a fork mix in the remaining ingredients to include the sweetcorn, clams, prawns and lobster tails if using.

6  Replace the cartouche and lid, place into the oven and continue cooking until all the stock has been absorbed, about a further 8 minutes.

7  Once the rice is cooked remove the bouquet garni and discard. Stir a knob of butter into the rice and any further seasoning, garnish with a sprig of chive and serve.

# Eggs

## NUTRITIONAL INFORMATION

Eggs are referred to as nature's functional food because they contain so many nutrients. They are relatively low in saturated fats and contain about 80 kcals, depending on their size. They contain vitamins:

A  essential for normal growth and development

B  vitamins that perform many bodily functions

D  for mineral absorption and good bone health

E  gives some protection against heart disease and certain cancers

Minerals and trace elements:

Iodine  production of thyroid hormones and phosphorous, for healthy teeth and bones

Zinc  improved immunity

Iron  for red blood cell production.

## TYPES OF EGG

Although the vast majority of eggs that we consume are chicken eggs almost any egg can be eaten. Millennia ago man lived as hunter-gatherers and the eggs of all animals were fair game and an essential part of the diet. The eggs used by the professional chef today are:

- Chicken
- Goose
- Duck
- Quail

When a recipe is constructed using eggs, the size of egg is a very important factor to consider. As recipes are scaled up for larger portions the difference becomes greater. The chef should have a plus or minus factor in their mind and generally err on the side of caution. In this chapter all recipes are for medium eggs (size three eggs). For mass production recipes we usually use egg quantities by weight and not by unit.

### Egg Sizes

If you see a recipe with egg numbers instead of sizes, this guide will help with conversion. Eggs are now sold in four different sizes: small, medium, large and very large (these replace the old sizes 0 to 7).

| NEW SIZE | WEIGHT | OLD SIZE |
|----------|--------|----------|
| Very large | 73g and over | Size 0<br>Size 1 |
| Large | 63–73g | Size 1<br>Size 2<br>Size 3 |
| Medium | 53–63g | Size 3<br>Size 4<br>Size 5 |
| Small | 53g and under | Size 5<br>Size 6<br>Size 7 |

# Quality

There are three grades of eggs.

Grade A   Shell eggs that are clean and internally perfect with an air sac that is no more than 6mm deep

Grade B   These eggs are removed from the shells and pasteurised

Industrial   Rejected eggs that are used in the production of soaps and shampoos.

Because eggshells are porous they take in a small amount of air each day. There are two simple methods to test this:

1   Put some water in a jug or tumbler and place the egg into the tumbler. A day-old egg will lie almost flat on the bottom, a week-old egg will be more upright and as the egg ages it will become more upright until after

## QUALITY POINTS

- Look for a quality mark on the egg shell and egg box such as the red lion, it shows that the eggs have been produced to the highest standards of food safety including a programme of vaccination against *Salmonella enteritidis*.

- Buy eggs from a reputable retailer where they will have been transported and stored at the correct temperature (below 20°C).

- Keep eggs in the fridge in their box after purchase at no more than 10°C.

- Store eggs separately from other foods.

- Make sure you use eggs by the 'best before' date shown on the egg or box.

- Wash hands before and after handling eggs.

- Discard dirty or cracked eggs.

- Eat cooked egg dishes as soon as possible after cooking.

about three weeks it will start to float. At this point the egg should be discarded.

2 As an egg ages the proteins in the white and yolk become compromised and they lose their strength. A new laid egg has a proud yolk and compact white. As the egg ages you will see that the yolk flattens and the white will spread.

## Purchasing

In the UK more than 10 billion eggs are used annually, approximately 20 per cent of those are used by the catering industry. Because of the vast quantities used it is important that the professional chef has an understanding of production and specifications.

There are four main types of production that can effect flavour, appearance and quality.

## How the Hens are Kept

1 *Laying cages* are the most common method of commercial egg production in the UK representing around two-thirds of egg production. Typically a laying cage system consists of a series of at least three tiers of cages. The cages have sloping mesh floors so that the eggs roll forward out of the reach of the birds to await collection. Droppings pass through the mesh floors onto boards, belts, the floors of the house or into a pit to await removal. This system allows for very little movement of the hens and a poor quality of life.

2 *Barn System* Around 7 per cent of UK eggs are produced in this way. In the barn system the hen house has a series of perches and feeders at different levels. The Welfare of Laying Hens Directive stipulates a maximum stocking density of nine hens per square metre of useable floor space. This system allows for some movement of the bird and a better quality of life.

3 *Free Range System* accounts for around 27 per cent of all eggs produced in the UK. The Welfare of Laying Hens Directive stipulates that for eggs to be termed 'free range', hens must have continuous daytime access to runs, which are mainly covered with vegetation and with a maximum stocking density of 2,500 birds per hectare. The hen house conditions for free range hens must comply with the regulations for birds kept in barn systems, or deep litter stocked at seven birds per square metre when no perches are provided. Free range eggs have more flavour than battery eggs.

4 *Organic System* Hens producing organic eggs are always free range. In addition, they must be fed an organically produced diet and ranged on organic land. Organic eggs are produced in the UK according to criteria set by the Advisory Committee on Organic Standards (ACOS) – which sets basic standards for organic production in the UK, in line with EU

legislation. Members of ACOS include the Soil Association, Organic Farmers and Growers and Organic Food Federation. All adhere to ACOS's basic standards, but may introduce higher standards in certain areas for their members.

There is a large range of egg products available to the chef and food manufacturers. For example, eggs are available:

1 Liquid

2 Frozen

3 Dried

4 Fried, poached, boiled, scrambled eggs and omelettes are available cooked and ready to serve.

5 Extended shelf life egg. In the past, liquid egg would only have a life of around one week. Now, as in the dairy industry, it is possible to pasteurise the egg at higher temperatures for a short time. This type of egg will typically have a quality symbol and is subject to rigorous audits by an independent monitoring agency to ensure they meet the standards of the Code of Practice.

## Cooking and Holding Temperatures

The protein in the white of an egg and the yolk start to cook at different temperatures.

*White (albumen)* contains up to 67 per cent of the liquid weight of an egg. Fresh egg whites coagulate at a temperature range of 62–64°C, but this can decrease in older eggs. If the egg white is set and the yolk has started to cook it is safe to eat as the killing temperature of 60°C for salmonella has been passed.

*Yolk* (the yellow portion of the egg) makes up about 33 per cent of the liquid weight of the egg. It contains all of the fat in the egg and slightly less than half of the protein.

Awareness of these temperatures when cooking will prevent the yolk temperature from getting too high. At about 70°C hydrogen sulphide generated by the white reacts with iron in the yolk causing a harmless grey-green film of ferrous sulphide to form on the surface of the yolk.

All egg dishes should be served as soon as possible after cooking and kept at a minimum temperature of 63°C.

# RECIPES

## Boiled eggs

| INGREDIENTS | 4 PORTIONS | 10 PORTIONS |
|---|---|---|
| Medium eggs | 4–8 | 10–20 |

### Method of work

1. Place the eggs into boiling salted water.
2. Allow to simmer for approximately 4 minutes for soft, 6 minutes for medium and 10–12 minutes for hard-boiled eggs.
3. Either serve immediately in an egg cup or refresh, peel and use as required.

> **CHEF'S TIP**
>
> If the eggs are at room temperature before they are placed in water they are less likely to crack.

## Poached eggs

| INGREDIENTS | 4 PORTIONS | 10 PORTIONS |
|---|---|---|
| Medium eggs | 4 | 10 |
| White wine vinegar | 10ml | 10ml |
| Good-quality salt and pepper | To taste | To taste |

### Method of work

1. Three-quarters fill a pan approximately 10cm deep with **acidulated**, seasoned water.
2. Bring to a gentle rolling boil.
3. Add the eggs one at a time and allow to gently poach until the whites are set with the yolks still soft.
4. If for immediate use trim the eggs.
5. If for storage the poached eggs can be placed into iced water and refreshed. They must be kept at 4°C and used within 48 hours.

*Place the egg into simmering water*

*Carefully remove the eggs*

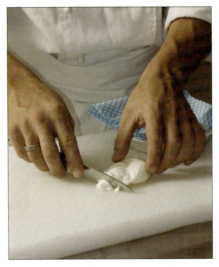

*Trim the eggs before service*

# Poached eggs Benedict

*Place the eggs onto the tongue*

| INGREDIENTS | 4 PORTIONS | 10 PORTIONS |
|---|---|---|
| Poached eggs | 8 | 20 |
| Sliced ox tongue | 200g | 500g |
| English muffins | 4 | 10 |
| Hollandaise sauce (see recipe on p. 124) | 200ml | 500ml |
| Butter | 40g | 100g |
| Good-quality salt and pepper | To taste | To taste |

## Method of work

1 Cut the muffins in half, toast until a light golden brown and butter lightly.
2 Place a slice of tongue on top and place a warmed egg on top of each half.
3 Season, coat with hollandaise and glaze under a salamander.

# Poached eggs Dauphinoise

*Pané the eggs*

| INGREDIENTS | 4 PORTIONS | 10 PORTIONS |
|---|---|---|
| Poached eggs | 8 | 20 |
| Flour | | |
| Eggwash | | |
| Breadcrumbs | | |
| Plum tomato coulis (see recipe on p. 126) | 200ml | 500ml |
| Good-quality salt and pepper | To taste | To taste |

## Method of work

1 Pané the poached egg in flour, eggwash and breadcrumbs.
2 Deep fry until golden brown.
3 Serve with a cordon of tomato sauce.

**CHEF'S TIP**

Make sure the eggs are well chilled and dry when they are **dusted** with flour during the pané process.

**HEALTH & SAFETY**

Care should be taken when deep frying the eggs. Always allow the eggs to fall into the oil away from you.

# Poached eggs Italienne

| INGREDIENTS | 4 PORTIONS | 10 PORTIONS |
|---|---|---|
| Poached eggs | 8 | 20 |
| Spaghetti Milanaise (see recipe on p.368) | 200g | 1kg |
| Plum tomato coulis (see recipe on p. 126) | 100ml | 500ml |
| Shaved Parmesan | 100g | 500g |
| Good-quality salt and pepper | To taste | To Taste |

## Method of work

1 Heat the spaghetti in a thick-bottomed pan and heat the eggs and sauce.
2 Arrange the spaghetti on a dish and place the egg on top.
3 Coat with the tomato sauce and serve with shaved Parmesan on the side.

# Moulded eggs

| INGREDIENTS | 4 PORTIONS | 10 PORTIONS |
|---|---|---|
| Medium eggs | 4 | 10 |
| Butter | 20g | 50g |
| Good-quality salt and pepper | To taste | To taste |

## Method of work

1 Lightly butter a **dariole** mould or ramekin, season the mould and add the egg.
2 Cover with a lid.
3 Poach in a bain marie for 8–10 minutes until the white is set and the yolk is still soft.
4 Turn out onto a plate and garnish in the same fashion as boiled eggs or poached eggs.

### CHEF'S TIP

For **á la carte** service store the egg in cold water and reheat in a chauffant for 3–5 minutes.

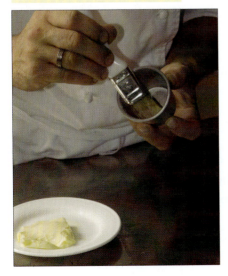

Lightly butter a dariole mould or ramekin

Break the egg into the mould

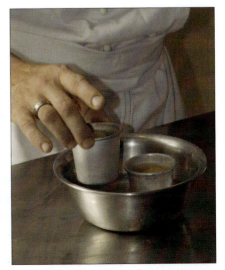

Poach in a bain marie

# Eggs en cocotte

| INGREDIENTS | 4 PORTIONS | 10 PORTIONS |
|---|---|---|
| Medium eggs | 4 | 10 |
| Butter | 40g | 100g |
| Good-quality salt and pepper | To taste | To taste |

## Method of work

1  Butter and season a ramekin or **cocotte** dish.
2  Beak and egg into the dish and cook in a bain marie for 5–6 minutes until the white is just set.
3  Serve in the dish.

> ### CHEF'S TIP
>
> The bain marie creates a barrier around the dish and allows the sides to cook without colour.

*Place into a bain marie*

# Eggs Florentine

| INGREDIENTS | 4 PORTIONS | 10 PORTIONS |
|---|---|---|
| Hard boiled | 4 | 10 |
| Mornay sauce (see recipe on p. 114) | 200ml | 500ml |
| Grated parmesan | 80g | 200g |
| Spinach | 400g | 2kg |
| Butter | 20g | 50g |
| Grated Nutmeg | | |
| Mill pepper and good-quality salt | To taste | To taste |

## Method of work

1  Blanch and refresh the spinach.
2  Allow to drain thoroughly.
3  Season with salt, pepper and nutmeg and gently reheat in the butter.
4  Halve and remove whilst the egg is still hot.
5  Place the spinach in a buttered ovenproof dish and place the eggs on top, cut side down.
6  Coat with the Mornay sauce.
7  Sprinkle with finely grated Parmesan and glaze under a salamander or in a hot oven.
8  Serve immediately.

*Cover the eggs with the Mornay sauce*

# Eggs en cocotte Alsace style

| INGREDIENTS | 4 PORTIONS | 10 PORTIONS |
|---|---|---|
| Medium eggs | 4 | 10 |
| Butter | 40g | 100g |
| Sauerkraut | 80g | 200g |
| Garlic sausage | | |
| Good-quality salt and pepper | To taste | To taste |

## Method of work

1 Butter and season a ramekin or cocotte dish.
2 Place 20g of sauerkraut into the bottom of each ramekin.
3 Beak an egg into the dish and cook in a bain marie until just set.
4 Garnish with either a sautéed julienne or pan-fried slice of garlic sausage.
5 Serve in the dish.

# Eggs en cocotte with asparagus

| INGREDIENTS | 4 PORTIONS | 10 PORTIONS |
|---|---|---|
| Medium eggs | 4 | 10 |
| Butter | 40g | 100g |
| Asparagus spears | 8 | 20 |
| Cream sauce (see recipe on p. 115) | 100ml | 250ml |
| Double cream | 40ml | 100ml |
| Good-quality salt and pepper | To taste | To taste |

**CHEF'S TIP**

The sauce can be varied by using a jus, demi glace or tomato sauce.

**HEALTH & SAFETY**

For a healthier option steam the asparagus.

## Method of work

1 Peel and slice the asparagus taking care to keep the heads intact for garnish.
2 Gently cook the asparagus in the butter, season and cohere with half the sauce.
3 Divide the asparagus equally into the bottom of each ramekin or cocotte.
4 Beak and egg into the dish and cook in a bain marie until just set.
5 Warm the sauce and add the cream.
6 Garnish with the asparagus heads and cream sauce.
7 Serve in the dish with a twist of mill pepper.

# Eggs sur le plat

| INGREDIENTS | 4 PORTIONS | 10 PORTIONS |
|---|---|---|
| Medium eggs | 4 | 10 |
| Butter | 40g | 100g |
| Good-quality salt and pepper | To taste | To taste |

## Method of work

1 Butter and season an egg dish.
2 Break an egg into the dish and cook on the side of the stove or in the oven until just set.
3 Serve in the dish.

*Start the cooking process on the stove top*

# Eggs en cocotte with chicken

| INGREDIENTS | 4 PORTIONS | 10 PORTIONS |
| --- | --- | --- |
| Medium eggs | 4 | 10 |
| Butter | 40g | 100g |
| Cooked chicken suprême | 100g | 250g |
| Chicken velouté | 100ml | 250ml |
| Tarragon | 10g | 25g |
| Double cream | 40ml | 100ml |
| Good-quality salt and pepper | To taste | To taste |

### CHEF'S TIP

The cream should not be heated prior to being added to the eggs. Part of the function of the cream in this recipe is to stop the cooking process as well as enriching the dish.

## Method of work

1 Dice the chicken and gently cook in the butter, season, add the chopped tarragon and cohere with half the sauce.
2 Divide equally into the bottom of each dish.
3 Break an egg into the dish and cook on the side of the stove or in a hot oven until just set.
4 Heat the remainder of the sauce, add the cream and drizzle over the top of the egg.
5 Garnish with slices of sautéed chicken.

# Fried eggs

| INGREDIENTS | 4 PORTIONS | 10 PORTIONS |
| --- | --- | --- |
| Medium eggs | 4–8 | 10–20 |
| Butter | 80g | 200g |
| Vegetable oil | | |
| Good-quality salt and pepper | To taste | To taste |

## Method of work: 1

1 Add a thin layer of oil to a thick-bottomed frying pan.
2 When slightly hot add half the butter.
3 Break an egg into a shallow dish and slide into the pan.
4 Allow to cook gently until the white has set and the yolk is still runny.
5 Add the remainder of the butter and allow to melt.
6 Season the egg(s), remove from the pan and place on a plate.
7 Quickly allow the butter to foam without colour.
8 Pour a little of the butter onto each egg.

*Allow the white to set*

### HEALTH & SAFETY

Crack the eggs into a dish to ensure that there will be no splashing of hot oil.

## Method of work: 2

1 Add a thin layer of oil to a hot frying pan or onto a medium temperature griddle.
2 Break the required amount of eggs into either the pan or the griddle.
3 Allow to cook gently.

# Scrambled eggs

| INGREDIENTS | 4 PORTIONS | 10 PORTIONS |
|---|---|---|
| Medium eggs | 4–8 | 10–20 |
| Butter | 80g | 200g |
| Cream | 40–80ml | 100–200ml |
| Good-quality salt and pepper | To taste | To taste |

**HEALTH & SAFETY**

Use unsalted butter and low sodium salt.

**VIDEO CLIP**
Scrambling eggs

## Method of work

1 Melt the butter in a thick-bottomed sauté pan.
2 **Beat** the eggs in a basin and season.
3 Add to the pan and cook very gently.
4 When they begin to set, add the cream, remove from the heat and continue to stir until lightly set (baveuse).
5 Serve immediately.

# Scrambled eggs with smoked salmon

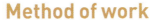

| INGREDIENTS | 4 PORTIONS | 10 PORTIONS |
|---|---|---|
| Medium eggs | 4–8 | 10–20 |
| Butter | 40–80g | 100–200g |
| Smoked salmon | 80–160g | 100–200g |
| Cream | 40–80ml | 100–200ml |
| Good-quality salt and pepper | To taste | To taste |

## Method of work

1 Cut the smoked salmon into a fine julienne.
2 Melt the butter in a thick-bottomed sauté pan.
3 Beat the eggs in a basin and season.
4 Add to the pan and cook very gently.
5 When they begin to set, add the salmon and the cream, remove from the heat and continue to stir until lightly set (baveuse).
6 Serve immediately.

*Cut the salmon into julienne*

**CHEF'S TIP**

Use smoked trout or smoked eel to replace the salmon.

# Scrambled eggs with herbs

| INGREDIENTS | 4 PORTIONS | 10 PORTIONS |
|---|---|---|
| Medium eggs | 4–8 | 10–20 |
| Butter | 40–80g | 100–200g |
| Cream | 40–80ml | 100–200ml |
| Shallots | 40–80g | 100–200g |
| Garlic | 1–2 cloves | 2–4 cloves |
| Parsley | 10–20g | 25–50g |
| Sage | 10–20g | 25–50g |
| Good-quality salt and pepper | To taste | To taste |

## Method of work

1  Chop the shallots and garlic.
2  Finely chop the herbs.
3  Melt the butter in a thick-bottomed sauté pan.
4  Add the shallots and garlic and allow to sweat.
5  Beat the eggs in a basin and season.
6  Add to the pan and cook very gently.
7  When they begin to set, add the herbs and the cream, remove from the heat and continue to stir until lightly set (baveuse).
8  Serve immediately.

**VIDEO CLIP**
Making omelettes

# Omelette  *basic recipe*

| INGREDIENTS | PER PORTION |
|---|---|
| Medium eggs | 3 |
| Butter | 10g |
| Oil | 5ml |
| Good-quality salt and pepper | To taste |

## Method of work

1  Break the eggs into a basin, season and beat lightly with a fork.
2  Heat a seasoned omelette pan, add the butter and oil, continue to heat until foaming but not brown (the oil helps prevent burning).
3  Add the eggs and cook quickly moving the eggs with a fork. Do not let them settle in one part of the pan as this can cause excess browning.
4  Remove from the heat and fold the omelette using the fork.
5  Tap the handle of the pan with your palm to bring the other side of the omelette up.
6  Turn the pan over the service dish or plate and allow to fall in a neat oval.
7  Neaten the shape and serve.

**HEALTH & SAFETY**

Extreme care should be taken when seasoning an omelette pan as the temperatures of the pan can be very high with no visual evidence of heat such as steam.

Tilt the pan and allow the omelette to roll

# Cheese omelette

| INGREDIENTS | PER PORTION |
|---|---|
| Medium eggs | 3 |
| Butter | 10g |
| Oil | 5ml |
| Grated cheese | 60g |
| Good-quality salt and pepper | To taste |

*Fold the omelette*

## Method of work

1 As in the preceding recipe.
2 Add the cheese to the omelette just before you start the folding process.

> 🍴 **CHEF'S TIP**
>
> Almost any type of cheese can be used in an omelette. This gives great range on the menu.

# Brown shrimp omelette

| INGREDIENTS | PER PORTION |
|---|---|
| Medium eggs | 3 |
| Butter | 10g |
| Oil | 5ml |
| Peeled brown shrimps | 50g |
| Tomato sauce | 50ml |
| Good-quality salt and pepper | To taste |

*Make an incision in the omelette*

## Method of work

1 Heat the shrimps in a pan and keep warm.
2 Make a plain omelette, turn it out onto a service dish and neaten the shape.
3 Cut an incision in the top of the omelette and spoon in the shrimp and tomato sauce mix.

> 🍴 **CHEF'S TIP**
>
> Use cooked peeled prawns instead of brown shrimp.

# Ham omelette

*Adding the eggs*

| INGREDIENTS | PER PORTION |
|---|---|
| Medium eggs | 3 |
| Butter | 20g |
| Oil | 5ml |
| Cooked ham | 50g |
| Chopped shallots | 25g |
| Good-quality salt and pepper | To taste |

## Method of work

1 Sweat the shallots in a little of the butter.
2 Dice the ham and add to the shallots.
3 Add the ham and shallots to the omelette pan at the same time as the eggs and proceed as for a plain omelette.
4 Garnish with a julienne of cooked ham.

**CHEF'S TIP**

This dish can be served as a breakfast item.

# Spanish omelette *tortilla*

| INGREDIENTS | 4 PORTIONS | 10 PORTIONS |
|---|---|---|
| Medium eggs | 12 | 30 |
| Olive oil | 100ml | 250ml |
| Peeled potatoes | 400g | 1kg |
| Peppers (red and green) | 2 | 5 |
| Chopped onions | 200g | 500g |
| Good-quality salt and pepper | To taste | To taste |

## Method of work

1 Slice the potatoes and gently fry them in the oil. Do not allow them to over-brown.
2 Dice the peppers and add to the potatoes, allow to cook until tender.
3 Beat the eggs and add to the pan, stir gently, cover with a lid and allow to cook very gently until set (approximately 10 minutes).
4 Turn the omelette using a plate or the lid.
5 Slide onto a service dish and serve.

## Assessment of knowledge and understanding

Now that you have learned about the preparation and cookery of egg dishes, to test your level of knowledge and understanding, answer the following short questions. These will help to prepare you for your summative (final) assessment.

**1** List three Quality points you should look for when receiving eggs.

i) _____ ii) _____

iii) _____

**2** State why it is important to use fresh eggs when preparing and cooking egg dishes.

_____

Explain why it is important to use clean equipment when preparing egg dishes.

_____

How and where should eggs be stored?

_____

Explain why eggs en cocotte are cooked in a bain marie.

_____

Explain the term 'eggs sur le plat'.

_____

Explain why it is important to season an omelette pan.

_____

List two safety points when frying eggs.

i) _____

ii) _____

## Research Task

Complete the following chart describing how to use, clean and maintain the following items of equipment and the safety considerations associated with them.

| | CLEANING | STERILISING | STORING | SAFETY PROCEDURES |
|---|---|---|---|---|
| Omelette pan | | | | |
| Dariole mould | | | | |
| Hand-held stick blender | | | | |

# CHEF'S PROFILE

**Name: DAVID MULCAHY**

**Position:** Craft and Culinary Development Director, Sodexho UK & Ireland

**When did you first realise you wanted to pursue a career in the catering and hospitality industry?** I wanted to do so from an early age as my grandmother and mother were keen cooks and so a significant influence. A range of part-time jobs in kitchens in Ireland and USA also provided an insight to the industry. After completing my A levels, I went to catering college in Galway for two years, gaining valuable work experience and training before being contacted by a hotel in UK.

**What do you find rewarding about your job?** In the early days, it was a combination of achieving success and recognition for a job well done and the variety and challenges that every day and every event brought. In addition it was the opportunities to excel through sheer hard work and the team spirit that existed among fellow chefs. By being flexible as a person I gained a huge amount of experience and was fortunate to have been part of many exciting projects. Once I became a head and executive chef, the rewards were about managing a well-run kitchen and operation as well as managing and developing a team of chefs. It was their success that became rewarding as I felt that I had either exposed, encouraged or supported their abilities for them to develop further. Now it is great to see many of those chefs running their own kitchens, operations or restaurants.

**What do you find most challenging about the job?** The challenge is finding the balance between making money for an organisation and continuing to invest in training and development. Other challenges include the changing market needs, and that people have to change or be retrained to meet current trends and needs.

**What advice would you give to students just beginning their career?** The food industry is wide and varied. Working in today's kitchen is about being able to run a business. So be aware of the importance of other skills involved such as communication and attention to detail.

**Who is your mentor or main inspiration?** Inspiration has come from people with passion and commitment to succeed. Many of my friends and colleagues inspire me. My children inspire me. I was inspired by my grandmother and mother, and chefs I worked with in my early days like Anton Mosimann, Raymond Blanc, Pierre Koffman and Paul Gaylor. Omero Gallucci, a great friend and mentor, and Chris Galvin, who is infectious with his passion for food. Having developed the Junior Chefs' Academy in many colleges across the UK, I find true inspiration in the potential of our next generation of young chefs.

**Can you give one essential kitchen tip or technique that you use as a chef:** When taking pomegranate seeds from a pomegranate, break the fruit into chunks and don't scoop the seeds out as they will break and the colour will leach out. Instead take a large spoon, and holding the fruit over a bowl, bang the skin side to allow the seed pearls to fall unbroken into the bowl.

**Secrets of a successful chef:** Patience, the ability to listen, a positive approach, being a team player, adopting a strong work ethic, dedication and focus, and finally a love of food.

**A brief personal profile of achievements:** The most prominent would be:
- Being elected National Chairman of The Craft Guild of Chefs for three years.
- Having won gold medals at the Culinary World Cup and Culinary Olympics.
- Developing and expanding The Junior Chefs Academy.
- Giving a significant involvement and support to The Hoxton Apprentice Restaurant, training disadvantaged young people for the industry.

# CHEF'S RECIPE

# Baked vegetable frittata, lemon crème fraîche, balsamic braised roots, herb and root oils

## *Beetroots*

| INGREDIENTS | 6 PORTIONS |
|---|---|
| Fresh beetroot | 500g |
| Extra virgin olive oil | 100ml |
| Malden salt and cracked pepper | pinch |
| Garlic cloves | 2 |
| Lemon juice | 1tsp |
| Aged balsamic vinegar | 60ml |
| Fresh thyme | sprigs |

## Method of work

1 Preheat the oven to 180°C.
2 Wash and trim the beetroots.
3 Season with salt, pepper, sliced garlic and thyme.
4 Individually wrap each beetroot in foil brushed with a little of the olive oil.
5 Place on a baking tray and cook for 45 minutes.
6 Test by inserting knife. The flesh should be soft.
7 Remove, peel and cut into wedges.
8 Toss in a pan with a coating made from the balsamic and olive oil. Add lemon juice and keep warm until required.

To serve, slice the warm fritata and place in the centre of the plate. Spoon the beetroots and herb oil around before placing a quenelle of the lemon crème fraîche on top.

## *Frittata*

| INGREDIENTS | 6 PORTIONS |
|---|---|
| Organic eggs | 6 |
| Olive oil | 100ml |
| Fresh basil leaves | 10 |
| Thyme leaves | ½ tsp |
| Parmesan | 80g |
| Sweet potato | 200g |
| Spinach | 150g |
| Aubergine | 150g |
| Red pepper | 125g |

| INGREDIENTS | 6 PORTIONS |
|---|---|
| Yellow pepper | 125g |
| Red onion – thinly sliced | 80g |
| Courgette | 120g |
| Spring onion | 60g |
| Vine tomato, sliced | 80g |
| Sundried tomato, sliced | 80g |
| Salt, mill pepper | |

## Method of work

1 Peel, slice and lightly cook the sweet potato in seasoned boiling water.
2 Once cooked, drain and reserve.
3 Wash and wilt spinach. Drain and reserve.
4 Place peppers under a hot grill and turn them occasionally until their skin colours and blisters.
5 Place peppers in a plastic bag and allow to cool. Peel off the skin and cut peppers into wedges.
6 Heat a pan and add a little olive oil. Add a clove of garlic to infuse flavour and remove it.
7 Season and lightly sear the courgettes, aubergine, red onion, peppers, spring onion and vine tomatoes, adding a little oil as necessary.
8 Beat eggs and add seasoning, parmesan and herbs.
9 Use an ovenproof dish approx 4cm deep, layer the vegetables adding a little egg mixture until dish is complete and all the egg mixture is used.
10 Press firmly to ensure everything is compact and even. The egg mixture should come just above the top layer of vegetables.
11 Cook in the oven until the dish is lightly set, approx 30 minutes.
12 Remove from the oven and allow to rest for 5 minutes.

# 9

# Fish and shellfish

## LEARNING OBJECTIVES

The aim of this unit is to enable the candidate to develop skills and apply knowledge in the preparation and cookery principles of fish and shellfish. This will also include materials, ingredients and equipment.

At the end of this chapter you will be able to:

- Identify each fish and shellfish variety
- Understand the use of relative ingredients in fish and shellfish cookery and their quality points
- State the quality points of various fish and shellfish commodities
- Prepare and cook each type of fish and shellfish variety
- Identify the storage procedures for fish and shellfish
- Identify the correct tools and equipment to utilise during the preparation and cooking of fish and shellfish
- Recognise potential alternative healthy eating options
- Show competence at preparing and cooking a range of fish and shellfish-based dishes

# Fish

## INTRODUCTION

Fish has become a major feature on the majority of menus across the world, as professional chefs find new and appealing ways to cook and present it. Its versatility makes fish a healthy, flavoursome and colourful choice for any menu. Fish is considered a delicate commodity requiring expertise and great care in its preparation. It is essential to have a lightness of touch at all stages of preparation to help ensure that the natural flavour and quality of the fish is not overwhelmed with heavy and incompatible garnishes.

Usually fish is featured on the menu as part of the main course selection. Its honourable place is as an intermediate course directly before the main course of meat or poultry. Alternatively, fish is used in other sections of the menu such as canapés, starters, hors d'oeuvre, garnishes for pasta and rice, salads and savouries.

Fish fall into five categories:

1 Flat white            4 Freshwater

2 Round white           5 Miscellaneous.

3 Oily

These different categories are formed due to the derivative of the species, environment caught, shape and size of the fish, as seen in the table overleaf.

**VIDEO CLIP**
Billingsgate fish market

**CHEF'S TIP**

Fresh fish should be purchased on a daily basis if at all possible. A really fresh fish should retain its natural colouring and be bright in its appearance. The colours fade as the fish loses its freshness.

## CATEGORIES OF FISH

| FLAT WHITE FISH | ROUND WHITE FISH | OILY FISH | MISCELLANEOUS | FRESHWATER FISH |
|---|---|---|---|---|
| Sole | Whiting | Salmon | Grouper | Zander |
| Plaice | Cod | Trout | Swordfish | Perch |
| Turbot | Grey mullet | Mackerel | Shark | Rainbow trout |
| Flounder | Pollack | Sardines | Skate | Pike |
| Halibut | Hake | Sprats | Monkfish | Carp |
| Brill | Haddock | Herrings | Red snapper | Eel |
| Megrim | Sea bass | Tuna | John Dory | Tilapia |

## QUALITY POINTS

- When buying fresh fish it is important to consider a range of quality points to help determine absolute freshness and good condition.

### Smell

- *Fresh* – there should be a delicate, pleasant odour reminiscent of the sea.
- *Not fresh* – unpleasant, fishy and strong smell, sometimes a sour and ammonia smell will be apparent.

### Appearance

- *Fresh* – shiny, slippery, moist, glistening skin and the presence of sea slime.
- *Not fresh* – dull, colourless, dry appearance.

### Scales

- *Fresh* – strong, attached, shiny in appearance.
- *Not fresh* – loose, easy to remove or partially removed.

### Skin

- *Fresh* – taut, colourful, glistening and adhered to fish.
- *Not fresh* – puckered, dry and easily damaged.

### Eyes

- *Fresh* – clear, bright, transparent and protruding eyes.
- *Not fresh* – flat, glassy, opaque, sunken and dry.

### Gills

- *Fresh* – moist, shiny, deep red flush with aerated blood.
- *Not fresh* – dry, grey and indistinct.

### Flesh

- *Fresh* – firm flesh, translucent, white or pink with a gleaming brightness.
- *Not fresh* – separates into large chunks, very soft, red or brown flecks, dry fillets at the edges and limp.

# YIELDS OF FISH

Accepting cheap and poor quality fish will only give the chef an unsatisfactory end result, regardless of what masking takes place when cooking and finishing the dish.

The wastage obtained from cutting fillets is approximately 50 per cent for round fish and 60 per cent loss on flat fish. This can be reduced slightly by using whole fish to cook where possible, cutting tronçons of large flat fish and darnes of round fish. Fish wastage means the amount of fish that is inedible when being prepared, such as the head, bones, intestines, tail and fins.

| PERCENTAGES OF USABLE FLESH IN FISH | |
| --- | --- |
| Cod | 45 |
| Monkfish | 30 |
| Whiting | 55 |
| Sole | 50 |
| Salmon | 45 |
| Pike | 45 |
| Turbot | 50 |
| Trout | 60 |

It is unusual to have over 60 per cent of usable flesh when preparing filleted fish. If serving round fish for grilling there will be an approximate 5 per cent weight loss from the discarding of the trimmed fins and the gutting, with a further 10 per cent if the head is removed.

To estimate the weight loss of fish, the calculation below should be applied:

$$\frac{\text{Total waste weight}}{\text{total original fish weight}} \times 100 = \% \text{ wastage}$$

The percentage of weight loss should be taken into account when pricing dishes.

# ETHICAL FISHING

The consumption of fish has increased steadily over the past few years. This is generally due to increased customer awareness of the healthy benefits afforded from fish and its growing appreciation as an international delicacy. This popularity has had the consequence of improving the vast array of fish available throughout the year. Modern transport is quick and efficient and the use of air transport now provides us with the ability to purchase quality fish from all over the world such as swordfish and grouper.

*Tropical fish*

*Flat fish*

*Freshwater fish*

Because the UK is an island it is seen as having abundant supplies of fish. Nonetheless, pollution and over-fishing are starting to have a damaging effect on the stock of certain fish. The contamination in some sea areas and rivers has affected the supply and fitness of certain fish and shellfish for human consumption. This is one of the reasons that the chef should be attentive in checking the quality of the fish they purchase and should also be concerned with the origin of the fish. Fish farms have been established to contribute to the demand of the customer. Stocks of wild salmon, cod and haddock are on a steady decline largely due to over-fishing. Although these farms are a welcome addition to the food supply chain (especially those that are organic and responsible to the environment) it is important that the chef is sensitive to this issue and looks at purchasing lesser known fish such as pollack, hake and red fish.

> **CHEF'S TIP**
>
> Oily fish contain a large amount of polyunsaturated fatty acids which helps to fight against heart disease.

# NUTRITION

Fish is an excellent source of easily digestible protein. White fish is very low in fat content and the fat itself is unsaturated. Oily fish contains a higher fat content and is not as easily digested as white fish. However, it is an excellent source of vitamins A and D and contains the essential fatty acids omega 3 and 6 which can help fight heart disease. Cod liver also has these attributes. The edible bones of whitebait and sardines can provide additional calcium. Generally fish is a good provision for building immune systems.

# PREPARATION TECHNIQUES

In this section we explore the preparation techniques that lead to a choice of cooking methods. Such techniques use skills which are compatible when handling round or flat fish. For example, most round or flat fish are filleted using similar techniques.

# PREPARATION OF ROUND WHITE FISH

Round white fish have delicately flavoured flesh that requires simple and fast cookery methods. Fish such as cod and haddock have been intensely fished to the point that natural stocks are being depleted. The modern chef should take these facts into consideration when planning menus and look to include underused fish such as hake, ling, whiting, pollock and coley.

## Step-by-step fillet of round white fish

1  Cut through the stomach of the fish by making a shallow incision along the underside of the fish. Remove the guts (viscera) and then cut off the gills. Rinse the cavity under cold running water to remove any remaining blood and guts.

2  De-scale the skin with the back of a knife and trim the fish of any fins. Using a filleting knife, cut into the fish at the head just behind the gills until the backbone is reached.

3  Cut the fish down the length of the back, cutting along the top side of the backbone, and working from head to tail continue cutting over the bone to remove the fillet completely.

4  Turn over the fish and remove the second fillet in the same way. Trim both fillets to the required shape and size.

5  Skin the fillet by inserting the filleting knife near the tail end cutting through the flesh to the skin. Run the blade along the skin pulling the flesh away from it as the cut is made.

**VIDEO CLIP**
Trimming and gutting a round white fish

**CHEF'S TIP**

If you need to keep the fish intact whilst gutting, you can remove the guts from the gill slits, although this is quite an advanced and time-consuming technique. It is used for fish that is to be poached whole because it retains the natural shape of the fish.

*Removing fins from a cod*

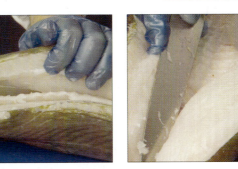

*Filleting by running the knife along the backbone*

*Easing the fillet away from the bones*

*Trimming and removing bones*

*Skinning the fillet*

*A fillet of cod*

*Portioning of cod fillet*

## Preparation of suprême of white round fish

1 Using a sharp and semi-flexible knife cut along the backbone until you reach the ribs.

2 Stand the fish on its belly and continue to cut down until the fillet is removed.

3 Cut the pinbones from the fillet into a V shape.

4 Remove the thicker suprêmes (also known as **pavé**) and then the flatter suprêmes. Average weight should be 150g.

# PREPARATION OF FLAT WHITE FISH

Because of their flatness, these categories of fish are usually fried, poached or grilled. They cook very quickly and are very unforgiving because they can change from succulent to dry in a very short time during the cooking process. Examples are Dover sole, lemon sole, plaice, megrim, witch sole and dabs. The exceptions to this are brill, turbot and the largest of the true flat fish, halibut. Because they are such large flat fish they can be prepared into tronçons and suprêmes.

## Step-by-step single filleting

*Removal of the single fillets from a plaice*

*Continue to remove the single fillets*

*Removing the skin from a single fillet of plaice*

*Single fillets of plaice*

# Step-by-step cross-cut filleting

Economically, a blocks-man would not have the time to fillet fish in the same fashion as a chef. They have to balance the waste against the time it takes to fillet the fish, although they are generally highly skilled people and usually have little or no waste.

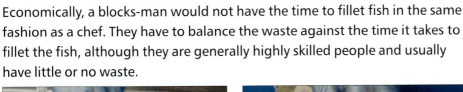

**CHEF'S TIP**

A blocks-man is a professional fishmonger who fillets and prepares fish commercially.

*Cut an incision just behind the head and slide the knife along the bone*

*Push the tip of the knife over the backbone and fillet the rear end of the fish*

*Continuing across the fish to remove the double fillet*

*Cutting fillet to make a plait of plaice*

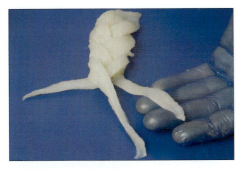

*Plaiting the fillet of plaice*

*A plait of plaice*

# Step-by-step fillet of plaice en tresse (plait)

1 Skin the fillet.

2 Being careful not to cut along the entire fillet make an incision 1 cm from thickest end of the fillet. Repeat this until you have three equal strips.

3 Plait the strips until they come to a point at the end of the fillet. Fish prepared en tresse can be steamed or breaded and fried.

## Preparing goujons of flat fish

1 Cut the fillets into strips approximately 6cm × 0.5cm.

2 Pass through seasoned flour, beaten egg and breadcrumbs (pané) and roll.

*Plaice fillets cut into goujons*

**VIDEO CLIP**
Skinning a Dover sole

## Step-by-step preparing a Dover sole

*Remove the fins from the sole*

*Carefully make a knife incision at the tail end of the sole and begin to pull the skin towards the head*

*Remove the skin in one piece by gently pulling*

*Trim the sole after both sides have been skinned*

*Finally remove the eyes and wash the finished Dover sole*

*The trimmed Dover sole*

**CHEF'S TIP**

Paupiettes can be produced individually using single fillets of fish such as sole, plaice or megrim.

## Step-by-step paupiettes of sole

A **paupiette** is a rolled fillet of flat fish, however in modern cuisine they are usually filled with mousseline or fine **forcemeat**.

Paupiettes can also be prepared with four fillets wrapped and filled with a mousseline to create a sausage shape.

*Lay the fillets on top of the plastic film with the presentation side down. Lightly bat out the fillets*

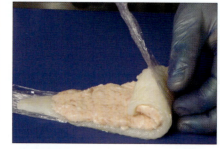

*Pipe or spread a mousse or forcemeat (in this case a crab and salmon mousse) and then roll up the fillet to obtain a roulade effect*

*Wrap the collars around the paupiettes*

# Step-by-step délice of sole

As with paupiettes, traditionally a délice is a folded fillet of flat fish. However, this is folded into two or three with the seam facing down. In modern cookery these are almost always stuffed with a mousseline or fine **farce**.

1 Lightly bat out and lay the fillets as you would with a paupiette but ensure the pointed end of the fillet is facing away from you.

2 Pipe a filling from the halfway point, starting with a deep fill and tapering to a shallow fill. Fold the thin end over to the middle and then the thicker end should be folded into the middle before ensuring that the sides are neat.

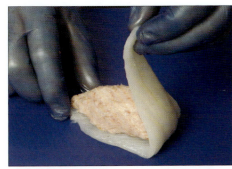

Folding a délice of sole stuffed with a mousseline

Délice of sole

# Step-by-step tronçon of large flat fish

A tronçon is a cut of flat fish on the bone. It is a cut that can be quite practical from a costing standpoint as the bone is still attached to an expensive fish.

Trim the outer fins

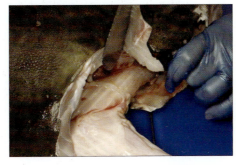

Remove the head with a large heavy knife

Cut the fish in half along the lateral line

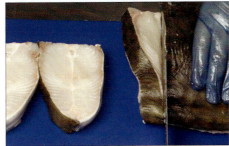

Cut the tronçon across at equal spaces to the desired weight (usually 180–250g)

**CHEF'S TIP**

A tronçon of turbot should always weigh more per portion than other cuts to allow for the bone weight.

**VIDEO CLIP**
Cutting tronçons

**VIDEO CLIP**
Cutting suprêmes

# PREPARATION OF OILY FISH

## Suprême of salmon

1 Gut, wash, de-scale and remove the head, trim the fins.

2 Cut just above the backbone so that the knife rests on the bone, insert the knife over the bone structure below the anal vent and allow the knife to follow the contours of the fish until it removes the bottom end of the fillet.

3 Remove the rib bones and any cartilage by cutting along each side and underneath until all the central backbone is clear.

4 Remove the pinbones using a pair of sterile fish pliers.

5 There are two excepted techniques associated with suprêmes of salmon.

   ■ The modern method where the suprêmes are cut at a straight angle with the skin still attached.

   ■ The traditional method where the fillet is skinned and the suprême is cut at 45° angle.

*Cleaning the cavity*

*Scaling a salmon*

*Removing head of a salmon*

*Clear the fillet from the rib bones of the salmon*

*Removing pinbones from the side of a salmon*

*Suprême of fish*

## Step-by-step darne of salmon and variations

1 Scale, wash, gut and remove the head.

2 Cutting from the top of the fish, slice darnes at the required weight (usually 180–225g).

3 Pinch the belly until a natural round shape is formed and cut off the surplus belly.

4 Tie with a gentle knot, ensuring that there is sufficient string to allow a slipknot to be tied. This allows for a smooth service because the string doesn't need to be cut away and cause potential damage the darne.

**VIDEO CLIP**
Cutting darnes

## CHEF'S TIP

Certain fish such as grouper, snapper, weever and sea bass have sharp, spiny fins or spines and care should be taken when preparing these fish.

- Method 2 is to tie at the natural round line.
- Method 3 is to remove the bone and stuff the darne with a fish farce before tying up.

Cutting a darne from a salmon

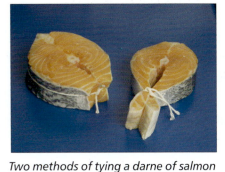
Two methods of tying a darne of salmon

Tying a stuffed darne of salmon

# PREPARATION OF SMALL OILY FISH

Fish such as sardines, mackerel, trout and herrings that are small enough to be served whole can be prepared in the following fashion.

1 Gut the fish by inserting the knife into the anal cavity and cutting through the skin up to the head. Pull out the intestines and any blood lying next to the back bone and wash the cavity well with clean water.

2 Trim off the fins and remove the head. (If the head is to be retained, the gills and eyes should be removed.)

3 Place the fish onto a chopping board and press along the backbone until you feel the bone separating from the flesh. Turn over and gently remove the entire backbone.

4 Make sure that all bones are removed. The fish is now ready for cooking. It can be stuffed or just **scored** on the skin with a sharp knife, seasoned, brushed with oil and simply grilled.

Removing the guts of the trout

Pressing down backbone of trout to loosen it from flesh for removal

Removing bones from the trout

Trout with head and bones removed

**HEALTH & SAFETY**

Fish bones, offal and heads are a high contamination risk and must not be mixed with raw prepared fish.

## Step-by-step butterfly filleting

If a fish is small enough to be used as a single portion it may be **butterfly** filleted without removing the guts.

1  Cut along the fish just above the ribs and inside, along the backbone until you reach the back skin; be careful not to pierce the skin. Turn the fish over and repeat the operation.

2  Holding the fish, cut under the hand and remove the bones with the guts still intact. This yields a butterfly fillet that can be used as any other fillet or stuffed and folded.

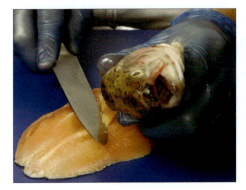
*Removing double fillet from bone*

*Double fillet of trout*

# STORING AND PRESERVING FISH

Fresh fish should be used on the day of purchase where possible, although this may not always be practical so care should be taken when storing fresh fish. Fish should be stored at 1°C in a refrigerator that is only used to store fish and shellfish. It should be kept covered with a clean, damp cloth and under crushed ice. The cloth barrier is to maintain the low temperature and prevent the flesh from drying out for as long as possible. It is important that under these conditions the fish is used quickly and is checked on a day by day basis to ensure its freshness. Ideally fish should be bought whole and on the bone, this way the freshness can easily be determined and the cost can be reduced by preparing the fish yourself.

Frozen fish is usually frozen at sea in long-range fish processing trawlers that can stay out fishing for long periods of time. It is always best to freeze fresh fish as quickly as possible with the use of a blast freezer to help prevent spoilage and deterioration of the flesh. This rapid process ensures that the ice crystals within the flesh are tiny, which allows for minimum water absorption and deterioration of the flesh. If freezing fresh fish in the kitchen, certain aspects will need to be observed by the chef. All frozen fish whether prepared whole, in fillets or darnes should be evenly coated with a thin layer of clean ice. Vacuum packing individual portions before freezing will help to prevent dehydration and **freezer burn**. As mentioned earlier, the rapid freezing of the flesh will also help maintain the fish in a good condition. Frozen fish must be stored at a maximum of −18°C in a deep freeze cabinet. Although in order to produce sashimi, the Japanese freeze yellow tail tuna to temperatures of about −60°C. This helps to maintain the delicate colour of the fish but will also kill off parasites which would usually hibernate when frozen under normal conditions and will help the chef when cutting very fine slices of the fish. Defrosted fish should *never* be refrozen as this can be a significant health hazard. When the frozen fish is required it should be defrosted in a refrigerator and not come into contact with any other ingredients.

# Curing

Most methods for curing seafood are usually to incorporate flavour to the fish rather than to maximise the storage. There are different methods for curing fish that reveal a diversity of textures, flavours and overall end results.

- *Ceviche*. This technique derives from Mexico and it involves the marinating of fish in fresh lemon or lime juice with the addition of herbs and aromatic vegetables. Fish and shellfish such as salmon, turbot and scallops are ideal for this method where they can be thinly sliced before marinating takes place.

- *Escabeche*. This is a popular way of curing used by South American countries and the Mediterranean regions. Fish is filleted and then shallow fried before being marinated with aromatic vegetables, fresh herbs and lemon juice or vinegar.

- *Pickling*. Herrings and shellfish such as whelks, prawns and cockles can be pickled in vinegar. Usually white vinegar is used with the addition of peppercorns and aromatic vegetables. The seafood must be cleaned before pickling commences and sealed jars are utilised to help the preservation process. Herrings that have been cleaned, filleted and rolled up are pickled in vinegar and recognised as rollmops.

- *Salting*. This is primarily used for white, round fish such as cod. The fish is covered with a good quality sea salt to draw out the moisture. It is then dried to preserve it. The fish is always soaked in water to reconstitute it before cooking. Salted cod is the main ingredient in brandade. Caviar is also slightly salted and comes from the roe of the sturgeon. It is carefully processed, tinned and refrigerated before being served on crushed ice with buckwheat cakes called blinis.

- *Smoking*. Fish that is smoked can be prepared and gutted or left whole. After soaking in a solution of salt and other additional ingredients to help the flavour, it is then drained and washed before being hung on racks and placed into a smoking chamber. Hot smoking fish is cured at between 70–80°C and it cooks the fish as it is being smoked. As it is only partially preserved it can only be kept for a few days in refrigeration. Cold smoking

**CHEF'S TIP**

Aromatic vegetables are used to present flavour to fish dishes, court bouillons and sauces. These include onions, carrots, shallots, fennel and celery.

**CHEF'S TIP**

Poaching fish in a court bouillon or white wine and fish stock improves the overall flavour of the fish.

**VIDEO CLIP**
Deep poaching a darne of salmon

**VIDEO CLIP**
Steaming fish

takes place at temperatures of no more than 33°C and will cure the fish over a period of time (usually 5–6 hours). This process has a drying characteristic to aid preservation.

■ *Canning*. Oily fish such as sardines, tuna, anchovies, herring and salmon are usually canned. The fish is preserved in its own juices, oil, **brine** or a sauce (such as tomato). This process is documented in greater detail in Chapter 6 in this book.

# COOKING METHODS FOR FISH

## Boiling

Whole fish such as salmon and turbot are suitable for this method of cookery. Whole fish should be placed into a cold cooking liquid which can be water, milk, or a **court bouillon**. Cuts of fish on the bone should be placed into simmering liquid. This will help to prevent the juices from escaping and coagulating into a white coating on the surface of the fish. The fish should be completely immersed in the cooking liquid. It is not recommended that fish be boiled rapidly as this will damage the texture and may eventually break up the shape of the fish. The cooking liquid should barely move and retain the heat at 90–95°C. On occasion a fish kettle may be employed.

## Poaching

Fish may be poached in shallow or deep liquid. With shallow poaching the cooking liquid is usually retained for the sauce. The fish can be barely covered with the liquid and buttered baking parchment and then cooked in a moderately heated oven. The cooking liquid used for shallow poaching can be fish stock, with addition of a little white wine.

## Steaming

Fish that is suitable for boiling and poaching may also be cooked by steaming. The preparation techniques are the same as for poaching and the fish is placed onto a buttered tray, seasoned lightly and covered with buttered baking parchment. It is an easy method of cooking and is accepted as a good method of cookery for large-scale operations such as banquets. Cooking by steam is rapid and will therefore help to retain flavour, nutrients and colour.

## Baking

Whole, filleted or portioned fish can be baked in an oven. Care must be taken to ensure that the direct heat does not overcook or burn the fish. Whole fish may be stuffed with a mousseline or forcemeat and brushed with oil or butter before baking. In Portugal whole fish is covered with sea salt and baked to help retain flavour and moisture. Another way of protecting the fish during baking is to wrap it in pastry such as puff paste or filo paste. Portions of fish can be baked in buttered dishes and basted frequently or herb crusts can be made to cover the fish portions.

# Grilling

Whole small fish and most cuts and types of fish are suitable for grilling. They need to be seasoned, passed lightly through flour and brushed with oil before being grilled on both sides under a salamander or cooked over heat on the bars of a char grill.

# Stewing

The usual method is to cook a variety of fish and shellfish with vegetables, aromatic herbs, fish stock and wine. The best known type of stewed fish dish is Bouillabaisse.

# Shallow Frying

Whole small fish, a variety of cuts and fillets are suitable for shallow frying. The term 'meuniere' can be used to indicate fish cooked by shallow frying. The fish is passed through seasoned flour and then shallow fried presentation side first in clarified butter before turning over to complete the cooking process. The cooked fish is then served with nut-brown butter flavoured with a little lemon juice and freshly chopped parsley.

# Deep Frying

Whole small round and flat fish, fillets and goujons are suitable for deep frying. The fish must be coated before frying with one of the following combinations:

- Seasoned flour, beaten egg and breadcrumbs
- Milk and flour
- Seasoned flour and batter
- Seasoned flour and beaten egg

The coating forms a protective layer to prevent the fish absorbing too much fat from the deep frying process. Deep fried fish is usually served with deep fried fresh sprigs of parsley, a quarter of a lemon and a suitable sauce (e.g. sauce tartare or sauce remoulade).

# Roasting

Thick cuts of fish such as sea bass and cod are suitable for roasting. The fish is usually portioned and the skin is left on before being lightly seared on both sides in a hot pan with oil. It is then roasted in the oven for a few minutes. Finely chopped vegetables and herbs may be placed under the fish on the roasting tray so that after the fish has been cooked any residual flavour in the bottom of the tray can be deglazed to help form the basis of a sauce.

**CHEF'S TIP**

Oily fish are ideal for baking because they remain moist whilst in the oven. Lean whole fish will require **basting** during cooking to prevent them from drying out in the heat of the oven.

**CHEF'S TIP**

Thin fillets of fish will only require approximately 2 minutes of cooking per side. It is important not to overcook the fish otherwise nutrients and the flavour and texture of the fish will be lost.

**CHEF'S TIP**

The addition of sesame seeds, grated lemon or lime zest, oats and desiccated coconut to breadcrumbs before passing through seasoned flour and beaten egg will enhance the flavour and appearance of the finished dish.

**VIDEO CLIP**
Seering and pan frying fish

**VIDEO CLIP**
Deep frying fish in batter

**CHEF'S TIP**

If roasting fish without the skin on, a crust of breadcrumbs mixed with olive oil, chopped herbs or a duxelle of mushrooms can be used to help protect the fish during the roasting process under higher temperatures and to add further flavour and texture nuances.

# RECIPES

## Baked trout with wilted spinach and spiced tomato salsa

*Buttered tin foil with the trout and lemon slices*

| INGREDIENTS | 4 PORTIONS | 10 PORTIONS |
|---|---|---|
| Trout fillets | 8 × 60g | 20 × 60g |
| Lemon slices | 8 | 20 |
| White wine | 4tbspp | 10tbspp |
| Fresh coriander | 4 sprigs | 10 sprigs |
| Washed spinach leaves | 200g | 500g |
| Butter | 100g | 250g |
| Plum tomatoes (concassé) | 4tbspp | 10tbspp |
| Finely diced red onion | 2tbspp | 5tbspp |
| Finely diced red chilli (preferably jalapeño) | ½ | 1 |
| Tomato ketchup | 1tbspp | 4tbspp |
| Tabasco sauce | To taste | To taste |
| Tomato juice | 2tbsp | 5tbsp |
| Olive oil | 20ml | 50ml |
| Red wine vinegar | 10ml | 25ml |
| Good-quality salt and pepper | To taste | To taste |

## Method of work

1 Preheat an oven at 180°C.

2 Fillet the trout, trimming the fins before filleting.

3 Brush a sheet of tin foil with melted butter and place the fish, seasoning, lemon slices and fresh coriander on top.

4 Place in the oven to bake for approximately 9 minutes.

5 Melt the remaining butter in a saucepan and place the washed and dried spinach into the pan cooking quickly for a few seconds until the spinach leaves have wilted.

6 To make the salsa, mix the tomato concassé, ketchup, Tabasco sauce, finely diced and deseeded chilli and finely diced red onion together. Season well and reserve to one side.

7 To make the tomato vinaigrette, combine the tomato juice, olive oil and red wine vinegar together using a whisk. Season to taste and reserve to one side.

8 To test that the fish is cooked gently lift the fillet to see if the colour of the flesh has changed from dark and translucent to light and opaque.

9 To serve, arrange the warm spinach on the plate with the trout carefully placed on top. Finish with the tomato salsa and the vinaigrette dressing.

# Cod fish pie

| INGREDIENTS | 4 PORTIONS | 10 PORTIONS |
|---|---|---|
| Cod fillet, skinned, pinboned | 400g | 1kg |
| Fish cream sauce (50% fish stock, 50% double cream reduced by half) | 200ml | 500ml |
| Fresh dill | ¼ small bunch | ½ small bunch |
| Baby spinach | 100g | 250g |
| Butter | 100g | 250g |
| Shallots (thinly sliced into rings) | 4 shallots | 10 shallots |
| Mashed potato | 400g | 1kg |
| Egg yolks | 2 | 5 |
| Good-quality salt and white pepper | To taste | To taste |
| Fresh milk (infused with bay leaf, parsley stalks and white peppercorns) | 300ml | 750ml |

## Method of work

1 Preheat an oven to 160°C.

2 Warm the milk **infusion** in a saucepan and add the prepared cod. Simmer for 6 minutes and remove the fish, leaving to drain on a tray. Break the cod into 2cm pieces, season with some salt and pepper and place into a stainless steel bowl.

3 Melt half of the butter in a saucepan and add the sliced shallots. Sweat until tender and then add the washed and dried baby spinach and continue cooking lightly until the spinach has wilted.

4 Chop the fresh dill and add to the fish with the baby spinach and then carefully fold in the fish cream sauce, season to taste.

5 Transfer the fish mixture into individual pie dishes and place in a refrigerator to chill.

6 Warm the mashed potato either in a microwave oven or in a saucepan, stirring constantly to prevent burning. Remove from the heat and beat in the egg yolks. Season well and transfer the potato into a piping bag with a 8mm star tube.

7 **Pipe** the potato on top the fish mixture in the pie dishes and then brush the top with melted butter.

8 Place in the oven and bake for approximately 12 minutes or until the centre has reached a minimum of 63°C.

9 Finish the fish pie under a salamander to colour the surface to a light golden finish if required just before serving.

*Poaching the cod in the infused fresh milk*

### CHEF'S TIP

Instead of finishing the pie with piped potato an alternative is to cover the top with puff pastry, eggwash and bake this through the oven at 180°C until the pastry has a golden brown colour.

# Baked whiting with a herb crust and a cream sauce

**CHEF'S TIP**

This dish works well during the summer served with a tossed salad and a sun-dried tomato coulis.

| INGREDIENTS | 4 PORTIONS | 10 PORTIONS |
|---|---|---|
| Whiting fillets, skinned and pinboned | 4 × 120g fillets | 10 × 120g fillets |
| Mashed potato | 8tbsp | 20tbsp |
| Egg yolks | 2 | 4 |
| Unsalted butter | 100g | 250g |
| Fresh parsley | 10g | 20g |
| Fresh dill | 10g | 20g |
| Fresh chervil | 10g | 20g |
| Fresh mint | 5g | 10g |
| Breadcrumbs | 100g | 250g |
| Finely grated lemon zest | 1 lemon | 2 lemons |
| Fish cream sauce | 150ml | 375ml |
| Tomato concassé | 40g | 100g |
| Good-quality salt and white pepper | To taste | To taste |

## Method of work

1 Preheat an oven to 180°C.

2 Place the washed and dried herbs, breadcrumbs and finely grated lemon zest into a food processor and blend until a fine green-coloured crumb has been produced.

3 Add the unsalted butter and blend until completely smooth and amalgamated.

4 Place this mix in between two sheets of plastic film and roll out to 5mm thick. Chill in a refrigerator until hardened.

5 Prepare the whiting fillets, season and lay onto a baking tray brushed with a little oil.

6 Bake the whiting in the preheated oven until tender to the touch (approximately 8 minutes) and then place on top a square of herb crust.

7 Set under a salamander until the crust begins to bubble and colour slightly. Reserve to one side to rest, keeping the fish hot.

8 Heat the fish cream sauce and add the tomato concassé to it. Season well and adjust the consistency.

9 Heat the mashed potato either in a microwave oven or in a saucepan, stirring constantly to prevent burning. Remove from the heat and beat in the egg yolks. Season well and transfer the potato into a piping bag with an 8mm plain tube.

10 Quickly pipe the potato mash onto the presentation plate.

11 Position the whiting and finish with the fish cream sauce around the plate. Serve immediately.

*Rolling out the herb crust*

*Placing the herb crust onto the whiting*

*The grilled herb crust on the whiting*

# Baked sea bass stuffed with apple and thyme

| INGREDIENTS | 4 PORTIONS | 10 PORTIONS |
|---|---|---|
| Sea bass fillets, pinboned and trimmed | 8 × 70g | 20 × 70g |
| Grated Cox's orange pippin apple | 1 | 2 |
| Finely chopped onion | 2tbsp | 5tbsp |
| Chopped fresh thyme | 1tbsp | 2tbsp |
| White breadcrumbs | 100g | 250g |
| Unsalted butter | 100g | 250g |
| Finely grated lemon zest and juice | 1 lemon | 2 lemons |
| Small baby gem lettuce leaves | 4 | 10 |
| Small curly endive leaves | 4 | 10 |
| Small radicchio leaves | 4 | 10 |
| Olive oil | 4tbsp | 10tbsp |
| Fresh chives cut into 2cm strips | 5g | 15g |
| Good quality salt and white pepper | To taste | To taste |
| Roasted new potatoes | 160g | 400g |
| Natural yoghurt | 75g | 150g |
| Powdered cumin | A pinch | A pinch |

*Stuffing the sea bass fillets*

### CHEF'S TIP

The dish can be made using small whole sea bass or fillets of different fish such as red mullet.

## Method of work

1   Preheat the oven to 180°C.

2   Prepare the sea bass by filleting and trimming each fillet. Ensure each fillet retains the skin and weighs approximately 70 grams each.

3   Melt the butter in a saucepan and add the chopped onion, lemon zest, fresh thyme and grated apple. Cook carefully without letting them colour for 4 minutes.

4   Remove from the heat and fold in the breadcrumbs. Season and leave in a refrigerator to chill slightly.

5   Place one fillet onto a buttered baking tray, season and spoon some of the apple filling on top. Place another fillet directly on top to encase the filling in a sandwich. Season the top fillet.

6   Meanwhile, ensure that the new potatoes are roasting by pan frying them in a little goose fat to begin colouring them. Season them and place into the oven to roast.

7   Mix together the natural yoghurt, ground cumin and a little olive oil to adjust the consistency to a runny texture. Reserve to one side.

8   Place the sea bass into the oven and bake for 12 minutes until tender and fully cooked.

9   Clean and dry the salad leaves. Lightly toss with some olive oil.

10  Lay the roasted new potatoes into the centre of the plate and rest the sea bass on top. Garnish with the lightly dressed salad leaves, chives, olive oil and the yoghurt dressing.

# Grilled sea bream on minted crushed peas

| INGREDIENTS | 4 PORTIONS | 10 PORTIONS |
|---|---|---|
| Sea bream fillets | 4 × 120g fillets | 10 × 120g fillets |
| Frozen or fresh green peas | 200g | 500g |
| Chopped shallots | 2 | 5 |
| Fresh mint leaves | 10 leaves | 20 leaves |
| Butter | 50g | 125g |
| Plain flour | 50g | 125g |
| Natural yoghurt | 50ml | 125ml |
| Sunflower oil | 50ml | 125ml |
| Good-quality salt and white pepper | To taste | To taste |
| Blanched lemon zest to garnish | 1 lemon | 2 lemons |

## Method of work

1. Prepare the sea bream by filleting and trimming it ready to be grilled.

2. Place enough water into a saucepan to totally cover the peas and bring to the boil. Then add the peas and chopped shallots and season well with salt.

3. Add the fresh mint two minutes before cooking is complete and then drain the water. Lightly crush the peas using the back of a spoon and mix well whilst aiming to keep some texture.

4. Lightly season and flour the fish fillets. Brush with melted butter and a little sunflower oil.

5. Place under a preheated salamander and cook the sea bream on both sides until slightly golden in colour and tender to the touch.

6. Beat the yoghurt and spoon onto the serving plate.

7. Place the crushed peas into the centre.

8. Position the grilled sea bream on top. Finish with a little extra crushed peas and the lemon zest for garnish.

*Crushing the peas*

# Grilled cod with shaved fennel and black olives

*Scoring the fillets of cod on the skin*

| INGREDIENTS | 4 PORTIONS | 10 PORTIONS |
|---|---|---|
| Cod fillets, trimmed and washed | 4 × 140g scored skin | 10 × 140g scored skin |
| Fresh fennel shavings | 200g | 500g |
| Chopped fresh dill | 2tbsp | 5tbsp |
| Tomato concassé | 2tbsp | 5tbsp |
| Finely diced shallots | 1 | 2 |
| Diced black olives | 4tbsp | 10tbsp |
| Sliced carrot | 100g | 250g |
| White wine vinegar | 100ml | 250ml |
| Olive oil | 50ml | 125ml |
| Good-quality salt and white pepper | To taste | To taste |
| Balsamic vinegar | 4tbsp | 10tbsp |
| Lemon juice | ½ lemon | 1 lemon |

## Method of work

1  Preheat an oven to 180°C.

2  Thinly shave the fennel carefully, using a mandolin. Finely slice the carrot and then mix the two vegetables together with some lemon juice, white wine vinegar and half the tomato concassée. Cover with plastic film and allow the vegetables to marinade at room temperature for one hour.

3  Combine the remaining tomato concassé with the black olives, oil and balsamic vinegar. Set aside.

4  Prepare and trim the cod fillets, scoring the skin with short incisions using a sharp knife.

5  Brush each fillet with oil and then place under the salamander skin side up and allow the scored marks to open slightly.

6  Transfer the fish to the oven to keep warm and finish the cooking process for 3 minutes.

7  Place the vegetable mixture into a saucepan and bring to the boil. Set aside and keep warm for 4 minutes to keep the vegetables warm but still crisp.

8  Lay the vegetables onto the centre of the plate, rest the gilled cod on top and set some shaved fennel on top of the cod with a sprig of fresh dill.

9  Spoon the olive and tomato concassé mix around the plate and serve.

# Grilled Dover sole with parsley butter

*Marking the Dover sole with a griddle*

| INGREDIENTS | 4 PORTIONS | 10 PORTIONS |
|---|---|---|
| Skinned, trimmed Dover sole | 4 × 500g | 10 × 500g |
| Unsalted butter | 200g | 500g |
| Plain flour | 100g | 250g |
| Sliced fennel | 200g | 500g |
| Chopped fresh parsley | 2tbsp | 5tbsp |
| Fresh lemon | 1 lemon | 3 lemons |
| Good-quality salt and white pepper | To taste | To taste |
| Lemon juice and finely grated zest | 1 lemon | 2 lemons |

## Method of work

1 Preheat the oven to 180°C.
2 Prepare the sole for grilling by trimming the fins and skinning the fish on both sides.
3 Lightly season and flour the sole, then brush with melted butter.
4 Place in a refrigerator for a few minutes to chill.
5 Meanwhile, beat the unsalted butter and add the lemon juice, finely grated zest and chopped parsley, mixing well until all the ingredients have been incorporated.
6 Transfer the butter into a piping bag with a 6mm star tube and pipe into neat rosettes onto a tray lined with silicone paper. Place in a refrigerator to chill.
7 Prepare the lemon by cutting into quarters, removing any seeds and trimming any white pith.
8 Heat an iron bar, metal skewer or solid griddle pan until it is very hot. Carefully mark the Dover soles in a quadrilateral pattern.
9 Lay the sliced fennel onto a greased baking tray, rest the Dover sole on top and place under the salamander to begin grilling for a few minutes, until the flesh begins to colour slightly.
10 Place the Dover sole in the oven and continue to cook for approximately 12 minutes.
11 Serve either on or off the bone with the parsley butter and a lemon quarter.

## CHEF'S TIP

Cooking times may vary according to the size and thickness of the fish. Thinner fillets (about 1cm thick) may take up to 2 minutes each side and thicker fillets (about 2.5cm thick) or whole fish may take up to 6 minutes per side. Thicker fillets should be grilled at a greater distance from the direct source of heat and may need further brushing with fat or oil from time to time.

# Poached halibut with a cherry tomato confit and vegetable julienne crisps

| INGREDIENTS | 4 PORTIONS | 10 PORTIONS |
| --- | --- | --- |
| Halibut suprêmes | 4 × 120g | 10 × 120g |
| Vine-ripened cherry tomatoes | 200g | 500g |
| Olive oil | 100ml | 250ml |
| White pepper | To taste | To taste |
| Sea salt | 2tsp | 5tsp |
| Chopped fresh garlic | 1 clove | 3 cloves |
| Dry white wine | 50ml | 125ml |
| Fresh bay leaves | 1 | 2 |
| Julienne of carrot | 100g | 250g |
| Julienne of leek | 100g | 250g |
| Finely sliced onion | 2 small onions | 5 small onions |
| Butter | 50g | 125g |
| Fish stock | 200ml | 500ml |

**CHEF'S TIP**

When poaching or boiling whole fish do not allow the liquid to boil as it will cause the fish to break.

**CHEF'S TIP**

Poach fish for approximately 5–7 minutes for a thickness of 2.5cm starting in hot liquid (or until the core temperature of the fish is 63°C). Reserving the poaching liquid and turning it into a sauce to accompany the halibut will add another element to this dish.

## Method of work

1 Preheat a deep fat fryer to 160°C and an oven to 170°C.
2 Cut the carrot and leek into julienne. Place onto a sheet of silicone paper and dry in an oven at 110°C or under heat lamps for 30 minutes.
3 Carefully deep fry the julienne carrot and leek separately, moving constantly in the hot fat to maintain an even cooking of the vegetables. Remove from the fat and dry on absorbent paper.
4 Place back under the heat lamps or the oven again and dry for a further 30 minutes.
5 Prepare a dish to poach the halibut in by brushing the base with butter and set the onion on the bottom.
6 Place the halibut on top, season well and drizzle the dry white wine over. Add the bay leaf and warm fish stock. Cover with tin foil and poach for approximately 15 minutes in the oven, until tender and just cooked.
7 Heat the oil and a pan and add the garlic and some salt. Add the tomatoes, cook for 30 seconds and remove from the heat. Carefully remove the tomatoes and leave to one side to rest for a few minutes.
8 To serve, set the tomato confit on the centre of the plate and rest the halibut on top. Garnish with the vegetable julienne crisps.

# Paupiette of lemon sole with a leek confit and sauce Duglére

| INGREDIENTS | 4 PORTIONS | 10 PORTIONS |
|---|---|---|
| Prepared lemon sole paupiettes | 8 | 20 |
| Dry white wine | 50ml | 125ml |
| Finely chopped shallots | 20g | 45g |
| Good-quality salt and white pepper | To taste | To taste |
| Tomato concassé | 200g | 500g |
| Double cream | 200ml | 400ml |
| Butter | 45g | 100g |
| Fish stock | 100ml | 200ml |
| Lemon juice | ¼ lemon | ½ lemon |
| Chopped flat leaf parsley | 2tbsp | 6tbsp |
| Whole leek | 1 | 3 |
| Olive oil | 4tsp | 9tsp |
| Lime juice | ½ lime | 1 lime |

*Paupiettes ready for poaching*

## Method of work

1  Preheat an oven to 180°C.

2  Prepare the paupiettes of sole as mentioned on page 190 of this chapter.

3  Lightly butter a poaching pan or tray and sprinkle the chopped shallots over. Place the paupiettes on top with three-quarters of tomato concassé and half of the chopped flat leaf parsley. Season well.

4  Add the white wine and the fish stock and cover with a buttered piece of baking parchment.

5  To prepare the confit of leek, carefully cut the leek into julienne and place into a baking tin with the olive oil and lime juice. Season well and place in the oven to cook to a confit for approximately 45 minutes. Remove from the oven, add the rest of the chopped flat leaf parsley and drain the leek oil from the confit. Retain the confit and the oil separately in a warm place.

6  Place the paupiettes into the oven to poach for approximately 10 minutes.

7  Remove the paupiettes, drain and reserve in a warm place covered with the buttered baking parchment.

8  Pass the cooking liquor into a small pan and reduce by two-thirds.

9  Add the double cream and once again reduce the liquid to a smooth coating consistency. Incorporate the butter by whisking in off the direct heat (**monter au beurre**) until completely blended into the sauce. Correct the consistency and seasoning. Add any remaining fresh chopped parsley to the sauce at this point.

10  To serve, arrange the leek confit in the centre of the plate and position two paupiettes per portion on top. Spoon some of the sauce Duglére over the fish and the rest around the plate. Drizzle the leek oil around the plate and put the remaining tomato concassée on top.

# Steamed délice of plaice with a champagne cream sauce

| INGREDIENTS | 4 PORTIONS | 10 PORTIONS |
|---|---|---|
| Plaice fillets, skinned | 8 | 20 |
| Julienne of carrot | 50g | 125g |
| Julienne of mooli | 50g | 125g |
| Julienne of leek | 50g | 125g |
| Julienne of courgette | 50g | 125g |
| Fish velouté | 100ml | 250ml |
| Double cream | 25ml | 75ml |
| Champagne | 50ml | 125ml |
| Butter | 100g | 250g |
| Good-quality salt and white pepper | To taste | To taste |

## Method of work

1 Prepare the fillets of plaice, skin and trim them accordingly ensuring each portion weight is the same.

2 Melt the butter in a small saucepan and the vegetables cut into julienne. Cook the vegetables without letting them colour, aiming to keep a little firmness to the texture of the vegetables. Drain and keep aside to remain warm.

3 Put the plaice onto a plate, season and pour a little champagne over the fillets. Cover with plastic film.

4 Place the fillets on the sealed plate into the steamer and cook for 5 minutes or until tender.

5 When cooking has been completed, drain the cooking liquor into a saucepan and add the fish velouté, the heated double cream and the rest of the champagne. Bring to the boil and then pass through a fine chinois. Correct the seasoning and consistency.

6 To serve, position the plaice fillets in the centre of the plate and set the julienne of vegetables on top. Spoon the champagne sauce around the fish.

# Monkfish wrapped in pancetta with salsa verde

**CHEF'S TIP**

The salsa verde is best made 30 minutes before service to give the most vibrant colour and flavours possible. Always ensure that the fresh herbs are washed carefully in plenty of cold water. Dry them by gently shaking the water off and patting dry with a cloth.

| INGREDIENTS | 4 PORTIONS | 10 PORTIONS |
| --- | --- | --- |
| Monkfish tail fillets | 4 × 120g | 10 × 120g |
| Thinly sliced unsmoked pancetta | 12 slices | 30 slices |
| Fresh chervil | 4 sprigs | 10 sprigs |
| Good-quality salt and white pepper | To taste | To taste |
| Chopped garlic | 1 clove | 3 cloves |
| Chopped fresh flat leaf parsley | 2tbsp | 5tbsp |
| Chopped fresh coriander | 2tbsp | 5tbsp |
| Chopped fresh chives | 1tbsp | 3tbsp |
| Finely sliced spring onion | 1 | 2 |
| Olive oil | 100ml | 250ml |
| Lime juice and zest | 2 limes | 5 limes |
| Chopped fresh mint | 1tbsp | 2tbsp |
| Dijon mustard | 2tsp | 5tsp |
| Finely diced shallots | 1 shallot | 3 shallots |
| White wine vinegar | 2tbsp | 5tbsp |

## Method of work

1 Prepare the monkfish tail into fillets by removing the bone and trimming each fillet, ensuring the weight of 120g per portion is maintained.

2 Lay the pancetta onto a sheet of plastic film, slightly overlapping, and then place the monkfish on top. Season the monkfish with salt and pepper.

3 Fold over the pancetta and the plastic film to encase the monkfish fillet inside.

4 Continue to roll the fillet into a sausage shape and then place in a refrigerator to chill for at least 30 minutes.

5 To make the salsa verde, mix all the chopped herbs, spring onion, garlic, shallots, olive oil, vinegar, lime juice and mustard carefully together and leave to one side after seasoning with a little salt.

6 Place the wrapped monkfish into a steamer and cook for 7 minutes. Remove and rest for 2 minutes still inside the plastic film.

7 Heat some olive oil in pan. Remove the plastic film then fry the monkfish to crisp the pancetta on all sides and to add colour.

8 To serve, slice the monkfish in half at an angle and position the monkfish on the centre of the plate, spoon the salsa verde on top with the picked chervil sprig.

Lay the monkfish fillet onto the pancetta and plastic film and roll

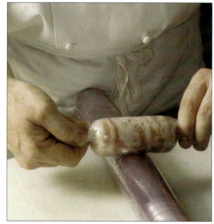
Rolling into a sausage shape in the plastic film

Colouring the pancetta after steaming

# Sesame tuna with hoi sin sauce and pak choy

| INGREDIENTS | 4 PORTIONS | 10 PORTIONS |
|---|---|---|
| Tuna fish, prepared into steaks | 4 × 120g circular slices | 10 × 120g circular slices |
| Sesame seeds | 4tsp | 10tsp |
| Hoi sin sauce | 4tbsp | 10tbsp |
| Pak choy | 200g | 500g |
| Finely chopped garlic | 1 clove | 3 cloves |
| Grated fresh ginger | 1tsp | 3tsp |
| Dark soy sauce | 2tbsp | 5tbsp |
| Finely chopped red chilli | ¼ chilli | ½ chilli |
| Finely sliced spring onions | 2 | 5 |
| Groundnut oil | 4tbsp | 10tbsp |
| Good-quality salt and black pepper | To taste | To taste |

*Roll the sides of the tuna steak in the sesame seeds*

## Method of work

1 Prepare the tuna by cutting into steaks.

2 Brush the sides of the tuna steaks with a little of the hoi sin sauce and then roll the sides into the sesame seeds to give a coating around the edges.

3 Place in a refrigerator to chill for 30 minutes.

4 Using a wok or a steep-sided pan for stir frying heat the groundnut oil, spreading it evenly throughout the pan.

5 When the oil is very hot add the spring onions, red chilli, ginger and garlic. Quickly toss these ingredients to prevent burning.

6 Add the pak choy and move the ingredients continuously from the centre of the pan to the sides. Quickly add the soy sauce and a few drops of water and cover the pan for a minute to complete the cooking. This final steaming of the food, combined with the initial stir frying, will finish the process perfectly.

7 Brush any remaining hoi sin sauce decoratively on service plates, as a presentation option.

8 Sear the tuna for approximately 2 minutes on each side to ensure that the tuna steak maintains a pink centre.

9 To serve, arrange the pak choy on the plate and set the tuna steak on top.

### CHEF'S TIP

The tuna can be replaced with swordfish or salmon. Ensure the tuna is extremely fresh as this gives a better flavour and colour and reduces the risk of bacterial poisoning.

# Skate with capers and black butter

*Shallow fry the skate to a golden colour*

| INGREDIENTS | 4 PORTIONS | 10 PORTIONS |
| --- | --- | --- |
| Skate wings, filleted, trimmed and skinned | 4 × 100g | 10 × 100g |
| Butter | 200g | 500g |
| Plain flour | 100g | 250g |
| Capers or caperberries | 4tbsp | 10tbsp |
| Lemon juice and zest | 2 lemons | 5 lemons |
| Chopped fresh parsley | 4tbsp | 10tbsp |
| Sunflower oil | 50ml | 100ml |
| Good-quality salt and white pepper | To taste | To taste |

## Method of work

1 To prepare the skate; cut fillets from the wings and remove the skin, trimming as required. Cut into equal-sized portions.

2 Lightly flour and season the skate and then in a frying pan heat the oil and a little butter.

3 Shallow fry the skate, presentation side down first until golden, before turning over to cook the other side.

4 Remove from the pan and allow to drain briefly on absorbent paper before keeping in a warm place for service.

5 Wipe the pan clean then add the remaining butter over the heat and allow to melt and begin to foam.

6 Continue to cook until a dark brown colour is achieved then add the capers, lemon zest and juice and the chopped parsley

7 Place a fillet of the skate onto a serving plate before spooning the butter and the capers on top. Serve with some additional fresh lemon.

### CHEF'S TIP

An alternative way of cooking skate is to poach the prepared wings in a court bouillon and drain well before making the caper and black butter sauce to spoon over the finished dish.

# Pan-fried red mullet with a black olive tapenade

### CHEF'S TIP

To test if the red mullet is cooked correctly, insert a thin-bladed knife into the centre of the fish. Then touch the tip of the knife with your thumb or forefinger. If the knife tip is warm, the fish is ready.

| INGREDIENTS | 4 PORTIONS | 10 PORTIONS |
| --- | --- | --- |
| Red mullet fillets | 4 × 80g | 10 × 80g |
| Chopped black olives | 2tbsp | 5tbsp |
| Chopped garlic | 1 clove | 2 cloves |
| Chopped anchovies | 1tbsp | 2tbsp |
| Dijon mustard | 1tsp | 2tsp |
| Olive oil | 50ml | 125ml |
| Plum tomato concassé | 8 tomatoes | 20 tomatoes |
| Finely chopped shallots | 1 | 2 |
| Chopped fresh thyme | 2tbsp | 4tbsp |
| Fresh chervil | 4 sprigs | 4 sprigs |
| Good-quality salt and white pepper | To taste | To taste |
| Chopped fresh dill | 1tbsp | 3tbsp |

*Shallow fry the red mullet*

## Method of work

1 Scale, remove the fins and cut the fillets off the red mullet. Trim and remove any pinbones as necessary. Run the back of a knife over the skin to ensure that all scales are removed.

2 Mix the black olives, anchovies, garlic, mustard and a little olive oil to form the tapenade. Retain at room temperature.

3 Combine the remaining olive oil, tomato concassé, chopped thyme and dill and add to a saucepan. Gently cook on a slow heat for 1 hour until it breaks down and thickens to a jam-like consistency. Check the seasoning.

4 Heat some oil in a shallow pan and season the fillets of red mullet before cooking them skin side down for 2 minutes. Turn over each fillet and finish the cooking process.

5 Spoon the tapenade onto the serving plate and then lay the fillet on top.

6 Spoon the rest of the tomato concassée onto the fish and garnish with a sprig of chervil.

# Roasted pollack with dill crème fraîche and Lyonnaise potatoes

| INGREDIENTS | 4 PORTIONS | 10 PORTIONS |
|---|---|---|
| Pollack fillets | 4 × 120g | 10 × 120g |
| Crème fraîche | 4tbsp | 10tbsp |
| Fresh chopped dill | 1tsp | 2tsp |
| Sliced onion | 1 | 3 |
| Cooked potatoes with skins removed (Cara or Maris Piper) | 300g | 850g |
| Clarified butter | 70g | 170g |
| Plain flour | 100g | 250g |
| Olive oil | 50ml | 125ml |
| Butter | 50g | 125g |
| Good-quality salt and white pepper | To taste | To taste |

## Method of work

1 Preheat an oven to 180°C.

2 Prepare the pollack by scraping off the scales with the back of a knife, washing and removing the fins. Carefully cut fillets from both sides of each fish and trim as required.

3 Lightly season and flour the fillets and then heat a little oil on a metal baking or roasting tin.

4 Place in the lightly floured pollack onto the oiled surface and put into the oven to roast for approximately 12 minutes, turning over the fillet from time to time and basting to keep the fish moist and prevent the dry heat from burning the fish.

5 Slice the cooked potatoes and heat some clarified butter in a heavy frying pan. Add the potatoes and sauté to a golden brown colour, tossing occasionally. Season well and place into a tray to keep warm.

6 Clean the pan and using the remaining clarified butter, sauté the sliced onions with a little colour before adding the potatoes and tossing to mix them well together.

7 Combine the freshly chopped dill with the crème fraîche and chill in a refrigerator for 5 minutes.

8 Lay the Lyonnaise potatoes onto the serving plate. Set the roasted pollack on top of the potatoes and quenelle the crème fraîche on to the fish.

### CHEF'S TIP

Pollack is from the cod family and is sometimes known as greenfish or lythe. It is recognised by its slender green-brown body and can weigh up to 9kg whole. Coley is another alternative fish which is also from the cod family and can be known as pollock or coalfish. Its flavour is not as pronounced as cod but as a cheaper and more conservation-friendly option it certainly has its value.

# Salmon fish cakes with a citrus mayonnaise

| INGREDIENTS | 4 PORTIONS | 10 PORTIONS |
|---|---|---|
| Salmon trimmings | 300g | 750g |
| Mashed potato | 150g | 375g |
| Finely diced shallots | 50g | 125g |
| Grated cheddar cheese | 50g | 125g |
| Lime juice and zest | 1 lime | 3 limes |
| Pasteurised egg | 80g | 200g |
| Plain flour | 100g | 250g |
| White breadcrumbs | 100g | 250g |
| Finely grated zest and juice of lemon | 1 | 3 |
| Mayonnaise | 100ml | 250ml |
| Fresh chopped parsley | 4tbsp | 8tbsp |
| Curly endive | A few leaves for garnish | A few leaves for garnish |
| Vinaigrette | 2tbsp | 5tbsp |
| Good-quality salt and white pepper | To taste | To taste |

## Method of work

1 Ensure that all the skin and bone have been removed from the salmon trimmings.

2 Place the salmon trimmings into a steamer with the lime juice and zest for 8 minutes to completely cook through.

3 Take out of the steamer and leave to cool.

4 Flake the salmon flesh into a bowl and add the mashed potato, chopped shallots and grated cheese. Combine these ingredients well, season and leave to rest covered in plastic film in a refrigerator.

5 Using a round 6cm pastry cutter as a mould, fill the salmon mixture inside to form a large cake.

6 Pass the salmon cake through seasoned flour, beaten egg and then the breadcrumbs. Utilising a palette knife press the crumbs into the cake and redefine the circular shape if required. Leave in a refrigerator to rest for 15 minutes.

7 Mix the mayonnaise with the grated zest and juice of the lemon. Season to taste and reserve for service.

8 Wash the curly endive well and carefully pat dry. Dress with the vinaigrette and set aside.

9 Deep fry each salmon cake at 180°C until golden brown. Drain the cakes on kitchen paper and then serve with the dressed curly endive on top of each cake and the lemon mayonnaise.

*Passing the cake through seasoned flour*

*Pass the cake through beaten egg*

*Pass the cake through the white breadcrumbs*

# Deep-fried haddock with mushy peas and thick-cut chips

*Deep fry the haddock until golden brown in colour*

### CHEF'S TIP

When deep frying always place fish in the oil away from you so as to prevent splashes of hot oil.

| INGREDIENTS | 4 PORTIONS | 10 PORTIONS |
|---|---|---|
| Haddock fillets | 4 × 140g | 10 × 140g |
| Plain flour | 100g | 250g |
| Baking powder | Pinch | 5g |
| Good brown ale | 125ml | 300ml |
| Egg | 1 | 2 |
| Dried marrowfat peas | 100g | 250g |
| Small chopped onion | 1 | 2 |
| Fresh bay leaves | 1 | 2 |
| Crushed garlic | 1 | 2 |
| Bicarbonate of soda | 1tsp | 2tsp |
| Potatoes (preferably Bintje or Maris Piper) | 600g | 1.5kg |
| Good-quality salt and white pepper | To taste | To taste |
| Lemon | 2 | 5 |

## Method of work

1 Soak the marrowfat peas in cold water for a minimum of two hours.

2 Drain and wash the peas. Place them into a saucepan with the chopped onion, crushed garlic, bay leaf and the bicarbonate of soda. Cover with cold water and then season with salt before slowly bringing the contents of the saucepan to the boil. Simmer for approximately three-quarters of an hour or until the peas begin to break down.

3 Remove the bay leaf, correct the seasoning and hold the peas warm on the side of a stove, covered with a lid.

4 To make the batter for the fish, mix the flour, baking powder, egg and the beer using a whisk until a smooth consistency has been obtained. Season with salt and allow to rest for at least 1 hour before using.

5 Peel, wash and cut the potatoes into straight sided batons approximately 6cm long and 2cm thick. Wash and dry well. Place into frying baskets and blanch in cool oil at 160°C without letting them colour until cooked through and soft. Drain on kitchen paper on trays until required.

6 Prepare the fish by removing the fillets and trimming. Wash well and dry before seasoning with salt and pepper and passing through flour and then the batter.

7 Carefully place the fish into the deep fryer and fry at 180°C until golden and cooked through, which will take approximately 5 minutes. Drain the fried fillet well on kitchen paper.

8 Place the blanched potatoes into a frying basket and cook at 180°C until crisp and golden brown in colour. Drain well on kitchen paper, season lightly with a little salt.

9 Serve the fish with the chipped potatoes, mushy peas and a wedge of lemon to accompany.

# Hot smoked jasmine and green tea salmon with wilted baby gem lettuce

*Lay the salmon onto the rack over the tea*

| INGREDIENTS | 4 PORTIONS | 10 PORTIONS |
|---|---|---|
| Salmon fillets with the skin left intact | 4 × 140g | 10 × 140g |
| Jasmine tea | 10g | 30g |
| Green tea leaves | 10g | 30g |
| Long grain rice | 100g | 250g |
| Granulated sugar | 50g | 125g |
| Baby gem lettuce | 4 | 10 |
| Fish cream sauce (50% fish stock, 50% double cream reduced by half) | 150ml | 375ml |
| Butter | 50g | 125g |
| Good-quality salt and white pepper | To taste | To taste |
| Finely chopped shallots | 1 | 2 |
| White wine vinegar | 1tbsp | 2tbsp |
| Dry white wine | 4tbsp | 10tbsp |
| Cold fish stock | 2tbsp | 5tbsp |
| Unsalted butter, chilled and diced | 200g | 500g |
| Lemon juice | 1tsp | 2tsp |

## Method of work

1 Prepare the salmon by cutting into suprêmes, trimming, washing and drying well.

2 Place the rice, both loose teas and the sugar into the bottom of a roasting tray and mix well; put into a hot oven at 200°C and bake until smoke begins to form.

3 Rest a cooling rack over the top of the tray, place the prepared salmon onto it and cover loosely with tin foil.

4 Lower the oven heat to 165°C and cook for approximately 12 minutes.

5 Wash and remove the leaves from the baby gem lettuce. Melt the butter in a pan and add the leaves, slowly wilting the gems and seasoning with salt and pepper.

6 To make the fish beurre blanc, place the chopped shallots, vinegar and wine into a pan and bring to the boil. Lower the heat and reduce for approximately 2 minutes until only 1 tbsp of liquid remains.

7 Over a gentle heat, add the fish stock and then whisk in the unsalted butter a little at a time until the ingredients have emulsified to produce a buttery sauce. Season well and add the lemon juice. Pass through a fine sieve and correct the consistency before serving.

8 To serve, place the wilted baby gems in the centre of the plate and rest of the salmon on top. Spoon the sauce around the plate.

## CHEF'S TIP

The smoking process gives a subtle flavour to the salmon. Other teas can be used such as Earl Grey, Keemun and various black teas. Oils, essences and spices can be added to the mix to give a deeper flavour. Sometimes the salmon can be marinated for 12 hours before smoking to create a stronger flavour and colour.

# Soused herring on a Waldorf salad

| INGREDIENTS | 4 PORTIONS | 10 PORTIONS |
|---|---|---|
| Herring fillets | 8 × 100g | 20 × 100g |
| Thinly sliced onions | 40g | 100g |
| Thinly sliced carrots | 40g | 100g |
| Black peppercorns | 4 | 10 |
| Parsley stalks | 5g | 10g |
| White wine | 40ml | 100ml |
| White wine vinegar | 80ml | 500ml |
| Water | 50ml | 400ml |
| Mustard seeds | 2 | 5 |
| Fresh bay leaf | 1 | 2 |
| Caster sugar | 5g | 20g |
| Diced celeriac | 40g | 100g |
| Diced red apple (such as Gala, Spartan or Cox's orange pippin) | 80g | 400g |
| Diced celery | 40g | 100g |
| Shelled, peeled and chopped walnuts | 30g | 100g |
| Lemon juice | 1tbsp | 3tbsp |
| Mayonnaise | 70g | 250g |
| Good-quality salt and white pepper | To taste | To taste |

## Method of work

1  Preheat an oven to 160°C.
2  Prepare the herring by removing the heads and the guts. Cut fillets from each fish, trim, scale the skin and wash well. Place the fillets into a deep baking tray.
3  Place the white wine, vinegar, water, carrots, onions, bay leaf, parsley stalks, mustard seeds, sugar and peppercorns into a saucepan and bring to the boil.
4  Season the herring fillets with salt and pepper and then pour over the hot liquid.
5  Cover the herring fillets with greaseproof paper and put into the oven to slowly bake for approximately 10 minutes.
6  Remove from the oven to cool in the cooking liquor.
7  To make the Waldorf salad, wash and dice the celeriac, celery and apple into 1cm dice. Peel the walnuts by blanching in a little milk or water and then drying out before removing the skins. Roughly chop the walnuts.
8  Combine the lemon juice, mayonnaise, diced celeriac, celery, walnuts and apple together. Season with a little salt.
9  Arrange the Waldorf salad on the serving plate and rest two herring fillets per portion on top. Spoon a little of the soused herring cooking liquor over the top and decorate with a little of the cooked sliced onion.

### CHEF'S TIP

Soused herrings can be served warm or cold and can be presented as a starter or fish course. Mackerel or trout are alternative fish that can also be served in this way.

## Assessment of knowledge and understanding

You have now learned about the use of the different categories of fish and how to produce a variety of fish dishes utilising a range of commodities, preparation and cooking techniques.

To test your level of knowledge and understanding, answer the following short questions. These will help to prepare you for your summative (final) assessment.

# Quality Identifications

List three examples of flat white fish.

i) _____     ii) _____

iii) _____

List three examples of round white fish.

i) _____     ii) _____

iii) _____

List three examples of oily fish.

i) _____     ii) _____

iii) _____

List two examples of fresh waterfish.

i) _____     ii) _____

List five quality points when purchasing whole fresh fish.

i) _____     ii) _____

iii) _____     iv) _____

v) _____

# Materials and storage

1 Describe the storage procedure for raw fish.

_____

_____

2 State which of the fish named below is the odd one out and give the reason for your answer.

(a) Herring _____

(b) Cod _____

(c) Haddock _____

(d) Hake _____

# Preparation

1 List three fish that are suitable for smoking.

i) _____     ii) _____

iii) _____

# Shellfish

## INTRODUCTION

Shellfish is a collective term for crustacean, mollusc and other types of seafood such as octopus. Each category has its own variations and consequently they will have differing methods of preparation. Shellfish are usually cooked by boiling, poaching and steaming, however some crustaceans can also be grilled and many molluscs are served raw. Shellfish are suitable for lunch and dinner service and can be utilised as a main course in its own right, as a intermediate course or as a garnishing role for starters, hors d'oeuvre, salads, fish dishes and meat and poultry dishes.

- **Molluscs**   Can have a single shell (univalve)
   Can have a pair of shells (bivalve)
   Can have no shell (cephalopods)
- **Crustaceans**   Have an external skeleton (shell) and jointed limbs.

### CLASSIFICATION OF SHELLFISH

| UNIVALVE | BIVALVE | CRUSTACEAN | CEPHALOPODS |
|---|---|---|---|
| Limpets | Cockles | Lobsters | Octopus |
| Whelks | Mussels | Crabs | Cuttlefish |
| Winkles | Razor shell clams | Crayfish | Squid |
| Sea urchin | Scallops | Prawns | |
| Tusk shell | Oysters | Shrimps | |
| Abalone | Clams | Langoustine | |
| Conch | | Crawfish | |

> **CHEF'S TIP**
>
> Fresh mussel shells may be open slightly when first purchased. They should close immediately when tapped. If this does not happen, either do not buy the molluscs, or if already purchased discard them.

### QUALITY POINTS

- All shellfish are best if purchased live. This will help to ensure that they are maximum freshness and that there can be no possibility of contamination from pollutants that the shellfish may have absorbed. It is accepted that shellfish items such as prawns are usually purchased in a frozen or a cook-chilled format.

- On delivery, lobsters, crabs, crayfish and crawfish should be evidently alive and they should feel heavy in relation to their size. It is important to touch and handle these crustaceans to check this. Also check for signs of damage such as claws that are missing and that they are generally of a good size.

- Bivalve molluscs should have shells that are tightly closed, mostly free of barnacles and mud. They should feel heavy in relation to their size and any shells that remain open after being moved or slightly tapped should be immediately discarded. Any signs of a foul smell, rather than a fresh, sweet, seawater smell, should also be rejected. If any of the shells have broken it is also important to discard these too.

- All shellfish will deteriorate quickly, raw and cooked, and so should be purchased for immediate consumption.

*Landing a catch from a short range crab and lobster boat in north Norfolk*

# TRANSPORTATION AND STORAGE

The best transportation and storage for live crustaceans is to use a seawater or freshwater tank. For shellfish to be transported in these conditions the following points should be observed:

■ Controlled water temperature within the tanks

■ Good aeration of the water

■ Suitable water quality depending on the type of crustacean or mollusc

■ Species should be separated into independent tanks.

However, this method is costly and only catering establishments that specialise in serving shellfish will have this facility. Fish and shellfish suppliers will also have this facility on their own premises, but generally when making deliveries crustaceans such as lobster, crabs and crayfish will be packed in cases (usually polystyrene), covered with wet cloths and kept in a refrigerated environment.

Follow these guidelines when storing fresh shellfish:

1 Keep the shellfish at a temperature of between 2°C and 8°C.
2 Keep shellfish in its packaging until preparation, this is to avoid moisture loss.
3 Ensure that all shellfish remain moist.
4 Molluscs should be kept in a container embedded in ice. The round side of the shell should face downwards to help collect and retain the natural juices.
5 Check regularly to make sure that they are still alive. Reject any dead or dying specimens.

Follow these guidelines when storing cooked shellfish:

1 The shells of cooked shellfish should be intact with no cracks.
2 The shells should not release copious amounts of liquid when shaken.
3 The cooked product should exhibit no signs of discolouration and there should be no odours indicative of spoilage.
4 Freshly cooked prawns and shrimps should be firm to the touch and should be chilled immediately.

# SHELLFISH ALLERGY

Allergy to shellfish is quite common and people who are sensitive can react to a number of different types of shellfish, such as shrimps, prawns, lobsters, crabs, crayfish, oysters, scallops, mussels and clams.

People who are allergic to one type of shellfish often react to others. Shellfish allergy can often cause severe reactions, and some people can react to the vapours from shellfish that is being cooked.

Since November 2005, prepacked food sold in Europe must show clearly on the label if it contains crustaceans including lobster, crab, prawns and langoustines. However, other groups of shellfish, such as molluscs (including mussels, scallops, oysters, and whelks), cephalopods (squid and octopus) or gastropods (snails) do not need to be labelled individually.

When these reactions occur, the cause could be the shellfish themselves, or from associated bacteria, viruses or naturally occurring toxins. It is therefore crucial that people who believe they have a food allergy get confirmatory diagnostic tests done so the right food is avoided in the future. The only treatment for seafood allergies is avoidance of the known food which induces the symptoms.

# UNIVALVE SHELLFISH

## Whelks

Whelks resemble pointed snails when fresh, and are usually sold already cooked and without their shell. After scrubbing only keep the good whelks and discard any damaged or dead ones. They can also be purged by placing into a large bowl with clean water and some polenta and then left to soak overnight in a refrigerator. (The shellfish will eat the polenta and expel any sand and grit.) These can be served as part of a seafood platter with other shellfish or cooked in the shell by simmering in salted water or a court bouillon. They can be used to garnish soups or fish stews.

## Winkles

Winkles are known as 'black sea snails' and are served as appetisers. They are usually sold cooked without their shells. They should be steamed in white wine for a couple of minutes and then served simply seasoned with fresh parsley. If purchased in shells the meat is easily removed with a pin from the shells once cooked and should taste salty, slightly chewy and juicy.

# BIVALVE SHELLFISH

If these crustaceans are purchased live, ensure the shells are intact and not broken. Remove any mud and grit by washing thoroughly in fresh water several times. Discard any dead bivalves before cooking by tapping the open shells with your finger until they close: if they stay open they should be discarded at once. There is a connective hair-like substance which hangs out of many shells, especially mussels, which is called the **beard**. This also should be removed prior to cooking, along with any barnacles, by scraping with the back of a knife and then rinsing in cold water. Place the cleaned mussels in a bowl of cold water then remove any that float to the top. After cooking, any shells that remain closed should also be discarded.

# Clams

There are two main types of clams: hard shell (such as carpet shell and venus) and soft shell (razor shell clams). Clams are well known for the classical dish clam chowder, associated mainly with the east coast of America. All clams should be well scrubbed and they may need to be purged too. They can be opened and eaten raw (if very fresh) or cooked by boiling or steaming.

# Cockles

Cockles are not readily available in fishmongers and usually require a little notice when ordering from the suppliers. They are a salty and juicy shellfish which can often be found preserved in vinegar or brine. They have a pink and yellow-beige-coloured shell and are quite uniform in shape and size. Cockles should be purged in the same way as whelks.

# Scallops

Scallops are highly regarded and expensive. The shells are rounded and fan-shaped; varying in size from the smaller queen scallop (7cm across) to the larger great scallop (up to 18cm across). The edible part is the round whitish muscle and the orange roe (called the coral). The frilly gills and mantle can be used for soup and stocks. Scallops can be opened by separating the shells with a knife. This can be done relatively easily once the basic techniques have been mastered. Because the scallop lives on the sea bed they will have grit and dirt inside the shells and will need to be purged or cleaned thoroughly upon opening.

## Step-by-step preparation of scallops

■ Hold the scallop shell firmly in hand with the flat shell uppermost.

■ Place a thick knife between the shells by the hinge and push up to break the connection.

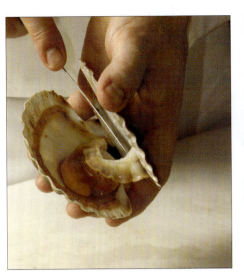 

■ Slide the knife along the inside of the flat shell, remove the flat shell and discard.

■ Work the knife under the skirt (frilly gills) and then under the white and coral to separate from the shell. Take care not to pierce the scallop meat.

■ Discard the skirt or save for making a stock.

■ Separate the white from the coral and gently wash both in clean water, store in a refrigerator until required.

If the scallops are exceptionally fresh, well prepared and in excellent condition they can be used raw for sashimi or simply marinated with an acidic dressing to gently denaturise the flesh.

Scallops can be purchased loose (in their shells) or already shelled and cleaned. The most expensive are diver-caught scallops; these are collected by divers by hand from the sea bed. The other way is by dredging the sea floor with a net, although this can cause damage to the shells.

## Razor Shell Clams

Razor clams are shaped like cut-throat razors. They can be caught by tipping salt onto the sandy shores of a beach: the shells pop out of the ground and are then carefully harvested. Treat in the same way as clams.

## Oysters

There are a variety of oyster species around the globe and therefore they come in a number of shapes and sizes. The best British oysters are known as 'natives' or 'flat'. Other British oysters include rock oysters. Natives are available from September to April, though they are at their best from late October to late February when the sea temperature is colder. Pacific oysters are available all year. Scrub the shells well before opening. To open the shells use an oyster knife because using a normal kitchen knife could be hazardous and may break easily.

# Step-by-step preparation of oysters

■ Hold the oyster in a thick cloth to protect the hand from the sharp edges of the oyster shell.

■ Keeping the oyster flat, use an oyster knife and place the blade between the shells by the hinge and using *gentle* force carefully twist the knife to open the shell.

■ Lift the top shell off and sever the muscle. Discard the top shell.

■ Slide the knife carefully under the oyster to free it. Take care not to cut into the oyster or spill any of the liquid inside the shell. Check for any loose shell and discard.

Any oysters that have an unusual smell should be discarded. Native oysters are best eaten raw as soon as possible after capture. Raw oysters are best served with freshly squeezed lemon or shallot vinaigrette. Cooked rock oysters can be served in chowders and stews.

# Mussels

**VIDEO CLIP**
Preparing mussels for cooking

These molluscs are often seen attached to rocks and wooden structures around the coastline worldwide and have a distinctive oval blue and black-coloured shell. The vibrant orange-coloured fish inside is sweet and salty to taste. Mussels should only be collected from unpolluted waters between September and March; they should be left alone during the summer months. Purchasing smaller or medium-sized mussels will help to ensure that they taste sweet and full of flavour. Approximately 450g should be enough per portion. Mussel beds are situated by estuaries which potentially filters clean water all year round. To prepare mussels it is important that they are scrubbed under cold running water to remove all grit and scrape off any barnacles using a small knife. Any beards should also be removed from the shells.

# CEPHALOPODS

## Squid

Squid is commonly referred to as 'calamari' and varies in size from small – 7cm – to larger ones of about 25cm. Squid is available all year round either fresh or frozen. It freezes very well and preparing squid is relatively straightforward. The ink, found in a small sac from the innards, is used to colour pasta and seafood sauces. There is a transparent flexible cartilage within the squid called the quill, which must be removed. Cooking must be either very quick or slowly braised; otherwise the flesh will become tough.

## Preparation of squid

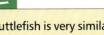

- Pull the head and tentacles away from the body (mantle). The eye and ink sac will come away with the tentacles.
- Cut the edible tentacles from the head, cutting just above the eye. Discard the head.
- Open the tentacles and pull out the beak in the centre (its mouth). Discard it and rinse the tentacles under cold running water.
- Remove the transparent quill from the body by pulling it out.
- Clean any excess membranes from inside the body. Rinse the insides under cold running water.

**CHEF'S TIP**

Cuttlefish is very similar to squid and is prepared in the same manner. It is slightly larger and the ink is much deeper in colour.

**VIDEO CLIP**
Preparing squid for cooking

# CRUSTACEANS

## Crab

There are restrictions to the size of crab that can be sold in the United Kingdom although there are no restrictions on the number, design or size of the traps used to catch them. Live crabs should be handled as little as possible after capture, and the claws may be shed quickly if not killed before cooking. They should be packed, in ventilated boxes, quite close together and preferably with wet seaweed or cloth in the bottom of the box. Live storage is difficult and crabs do not travel well. Where live storage is necessary, they should be tightly packed in baskets in aerated sea water.

Transit time should be as short as possible and preferably overnight, when air temperature is lower.

There are many varieties of crab and many regions throughout the world where crabs are abundant. Europe is well known for the brown crab and the spider crab: in the eastern USA the blue crab is caught. The Dungeness crab is caught on the Pacific coast off the USA.

The soft brown flesh from under the upper shell is strong and full-flavoured, this contrasts with the sweet, delicate white flesh found in the claws and body.

Male crabs often have larger claws and therefore more white flesh. However, females may have 'coral' – a red-coloured roe that is found on the underside of the body.

Brown crab from Europe is available all year, and reaches 20–25cm across with heavy front claws with almost-black pincers. Its shell is a rusty-red or brown colour.

The Atlantic blue crab grows to 20cm but is usually sold smaller. It has a blue-brown shell. When newly moulted these crabs are caught with soft shells and are prepared and shallow or deep fried for eating whole. This crab has plenty of white meat. The meat in the shell is also fine and notably different for its pale grey colour.

The spider crab is popular in France and Spain. It is a sweet-flavoured crab that resembles a large spider and has no large claws. One crab should be sufficient per person.

Purchase crabs that feel heavy for their size and smell fresh whether alive or cooked. If there is a hint of ammonia do not buy. Crabs are best bought alive and cooked fresh. There is approximately 115g of meat per portion; this is about 450g for a whole crab with the shell intact.

To prepare a cooked crab:

- Lay the crab on its back on a chopping board and remove the legs and claws by firmly twisting and pulling from the body. Lift the triangular flap (called the apron) on the underside of the crab, twist it off and discard.
- Hold the belly of the crab by the eyes and pull downwards, the underside will be prised off in one piece. Remove any white meat from this area using a teaspoon.
- Inside you will see the gills (dead man's fingers) and a sac behind the eyes, discard all of these.
- Spoon out the meat from the shell and reserve it to serve with the white meat (keep the brown and white meat separate).
- Crack each leg with poultry shears and using a lobster pick, remove the white meat.
- The inside of the claws can be accessed by cracking the shell with the back of a knife or by using lobster crackers and then carefully peeling the shell away to reveal the white meat. Remove any membrane from the meat.
- Clean the main shell and dry before placing all the reserved meat back into the shell.

## Langoustine (Dublin Bay prawns)

Also known as Norway lobster and scampi, these orange-pink shellfish from the north-east Atlantic and Mediterranean resemble small, slim lobsters. They can be expensive with little meat, but are delicious if freshly caught and cooked. The best specimens can be bought from late spring to late autumn and are cooked in the same way as lobster. Because of their smaller size, they need less cooking. Usually only the tail is sold. In their shells 200g should be enough per portion, however removed from their shells, half this amount will be adequate. They are available frozen all year round.

To prepare a cooked langoustine:

- Pull the heads from the bodies (save for stock).
- Snip underneath the belly of the tail with a pair of scissors, taking great care not to pierce the flesh.
- Remove the legs and peel the shells carefully.
- Make an incision along the back of the tail and remove the dark intestinal vein running along the back.
- Rinse under clean water and pat dry.

## Prawns

One method used for the transportation of prawns is in plastic tubes. It seems that although the tubes are open-ended, the prawn stays inside of its own accord, as though it were hiding on the sea bed. The tubes are put into the hold of a long-range fish trawler and refrigerated sea water is pumped around the hold.

There are many prawn species and they vary in size from 5–18 cm long. King prawns grow even larger at up to 23cm. Shrimps are very small and require boiling before serving whole as an appetiser. Prawns come in many colours, from the familiar common pink prawns to the brown-blue tiger prawns.

Prawns are available all year round, though usually frozen in the UK. Fresh raw prawns are the tastiest. They should be firm and springy with bright shells. If they are limp, soft or have an ammonia smell then discard them. Ensure frozen prawns are properly defrosted before using.

Prawns can be prepared the same as langoustines but do not require the scissor cut to peel as the shells are softer.

**VIDEO CLIP**
Preparing prawns for cooking

# RECIPES

## Cockles with red wine and tomato with toasted ficelle

| INGREDIENTS | 4 PORTIONS | 10 PORTIONS |
|---|---|---|
| Washed and prepared cockles | 1.2kg | 3kg |
| Chopped plum tomatoes | 8 | 20 |
| Chopped red chilli | ½ | 1 |
| Chopped onion | 50g | 200g |
| Chopped garlic | 2 cloves | 4 cloves |
| Red wine | 50ml | 125ml |
| Olive oil | 4tbsp | 10tbsp |
| Ficelle bread | 1 stick | 2½ sticks |
| Fresh chopped parsley | 2tbsp | 4tbsp |
| Fish stock | 100ml | 250ml |
| Lemon juice and zest | 1 | 2 |
| Good-quality salt and white pepper | To taste | To taste |

*The cockles have opened after cooking in the pan*

## Method of work

1 Prepare the cockles by washing and scrubbing them clean. Purge over night in clean salted water in a refrigerator with a little oatmeal added.

2 Using a large saucepan, heat the olive oil, and then add the chopped onion, garlic, finely chopped chilli pepper and sweat without letting them colour for 4 minutes.

3 Add the cockles, chopped plum tomato, red wine, lemon zest and the fish stock.

4 Cover the pan with a tight-fitting lid and cook for 3 minutes until the shells open. Discard any closed shells after cooking.

5 Slice the ficelle bread stick into long slices and toast on both sides to accompany the cockles.

6 Finally add the freshly chopped parsley and lemon juice to the cockles and season well.

7 Serve the cockles in a bowl with the sliced and toasted ficelle.

# Deep-fried clams in lemon crumb with a baby leaf and caper salad

*The deep-fried clams*

| INGREDIENTS | 4 PORTIONS | 10 PORTIONS |
|---|---|---|
| Fresh clams | 12 | 30 |
| Finely grated lemon zest | 2 | 5 |
| Fresh white breadcrumbs | 100g | 250g |
| Flour | 50g | 125g |
| Pasteurised egg | 100ml | 250ml |
| Assorted baby lettuce leaves | 100g | 250g |
| White wine vinegar | 4tbsp | 10tbsp |
| Olive oil | 50ml | 125ml |
| Capers | 8tbsp | 20tbsp |
| Caster sugar | Pinch | Pinch |
| Good-quality salt and white pepper | To taste | To taste |
| Fresh chives | For garnish | For garnish |

## Method of work

1 The fresh clams should be washed and scrubbed well and they may require purging if they are very gritty.

2 Open each clam very carefully using a knife to work in between the top and bottom shells. Twist the knife upwards to open the clam.

3 Carefully slide the knife under the clam to separate it from the shell. Remove any dark membrane from the clam.

4 Mix the white breadcrumbs and finely grated lemon zest together.

5 Pass the raw clams through seasoned flour, egg and breadcrumbs with lemon zest mixed in. Repeat this step again to double-coat the clam for protection against the hot fat when cooking.

6 Prepare the caper dressing by blending the capers with a little olive oil and the caster sugar to taste. Add the white wine vinegar and the rest of the olive oil.

7 Dress the washed baby leaves with the caper dressing and then arrange on the serving plate.

8 Deep fry the clams at 185°C until golden and arrange 3 per portion.

9 Garnish with the fresh chives and spoon any remaining caper dressing around the baby leaves.

# Pernod butter mussels with walnut bread

| INGREDIENTS | 4 PORTIONS | 10 PORTIONS |
|---|---|---|
| Fresh mussels | 2kg | 5kg |
| Chopped shallots | 100g | 300g |
| Chopped garlic | 2 cloves | 5 cloves |
| Fresh chopped flat leaf parsley | 3tbsp | 7tbsp |
| Pernod | 200ml | 550ml |
| Unsalted butter | 200g | 425g |
| Good-quality salt and white pepper | To taste | To taste |
| Walnut bread | 4 large slices | 10 large slices |

## Method of work

1 Scrub the mussels under running cold water to remove any grit. Remove the beards and scrape off any barnacles with a sharp knife.

2 Finely chop the shallots. Purée the garlic and then chop the flat leaf parsley.

3 Sweat the shallots with the garlic in a little of the unsalted butter, add a little cold water at the end and season well.

4 Add the prepared mussels and place a tight-fitting lid on the saucepan, cook for 4 minutes.

5 Pour the Pernod into the pan and ignite to flambé. Allow the alcohol to burn away before removing the mussels and retaining in an oven to keep warm.

6 Stir in the butter to the cooking liquor to make an emulsification and add the chopped parsley. Correct the seasoning and the consistency.

7 Place the mussels into a dish and pour the sauce over; serve with the bread.

### CHEF'S TIP

This dish is quite strong in flavour, so substitute half of the Pernod content for white wine instead if required.

Cook the mussels until they open

Add the Pernod and flambé

Remove the mussels and finish the sauce with the butter

# Linguine of brown shrimps with a chive and mustard sauce

| INGREDIENTS | 4 PORTIONS | 10 PORTIONS |
|---|---|---|
| Fresh or dried linguine pasta | 400g | 1kg |
| Brown shrimps | 300g | 750g |
| Grain mustard | 4tbsp | 10tbsp |
| Fish velouté | 200ml | 500ml |
| Double cream | 50ml | 100ml |
| Finely chopped fresh chives | 3tbsp | 6tbsp |
| Grated Parmesan cheese | 75g | 175g |
| Unsalted butter | 50g | 125g |
| Finely chopped shallots | 2 | 5 |
| Good-quality salt and white pepper | To taste | To taste |

### CHEF'S TIP

Keep leftover prawn, shrimp, crab and lobster shells for making bisques and shellfish stocks. They should be washed and used as quickly as possible.

## Method of work

1. Prepare the shrimps by removing the heads and shells until only the tail remains. Wash in cold water and dry.
2. Melt the butter in a saucepan, add the chopped shallots and sweat without letting them colour.
3. Add the shrimps and cook for 1 minute.
4. Add the fish velouté, mustard and the double cream. Simmer for 2 minutes and season well.
5. Cook the linguine pasta in plenty of boiling salted water for 4 minutes. Drain well and then add to the shrimp sauce.
6. Add the freshly chopped chives.
7. Fold in the Parmesan cheese and serve garnished with chives.

# Brochette of tiger prawns with herb and garlic couscous

| INGREDIENTS | 4 PORTIONS | 10 PORTIONS |
|---|---|---|
| Tiger prawns | 12 | 30 |
| Butter | 100g | 250g |
| Chopped garlic | 2 cloves | 5 cloves |
| Lime juice and zest | 1 | 3 |
| Cous cous | 100 g | 250g |
| Water | 250ml | 550ml |
| Olive oil | 4tbsp | 10tbsp |
| Fresh chopped coriander | 2tbsp | 4tbsp |
| Fresh chopped parsley | 2tbsp | 4tbsp |
| Fresh chopped mint | 2tbsp | 4tbsp |
| Herb oil | 4tbsp | 10tbsp |
| Finely chopped red onion | 50g | 140g |
| Good-quality salt and white pepper | To taste | To taste |

## Method of work

1   Prepare the tiger prawns by peeling off their shells and deveining them by cutting a small incision along the back to expose the dark intestinal vein. Remove the vein with a knife and wash the prawns well under running water. Ensure that heads remain intact.

2   Place three prawns per portion onto a bamboo skewer (for a starter or appetiser portion).

3   Melt the butter and mix with the chopped garlic and lime zest and juice.

4   Brush this over the prawns and leave for 20 minutes to marinate.

5   Bring the water to the boil and pour onto the cous cous with the oil. Cover and leave to stand for 4 minutes.

6   Use a fork to break up the cous cous. Add the freshly chopped herbs, red onion and season well.

7   Shallow fry the prawns quickly on both sides in a little butter until they are tender and change colour to a pinkish-orange.

8   Arrange the cous cous on the serving plate with the prawns on top and some herb-infused oil to garnish.

# Grilled scallops with soy and ginger

| INGREDIENTS | 4 PORTIONS | 10 PORTIONS |
|---|---|---|
| King scallops | 12 | 30 |
| Dark soy sauce | 80ml | 200ml |
| Fresh ginger | 40g | 100g |
| Pak choy | 800g | 2kg |
| Olive oil | 20ml | 50ml |
| Good-quality salt and black pepper | To taste | To taste |

## Method of work

1   Prepare the scallops by holding the scallop shell firmly in your hand with the flat shell uppermost.

2   Place a thick knife between the shells by the hinge and push up to break the connection, remove the flat shell and discard.

3   Work the knife under the skirt (frilly gills) and then under the white and coral to separate from the shell. Take care not to pierce the scallop meat.

4   Discard the skirt or save for making a stock.

5   Separate the white from the coral and gently wash both in clean water, store in a refrigerator until required.

6   Peel and finely chop the ginger and make a paste with the soy sauce.

7   Dip the scallops in the mixture and lightly grill them under a salamander or on a chargrill until golden brown on the presentation side. Adjust seasoning.

8   In a separate pan, slightly wilt the chopped pak choy and season well.

9   Serve the scallops on a bed of pak choy. The remaining marinade can be heated and served as a dipping sauce.

# Prawns en papilotte  *Crevettes en papilotte*

| INGREDIENTS | 4 PORTIONS | 10 PORTIONS |
|---|---|---|
| King prawns | 20 | 50 |
| Carrots cut into julienne | 100g | 275g |
| Leek cut into julienne | 100g | 275g |
| Onion cut into julienne | 100g | 275g |
| Soy sauce | 40ml | 90ml |
| Sweet chilli sauce | 40ml | 90ml |
| Coconut milk | 50ml | 100ml |
| White wine | 50ml | 100ml |
| Good-quality salt and black pepper | To taste | To taste |

*Placing the prawns onto the bed of julienne vegetables on the foil*

## Method of work

1  Preheat an oven to 190°C.

2  Slice the carrots, onions and leeks into a julienne, sweat them down in a pan with a little vegetable oil and season well. Leave to one side.

3  Take a sheet of aluminium foil and cut into 10 × 10cm squares, for one portion. Repeat this process depending on the number of portions needed.

4  Brush some butter on top of the foil, then add the cooked vegetables, followed by the prawns.

5  Add a splash of soy sauce, sweet chilli sauce, white wine and coconut milk. Season well and then fold over the foil and crimp the open edges to make a secure seal.

6  Place the papilotte into the preheated oven for 6 minutes.

7  Serve by placing the parcels onto serving plates and allowing each guest to open their own parcel.

### CHEF'S TIP

Any combination of fish and shellfish can be added to this recipe (such as salmon and squid combined with the prawns) and served as a main course or starter. The recipe explains how to cook shellfish in a parcel. The traditional **en papilotte** method makes use of baking parchment; however, tin foil and banana leaves work well too.

# Prawn and crab cakes with mango salsa

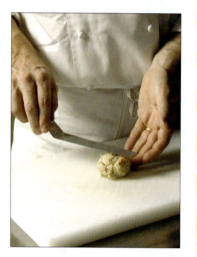

*Shaping the cakes with a palette knife*

| INGREDIENTS | 4 PORTIONS | 10 PORTIONS |
|---|---|---|
| Cooked prawns | 280g | 700g |
| White crab meat | 280g | 700g |
| Mayonnaise | 2tbsp | 5tbsp |
| White breadcrumbs | 200g | 450g |
| Fresh chopped dill | 3tbsp | 6tbsp |
| Grain mustard | 1tbsp | 2tbsp |
| Finely chopped shallots | 50g | 100g |
| Flour | 60g | 160g |
| Pasteurised egg | 75g | 200g |
| Finely chopped red chilli | ½ | 1 |
| Lime juice and zest | 1 lime | 3 limes |
| Diced mango | ½ mango | 1½ mangoes |
| Shishu cress | ½ punnet | 1½ punnets |
| Rocket leaves | 50g | 125g |
| Tomato concassé | 80g | 200g |
| Fresh chopped coriander | 4tbsp | 8tbsp |
| White wine vinegar | 20ml | 45ml |
| Butter | 50g | 125g |
| Olive oil | 20ml | 45ml |
| Good-quality salt and white pepper | To taste | To taste |

## CHEF'S TIP

An alternative to using white breadcrumbs is polenta, cornmeal or wholemeal breadcrumbs. Care must be taken when shallow frying that the core temperature is sufficiently high. This is the temperature in the centre of the item being cooked. To test the core temperature, a temperature probe is inserted into the centre. The electronic reading then displays the temperature in the centre of the food, telling you if the item has reached a safe temperature to kill bacteria, making the food safe to eat.

## Method of work

1 Mix the cooked prawns, white crab meat, half of the breadcrumbs, the chopped shallots, mayonnaise, grain mustard and freshly chopped dill together in a bowl. Season well and cover with cling film before placing into a refrigerator to chill for 30 minutes.

2 Divide the mix equally with two balls per portion.

3 Flatten each ball and use a palette knife to form discs of approximately 5cm in diameter and 1.5cm thick.

4 Pass through seasoned flour and then into the pasteurised egg before coating in breadcrumbs and placing onto a tray. Cover with cling film and chill in a refrigerator.

5 Combine the chilli, lime, mango, tomato concassé and fresh coriander with the vinegar and oil.

6 Melt some butter and a little oil in a shallow pan. Shallow-fry the cakes until golden and heated through.

7 Serve the rocket, cress and salsa tossed together and arrange on a serving plate before resting the prawn and crab cakes on top.

# Tempura of crayfish tails with basil mayonnaise

| INGREDIENTS | 4 PORTIONS | 10 PORTIONS |
|---|---|---|
| Prepared and cooked crayfish tails | 28 | 40 |
| Tempura flour (see chef's tip) | 200g | 350g |
| Iced water | 75g | 110g |
| Mayonnaise | 100g | 250g |
| Chiffonade of fresh basil | 2tbsp | 4tbsp |
| Sea salt | Pinch | Pinch |
| Roasted red peppers | ¼ of a pepper | ½ of a pepper |
| Red chard | 50g | 125g |
| White pepper | To taste | To taste |

## CHEF'S TIP

To prepare a tempura flour combine the following ingredients together, sieve and store in an airtight container:

- 75g cornflour
- 375g soft flour
- 2tsp baking powder
- 1tsp sea salt

## Method of work

1 Preheat the deep fryer to 190°C.
2 Prepare the cooked crayfish tails by breaking off the head and gently squeezing the tail to break the shell. Remove the tail by pulling off the sides of the shell. Devein with a sharp knife as for preparing prawns.
3 Mix together the chopped fresh basil and the mayonnaise. Season to taste and reserve to one side for service.
4 Mix the tempura flour ingredients together and sieve once. Combine the appropriate amounts with the ice water to form a batter (it should be slightly thinner than a usual batter).
5 Season and lightly flour the crayfish and pass through the tempura batter.
6 Deep fry for at least 2 minutes until a light golden colour has been achieved and there is a crisp appearance.
7 Roast, peel, deseed and cut the red pepper into julienne.
8 Mix with the chard and arrange on the service plate.
9 Place the crayfish on the plate and sprinkle with the sea salt. Serve with the basil mayonnaise.

Adding the iced water to the tempura flour

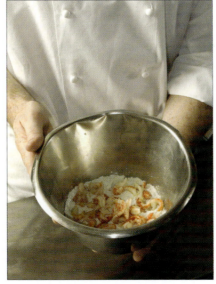
Lightly flouring the crayfish tails

Passing the crayfish tails in the tempura batter

# Oyster tempura on a shaved fennel and tarragon carrot purée

| INGREDIENTS | 4 PORTIONS | 10 PORTIONS |
|---|---|---|
| Tempura flour (see recipe on p. 285) | 200g | 350g |
| Good-quality salt and white pepper | To taste | To taste |
| Iced water | 75g | 110g |
| Olive oil | 40ml | 100ml |
| Fresh fennel | 1 head | 3 heads |
| Fresh tarragon | 1 small bunch | 3 small bunches |
| Carrots | 3 large | 7 large |
| Unsalted butter | 50g | 125g |
| Double cream | 100ml | 250ml |
| Live oysters | 4 (starter) 12 (main) | 10 (starter) 30 (main) |

## CHEF'S TIP

The fennel needs to be finely sliced so that the aniseed flavour becomes more subtle. Oysters are always calculated by number and will vary from 5–6 per portion for a starter and 10–12 per portion for a main course.

## Method of work

1  Preheat a deep fryer to 190°C.

2  Make the tempura batter as in the previous recipe; keep it refrigerated until required.

3  Slice the fennel very finely on a mandoline.

4  Heat the olive oil in a saucepan and add the shaved fennel. Sweat for 5 minutes without letting it colour, check the seasoning and reserve to one side.

5  Peel, wash and cut the carrot into even-sized pieces and cook in boiling salted water.

6  Purée the cooked carrot and add chopped tarragon, double cream and season well.

7  Prepare the oysters by removing them from their shells. Boil the shells for 30 minutes, leave to dry for a later use.

8  Coat the oyster in seasoned flour and pass through the tempura batter.

9  Fry in the deep fat fryer for 3 minutes until the tempura batter has turned a crisp texture.

10  Place the fennel and a small amount of the carrot purée in each cleaned shell with the oyster resting on top.

# Assessment of knowledge and understanding

You have now learned about the use of the different categories of fish and shellfish and how to produce a variety of dishes utilising a range of commodities, preparation and cooking techniques.

To test your level of knowledge and understanding, answer the following short questions. These will help to prepare you for your summative (final) assessment.

1 List two types of oysters.

i) _____

ii) _____

2 Explain the difference between crustaceans and molluscs.

_____

_____

3 List two members of the cephalopod family.

i) _____

ii) _____

4 List two methods of ensuring that mussels are fresh and alive during storage.

i)

ii)

5 State how mussels are prepared before cooking.

_____

_____

6 Explain how you could purge a clam of grit.

_____

_____

7 List three methods of cooking shellfish.

i) _____  ii) _____

iii) _____

8 At what time of year should you refrain from eating raw native oysters?

_____

_____

9 Explain why shellfish is not recommended for hospital patients.

_____

_____

# CHEF'S PROFILE

**Name: STEVEN MUNKLEY**

**Position:** Executive Chef, Royal Garden Hotel

**Main responsibilities:**

1. Total food production and Back of House Service
2. Management for the Hotel
   120 Seat A la Carte Restaurant
   100 Seat 24 Hour Lounge and Bar Restaurant
3. Banqueting facilities to 300 covers plus delegate boardrooms
4. Room Service for the 603 Bedrooms
5. Staff Cafeteria for 300 Personnel
6. Brigade of 20 Chefs, 20 Stewards, 2 Cafeteria Staff and 2 Storepersons

**Training:** City & Guilds 705, Credit and Distinction; 706/1/2/3, Credit and Distinction; 707/1/3, Distinction and Distinction; College Diploma Trainers Certificate, Distinction

**Key strengths as a chef:**

1. Good man management skills at all levels, actively communicating, training and counselling
2. Experienced problem-solving skills throughout the Hotel
3. Ability to organise and prioritize work load for myself and team effectively
4. Setting and managing of procedures to attain consistent high quality products
5. Never losing sight of my love for experimenting with dishes, creating items that can be served for 2 persons or 500 persons to the highest standards
6. Production of creative, balanced, cost effective customer profile related menus

# Ravioli of halibut with shiitake mushrooms, shellfish velouté and pink ginger foam

### Coriander pasta

| INGREDIENTS | 10 PORTIONS |
|---|---|
| Flour | 250g |
| Whole egg | 1 |
| Yolks | 2 |
| Olive oil | 10ml |
| Coriander chlorophyll | 60g |
| Salt | |

### Ravioli filling

| INGREDIENTS | 10 PORTIONS |
|---|---|
| Halibut suprêmes | 10 × 80g |
| Shiitaki mushrooms sliced and sautéed | 100g |

### Garnish

| INGREDIENTS | 10 PORTIONS |
|---|---|
| Pak choy or bok choy or choy sum | 500g |
| Shredded pickled pink ginger | 25g |
| Shellfish bisque | 500ml |
| Fish cream sauce [fish stock reduction with cream] | 150ml |
| White wine | 25ml |
| Pink pickled ginger | 10g |
| Oysters | 10 each |
| Saffron mustard batter | 100ml |

## Method of work

1 Make the pasta in the normal manner.

2 Cut the halibut suprême in half, season and sandwich with the mushrooms.

3 Dry the fish on muslin before encasing it in pasta. To do this roll out the pasta to no. 1 on the roller. Place one piece of pasta on the table then lay fish spread out on top of it. Brush around the fish with eggwash, then cover with the second piece. Cut out with a large round cutter and shape as shown in the picture.

4 Blanch the green vegetable whole with the core attached and refresh. Drain well and dry on muslin.

5 To finish the pink ginger sauce, place the fish sauce on the stove to heat with wine and ginger, allow to infuse for gently for 15 minutes then liquidise with a hand blender and strain through a fine chinois. For service keep this in a soda siphon in a water bath.

6 Reheat the shellfish sauce and reserve for service.

7 Shape the green vegetable in to a circular disc and reheat in a flat pan in a little water, butter, seasoning and the shredded pink ginger.

8 Cook the ravioli in boiling salted water with a little oil for 8 minutes.

9 Dip the oysters in flour then the saffron batter and deep fry.

10 To serve place the green vegetables in the centre of a plate, drain the ravioli and place on top. Drizzle the shellfish bisque around the outside, place the oyster beignet on top and foam with the ginger sauce.

### Recipe for saffron mustard batter

| INGREDIENTS | 100 OYSTER BEIGNETS |
|---|---|
| Plain flour | 1.2kg |
| Cornflour | 525g |
| Baking powder | 150g |
| Iced water | 1.7l |
| Seasoning | |
| Grain mustard | 100g |

## Method of work

1 Mix all dry ingredients together, then slowly whisk in the water.

2 Now add the mustard and leave to ferment for 2 hours before using.

### Coriander chlorophyll

To make the chlorophyll, blend a bunch of fresh coriander leaves with a little water until as fine as possible. Pass the liquor through a fine strainer and place on the side of the stove to heat but not boil. The residue that comes to the top is skimmed of and this is the chlorophyll.

# 10
# Poultry

## LEARNING OBJECTIVES

At the end of this chapter you will be able to:

- Identify each type of poultry
- Prepare basic poultry dishes
- State the quality points of fresh poultry
- Prepare each type of poultry for cooking
- Be competent at cooking poultry for basic dishes

## INTRODUCTION

When we refer to poultry we describe birds specifically reared for the table. They include chicken, guinea fowl, turkey, goose and duck.

# Chicken

**VIDEO CLIP**
Smithfield poultry

Chicken is the world's most popular meat and until the mid twentieth century it was considered to be a luxury meat, on a par with sirloin steak both in terms of quality and cost. This came to an end when intensive rearing methods were developed. Today battery-reared broilers (the industry term for a chicken reared specifically for the table) are the most economical and versatile of all products used in the professional kitchen.

In the UK more than 98 per cent of chickens are battery reared. Because of intensive husbandry, the birds are bred to achieve slaughter weight at 6 weeks, are rather tasteless and have a tough texture. For this reason, modern chefs impose flavours upon them.

Free range and especially organic chickens are allowed to forage in the open and have space to develop muscle and a stronger bone structure. They are usually slow-growing breeds that can take around 20 weeks to reach slaughter weight. There are several labelling systems in use for these birds for example soil association, little red tractor. One British company has adopted a system of labelling similar to the French *Label Rouge*. The name is 'label Anglaise', a producer that uses older breeds and free range/organic methods of rearing. The label is featured on menus and assures the guests that the chicken has been well reared and is flavourful.

Corn-fed chickens are fed on a diet of either corn or a proportion of corn. This does not guarantee any kind of quality assurance. The distinctive yellow colouring of the skin is gained by the introduction of a yellow dye into the feed and not by the corn itself. The flavour may sometimes be only marginally better than that of a broiler.

## QUALITY POINTS

When buying chickens we should be able to identify the quality points associated with them:

- Clear skin with no blemishes (the colour varies from breed to breed, But the most common battery reared breeds, the hybrids, Ross and Cobb have a pale creamy colour

- Flesh should be firm and pliable

- Not too much fat. Check the abdominal cavity for excess

- No bruising, blood clots, ammonia sores on the legs or cuts

- The breastbone should be pliable (this is for younger birds that are destined to be grilled, roasted or sautéed)

Grades of poultry. Left to right – battery chicken, free range, corn-fed.

Types of chicken

Turkey

## PURCHASE SPECIFICATIONS

■ For the modern chef it is important to be able to tell your supplier exactly what you require from them. If a supplier has an understanding of your requirements, they will be only too happy to oblige. Constant dialogue between the chef or the Garde-manger and the poultry supplier leads to a more harmonious relationship.

Chicken weight specification

| TYPE | AVERAGE WEIGHT |
| --- | --- |
| Poussin | 250–400g |
| Spring chicken | 1–1.25kg |
| Chicken | 1–2kg |
| Boiling fowl | 2–4kg |
| Capon (desexed cockerels) | 2–4kg |

## Turkey

The Aztecs and Mexicans domesticated the turkey and it was introduced to Europe by the Spanish, becoming popular because of its delicate flavour. The term 'turkey' is said to have come from the belief that the Spanish imported them from Turkey. The Spanish referred to them as 'Indian chickens' because even though they were in Mexico they believed they were still in the West Indies.

When the colonists settled in America they relied on turkeys to stave off famine, and the turkey is still the festive bird used at Thanksgiving. Turkeys are mainly battery farmed, but it is well worthwhile sourcing and using organic and free range birds should budgets permit.

Turkey is available in a vast array of weights from 4–15kg depending on requirements. In percentage terms, the larger the bird, the greater the yield.

## QUALITY POINTS

■ Cock birds have a tendency to be drier and tougher than hens

■ Bronze birds can have residual dark feather stubs; these can be removed with duck tweezers

■ The flesh should be dry to the touch without excess blemishes

■ If the windpipe is still intact, it should be pliable and not rigid

■ The breast should be plump in domesticated birds and slightly leaner in the rarer wild variety

# Duck

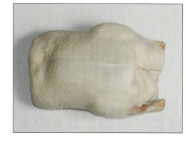

Duck is a web-footed waterfowl, originally domesticated by the Chinese about 2000 years ago. It is highly appreciated in Europe for its rich moist meat. Although intensive farming produces 20 million, it is a type of meat that can still be **palatable** and requires less intervention by the chef to make an acceptable meal. It is worth noting that the type and breed of duck should be taken into account when purchasing for specific reasons, e.g. Barbary duck yield excellent suprême portions whilst Aylesbury are ideal for roasting.

## QUALITY POINTS

When buying duck, check that the birds are:

- Pale skinned (except with wild varieties, see game section)
- Fresh pleasant smell
- Moist but not sticky
- Free from bruises, feathers and blemishes

**Breeds**

- Aylesbury, a small bird with white feathers and delicate flesh
- Gressingham, a cross between a domesticated duck and a mallard, a highly prized breed with a low fat content and rich flesh
- Norfolk, from the county of Norfolk, a domesticated fowl with similar attributes to Aylesbury
- Barbary, firm, lean flesh with a stronger flavour
- Nantes, small and slightly fatty with delicate flesh

# Guinea Fowl

Originally from West Africa, guinea fowl has been raised for the table for many centuries. It is an excellent alternative to battery-farmed chicken in that the flesh is comparable to organic free range chickens. It can have a tendency to be dry so care must be taken when cooking this bird. All recipes that apply to chicken also apply to guinea fowl.

# Goose

This traditional festive bird fell out of favour when turkey became popular, mainly because it has resisted intensive rearing. This makes the cost high in comparison to other poultry.

Goose has a rich dark flesh with a copious covering of fat which means that it will very rarely dry out during cooking. Birds can weigh anything from 2.5–12kg, depending on whether they were used for the production of foie gras or not. Goose should have the same quality points as duck and when not in season can be purchased frozen.

During this chapter, various techniques for the preparation of poultry will be demonstrated. It should be noted that the structure of poultry birds is very similar and the techniques used can be transferred between each type.

# KEY PREPARATION TECHNIQUES FOR POULTRY

## Step-by-step preparation of chicken for sauté

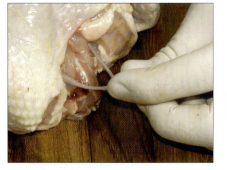

*Remove wishbone*

*Remove the wing by cutting around the bone just away from the breast*

*Remove the legs by cutting through the skin between the leg and the breast*

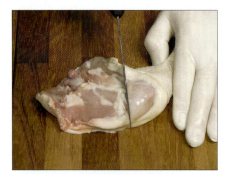

*Cut the leg in half at the kneejoint*

*The thigh and the drumstick*

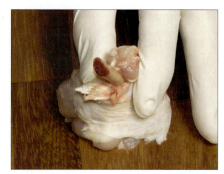

*Remove the knuckles from the drumstick*

*Twist the sinews into the drumstick to form a neat compact shape*

*Remove the petit suprême by cutting 2–3cm on either side of the breast, straight down and leaving the wing bone on the suprême*

*The petit suprême removed*

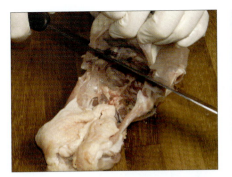

Remove the breast by cutting through the rib cage just below the breast

Dissect the breast in half at the highest point of the breast bone

Chicken prepared for sauté

# Step-by-step preparation of chicken suprême for Kiev

Remove the fillet

Remove bone from the suprême

Cut an incision in the suprême

Open it out

Place between two layers of plastic with the fillet and gently bat out

Carefully place the butter down the centre of the suprême

Fold over the meat to contain the butter

# Step-by-step preparation of chicken for roasting

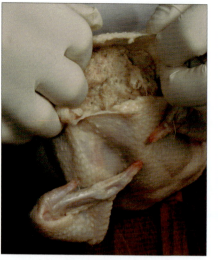

*Remove the wishbone and add the stuffing if required*

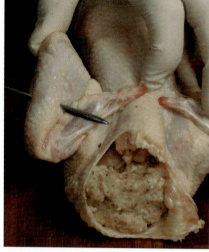

*Truss the chicken by threading a trussing needle with string and pulling it through the wings after they have been pushed behind the back*

*Thread the needle through the skin flap of the neck to seal in the stuffing*

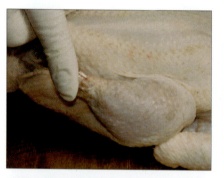

*Push the legs back in towards the breast*

*Push the needle through the legs*

*Tie off with a firm knot*

*Secure the legs by pushing the needle through the bird at the bottom of the thighs*

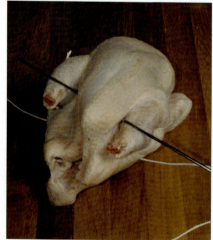

*Bring the needle over the drumsticks and below the breast*

*Tie off just tight enough to keep the legs in place*

 **VIDEO CLIP**
Prepare and tie turkey for roasting

 **VIDEO CLIP**
Prepare and tie a turkey breast for roasting

# RECIPES

## Chicken chasseur

| INGREDIENTS | 4 PORTIONS | 12 PORTIONS |
|---|---|---|
| Chicken (1.3–1.6kg) | 1 | 3 |
| Shallots | 100g | 300g |
| Tomato concassé | 200g | 600g |
| Button mushrooms | 200g | 600g |
| Demi glace | 200ml | 600ml |
| Oil or butter | | |
| White wine | 100ml | 300ml |
| Chopped tarragon | 1tsp | 1tbs |
| Heart-shaped croûtons (see recipe on p. 376) | 4 | 12 |
| Good-quality salt and white pepper | To taste | To taste |

### HEALTH & SAFETY

Be sure to keep your hand flat on the back of the knife to prevent cuts.

### CHEF'S TIP

Use a sharp heavy knife to remove the knuckle from the leg. This minimises bone splinters.

### VIDEO CLIP
Chicken chasseur

### Method of work

1 Melt the butter in a sauté pan.
2 Season and add the chicken in a sequence that takes into account the density of the flesh e.g. thighs first then drumsticks, breast, suprême and finally the carcass.
3 Sauté until completely cooked and the meat juices run clear.
4 Remove from the pan and keep hot.
5 Add the shallots and the sliced mushrooms and allow to cook.
6 Add the wine and reduce by half.
7 Add the tomato concassé and demi glace.
8 Correct the seasoning and consistency and serve on a plate or service dish, garnished with heart-shaped croûtons.

## Chicken sauté with onions

| INGREDIENTS | 4 PORTIONS | 12 PORTIONS |
|---|---|---|
| Chickens cut for sauté (1.3–1.6kg) | 1 | 3 |
| Sautéed onions | 300g | 900g |
| Bacon lardons (cooked) | 100g | 300g |
| Jus lie or demi glace | 100ml | 300ml |
| Oil or butter | | |
| Red wine | 100ml | 300ml |
| Good-quality salt and white pepper | To taste | To taste |

*Add the chicken to the pan*

## Method of work

1 Melt the butter in a sauté pan.
2 Add the chicken and sauté until cooked.
3 Remove from the pan and keep hot.
4 Deglaze the pan with the wine and reduce by half before adding the demi glace and bringing back to the boil. Add the onions and lardons to reheat.
5 Correct the seasoning and consistency of the sauce
6 Serve the chicken coated with the sauce.

### CHEF'S TIP

The carcass section of the chicken is used to intensify the sauce's flavour.

# Chicken Fricassée

| INGREDIENTS | 4 PORTIONS | 12 PORTIONS |
| --- | --- | --- |
| Chickens cut for sauté (1.3–1.6kg) | 1 | 3 |
| Button onions, cooked | 80g | 240g |
| Sautéed button mushrooms | 80g | 240g |
| Butter | 60g | 180g |
| Plain flour | 40g | 120g |
| Chicken stock | 500ml | 150m |
| Double cream | 100ml | 300ml |
| Egg yolks | 2 | 6 |
| Oil or butter | | |
| Good-quality salt and white pepper | To taste | To taste |

## Method of work

1 Remove the skin from the chicken pieces.
2 Melt the butter in a sauté pan.
3 Season the chicken sauté the chicken until cooked without colour.
4 Add the flour to make a loose roux.
5 Add the stock, bring to the boil and simmer very gently until cooked.
6 Add the onions and mushrooms.
7 Mix the yolks and cream together, add a little of the sauce to the liaison and then add the liaison back to the sauce. This makes the sauce into a velouté. Do not allow the sauce to reboil.
8 Serve the chicken coated with the sauce and garnished with some chopped parsley.

*Remove the skin from the chicken*

Note: this fricassée can be made using 200g of diced chicken per portion instead of chicken cut for sauté.

# Chicken sauté Hungarian style

| INGREDIENTS | 4 PORTIONS | 12 PORTIONS |
|---|---|---|
| Chickens cut for sauté (1.3–1.6kg) | 1 | 3 |
| Diced onions | 200g | 600g |
| Tomato concassé | 200g | 600g |
| Jus lie or demi glace | 100ml | 300ml |
| Tomato purée | 40g | 120g |
| Sweet paprika | 20g | 60g |
| Soured cream | 80ml | 240ml |
| Potatoes (Maris Bard or Nadine) | 400g | 1.2kg |
| Oil or butter | | |
| Good-quality salt and white pepper | To taste | To taste |

## Method of work

1  Melt the butter in a sauté pan.
2  Season the chicken with the paprika and sauté the chicken until cooked.
3  Meanwhile, turn and steam the potatoes.
4  Remove the chicken from the pan and keep hot, add the onions and tomato concassé and allow to cook.
5  Deglaze the pan with demi glace, and add the tomato purée. Correct the seasoning.
6  Serve the chicken coated with the sauce and garnish with sour cream and steamed potatoes.

**HEALTH & SAFETY**

Replace the cream with yoghurt for a healthier option.

*Dust the chicken with the paprika*

*Shape the potatoes*

*Drizzle sour cream over the chicken*

# Coq au vin *Chicken in red wine*

| INGREDIENTS | 4 PORTIONS | 12 PORTIONS |
|---|---|---|
| Chickens cut for sauté (1.3–1.6kg) | 1 | 3 |
| Button onions, cooked | 80g | 240g |
| Sautéed button mushrooms | 80g | 240g |
| Lardons | 80g | 240g |
| Diced shallots | 40g | 120g |
| Red wine | 250ml | 750ml |
| Heart-shaped croûtons | 4 | 12 |
| Demi glace | 400ml | 120ml |
| Oil or butter | | |
| Good-quality salt and white pepper | To taste | To taste |
| Butter | 60g | 180g |

**CHEF'S TIP**

Coq au vin was traditionally made using cockerels, however hen chickens are now used as much as cocks.

## Method of work

1 Melt the butter or oil in a sauté pan.
2 Season the chicken and sauté until cooked.
3 Remove from the pan and keep hot.
4 Add the shallots and lardons and continue to cook.
5 Add the demi glace, bring to the boil and simmer very gently until cooked. Correct the seasoning.
6 Return the chicken to the pan with the mushrooms and button onions.
7 Serve the chicken coated with the sauce and garnished with the croûtons and chopped parsley.

# Chicken Kiev

| INGREDIENTS | 4 PORTIONS | 10 PORTIONS |
|---|---|---|
| Chicken suprêmes | 4 | 10 |
| Butter | 200g | 500g |
| Lemon juice | ½ lemon | 2 lemons |
| Chopped parsley | 1tsp | 1tbs |
| Crushed garlic | 2 cloves | 5 cloves |
| Good-quality salt and black pepper | To taste | To taste |
| Flour | | |
| Eggwash | | |
| Breadcrumbs | | |

## Method of work

*Pané the chicken*

1 Beat the butter, lemon juice, parsley and garlic to form a smooth paste. Put to one side.
2 See p. 243 for the step-by-step guide for preparing chicken suprêmes for Kiev.
3 Pass through seasoned flour, eggwash and breadcrumbs and allow to set in a refrigerator for at least 30 minutes.
4 Deep of shallow fry until golden brown and with a core temperature of 75°C.
5 Place onto clean kitchen paper to drain from excess fat and then serve.

# Chicken Maryland

*Check the core temperature*

| INGREDIENTS | 4 PORTIONS | 10 PORTIONS |
|---|---|---|
| Chicken suprêmes (skinless) | 4 | 10 |
| Bacon rashers | 4 | 10 |
| Bananas | 2 | 5 |
| Small tomatoes | 4 | 10 |
| Tinned sweetcorn niblets | 100g | 250g |
| Flour | 160g | 400g |
| Egg | 1 | 2–3 |
| Water | 200ml | 500ml |
| Plum tomato coulis (recipe on p. 126) | | |
| Flour eggwash and breadcrumbs | | |
| Good-quality salt and mill pepper | To taste | To taste |

## Method of work

1 Pass the chicken through seasoned flour, eggwash and breadcrumbs and place in a refrigerator until required.
2 Prepare the tomatoes for grilling by cutting a cross in the top of each one and removing the core. Place on an oiled baking sheet.
3 Make a light batter with the eggs, milk and seasoned flour. Add the sweetcorn and put to rest in the refrigerator.
4 Shallow fry the chicken until golden brown and with a core temperature of 75°C.
5 Meanwhile grill the tomatoes and bacon.
6 Heat some oil on a griddle plate or a thick-bottomed pan; divide the pancake batter and fry the corn fritters (galette) until golden brown on both sides.
7 Heat another pan and fry the halved bananas until heated through.
8 Arrange all the items on a plate and serve with a cordon of tomato coulis.

> ### 🄻 CHEF'S TIP
>
> There are as many variations to this dish as there are homes in Maryland USA. Some recipes spice up the breadcrumbs, some use batter or plain flour to coat the chicken. Each kitchen and chef will have their own variation.

# Poached chicken duxelle

| INGREDIENTS | 4 PORTIONS | 10 PORTIONS |
|---|---|---|
| Chicken suprêmes (skinless) | 4 | 10 |
| Diced shallots | 100g | 250g |
| Button mushrooms | 200g | 500g |
| Butter | 20g | 100g |
| Dry white wine | 50ml | 125ml |
| Chicken stock | 100ml | 250ml |
| Suprême sauce (see recipe on p. 117) | 100ml | 250ml |
| Good-quality salt and ground white pepper | To taste | To taste |

## Method of work

1  Finely dice the shallots and mushrooms.
2  Cook in the butter until brown and the moisture has evaporated.
3  Add half the wine and continue to cook until it has evaporated. Season and allow to cool. This is the basic preparation called duxelle.
4  Remove the fillet from the suprême and bat out until thin but not broken.
5  Make an incision in the suprême. Stuff with the duxelle and secure with the fillet. Reform to its original shape.
6  Pour the stock and the remainder of the wine into a shallow dish.
7  Place the suprême in the poaching dish.
8  Cover with a lid and shallow poach for 20 minutes.
9  Remove from the poaching liquor and keep warm for service.
Note: only touch the chicken by the bone as the outer layer of the suprême is delicate.
10  Pour the liquor into a heavy hot pan and reduce to a syrupy consistency, add the suprême sauce and strain.
11  Serve the chicken on a plate or service dish carved across the centre.

*Stuff the suprême with the duxelle*

# Traditional chicken and ham pie

| INGREDIENTS | 4 PORTIONS | 10 PORTIONS |
|---|---|---|
| Diced cooked chicken | 600g | 1.5kg |
| Diced cooked ham | 200g | 500g |
| Button mushrooms | 100g | 250g |
| Onions | 100g | 250g |
| Chopped parsley | 1tbs | 2–3tbs |
| Béchamel sauce | 400ml | 1 litre |
| Butter | 40g | 100g |
| Good-quality salt and black pepper | To taste | To taste |
| Puff pastry (see recipe on p. 501) | 500g | 1kg |
| Eggwash | | |

*Decorating the pie*

## Method of work

1 Peel and dice the onions, quarter the mushrooms and sweat in the butter. Allow to cool.
2 Combine the chicken, ham, vegetables, herbs and sauce and place the mixture in a pie dish.
3 Roll the pastry on a floured board to 4–5mm thickness and larger than the pie dish.
4 Cut a strip to go around the edges of the pie dish.
5 Brush the edge of the dish with eggwash and attach the strip.
6 Lay the pastry loosely over the top of the pie dish. Press the edges and remove the excess with a sharp knife.
7 Crimp the edges and make a hole in the centre to allow steam to escape.
8 Decorate the pie with the leftover pastry.
9 Brush well with the eggwash and bake in the oven for 30–40 minutes until the pastry is risen and golden brown.

Note: a core temperature of 83°C must be achieved with reheated food.

### CHEF'S TIP

If the core temperature has not reached 83°C by the time the pastry is cooked, turn the oven temperature down to 130°C and continue to cook until an 83°C core temperature has been achieved.

# Roast chicken English style

| INGREDIENTS | 4 PORTIONS | 12 PORTIONS |
|---|---|---|
| Spring chicken 1.3kg | 1 | 3 |
| Butter | 80g | 240g |
| Onions | 80g | 240g |
| Fresh breadcrumbs | 120g | 360g |
| Chopped parsley | 1tsp | 3tsp |
| Chopped thyme | 1tbs | 3tbs |
| Good-quality salt and black pepper | To taste | To taste |
| Chicken livers | 1 | 3 |
| Chicken giblets | 1 | 3 |
| Carrot, onion, celery, leek | 500g | 1.5kg |
| Chipolata sausages | 4 | 12 |
| Streaky bacon rashers | 4 | 12 |
| Bread sauce (see recipe on p. 122) | 150ml | 450ml |
| Watercress | I bunch | 3 bunches |
| Brown chicken stock | 300ml | 900ml |
| Game chips (see recipe on p. 424) | 40g | 120g |

## Method of work

1  Cut the onion for the stuffing into a fine brunoise and sweat in the butter until cooked.

2  Add to the breadcrumbs along with the parsley and thyme and allow to cool.

3  Crush the livers and add to the stuffing

4  Remove the wishbone from the chicken and place the stuffing in the neck cavity (the crop). See page 296 for step by step guide to preparing chicken for roasting.

5  Chop the vegetables into a rough mirepoix and place them in a roasting pan.

6  Place the chicken on the bed of roots; brush with a little oil and put into an oven at 260°C to caramelise. When this is achieved turn the chicken and caramelise the breast.

7  Turn the heat down to 130°C and continue to cook until a core temperature of 75°C is reached and the juices run clear when the thigh is pierced.

8  Remove from the dish, drain any juices from the cavity and allow the chicken to rest in a warm place (above 63°C).

9  Meanwhile grill the chipolatas and bacon.

10 Place the roasting pan with the chicken juices onto a high heat and begin to cook to a nut-brown colour. The juices should reduce to a thicker consistency.

11 Add the stock and boil rapidly until the pan has been completely deglazed.

12 Strain into a clean pan and remove any fat from the gravy. Reduce to the required quantity and adjust the seasoning.

13 Serve the chicken accompanied by roast gravy, bread sauce, chipolatas, bacon, game chips and watercress.

## CHEF'S TIP

If the stuffing seems dry it can be moistened with some chicken stock.

# Hot and spicy chicken wings

| INGREDIENTS | 4 PORTIONS | 10 PORTIONS |
|---|---|---|
| Chicken wings | 24 | 60 |
| Blackened Cajun seasoning | 20g | 50g |
| Juice and grated zest of lemon | 1 | 2 |
| Good-quality salt | To taste | To taste |
| Oil | 20ml | 50ml |
| Garlic mayonnaise | 80ml | 200ml |

## Method of work

1 Remove the wingtips from the wings and cut in half at the joint.
2 Place the wings in a bowl and pour on the oil and lemon juice and mix until they are coated.
3 Add the spices, lemon zest and season lightly with salt and mix until all the wings have a light dusting. Increase the amount of Cajun spices as necessary.
4 Marinate for 3–4 hours.
5 Grill until thoroughly cooked.
6 Serve accompanied by garlic mayonnaise and a variety of salads.

**HEALTH & SAFETY**

Chicken wings can be quite fatty so use long tongs at the grill to prevent burning from flame bursts.

# Baked suprême of chicken with mozzarella and tomatoes

| INGREDIENTS | 4 PORTIONS | 10 PORTIONS |
|---|---|---|
| Chicken suprêmes | 4 | 10 |
| Mozzarella balls | 2 | 2–3 |
| Vine-ripened tomatoes | 4 | 10 |
| Olive oil | | |
| Fresh basil | 1 bunch | 2 bunches |
| Good-quality salt and black pepper | To taste | To taste |

## Method of work

1 Season and brush the suprêmes with a little oil.
2 Slice the mozzarella and season well with Good-quality salt and white pepper.
3 Slice the tomatoes and season with salt.
4 Cut the basil leaves into a fine julienne and mix with the oil.
5 Coat the suprêmes with the basil.
6 Layer the cheese and the tomatoes on top of the chicken.
7 Bake in an oven set to 180°C until the chicken is cooked and golden in colour. Present on the appropriate service plate.

*Arrange the cheese and tomatoes on the chicken*

# Chicken korma

| INGREDIENTS | 4 PORTIONS | 10 PORTIONS |
|---|---|---|
| Diced chicken | 800g | 2kg |
| Grated ginger | 20g | 100g |
| Thick yoghurt | 120ml | 300ml |
| Onion | 100g | 250g |
| Mild chillies | 2 | 4 |
| Oil | 40ml | 100ml |
| Ground coriander | 10g | 25g |
| Garam masala | 10g | 25g |
| Ground turmeric | 10g | 25g |
| Chicken stock | 120ml | 300ml |
| Creamed coconut | 100g | 250g |
| Ground almonds | 40g | 100g |
| Lemon juice | ½ lemon | 2 lemons |
| Good-quality salt and white pepper | To taste | To taste |

## Method of work

1   Mix the chicken with the ginger and yoghurt and marinate for at least 2 hours.
2   Finely chop the onions, garlic and chillies and sweat with the sliced onions in the oil.
3   Remove from the pan and purée.
4   Add the spices to the pan and cook until the spices release their fragrance.
5   Add the chicken and cook on a low heat for a few minutes.
6   Add the purée and continue to cook for 5–6 minutes.
7   Stir in the stock and coconut milk, season and continue to simmer for 15 minutes.
8   Stir in the almonds and lemon juice and serve.

*Mix the chicken with the marinade*

### CHEF'S TIP

The addition of 5g of sodium bicarbonate to 1kg of chicken helps it to absorb the marinade.

# Chicken Madras

| INGREDIENTS | 4 PORTIONS | 10 PORTIONS |
| --- | --- | --- |
| Diced chicken | 800g | 2kg |
| Oil | 80ml | 100ml |
| Chopped onions | 200g | 500g |
| Chopped garlic | 40g | 100g |
| Dried chillies | 4 | 10 |
| Crushed garlic | 2 cloves | 5 cloves |
| Fresh green chillies | 1 | 3 |
| Chopped beef tomatoes | 200g | 500g |
| Ground cumin | 20g | 50g |
| Ground coriander | 10g | 25g |
| Ground turmeric | 10g | 25g |
| Chicken stock | 200ml | 500ml |
| Garam masala | 10g | 25g |
| Good-quality salt | To taste | To taste |

## Method of work

1 Sweat the onions, garlic and dried chillies in half the oil until the onions are translucent.
2 Heat the remaining oil and fry the chicken, garlic and green chillies until the garlic begins to colour.
3 Add the tomatoes and cook for 2–3 minutes.
4 Add the cumin, coriander, chilli powder and turmeric and simmer for 6–8 minutes.
5 Add the stock and continue to cook for 20 minutes.
6 Stir in the garam masala and serve.

# Ballotine of turkey

| INGREDIENTS | 4 PORTIONS | 10 PORTIONS |
|---|---|---|
| Turkey thighs | 1 × 400g | 4 × 500g |
| Turkey sausagemeat | 100g | 250g |
| Crepinette | ½ sheet | 1 sheet |
| Good-quality salt and white pepper | To taste | To taste |

## Method of work

1 Steam the ballotine until a core temperature of 75°C is reached.
2 Chill and slice.
3 Pan fry and serve with a suitable sauce e.g. Reform, Cumberland, or a jus with cranberries and a selection of vegetables.

*Lightly bat out on the flesh side*

*Lay the sausagemeat along one thigh*

*Roll in crepinette and then plastic film*

**CHEF'S TIP**

This is an excellent method of using turkey legs and getting the optimum number of portions.

*Pan fry the ballotine*

# Escalope of turkey stuffed with a duo of cheeses and served with blackberry and redcurrant sauce

| INGREDIENTS | 4 PORTIONS | 10 PORTIONS |
|---|---|---|
| Turkey escalopes | 4 × 125g | 10 × 125g |
| Gruyère cheese | 4 × 25g slices | 10 × 25g slices |
| St Agur cheese | 4 × 25g slices | 10 × 25g slices |
| Milled white pepper | To taste | To taste |
| Flour | | |
| Eggwash | | |
| Breadcrumbs | | |
| Demi glace (see page 120) | 200ml | 500ml |
| Redcurrant jelly | 1tsp | 1tbs |
| Redcurrants | 50g | 125g |
| Blackberries | 20 | 50 |

**CHEF'S TIP**

The lack of fat in turkey breast can make it very dry on the palate. The use of a barrier such as breadcrumbs helps to keep in the moisture.

**VIDEO CLIP**
Prepare and cook escalope of turkey

## Method of work

1 Pané with the seasoned flour, eggwash and breadcrumbs.

2 Shallow fry the turkey escalope until golden on both sides and thoroughly cooked in the centre. Remove from the pan and leave to rest on some clean kitchen paper in a warm place.

3 Place the berries into a saucepan and slowly heat through to release the juices. Add the redcurrant jelly and heat until it begins to bubble before deglazing the saucepan with the demi glace. Bring to the boil and simmer for 5 minutes before adjusting the consistency and seasoning.

4 Place the escalope on a service plate and serve a cordon of the berry sauce to accompany.

Place the cheeses onto the escalope

Fold and shape the escalope to form a 'D' shape

Quadrillage the escalopes with the back of a knife

# Suprême of turkey wrapped in bacon

| INGREDIENTS | 10 PORTIONS | 10 PORTIONS |
|---|---|---|
| Turkey suprême | 4 × 150g | 10 × 150g |
| Streaky bacon (green) | 8 rashers | 20 rashers |
| Black pepper | To taste | To taste |
| Turkey jus (see recipe on p. 124) | | |

## Method of work

1   Layer the bacon on cling film to the size of the suprême.

2   Wrap the suprême with the bacon and roll in several layers of cling film.

3   Secure each end by twisting and tying if necessary.

4   Steam in a steaming oven or simmer in boiling water for 30 minutes.

5   Remove, cut away the cling film and roast at 150°C for approximately a further 30 minutes until the bacon has browned but not crisped and a core temperature of 75°C has been achieved.

6   Place in a clean pan and cover with plastic film for 10–15 minutes to allow the meat to rest.

7   Carve across the grain and serve accompanied by the jus and traditional roast turkey garnish.

# Roast duckling à l'orange

*Carve the duck*

| INGREDIENTS | 4 PORTIONS | 10 PORTIONS |
|---|---|---|
| Duckling | 1 | 2 |
| Chopped shallots | 80g | 200g |
| Oranges | 3 | 7 |
| Sugar | 20g | 50g |
| Wine vinegar | 20ml | 50ml |
| Demi glace (page 120) | 200ml | 500ml |
| Straw potatoes (page 422) | 80g | 200g |
| Carrot | 80g | 200g |
| Onion | 80g | 200g |
| Celery | 40g | 100g |
| Leek | 80g | 200g |
| Thyme | Sprig | Sprig |
| Parsley stalk | Sprig | Sprig |
| Good-quality salt and white pepper | 4g | 10g |

## Method of work

1 Wash and peel the vegetables, cut into very rough dice and place into a roasting pan.
2 Place the duckling breast side down and roast at 260°C until golden brown, turn over and brown the breast.
3 Lower the temperature to 130°C and continue to cook until the juices run clear when the thigh is pierced.
4 Remove the duck from the roasting pan and allow to rest.
5 Finely dice the shallots and segment the oranges, allowing half an orange per portion.
6 Create a caramel with the sugar and vinegar, add the chopped shallots, juice of the oranges and demi glace. Reboil and correct the consistency and seasoning.
7 Carve the duckling and serve with straw potatoes.

### CHEF'S TIP

An alternative to serving duck with an orange sauce is to serve it with a demi glace based cherry sauce. Replace the oranges with pitted black cherries.

# Pan-fried suprême of duck with sauté potatoes

| INGREDIENTS | 4 PORTIONS | 10 PORTIONS |
|---|---|---|
| Suprême of duck | 4 | 10 |
| Boiled potatoes | 400g | 1kg |
| Red peppers | 1 | 2 |
| Shallots | 1 | 2 |
| Garlic cloves | 1 | 2 |
| Tomato concassé | 100g | 250g |
| Thin demi glace (page 120) | 160ml | 400ml |
| Good-quality salt and black pepper | To taste | To taste |

*Fry the duck skin side down*

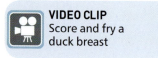

**VIDEO CLIP**
Score and fry a
duck breast

## Method of work

1 Slice the potatoes and finely dice the vegetables.

2 Season the suprêmes and pan fry skin-side down over a gentle heat until the skin has rendered most of its fat and has become golden brown. Turn the suprêmes and continue to cook to the desired degree of doneness.

3 Place in a warm place to rest.

4 Heat the duck fat in the pan and add the potatoes, sauté until golden brown and season.

5 Remove the potatoes with a slotted spoon and drain on dish paper.

6 Add the garlic, peppers and shallots and fry until lightly browned.

7 Add the tomato and demi glace, bring to the boil, add the potatoes and remove from the stove.

8 Drain the duck juices that have formed, slice the suprêmes and present them on top of the potatoes.

# Confit of duck leg

| INGREDIENTS | 4 PORTIONS | 10 PORTIONS |
|---|---|---|
| Duck legs | 4 | 10 |
| Rock salt | 20g | 100g |
| Sugar | 10g | 50g |
| Star anise | 1 | 2 |
| Orange zest | 1 | 2 |
| Thyme | 2 sprigs | 5 sprigs |
| Rosemary | 2 sprigs | 5 sprigs |
| Duck fat (sufficient to cover the legs) | 500g | 1kg |

## Method of work

1 Remove the thighbone from the legs and lightly score the thigh meat.

2 Coat the thighs in salt, then add the remainder of the ingredients and allow to cure in a non-metallic container for at least 24 hours and up to 48 hours.

3 At this stage some brine will have formed. Discard this and pat the legs dry with a clean cloth or paper towel.

4 Place the duck fat in a casserole or crockpot and melt.

5 Add the duck legs together with the aromatic ingredients and very gently simmer in the fat for 3–4 hours, taking care not to let the fat become so hot that the legs begin to fry.

6 Remove from the heat and cool.

7 Store in a cool larder or refrigerator covered with the fat until required (up to 2 months).

8 Serve hot or cold with salad or a pulse vegetable such as Puy lentils.

**HEALTH & SAFETY**

If the confit is to be stored ensure that it is completely covered and that the utensils are thoroughly sterilised.

**CHEF'S TIP**

This method of cookery was traditionally used to preserve the geese that were used for foie gras and it was said that the flavour and texture of a confit took 6 months to mature.

# Assessment of knowledge and understanding

You have now learned about the use of different types of poultry and how to produce a variety of poultry dishes utilising an array of commodities and cooking techniques.

To test your level of knowledge and understanding, answer the following short questions. These will help to prepare you for your summative (final) assessment.

**1** Discuss the main difference between battery-reared and free range chickens.

_____

_____

**2** Give three guidelines as to how you can identify a good quality fresh chicken.

i) _____  ii) _____

iii) _____

**3** Explain how you can best retain roast chicken hot for service and at what temperature it should ideally be maintained.

_____

_____

**4** Explain how cross-contamination might occur in the preparation of chicken.

_____

_____

**5** Give one example of how you are able to tell if chicken is cooked through.

_____

_____

**6** State the differences between pot roasting and braising.

_____

_____

**7** State why it is important to consider cooking a suprême of duck skin-side down to render excess fat.

_____

_____

# CHEF'S PROFILE

**Name: MARTIN BLUNOS**

**Position:** Chef/Director

**Establishment:** FOODEAZE (Exeter, UK)

**Current job role and main responsibilities:**
1. Development and implementation of all food offerings within the group
2. Training
3. The general overseeing of the operation

**When did you realise that you wanted to pursue a career in the catering and hospitality industry?**
Before leaving school at 16

**Training:** I attended college in Cheltenham and Cambridge, attaining the old 706/1 and 706/2 certificates.

**Experience:** Worked in various establishments in this country and abroad, from hotels to restaurants.

**What do you find rewarding about your job?**
The satisfaction of providing pleasure to people through food.

**What advice would you give to students just beginning their career?**
Be either: the best, a winner or first.

**Who is your mentor or main inspiration?**
Pierre Koffman

**Secrets of a successful chef?**
If in doubt, don't do it!

**Some achievements to date:**
2** Michelin stars and cooking for HRH the Queen.

**Can you give one essential kitchen tip or technique that you use as a chef?**
Listen and be heard.

# Roast chicken with lemon and garlic

| INGREDIENTS | |
|---|---|
| Chicken | 1 × 1.8kg |
| Head garlic | 1 large |
| Lemon | 1 large |
| Sprig thyme | 1 |
| Olive oil | 1tbsp |
| Unsalted butter | 20g |
| Salt | |
| White pepper, coarse crushed | |
| Fresh-squeezed lemon juice | |
| Chopped curly parsley | 1tbsp |

## Method of work

1   Pre-heat oven to 200°C.

2   Remove wishbone from chicken (this will help with carving).

3   Cut head of garlic in half and place in chicken cavity.

4   Cut lemon in half and place in cavity.

5   Put sprig of thyme in cavity of bird.

6   Heat deep roasting tray on stove and add the oil and butter.

7   Season the chicken well with salt and pepper.

8   Sear in tray on all sides to colour until golden.

9   Leave chicken on its breasts and roast in the oven for 30 minutes.

10  Then turn the bird onto its back and roast for a further 25 minutes, basting from time to time with the juices, oil and butter.

11  Remove from the oven and turn bird back onto its breasts and cover loosely with foil. Rest the chicken for at least 20 minutes in a warm place.

12  Carve chicken and set aside.

13  Press garlic and lemon to extract juices then pass all plus cooking liquor into a pan.

14  Boil and adjust seasoning with salt and pepper and a little more fresh-squeezed lemon juice, if needed.

15  Add chopped parsley and pour over the set-aside chicken pieces. Serve.

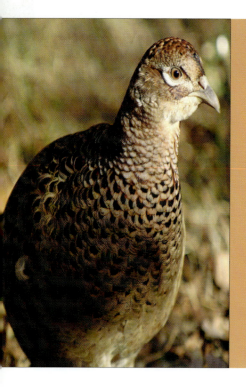

# 11
# Game

## LEARNING OBJECTIVES

The aim of this unit is to enable the candidate to develop skills and implement knowledge in the preparation and cookery principles of basic game dishes. This will also include materials, ingredients and equipment.

At the end of this chapter you will be able to:

- Identify each variety of both feathered and furred game and their finished dish

- Understand the use of relative ingredients in game preparation and cookery

- State the quality points of various game items and dishes

- Prepare and cook each type of game variety

- Identify the storage procedures of all types of game, both raw and cooked

- Have a good knowledge of preparing and cooking a range of basic game-based dishes

# BACKGROUND

Game is one of the only really seasonal products in this country, and in the culinary world it remains very much unchanged in seasonality today.

This is because it is very difficult to rear wild animals in farms to the same standard they develop to naturally in the wild. This gives game items their distinct and intense flavour.

The hunting and gathering of wild animals has always been part of human existence, so to know that this continues today makes game items that little bit more special.

The hunting season starts from 12 August each year in the United Kingdom – it is more commonly known as the 'Glorious Twelfth' because this is the start of the grouse shooting season.

The hunting and shooting season varies depending on the type of game you require. The table below indicates approximate hunting times during the year (for Scotland, England and Wales), when the various types of game are in their correct season.

## FURRED GAME

| SPECIES | SCOTLAND | ENGLAND AND WALES |
|---|---|---|
| Red stag | 1 July – 20 October | 1 August – 30 April |
| Red hinds | 21 October – 15 February | 1 November – 28/29 February |
| Fallow buck | 1 August – 30 April | 1 August – 30 April |
| Fallow doe | 21 October – 15 February | 1 November – 28/29 February |
| Roe buck | 1 April – 20 October | 1 April – 31 October |
| Roe doe | 21 October – 31 March | 1 November – 28/29 February |
| Sika stags | 1 August – 30 April | 1 August – 30 April |
| Sika hinds | 21 October – 15 February | 1 November – 28/29 February |

## GAME BIRDS

| SPECIES | SCOTLAND | ENGLAND AND WALES |
|---|---|---|
| Grouse | 12 August – 10 December | 12 August – 10 December |
| Red grouse | 12 August – 10 December | 12 August – 10 December |
| Snipe | 12 August – 31 January | 12 August – 31 January |
| Partridge | 1 September – 1 February | 1 September – 1 February |
| Wild duck and geese (inland) | 1 September – 31 January | 1 September – 31 January |
| Mallard, teal and widgeon | 1 September – 31 January | 1 September – 31 January |
| Wild duck and geese (below high water mark) | 1 September – 20 February | 1 September – 20 February |
| Woodcock | 1 October – 31 January | 1 October – 31 January |
| Pheasant | 1 October – 1 February | 1 October – 1 February |

### HEALTH & SAFETY

It is good practice to wear disposable gloves where possible when handling raw meat.

### CHEF'S TIP

Wrapping game items in bacon, pork fat or pig's caul will help keep them moist as they are very lean and do not have much, if any, fat on them to aid this.

The only exceptions to this rule, due to their breeding habits, are hares and rabbits which can be hunted all year round.

Furthermore, there are now some very good venison farms, which again enables this type of game to be available all year round. The farming of some game items will help create the same natural environment for the animal to exist, and can have higher quality results in respect of good availability and consistency of meat than wild game.

Having set periods to hunt and understanding the seasonality can help maintain wild game numbers and stop over-hunting, thus reducing the possibility of eliminating certain breeds.

As the season is relatively short for each type of game, this immediately makes these meats more appealing to both chefs and customers alike. Game helps to make menus seem that little bit more interesting. It shows customers that the menu is not just the same all year and that fresh local produce can be a major factor to a strong menu.

As game is generally wild birds and animals, they have very little apparent fat making it a healthy meat to eat, as well as being unique in their flavour. One difficulty with game, however, can be that because they are so active their muscles undertake a lot of work and this may result in tougher-textured meat.

However, the tougher the actual meat the more flavour it has because of the red cells produced in working muscles. This is why venison will have a stronger flavour than beef.

The purpose of **hanging** game is to give the meat time to relax into a less rigid state. When any muscle is consistently used, the fat marbling is less and muscle fibres and connective tissue become tougher. If the animal or bird is killed while it is in action, the meat will be very firm. Hanging the meat gives it time to drain of the blood, making the muscles relax again. The older the animal is, the longer it will have to be hung so that this slow disintegration process can compose the meat to a softer and more edible texture. All game should be hung by its feet with its head to the ground so gravity can naturally cause the blood to flow down towards the head and away from the areas of flesh that will be cooked.

# TYPES OF GAME

## Feathered Game

*Pheasant*  Pheasants are not, as many of us think, a native of the British Isles but were introduced into this country by the Romans, who even left detailed accounts of rearing methods and cooking recipes.

Many cross-breeds have been released by shooting estates in order to produce larger, higher-flying and faster birds. Pheasants live around woodland and open farmland, eating all kinds of vegetable matter and insect life.

Males, called cocks, have rich chestnut, golden-brown and black markings on their body and tail, with a dark green head and red face wattling. Females are smaller and mottled pale brown and black.

*Red-legged partridge*  The French, or red-legged partridge, as it is more commonly known, is not native to the British Isles: its origins are in the semi-arid regions of the Mediterranean. This type of game mainly feed on vegetable matter and are therefore found in many agricultural areas.

Males (cocks) and females (hens) are hard to differentiate as both are grey in colour with a white throat, black and brown flecks and have a red beak and legs. The only real difference is that the males have small spurs and are slightly larger in size.

*Grey-legged partridge*  The grey partridge is native to the UK. Unfortunately its numbers have been in decline due to changes in farming methods and the wide use of pesticides which are killing off insects, that are important in the diet of its chicks.

More recently they have started to make a very slow comeback in some areas, owing to the increasing popularity of organic farming. They thrive best in large areas of open agricultural land and during winter months live in large groups called coveys.

**CHEF'S TIP**

When stuffing game items with a mousse it is easier to use pork or chicken as they have a flavour that can easily be managed much easier with other flavourings.

*Pheasant cock (top) and female (bottom)*

*Grey (top) and red-legged (bottom) partridge*

**CHEF'S TIP**

Using a flavoured butter underneath the skin when cooking feathered game can aid flavour and stop the item from drying out.

**CHEF'S TIP**

If you are finding it hard to pluck feathered game, a useful trick to make this easier is to plunge the bird quickly into boiling water for a few seconds so that the skin loosens. The feathers should then come away without too much effort.

*A snipe*

*Wood pigeon*

It is hard to differentiate between males and females. Both have an orange/red head and a red/brown heart in the middle of a grey breast; the only real difference is that the males are very slightly larger.

*Red grouse* The red grouse is considered the only truly wild game bird found in the UK. The opening of grouse shooting season in the UK is 12 August (referred to as the Glorious Twelfth). The red grouse is a species unique to the British Isles and is generally found in the uplands of the country, particularly the north of England, Scotland and the northern part of Ireland. Other members of the same family are blackcock, ptarmigan and capercaille.

Grouse moors must be carefully managed, with the burning away of old heather to give rise to new growth which is a vital food source. Males are a reddish brown colour and have two scarlet combs which are particularly prominent during springtime courtship. The female, hen bird is duller and without combs. Both sexes have feathered feet.

*Snipe* The snipe is one of Britain's most striking game birds, living in areas of moorland fringe – heather moorland and pine tree areas. It is closely related to the woodcock.

*Quail* Quail live on open grassland and cereal fields where they eat seeds and insects. They live solitary lives, coming together only to breed and migrate through southern Europe. It is illegal to hunt wild quail in Britain due to its declining numbers, but farm-bred birds close to the wild variety are available.

Being a small game bird, the combination of its stocky body and long, pointed wings makes it quite distinctive. It has a brown back streaked and barred with buff, whilst its breast is a warm orange.

*Wood pigeon* The wood pigeon is not considered a game bird but more of a pest: hence they are in season all year round. The wood pigeon is the UK's largest and most common pigeon. Farmers are constantly at war with the wood pigeon as crops such as cabbages, sprouts, peas and grain are a staple part of its diet and they contribute towards destroying these.

Wood pigeons are easily identifiable birds, grey with a patch of white on the neck and wings (making it clearly visible in flight) and a rosy coloured breast.

# BASIC GAME BIRD PREPARATION

## Removal of the Wishbone

Once the birds have been plucked and drawn, the wishbone should be removed to facilitate carving (when cooked) or any type of portioning or preparation. The only exceptions to this rule are snipe and woodcock. These two birds can be cooked whole and with the intestines intact, and require no preparation other than plucking and removal of the gizzard.

The wishbone is situated at the neck end and you will find that it runs either side of the cavity left by the crop and ends up meeting at the top of the breastbone. Place the tip of your knife on the board and use the blade to scrape along the bone on each side.

**VIDEO CLIP**
Removing the wishbone in game birds

**HEALTH & SAFETY**

When working with raw meat always ensure that it is only out of a refrigerator for a short period of time. If not needed straight away, always refrigerate.

1 Expose the bone so that it can be seen. It will be attached in three places: (i) at the tip where it meets the breastbone; (ii and iii) at the base attached to the wing bones either side of the neck.

2 Slip the blade of your knife behind the bone and cut downwards to release the bottom of the wishbone. Repeat this on the other side.

3 Once the bottom of the wishbone has been released, take hold of it, carefully twist it three or four times and pull it away from the tip of the breastbone.

## Removing Legs and Breasts

The legs on most game birds are very sinewy and tough and consequently require longer cooking methods than the breast. They have a very rich gamey flavour because of this and can be very good for enriching game stock to make a strong flavoured jus. The breast, on the other hand, can be cooked quickly and have only one piece of sinew which runs along the inner fillet. This sinew can be removed carefully if you are to pan fry or grill the breast. Before starting, remove the wishbone.

Pull the leg away from the body and cut into the thigh muscle, making sure to cut around the oyster

To remove the breasts, cut along one side of the breast bone from the neck end of the carcass to the vent

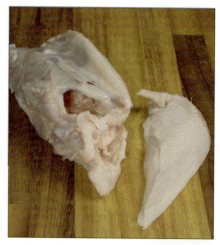

When you get down as far as the wing bone, cut through the joint leaving the bone on the breast. Repeat this process on the other side

Clean the wing bone by scraping the flesh and chopping the end of the bone

The bone and skin may be removed depending on how the breast is to be used

**VIDEO CLIP**
Removing the breast from large game birds

# Trussing Whole Birds for Pot Roasting or Roasting

Trussing is a way of tying game birds and poultry so that they become a tight uniform package. This aids the cooking because the carcass cooks evenly and at the same time. If a bird is not trussed, the legs tend to cook before the breast so that by the time the breast is cooked the legs are dry and inedible. Before you start, remove the wishbone.

Thread a trussing needle with some butcher's twine

If the wing is still intact, push the needle between the bones in the wing just after the first joint from the tip, then push the needle through the fleshy part of the wing bone as in the picture

Push the needle through the carcass under the breast meat and emerging out the other side

Pierce the wing bone on the other side.
Pull the butcher's twine through,
leaving enough line on the other side to
tie off

Pull the legs back and place the needle
under the bone at the first joint

## Splitting and Flattening Small Game Birds for Grilling

Small birds can have their backbones removed and be flattened out –
spatchcocked – so they can be grilled under a salamander or on a barbeque
grill. This works well with partridge, quail, woodcock, snipe and pigeon.
With birds that are not drawn, the intestines can be removed after the
backbone is cut out, the legs turned around and pushed through an incision
cut above the vent. Most game supplied to the catering industry are already
drawn through the vent and because of this you will not be able to secure
the legs as mentioned. Below is a step by step way to prepare birds that have
been already drawn by securing the legs with a skewer.

Before starting, remove the wishbone.

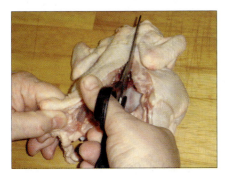

Place the poultry scissors into where
the crop would be. Cut along the
backbone to the vent. Repeat this on
the other side and remove the
backbone

Turn the bird over and using the palm
of your hand flatten the breast, pulling
the legs around to either side of the
breast. Push a skewer under the leg
bone at the first joint. Go through the
breast and out the other side. This will
hold the legs and breast together and
will allow the bird to cook evenly

## Shot Damage

Great care needs to be taken when buying game birds. Because of the way
birds are shot with shotgun cartridges, some damage is inevitable, but be
aware that excessive bruising can ruin the colour of the meat and the flavour
of any sauce made from the bones.

## Small Furred Game

*Wild rabbit* Rabbits originate from the west Mediterranean and were introduced to Britain by the Normans in the twelfth century to provide meat and fur.

They are now widespread throughout Britain and Ireland and in the UK are considered somewhat of a pest as they eat crops and spoil large areas of pasture land meant for farm animals. However, in the rest of Europe the rabbit is a highly prized game species. Rabbits in southern Europe live on rocky mountainous ground and tend to eat wild thyme which greatly flavours their meat.

*Brown hares* These were most probably introduced to the UK, since there is no evidence of their presence in Britain before Roman times and they are now widespread on low ground throughout England.

Brown hares live in very exposed habitats, relying highly on their acute senses and being able to run at speeds of up to 45mph to evade predators. Hares do not use burrows, but instead make small depressions in the ground among long grass, commonly known as a 'form'.

# PREPARATION OF SMALL GROUND GAME

## Rabbits and Hares

In this country we tend to under-use these two wonderful commodities. They are abundant at certain times of year and can be relatively cheap.

The difference between rabbits and hares is obvious, and when they are seen together you are able to see just how much larger a hare is: they can weigh up to 5kg. The following guidelines concentrate on brown hares, but there is another species, blue or white hares, which come from the highlands of Scotland. These are smaller than brown hares and are not as gastronomically prized as their larger cousins.

1  The rabbit can be seen at the top of the bottom left photo and is visibly much smaller than its cousin the hare.

2  The hare has a reddish-brown fur which will become flecked with grey as the animal gets older. The rabbit tends to be a light or in some cases dark grey colour.

3  Another distinguishing feature is the ears. The hares' are large with black points whereas rabbits are smaller and grey.

4  The meat of rabbits and hare is very different. Hare is very red in colour, not unlike venison. It has a rich flavour and, if roasted, should be served under-done because, like venison, it has very little fat and if over-cooked

### CHEF'S TIP

As game can be very strong in flavour, game stocks or liquors can be too pungent when reduced or used. It is best to have a brown chicken or veal stock to hand as the flavour of these is much more subtle and will dilute the game flavour enough for you to be able to achieve the end result you require.

*Rabbit in fur*

*Hare in fur*

*Difference in size between a rabbit (below) and hare (top)*

will dry out. Rabbit has a much lighter colour and flavour and as it is a white meat should not be over-cooked. Unlike the hare it should be just cooked if roasted.

**VIDEO CLIP**
Skinning and preparing a rabbit for dissecting

# JOINTING SMALL GROUND GAME

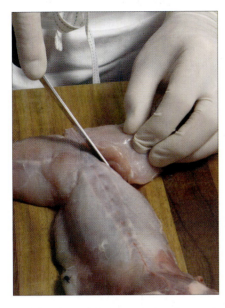

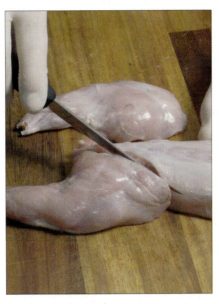

**VIDEO CLIP**
Dissecting a rabbit

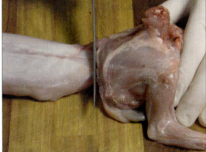

*Feel for the pelvic bone and make a cut around it leaving the pelvis attached to the saddle*

*After cutting around the top side of the leg, turn the carcass over and cut at the same angle on the inside of the leg as shown. Once the meat has been cut away, pop the ball and socket joint to release the leg. When cutting around the hip bone stay as close to the bone as you can. You will end up with a 'V' shape at the bottom of the saddle once both legs are removed*

*Counting from tail to head, find the second rib bone and make a cut between the second and third rib bones outwards, away from the loin, then turn the carcass around and carefully with one sweeping cut, cut through the loin and stop at the backbone. Again do the same on the other side of the carcass and then chop through the backbone*

*After cutting away the first membrane you will see another thicker membrane in place around the loins. To remove this start at one end and using a thin sharp filleting knife place the tip of the knife under the membrane and keeping it as close to its underside as possible. Push the knife up to the top. Once the knife comes out the other end, angle it upwards and cut around the loin and downwards*

*This picture shows five pieces (one leg is not dissected in half). By cutting the saddle into three pieces the end result would be eight pieces or four good portions. The best end, the neck and the head, should all be added to jugged hare as should the blood*

**VIDEO CLIP**
Venison being delivered

# Large Furred Game

*Red deer*  Our largest deer species, red deer can be up to 1.2 metres in height at the shoulder. In Britain most red deer are found on the open moorlands of the Highlands and Islands of Scotland, although scattered populations are also found in places such as north-west England, East Anglia and Exmoor. Red deer lend themselves well to farming.

During the summer, red deer are dark red or brown with a lighter cream underbelly, inner thighs and rump. In winter the pelage changes to a darker brown or grey. Lowland red deer stags grow larger antlers with more points than highland deer, which tend to stop at 12 points and are known as 'royal stags'.

*Fallow deer*  Fallow deer were abundant in prehistoric times but became extinct during the Ice Age. The Norman nobility reintroduced them to Britain around the end of the eleventh century.

Fallow deer have the widest variation of coat colour or pelage of any wild British deer, ranging from very dark black to white.

The summer coat of the common fallow deer is deep chestnut in colour with white spots, which in winter turns to a dark brown and the spots fade. Fallow bucks' antlers are flattened unlike those of the red deer which are pointed.

# HOW TO DEFINE AGE IN GAME

## Feathered Game

There are three main indications as to the age of game birds:

1 *Spurs* – in cock (male) birds the spurs get longer as the bird gets older.
2 *Beaks* – the younger the bird, the more pliable the beak will be.
3 *Feet* – in younger birds with webbed feet the webbing will tear more easily.

**QUALITY POINTS**

- Age is a very important factor to take into account when considering the quality of game and its suitability for certain dishes and cooking methods.

- Older animals are better suited for braising, stewing and boiling, whereas younger animals lend themselves well to roasting, grilling, pan-frying, pot roasting and griddling.

Game birds should not have any broken limbs or any tears or breaks to the skin and should not be slimy to the touch. They should smell strong in flavour but not be pungent or off-putting. The breast should be prominent and have a good shape and along with the legs, should not have darkened patches, bruising or major shot damage. These factors can be harder to spot if the birds are in feather, but all animals should be thoroughly inspected before purchasing or receiving.

With most game birds the meat will be dark in colour, but the meat should not be too dark as this could mean there is excess blood in the meat where it may not have been hung properly or can also indicate bruising. Bear in mind the size of the animal you are using as you will not always get a great yield from certain game birds, so check its meat to bone ratio to see if the bird is of good quality.

# Furred Game: Small

There are three main indications of age in small ground game.

1 *Teeth* – in young rabbits and hares the two front teeth should be quite white, clean and not protrude from the mouth.
2 *Feet* – in rabbits and hares the longer the claws are, the older the animal.
3 *Ears* – the ears on young rabbits and hares will tear more easily.

With rabbits, hare, and other small game animals the main things to consider are that when in fur, they should not have excess blood on the fur, should have no tears or breaks in the fur or skin and again should have no major shoot damage or injuries.

The meat on rabbits should be pale pink in colour with no major bruising or dark blood spots. Unlike game birds or hares rabbits should have a fresh smell and not be tacky to the touch.

# Furred Game: Large

Apart from size, there are three further factors to consider when choosing large game.

1 *Time of year* – bucks or stags (male deer) are at their best just before the 'rut' (breeding season) starts as they have built up fat reserves to give them strength and vitality at this time of year. The same applies to does or hinds (female deer) as at this time of year the pickings will have been rich and allowed them to prepare for the winter. This small amount of fat adds to the quality of the meat. The meat in younger animals that have not bred is of much better quality than older ones, although these younger deer do not have the meat yield of older specimens.

*Shot damage*

2 *Shot damage* – because all game (with the possible exception of some farmed venison) will be killed with a shotgun or rifle, you should look for damage caused by the shot entering the animal. With game shot using a shotgun, the damage can be quite severe if it is shot at close range and these animals should not be accepted. With rifle shot game, look at the entrance and exit wounds: if it has been shot in the wrong place, large areas of the carcass can be lost.

The meat itself should be a deep red in colour, like beef or duck. It should smell strong but not off – there is a noticeable difference between the two. Venison only has about 5 per cent fat compared to other meats that average between 18 to 22 per cent and should therefore not have excess fat or marbling.

## STORAGE OF GAME

Storage of game animals can be an issue for several reasons. As they are classed as 'wild' the rules enforced by Environmental Health state that unless premises are a learning environment or teaching area, feathered and furred game should not enter a food preparation area.

As noted earlier, game animals should be hung from their feet ideally in an ambient temperature and should not be plucked or drawn. Furthermore, they should also be stored away from prepared meat and poultry items and if possible they should have their own designated area or fridge. Prepared game items that have been de-furred and feathered should be stored with the same general hygiene rules of below 5°C, labelled and dated.

**CHEF'S TIP**

As game only has a short season, items such as pigeon, venison, pheasant and rabbit can be hot- or cold-smoked very easily to help preserve them. This of course is as well as cooking and settling them in duck or goose fat as for confits or rillettes.

# RECIPES

## Confit crown of pigeon with vegetables à la grecque

*Draining the ingredients from the cooking liquor*

| INGREDIENTS | 4 PORTIONS | 10 PORTIONS |
|---|---|---|
| Crowns of pigeon | 4 | 10 |
| Water | 250ml | 600ml |
| Olive oil | 50ml | 130ml |
| Lemon, juice | 1 | 2 |
| Bouquet garni | 1 | 1 |
| Button onions | 200g | 500g |
| Celery, peeled and cut into small batons | 150g | 400g |
| Good-quality salt and white pepper | To taste | To taste |

### Method of work

1 Place the all the ingredients, except the onion and celery, into a saucepan and bring up to a very light simmer. Leave for about 1 hour or until the flesh on the pigeon is very tender.

2 Add the vegetables and continue to cook until the vegetables are slightly tender but still have a little bite.

3 Drain and serve along with the cooking liquor.

4 Best served cold but can also be served warm.

### CHEF'S TIP

If serving the dish cold, once the vegetables are cooked in the liquid remove from the heat and allow them to infuse in the cooking liquid until cold then serve along with some of the unstrained liquor.

## Spatchcock pigeon with lemon and basil butter

| INGREDIENTS | 4 PORTIONS | 10 PORTIONS |
|---|---|---|
| Pigeons prepared for spatchcock | 4 | 10 |
| Unsalted butter | 125g | 250g |
| Basil leaves, roughly chopped | 10g | 20g |
| Lemon, fine grated zest and juice | ½ | 1 |
| Good-quality salt and white pepper | To taste | To taste |

### Method of work

1 To make the butter, soften the butter and add the basil, lemon juice and zest.

2 Roll out cling film and mould the butter into a log. Wrap tightly and chill.

3 On a lightly greased and seasoned tray place the pigeons and grill, making sure they are turned during cooking.

4 Once cooked remove any skewers holding the pigeon in place and serve topped with a couple of slices from the butter log.

### CHEF'S TIP

When grilling using wooden skewers always soak them in water first to stop them from burning, which would in turn taint the food.

# Pheasant breast stuffed with black pudding and mushroom farce

*Piping the mousse onto the breast*

| INGREDIENTS | 4 PORTIONS | 10 PORTIONS |
|---|---|---|
| Pheasants whole, broken down into two breasts and using the remaining meat to make a pheasant mousse | 2 | 5 |
| Pheasant mousseline | 200g | 500g |
| Black pudding | 50g | 100g |
| Field mushrooms, finely chopped | 1 | 3 |
| Shallots, chopped | 1 | 3 |
| Crepinette | 4 sheets | 10 sheets |
| Garlic, chopped | 30g | 50g |
| Rosemary, chopped | 1 sprig | 2–3 sprigs |
| Good-quality salt and white pepper | To taste | To taste |

## Method of work

1 Sweat the shallots, garlic, rosemary and mushrooms in a little butter in a saucepan. Once sweated for a few minutes, add the black pudding, cook for a few minutes then allow to cool.

2 Once cooled, mix together with the pheasant mousse.

3 Butterfly open the pheasant breasts and place on a large piece of crepinette. Using a piping bag, pipe the pheasant mousse down the middle of the breasts.

4 Fold the breasts back over and wrap in the crepinette and chill.

5 To cook, in a frying pan with a little oil fry over a medium heat and once lightly coloured to both sides, place in a preheated oven at 180°C to finish cooking through.

6 Serve with appropriate vegetables and a light game jus.

# Pot-roasted saddle of rabbit with lemon thyme

| INGREDIENTS | 4 PORTIONS | 10 PORTIONS |
|---|---|---|
| Prepared saddle of rabbit | 1 | 3 |
| Leek | 50g | 100g |
| Celery | 50g | 100g |
| Onion | 50g | 100g |
| Bouquet garni | 1 | 1 |
| Lemon thyme | 30g | 50g |
| Red wine | 200ml | 400ml |
| Chicken stock | 500ml | 1 litre |
| Butter, cold and cut into small pieces | 250g | 500g |
| Double cream | 100ml | 250ml |
| Good-quality salt and white pepper | To taste | To taste |

## Method of work

1  Season the saddle with salt and pepper. In a thick bottomed ceramic casserole dish gently brown the saddle and then remove, place in a separate dish and keep warm.
2  Add the vegetables, bouquet garni and half of the herbs and sweat gently for a few minutes.
3  Make a bed on the bottom of the pan with the white mirepoix and place the saddle on top followed by the rest of the herbs and half of the wine. Brush the saddle with a little melted butter and cover with a lid.
4  Place the dish into a hot oven at 200°C and cook for approximately 15–20 minutes, basting frequently.
5  Once cooked remove the saddle and any liquid left in the pot and allow to rest for 10 minutes.
6  Place the pot over a high heat and colour the vegetables for a few minutes. Add the rest of the wine, any juices taken earlier and reduce by half.
7  Add the stock and reduce by half. Add the cream and reduce by a further half. Now whisk in the butter until all has amalgamated with the sauce and the sauce has a glossy finish.
8  To serve, carve the loins off the rabbit saddle and slice then cover with a good amount of the sauce.

# Partridge and ale pie

| INGREDIENTS | 4 PORTIONS | 10 PORTIONS |
|---|---|---|
| Diced partridge | 500g | 1.2kg |
| Butter | 50g | 100g |
| Flour | 50g | 100g |
| Dark ale | 500ml | 1.5 litres |
| Button mushrooms | 100g | 500g |
| Button onions | 100g | 500g |
| Garlic | 1–2 cloves | 3–4 cloves |
| Fresh thyme | 1–2 large sprigs | 3–4 large sprigs |
| Puff pastry (see recipe on p. 501) | 250g | 500g |
| Good-quality salt and white pepper | To taste | To taste |

## Method of work

1 Place the diced meat into a suitable and clean plastic container along with the garlic, herbs and ale, and allow to marinate for 24 hours.

2 Roll out the puff pastry on a floured surface to about 5mm thick and long enough to fit over the pie dish. Rest the rolled pastry in the fridge for 20 minutes.

3 Drain the meat from the marinade and in a large frying pan sauté over a high heat until golden all over. Remove from the pan and sauté the mushrooms and onions, also until golden, then remove.

4 In the same pan add the butter and allow to melt before adding the flour. Cook out the flour to a second stage (blond) roux before slowly adding the marinade to the pan to form the cooking sauce for the meat.

5 Combine the cooking sauce and the meat together in the same saucepan and allow to simmer gently on the stove for 20 minutes before transferring into your chosen pie dish. Allow the filling to cool before placing the pastry lid on top, to prevent the pastry sweating and shrinking.

6 Once cool, lay the rested pastry over the dish and use a little eggwash to stick the pastry to the sides. Then eggwash and lightly score the top ensuring you do not pierce the pastry.

7 Bake in a hot oven at 200°C until the filling is piping hot. If the pastry colours too quickly, reduce the temperature to suit.

# Venison bitok Lyonnaise

| INGREDIENTS | 4 PORTIONS | 10 PORTIONS |
|---|---|---|
| Minced venison | 500g | 1.3kg |
| Onion | 2 half dice/half sliced | 5 half dice/half sliced |
| Dried mixed herbs | 40g | 100g |
| Egg yolks | 3 | 6 |
| Dried breadcrumbs | 100g | 300g |
| Butter | 30g | 60g |
| Flour | 30g | 60g |
| Game or beef stock | 500ml | 1 litre |
| Good-quality salt and white pepper | To taste | To taste |

## Method of work

1 To make the burgers mix the mince, herbs, egg yolks, breadcrumbs and diced onion together, then using your hands and a palette knife shape into burger patties.

2 To make the Lyonnaise sauce: using the butter, sweat the sliced onions for about 15 minutes over a medium heat until golden.

3 Add the flour to the onions and cook the flour out for approximately 2 minutes before slowly adding the stock to form a sauce.

4 Pan fry, grill or bake the patties and serve together with the Lyonnaise sauce.

Mixing the ingredients

Moulding the burgers

Sauté the onions for the Lyonnaise sauce

# Partridge and plums in mulled wine

| INGREDIENTS | 4 PORTIONS | 10 PORTIONS |
|---|---|---|
| Partridge legs | 4 | 10 |
| Plums | 500g | 1kg |
| Red wine | 1 litre | 2 litres |
| Mulled wine spices e.g. cinnamon, nutmeg and cloves | To taste | To taste |
| Pieces of orange without pith | 1 orange | 2 oranges |
| Sugar | 50g | 150g |
| Juniper berries | 1tbs | 2tbs |
| Butter | 10g | 30g |
| Flour | 10g | 30g |
| Good-quality salt and white pepper | To taste | To taste |

## Method of work

1   Joint the partridge leg into drumsticks and thighs then remove the thigh bone from each and trim the drumstick as for sauté.

2   Halve or quarter the plums dependent on size and remove the stone from the middle of the plum.

3   Add the wine, spices, orange, juniper berries and sugar to a saucepan and bring up to the boil. Once boiling, add the halved or quartered plums (depending on size).

4   Add the partridge drumsticks and thighs to the boiled cooking liquor and poach gently until the meat is cooked and the plums tender.

5   One cooked through, remove the plums, drumsticks and thighs from the liquor and strain.

6   Using a wooden spoon, combine the butter and flour together to make beurre manie and whisk into the hot liquor to thicken.

7   To serve, carve the thigh into thin slices, arrange in a fan around the drumstick and garnish with the plums and the sauce.

# Fricassée of rabbit with orange and chive

Deglazing the pan for rabbit

| INGREDIENTS | 4 PORTIONS | 10 PORTIONS |
|---|---|---|
| Rabbit, cut into large dice | 500g | 1.5kg |
| Double cream | 500ml | 1 litre |
| Orange, zest and juice | 1 | 3 |
| Chicken stock | 100ml | 300ml |
| White wine | 100ml | 300ml |
| Chives, chopped | 30g | 80g |
| Good-quality salt and white pepper | To taste | To taste |

## Method of work

1 Season the meat with salt and pepper and sauté quickly in a very hot frying pan until golden. Remove the meat from the pan and keep warm.

2 Deglaze the pan with the white wine and reduce by half, then pour into a saucepan along with the orange zest and juice and the chicken stock and reduce by a further half.

3 Add the cream followed by the sautéed rabbit and any juice that may be in the bottom of the pan.

4 Continue to simmer gently over a medium heat until the meat is tender and the sauce has thickened.

5 Garnish with chopped chives and serve.

# Spiced tempura quail breasts with chilli dipping jam

| INGREDIENTS | 4 PORTIONS | 10 PORTIONS |
|---|---|---|
| Quail breast | 12 | 30 |
| Chilli powder | 1tsp | 2tsp |
| Soft flour | 50g | 125g |
| Rice flour | 50g | 125g |
| Cornflour | 50g | 125g |
| Egg whites | 3 | 6 |
| Iced sparkling mineral water | 500ml | 1 litre |
| Red chilli | 1 | 2 |
| Honey | 30ml | 90ml |
| White wine | 90ml | 220ml |
| Good-quality salt and white pepper | To taste | To taste |

## Method of work

1  In a bowl combine all the flours together with the chilli powder and salt.
2  Whisk in the sparkling water to form a smooth batter.
3  Whisk the egg whites to form stiff peaks and fold into the batter.
4  In a small saucepan sweat the diced red chilli before adding the wine and honey and then reduce until slightly thickened.
5  Season the breasts and pass through flour and tempura batter, and deep fry until the batter is crispy and golden.
6  Serve the deep-fried tempura-coated breasts with the chilli dip.

# Grilled tournedos of venison with pan-fried foie gras

*Cooking the steak*

| INGREDIENTS | 4 PORTIONS | 10 PORTIONS |
|---|---|---|
| Venison loin steaks wrapped in streaky bacon | 4 | 10 |
| Foie gras (50g slices) | 4 | 10 |
| Wild mushroom | 250g | 750g |
| Game or good beef jus | 150ml | 500ml |
| Madeira | 10ml | 50ml |
| Croûtons (1 × 4cm disc per portion) | 4 | 10 |
| Good-quality salt and white pepper | To taste | To taste |

## Method of work

1  Sauté the wild mushrooms and flambé with the Madeira until golden and softened. Add to a saucepan with the jus and reduce until thickened.
2  Season the steaks and rub with a little oil, then grill to medium or however liked and allow to rest.
3  Very quickly in a hot pan, fry the foie gras slices until golden on each side.
4  To serve, place the steak onto the plate topped with some of the wild mushrooms in the jus, then the foie gras on top. Spoon any remaining jus over the top.

**CHEF'S TIP**

Keep the foie gras in the fridge until the very second it is needed as it will go very soft quickly which will make it impossible to fry.

## Assessment of knowledge and understanding

You have now learned about the use of the different types of feathered and furred game, how to produce a variety of dishes utilising an array of commodities and the cooking techniques used.

To test your level of knowledge and understanding, answer the following short questions. These will help to prepare you for your summative (final) assessment.

1 Name two features to identify on game birds that have been plucked to establish if they are of edible quality.

i) _____ ii) _____

2 Explain what the 'Glorious Twelfth' is.

_____

_____

3 When roasting game there are various ways in which you can help to enhance flavour. Give three different examples of how this can be achieved.

i) _____ ii) _____

iii)_____

4 Explain why it is easier to cut venison loin into steaks if tightly wrapped in cling film and refrigerated first.

_____

_____

5 Discuss the importance of removing the wishbone prior to cooking or preparing.

_____

_____

6 Explain the benefits of cooking game items on the bone and give one reason why this is beneficial.

_____

_____

7 Explain the benefits of pot roasting or braising tougher cuts of game.

_____

_____

8 Explain why all furred and feathered game still in coats should not be stored within a kitchen or prepared meat fridges.

_____

_____

9 List four rules that should be taken into consideration before accepting/purchasing game from a supplier.

i) _____ ii) _____

iii)_____ iv)_____

# CHEF'S PROFILE

**Name: ANDREW PERN**

**Position:** Chef/Owner

**Establishment:** The Star Inn, Harome, Helmsley, North Yorkshire

**Current job role and main responsibilities:** As Chef Patron I have many responsibilities – menus, cooking, recruiting, publicity – the whole running of the business involved with the Star Inn. Our butchers, café and accommodation are all part of our 'little industry'. We buy direct from a farmer who supplies our butchers, who then supplies us – giving a complete field to fork experience.

**When did you realise that you wanted to pursue a career in the catering and hospitality industry?** From a young age! I cooked at home from when I was about 8 years old, as my mother has MS. We were a very sociable family, with dinner parties and Sunday lunch always playing a part. This led me to catering college eventually, having worked at local pubs washing up and helping with the food. My story is of a 'local lad' from Whitby, who has done well on his own doorstep.

**Training:** I spent 3 years at Scarborough Technical College (now Yorkshire Coast College), gaining 207,1,2,3, Pastry, Bakery and Food Beverage Exams. I gained invaluable experience by going to France on placements, where I had access to Rungis market and by taking a two-month summer job working for HM Forces, cooking and washing up for 600 squaddies a day.

**Experience:** After leaving college I worked at two small country inns before buying the Star Inn at the age of 26 years. Buying our own place, we worked for 20 months, seven days a week from 7.30 am to 2.30 am! This ordeal built the foundations to the success we have today.

**What do you find rewarding about your job?** I always say it is a hobby to me and a lifestyle. All four of our children have been born whilst we have been at The Star, so it is more of a home to us than a business, where we welcome guests into our own little world. We have been well rewarded with the many awards and accolades we have gained, which has allowed us to carry on doing various projects to a very high level. Offering hospitality and allowing our guests to enjoy themselves is the main aim of the game.

**What do you find the most challenging about the job?** Keeping our high standards day in, day out. If you do your best every time then hopefully the customer will benefit. If you don't, you are letting the customer and yourself down.

**What advice would you give to students just beginning their career?** Be prepared! The more you give to the job, the more you will get back. Also enjoy what you do and do it to the best of your ability!

**Who is your mentor or main inspiration?** In my early twenties I did the Roux Scholarship and Albert and Michael Roux had a big influence in my college days. Marco Pierre White published *White Heat* when I was at college, which opened my eyes to new ways of presenting the old classics. Then people like Paul Heathcote, Terry Laybowne and the late Denis Watkins from the Angel Inn have inspired my northern food ethos.

**Secrets of a successful chef:**
1   Have an open mind about everything that people offer to teach you.
2   Stamina.
3   Eye for presentation.
4   Be a good team member.
5   Don't be lazy!

**A brief personal profile:** My family are all from a farming background, so I am the odd one out! However, this has set me up for my style of cookery, which is very seasonal and very local, using produce from the North Sea, game from the moor and meat from our own butchers. I have had a Michelin star for five years. We have won 3 Cateys, 'the Oscars of the catering industry', and many other awards such as Gastro Pub of the Year. We now own The Star Inn, The Star at Scampston (a café in a 4½ acre walled garden), Cross House Lodge (private dinning and accommodation), Black Eagle Cottage (three self-catering suites), The Farmhouse (where a chalet style chef cooks in a part-thatched farm house for families/groups), Pern's of Helmsley (butcher/deli) and the Corner Shop (deli/crockery shop).

**Can you give one essential kitchen tip or technique that you use as a chef:** Communication, be it with suppliers, chefs, Front of House, customers or guests. It is always good to communicate.

# Pot roast Rievaulx shot partridge with Fadmoor beetroot, creamed curly kale, smoked bacon and thyme juices

| INGREDIENTS | 2 PORTIONS |
|---|---|
| Partridge (grey or red-legged, depending on availability) | 2 |
| Rashers of smoked bacon | 2 |
| Turned barrel-shaped beetroot cooked in red wine with a little seasoning | |
| Baby onions | 8 |
| Picked curly kale off the stalks | 500g |
| Double cream | 100g |
| Grated mature Lancashire cheese | 65g |
| Creamed mashed potato with fresh thyme | 200g |
| Cooked bacon lardons | 10 |
| Good game stock | 300ml |
| Redcurrant jelly | 1tsp |
| Fresh thyme leaves | Pinch |

Pre-heat the oven to 200°C, 425F, gas mark 7

## Method of work

1 Cover the breasts of the bird with the bacon streaks and cook for 14 minutes.

2 While the bird is cooking, reduce the stock. Once syrupy, add the baby onions, bacon and beetroot to reheat gently.

3 Warm cream. When reduced by ½, add the cheese, curly kale and seasoning.

4 Take the partridge out of the oven and rest it in a warm place.

5 Pipe the potato in a swirl shape onto hot plates and carve the bird onto the mash. Spoon the creamed kale into a little pot or onto the plate with the beetroot alongside. Sprinkle the thyme leaves into the sauce. Check seasoning, spoon over and serve immediately.

# 12

# Meat and offal

UNIT 209
1. **Prepare meat and offal**
2. **Cook meat and offal**

## LEARNING OBJECTIVES

By the end of this chapter you will be able to:

- Demonstrate a range of skills related to the preparation of meat and offal

- Demonstrate cookery skills using meat and offal as the principal ingredient

- Identify quality points of beef, lamb and pork and various offal items and dishes

- List health and safety regulations relating to the preparation, cooking and storage of both raw and cooked meat and offal, and meat and offal dishes

- Identify the different cuts of meat and variety of offal and relate appropriate cookery methods for them

- Identify healthy options with the preparation and cookery of meat dishes

# Meat

**VIDEO CLIP**
Smithfield meat market

# INTRODUCTION

Meat for the catering industry is the flesh of any animal reared for the table, most commonly beef, pork and lamb.

There have been few societies in history that haven't recorded meat in their diet: in relative terms vegetarianism is a recent phenomena. Historically meat, a rich source of high-quality protein, has been an important factor in the nutritional requirements of man.

Meat has three distinctive parts: muscle, fat and connective tissue.

## Muscle

Most of the meat we consume is the muscle of the animal: the fat is usually trimmed to lessen calorific intake and lower the consumption of saturated fats (a major factor in high cholesterol levels).

Muscle fibres are made up of long thin threads that are not usually visible. In themselves they are not strong enough to do the work, so they are gathered in bundles similar to ropes. A sheath of connective tissue holds the bundles together, adding even greater strength. Muscle fibres split easily along the grain but not across. That is why we carve across the grain with a sharp knife, allowing the customer to easily cut the meat with a dinner knife.

Some muscles do more work than others, making the fibres thicker and requiring them to be cooked for a longer period of time than the more tender and fine-fibred muscles. Leg and neck muscles do most work whereas loin muscles are there mainly to protect the backbone. (See the usage charts and anatomical diagrams p. 290–97.) Hard-working muscles are more flavourful than the finer textured muscles, so the chef must take this into consideration when deciding upon cooking techniques.

## Fat

If you completely remove all traces of fat from meat it is almost impossible to detect the true characteristics of the type of meat that is being eaten. (If you add minced pork fat into very lean minced beef it will taste like pork and not beef.) The flavour is in the fat and even in our culture of almost zero fat consumption we still need a vestige of fat to add flavour, succulence and necessary nutrition.

Very lean meat dishes usually have added fat, for example by braising beef topside and adding cheese and ham to pork escalope dishes.

IMAGES COURTESY OF QUALITY MEAT SCOTLAND

*Subcutaneous fat*

*Intramuscular fat*

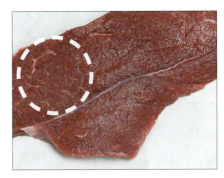
*Intermuscular fat (marbling)*

There are three types of fat:

1 Subcutaneous: fat that is under the skin and surrounds the muscle

2 Intramuscular: fat that is in-between muscles

3 Intermuscular: fat that is inside the muscle (marbling).

## Connective tissue

There are three types of tissue that can be described as connective tissue:

1 **Collagen**, which converts to gelatine when it is cooked for a long period of time. It is essential when making clarifications for consommés. It is also known as white connective tissue.

2 **Elastin**

3 **Reticulin**.

Both elastin and reticulin remain tough no matter how long they are cooked.

## Meat ageing

The **ageing** of meat is a complex series of chemical processes that alter fats and proteins, develop flavour compounds, and tenderise the meat.

If you cooked the meat of a freshly slaughtered animal it would be tough and flavourless, practically inedible, because muscles tighten after slaughter and do not begin to relax for 24 hours, but then continue to relax for about 6 days.

Beef should be aged for at least 10 days and up to 42 days, although after 21 days the benefits of continued ageing are negligible. Mutton should be aged for 1 week. Lamb and pork need little ageing because they are from young animals with little fat and connective tissue.

There are two types of ageing:

1 *Dry ageing* takes place in refrigerators at 1–2°C with controlled humidity. The meat is usually hung to allow air to circulate. If the meat is hung by the aitch-bone, the resultant stretching of the muscles leads to greater tenderness. This is not a very common practice due to the extra space that is required in the refrigerators.

2 *Wet ageing* takes place in vacuum pouches but has the disadvantages of producing a lower intensity of flavour and increased expense of storage.

*Block scraper, steel butcher's knives, a boning knife and meat bat*

*Butcher's saw, chain mail glove and cut proof glove*

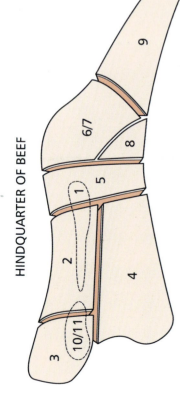

## Storage

Meat should always be covered by plastic wrap when stored in a refrigerator to help prevent oxidation of protein. The temperature should be 1–4°C and meat should always be used as quickly as possible. Frozen meat should be covered to prevent freezer burn and kept at –18°C. The thawing of meat should take place in a refrigerator.

## Equipment

When preparing meat all equipment must be cleaned and sprayed with an antibacterial spray after each use. Whilst the meat itself may not be contaminated, it is an ideal medium in which pathogens can multiply. All manufacturer safety guidelines must always be followed. It is recommended that a chain mail or cut-proof glove be worn when cutting meat.

## Quality

The idea of first and second quality of meat is an incorrect assumption. The quality of meat is directly related to the cookery method. If a tender fillet steak is stewed for 2 hours it will completely disintegrate in the sauce, if chuck beef is used it will be tender and succulent. On the other hand if you grilled the chuck beef it would be almost impossible to chew. Careful consideration should be made when marrying cookery techniques and cuts of meat. Prime cuts of meat are the more tender muscles that lend themselves to dry cookery methods such as frying and grilling.

## Beef Hindquarter

### BREAKDOWN OF A HINDQUARTER OF BEEF

| JOINT | USE | AVERAGE WEIGHT |
|---|---|---|
| 1 Fillet | Grilling, roasting, frying | 3–3.5kg |
| 2 Sirloin | Grilling, roasting, frying | 12–14kg |
| 3 Wing rib | Grilling, roasting, frying | 3–4kg |
| 4 Thin flank | Braising, stewing | 8–10kg |
| 5 Rump | Frying, roasting, braising | 10 kg |
| 6 Topside | Braising, stewing, slow roasting | 9–10kg |
| 7 Thick flank | Braising, stewing | 10–11kg |
| 8 Silverside | Pickling, boiling | 12–14kg |
| 9 Shin | Consommé, braising | 6–7kg |
| 10 Kidney | Pies, puddings | 1–2kg |
| 11 Fat (suet) | Suet pastry, rendering | 5–6kg |

# Beef Forequarter

Average weight 75–80kg

**VIDEO CLIP**
Technique for producing a fore rib of beef for roasting

## BREAKDOWN OF A FOREQUARTER OF BEEF

| JOINT | USE | AVERAGE WEIGHT |
|---|---|---|
| 1 Fore rib | Roast, grilling, frying | 6.5kg |
| 2 Middle rib | Braising, roasting | 8.5kg |
| 3 Chuck rib | Stewing, braising | 13kg |
| 4 Sticking piece | Stewing, mincing | 7kg |
| 5 Plate | Stewing, mincing, boiling | 8.5kg |
| 6 Brisket | Brining, boiling | 16kg |
| 7 Leg of mutton cut | Braising steaks, paupiettes, stew, mince | 9kg |
| 8 Shin | Clarification, mince | 5kg |

**BREAKDOWN ON A FOREQUARTER OF BEEF**

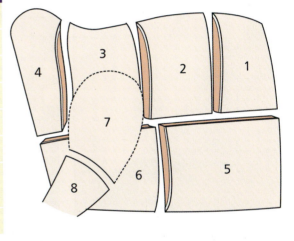

Step-by-step: **Preparation of a leg of mutton cut of beef into steaks and carbonnade**

**STEP 1** Cut away the leg of mutton cut (LMC) of all silver gristle and fat

**STEP 2** Remove thin muscle

**STEP 3** Remove outer muscle

**STEP 4** Remove silver gristle

**STEP 5** Main muscle, secondary muscle and trimmings

**STEP 6** Slice main muscle into steaks

**STEP 7** Slice the secondary muscle into carbonarde

**STEP 8** Bat out carbonarde

**STEP 9** Steaks and carbonarde

## Veal

Veal is the meat from milk-fed calves that are slaughtered at around 4 months. The meat is very pale in colour, although a calf of 2½ months is highly prized for its white flesh. The meat is usually from the male offspring of dairy cattle, as they would not make high quality beef. There is a growing fondness for 'pink' or 'rose' veal that has a little time to graze before slaughter, this gives a deeper flavour than the purely milk fed variety.

Almost all the joints of veal are tender and can be cooked in a short time. It is by nature a very lean meat, which lends itself to cream sauces, the addition of cheese and cooking using barriers of flour, eggs or pané.

## QUALITY POINTS

- The fat is white, pleasant to smell and mainly situated around the kidneys
- The muscles should not feel sticky to the touch
- The flesh is very lean and a pale pink colour except when a rose colour is specifically ordered

BREAKDOWN ON A SIDE OF VEAL

### BREAKDOWN OF A SIDE OF VEAL

| JOINT | USE | AVERAGE WEIGHT |
| --- | --- | --- |
| 1 Scrag | Stews, mince | 1.25kg |
| 2 Neck | Braising, stew mince | 1.5kg |
| 3 Best end | Roasting, pot roasting, cutlets, frying | 1.5kg |
| 4 Loin | Roast, grilling, frying | 1.5kg |
| 5 Rump | Roast, grilling, frying | 1kg |
| 6 Leg | Pot roast, frying, grilling | 4kg |
| 7 Knuckle/shank | Mince, stew, osso bucco | 2kg |
| 8 Shoulder | Braising, stewing, forcemeats | 2.5kg |
| 9 Breast | Stewing, braising | 2kg |

Step-by-step: **Preparation of veal escalopes**

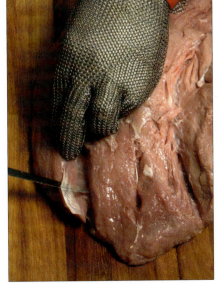

STEP 1 Trim any fat

STEP 2 Remove any membrane

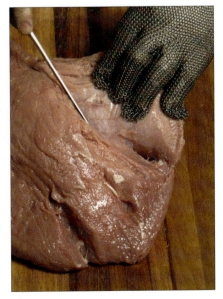

STEP 3 Remove any muscle groups

**STEP 4** Slice the veal across the grain

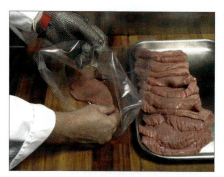

**STEP 5** Place the escalopes into heavy plastic

**STEP 6** Bat out with a meat bat

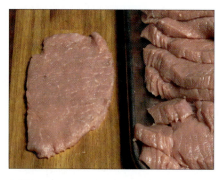

**STEP 7** An escalope of veal

**STEP 8** Add a stuffing, in this case cheese and ham

**STEP 9** Fold into a D shape

# Lamb and Mutton

Lamb is the meat from farmed sheep less than 12 months old. Over the age of 12 months the meat is technically described as mutton. The flesh can vary in colour and flavour depending on the breed, feeding regime and age of slaughter.

 **VIDEO CLIP** Technique for producing a leg of lamb for roasting

### BREAKDOWN OF A SIDE OF LAMB/MUTTON

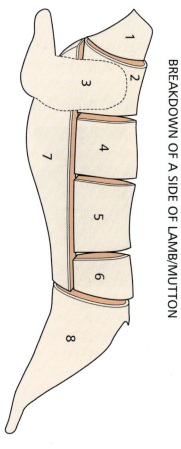

BREAKDOWN OF A SIDE OF LAMB/MUTTON

| JOINT | USES | AVERAGE WEIGHT |
|---|---|---|
| 1 Scrag | Stewing, broths | 1kg |
| 2 Middle neck | Stewing | 2kg |
| 3 Shoulder | Roasting, stewing | 2 × 2kg |
| 4 Best end | Roasting, grilling, frying (cutlets, racks) | 2kg |
| 5 Saddle | Roast, frying, grilling (chops, cannon, filet mignon) | 2kg |
| 6 Rump | Braising, roast | 2kg |
| 7 Breast | Slow roasting, stewing, steaming | 2kg |
| 8 Leg | Roasting, frying (steaks), braising (shanks) | 2 × 2.5kg |

## QUALITY POINTS

- The lean flesh should be a ruddy red colour
- The fat should be evenly distributed, dry to the touch and flaky in texture
- The smell of lamb is pleasing and characteristic to the animal
- The bones should be porous and have a small degree of blood present
- It is important to keep lamb cold when cutting the meat as otherwise the fat becomes greasy and knife handles become slippery

Step-by-step: **Preparation of a shoulder of lamb**

**STEP 1** Shoulder of lamb

**STEP 2** Trim excess fat

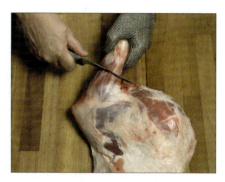
**STEP 3** Trim the end of the shank

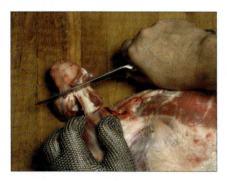
**STEP 4** Scrape the flesh from the bone

**STEP 5** Saw the end of the bone

**STEP 6** Cut along the shoulder blade

**STEP 7** Pull out the shoulder blade

**STEP 8** Cut along the humerus bone and remove

**STEP 9** Add the stuffing

**STEP 10** Tie at 2cm intervals

BREAKDOWN OF A SIDE OF PORK

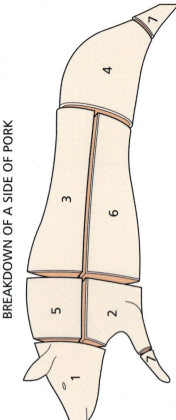

# Pork

Pork is the meat from pigs which are usually slaughtered between 10–12 months old. Intensively farmed pigs are usually quite large for their age and the main breeds for this type of farming are Danish Landrace, Belgian Pietrain and Western Whites. However, older breeds are now becoming more popular using less intensive methods of farming, such as Gloucester Old Spot and Tamworth.

Pork is usually supplied in sides.

**VIDEO CLIP**
Technique for producing a loin of pork into chops and medallions

## BREAKDOWN OF A SIDE OF PORK

| JOINT | USES | AVERAGE WEIGHT |
|---|---|---|
| 1 Head | Brawn, stuffing, buffet centre pieces | 4kg |
| 2 Shoulder | Sausages, pies, stewing | 3kg |
| 3 Loin | Frying (chops), grilling, roasting, sauté | 5kg |
| 4 Leg | Roasting, frying, stir-frying | 4 kg |
| 5 Spare rib | Sausages, stewing | 2kg |
| 6 Belly | Braising, curing, boiling | 3kg |
| 7 Trotters | Boiling, stocks | .5kg |

Step-by-step: **Preparation of a rolled belly of pork**

**STEP 1** Belly of pork

**STEP 2** Singeing hairs

**STEP 3** Uncovering the floating ribs

**STEP 4** Removing the floating ribs

**STEP 5** Cutting under the ribs

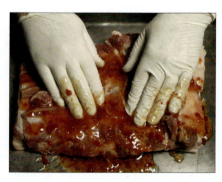

**STEP 6** Rubbing in the marinade

**STEP 7** Scraping excess marinade      **STEP 8** Rolling the belly      **STEP 9** Rolled belly of pork

## QUALITY POINTS

- Pale pink flesh with a fine texture

- Skin should be free of bristle and not wet to the touch

- There should be a covering of fat that is not excessive

- The bones should be small an pink

- There should not be excessive connective tissue

# Bacon

The meat from the pig to produce bacon is cured in salt brine or smoked. The cured bacon is commonly referred to as green bacon. The flesh should be firm to the touch and a dark pink colour with a slightly creamy fat colour, unless it has been smoked whereby the fat colour will have a light caramel colour to it.

**BREAKDOWN OF A SIDE OF BACON**

| JOINT | USES | AVERAGE WEIGHT |
|-------|------|----------------|
| 1 Gammon | Boiling, grilling (gammon steaks) | 7–8kg |
| 2 Back | Grilling, frying | 9–10kg |
| 3 Collar | Boiling | 4–5kg |
| 4 Hock | Boiling | 4–5kg |
| 5 Belly | Boiling, grilling | 4–5kg |

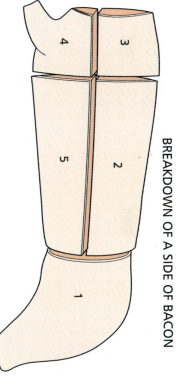

BREAKDOWN OF A SIDE OF BACON

## QUALITY POINTS

- The lean muscle should be pink, firm and not sticky to the touch

- The fat should be white and not excessive

- The rind must be free from wrinkles and not sticky

- The bacon in general should not feel wet or sticky to the touch

# BEEF RECIPES

## Brown beef stew

| INGREDIENTS | 4 PORTIONS | 10 PORTIONS |
| --- | --- | --- |
| Diced chuck beef | 600g | 1.5kg |
| Carrots | 80g | 200g |
| Celery | 1 stick | 2 sticks |
| Onion | 80g | 200g |
| Bouquet garni | 1 small | 1 large |
| Garlic | 1 clove | 2–3 cloves |
| Oil | 40ml | 100ml |
| Flour | 40g | 100g |
| Brown beef stock | 800ml | 2 litres |
| Tomato purée | 40g | 100g |
| Good-quality salt and white pepper | To taste | To taste |

*Removing the sinews*

### Method of work

1. Remove sinews and excess fat from the beef and cut into a 2cm dice.
2. Peel and chop the carrot, onion, celery and garlic into a large dice.
3. Heat the oil in a pan and sear the meat until brown on all sides.
4. Add the mirepoix and continue to brown.
5. Add the flour and cook for 1–2 minutes, remove from the heat and allow to cool slightly.
6. Add the tomato purée and stock and stir with a wooden spoon or spatula. Ensure that there are no lumps then add the bouquet garni, season and cover with a lid.
7. Simmer gently for 2–2½ hours.
8. Skim any fat from the surface and remove the meat to a clean pan.
9. Pass the sauce onto the meat.
10. Correct the seasoning and serve.

## Chilli con carne

| INGREDIENTS | 4 PORTIONS | 10 PORTIONS |
| --- | --- | --- |
| Chuck beef | 600g | 1.5kg |
| Onions | 80g | 200g |
| Chillies | 2 | 5 |
| Garlic cloves | 2 | 5 |
| Canned tomatoes | 400g | 1kg |
| Canned red kidney beans | 200g | 500g |
| Brown beef stock (approximately) | 200ml | 500ml |
| Sugar | ½ tsp | 2tsp |
| Good-quality salt and black pepper | To taste | To taste |
| Oil | 40ml | 100ml |

## Method of work

1 Trim the beef of excess fat and connective tissue, cut into large dice and pass through a medium plate of a mincer.

2 Crush the garlic, chop the onion and chillies. Fry the beef in the oil stirring continuously to break it up.

3 Add the onions, garlic and chillies. Continue to cook until they are well sweated.

4 Add the sugar, tomatoes and enough stock to moisten.

5 Bring to the boil and simmer very gently for 1–2 hours. Add more stock when necessary and skim.

6 Serve with plain boiled rice and flour tortillas.

# Steak and kidney pudding

| INGREDIENTS | 4 PORTIONS | 10 PORTIONS |
|---|---|---|
| Diced chuck beef | 500g | 1.25kg |
| Ox Kidney | 100g | 250g |
| Worcestershire sauce | To taste | To taste |
| Onion (chopped) | 1 | 2–3 |
| Flour | 40g | 100g |
| Beef stock | 160ml | 400ml |
| Good-quality salt and white pepper | To taste | To taste |
| Suet paste (see p. 504) | 300g | 750g |

*Adding the kidney*

## Method of work

1 Remove the core from the kidney and dice.

2 Line a greased pudding basin with three-quarters of the paste.

3 Mix the remainder of the ingredients and place in the bowl.

4 Roll out the remainder of the paste, moisten the paste in the basin and cover.

5 Cover with a lid of cling film reinforced with tin foil.

6 Steam for 3–4 hours.

7 Allow to rest for 30 mins in a warm place then turn out onto a serving dish and serve.

### CHEF'S TIP

Vegetable suet can be used as a substitute for beef suet.

*Forming the top*

# Steak and kidney pie

*Covering the pie*

| INGREDIENTS | 4 PORTIONS | 10 PORTIONS |
|---|---|---|
| Diced chuck beef | 500g | 1.25kg |
| Ox kidney | 100g | 250g |
| Flour | 40g | 100g |
| Onion concassé | 1 | 2–3 |
| Carrot concassé | 1 | 2 |
| Brown beef stock | 160ml | 400ml |
| Worcestershire sauce | To taste | To taste |
| Good-quality salt and white pepper | To taste | To taste |
| Puff pastry (see p. 468) | 200g | 500g |

## Method of work

1 Dust the beef with the flour, sear in the oil and allow to cool.
2 Mix with the remainder of the ingredients and place in a pie dish that allow the mixture to come almost to the top.
3 Roll out the pastry and put onto the moistened dish.
4 Allow to rest in the refrigerator for 2–3 hours.
5 Eggwash and place in an oven at 175°C for 15 minutes until the pastry has begun to colour.
6 Reduce the temperature to 130°C and continue to cook for a further 2 hours.
7 Clean the rim of the pie dish and serve.

### CHEF'S TIP

The filling can be precooked and chilled to allow the pies to be cooked in an à la carte situation.

# Boiled salt beef with carrots and dumplings

*Forming the dumplings*

| INGREDIENTS | 4 PORTIONS | 10 PORTIONS |
|---|---|---|
| Salted silverside of beef | 800g | 2kg |
| Small carrots | 8 | 20 |
| Onions | 8 | 20 |
| Suet paste (see p. 504) | 40g | 1kg |
| Good-quality salt and white pepper | To taste | To taste |

## Method of work

1 Place the meat in cold water and bring to the boil.
2 Remove to a clean pan and cover with some more clean water.
3 Bring to the boil again and simmer for 1½ hours.
4 Add the carrots and simmer for a further 20 minutes.
5 Divide the suet paste into even pieces and add to the cooking liquor.
6 Simmer for a further 20 minutes.
7 Serve carved onto a plate or service dish garnished with the vegetables and dumplings.

### CHEF'S TIP

The salt beef can be soaked overnight in cold water to remove excess salt. This cuts down on the cooking time.

# Braised beef in beer and onions *Carbonnade of beef*

| INGREDIENTS | 4 PORTIONS | 10 PORTIONS |
|---|---|---|
| **Lean beef** (topside or trimmed leg of mutton cut) | 600g | 1.5kg |
| **Sliced onions** | 300g | 750g |
| **Brown beef stock** | 400ml | 2 litres |
| **Ale** | 300ml | 750ml |
| **Flour** | 40g | 100g |
| **Sugar** | 10g | 25g |
| **Oil** | | |
| **Good-quality salt and white pepper** | To taste | To taste |

*Beating the flour into the beef*

> **CHEF'S TIP**
>
> Rump beef or LMC beef are ideal for this dish as they have very little fat and no gristle.

> **CHEF'S TIP**
>
> LMC refers to the leg of mutton cut of beef. There can be confusion with telesales people and sometimes a leg of mutton will be delivered. Use the term 'LMC beef' to overcome this confusion.

## Method of work

1. Cut the meat into thin slices and bat out to 2mm in thickness.
2. Dust the beef in flour and season and beat it in with the back of a knife.
3. Fry quickly in hot fat and place in a casserole.
4. Add the onions to the pan and sauté to a light brown colour.
5. Add to the beef with the beer and stock.
6. Cover and cook in the oven for approximately 1½ hours.
7. Serve with parsley potatoes and root vegetables.

# Beef stroganoff

| INGREDIENTS | 4 PORTIONS | 10 PORTIONS |
|---|---|---|
| **Beef fillet** (tail) | 600g | 1.5kg |
| **Shallots** | 1 | 2 |
| **Button mushrooms** | 100g | 250g |
| **Butter** | 50g | 125g |
| **Brandy** | 20ml | 100ml |
| **Double cream** | 150ml | 350ml |
| **Lemon** | ½ | 1½ |
| **Good-quality salt and white pepper** | To taste | To taste |
| **Pilaff rice** (see p. 167) | 4 portions | 10 portions |

*Flambé the beef*

## Method of work

1  Cut the beef into fingers 4cm x ½ cm.
2  Cut the shallots into a fine brunoise and finely slice the mushrooms.
3  Heat the butter in a sauté pan until foaming but not browning. Add the beef and sauté briskly over a high heat.
4  Add the shallots and mushrooms and continue to cook for 1 min. Season.
5  Add the brandy and set alight. When the flames have gone add the cream.
6  Allow the cream to come to the boil and add the lemon juice.
7  Serve with pilaff rice.

# Stir fried beef with oyster sauce

*Cutting the meat into ribbons*

| INGREDIENTS | 4 PORTIONS | 10 PORTIONS |
|---|---|---|
| *Oyster sauce marinade* | | |
| Soy sauce | 1tbsp | 2tbsp |
| White wine | 2tsp | 2tbsp |
| Salt | To taste | To taste |
| Sugar | 1tsp | 1tbsp |
| Baking powder | ¼ tsp | ½ tsp |
| Ground black pepper | ¼ tsp | ½ tsp |
| Water | 1tbsp | 2tbsp |
| Cornflour | 2tsp | 2tbsp |
| Oil | 2tbsp | 4tbsp |
| *The recipe* | | |
| Lean beef | 400g | 1kg |
| Oyster sauce | 2tbsp | 4tbsp |
| Salt | To taste | To taste |
| Sugar | 1tsp | 1tbsp |
| Spring onions | 2 | 4–5 |

## Method of work

1  Mix all the ingredients for the marinade together.
2  Slice the meat into thin slices and then into ribbons, add to the marinade and marinate for 4–6 hours.
3  Remove from the marinade and **stir fry** in a hot wok for 1 minute.
4  Pour off the oil and add the spring onions, oyster sauce, salt and sugar.
5  Continue to cook for a further 1 minute and serve with rice.

# Italian meatballs with pepperonata

| INGREDIENTS | 4 PORTIONS | 10 PORTIONS |
|---|---|---|
| Minced beef | 400g | 1kg |
| Fresh breadcrumbs | 50g | 125g |
| Finely chopped Parma ham | 40g | 100g |
| Grated Parmesan | 30g | 75g |
| Eggs | 2 | 5 |
| Dried oregano | 1tsp | 1tbsp |
| Grated nutmeg | Pinch | 2 pinches |
| Smoked paprika | Pinch | 2 pinches |
| Vegetable oil for frying | | |
| Good-quality salt and black pepper | To taste | To taste |
| *Pepperonata* | | |
| Olive oil | 40ml | 100ml |
| Sliced onion | 80g | 200g |
| Sliced red pepper | 2 | 5 |
| Sliced yellow pepper | 2 | 5 |
| Ripe plum tomatoes | 4 | 10 |
| Good-quality salt and black pepper | To taste | To taste |
| Chopped parsley | | |

## Method of work

1 Place half the breadcrumbs and all the ingredients for the meatballs in a bowl and mix thoroughly.

2 Divide into 16 or 40 equal pieces and shape into smooth balls.

3 Roll the meatballs in the breadcrumbs.

4 Allow to chill for 1–2 hours.

5 Make the pepperonata. Sweat the onion in the oil, add the peppers and continue to cook for 3–4 minutes.

6 Add the spices and herbs and tomatoes.

7 Season, cover with a lid and simmer for 10 minutes.

8 Uncover and reduce until thick.

9 Fry the meat balls in 2cm of oil, turning frequently until a core temperature of 75°C has been reached.

10 Serve with the pepperonata.

# Beef goulash

| INGREDIENTS | 4 PORTIONS | 10 PORTIONS |
|---|---|---|
| Diced chuck beef | 600g | 1.5kg |
| Carrots | 80g | 200g |
| Celery | 1 stick | 2 sticks |
| Onion | 80g | 200g |
| Bouquet garni | 1 small | 1 large |
| Garlic | 1 clove | 2–3 cloves |
| Oil | 40ml | 100ml |
| Flour | 40g | 100g |
| Brown beef stock | 800ml | 2 litres |
| Tomato purée | 40g | 100g |
| Paprika | 1tsp | 1tbsp |
| Gnocchi Romaine (see p. 212) | 4 portions | 10 portions |
| Boiled turned potatoes | | |
| Good-quality salt and white pepper | To taste | To taste |

## Method of work

1 Remove sinews and excess fat from the beef and cut into a 2cm dice.
2 Peel and chop the carrot, onion, celery and garlic into a large dice.
3 Heat the oil in a pan and sear the meat until brown on all sides.
4 Add the mirepoix and continue to brown.
5 Add the flour and paprika. Cook for 1–2 mins, remove from the heat and allow to cool slightly.
6 Add the tomato purée and stock and stir with a wooden spoon or spatula ensuring that there are no lumps, add the bouquet garni, season and cover with a lid.
7 Simmer gently for 2–2½ hours.
8 Skim any fat from the surface and remove the meat to a clean pan.
9 Pass the sauce onto the meat.
10 Correct the seasoning and serve accompanied by the gnocchi and potatoes.

*Searing the meat*

*Add the stock*

*Passing the sauce*

# Roast beef and Yorkshire pudding

| INGREDIENTS | 4 PORTIONS | 10 PORTIONS |
| --- | --- | --- |
| **Sirloin, fillet or rib of beef** (allow 150g per portion off the bone and 200g on the bone) | 800g | 2kg |
| **Salt and pepper** | To taste | To taste |
| **Brown beef stock** | 160ml | 400ml |
| **Beef bones** | 1kg | 2kg |
| **Watercress** | 1 bunch | 2 bunches |
| **Horseradish sauce** | 4 portions | 10 portions |
| **Yorkshire puddings** (see p. 358) | 4 | 10 |

## Method of work

1   Prepare the beef.

2   Season with salt and pepper.

3   Place the forerib on the bones in a roasting dish.

4   Place in a hot oven to brown.

5   Turn the heat down to 130°C and continue to cook until the joint is done as requested. The centre temperature should be:

| | |
| --- | --- |
| 55°C | Rare |
| 63°C | Medium rare |
| 68°C | Medium |
| 75°C+ | Well done |

6   Remove the meat, cover with tin foil and rest for 20–30 minutes.

7   Pour off the excess fat, remove the bones and place on a hot stove.

8   Allow the sediment to brown taking care not to burn it.

9   Pour on the stock, deglaze the pan and allow to simmer for 10 minutes.

10  Strain into a clean pan, season if necessary and degrease.

11  Carve the meat across the grain accompanied with gravy, horseradish sauce, watercress and Yorkshire puddings.

*Trimming forerib*

*Cutting onto the ribs to remove the chine bone*

*Removing the chine bone*

*Removing the bones prior to carving*

*Carving the meat across the grain*

# Yorkshire pudding

| INGREDIENTS | 4 PORTIONS | 10 PORTIONS |
|---|---|---|
| Milk | 100ml | 250ml |
| Eggs | 100ml | 250ml |
| Flour | 100g | 250g |
| Good-quality salt and white pepper | To taste | To taste |
| Oil or beef dripping | 100ml | 250ml |

## CHEF'S TIP

In this case the golden rule for Yorkshire pudding is that the capacity is the same. It doesn't matter if it is in cups, pints or litres.

## Method of work

1  Sift the flour and seasoning into a bowl.
2  Combine the eggs and milk.
3  Make a well in the centre of the flour, add the liquids and mix to a light batter.
4  Allow to rest in a refrigerator for at least 1 hour.
5  Pour 25ml of oil into each of the pudding moulds and place in a hot oven until almost smoking (190°C).
6  Pour in the batter and place into the oven until well risen and crispy.
7  When the puddings are brown and well risen test by lifting one: if it feels light it is cooked, if not, return to the oven at 130°C until light and crisp.

# Mexican beef fajitas

*Rolling the tortilla*

| INGREDIENTS | 4 PORTIONS | 10 PORTIONS |
|---|---|---|
| Topside beef | 400g | 1kg |
| Crushed garlic | 1 clove | 2 cloves |
| Jalapeno peppers | 1 | 2 |
| Oil | 50ml | 125ml |
| Dry sherry | 40ml | 100ml |
| Chilli flakes | 1tsp | 1tbsp |
| Ground cumin | 1tbsp | 2tbsp |
| Flour tortilla | 4 | 10 |
| Grated cheese | 100g | 250g |
| Tomato concassé | 100g | 250g |
| Shredded iceberg lettuce | 100g | 250g |

## CHEF'S TIP

The intensity of a vindaloo relies upon the strength of the chillies. If it is too hot advise your guests to eat some yoghurt to nullify the capsaicin from the chilli.

## Method of work

1  Purée the garlic, jalapenos, chilli flakes, cumin and sherry until smooth.
2  Add the beef, cut into strips, and marinate for 24 hours.
3  Drain the beef and sauté in the oil for 2–3minutes.
4  Add the marinade and simmer until cooked.
5  Serve in the tortillas with the cheese, lettuce, tomato and salsa verde.

# Beef bourguignon

| INGREDIENTS | 4 PORTIONS | 10 PORTIONS |
|---|---|---|
| Beef | 600g | 1.5kg |
| Demi glace (see p. 120) | 400ml | 1 litre |
| Red wine | 200ml | 500ml |
| Oil | 20ml | 50ml |
| Button mushrooms | 100g | 250g |
| Dry-cured streaky bacon | 100g | 250g |
| Button onions | 100g | 250g |
| Good-quality salt and white pepper | To taste | To taste |
| Sugar | Pinch | ½ tsp |

## Method of work

1 Remove sinews and excess fat from the beef and cut pieces 2cm × 2cm × 1cm.

2 Remove the rind from the bacon and cut into 2cm dice (lardons).

3 Heat the oil in a pan and sear the meat until brown on all sides

4 Add the demi glace and red wine and cover with a lid. Simmer gently for approximately 2–2½ hours.

5 Blanch the onions and lardons in boiling water.

6 Fry the bacon (lardons) in a little oil. Add the mushrooms and onions, sprinkle with a pinch of sugar and sauté until cooked, season with salt and pepper.

7 Serve the beef accompanied by the garnish.

*Meat cut for bourguignon*

*Cutting the streaky bacon into lardons*

*Sauté the garnish*

# Grilled steaks and their garnishes

Types of beefsteak:

■ *Fillet steak* Taken from the fillet of beef

■ *Tournedos* From the centre of the fillet and can sometimes be barbed with fat bacon

■ *Rump* From the rump of beef. Popular as a grill steak in pubs

■ *Sirloin steak* Cut from a boned sirloin after the rump piece

■ *Minute steak* Cut from the sirloin or rump and batted to ½ cm thickness

■ *Rib eye steak* Taken from a boned-out forerib of beef or the rib end of a sirloin and usually has the outer fat removed

■ *T-bone* Cut from across the rump end.

Step-by-step: **Stages of preparation of sirloin steaks**

**STEP 1** Boneless 2 rib sirloin

**STEP 2** Remove the chin

**STEP 3** Remove visible gristle and connective tissue

**STEP 4** Remove back strap (5cm wide) and trim the tail (2cm from the tip of the eye muscle)

**STEP 5** Trim fat to a maximum depth of 15mm

**STEP 6** Remove 3–4 steaks from the rump end until gristle in the centre of the steak has disappeared

**STEP 7** Remainder of the sirloin to be cut into steaks 2cm thick

**STEP 8** Steaks to be of even thickness (not wedge shape)

# Steak Cuts

*LMC slices*

*Brisket steak blocks*

*Rib cutlets*

*Rib eye*

*Chuck steaks*

*Shin steaks (Osso Bucco)*

*Feather steaks*

*Under blade muscle steaks*

*Shin boneless*

| INGREDIENTS | 4 PORTIONS | 10 PORTIONS |
|---|---|---|
| Beef steak | 4 x 150g | 10 x 150g |
| Oil | | |
| Good-quality salt and white pepper | To taste | To taste |
| Straw potatoes  (see p. 422) | 4 portions | 10 portions |
| Named garnish or sauce | 4 portions | 10 portions |

## Method of work

1  Brush the steaks with oil.

2  Place on a hot grill, griddle or frying pan and allow to sear.

3  Turn and cook on the other side until the steak is cooked to the desired degree.

The degree that a steak is cooked to is purely a matter of personal preference, and the opinion of the customer. As a chef you must try to interpret a customer's desires. With experience simply touching a steak can tell you how well it is done.

# Cooking Specifications for Steak

Blue – core temperature up to 29°C

Rare – core temperature up to 51°C

Medium rare – core temperature 57–63°C

Medium – core temperature 63–68°C

Medium well – core temperature 70–75°C

Well done – core temperature 77°C or above

**CHEF'S TIP**

Cook the steaks from room temperature, this allows the meat to relax quicker and has less blood loss after cooking.

## Garnishes and named sauces

- *Steak au poivre* Pepper sauce
- *Chasseur* Chasseur sauce
- *Champignon* Mushroom sauce
- *Vin rouge* Red wine sauce
- *Bordelaise* Red wine sauce and poached bone marrow
- *Vert pre* Watercress and straw potatoes
- *Béarnaise* Watercress and béarnaise sauce
- *Lyonnaise* Served with sauté onions

# Paupiettes of beef

| INGREDIENTS | 4 PORTIONS | 10 PORTIONS |
|---|---|---|
| Beef topside (trimmed) | 400g | 1kg |
| Sausagemeat | 200g | 500g |
| Tomato purée | 20g | 100g |
| Mirepoix (carrot, onion, celery leek) | 200g | 500g |
| Brown sauce (see p. 119) | 240ml | 600ml |
| Brown beef stock | 400ml | 1 litre |
| Ripe plum tomatoes | 2 | 5 |
| Oil for frying | | |
| Good-quality salt and white pepper | To taste | To Taste |

## Method of work

1  Slice the beef into 4 or 10 slices, each 100g.
2  Bat out the beef between plastic until very thin.
3  Divide the sausagemeat and roll the beef around it.
4  Tie with string or secure with skewers.
5  Sear in a hot pan with just enough oil to coat the base.
6  Remove and add the mirepoix, brown in the pan.
7  Place the mirepoix, tomatoes and tomato purée in a pan that has a tight fitting lid.
8  Place the paupiettes on the mirepoix.
9  Deglaze the pan with the stock and add to the braising pan. Add the brown sauce.
10  Cover with a lid and bring to the boil. Place in an oven at 175°C for approximately 1½ hours.
11  Remove the paupiettes.
12  Strain the sauce and reduce to the desired consistency. Season well.
13  Serve accompanied with seasonal vegetables and potatoes.

*Batting the meat*

*Adding the stuffing*

*Rolling the paupiettes*

# LAMB RECIPES
## Navarin of lamb

| INGREDIENTS | 4 PORTIONS | 10 PORTIONS |
|---|---|---|
| Middle neck of lamb | 600g | 1.5kg |
| Carrots | 80g | 200g |
| Celery | 1 stick | 2 sticks |
| Onion | 80g | 200g |
| Bouquet garni | 1 small | 1 large |
| Garlic | 1 clove | 2–3 cloves |
| Oil | 40ml | 100ml |
| Flour | 40g | 100g |
| Brown stock | 800ml | 2 litres |
| Tomato purée | 40g | 100g |
| Good-quality salt and white pepper | To taste | To taste |

## Method of work

1 Remove sinews and excess fat from the lamb. Cut with a meat saw at the point where the ribs meet the chine bone and cut into uncovered cutlets.

2 Peel and chop the carrot, onion, celery and garlic into a large dice.

3 Heat the oil in a pan and sear the meat until brown on all sides.

4 Add the mirepoix and continue to brown.

5 Add the flour and cook for 1–2 mins, remove from the heat and allow to cool slightly.

6 Add the tomato purée and stock and stir with a wooden spoon or spatula ensuring that there are no lumps. Add the bouquet garni, season and cover with a lid.

7 Simmer gently for 2–2½ hours.

8 Skim any fat from the surface and remove the meat to a clean pan.

9 Pass the sauce onto the meat.

10 Correct the seasoning and serve.

Remove the back strap

Sawing through the ribs to remove the chine bone

Cutting the uncovered cutlets

# Cornish pastie

| INGREDIENTS | 4 PORTIONS | 10 PORTIONS |
|---|---|---|
| Diced potato | 80g | 200g |
| Diced swede | 80g | 200g |
| Small dice of lamb | 100g | 250g |
| Chopped onion | 40g | 100g |
| Short paste (see p. 496) | 240g | 800g |
| Good-quality salt and white pepper | To taste | To taste |
| Eggwash | | |

## Method of work

1 Divide the pastry and roll out to 15cm discs.
2 Mix the filling and moisten if necessary.
3 Place the filling on each round.
4 Moisten the edges of each piece of pastry.
5 Fold in half and crimp the edges to resemble a knot.
6 Brush with the eggwash and bake in the oven at 150°C for approximately 1 hour until cooked through and golden brown.
7 Serve hot or cold.

# Lancashire hotpot

| INGREDIENTS | 4 PORTIONS | 10 PORTIONS |
|---|---|---|
| Diced middle neck of lamb | 800g | 2kg |
| Potatoes | 400g | 1kg |
| Onions | 200g | 500g |
| Celery | 100g | 250g |
| Leek | 200g | 500g |
| Fresh thyme | 4 sprigs | 10 sprigs |
| Parsley stalks | 4 | 10 |
| Bay leaf | 1 | 2 |
| White chicken or lamb stock | 1 litre | 2.5 litres |

## Method of work

1 Place the diced lamb into a saucepan and fill with cold water. Bring to the boil to blanch the meat and then refresh under cold running water. Heat some fat in a frying pan, season the lamb and fry without letting it colour too much.
2 Slice the potatoes into 2–3mm slices.
3 Mix the remaining ingredients with the lamb and season.
4 Place one third of the lamb into earthenware dishes.
5 Arrange a layer of potatoes on top of the lamb.
6 Repeat this process twice, finishing with a neat layer of potatoes on top.
7 Brush with melted butter and bake at 150°C until the meat is tender and there is a light golden brown finish to the potatoes.

## CHEF'S TIP

Ensure that the lamb is very lean and of the same quality with no fat or gristle.

# Roast leg of lamb

| INGREDIENTS | 8 PORTIONS |
|---|---|
| Leg of lamb | 1 |
| Carrot | 100g |
| Onion | 100g |
| Celery | 100g |
| Leek | 100g |
| Rosemary | 4–5 sprigs |
| Garlic | 2 cloves |
| Buttered new potatoes (see p. 426) | 8 portions |
| Oil | |
| Good-quality salt and white pepper | To taste |
| Mint sauce | 8 portions |
| Brown lamb stock | 400ml |

## Method of work

1 Prepare the leg of lamb by uncovering the knuckle and sawing the end of the leg. Remove any marrow and reserve for the sauce.

2 Remove the 'H' bone and tie the leg at 3cm intervals.

3 Peel and roughly chop the vegetables and place in a roasting dish with the garlic and rosemary.

4 Rub the lamb with a light coating of oil and season with salt and pepper.

5 Place the lamb on the bed of roots and place in an oven at 260°C until caramelised. Lower the temperature to 130°C and allow to cook to the required temperature (see p. 305).

6 Remove from the pan and rest in a warm place for 15–20 minutes.

7 Place the pan on a hot stove and caramelise the vegetables.

8 Add the stock and cook out until the pan is deglazed.

9 Strain the gravy into a clean sauce pan and allow to simmer.

10 Degrease and correct the seasoning.

11 Serve the lamb with the gravy, mint sauce and new potatoes.

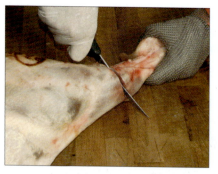

*Trimming the leg*

*Sawing the leg*

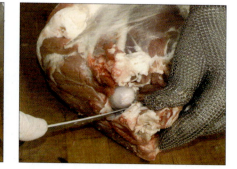

*Removing the aitch bone*

# Shepherd's pie

| INGREDIENTS | 4 PORTIONS | 10 PORTIONS |
| --- | --- | --- |
| Minced lamb | 500g | 1.25kg |
| Diced onions | 100g | 250g |
| Oil | 40ml | 100ml |
| Demi glace (see p. 120) | 200ml | 500ml |
| Duchesse potatoes (see p. 420) | 500g | 1.25kg |
| Good-quality salt and white pepper | To taste | To taste |

## Method of work

1. Cook the lamb and onions in the pan until browned and well broken up.
2. Add the demi glace and allow to simmer for 30 minutes, correct the seasoning.
3. Place in either individual bowls or earthenware dishes
4. Pipe the potato on top and bake until golden brown.

# Moussaka

| INGREDIENTS | 4 PORTIONS | 10 PORTIONS |
| --- | --- | --- |
| Minced lamb | 400g | 1kg |
| Aubergines | 600g | 1.5kg |
| Olive oil | 80ml | 200ml |
| Peeled chopped plum tomatoes | 4 | 10 |
| Sliced onions | 150g | 425g |
| Tomato purée | 40g | 100g |
| Chopped parsley | 20g | 50g |
| White wine | 80ml | 200ml |
| Sauce Mornay (see p. 114) | 500ml | 1.25 litres |
| Good-quality salt and black pepper | To taste | To taste |
| Toasted breadcrumbs | 40g | 100g |

## Method of work

1. Slice the aubergines, layer them with salt in a colander and leave for 1 hour.
2. Wash in several changes of fresh water and allow to dry on a clean cloth.
3. Fry the aubergines until golden brown and drain on dish paper.
4. Fry the lamb and onions in a little oil until the lamb is broken up.
5. Add the remainder of the ingredients, bring to the boil and simmer for 30 minutes.
6. Arrange alternating layers of meat and aubergines finishing with a layer of aubergines. Pour on the sauce, sprinkle with the breadcrumbs and bake in the oven at 180°C for 45–50 minutes until the surface is golden brown.
7. Serve hot with green salad.

# Lamb cutlets Milanese

| INGREDIENTS | 4 PORTIONS | 10 PORTIONS |
|---|---|---|
| Lamb cutlets | 12 | 30 |
| Flour | | |
| Eggwash | | |
| Seasoned breadcrumbs | | |
| *Spaghetti Milanese* | | |
| Spaghetti | 100g | 200g |
| Grated parmesan | 25g | 50g |
| Plum tomato coulis | 125ml | 250ml |
| Ham, tongue and cooked mushroom into julienne | 25g | 50g |
| Good-quality salt and black pepper | To taste | To taste |
| Clarified butter | 50g | 125g |

## Method of work

1 Using a saw or heavy knife chine the best end by cutting through the ribs where they join the chine bone, being careful not to cut into the meat.

2 Cut away the flesh from the bone to leave 2–3cm of bone exposed.

3 Remove the outer skin from the best ends (bark).

4 Scrape the bones until they are clean, Using the tip of the knife, gently push the meat from the bone.

5 Push the sheet of flesh from the bones and cut away at the bottom.

6 Cut between each bone to achieve lamb cutlets.

7 Trim the cutlets by removing any elastin and flatten with a meat bat.

8 Pass through flour, eggwash and breadcrumbs.

9 Fry in clarified butter until cooked and golden brown.

10 Cook the spaghetti in boiling salted water.

11 Drain well in a colander, return to a clean pan and add the tomato coulis.

12 Correct the seasoning and add the julienne garnish.

13 Serve the lamb on top of spaghetti Milanese, with the parmesan.

*Chining*

*Peeling the meat away from the bones*

*Trimming and removing elastin*

# Mixed grill

| INGREDIENTS | 4 PORTIONS | 10 PORTIONS |
|---|---|---|
| Lamb chops | 4 | 10 |
| Chipolata sausages | 4 | 10 |
| Lambs kidney | 4 | 10 |
| Gammon steak 60–80g | 4 | 10 |
| Beef tomatoes | 2 | 5 |
| Flat mushrooms | 4 | 10 |
| Minute steak 60–80g | 4 | 10 |
| Parsley butter | | |
| Straw potatoes (see p. 422) | 4 portions | 10 portions |

## Method of work

1 Prepare the chops.
2 Cut the kidneys in half and remove the core.
3 Brush the meat and vegetables with oil.
4 Grill all the items until cooked and serve with straw potatoes and parsley butter.

# Lamb meatballs with spaghetti

| INGREDIENTS | 4 PORTIONS | 10 PORTIONS |
|---|---|---|
| Middle neck of lamb | 400g | 1kg |
| Soaked breadcrumbs | 50g | 125g |
| Dried basil | 1tsp | 1tbsp |
| Finely diced onions | 100g | 250g |
| Crushed garlic | 1 clove | 2 cloves |
| Finely diced carrot | 40g | 100g |
| Finely diced celery | 40g | 100g |
| Chopped ripe tomatoes | 200g | 500g |
| White wine vinegar | | |
| Sugar | 1tsp | 1tbsp |
| Good-quality salt and black pepper | To taste | To taste |
| Buttered spaghetti | 4 portions | 10 portions |
| Shaved Parmesan | 120g | 300g |

## Method of work

1 Remove the meat from the bone. Remove all sinew and excess fat. Slice into pieces, dice then pass through a fine mincer.
2 Mix half the onions, soaked breadcrumbs (bread panada), dried basil, garlic and minced lamb together.
3 Form into 25g meatballs.
4 Shallow fry the meatballs until brown on the outside.
5 Remove the meatballs and add the onions, carrot and celery: allow to sweat.
6 Add the sugar and vinegar and allow the vinegar to reduce until the acid is evaporated.
7 Add the tomatoes and meatballs. Bring to the boil and simmer on top of the stove or in the oven for 20–30 minutes.
8 Serve on a bed of buttered spaghetti with shaved Parmesan.

### CHEF'S TIP

The use of vinegar and sugar to make a gastrique counteracts the acidity in the tomatoes.

# PORK RECIPES

## Roast loin of pork with caramelized apple sauce and parsnip mash

| INGREDIENTS | 4 PORTIONS | 10 PORTIONS |
|---|---|---|
| Loin of pork on the bone | 800g | 2kg |
| Apple sauce | 4 portions | 10 portions |
| Carrots, onion, leeks, celery (mirepoix) | 200g | 500g |
| Brown stock | 400ml | 1 litre |
| Vinegar | 1tsp | 1tbsp |
| Mashed parsnips | | |
| Good-quality salt and white pepper | To taste | To taste |

## Method of work

1  Remove the rind from the loin and score with a sharp knife.

2  Remove the chine bone from the loin and trim the bones until clean.

3  Rub the rind with vinegar and a little salt.

4  Tie the rind back onto the loin and place it on the mirepoix.

5  Place in a hot oven, 260°C, until brown.

6  Turn down the heat and continue to roast until a core temperature of 75°C is achieved.

7  Remove from the oven, remove the rind and place it back into a hot oven to crisp up for crackling.

8  Allow the loin to rest in a warm place.

9  Pour off the excess fat from the roasting pan and place it on the stove to caramelise.

10  Deglaze with the stock and boil for a few minutes.

11  Strain the gravy into a clean pan and thicken with a little arrowroot if necessary, correct the seasoning.

12  Serve with apple sauce, gravy, roast potatoes and crackling.

Removing chine bone

Trimming flesh from the rib

Tying the rind on

# Boiled gammon with parsley sauce

| INGREDIENTS | 4 PORTIONS | 10 PORTIONS |
|---|---|---|
| **Boned and rolled gammon** (allow 150g of cooked gammon per portion) | 4 | 10 |
| **Parsley sauce** (see p. 114) | 4 portions | 10 portions |

## Method of work

1 Soak the gammon for 24 hours in cold water.

2 Place into a pan and cover with fresh cold water.

3 Bring to the boil and simmer for 3½–4 hours until cooked.

4 Test by pushing a skewer into the thickest part. There should be little resistance when the skewer is withdrawn.

5 Remove the rind and carve into thin slices. Serve coated with parsley sauce.

# Barbecued baby back ribs

| INGREDIENTS | 4 PORTIONS | 10 PORTIONS |
|---|---|---|
| **Baby back ribs** | 2 sheets | 5 sheets |
| **Robert sauce** (see p. 123) | 200ml | 500ml |
| **Oil** | 20ml | 50ml |
| **White wine** | 40ml | 100ml |
| **Honey** | 20ml | 50ml |
| **Star anise** | 2 | 5 |
| **Water** | 40ml | 100ml |
| **Hoi sin sauce** | 20ml | 50ml |
| **Soy sauce** | 20ml | 50ml |
| **Chopped chilli** | 20g | 50g |

## Method of work

1 Combine the ingredients for the marinade and marinate the ribs for 24 hours turning from time to time.

2 Place the ribs in a covered dish, in an oven set at 150°C for 1 hour.

3 Cut the sheets of ribs in half and brush each with half of the Robert sauce.

4 Grill until glazed, reduce the marinade and add to the remainder of the sauce.

5 Coat the ribs with the sauce and serve.

## CHEF'S TIP

Be sure to give the ribs their full time in the oven before grilling: they will not be tender enough after a shorter cooking, but when they are well cooked and used later they are both tender and succulent.

# Toad in the hole

| INGREDIENTS | 4 PORTIONS | 10 PORTIONS |
|---|---|---|
| Pork sausages | 8 | 20 |
| Yorkshire pudding batter | 200ml | 500ml |
| Oil | 20ml | 50ml |

## Method of work

1 Fry the sausages until golden brown.

2 Heat the oil in a individual dish or roasting pan.

3 Add the sausages and pour over the batter.

4 Place in a hot oven, 220°C, for 20–30minutes until the batter has risen and is a golden brown.

5 Serve with onion gravy.

# Pork medallions with Madeira sauce

| INGREDIENTS | 4 PORTIONS | 10 PORTIONS |
|---|---|---|
| Pork fillets | 2 | 5 |
| Flour | To dust | To dust |
| Good-quality salt and pepper | To taste | To taste |
| Butter | 40g | 100g |
| Chopped shallots | 40g | 100g |
| Madeira | 40ml | 100ml |
| Madeira sauce (see p. 122) | 4 portions | 10 portions |

## Method of work

1 Slice the fillets into medallions 1cm thick.

2 Season and dust lightly with flour.

3 Heat the butter in a pan until it starts to foam.

4 Add the medallions and shallow fry for 3–4 minutes on each side until thoroughly cooked.

5 Remove from the pan and add the shallots, sweat for 2–3 minutes and add the Madeira to deglaze the pan. Allow to reduce.

6 Add the sauce and reboil.

7 Serve coated with the sauce.

*Trimming the pork fillet*

*Slicing the medallions*

*Dusting the meat with flour and flattening the medallions*

# Pork cutlets with cranberries

| INGREDIENTS | 4 PORTIONS | 10 PORTIONS |
|---|---|---|
| Pork cutlets | 4 x 180g | 10 x 180g |
| Fresh or frozen cranberries | 160g | 400g |
| Demi glace (see p. 120) | 240ml | 600ml |
| Sugar | To taste | To taste |
| Brown chicken or beef stock | 40ml | 100ml |
| Shallots | 80g | 100g |
| Good-quality salt and black pepper | To taste | To taste |
| Oil | 40ml | 100ml |
| Flour for dusting | | |

## Method of work

1 Cut the cutlets from a chined loin of pork.
2 Trim the bones and scrape clean.
3 Peel and cut the shallots into a fine brunoise.
4 Heat the oil in a thick-bottomed frying pan.
5 Season the flour and dust the pork cutlets.
6 Fry the cutlets in the oil until golden brown. Place on a tray and put into oven at 130°C.
7 Add the shallots to the pan and sweat without letting them colour.
8 Add the cranberries and stock, cover with a lid and cook until the cranberries split.
9 Add the demi glace, bring to the boil, adjust the seasoning and add the sugar as desired.
10 Return the cutlets to the pan and simmer gently until the cutlets are cooked.
11 Serve with creamed potatoes and seasonal vegetables.

Finished cutlets

# Sausage and mash with Lyonnaise sauce

| INGREDIENTS | 4 PORTIONS | 10 PORTIONS |
|---|---|---|
| Pork sausages | 12 x 40g | 30 x 40g |
| Lyonnaise sauce (see p.332) | 4 portions | 10 portions |
| Mashed potatoes (see p. 419) | 4 portions | 10 portions |
| Oil for frying | | |

## Method of work

1 Shallow fry or grill the sausages until golden brown.
2 Transfer to an oven to finish cooking. Achieve a core temperature of 75°C.
3 Serve on the mashed potatoes with the Lyonnaise sauce on top.

# VEAL RECIPES

## Fricassée of veal

| INGREDIENTS | 4 PORTIONS | 10 PORTIONS |
|---|---|---|
| Diced veal | 600g | 1.5kg |
| Butter | 80g | 200g |
| Flour | 40g | 100g |
| White veal or chicken stock (see p. 112) | 600ml | 1.5 litres |
| Double cream | 100ml | 250ml |
| Chopped parsley | 1tsp | 1tbsp |
| Egg yolks | 2 | 4–5 |

### Method of work

1 Melt the butter in a thick-bottomed pan.
2 Add the veal and cook until all sides of the meat have been sealed without colour.
3 Add the flour and cook out until a blond roux has been formed.
4 Add the stock and bring to the boil.
5 Simmer until the meat is tender.
6 Strain the meat and put to one side.
7 Mix the cream and the yolks.
8 Boil the sauce and pour a little onto the cream and yolks. Mix well.
9 Add the yolks, cream and sauce (liaison) back into the sauce and mix thoroughly. DO NOT ALLOW TO REBOIL.
10 Correct the seasoning and pour over the cooked veal.
11 Garnish with chopped parsley and serve with pilaff rice.

*Making the liaison*

## Escalope of veal Cordon Bleu

| INGREDIENTS | 4 PORTIONS | 10 PORTIONS |
|---|---|---|
| Veal escalopes × 100g | 4 | 10 |
| Slice of cooked ham 40g | 4 | 10 |
| Slices of Gruyère cheese 20g | 4 | 10 |
| Flour | For pané | For pané |
| Eggwash | For pané | For pané |
| Breadcrumbs | For pané | For pané |
| Butter | 40g | 100g |
| Plum tomato coulis (see p. 126) | 4 portions | 10 portions |

## Method of work

1 Bat out the escalopes until they are 150mm round.
2 Place a slice of ham on each escalope.
3 Lace a slice of Gruyère cheese on half of each escalope.
4 Fold in half to make a 'D'-shape, season each side with salt and pepper.
5 Pané with flour eggwash and breadcrumbs, and reshape to a neat oval.
6 Heat the butter in a pan until foaming but not starting to colour.
7 Pan fry the escalopes until golden brown on each side.
8 Serve with tomato coulis.

# Fillet of veal with orange and tarragon sauce and grain mustard mash

| INGREDIENTS | 4 PORTIONS | 10 PORTIONS |
|---|---|---|
| Fillet of veal | 2 | 2.5 |
| Flour for dusting | | |
| Oranges | 1 | 2.5 |
| Tarragon | 1tbsp | 2tbsp |
| Double cream | 100ml | 250ml |
| Butter | 40g | 100g |
| Creamed potatoes | 4 portions | 10 portions |
| Wholegrain mustard seeds | 1tsp | 1tbsp |
| Good-quality salt and white pepper | To taste | To taste |

*Frying the veal*

## Method of work

1 Prepare the veal by cutting fillet in half, wrap in several layers of cling film and chill for no less than 2 hours.
2 Slice into equal portions. Preheat the oven to 180°C.
3 Fry the slices in the butter on each side until golden brown, season to taste.
4 Place in the oven until cooked.
5 Grate the zest of the orange and squeeze in the juice. Pour this into a pan and reduce to a light syrup. Add the double cream and bring to the boil. Add the tarragon and correct the seasoning and the consistency.
6 Mix the mustard seeds with the creamed potatoes and serve the veal with the sauce on the mustard grain mash.

# Blanquette of veal with onions and mushrooms

*Blanquette de veau à l'Ancienne*

| INGREDIENTS | 4 PORTIONS | 10 PORTIONS |
|---|---|---|
| Diced veal | 500g | 1.25kg |
| Veal stock | 1 litre | 2.5 litres |
| Onion studded with cloves | 1 | 2 |
| Bouquet garni | 1 small | 1 large |
| Button onions | 20 | 50 |
| Button mushrooms | 20 | 50 |
| Lemon juice | ½ | 1 |
| Flour (for the roux) | 20g | 50g |
| Flour | 80g | 200g |
| Butter (for the roux) | 80g | 200g |
| Double cream | 80ml | 200ml |
| Egg yolks | 4 | 10 |
| Sliced bread | 4 | 10 |
| Butter for frying | 100g | 250g |

## Method of work

1  Blanch the veal in boiling water and refresh in cold water.

2  Place the blanched veal into the stock with the bouquet garni and onion clouté and simmer until tender (1–1½ hours).

3  Meanwhile cook the onions and mushrooms in a blanc (water mixed with the lemon juice, flour and seasoning).

4  Make a roux with the flour and butter.

5  Remove the meat from the stock and add the stock to the roux, cook for 20–25 minutes until the flour is cooked.

6  Make a liaison with the cream and yolks. Add a little sauce to the liaison and add this back to the sauce. DO NO ALLOW THE SAUCE TO REBOIL.

7  Meanwhile mix the cooked veal with the garnish and keep hot.

8  Cut the bread into heart-shaped croûtons and cook in clarified butter until a light golden brown.

9  Coat the meat with the sauce and serve.

Cut a V shape into the sliced bread

Cut each corner to form the heart shape

Cut a wedge into the top of the form to create a heart shape

# Assessment of knowledge and understanding

You have now learned about the use of the different varieties of meat and how to prepare and cook different meat dishes.

To test your level of knowledge and understanding, answer the following short questions. These will help to prepare you for your summative (final) assessment.

1 List three quality points you should look for when receiving beef.

i) _____     ii) _____

iii) _____

2 State why you should check for marbling in red meat.

_____

_____

3 Explain why it is important to use sharp knives when preparing cuts of meat.

_____

_____

4 Describe the process of making a paupiettes of beef.

_____

_____

5 Explain what a stew is.

_____

_____

_____

6 Explain the reason for resting roasted meats prior to carving.

_____

_____

_____

7 State the correct temperature for holding a meat dish hot for service.

_____

_____

## Research Task

Complete the following chart describing how to use, clean and maintain the following items of equipment and the safety considerations associated with them

| | CLEANING | STERILISING | STORING | SAFETY PROCEDURES |
|---|---|---|---|---|
| Raw meat chopping board | | | | |
| Boning knife | | | | |
| Electric mincing machine | | | | |

## CHEF'S PROFILE

**Name: NIGEL HAWORTH**

**Establishment:** Northcote Manor

**When did you realise you wanted to pursue a career in catering?** Halfway through my final year at school, I basically just woke up one morning and decided cooking was for me. It was weird and yet a very satisfying feeling. From that moment on I have been totally dedicated to a life of cookery.

**What do you find rewarding about your job?** I find the creative aspect the most rewarding part. Food is a love affair and if you care about the product you will produce quality on the plate. What other job allows you to use such incredible products that change with the seasons!

**What do you find the most challenging about the job?** The most challenging aspect of the job is to train people well. To pass on skills and to develop people to love and understand the beauty of quality ingredients. Cookery is a challenging job in all aspects both mentally and physically and today's chefs need to also be more business aware.

**What advice would you give to students just beginning their career?** I would advise students to look at where the food comes from, to understand the roots of their produce and then to follow the path of the product. Food with provenance is a very important aspect; to have knowledge and to understand is to respect a product.

**Who was your mentor or main inspiration?** I had two mentors. One was a food historian, Roy Shipperbottom, who has sadly passed away, but who inspired me to understand more about the heritage of food.

Michael Quinn, was my other inspiration. He was my college lecturer at Accrington & Rossendale College and went on to be the first English chef at the Ritz, and has remained a great friend.

**Secrets of a successful chef:** Dedication in the pursuit of perfection, an understanding of the craft and above all a real love for the raw material you are cooking. I believe without that you cannot become a great chef nor have a true understanding of cookery.

**Can you give one essential kitchen tip or technique that you use as a chef:** One essential tip is to cut an onion finely. This is the easiest way to detect whether a chef holds his knives in the correct manner and whether he has grasped the basics of learning how to cook.

# Butter puff pastry wrapped breast of partridge, butternut crush

| INGREDIENTS | |
|---|---|
| Partridge breasts | 4 |
| Stuffing | 100g |
| Cumbrian ham | 4 slices |
| Fine green beans | 4 handfulls |
| Salt and pepper | |
| Egg yolk (add a pinch of salt and mix well) | 1 |
| Butter puff pastry (roll out approximately 2mm thick, roll with lattice cutter and refrigerate) | 300g |
| Madeira sauce | |
| Stuffing | |
| Sliced button mushrooms | 100g |
| Butter | 50g |
| Finely diced onion | 50g |
| Finely diced bacon | 20g |
| Finely diced Cumbrian ham | 30g |
| Clove of baked garlic, peeled and puréed | 1 |
| Picked chervil, roughly chopped | 10g |
| Balsamic vinegar | 1½tsp |
| Salt to taste | |

## Method for stuffing

1 In a non-stick pan fry off the onion, bacon, mushrooms, garlic and Cumbrian ham for 3–4 minutes. Add the balsamic vinegar and salt. Reduce all of the liquid off.

2 Remove from the pan and allow to cool. Once cool, add the chervil. Finally, check the seasoning.

## Method of work

1 Take the partridge breasts and release the small fillet (that is, the fillet on the underside of the breasts) to one side of the breast. Make a small incision to the meatier side of the breast to form a small pouch.

2 Carefully place the stuffing into the pouch and fold the small fillet back over, closing the pouch.

3 Wrap a slice of Cumbrian ham around the breast.

4 Take the puff pastry and brush with the egg wash. Carefully cut the pastry into 4 squares and fold around the partridge breast opening lattice, work a little as you go. Cut off any excess pastry and tuck in well at all sides.

5 Bake in a hot oven at 200°C for 8 minutes. Remove and allow to rest for 5 minutes before serving.

6 Top and tail the green beans and cook for 2–3 minutes in boiling water. Remove from water and place into ice-cold water (to retain green colour). Re-heat with seasoning and butter in a small pan or a microwave.

### Butternut crush

| INGREDIENTS | |
|---|---|
| Butternut squash (cut in half, remove seeds and score) | 1 |
| Cloves garlic (crushed) | 3 |
| Olive oil to coat | |
| Salt and pepper | |

## Method of work

1 Score the squash with a sharp knife on the flesh side, rub on garlic and sprinkle with olive oil. Season with salt and pepper.

2 Bake at 180°C for 30–40 minutes until flesh is soft. Scoop out, check seasoning and reserve.

*To serve*
Take the partridge breast and slice in half on a slight slant, place on the plate at the top, put the butternut squash opposite, place the beans on top and sauce around with the Madeira sauce.

# Offal

## INTRODUCTION

The term offal refers to certain internal organs and other parts of an animal that should not be confused with the flesh (meat) of an animal. Offal has always been considered the cheapest of meat cuts and is known in France and other European countries as the 'fifth quarter'. This name comes from the fact that offal cuts are derived 'outside' of the four quarters of the animal and are removed from the carcass before the animal is broken down into the relative joints.

The reason these items are cheaper is because they are classed as an inferior cut of the animal. Historically these cuts were brought by poor customers and were thought of as a good way of adding flavour to soups and stews for little extra financial outlay. In addition to this, offal has a good nutritional value and was used to provide a cheaper alternative in creating a balanced diet.

In recent times, however, offal has appeared on menus used as a dish on its own or as a garnish. Once again this is partly due to the cost of offal – it is cheaper to purchase – but is also because of its defined and strong flavour. Offal is now used to create interesting dishes in its own right to add variety to modern menus.

Certain items of offal, such as duck or goose liver, can be quite expensive. Usually this is because of the increased labour which is required to prepare such delicacies as foie gras, or due to the fact that certain offal such as lamb sweetbreads can be hard to purchase from suppliers due to seasonality or lack of quality supply.

The variety of organs and tissues that are collectively known as offal generally contain more connective tissue than ordinary meat. Because of this they will benefit from a slow and moist cooking (stewing, braising) to dissolve the collagen. Certain offal such as liver contains relatively little collagen and because this organ experiences very little mechanical strain it is usually a delicate texture. If liver is slightly undercooked it will be tender and moist: if over-cooked it will become dry and crumbly.

Many offal cuts such as hearts and sweetbreads are often trimmed and cleaned before being blanched or covered with cold water and brought slowly to the boil. The blanching process will help to remove any waste materials from the organ and will lessen any strong smells on the meat surface.

More chefs are beginning to understand and realise the flexibility that using offal brings to an individual dish or menu. The more adventurous among us have fashioned reputations for using offal and this is beginning to bring the use of offal back into mainstream cookery.

**CHEF'S TIP**

Once offal has been soaked or prepared, one way to enhance its flavour is to marinate it in herbs, spices and oil.

**VIDEO CLIP**
Preparing lamb's heart

This chapter will begin to explore some modern ideas of preparing, cooking and presenting offal, but classical methods of preparation should also be understood as a basis for progression.

# BASIC TYPES OF OFFAL

There are two main types of offal: red and white. Red offal consists of liver, kidneys, heart, oxtail, lungs and tongue. White offal consists of sweetbreads, brain, bone marrow, tripe, the head, trotters and stomach. Other parts that have not been mentioned are classed as offal too, such as cheek and pig's ears.

The main offal items that are generally utilised are obtained from pork, beef, ox, calves, lambs, poultry, rabbit and some feathered game such as pheasant. Each type of animal or bird offal will have its own distinct flavours, textures and use. Therefore it is important that chefs have an understanding of the techniques and skills needed to obtain the finest flavours and eating quality from each product.

This chapter will concentrate on three main types of offal used in cooking: kidney, liver and sweetbreads.

## Liver

The liver is the largest organ in the body and most of the nutrients that the body absorbs from food will travel here first to be processed for distribution around the body, hence it has a sponge-like texture and is extremely delicate. Generally both the flavour and the texture of liver will become stronger and coarser with age.

Liver is one of the most versatile offal categories. It can be used shallow fried on its own, braised, made into pâtés, parfaits, terrines or farces. As liver has little fat (between 4–8 per cent), if it is not slightly under-cooked it can become very dry.

Because the texture of liver is delicate it is able to absorb flavours very well. Various herbs such as sage, thyme, rosemary and chives combine well with liver as do shallots, onions or smoked products like pancetta and cured bacon.

The composition of liver is up to 31 per cent protein. It has many nutrients such as iron and folate, a vitamin that is traditionally associated with helping to reduce the risk of heart disease.

When purchasing liver it is essential to check that it has a good even colouration throughout with no discoloured patches on the surface of the liver. It should be as fresh as possible and have no unpleasant odour or stickiness.

**CHEF'S TIP**

To add texture to a shallow-fried dish coat the offal in breadcrumbs, polenta, brioche crumbs or herbed breadcrumbs.

**VIDEO CLIP**
Preparing lamb's liver

**VIDEO CLIP**
Preparing lamb's kidney

# Kidney

Kidney has a very distinct but delicate flavour. The function of the kidneys is to purge the body from liquid waste materials, therefore care must be taken to ensure that they are correctly cleaned and prepared before use in cooking. The best way of cleaning kidneys is to soak them in milk as this helps to draw out the impurities and encourage the natural kidney flavour. Kidney has approximately 16–26 per cent protein, and 3–6 per cent fat content.

Veal kidney is the most respected of all the different varieties of kidney as they have a tender and full flavour. Because they are of such a delicate texture, they can be cooked using dry- and quick-cooking methods. Pork kidney has a smooth, larger appearance than veal kidney, and also has a stronger flavour. The kidney can be quite tough depending on the age of the animal, so quick-cooking methods may not always give the best results. Moist and slow methods such as braising will be best. Lamb's kidney is tender and light in colour. The kidneys have a subtle flavour and can be cooked by grilling and frying, but also can be cooked using moist methods of cookery such as stewing. Mutton kidney is darker in colour and has a stronger flavour than lamb's kidney. Ox kidney is thought to be the toughest-textured kidney available. It has a dark colour and strong flavour and is generally used mixed with beef for steak and kidney pudding. Calf's kidney has a light colour and a delicate flavour similar to that of veal. This is a product that has a diverse appeal because it can be used for a variety of dishes and methods of cookery.

## PURCHASE SPECIFICATIONS

For the purchase of kidney the chef should always look at the following factors:

- All kidneys should be as fresh as possible.
- Both ox and lamb's kidney should have a covering of fat to maintain their natural moisture. This should not be removed until just before preparation for cooking.
- The smell of the kidney and fat should not be overpowering. Any trace of an ammonia odour means that the kidney should be discarded.
- Storage temperature can be as low as −1°C for fresh kidney and should not really be stored for any longer than a maximum of three days.

**CHEF'S TIP**

In longer cooking processes such as braising or stewing, adding the kidney too early can result in them becoming tough through overcooking. It is best to seal them by shallow frying the kidneys separately and adding them towards the end of the cooking process to retain the texture and flavour.

# Sweetbreads

Sweetbreads are the soft-textured thymus and pancreas glands of calves and lambs and are a respected food commodity in gastronomic kitchens across the world. Although they are still under-utilised as a product or a dish in their own right, they can generally be found as an component of a dish or as a garnish. They are a light meat that is firm in texture. Veal sweetbreads are considered the best; beef sweetbreads are rather fatty and coarse, but if well prepared, they will taste similar to veal. Sweetbreads contain between 12–33 per cent protein content and approximately 3–23 per cent fat (of which most can be removed during the preparation stage).

Sweetbreads require a great deal of preparation before they can be used and cooked as they are a gland from either the throat or heart area and certain impurities that need to be removed by soaking and blanching before being pressed. Pressing is not always applicable with sweetbreads, however, as this depends on the cooking process to be used.

Sweetbreads should be soaked in cold salted water in a refrigerator for approximately 4 hours and then washed under cold running water to remove all traces of blood and return them to a white colour. When blanching, veal sweetbreads should be blanched for 5 minutes and lamb sweetbreads for about 3 minutes and refreshed immediately in cold water. This will aid the removal of the skin, which can be difficult in its raw state. All fat and gristle should be removed at this stage. Place on a tray between two clean and damp kitchen cloths before setting a lightly weighted tray on top. Leave in a refrigerator for 4 hours to become firm and slightly pressed.

**VIDEO CLIP**
Preparing lamb's sweetbread

*Various sweetbreads*

# STORAGE OF OFFAL

When storing any offal it is important to remember that because these are organs and parts of the body they may have blood retained inside them. It is necessary to ensure that offal is stored in deep containers (minimum 8cm depth) with a filter tray or absorbent paper underneath to soak or easily remove discarded fluids and blood.

Refrigeration temperatures can be adjusted to as low as −1°C for the storage of fresh offal so that deterioration is slowed. Offal should be regularly checked during storage for signs of decline.

The following information will give a brief summary of the various offal products, detailing their French terminology, how to recognise the item by appearance and how best to prepare the product for cooking.

## Beef/ox liver

- *French term* – Foie de boeuf
- *Appearance* – Should be large in size, deep red in colour and will have a strong smell, although not too pungent. The product should look moist but not slimy and have no tearing, cuts or dark spots on the flesh.
- *Preparation* – Care must to be taken not to dissect the liver too much. Remove the outer skin membrane with a sharp knife making sure you do

*Use the hand to release the membrane*

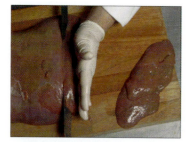

*Slicing the ox liver*

not pierce the flesh, at the same time trimming off any excess fat and removing any sinews and tubes.

Beef/ox livers can be left whole but this is no longer a general procedure. The preference today is to cut the product into slices or thin strips or dice depending on the dish to be produced.

Following this procedure the product can then be stored as mentioned earlier, or utilise the milk soaking process to further remove any impurities.

## Beef/ox kidney

■ *French term* – Rognon de boeuf

■ *Appearance* – Bright and a deep red, it should not have an overpowering smell and should be evenly coloured with no dull or dark spots on the flesh. It should be moist and not dry, with unbroken skin and without any cuts. If there is any fat around the kidneys, it should be white in colour and not an off-yellow.

■ *Preparation* – Remove the outer membrane with a sharp knife, making sure you do not pierce the flesh, at the same time trimming off any excess fat and removing any tubes.

Beef/ox kidney can be left whole or cut in half lengthways, with the cortex and white fat part being removed following which they can then be sliced into bundles and cooked.

If not being prepared for immediate use, the kidneys should be soaked in milk to remove any impurities.

These items are generally diced and sliced then placed into pies and puddings.

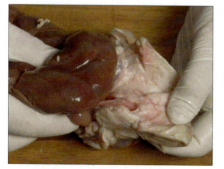

*Remove the fat and outer skin membrane from the kidney*

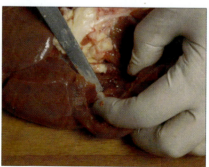

*Remove the cortex from the kidney*

*Soaking kidneys in milk*

## Pig liver

■ *French term* – Foie de porc

■ *Appearance* – A bright red-brown colour, this product will be firmer to the touch and have quite a strong smell. Should be moist but not slimy with no cuts, tearing or dark spots on the surface of the flesh.

- *Procedure* – Remove outer skin with a sharp knife, making sure you do not pierce the flesh. Trim off excess fat if necessary and remove any sinews and tubes.

  This product can be left whole or cut into slices, diced or cut into strips depending on the dish.

  Following this procedure the product can then be stored as normal meat and poultry would, or if storing in raw state it is best to utilise the milk soaking process.

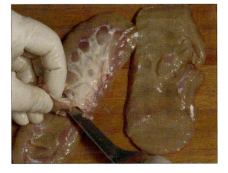
*Trim off any excess fat*

*Cutting into strips*

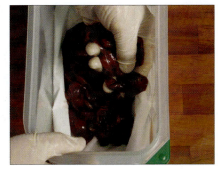
*Storing in a deep plastic container with absorbent paper underneath*

# Pig kidney

- *French term* – Rognon de porc

- *Appearance* – Red, should not have an overbearing acidic smell. Should be evenly coloured and have no dull or dark spots on its flesh, moist and not dry. The flesh should not be broken or have any cuts and if there is any fat around the kidney it should be white in colour and not off-yellow in appearance.

*Cut the kidneys in half lengthways*

- *Procedure* – Remove the outer membrane with a sharp knife making sure you do not pierce the flesh. Trim off any excess fat and remove any tubes. The kidney can be left whole or cut in half lengthways and the cortex removed.

  They can also be cut along the thicker edge of the kidney, not cutting all the way through, and opened up into a round shape.

  If not being prepared for immediate use, they should be soaked in milk to remove any impurities. These items are generally diced and sliced then placed into pies and puddings.

*Opening the cut kidney into a round shape*

# Lamb/mutton liver

- *French term* – Foie d'agneau

- *Appearance* – Deep red in colour and should not smell strong. This will be of a medium size compared to veal or ox. It should have a moist texture

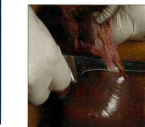

*Trim any excess fat from the liver*

*Cutting the liver into dice*

*Soak the sweetbreads in water*

but not be slimy to the touch. The product should be in one whole piece with no tearing or cuts to the flesh.

■ *Procedure* – Remove the outer skin with a sharp knife, making sure you do not pierce the flesh. Trim off any excess fat if necessary and remove any sinews and tubes.

Can then be left whole or cut into slices, diced or into strips depending on the dish.

The product can be stored as normal meat and poultry would, but if storing in raw state it is best to utilise the milk soaking process.

# Lamb/mutton kidney

■ *French term* – Rognon d'agneau

■ *Appearance* – Pale red, not purple, and should not have an acidic smell. Lamb/mutton kidneys should be evenly coloured and have no dull or dark spots on the flesh, which should also be moist, not dry. The skin should not be broken or have any cuts. If there is any fat around the kidneys it should be white in colour and not an off-yellow.

■ *Procedure* – Remove the outer membrane with a sharp knife making sure you do not pierce the flesh. Trim off any excess fat and remove any tubes. Can be left whole or cut in half lengthways and the cortex removed.

They can be slit along the thicker side, not all the way through, and opened up into a round shape. If not being prepared for immediate use, soak in milk to remove any impurities.

# Lamb sweetbreads

■ *French term* – Ris d'agneau

■ *Appearance* – Should be plump and firm to the touch and pale-white in colour. May sometimes be bloody in appearance but this should wash out with soaking and washing. There are two types – thymus and pancreas glands – so the shape will vary. These are from two areas of the animal – the throat, and nearer the heart, which is rounder in shape.

■ *Procedure* – Soak in water to remove blood or impurities and to whiten them in colour. Blanch and refresh in iced water. They can then be trimmed of any sinews or fat.

Press between two clean trays and clean/damp kitchen cloths for approximately 4 hours in a refrigerator. Use whole or slice for cooking.

Blanching the sweetbreads and refreshing them in cold water

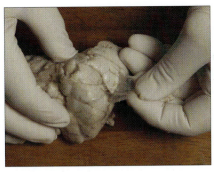

Trim and remove any fat and sinew

Pressing the sweetbreads between two trays

# Veal liver

- *French term* – Foie de veau
- *Appearance* – Should be pale pink or rose red in colour and will be quite large in size. They should be moist but not slimy and have no cuts or blemishes to the flesh.
- *Procedure* – Remove the outer membrane with a sharp knife making sure you do not pierce the flesh. Trim off any excess fat and remove any sinews and tubes. They can be left whole or cut in half lengthways and the cortex removed. Can be slit along the thicker side, not all the way through, and opened up into a round shape. If not being prepared for immediate use, soak in milk to remove any impurities.

# Veal kidney

- *French term* – Rognon de veau
- *Appearance* – Pale red, not purple, and should not have an acidic smell. Evenly coloured with no dull or dark spots on the flesh, which should also be moist and not dry. The skin should not be broken or have any cuts. If there is any fat around the kidneys it should be white in colour and not an off-yellow.
- *Procedure* – Remove the outer membrane with a sharp knife making sure you do not pierce the flesh. Trim off any excess fat and remove any tubes. Can be left whole or cut in half lengthways and the cortex removed. If not being prepared for immediate use, soak in milk to remove any impurities.

# Veal sweetbreads

- *French term* – Ris de veau
- *Appearance* – Plump and firm to the touch, evenly shaped and pale (white) in colour. May sometimes be bloody in appearance but this should wash out with soaking. As with lamb's sweetbreads, there are two types so the shape and size will vary.

■ *Procedure* – From two areas of the animal – the throat, and nearer to the heart, which is rounder in shape. Soak in water to remove blood and impurities and to whiten the colour. Blanch and refresh in iced water. They can then be trimmed of any sinews or tubes, and pressed as shown with the lamb's sweetbreads.

## Chicken/duck liver

■ *French term* – Foie de volaille/foie de caneton

■ *Appearance* – Should be brown- and red-coloured offal, quite pale and reasonably small in size.

Due to the delicate nature of the livers, they may sometimes be broken or torn. They will be soft to the touch, should be moist but not slimy and smell fresh and not strong. Any green-coloured residue or flesh should be removed.

■ *Procedure* – Remove the gallbladder if attached, taking care that it does not burst or split. Trim any excess yellow-coloured strands. It can then be left whole or cut into small pieces. If not prepared for immediate use, soak in milk to remove any toxins or impurities.

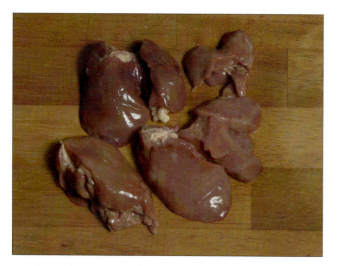

*Chicken livers*

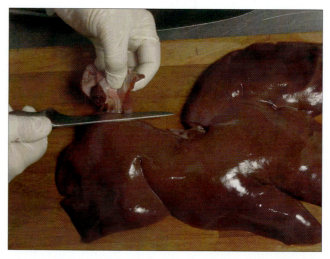

*Trim any excess fat or yellow tissue from the chicken liver*

# RECIPES

## Calves' liver stroganoff

*Stirring in the soured cream or crème fraîche*

| INGREDIENTS | 4 PORTIONS | 10 PORTIONS |
|---|---|---|
| Butter | 100g | 250g |
| Paprika | 50g | 100g |
| Calves liver, sliced into strips | 400g | 1kg |
| Onion, sliced | 150g | 275g |
| Beef or vegetable stock | 45ml | 100ml |
| Button mushrooms, thinly sliced | 200g | 400g |
| Soured cream or crème fraîche | 250ml | 525ml |
| Chopped fresh parsley | 2tbsp | 5tbsp |
| Good-quality salt and white pepper | To taste | To taste |

## Method of work

1 In a large bowl season the liver with salt and pepper making sure it is covered evenly. Lightly flour each slice of liver.

2 Over a high heat sauté the calves' livers in oil until golden in colour then remove from pan.

3 Now add the onions, paprika, salt and pepper, cook until brown and softened then remove from pan.

4 Deglaze the pan with the beef or vegetable stock to remove the residue from the bottom of the pan and bring to the boil.

5 Sauté the mushrooms and cook until softened, then add the onions, mushrooms and liver can be added back to the pan with the cooking juices.

6 Simmer for a few minutes before adding the parsley and correcting the seasoning. Remove from the heat and cool slightly before stirring in the soured cream or the crème fraîche.

# Lamb's liver with balsamic-glazed onions and salt-roasted walnuts

| INGREDIENTS | 4 PORTIONS | 10 PORTIONS |
|---|---|---|
| Lamb's liver, sliced into 80g sized pieces | 8 | 20 |
| Flour | 4tbsp | 10tbsp |
| Mustard powder | 1tsp | 3tsp |
| Button onions | 200g | 500g |
| Butter | 50g | 125g |
| Balsamic vinegar | 120ml | 250ml |
| Soft brown sugar | 2tbsp | 5tbsp |
| Walnut halves | 100g | 200g |
| Good-quality salt | 1tbsp | 3tbsp |
| White pepper | To taste | To taste |
| Olive oil | 30ml | 80ml |

## Method of work

1   Preheat an oven to 170°C. Blanch the walnuts in boiling water for 3 minutes and leave to dry. Remove the skins of the walnuts.

2   In a sauteuse melt the butter and add the button onions, sauté until lightly coloured and softened before adding the balsamic vinegar and sugar. Allow to the contents to caramelise and glaze the onions. Leave to one side keeping them covered and warm.

3   In a shallow frying pan add the olive oil and heat until almost smoking, add the walnuts and salt and toss for one minute off the heat. Place into the oven for 5 minutes or until lightly coloured, remove from the oven and pan and leave to cool.

4   Mix the flour and mustard powder together in a bowl then coat the slices of liver lightly in the flour mixture. Pat any excess flour off each slice and season well.

5   Shallow fry the liver slices in a frying pan on both sides until light golden brown and medium in cooking degree. Allow to rest for 2 minutes.

6   To serve the lamb's liver place the slices on a bed of the balsamic onions, sprinkle the walnuts around the plate and with any remaining glaze decorate over the liver and around the plate.

# Ca___' sweetbread fricassée with whisky and wh___grain mustard

| INGREDIENTS | 4 PORTIONS | 10 PORTIONS |
|---|---|---|
| Calves sweetbreads soaked in iced water overnight | 500g | 1.25kg |
| Beef stock | 500ml | 1.25 litres |
| Onion, finely chopped | 75g | 200g |
| Fresh sage leaves, chopped | 10g | 25g |
| Whisky | 100ml | 200ml |
| Double cream | 600ml | 1.5 litres |
| Wholegrain mustard | 1tbsp | 2½tbsp |
| Butter | 50g | 125g |
| Garlic, finely chopped | 1 clove | 3 cloves |
| Good-quality salt and white pepper | To taste | To taste |

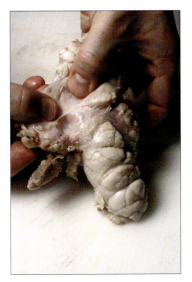

Peeling membrane away from the poached sweetbread

## Method of work

1 Rinse the sweetbreads until the water runs clear, drain and pat dry with a clean kitchen cloth.
2 Gently poach the sweetbreads for 3–4 minutes in water before peeling the membrane away, removing any excess fat and slicing into small even pieces.
3 Sweat the chopped onion, sage and finely chopped garlic in the butter until softened.
4 Add the whisky and flambé to remove the alcohol before returning the sweetbreads to the pan and turning over in the cooking liquor for a minute.
5 Add the hot beef stock and reduce gently until only about 100ml remains.
6 Add the double cream and mustard. Cook out gently for approximately 1 hour or until the sweetbreads are tender. Correct the seasoning and serve.

# Skewers of chorizo and marinated pork kidney

| INGREDIENTS | 4 PORTIONS | 10 PORTIONS |
|---|---|---|
| Pork kidney, 2cm dice | 400g | 1kg |
| Chorizo, 2cm dice | 200g | 500g |
| Wooden skewers | 4 | 10 |
| Olive oil | 50ml | 125ml |
| Fresh parsley | 10g | 25g |
| Fresh basil | 10g | 25g |
| Garlic, chopped | 1 clove | 2 cloves |
| Fresh coriander | 10g | 25g |
| Good-quality salt and white pepper | To taste | To taste |

*Placing the items on skewers*

## Method of work

1 Blend the chopped fresh herbs and garlic with the olive oil to create the marinade.

2 Carefully skin the kidneys, trimming off any excess fat and the cortex, cut into large 2cm dice, season and coat in the marinade. Leave covered in a refrigerator for a minimum of 30 minutes.

3 Using the skewers, place alternate pieces of the kidney and chorizo on to these ensuring an even portion size between each skewer.

4 Brush the skewers with a little marinade and either grill lightly under a salamander, griddle, bake or shallow fry until cooked.

# Pan-fried lamb's sweetbreads with rosemary and lemon butter

| INGREDIENTS | 4 PORTIONS | 10 PORTIONS |
| --- | --- | --- |
| Lamb sweetbreads, soaked overnight in iced water | 500g | 1.25kg |
| Flour | 100g | 250g |
| Lamb stock | 500ml | 1.25 litres |
| Butter | 200g | 500g |
| Lemon | 1 | 2 |
| Fresh rosemary, finely chopped | 10g | 25g |
| Good-quality salt and white pepper | To taste | To taste |

## Method of work

1 Soak the sweetbreads for 4 hours, rinse until the water runs clear and drain.

2 In the stock, gently poach the sweetbreads for 3–4 minutes, remove, drain and cool before removing the membrane and fat from the outside of the sweetbreads. Press the sweetbreads between two trays lined with a clean kitchen cloth for 4 hours and leave in a refrigerator.

3 Once pressed, slice, season and pass through the flour. Melt 50g of the butter and gently shallow fry until golden on both sides, drain and place on a serving plate.

4 Add the rest of the butter to a hot pan and allow to bubble until a nutty brown colour begins to appear and the bubbles have disappeared. Squeeze in the lemon juice and add the rosemary before pouring directly over the sweetbreads and serving.

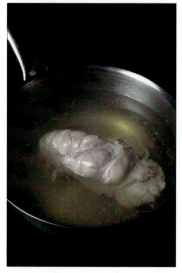

*Poaching sweetbreads*

# Lamb's kidney and liver mixed grill

| INGREDIENTS | 4 PORTIONS | 10 PORTIONS |
|---|---|---|
| Lambs' kidneys | 4 | 10 |
| Pork sausages | 4 | 10 |
| Bacon | 4 | 10 |
| Tomato | 4 | 10 |
| Large flat mushrooms | 4 | 10 |
| Lambs' livers (60g slices) | 4 | 10 |
| Picked and washed watercress | 50g | 100g |
| Good-quality salt and black pepper | To taste | To taste |

*Preparing kidneys for grilling*

## Method of work

1 Season the sausages and cook on a griddle plate until thoroughly cooked with the bar marking effect. To test the cooking place a probe into the centre of each sausage to check the core temperature.

2 Prepare kidneys for grilling by cutting in half lengthways and remove the cortex and any excess fat. Season and grill the kidneys on both sides.

3 Wash, season and brush the mushrooms with melted butter. Place under a salamander and turn regularly until cooked and slightly coloured.

4 Wash, prepare and slice the lambs' livers. Season and pan-fry the lambs' livers until they are slightly pink and under-cooked inside.

5 Wash the tomatoes, score the top with a sharp knife, season and brush with butter. Place under a salamander until cooked and slightly coloured.

6 Season and grill the bacon under a salamander until cooked and crisp.

7 Serve all of the cooked pieces of meat and garnish together with the washed watercress.

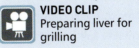 **VIDEO CLIP** Preparing liver for grilling

 **VIDEO CLIP** Preparing kidneys for grilling

# Lamb's liver bhajis

| INGREDIENTS | 4 PORTIONS | 10 PORTIONS |
|---|---|---|
| Lamb's liver, sliced into thin strips | 400g | 1kg |
| Onion, sliced | 100g | 200g |
| Curry powder/garam masala | 60g | 140g |
| Flour | 120g | 260g |
| Milk | 300ml | 700ml |
| Fresh chopped coriander | 2tbsp | 5tbsp |
| Wild cress | 160g | 350g |
| Yoghurt dressing | 120ml | 270ml |
| Good-quality salt and white pepper | To taste | To taste |

## Method of work

1 Season the liver and mix in a bowl with the sliced onions, curry powder, flour, milk and chopped coriander to form a thick paste.

2 Mould into 50g size balls and then flatten slightly so they have a better surface area.

3 In a frying pan with a drop of oil, cook them for approximately 5 minutes or until golden brown on both sides. They may require finishing in an oven at 180°C for a few minutes to ensure the core of each bhaji is cooked through.

4 Remove from the pan or oven and place onto kitchen paper or greaseproof to remove the excess fat.

5 Serve with a wild cress salad and yoghurt dressing.

# Chicken liver stir fry

| INGREDIENTS | 4 PORTIONS | 10 PORTIONS |
|---|---|---|
| Chicken livers, cleaned and sliced | 300g | 750g |
| Bean sprouts | 150g | 375g |
| Mooli, thinly sliced | 100g | 250g |
| Carrot, thinly sliced | 1 | 3 |
| Chinese cabbage | 100g | 250g |
| Mixed peppers, sliced | 100g | 250g |
| Soya sauce | 1tbsp | 3tbsp |
| Spring onion, chopped | 1 | 3 |
| Sesame oil | 100ml | 200ml |
| Garlic, finely chopped | ½ tsp | 1tsp |
| Fresh ginger, finely chopped | ½ tsp | 1tsp |
| Good-quality salt and white pepper | To taste | To taste |

## Method of work

1 Using a hot wok or shallow pan quickly stir fry the garlic, ginger and livers in the sesame oil.

2 Add the prepared carrot and peppers and continue to stir fry for two minutes.

3 Add the mooli and bean sprouts, continue to stir fry for another minute.

4 Prepare the cabbage by washing and slicing thinly. Add the cabbage, spring onion, soy sauce and correct the seasoning before serving.

*Stir frying livers with ginger and garlic*

# Pig liver escalopes stuffed with lemon and caper butter

| INGREDIENTS | 4 PORTIONS | 10 PORTIONS |
|---|---|---|
| Pig liver, large slices | 4 | 10 |
| Slightly salted butter, softened | 50g | 125g |
| Capers, chopped | 1tbsp | 3tbsp |
| Parsley, chopped | 1tbsp | 3tbsp |
| Lemon, zest and juice | ½ lemon | 2 lemons |
| Flour | 50g | 125g |
| Whole eggs, beaten | 3 | 7 |
| White breadcrumbs | 150g | 375g |
| Good-quality salt and white pepper | To taste | To taste |

## Method of work

1 Mix the capers, butter, lemon and parsley together to create the stuffing for the liver, season and chill in a refrigerator to set slightly.

2 Prepare the sliced liver. Place a large slice of the butter into the centre of the liver and fold in half.

3 Season the stuffed liver and pass through the flour, egg and breadcrumbs.

4 Melt some butter in a shallow pan, shallow fry the breadcrumbed stuffed liver and serve.

Stuffing and folding the slices of liver

# Ox liver and pancetta hotpot

| INGREDIENTS | 4 PORTIONS | 10 PORTIONS |
|---|---|---|
| Ox liver, cut into large dice | 500g | 1.2kg |
| Pancetta lardons | 125g | 320g |
| Seasoned flour | 60g | 150g |
| Large onions, sliced | 3 | 8 |
| Carrot chopped | 1 carrot | 3 carrots |
| Celery | 1 stick | 3 sticks |
| Swede, peeled and cut into large dice | 100g | 200g |
| Fresh thyme | 2 sprigs | 5 sprigs |
| Beef stock | 400ml | 1 litre |
| Worcester sauce | 1tsp | 2tsp |
| Potatoes in thick slices (Maris Piper) | 1kg | 2225g |
| Butter or dripping | 40g | 100g |
| Good-quality salt and white pepper | To taste | To taste |

*Layering potatoes onto the vegetables and liver*

## Method of work

1  Preheat an oven 170°C. Sauté the lardons of pancetta in a in a little oil until golden in colour.

2  Using a saucepan sweat and lightly colour the chopped carrot, celery, swede and sliced onion with the fresh thyme and a little butter.

3  Season the liver, dust with flour and place into the bottom of a casserole dish along with the lardons and sweated off vegetables.

4  Add the Worcester sauce and a layer of overlapped washed and sliced potatoes with enough beef stock to just cover the vegetables. Top with another layer of potatoes, season and brush with the butter or dripping.

5  Cover with a lid or foil and bake for approximately 2 hours. Remove the lid, turn up the heat to 200°C and place in the oven to crisp and colour the potatoes.

6  Serve the hotpot in its cooking dish at the table.

## Assessment of knowledge and understanding

You have now learned about the use of the different types of offal, both red and white, and how to produce a variety of dishes utilising an array of commodities and cooking techniques.

To test your level of knowledge and understanding, answer the following short questions. These will help to prepare you for your summative (final) assessment.

1  Name two quality points to look for when purchasing lambs' kidneys.

 i) _____  ii) _____

2  Give two reasons why pork liver may not be the quality that is required.

 i) _____  ii) _____

3  Quality points of the sweetbread should be taken into consideration when using this product. Name two factors and the reasons why they need to be considered.

 i) _____  ii) _____

4  Explain how to prepare chicken livers for sauté.

 _____
 _____

5  Liver is best cooked pink. Explain what this means and why it is cooked this way.

 _____
 _____

6  Generally offal should be soaked prior to use. Explain why this is and how best it could be carried out.

 _____
 _____

# 13

# Vegetables, fruit and pulses

## LEARNING OBJECTIVES

The aim of this unit is to enable the candidate to develop skills and apply this knowledge in the preparation and cookery principles of vegetables, fruits, pulses and vegetable protein. This will also include information on materials, ingredients and equipment.

At the end of this chapter you will be able to:

- Identify each vegetable and pulse variety and finished dish
- Understand the use of relative ingredients in vegetable and pulse cookery
- State the quality points of various vegetable, fruit and pulse commodities and dishes
- Identify the correct tools and equipment to utilise during the production of each variety
- Identify the storage procedures for vegetables, fruits and pulses
- Be competent at preparing and cooking a range of vegetable, fruit, pulse and vegetable protein-based dishes
- Identify the various types of vegetable protein at a basic level and explain their health advantages

# Vegetables and fruit

## INTRODUCTION

Edible plants have been a major part of our diet since the beginning of mankind. It is believed that the first evidence of farming wheat and barley dates from 8000 BC in the Middle East. The discovery of edible plants was then developed into the farming and crop harvesting we recognise today. Lettuce, peas and beans were amongst the first vegetables farmed in Greece and formed a staple part of the country's diet, they were easy to grow and ideal for storing once dried. In Rome lettuce was served both at the beginning and end of meals, and fruit as dessert. Fruits were preserved whole in honey and the Roman gastronome Apicius gave a recipe for pickled peaches. Onions and garlic were favoured in Egypt and were cultivated expertly.

On Marco Polo's travels to Eastern Asia he returned to Europe with a variety of aromatic spices such as cinnamon, cloves and nutmeg. The European appetite for Asian spices was an important aspect in the development of Spain, Portugal, Italy, France, Holland and England into major sea powers. This introduced the exportation of vanilla and chillies from the West Indies and Christopher Columbus returned from his travels with potatoes, squash, tomatoes and peppers. These commodities eventually became staple ingredients in the new cuisines of the old world.

During the seventeenth and eighteenth centuries the cultivation and breeding of plants, fruits and vegetables was of greater significance as cooks began to take a new interest and began to use them in recipes with greater refinement. Plants, fruits and vegetables were now grown locally in larger quantities and had to be eaten quickly or preserved by drying or pickling.

With the industrialisation of developed countries in the early nineteenth century supply routes became more reliable and faster (the advance in rail transportation, for instance). The introduction of both canning and refrigeration also helped the transportation of supplies.

Today we can purchase exactly what we want, when we want, due to an excellent world transportation system. This has positive and negative points: fruits and vegetables are now available to purchase nearly all year long because growers are breeding and cultivating fruits and vegetables to withstand the rigours of technical harvesting, transport and storage. They are often harvested whilst still hard and under-ripe because it can be weeks before they were sold and eaten. These varieties often have a poor flavour value. This situation has stimulated the trend to eat food 'out of season' which can also be extremely expensive due to transportation costs when purchasing from long distance. The flavour and quality of fresh seasonal fruit and vegetables is second to none.

**VIDEO CLIP**
Covent Garden vegetable market

The rediscovery of the traditional system of food production and the enjoyment of consuming locally grown and sold products in the form of farmers markets and farm shops is now on the increase. Organic practices also represent an essential alternative to industrial farming as it encourages attention to the quality and sustainability of agricultural produce once more. Chefs are now becoming more conscious with respect to their locality and the produce and purchase of locally grown commodities. This emphasis is being encouraged by leading associations such as the Academy of Culinary Arts and the Craft Guild of Chefs who have developed support campaigns to promote this development.

IMAGE COURTESY OF WWW.THINKVEGETABLES.CO.UK

# NUTRITION IN VEGETABLES

Experts recommend we eat at least five portions of fruit or vegetables a day. The nutritional values of vegetables depend on a number of factors, such as the type, size, season, freshness, preparation method and cooking techniques used.

Vegetables are a main source of vitamin C, as well as some of the B group vitamins. The body will be able to produce vitamin A if vegetables such as carrots, tomatoes and peppers (which contain beta-carotene, an antioxidant) are consumed.

The majority of vegetables contain folic acid, iron, magnesium, calcium and potassium as well as other minerals in smaller amounts.

Vegetables with a high starch content (potatoes) contain carbohydrates which produce energy as well as fibre.

The vitamin and mineral content in vegetables is at their highest when just picked but begin to disappear when the produce is exposed to sunlight or left to wane slowly in uncontrolled storage conditions. The majority of the nutrients are found in the skin or the layer just below the skin, so where possible in preparation simply wash the vegetables to achieve the maximum nutritional benefit.

Vitamins B and C are water soluble which means they are lost when exposed to hot water (boiled, stewed or steamed).

The smaller the cut of vegetables the greater the loss of vitamins and minerals because the surface area becomes larger.

Vitamin C is destroyed by long cooking processes, so where possible attempt to use quick methods of cookery to retain the nutritional value. As the cooking liquor will undoubtedly absorb some vitamins and nutrients it can be used to make sauces, which will return some of the nutrients back to the dish.

Trace chemicals called phytochemicals that are found in plants, including herbs and spices, have beneficial effects on health and disease prevention. They have a wide-ranging effect on the avoidance of damage to various body mechanisms such as the heart, blood, eyes and the prevention of cancer cells.

The following table gives a simple guide to which vegetables are high in specific vitamins.

| VITAMIN | RECOMMENDED DAILY ALLOWANCE | WHAT IS IT NEEDED FOR? | STRONG SOURCE | USEFUL SOURCE |
|---|---|---|---|---|
| A Retinol | 600µg/day women 700µg/day men | Growth, development, healthy skin and eyes. Important for a healthy immune system. | Pak choy, peppers, sweet potato | Pumpkin, Brussels sprouts, red cabbage, carrots, spinach, butternut squash |
| B1 Thiamine | 0.8mg/day women 1.0mg/day men | Maintain a healthy nervous system. | Sweetcorn, onions, potatoes | Broad beans, cauliflower, leeks, garlic, swede, parsnips, courgettes, celery |
| B2 Riboflavin | 1.1mg/day women 1.3mg/day men | The release of energy from food. | | Asparagus, watercress, leeks, mange tout, mushrooms, peppers, tomatoes |
| B5 Pantothenic acid | None set | Energy production. | | Green cabbage, carrots, broad beans, asparagus, broccoli, cauliflower |
| B6 Pyridoxine | 1.2mg/day women 1.4mg/day men | Healthy nervous system and production of red blood cells. | Potatoes | Aubergine, peppers, shallots, okra, brown onion, butternut squash |

| VITAMIN | RECOMMENDED DAILY ALLOWANCE | WHAT IS IT NEEDED FOR? | STRONG SOURCE | USEFUL SOURCE |
|---------|------------------------------|-------------------------|----------------|----------------|
| C Ascorbic acid | 40mg/day women 40mg/day men | Creates collagen – a protein necessary for healthy bones, teeth, gums, blood and all connective tissue. Acts as powerful antioxidant and helps protect against certain types of cancer and coronary heart disease. Has an important role in the healing of wounds. | Cauliflower, spring greens, kale, broccoli, peppers, red cabbage | Swede, spinach, potatoes, mange tout, savoy cabbage, aubergine, courgette, tomatoes |
| E Tocopherols | None set | Powerful antioxidant. Helps protect against heart disease and cancer. | Broccoli | |
| Beta-carotene | None set | The body can convert beta-carotene into vitamin A but beta-carotene also acts as an antioxidant, protecting cells from damage. Can help to prevent heart disease and certain types of cancer. | Peppers, sweet potato | Spring greens, Brussels sprouts, butternut squash, pumpkin, spinach, carrots, tomatoes |
| Biotin | None set | Release of energy from foods. | | Cauliflower, broccoli, Brussels sprouts, carrots, broad beans |
| Folate | 200µg/day women 200µg/day men. | Production of red blood cells and the release of energy from food. Essential during pregnancy for folic acid. | Baby corn, asparagus | Beetroot, kale, leeks, cauliflower, spinach, broccoli, spring greens, aubergine, potatoes, Chinese leaf |
| B3 Niacin | 13mg/day women 17mg/day men | Release of energy from food and a healthy nervous system. | Broad beans | Artichokes, watercress, red cabbage, savoy cabbage, sweet potato, spring greens, leeks, marrow, courgette |

# CLASSIFICATIONS

Vegetables are classified into the following varieties: roots, bulbs, flower heads, fungi, tubers, leaves, stems and shoots, seeds and pods, vegetable fruits and sea vegetables.

Over the next few pages we will break down the vegetable classifications and list possible cooking techniques.

## Roots

The root of the plant anchors itself into the ground; the roots absorb water and nutrients from the soil and transports them to the rest of the plant.

### PURCHASING SPECIFICATION

- Generally clean and free from soil.
- Firm, not soft, free from bruising and blemishes, evenly sized and shaped.

| EXAMPLES | PICTURE |
|---|---|
| **Parsnips** (boiled, roasted, creamed, fried, soup) | |
| **Turnips** (boiled, buttered, fried, glacé, soup) | |
| **Galangal** (with stir fried dishes and curries, used as a flavouring) | |
| **Celeriac** (similar flavour to celery but used blanched for salads, boiled, buttered, creamed, roasted or braised) | |
| **Swede** (boiled, buttered, fried, glacé, purée, soup) | |
| **Beetroot** (steamed, boiled, shredded, baby, salad, roast, soup) | |
| **Carrots** (buttered, glace, Vichy, purée, baby, soup) | |

IMAGES COURTESY OF WWW.THINKVEGETABLES.CO.UK

**VIDEO CLIP**
Turning and cooking carrots

## Brassicas/Flower Heads

This plant is allowed to develop so the main part of the vegetable emerges and forms a head above ground. The plant develops male pollen and female ovules which produce seeds.

## PURCHASING SPECIFICATION

■ Cauliflowers should have tight and firm flower heads that are white in colour.

■ Other brassicas should also have tight heads and bright colouring.

■ They should not feel limp and the stems should be strong.

| EXAMPLES | PICTURE |
|---|---|
| **Cauliflower** (boiled, buttered, fried, gratin, creamed, Mornay or cheese sauce, polonaise) | |
| **Broccoli** (boiled, buttered, fried, gratin, creamed, Mornay or cheese sauce, polonaise) | |
| **Calabrese** (boiled, buttered, fried) | |
| **Brussels sprouts** (boiled, fried, buttered) | |
| **Cabbage** (boiled, braised, stuffed, pickled) | |
| **Kale** (boiled, buttered) | |
| **Chinese cabbage** (boiled, buttered, fried) | |
| **Pak choy** (boiled, buttered, fried) | |
| **Spring greens** (boiled, buttered, braised) | |

# Tubers

This vegetable is grown beneath the surface from planting to harvesting. The roots feed the plant with water and nutrients.

## PURCHASING SPECIFICATION

■ Clean and free from soil. Firm and not soft or dried-out skin. Even size and shape with no bruising or blemishes.

| EXAMPLES | PICTURE |
|---|---|
| **Potato** (majority of cooking techniques can be used) |  |
| **Sweet potato** (as above) | |

# Bulbs

These are vegetables with a strong leaf top. They are formed with many layers and are packed with carbohydrates and water. The lower the temperature these vegetables are grown in the stronger the flavour will be.

> ## PURCHASING SPECIFICATION
>
> - Skin should not be damaged.
> - No bruising or blemishes.
> - Fennel should be crisp and firm, leeks should be predominantly clean and free from soil.

| EXAMPLES | PICTURE |
|---|---|
| **Onions** (braised, fried, chopped, sliced) | |
| **Garlic** (peeled, sliced, chopped, fried, marinated, soup) | |
| **Fennel** (boiled, buttered, gratin, Mornay, cheese sauce hollandaise) | |
| **Shallot** (peeled, chopped, sliced, soup) | |
| **Leek** (braised, buttered, boiled, gratin) | |

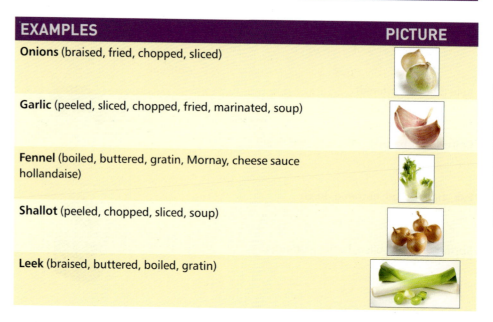

# Leaves

These vegetables, as the name suggests, are mostly leaf and green in colour. They grow using photosynthesis which is a process that uses water and sunlight to produce natural sugar and oxygen.

> ## PURCHASING SPECIFICATION
>
> - Should be fresh with leaves that are bright in colour, crisp and not wilted.

| EXAMPLES | PICTURE |
|---|---|
| **Spinach** (boiled, sautéed, creamed, wilted, purée, salad) | |
| **Chicory** (steamed, braised) | |
| **Lettuce** (salad, braised) | |
| **Watercress** (salad, soup) | |

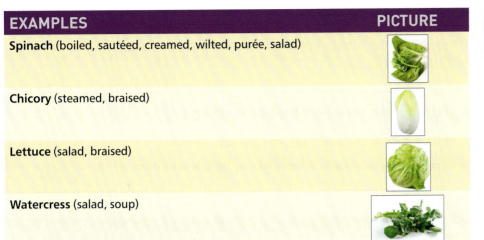

**VIDEO CLIP**
Preparing and cooking green vegetables

IMAGES COURTESY OF WWW.THINKVEGETABLES.CO.UK

# Seeds and Pods

These vegetables are eaten whole or as seeds. They grow from bushes and trees and hang so they are simple to harvest.

### PURCHASING SPECIFICATION

- Peas and beans should be crisp. If purchased in pods, peas should be full and beans not stringy.
- Good, bright colouration and no bruising or damage.

| EXAMPLES | PICTURE |
|---|---|
| **Okra** (boiled, buttered, fried, soup) | |
| **Sweetcorn** (boiled, buttered, fried, soup) | |
| **Peas** (boiled, buttered) | |
| **Broad beans** (boiled, buttered) | |
| **Runner beans** (boiled, buttered) | |
| **Sugar snaps** (boiled, sautéed) | |
| **Mange tout** (boiled, sautéed) | |

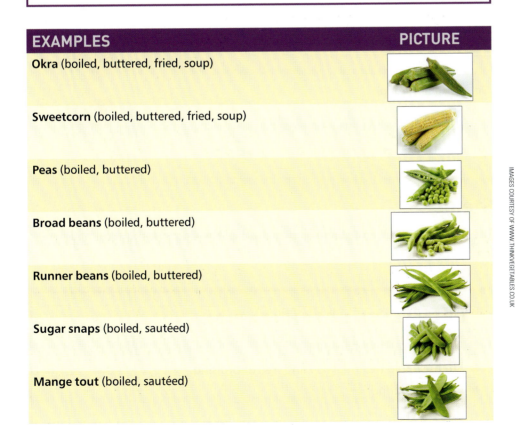

IMAGES COURTESY OF WWW.THINKVEGETABLES.CO.UK

# Vegetable Fruits

These vegetables usually grow from a stem and have seeds, they can be dry or juicy on the inside.

## PURCHASING SPECIFICATION

- Ripe, firm to the touch and not too soft.
- Good deep colouration without bruising or blemishes.

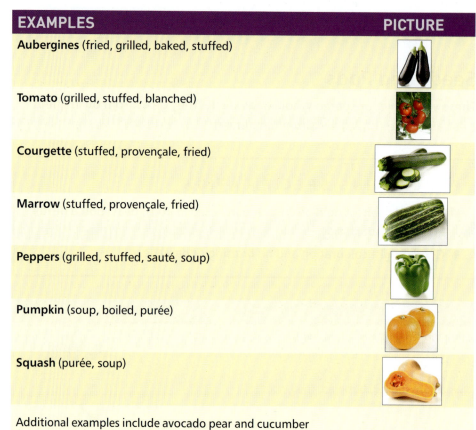

| EXAMPLES | PICTURE |
|---|---|
| **Aubergines** (fried, grilled, baked, stuffed) | |
| **Tomato** (grilled, stuffed, blanched) | |
| **Courgette** (stuffed, provençale, fried) | |
| **Marrow** (stuffed, provençale, fried) | |
| **Peppers** (grilled, stuffed, sauté, soup) | |
| **Pumpkin** (soup, boiled, purée) | |
| **Squash** (purée, soup) | |

Additional examples include avocado pear and cucumber

# Stems

These vegetables are rooted and grow out of the ground; they can have leaves too.

## PURCHASING SPECIFICATION

- Generally clean and free of soil.
- Stems should be firm, crisp and free of bruising.
- Bright colouring.

IMAGES COURTESY OF WWW.THINKVEGETABLES.CO.UK

| EXAMPLES | PICTURE |
|---|---|
| **Celery** (braised, soup) |  |
| **Asparagus** (tips, hollandaise, buttered, vinaigrette) | |
| **Globe artichokes** (boiled, fried) | |
| Additional examples include kohlrabi, sea kale and endive | |

# Fungi

Mushrooms/fungi are the only vegetables which do not grow from a green plant but in damp, dark, mossy conditions. They grow well cultivated and wild (care should be taken when harvesting wild mushrooms as some are toxic). Wild mushrooms are very delicate and care should be taken when handling and storing them.

## PURCHASING SPECIFICATION

■ Clean and free from grit, sand and soil.

■ Ensure that wild mushrooms are easily identifiable. No blemishes, bruising or early signs of wilting.

| EXAMPLES | PICTURE |
|---|---|
| **Button** (fried, grilled) | |
| **Chestnut** (fried, grilled) | |
| **Chanterelle** (fried) | |
| **Shiitake** (fried) | |
| **Oyster** (fried) | |
| Additional examples include trompette noir, morels, ceps, portabello and open mushrooms | |

# Sea Vegetables

These vegetables are becoming better known and used in modern day cooking. They tend to be purchased dried and require soaking to remove the high salt levels.

---

## PURCHASING SPECIFICATION

- Sea vegetables are usually purchased dried.
- Samphire should have a strong colour and feel firm without signs of deterioration such as a strong odour and weeping moisture.

---

| EXAMPLE |
| --- |
| **Arame** (Japanese miso soup) |
| **Kelp** (raw or fried) |
| **Nori** (sometimes known as laverbread) (sushi) |
| **Wakame** (fried) |
| **Hijiki** (simmered with other vegetables) |
| **Carragheen** (used for its gelling properties) |
| **Samphire** (boiled, poached and fried) |
| **Agar-agar** (vegetarian alternative to gelatine) |

## SEASONAL AVAILABILITY FOR VEGETABLES IN THE UK

| VEGETABLES | JAN | FEB | MAR | APR | MAY | JUN | JUL | AUG | SEP | OCT | NOV | DEC |
| --- | --- | --- | --- | --- | --- | --- | --- | --- | --- | --- | --- | --- |
| Asparagus | | | | | X | X | | | | | | |
| Aubergine | | | | | X | X | X | X | X | | | |
| Broad beans | | | | | X | X | X | X | X | | | |
| Broccoli | X | X | X | | | | | X | X | X | X | X |
| Brussels sprouts | X | X | X | | | | | | X | X | X | X |
| Cabbage | | | | | X | X | X | X | X | X | | |
| Carrots | X | X | X | | | X | X | X | X | X | X | X |
| Cauliflower | X | X | X | | | | X | X | X | X | X | X |
| Celery | | | | X | X | X | X | | | | | |
| Courgettes | | | | | | X | X | X | X | | | |

| VEGETABLES | JAN | FEB | MAR | APR | MAY | JUN | JUL | AUG | SEP | OCT | NOV | DEC |
|---|---|---|---|---|---|---|---|---|---|---|---|---|
| French beans | | | | | | X | X | | | | | |
| Leeks | X | X | | | | | | X | X | X | X | X |
| Lettuce | | | | | X | X | X | X | X | X | X | |
| Marrows | | | | | | | | X | X | X | | |
| New potatoes | | | | | X | X | X | X | X | | | |
| Onions | X | X | X | | | | | X | X | X | X | X |
| Parsnips | X | X | X | | | | | X | X | X | X | X |
| Peas | | | | | | X | X | | | | | |
| Potatoes | X | X | X | X | X | | | X | X | X | X | X |
| Pumpkin | X | X | X | | | | | X | X | X | X | X |
| Radish | | | X | X | X | X | X | X | X | X | X | |
| Runner beans | | | | | | | | X | X | X | X | |
| Spinach | | | | X | X | X | X | X | X | X | | |
| Spring onions | | | | | | X | X | X | X | X | X | |
| Swedes | X | X | X | | | | | X | X | X | X | X |
| Sweetcorn | | | | | | | | | X | X | | |
| Tomatoes | | | | X | X | X | X | X | X | X | | |
| Turnip | X | X | | | | | | | X | X | X | X |
| Watercress | | | | X | X | X | X | X | X | X | X | |

# STORAGE

The different types of vegetable may require different storage methods depending upon the shape, size and species.

Onions, garlic, shallots are stored in a cool environment (10–18°C) and preferably on their own as the smell can overpower any produce nearby. It is best to leave these products whole as cutting them will release the strong odour and they will lose flavour. All root vegetables should be removed from their sacks and stored in plastic bins or containers.

**VIDEO CLIP**
Preparing various fried potato dishes

Leeks and other green vegetables are best purchased as required and should be placed in a refrigerator if storage is necessary. In general they will last 2–3 days in good condition then deteriorate quickly after that, turning limp and losing colour. They should also be stored away from tomatoes because tomatoes release small quantities of ethylene gas which causes green vegetables to wilt. If green vegetables are damaged they will soon lose the vitamin C content.

Potatoes are best stored in cool, dark places as sunlight causes rapid deterioration of the skin. They should be kept clear of damp areas as this turns them mouldy. Paper bags or sacks are ideal units to store them in as it allows the potatoes to breathe; polythene simply causes humidity and moisture.

Hard vegetables such as carrots, swedes and parsnips are best kept in cool conditions in a refrigerator and will last for approximately 5–6 days until they begin to soften and the texture breaks down. As a general rule hard vegetables will store for longer periods of time and soft/leafy vegetables for only a day or two.

Fruit vegetables such as tomatoes can be purchased slightly unripe and left to ripen slowly at room temperature in the kitchen. The ethylene gas produced by tomatoes is a ripening agent, placing a ripe tomato with unripe ones in a bag helps to speed the ripening process. Salad vegetables should be placed into plastic containers and stored in a refrigerator.

In an ideal kitchen all the produce would be purchased on a daily basis and used immediately; this would increase the vitamin/nutrient content, flavours and textures and ensure only the freshest ingredients are served to the customer.

# POTATOES

These vegetables deserve a special section due to their versatility and every day use in a modern professional kitchen.

There are more than 400 different varieties of potato, approximately 20 of which are commonly available.

They fall into three main categories:

- New potatoes
- Main crop potatoes
- Exotic potatoes

Potatoes can be imported from Belgium, the Canary Islands, Egypt, Holland, Spain, France, Greece, Italy, North Africa and North America. The different varieties have different characteristics which mean that some are more suitable for certain methods of cookery than others.

| NEW POTATOES | MAIN CROP POTATOES | EXOTIC POTATOES |
|---|---|---|
| Carlingford (tight white flesh) | Desirée (pink skin, soft yellow flesh) | Purple Congo (rough dark skin, purple flesh) |
| Jersey Royals (kidney-shaped, pale yellow flesh, the best new potato available) | Estima (yellow flesh and pale skin) | Truffe de chine (knobbly dark skin, purple flesh) |
| Maris Bard (white flesh, waxy texture) | Golden Wonder (pale flesh, medium colour skin) | Sweet Potato (yellow/red skin, orange flesh with a sweet flavour) |
| Maris Peer (dry, firm flesh, waxy texture – good salad potato) | Kerr's pink (pink skin, creamy flesh) | |
| Charlotte (pale skin and yellow flesh, firm, waxy texture and good flavour) | King Edward (creamy-white colour with floury texture) | |
| | Bintje (white/yellow skin, yellow flesh) | |
| | Maris Piper (pale skin, creamy white flesh) | |
| | Pentland Dell (oval shape, floury texture) | |
| | Romano (red skin, creamy flesh) | |
| | Wilja (pale yellow flesh, waxy texture) | |
| | Cara (brown skin, pale flesh) | |
| | Pink Fir Apple (pink skin, yellow flesh) | |

# VEGETABLE/POTATO CUTS

*Julienne* thin matchsticks which measure 2mm × 2mm × 4cm long
*Brunoise* 2mm dice cut from julienne
*Gros brunoise* 4mm × 4mm dice
*Jardinière* batons measuring 4mm × 4mm × 1.5cm long
*Macedoine* 5mm dice cut from jardinière
*Paysanne* thinly sliced squares, rounds, triangles or rough-sided rounds all 1cm in diameter
*Mirepoix* roughly chopped root vegetables approximately 2cm × 2cm

**VIDEO CLIP**
Cutting brunoise, julienne, paysanne, jardinière and macedoine

Vegetables and potatoes should be washed well in clean water and then peeled as little as possible to retain as much nutritional value as you can. Sometimes the vegetables or potatoes may require a final wash after peeling. The peelings should be placed into a bowl to keep the work surface as hygienic as possible. Keep the workstation tidy at all times, dispose of the waste once each task is completed and sanitise the area thoroughly with hot water and a soft detergent.

# THE USE OF FRUIT IN DESSERTS

Fruits have always been available in variety and abundance. They are the world's first convenience food and although the early Greek and Roman writers include them as components of meat and fish dishes, traditionally fruits bring a meal to its conclusion.

Fruit provides a ready source of energy because it is rich in sugar (fructose), minerals and vitamins. It is also a good source of dietary fibre, both in the edible skin and in the water-soluble fibre called pectin found in certain fruits such as apples and quinces. Almost all fruit has a low calorie count.

> **CHEF'S TIP**
>
> Many fruits will ripen successfully in storage, but it is always best to buy fruit on a daily basis to ensure freshness. However, bananas, for example, are often sold immaculately pale yellow and tinged with green. These need to be ripened to a warm yellow and slightly marked with small brown streaks.

## PURCHASING AND STORAGE OF FRUIT

- Above all, fruit should look fresh and appetising. Plumpness and, firmness, without bruising and wrinkles, are signs of freshness and good moisture content in a fruit. Soft fruits, such as berries, should look dry on the outside and full. Avoid those with signs of mould or moisture, including any leakage in the packaging. Whether the fruit skins are edible or inedible always make sure that they are not bruised, split or broken or with signs of insect damage.

- Citrus fruit will keep well for a couple of weeks if necessary, but the skins will begin to toughen, dry out and wrinkle and they will lose some of their essential oils which help flavour many desserts. If the citrus fruit is purchased for its zest, then it must be used within a couple of days. Pineapples and melons are best eaten just chilled at 5°C; however, this causes a slight problem in storage because their scent is so penetrating that they must be well wrapped, or they will pass on their flavours to other refrigerated foods stored nearby.

- Odour is a good indication of ripeness. Fruit such as melon should smell fragrant. Although they will keep quite well for a week or so, they will not ripen if bought underripe. Hard fruit such as apples and pears, as long as they are purchased unblemished, will keep for a few weeks in the refrigerator. Any fruit stored at room temperature will ripen and deteriorate quicker than if stored in a cool place, because the water content gradually evaporates and with it the sweet moisture within the fruit. Some fruits are best purchased for immediate use. All the soft berry fruits come into this category. All fruits should be carefully washed before cooking and eating.

# FRUITS AND THEIR SEASONAL AVAILABILITY

It is important that we should recognise seasonality as much as possible and buy our commodities according to seasonal availability. If a fruit is available throughout the year it is generally recognised that it is purchased overseas. However, purchasing fruit within season and locally will help to ensure freshness because the storage time before purchase has been minimal. The travelling expense is kept to minimum because it is locally grown, which should also help lower the price of the fruit.

The list below is a general guide to the seasonal availability of fruit.

| NAME OF FRUIT | SEASON |
|---|---|
| Apple (pomme) | All of the year |
| Apricot (abricot) | May–September |
| Blackberry (mûre) | May–September |
| Cherry (cerise) | May–July. |
| Clementine (clémentine) | All of the year |
| Cranberry (airelle rouge) | November–January |
| Damson (prune de damas) | September–October |
| Fig (figue) | July–September |
| Gooseberry (groiselle à macquereau) | June–July |
| Greengage (Reine-Claude) | August–September |
| Grapefruit (pamplemousse) | All of the year |
| Grapes (raisin) | All of the year |
| Lemon (citron) | All of the year |
| Melon (melon) | May–October |
| Nectarine (Brugnon) | June–September |
| Peach (pêche) | June–September |
| Pear (poire) | All of the year (best in Autumn–Winter) |
| Plum (prune) | July-October |
| Pineapple (ananas) | All of the year |
| Raspberry (framboise) | June–October |
| Rhubarb (rhubarbe) | January–July |
| Strawberry (fraise) | June–September |

## DIFFERENT CATEGORIES OF FRUITS

| STONE FRUITS | HARD FRUITS | SOFT FRUITS | CITRUS FRUITS | TROPICAL FRUITS |
|---|---|---|---|---|
| Apricots | Apples | Bilberries | Clementines | Bananas |
| Cherries | Crab apples | Blackberries | Grapefruit | Cape goosberrries |
| Damsons | Pears | Blackcurrants | Kumquats | Carambola (star fruit) |
| Greengages | | Blueberries | Lemons | Dates |
| Nectarines | | Gooseberries | Mandarins | Figs |
| Peaches | | Loganberries | Limes | Granadillas |
| Plums | | Raspberries | Oranges | Guavas |
| | | Redcurrants | Tangerines | Kiwi fruit |
| | | Strawberries | Blood orange | Lychees |
| | | Tayberries | Satsuma | Mangoes |
| | | Whitecurrants | | Passion fruit |
| | | | | Papaya (paw paw) |
| | | | | Pineapples |
| | | | | Sharon fruit |
| | | | | Tamarillos |

*Other fruits:* cranberries, grapes, melons, rhubarb.

# PRESERVATION OF FRUIT

- *Drying* Apples, pears, apricots, peaches, bananas and figs can be dried. Plums when dried are called prunes, and currants, sultanas and raisins are produced by drying grapes. Also, fruit crisps can be produced by macerating thinly sliced fruits such as pineapple for a few minutes and then drying out in a low-heated oven.

- *Canning* Almost all fruits may be canned. Apples are packed in water and known as 'solid packed apples'. Other fruits are canned in a light syrup.

- *Bottling* Bottling is used domestically, but very little fruit is commercially preserved in this way. Cherries are bottled in maraschino.

- *Candied* Orange and lemon peels are candied. Other fruits with a strong flavour, such as pineapple, are preserved in this way. The fruit is covered in hot syrup, which is increased in sugar content from day to day until the fruit is saturated in a very heavy syrup. It is then allowed to dry slowly until it is no longer sticky and moist.

- *Glacé* The fruit is first candied and then dipped in fresh syrup to give a clear finish. This method is applied to cherries.

- *Crystallised* After the fruit has been candied it is left in fresh syrup for 24 hours and then allowed to dry very slowly until crystals form on the surface of the fruit.

- *Jam* Some stone and all soft fruits can be used to make jam. The fruits are boiled with sugar and pectin may added to help set the mixture.

- *Jelly* Jellies are produced from fruit juice and can be set with either gelatine or pectin.

- *Quick freezing* Strawberries, raspberries, loganberries, apples, blackberries, gooseberries, grapefruit and plums are frozen and must be kept below zero and preferably at −18°C.

- *Cold storage* Apples are stored at temperatures between 1–4°C, depending on the variety of apple. This suppresses the ripening of the fruit.

- *Gas storage* Fruit can be kept in a sealed storage room where the atmosphere is controlled. The amount of air is limited, the oxygen content of the air is decreased and the carbon dioxide increased, which controls the respiration rate of the fruit and preserves it for longer.

# COOKING

There are numerous ways to cook vegetables and fruits and the choice depends on the end result that is required.

- The most basic cooking technique is blanching. This involves cooking the vegetables in boiling salted water for a very short time, usually no more than a few seconds. They are then plunged into iced water to halt the cooking process immediately. Vegetables are blanched to set the colour, to loosen skin (as for tomato concassé) or to eliminate strong flavours.

■ **Parboiling**, which is to partially cook the vegetable to prepare it for alternative finishing such as deep frying, braising or roasting.

■ Cooking al dente, literally means 'to the tooth' and requires vegetables to be cooked until just firm, crisp and yet tender. This degree of cooking is applied to most green vegetables such as beans, mange tout and sugar snap peas.

■ Fully cooked means to cook the vegetable until tender and it is normally for root vegetables and potatoes which are usually cooked until fully done.

## Boiling and Steaming

As a guide, vegetables that grow beneath the ground should be placed into cold salted water and brought to the boil. Those vegetables that grow above the ground should be plunged into boiling salted water. This is so that they can be cooked as quickly as possible to retain as much of their flavour, colour and nutrients as possible. The exception to the rule is new potatoes, which should be plunged into boiling salted water. Vegetables grown above the ground should be added to the boiling salted water in small batches to prevent the temperature of the water from dropping too much.

All vegetables cooked by boiling can be cooked by steaming. They are prepared in the same way as for boiling, placed into steamer trays and seasoned with salt before cooking. Steaming vegetables results in a firmer and crisper vegetable because there has been no contact with liquid in the saucepan. In general, you can add seasonings to the steaming liquid, such as lemon zest or fresh herbs, which can impart flavour to the vegetables.

White vegetables which discolour once prepared or boiled, such as salsify and Jerusalem artichokes, should be cooked in **au blanc**. Their whiteness can be retained by cooking them in a liquid made up of water, flour, salt and a little lemon juice. Mix the flour with a little water to a smooth paste. Add the remaining water and lemon juice. Season with the salt and bring to the boil whilst stirring.

Ideally all boiled vegetables should be drained and served immediately. In practice that can create difficulties, especially where large numbers of customers are served over a long service period. Green vegetables will always discolour quickly and all vegetables will lose flavour if held for too long at hot temperatures. The reheating of boiled vegetables such as French beans, broccoli, peas, asparagus, kale, Brussels sprouts and cauliflower should follow these guidelines:

■ As soon as the vegetable is just cooked refresh in iced water as quickly as possible.

■ Drain thoroughly, place onto trays and store covered with plastic film in a refrigerator.

### CHEF'S TIP

Do not pierce the beetroot skin before baking as the beetroot will bleed and lose its valuable nutrients and flavour.

### CHEF'S TIP

Other vegetables which can be successfully roasted are asparagus, carrots, baby corn, mushrooms and parsnips.

### CHEF'S TIP

Use sunflower, canola, groundnut and olive oil for sautéeing. Butter (either clarified or whole) and goose fat will also add plenty of flavour when shallow frying. When using olive oil for sautéeing, ensure that it does not overheat. Olive oil has a lower smoke point than other oils and will burn easily.

■ When required for service, using one tray of vegetables at a time, place the required number of portions into a vegetable strainer and plunge into plenty of boiling salted water.

■ When the vegetables have just heated through, remove from the boiling water and drain thoroughly before presenting on hot dishes or plates to be served.

This method is economical because any vegetable not used for one service can be utilised for the next.

# Baking

This is a dry heat method where the vegetable is surrounded by very hot air in an oven chamber. The baking of vegetables and fruit will concentrate the natural flavours and will sometimes produce a slight natural caramelisation on the skin. Thick-skinned or hard vegetables and fruit are most suited to baking, for example potatoes, beetroot, aubergine and tomatoes, apples and pineapples. Potatoes are often baked in their skins and sometimes wrapped in aluminium foil. The oven temperature is usually around 200°C and the vegetables should be of an even size.

# Roasting

This is a similar method to baking, utilising the same heating technique. Generally the vegetables to be roasted will have been washed, peeled and prepared and placed into a roasting tray with a little fat and seasoning. At this stage additional flavours such as herbs, garlic, onions and spices can be added. The oven should be preheated to 200°C and during the roasting stage natural caramelisation will occur to the vegetable. This is to be encouraged to create further colour and flavour enhancements.

# Frying

Shallow frying is a quick method of cookery that uses small amounts of fat. The normal procedure consists of heating butter or oil in a frying pan until it just begins to brown before adding the vegetables, seasoning and cooking until lightly coloured on all sides.

Sautéeing is another alternative and is a similar method of cookery to shallow frying. The difference is that the amount of fat used to sauté is usually less and the vegetables are 'tossed' whilst cooking is being undertaken. Vegetables suitable for sautéeing include leafy greens, onions, mushrooms and beans. Sometimes both sautéeing and shallow frying is seen as a finishing step for vegetables that are parboiled.

Stir frying is a traditional Chinese method of cooking and is a variation of sautéeing. The technique consists of prepared vegetables being placed into a little very hot oil in a wok or heavy frying pan with curved sides. The cooking

is carried out quickly in as high a heat as possible whilst continuously stirring or 'tossing' the vegetables. The vegetables are cooked when they are judged to be still slightly crisp and firm. The quality points for a stir fried vegetable are crispness, firmness, the original colour is maintained and a good fresh flavour preserved.

Deep frying has a number of applications for vegetables such as fritters or tempura. With a few exceptions, vegetables should be cut into small pieces or florets, seasoned or marinated in a little flavoured oil or lime juice and fresh herbs and passed through the prepared batter.

Deep fry quickly at approximately 185°C, until golden brown in colour. Other vegetables can be passed through milk and then seasoned flour and deep fried or through seasoned flour and beaten egg before cooking. All deep fried vegetables should be thoroughly drained before serving and should not be covered with a lid as condensation will quickly make the vegetable become soft and soggy.

## Grilling

This is a healthy method of cookery because little or no fat is required. Most vegetables are suitable for this method of cookery although some, for example potatoes, fennel and carrots, may need to be parboiled first. Additional flavours can be added in the form of flavoured oils, herbs and spices, and left to marinate prior to grilling. Vegetables can be grilled under a salamander where the position of the rack is important to help ensure an even cookery and prevent burning. Alternatively, grilling on a chargrill will produce a direct heat via the hot bars. This will give attractive grilled bar marking on the vegetable surface.

## Stewing

Vegetables and fruits which have high moisture content such as courgette, aubergine and figs can be stewed successfully. For this method of cookery the vegetables or fruit are simmered in a stock or flavoured liquid for an extended period of time. Stewing can take place in the oven or on the stove top. A well-known stewed vegetable dish is ratatouille.

## Braising

This is a similar method of cookery to stewing but it uses less liquid and some of the recipes for braising do not call for sweating or browning any flavouring agents such as garlic before adding the vegetables. Cabbage, endive, leeks and celery are all vegetables that can be braised successfully.

When cooking with potatoes it is important to use the correct variety to give the best results.

### CHEF'S TIP

If there is no thermometer to measure the temperature of hot fat to deep fry heat the oil in a saucepan for 8 minutes. Drop a small piece of the vegetable that is going to be deep fried into the hot fat. If it floats to the top, the oil is at the correct temperature. If not continue heating and testing at 1 minute intervals.

### CHEF'S TIP

When preparing vegetables for grilling ensure that they are cut into equal-sized pieces so that they cook evenly.

# RECIPES

## Anna potatoes *Pommes Anna*

| INGREDIENTS | 4 PORTIONS | 10 PORTIONS |
| --- | --- | --- |
| **Vegetable oil** | 2tbsp | 5tbsp |
| **Potatoes** (Maris Piper) | 700g | 1.7kg |
| **Good-quality salt and white pepper** | To taste | To taste |
| **Butter** (clarified) | 50g | 125g |

### Method of work

1. Preheat the oven to 220°C.
2. Warm the oil and brush the inside of a clean Anna mould.
3. Wash and peel the potatoes, and cut to even cylindrical shapes with a plain cutter or large metal disc cutter.
4. Using a mandoline slice the potatoes into thin 1–2mm slices.
5. Place a layer of the potato slices in the bottom of the Anna mould, neatly overlapping. Butter and lightly season.
6. Continue to build up each layer in the same way until the mould is almost full.
7. Butter the top layer.
8. Heat the pans well on the stove until a sizzling sound can be heard from the Anna mould.
9. Place into the preheated oven and bake for 1 hour, occasionally pressing down on the potatoes and brushing with butter to help them to stick together.
10. When golden brown, remove from the oven, knock firmly to release the potatoes and allow to rest for 10 minutes.
11. Carefully turn out of the mould and cut into the required portions.

### 🥄 CHEF'S TIP

Do not wash the potato slices because the starch on the surfaces will help them to stick together to compact the potatoes together.

### 🥄 CHEF'S TIP

Heavy omelette pans can be used instead of Anna moulds. The pans should always be kept clean by wiping with kitchen paper or cloth and coating with a little clean fat.

*Brush each layer with clarified butter and season lightly*

# Mashed potatoes *Pommes purées*

| INGREDIENTS | 4 PORTIONS | 10 PORTIONS |
|---|---|---|
| Potatoes (King Edward Reds if possible) | 400g | 1kg |
| Butter | 40g | 100g |
| Milk | 50ml | 125ml |
| Good-quality salt and white pepper | To taste | To taste |

### CHEF'S TIP

King Edward Reds are excellent for mashed potatoes because the flesh does not break up during cooking, so the potatoes will not become wet and stodgy.

## Method of work

1 Wash, peel and cut the potatoes into an even size.
2 Rewash, place into a saucepan of cold salted water and bring to the boil.
3 Simmer until the potatoes are cooked. Remove from the heat and drain in a colander.
4 Return to a light heat in the saucepan without the water, cover with a lid and heat for 2 minutes to allow the potatoes to dry out.
5 Pass the potatoes through a mouli, potato ricer or mash by hand.
6 Add the butter and warm milk and mix to the required consistency.
7 Check the seasoning and use as required.

# Biarritz potatoes *Pommes Biarritz*

| INGREDIENTS | 4 PORTIONS | 10 PORTIONS |
|---|---|---|
| Mashed potato (see previous) | 600g | 1.5kg |
| 1cm diced cooked ham | 60g | 150g |
| 1cm diced cooked pimento | 30g | 75g |
| Finely chopped fresh parsley | 3tbsp | 7tbsp |
| Clarified butter | 40g | 100g |
| Good-quality salt and white pepper | To taste | To taste |

## Method of work

1 Take the hot mashed potato and add the ham, pimento and chopped parsley.
2 Ensure the ham and pimento are warm before adding or the final mix will be cold.
3 Mix well and arrange in a serving dish. Dip a palette knife in the clarified butter and make little decorative marks on top of the potatoes.
4 Briefly place under the salamander to raise the final temperature and serve immediately.

### CHEF'S TIP

Ensure the ham and pimentos are cut neatly and the ham is free from fat and gristle. The mix can be kept warm during service in a bain marie for up to 1 hour. Any longer and the pimento begins to bleed into the potato.

*Decorate with a palette knife*

# Duchesse potatoes *Pommes duchesse*

*Pipe the duchesse potatoes onto a buttered tray*

| INGREDIENTS | 4 PORTIONS | 10 PORTIONS |
|---|---|---|
| Mashed potato without the butter or milk | 600g | 1.5kg |
| Egg yolk | 2 | 5 |
| Butter | 30g | 75g |
| Whole egg | 1 | 2 |
| Good-quality salt and white pepper | To taste | To taste |
| Grated Nutmeg | To taste | To taste |

## Method of work

1 Wash, peel and rewash the potatoes, cut into even-sized pieces and place into boiling salted water.

2 Simmer gently for approximately 25 minutes until cooked. Drain well and return to the pan, placing on the stove, covered with a lid to dry out for 2 minutes.

3 Pass the potatoes through a potato ricer, mouli or pass through a medium sieve. Place into a clean bowl.

4 Beat in the egg yolk and add the butter. Season well with the salt, pepper and nutmeg.

5 Place the mixture into a piping bag with a large star tube.

6 Lightly butter a baking tray and then pipe neat spiral shapes no bigger than 2cm wide and 5cm tall. Allow two per portion.

7 Bake for 2 minutes at 140°C to give the outside a dry surface.

8 Beat the whole egg and brush over the potato spirals.

9 Return to the oven and bake at 220°C until golden brown.

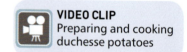

**VIDEO CLIP**
Preparing and cooking duchesse potatoes

### CHEF'S TIP

Duchesse potato is a basic mixture and is widely used in the preparation of many other potato dishes as well as being used to provide a garnish for fish and meat dishes.

### CHEF'S TIP

A little potato starch can be added to the mix if the end product is too wet to pipe and hold up, this will stiffen the mixture and the duchesse potatoes will hold up better.

# Marquis potatoes *Pommes Marquise*

| INGREDIENTS | 4 PORTIONS | 10 PORTIONS |
|---|---|---|
| Duchesse potato mixture (see p. 420) | 600g | 1.5kg |
| Plum tomatoes blanched, peeled, deseeded and neatly diced | 6 | 15 |
| Finely chopped shallots | 1 whole | 2 whole |
| Butter | 30g | 75g |
| Garlic chopped | 1 clove | 2 cloves |
| Finely chopped fresh parsley | 3tbsp | 8tbsp |
| Whole egg | 1 | 2 |
| Good-quality salt and white pepper | To taste | To taste |

### CHEF'S TIP

Any tomato mixture left can be chilled and reused or added to salads, sauces and used for garnishes.

## Method of work

1. Make the duchesse potato mixture as instructed on p. 420.
2. Place the duchesse mixture into a piping bag with a large star tube.
3. Pipe the potato onto a buttered baking tray into the form of round nests, approximately 5cm wide by 2.5cm tall. Allow two per portion.
4. Place into a hot oven for a few minutes to dry the outside of the potato. Brush with the beaten egg and return to the oven to colour golden brown.
5. Sweat the shallots and garlic in the butter and then add the parsley and tomato, season and cool.
6. Spoon the tomato mixture into the centre of the potato and return to the oven to heat through.

# Dauphine potatoes *Pommes Dauphine*

| INGREDIENTS | 4 PORTIONS | 10 PORTIONS |
|---|---|---|
| Duchesse potato mixture (p. 420) | 600g | 1.5kg |
| Choux paste (p. 503) | 140ml | 350ml |
| Soft flour | | |

## Method of work

1. Make the duchesse potatoes as instructed on p. 420.
2. Mix the duchesse potato mix with the choux paste thoroughly and place in a refrigerator to chill.
3. Mould into cylindrical shapes using the flour (2cm wide by 5cm long).
4. Place onto strips of oiled greaseproof paper and allow three pieces per portion.
5. Holding the paper firmly slide the potatoes into a deep fat fryer and fry at 180°C until golden, drain and serve.

*Roll the chilled mixture into cylindrical shapes*

### CHEF'S TIP

Ensure the formed shape before cooking is as neat as possible because the frying will exaggerate any imperfections. Dauphine potatoes can also be moulded into quenelle shapes using oiled tablespoons.

# Croquette potatoes *Pommes croquette*

| INGREDIENTS | 4 PORTIONS | 10 PORTIONS |
|---|---|---|
| Duchesse potato mix | 600g | 1.5kg |
| Flour | 100g | 250g |
| Whole egg | 6 | 15 |
| White breadcrumbs | 200g | 500g |
| Good-quality salt and white pepper | To taste | To taste |

## Method of work

1 Make the duchesse potatoes as instructed on p. 420.
2 Mould the duchesse mixture into 2cm by 5cm cylinders, allowing three per portion.
3 Place in a refrigerator to chill for 30 minutes.
4 Pass the potato cylinders through the seasoned flour, beaten egg and then the breadcrumbs.
5 Use a palette knife to remould the cylinders and pack the breadcrumbs in tightly.
6 Place into frying baskets and deep fry at 185°C until golden brown, drain and serve.

### CHEF'S TIP

As an alternative to breadcrumbs, use nibbed almonds instead. Prepare and cook as for this recipe, but with the coating of almonds this dish is named *Pommes amandines* (almond potatoes).

*Roll the duchesse mixture into cylindrical shapes of equal size*

# Straw potatoes *Pommes pailles*

| INGREDIENTS | 4 PORTIONS | 10 PORTIONS |
|---|---|---|
| Good frying potatoes (for example King Edward) | 200g | 500g |

## Method of work

1 Wash, peel and rewash the potatoes.
2 Cut the potatoes into julienne strips about 6cm long.
3 Wash well and drain, dry thoroughly in a clean kitchen cloth.
4 Deep fry at 180°C moving constantly to achieve a golden brown colour.
5 Drain well and season with a little salt.

### CHEF'S TIP

Straw potatoes are normally used as a garnish for grilled meats such as steaks and lamb chops. They are sometimes used in other dishes such as salads to give an added texture and flavour combination.

# Sauté potatoes *Pommes sautées*

| INGREDIENTS | 4 PORTIONS | 10 PORTIONS |
|---|---|---|
| Potatoes (Maris Piper for example) | 600g | 1.5kg |
| Vegetable oil | 100ml | 250ml |
| Butter | 50g | 120g |
| Good-quality salt and white pepper | To taste | To taste |
| Chopped parsley | 3tbsp | 6tbsp |

## Method of work

1 Wash the potatoes well and place onto steaming trays. Steam the potatoes until just cooked (approximately 12 minutes) then cool slightly and peel.
2 Cut into neat slices approximately 3mm thick.
3 Place the oil in a heavy frying pan and heat the oil. Add the sliced potatoes and gently fry until golden brown in colour. Toss occasionally to ensure that the potatoes are cooked on both sides.
4 Drain in a colander.
5 Heat the frying pan, add the potatoes, season and add the butter. Toss over and add chopped parsley then serve.

### CHEF'S TIP

The potatoes can be steamed or boiled in their skins. Always try to select even sizes to facilitate even cooking and uniformity of the end product.

# Sauté potatoes with onions *Pommes Lyonnaises*

| INGREDIENTS | 4 PORTIONS | 10 PORTIONS |
|---|---|---|
| Sauté potatoes | 600g | 1.5kg |
| Sliced onions | 200g | 500g |
| Butter | 50g | 125g |
| Good-quality salt and white pepper | To taste | To taste |
| Freshly chopped parsley | 3tbsp | 6tbsp |

## Method of work

1 Fry the onions separately in the butter until they begin to caramelise and turn golden brown.
2 Mix with the sauté potatoes, correct the seasoning and serve with some freshly chopped parsley.

### CHEF'S TIP

Slowly cooking with butter will give the onions a good flavour but it can be difficult to control the heat process and prevent the butter from burning. Use 50 per cent oil and 50 per cent butter to correct this problem and help raise the smoke point of the fat.

# Game chips and gaufrette potatoes *Pommes chips et pommes gaufrette*

| INGREDIENTS | 4 PORTIONS | 10 PORTIONS |
|---|---|---|
| **Good frying potatoes e.g.** (for example King Edward) | 200g | 500g |

## Method of work for game chips

1 Wash, peel and then rewash the potatoes. Trim into a cylindrical shape.
2 Using a mandoline slice the potatoes to 1mm thick. Wash again in plenty of cold water.
3 Drain and pat dry with a clean kitchen cloth.
4 Place the potatoes into a frying basket and deep fry at 180°C, moving the potatoes constantly until golden brown in colour.
5 Drain well, season with a little salt and serve as a garnish for roast poultry and game.

## Method of work for gaufrette potatoes

1 Once the potatoes are peeled, wash and trim into cylindrical shapes using the corrugated blade of the mandoline.
2 Give a half turn to the potato between each slicing action. This will produce a trellis pattern.
3 Cook in the same way as game chips.

**CHEF'S TIP**

Game chips and gaufrette potatoes are used for a garnish and can also be used as part of a canapé service within a cocktail bar setting. They are not served as a potato dish on its own. Care must be taken as they burn very quickly in the hot fat, especially if they are not well dried before placing them in the deep fryer.

# Matchstick potatoes *Pommes allumettes*

| INGREDIENTS | 4 PORTIONS | 10 PORTIONS |
|---|---|---|
| **Good frying potatoes** (for example King Edward) | 400g | 1kg |

## Method of work

1 Wash, peel and rewash the potatoes.
2 Trim the potatoes into a rectangular shape with even sides.
3 Cut slices measuring 4cm × 3mm.
4 Cut the slices into 3mm × 3mm matchsticks 4cm long.
5 Wash well and then dry with a clean kitchen towel.
6 Deep fry at 180°C moving them constantly to ensure an even cooking until golden.
7 Remove from the fryer and drain, season with salt and serve.

**CHEF'S TIP**

To help cook the deep fried matchstick potatoes evenly it is worthwhile to cut uniform sizes using a sharp knife. Matchstick potatoes are served in the same way as game chips.

# Mignonette potatoes *Pommes mignonettes*

| INGREDIENTS | 4 PORTIONS | 10 PORTIONS |
|---|---|---|
| **Good frying potatoes** (for example King Edward) | 600g | 1.5kg |

## Method of work

1. Wash, peel and rewash the potatoes.
2. Trim to give straight sides and cut into batons measuring 4cm × ½cm × ½cm.
3. Rewash, drain and dry in a clean kitchen cloth.
4. Deep fry at 180°C until golden in colour.
5. Drain well and season with salt.

> **CHEF'S TIP**
>
> Mignonette potatoes can be parcooked until soft at 165°C before service and when required plunged into a deep fryer at 180°C to complete the cooking process.

# Boulangère potatoes *Pommes boulangère*

| INGREDIENTS | 4 PORTIONS | 10 PORTIONS |
|---|---|---|
| **Potatoes** (Maris Piper are best) | 400g | 1kg |
| **Finely sliced onions** | 150g | 375g |
| **White vegetable or chicken stock** | 250ml | 625ml |
| **Butter** | 50g | 125g |
| **Chopped fresh parsley** (optional) | 2tbsp | 4tbsp |
| **Good-quality salt and white pepper** | To taste | To taste |

> **CHEF'S TIP**
>
> The use of a round cutter to achieve neat discs of potato to layer on top will give the finished dish a neater presentation.

## Method of work

1. Preheat an oven to 200°C.
2. Wash, peel and rewash the potatoes.
3. Cut the potatoes into 2mm thick slices. Reserve the best slices for finishing the dish.
4. Lightly cook the sliced onions without colour in a little butter.
5. Grease a deep baking tray and arrange the potatoes and onions layer by layer, seasoning with salt and paper between each tier of potatoes.
6. Neatly arrange the reserved potato slices on the top.
7. Pour in the stock barely covering the potatoes.
8. Add a few pieces of butter on the top of the potatoes.
9. Place in the oven for approximately 25–30 minutes to achieve a little colour.
10. Lower the heat to 170°C and press the potatoes down flat occasionally. Continue to cook for approximately 1 hour until the liquid has almost been absorbed. Brush with melted butter and serve with the chopped parsley if desired.

# Chipped potatoes (chips) *Pommes frites*

| INGREDIENTS | 4 PORTIONS | 10 PORTIONS |
|---|---|---|
| Good frying potatoes (for example King Edward) | 600g | 1.5kg |

## Method of work

1. Wash, peel and rewash potatoes.
2. Trim the potatoes to give straight sides.
3. Cut into neat batons measuring 5cm long by 1cm × 1cm.
4. Wash well and dry in a clean kitchen cloth.
5. Deep fry at 170°C to blanch until soft without colour.
6. Drain and place on tray and store in a refrigerator until required.
7. When required, deep fry at 180°C until golden in colour and crisp.
8. Remove from the fryer, drain and season with salt.

Cut the potatoes into batons

> ### CHEF'S TIP
>
> The UK's love of chips began in the nineteenth century and was first recorded in an 1854 cookbook called *Shilling Cookery*. Fish and chips were the only food items not to be rationed during the Second World War.

# Boiled potatoes *Pommes à l'Anglaise*

| INGREDIENTS | 4 PORTIONS | 10 PORTIONS |
|---|---|---|
| New potatoes | 600g | 1.5kg |
| Good-quality salt | To taste | To taste |
| Butter | To garnish | To garnish |

## Method of work

1. Wash and trim any blemishes from the new potatoes. Rewash and set aside.
2. Place a saucepan of salted water on the stove and bring to the boil.
3. Carefully add the new potatoes and simmer for 20 minutes until just cooked through.
4. Drain well and serve with a little butter, chopped fresh parsley or fresh mint if required.

Note: if you are using older potatoes these should be placed into *cold* water and brought to the boil.

> ### CHEF'S TIP
>
> Blackening after cooking is caused by acid and iron in the potato, or by the water in certain areas. A little lemon juice or vinegar added to the cooking water helps prevent this.

> ### HEALTH & SAFETY
>
> Whenever possible, cook potatoes in their skins to preserve the minerals and vitamin C which lay under the skin, peel after boiling if necessary.

# Pont-neuf potatoes (chips) *Pommes Pont-neuf*

| INGREDIENTS | 4 PORTIONS | 10 PORTIONS |
|---|---|---|
| **Good frying potatoes** (for example King Edward) | 600g | 1.5kg |

## Method of work

1 Prepare as for fresh chips (see p. 426).
2 Cut into large batons 6cm long × 2cm × 2cm.
3 Wash and dry in a clean kitchen cloth.
4 Deep fry at 170°C to blanch until soft without colour.
5 Drain and place on tray and store in a refrigerator until required.
6 When required, deep fry at 180°C until golden in colour and crisp.
7 Remove from the fryer, drain and season with salt.
8 Pont-neuf potatoes are usually served with grilled steaks as an accompaniment.

> **CHEF'S TIP**
>
> For service Pont-neuf potatoes should be stacked like building blocks onto the service plate. It is thought that the name for this dish may come from the Pont-Neuf, the oldest surviving bridge over the river Seine in the centre of Paris.

> **CHEF'S TIP**
>
> Peeled potatoes will blacken when exposed to the air. Cook them immediately if possible; if they have to be kept, cover with cold water.

# Fondant potatoes *Pommes fondantes*

| INGREDIENTS | 4 PORTIONS | 10 PORTIONS |
|---|---|---|
| **Potatoes** (preferably Maris Piper) | 900g | 2kg |
| **Butter** | 40g | 75g |
| **White vegetable or chicken stock** | 400ml | 1 litre |
| **Good-quality salt and white pepper** | To taste | To taste |

## Method of work

1 Preheat the oven to 200°C.
2 Wash, peel and rewash the potatoes.
3 Cut each potato into sections and turn the potatoes into barrel shapes with eight sides. Each should measure 5cm long and at the largest width 2cm thick. Allow three per portion.
4 Wash the potatoes and pat dry with a clean kitchen cloth.
5 Brush the potatoes with some melted butter and place in a deep baking tray.
6 Add sufficient stock so it reaches halfway up the potatoes.
7 Season and bake until the potato is just cooked and the stock is almost completely reduced. Spoon over the cooking stock occasionally during cooking.
8 Continue brushing with butter to help build up a nice glossy-looking potato dish.

> **CHEF'S TIP**
>
> Fondant potatoes can be cut into squares or rounds and then cooked. They can develop into an especially visual element to a dish and complement the main item very well.

*Turn the potatoes into barrel shapes*

# Château potatoes *Pommes château*

| INGREDIENTS | 4 PORTIONS | 10 PORTIONS |
|---|---|---|
| Maris Piper or good roasting potatoes | 600g | 1.5kg |
| Vegetable oil or goose fat | 50ml | 125ml |
| Good-quality salt and white pepper | To taste | To taste |

## Method of work

1. Preheat an oven to 200°C.
2. Wash, peel and rewash the potatoes.
3. Cut into even sections slightly larger than for the fondant potatoes (see recipe on p. 427).
4. Trim the potatoes into the same shape as for fondant potatoes; 5cm in length and allow three pieces per portion.
5. Place the potatoes into a pan of boiling salted water and cook for 3 minutes. Remove and drain in a colander. Dry with a clean kitchen cloth.
6. Heat the oil or goose fat in a roasting tray and then add the potatoes, season with the salt and pepper.
7. Lightly brown the potatoes evenly all over.
8. Place into an oven to roast for 35 minutes or until just cooked and golden in colour.
9. Drain off the fat and toss the potatoes in a little melted butter and serve.

### CHEF'S TIP

The potatoes can be cooked in goose fat for a richer flavour, or the addition of fresh rosemary will add an extra feature to the dish and overall aroma. Rissolée potatoes are half the size of château, but cooked using the same method for a shorter period of time because they are smaller. Cocotte potatoes are a quarter of the size of château and cooked for an even shorter period.

# Dauphinoise potatoes *Pommes dauphinoise*

| INGREDIENTS | 4 PORTIONS | 10 PORTIONS |
|---|---|---|
| Potatoes (Pentland Dell or other good baking varieties) | 600g | 1.5kg |
| Double cream | 350ml | 575ml |
| Chopped garlic | 2 cloves | 4 cloves |
| Grated Gruyère cheese | 70g | 175g |
| Good-quality salt and white pepper | To taste | To taste |

## Method of work

1 Preheat an oven to 200°C.
2 Place the double cream and the chopped garlic into a saucepan and bring to the boil.
3 Remove from the heat and leave to sit for 2 minutes to infuse the garlic flavour.
4 Wash, peel and rewash potatoes.
5 Cut the potatoes into 2mm slices.
6 Add the potatoes to the cream mix, season well and place back onto the stove to cook for 3 minutes.
7 Carefully deposit the potatoes and garlic cream into a buttered deep-sided baking tray and sprinkle the cheese on top.
8 Lay a sheet of silicone paper on top of the cheese and then place a weighted baking tray on top of it.
9 Bake for approximately 30 minutes, until the potatoes are cooked.
10 Remove from the oven and cool down. Place into a refrigerator and chill to set the potato mixture.
11 Remove the heavy tray and silicone paper. Cut out the potatoes into the desired portion size.
12 Reheat with a little extra cheese sprinkled on top. Ensure that the potato has heated through completely.

# Buttered asparagus *Asperges au beurre*

| INGREDIENTS | 4 PORTIONS | 10 PORTIONS |
|---|---|---|
| Medium asparagus | 20 spears | 60 spears |
| Butter | 100g | 250g |
| Good-quality salt and white pepper | To taste | To taste |

## Method of work

1 Wash the asparagus well to remove any sand and grit.
2 Hold the asparagus spears at the tip and base then snap in half. The hard root end should be discarded or used as flavouring in soups.
3 Remove all the small spurs from the top section of the asparagus with the back of a knife.
4 Thinly peel the base of the halved stem and wash well again.
5 Tie the asparagus in bunches of 3–6 spears and trim the base neatly.
6 Place the bundles carefully into boiling salted water and cook until the tips are just tender.
7 Remove from the water carefully, detach the string, cut in half if required and quickly toss in melted butter in a pan for one minute. Season and serve.

# Buttered globe artichoke *Fonds d'artichauts au beurre*

| INGREDIENTS | 4 PORTIONS | 10 PORTIONS |
|---|---|---|
| Globe artichokes | 4 | 10 |
| Lemon juice | 1 | 3 |
| Flour | 10g | 25g |
| Water | 400ml | 1 litre |
| Butter | 50g | 125g |
| Chopped fresh parsley | 3tbsp | 6tbsp |
| Good-quality salt and white pepper | To taste | To taste |

## Method of work

1 Cut the stalk of the artichoke off close to the base and remove the bottom layer of leaves.

2 Lay the artichoke on its side and cut through and leave 1½ cm remaining at the base.

3 Using a small, sharp knife, carefully trim all of the leaves leaving a neat circular disc.

4 Scoop out the furry centre using a small spoon. Rub well with half a lemon to help stop any discolouring.

5 Place the trimmed artichoke into acidulated water (use half the lemon juice) to prevent discolouration.

6 Prepare the blanc by mixing the flour and water together, then adding salt and the remaining lemon juice.

7 Bring the liquid to the boil stirring regularly.

8 Place the artichokes into the blanc and simmer until cooked, approximately 20 minutes. Remove the artichokes and refresh in cold water.

9 Cut the artichokes into six sections and heat the butter in a saucepan. Add the artichokes, season well and heat through.

10 Add chopped fresh parsley and serve.

### CHEF'S TIP

Globe artichokes can be stuffed with other vegetables or farces and baked.
To prepare artichokes whole simply remove the stalk, cut 2cm from the top and snip the remaining leaves with scissors, they can be cooked in acidic salted water for approximately 20 minutes then refreshed and the centre removed. Then add the farce or prepared vegetables.

Remove the outer leaves and discard them

Cut the artichoke across to remove the pointed end

Trim the outer edges

# Stuffed aubergines *Aubergine farcie*

| INGREDIENTS | 4 PORTIONS | 10 PORTIONS |
|---|---|---|
| Aubergines | 2 | 5 |
| Finely chopped shallots | 50g | 125g |
| Chopped garlic | 2 cloves | 4 cloves |
| Butter | 100g | 250g |
| Fresh wholemeal breadcrumbs | 8tbsp | 20tbsp |
| Tomato concassé | 2tbsp | 5tbsp |
| 1cm diced green, yellow and red peppers | ½ of each coloured pepper | 1½ of each coloured pepper |
| Grated Gruyère cheese | 50g | 125g |
| Olive oil | 4tbsp | 10tbsp |
| Good-quality salt and white pepper | To taste | To taste |

## Method of work

1  Preheat an oven to 170°C.

2  Remove the green parts of the aubergine and discard. Wash and cut the aubergines in half lengthways. Using a sharp knife, score the flesh in a criss-cross fashion without piercing the skin.

3  Drizzle over the olive oil and freshly chopped garlic.

4  Place onto a pan or baking tray and bake in the preheated oven until the flesh is soft.

5  Remove from the oven, and using a spoon carefully scoop out the flesh, leaving the empty skins to one side for later use. Chop the aubergine flesh into smaller pieces.

6  Sauté the chopped shallots and diced peppers in the butter and then add the aubergine.

7  Fold in the breadcrumbs and tomato concassé before seasoning with the salt and pepper. Cook gently until any excess moisture has evaporated.

8  Spoon the mix back into the aubergine skins.

9  Cover with grated Gruyère cheese and gratinate in a hot oven.

*Score the aubergine, drizzle with oil and rub in the garlic*

# Ratatouille

| INGREDIENTS | 4 PORTIONS | 10 PORTIONS |
|---|---|---|
| Aubergine 1cm dice | 200g | 500g |
| Courgettes 1cm dice | 200g | 500g |
| Onion 1cm dice | 50g | 125g |
| Chopped garlic | 3 cloves | 6 cloves |
| 1cm diced green, yellow and red peppers | ½ of each coloured pepper | 1½ of each coloured pepper |
| Tomato concassé 1cm dice | 200g | 500g |
| Chopped fresh parsley | 4tbsp | 6tbsp |
| Chopped fresh basil | 2tbsp | 4tbsp |
| White wine | 50ml | 125ml |
| Olive oil | 4tbsp | 10tbsp |
| Good-quality salt and white pepper | To taste | To taste |

## CHEF'S TIP

Ratatouille is a classical Provençal dish. The word is derived from the French word touiller (to mix or stir). Traditionally each vegetable is cooked separately before being combined and then stewed. This dish can be served with lamb, chicken or venison as well as braised fish dishes.

## Method of work

1 Wash the courgettes, aubergines and peppers well.

2 In a heavy-based saucepan heat the olive oil and cook the peeled and finely chopped onions and garlic without letting them colour.

3 Add the various coloured peppers and cook for a few minutes, then add the tomato concassé, mix together and set aside.

4 Heat some more olive oil in a saucepan, add the courgettes and cook for approximately 3 minutes. Remove from the pan and add to the cooked onions and peppers.

5 Add the aubergines to the saucepan with a little extra olive oil and cook again for 3 minutes. Remove from the pan and add to the onions, peppers and courgettes.

6 Pour in the white wine, season well and place back onto the stove to cook for approximately a further 6 minutes covered with a lid.

7 Remove from the heat and fold in the freshly chopped parsley and basil, correct the seasoning and serve.

# Buttered Brussels sprouts with grain mustard

*Chou de Bruxelles Dijonaise*

| INGREDIENTS | 4 PORTIONS | 10 PORTIONS |
|---|---|---|
| Brussels sprouts | 400 g | 1kg |
| Butter | 80g | 150g |
| Dijon mustard | 40g | 100g |
| Good-quality salt and white pepper | To taste | To taste |

## Method of work

1 Remove the outer leaves, trim the stalks and cut a cross in the base of the stalk so as to help ensure even cooking. Alternatively cut the Brussels sprouts in half. Wash well in cold water.

2 Place into boiling salted water and cook until tender.

3 Remove the Brussels sprouts from the water when cooked and toss in a pan with the butter gradually adding the Dijon mustard. Season with salt and pepper and serve.

# Braised celery *Céleri braisé*

| INGREDIENTS | 4 PORTIONS | 10 PORTIONS |
|---|---|---|
| Celery | 2 heads | 5 heads |
| Sliced onion | 100g | 250g |
| Sliced carrot | 100g | 250g |
| Vegetable stock | 300ml | 750ml |
| Bouquet garni | 1 small | 1 small |
| Demi glace (see p. 120) | 100ml | 250ml |
| Butter | 30g | 70g |
| Good-quality salt and white pepper | To taste | To taste |

## Method of work

1 Preheat an oven to 180°C.

2 Remove any outer stalks that are blemished. Wash, peel and trim the celery, keeping the root intact, and cut the tops off level ensuring the celery is trimmed to 12cm lengths.

3 Rewash and place into boiling salted water and blanch for 10 minutes. Refresh under cold running water.

4 Lay the sliced carrots and onions into a sauté pan with the already melted butter. Cut the celery in half lengthways and place on top.

5 Barely cover with the stock, season well and add the bouquet garni.

6 Cover with a cartouche and a lid and bake for approximately 1½ hours until tender.

7 Remove the celery from the pan and pass the liquor.

8 Reduce the liquor by half and add the demi glace. Cook out to the required consistency and adjust the seasoning.

9 Dress the celery and serve with the cooking liquor.

# Glazed carrots *Carottes glacées*

*Place the cartouche over the carrots in the saucepan of liquid*

| INGREDIENTS | 4 PORTIONS | 10 PORTIONS |
|---|---|---|
| Carrots | 450g | 1.2kg |
| Butter | 40g | 100g |
| Caster sugar | 5g | 10g |
| Chopped parsley | 2tbsp | 4tbsp |
| Good-quality salt | To taste | To taste |

## Method of work

1 Wash, peel and cut the carrots into even sections 3cm in long × 1cm thick.
2 Turn the carrots into barrel shapes and retain the trimmings for the use in soups, stocks or sauces as appropriate.
3 Place the carrots into a pan and barely cover with water, add the butter, sugar and a pinch of salt.
4 Cover with a cartouche and bring to the boil on the stove.
5 Simmer until the water evaporates and the carrots are just tender.
6 Remove the carrots and reduce the remaining liquid to a glaze. Add any extra butter at this point if required.
7 Return the carrots to the pan and toss with the parsley in the glaze.

# Deep fried courgettes *Courgettes frites*

| INGREDIENTS | 4 PORTIONS | 10 PORTIONS |
|---|---|---|
| Courgettes | 400g | 1kg |
| Plain flour | 100g | 250g |
| Milk | 100ml | 250ml |
| Good-quality salt and white pepper | To taste | To taste |

## Method of work

1 Remove the stalks and wash the courgettes.
2 Cut into slices on a mandoline cutting disc ½cm thick.
3 Pass the slices through the milk and then through the seasoned flour.
4 Shake off the surplus flour and deep fry at 180°C until golden in colour.
5 Drain well, season with a little salt and serve.

### CHEF'S TIP

Alternative coatings for the courgettes are to simply pass through seasoned flour, through batter or in breadcrumbs to give different textures.

# Stuffed mushrooms *Champignons farcis*

| INGREDIENTS | 4 PORTIONS | 10 PORTIONS |
|---|---|---|
| Large field mushrooms | 400g | 1kg |
| Chopped shallots | 30g | 75g |
| Chopped garlic | 2 cloves | 4 cloves |
| Fresh white or wholemeal breadcrumbs | 4tbsp | 10tbsp |
| Chopped fresh parsley | 2tbsp | 4tbsp |
| Butter | 50g | 125g |
| Crumbled Stilton cheese | 80g | 200g |
| Olive oil | 2tbsp | 5tbsp |
| Good-quality salt and white pepper | To taste | To taste |

## Method of work

1 Preheat an oven to 200°C.
2 Wash the mushrooms, peel the outer skin and remove the stalks. Carefully brush the insides of the mushrooms clean to remove any grit.
3 Place the mushrooms cup side up on a baking tray.
4 Melt the butter in a saucepan and sweat the garlic and onion until translucent.
5 Drizzle the mushrooms with some olive oil and place under a salamander until half cooked.
6 Mix the onion and garlic with the breadcrumbs, Stilton cheese and freshly chopped parsley.
7 Cover the mushrooms with the breadcrumb stuffing and place into the oven to bake until golden-coloured on the top.

### CHEF'S TIP

Do not leave the mushrooms to soak in the water when washing because they absorb moisture quickly and become spongy, losing texture and flavour. Always dry them with a clean kitchen towel after washing.

# Deep-fried onion rings French style *Oignons frits à la Française*

| INGREDIENTS | 4 PORTIONS | 10 PORTIONS |
|---|---|---|
| Onions | 600g | 1kg |
| Plain flour | 100g | 250g |
| Milk | 100ml | 250ml |
| Good-quality salt and white pepper | To taste | To taste |

## Method of work

1 Peel and slice the onions into 2mm thick rings.
2 Ensure the cut is against the grain to produce rings.
3 Separate the rings and pass through milk and then seasoned flour.
4 Shake off any excess flour.
5 Deep fry at 180°C until golden in colour.
6 Drain, lightly season and serve.

### CHEF'S TIP

The flour can be seasoned with a little turmeric to give a yellow tinge to the overall colour, or it can be flavoured with some cayenne pepper or curry powder for a slightly different flavour.

# Braised cabbage *Chou braisé*

| INGREDIENTS | 4 PORTIONS | 10 PORTIONS |
|---|---|---|
| Cabbage (savoy, green or sweetheart) | 400g | 1kg |
| Mirepoix carrot | 100g | 250g |
| Mirepoix onion | 100g | 250g |
| Vegetable stock | 300ml | 750ml |
| Bouquet garni | 1 small | 1 small |
| Demi glace (see p. 120) | 100ml | 250ml |
| Good-quality salt and white pepper | To taste | To taste |

### CHEF'S TIP

The addition of julienne carrot, leek and bacon mixed into the finely sliced cabbage centre will supplement the flavour of the dish. Never add bicarbonate of soda, as some suggest, to the boiling water to help maintain the bright green colour of the vegetable. The soda will soften the leaves and degrade the flavour.

## Method of work

1  Preheat an oven to 180°C.

2  Remove any blemished outer leaves and wash well. Cut the cabbage into quarters and remove the stalk. Rewash and drain off the water.

3  Place the cabbage into boiling salted water and blanch for 4 minutes.

4  Remove and refresh the cabbage.

5  Reserve the best leaves leaving one per portion. Lay onto a clean tea towel and dry.

6  Finely slice the remaining cabbage and press dry to remove any excess water.

7  Divide the finely sliced cabbage onto each leaf and season well. Using a clean kitchen cloth roll the cabbage balls tightly.

8  Using a sauteuse pan lay the onion and carrot on the bottom and rest the cabbage parcels on top. Pour over the vegetable stock halfway up the sides.

9  Add the bouquet garni and bring to the boil, cover with a cartouche and a lid then bake for about 60 minutes.

10  Remove the cabbage parcels and pass the liquid, return to a clean saucepan and reduce the quantity by half. Add the demi glace and correct the consistency and seasoning.

11  Return the cabbage to the sauce and use it to glaze the cabbage before serving.

Place the finely sliced cabbage onto the dried outer leaves

Blanch the cabbage in boiling salted water

Form a ball and carefully set the shape

# Braised red cabbage *Chou-rouge braisé*

| INGREDIENTS | 4 PORTIONS | 10 PORTIONS |
|---|---|---|
| Red cabbage | 300g | 750g |
| Sliced onions | 50g | 125g |
| Butter | 60g | 150g |
| Red wine | 80ml | 200g |
| Red wine vinegar | 60ml | 150g |
| Grated Cox's apples | 140g | 350g |
| Caster sugar | 20g | 50g |
| Streaky bacon | 50g | 125g |
| Good-quality salt and white pepper | To taste | To taste |

**CHEF'S TIP**

The bacon can be left out of this recipe for vegetarian diets. Sultanas or peeled chestnuts can be supplemented instead to enhance the sweetness if desired.

## Method of work

1 Preheat an oven to 175°C.
2 Remove any blemished outer leaves and wash the red cabbage. Cut into quarters and remove the cabbage stalks. Rewash and dry the cabbage.
3 Thinly slice the red cabbage and place into a heavy-based saucepan.
4 Add the wine, vinegar, chopped bacon, sliced onion and butter. Season well.
5 Cover with a cartouche and with a lid then braise in the oven for approximately 45–60 minutes.
6 Add the diced apple and caster sugar, re-cover and continue braising for another 40 minutes.
7 Remove from the oven once tender and cooked, correct the seasoning and serve.

# Swede purée *Rutabaga purée*

*Puréeing the swede using a mouli*

| INGREDIENTS | 4 PORTIONS | 10 PORTIONS |
|---|---|---|
| Swede | 400g | 1kg |
| Butter | 40g | 100g |
| Good-quality salt and white pepper | To taste | To taste |

## Method of work

1 Wash, peel and dice the swede.
2 Rewash and place in a steamer until just cooked and tender.
3 Remove and drain if necessary in a colander. Pass through a sieve or blend in a food processor or mouli.
4 Place in a saucepan and dry out over a gentle heat.
5 Add the butter, season and serve.

**CHEF'S TIP**

Carrots, celeriac, turnips and parsnips can be used for this recipe also. Puréeing with a mouli or a sieve will remove any fibres from fibrous vegetables such as swede or celeriac. If using a blender to purée it is best to then pass the mixture through a sieve to remove the fibres.

# Broccoli polonaise

| INGREDIENTS | 4 PORTIONS | 10 PORTIONS |
|---|---|---|
| Broccoli | 2 medium-sized heads | 4 medium-sized heads |
| Butter | 100g | 250g |
| Fresh white breadcrumbs | 100g | 250g |
| Chopped fresh parsley | 3tbsp | 6tbsp |
| Grated hard-boiled egg | 2 eggs | 5 eggs |
| Good-quality salt | To taste | To taste |

## Method of work

1 Wash the broccoli well and dry. Trim the broccoli heads into 2cm-sized florets.
2 Rewash and place into plenty of boiling salted water. Simmer until tender but slightly firm.
3 Drain the broccoli well and arrange in a serving dish.
4 Heat the butter in a frying pan and add the breadcrumbs. Fry until golden, add the freshly chopped parsley and grated egg.
5 Spoon over the broccoli and serve.

> **CHEF'S TIP**
>
> Care must be taken when cooking the broccoli as over-cooking will render the flowers mushy, broken and without colour. The water must be boiling and salted to cook as quickly as possible to retain the broccoli's green colour. Purple sprouting broccoli can also be cooked and presented in the same way.

Cut the broccoli into florets

# Shallow fried chicory *Endive meunière*

| INGREDIENTS | 4 PORTIONS | 10 PORTIONS |
|---|---|---|
| Chicory | 400g | 1kg |
| Sugar | ½tsp | 1tsp |
| Lemon juice | 1 lemon | 2 lemons |
| Butter | 80g | 200g |
| Chopped parsley | 2tbsp | 4tbsp |
| Good-quality salt and white pepper | To taste | To taste |

## Method of work

1 Preheat an oven to 180°C.
2 Wash the chicory, trim the stems and discard any brown outer leaves.
3 Place into a buttered ovenproof dish, season and add the sugar.
4 Add half the lemon juice and half the butter.
5 Pour in 2tbsp of water per portion. Season well.
6 Cover with a cartouche and a lid. Bake at 180°C for 45 minutes.
7 Once cooked remove from the ovenproof dish. Set aside.

8. Heat the butter in a shallow frying pan until it foams and just turns nut brown. Add the chicory. Fry until light brown colour is obtained on all sides.

9. Squeeze the lemon juice over the chicory and add the freshly chopped parsley.

> ### CHEF'S TIP
>
> The chicory could be placed in a sealed vacuum pack bag with butter, lemon, sugar and seasoning then steamed for 40 minutes to obtain a braised chicory. In this method, more of the nutrients and flavours are retained.

# Cauliflower Mornay *Chou-fleur Mornay*

| INGREDIENTS | 4 PORTIONS | 10 PORTIONS |
|---|---|---|
| Cauliflower | 1½ medium-sized | 3 medium-sized |
| Mornay (cheese) sauce | 275ml | 650ml |
| Grated cheddar cheese | 50g | 125g |
| Good-quality salt | To taste | To taste |

## Method of work

1. Remove the outer leaves, cut the stalks and wash the cauliflower.
2. Break the cauliflower into 3cm florets.
3. Place into plenty of boiling salted water and cook until tender but slightly firm.
4. Remove from the boiling water and drain well.
5. Arrange in a serving dish.
6. Coat with the hot Mornay sauce and top with grated cheese.
7. Place in the oven to gratinate or finish under the salamander.

Pull the cauliflower leaves back to expose the vegetable

Cut the leaves from the cauliflower

Cut into florets

# Creamed spinach purée *Purée d'epinards à la crème*

| INGREDIENTS | 4 PORTIONS | 10 PORTIONS |
|---|---|---|
| Spinach leaves | 1kg | 2.5kg |
| Double cream | 80ml | 200ml |
| Béchamel | 40ml | 100ml |
| Good-quality salt and white pepper | To taste | To taste |

## Method of work

1 Wash the spinach, pick the stalks from the leaves and discard.
2 Rewash the leaves several times in plenty of cold water and then drain.
3 Blanch in boiling salted water for a few seconds.
4 Remove and refresh in iced water to halt the cooking immediately.
5 Drain well and squeeze any excess water out of the spinach.
6 Place into a food processor and blend until puréed.
7 Place the spinach into a saucepan with the double cream and béchamel sauce.
8 Simmer, season with salt and pepper and serve.

 **CHEF'S TIP**

Ensure the spinach is very dry when adding the cream and béchamel, this can be done by drying the spinach in a hot pan allowing any excess moisture to evaporate.

# Braised Baby Gem lettuce *Laitue braisée*

| INGREDIENTS | 4 PORTIONS | 10 PORTIONS |
|---|---|---|
| Baby Gem lettuce | 2 each | 5 each |
| Sliced onion | 60g | 150g |
| Sliced carrot | 60g | 150g |
| Bouquet garni | 1 small | 1 small |
| Vegetable stock | 150ml | 375ml |
| Butter | 50g | 125g |
| Demi glace (see p. 120) | 40ml | 100ml |
| Chopped fresh parsley | 2tbsp | 4tbsp |
| Good-quality salt and white pepper | To taste | To taste |

## Method of work

1 Preheat an oven to 180°C.
2 Remove any outer blemished leaves and wash the lettuce. Blanch in boiling salted water for 2 minutes and then refresh in cold water.
3 Drain and pat the lettuce dry on a clean kitchen cloth.
4 Using a sauteuse lay the onion and carrot on the lightly buttered base.
5 Arrange the lettuce on top, barely cover with the stock and add the bouquet garni.
6 Cover with a cartouche and lid then braise for 30 minutes.
7 Remove the lettuce and cut in half lengthways.
8 Pass the cooking liquor and reduce by half.
9 Add the demi glace and then return the lettuce to the pan with the cooking sauce. Coat well and check the seasoning.

**CHEF'S TIP**

The braised lettuce can also be served with croûtons or the demi glace can be omitted to ensure the dish can be consumed by vegetarians.

# Roasted parsnips in honey and grain mustard

| INGREDIENTS | 4 PORTIONS | 10 PORTIONS |
|---|---|---|
| Parsnips | 400g | 1kg |
| Vegetable oil | 50ml | 125ml |
| Clear honey | 4tbsp | 10tbsp |
| Grain mustard | 2tbsp | 5tbsp |
| Good-quality salt and white pepper | To taste | To taste |

## Method of work

1 Preheat an oven to 185°C.
2 Wash, peel and rewash the parsnips.
3 Cut into 4cm lengths, split in half lengthways and remove the core.
4 Heat the oil in a roasting tray and add the parsnips.
5 Roast in the oven for approximately for 20 minutes.
6 Add the honey and grain mustard then return to the oven for a further 10 minutes.
7 Season and serve.

*Prepare the parsnips by cutting into lengths and removing the core*

### CHEF'S TIP

Parsnips that are in season and as fresh as possible will be less woody and have a sweeter flavour.

# Buttered samphire with sesame seeds

| INGREDIENTS | 4 PORTIONS | 10 PORTIONS |
|---|---|---|
| Samphire | 400g | 1kg |
| Unsalted butter | 50g | 125g |
| Sesame seeds | 1tbsp | 2tbsp |
| Sesame oil | 1tbsp | 2tbsp |
| Black pepper | To taste | To taste |

## Method of work

1 Soak the fresh samphire for five minutes and rinse with clean water to wash out any sand or grit. Discard any wilted stems.
2 Place a pan of salted water onto the stove and bring to the boil.
3 Blanch the samphire in boiling water for 5 minutes and then refresh immediately in iced water.
4 Carefully pull the samphire off each wooden stalk and discard the stalks.
5 Heat the butter and a little sesame oil in a wok.
6 Add the samphire and the sesame seeds. Toss in the hot fat for 2 minutes.
7 Season with a little black pepper and serve.

*Removing the wooden stalks from the samphire*

### CHEF'S TIP

Samphire can be quite salty because it grows near the sea shores and in salt water marshes. It must be washed thoroughly to remove salt deposits and any grit or sand.

# Stuffed tomatoes *Tomates farcies*

*Hollow out the tomatoes*

| INGREDIENTS | 4 PORTIONS | 10 PORTIONS |
|---|---|---|
| Medium-sized tomatoes | 8 each | 20 each |
| Finely chopped shallots | 20g | 50g |
| Chopped garlic | 1 clove | 2 cloves |
| Butter | 30g | 75g |
| Chopped fresh parsley | 3tbsp | 5tbsp |
| Fresh white or wholemeal breadcrumbs | 30g | 75g |
| Chopped sweated button mushrooms | 2tbsp | 5tbsp |
| Good-quality salt and white pepper | To taste | To taste |

## Method of work

1 Preheat an oven to 180°C.
2 Wash and remove the eyes from the tomatoes.
3 Cut off the top quarter from the tomato with a knife, pointing at an angle thus creating a lip.
4 Remove the seeds from the tomatoes carefully with a small spoon. Place the tomatoes onto a greased tray. Season inside the tomatoes.
5 Melt the butter in a sauteuse and sweat the garlic and shallots without letting them colour.
6 Add the breadcrumbs, cooked mushrooms, freshly chopped parsley and seasoning.
7 Fill the tomatoes and replace the lids.
8 Brush with a little melted butter and bake for 5 minutes or until just cooked.

## CHEF'S TIP

The filling can be enhanced with diced ham, alternative herbs, citrus zest and spices.

# Peas French style *Petits pois à la Française*

| INGREDIENTS | 4 PORTIONS | 10 PORTIONS |
|---|---|---|
| Peas (preferably in the pod, frozen are acceptable) | 800g | 2kg |
| Button onions | 12 each | 40 each |
| Lettuce | 1 medium | 2½ medium |
| Butter | 30g | 75g |
| Plain flour | 10g | 25g |
| Sugar | Pinch | Pinch |
| Good-quality salt and white pepper | To taste | To taste |

## Method of work

1 If the peas are fresh, shell and wash well in plenty of cold water.
2 Wash and peel the onions.
3 Mix the flour with an equal amount of butter to create the beurre manie.
4 Place the peas and onions together in a pan with the remaining butter, sugar and salt.

*Cook the peas, button onions, butter and sugar with the water*

5  Add the water, cover with a tight-fitting lid and cook until tender, approximately 30 minutes.
6  Cut the lettuce into a chiffonade and add to the peas.
7  Drop in small pieces of butter/flour mix and allow the liquid to thicken by stirring carefully.
8  Adjust the seasoning and serve.

> ### CHEF'S TIP
>
> Frozen peas are more commonly available at all times of the year. If they are to be used for this recipe the size and the quality needs to be taken into consideration and cooking times adjusted accordingly.

# Braised leeks *Poireau braisé*

*Fold the leeks in half and tie with string*

> ### CHEF'S TIP
>
> The leeks can be cut into large diamonds and cooked slowly in half water and half butter to give a glazed finish.

| INGREDIENTS | 4 PORTIONS | 10 PORTIONS |
|---|---|---|
| Leeks | 800g | 2kg |
| Sliced carrot | 60g | 150g |
| Sliced onion | 60g | 150g |
| Bouquet garni | 1 small | 1 small |
| Vegetable stock | 150ml | 375ml |
| Butter | 50g | 125g |
| Demi glace (see p. 120) | 40ml | 100ml |
| Good-quality salt and white pepper | To taste | To taste |

## Method of work

1  Preheat an oven to 180°C.
2  Wash and trim the root from the leeks along with any blemished outer leaves.
3  Cut lengthways and rewash the leeks thoroughly.
4  Fold over in half and tie together. Blanch in boiling salted water until tender.
5  In a pan place the butter, onion, carrot and bouquet garni.
6  Lay the leeks on top and pour in the stock, season well.
7  Cover with a cartouche and lid then braise for 45 minutes.
8  Carefully remove the leeks and snip the string off.
9  Strain the cooking liquid and reduce by a half. Add the demi glace and cook out.
10  Add the leeks and coat well with the cooking sauce, check the seasoning and serve.

## Assessment of knowledge and understanding

You have now learned about the use of the different types of vegetables and how to produce a variety of vegetable dishes utilising an array of commodities and cooking techniques.

To test your level of knowledge and understanding, answer the following short questions. These will help to prepare you for your summative (final) assessment.

1 Identify two types of tomatoes.

i) _____     ii) _____

2 Identify two different types of artichokes.

i) _____     ii) _____

3 Briefly define the following vegetable cuts:

(a) brunoise _____     (b) julienne _____

(c) macedoine _____     (d) jardinaire _____

(e) paysanne _____     (f) mirepoix _____

(g) chiffonade _____

4 Explain the reason for not storing potatoes in direct sunlight.

_____

_____

5 State two ways of retaining nutrients in potatoes during preparation.

i) _____     ii) _____

6 State the reason for green vegetables being cooked in boiling salted water without a lid.

_____

_____

7 When steaming vegetables state the precautions that should be taken.

_____

_____

8 Explain the reasons for removing excess moisture and water from vegetables before deep frying.

_____

_____

# CHEF'S PROFILE

**Name: ANDREW BENNETT**

**Position:** Executive Chef, The Sheraton Park Lane Hotel, London

**Current job role:** My job includes the overseeing of the entire Food and Beverage operation which involves traditional and specialist banqueting for up to 1500 covers and a one of only three venue's in London that have a Kosher licence to produce banquets within the hotel. I have a current head count of 75 full time staff not including casual labour and we turn over in the region of £7 million a year in food and beverage.

**Key responsibilities:** Training and development; Health and safety; Financial goals and targets for all departments. Marketing trends and analysis; Creating and delivering standards.

**When did you realise that you wanted to pursue a career in the hospitality industry?** I enjoyed cooking when I was at school, when I was the first boy to ever take, what was called then 'Domestic Science'. I felt a great achievement and excitement and intrigue to the possibilities of what could be achieved with such versatile products and everybody will always need feeding in some form so it had endless boundaries which could take you as far as you wanted to go anywhere in the world.

**Training:** I went to Barnfield College on a full time 2-year course in Luton and never really looked back after that. I took a position at Claridges Hotel as a commis chef for my first 4 years. It is always a huge growing up period for any young person leaving home for the first time when in those days you were not given placement and work experience oppportunities to ease you into big kitchen life.

**What do you find rewarding about your job?** It has to be the ultimate feeling that you produced good food and your customers have left with a good experience that they want to repeat, and you have given them reason to talk to friends and family about the quality and value for money that they received.

**What advice would you give to students just beginning their career?** Understand that to reach a high level in the trade takes hard work, commitment, and dedication and along with some common sense and a little creativity you will enjoy a wonderful career but be prepared to sacrifice a lot of social hours as you would in a lot of industries you only get out what you put in and you are only as good as your last meal.

**Who is your mentor or main inspiration?** There are many chefs and hospitality personnel that you take inspiration from. You take a little from them all and use it to mould your own style and personality.

On a professional level I would pick out Gunther Schlender who was the executive chef for Robert Carrier for 17 Years and Chef for the Michelin starred Rue St. Jacques Restaurant. Gunther had a great palette and taught you to always taste the food that you are preparing and criticise yourself and search for improvements at all times.

**Secrets of a successful chef?** Hard work, passion, dedication, common sense, respect, uncompromising your standards.

**Can you give one essential kitchen tip or technique that you use as a chef:** When you are soft poaching quails eggs break them into neat white wine vinegar and then gently place them altogether in simmer water and they don't fall apart.

# Roast crown and jambonette of corn fed chicken 'Grand Veneur'

| INGREDIENTS | 4 PORTIONS |
|---|---|
| Whole corn fed chicken | 1 × 3–4kg |
| Minced chicken breast | 250g |
| Whipping cream | 300ml |
| Egg white | 1 |
| Unsalted butter | 100g |
| Chopped tarragon | 1 batch |
| Good-quality salt and white pepper | |

## Method of work

1 Blitz the chicken breast in the robot coupe with the egg white and seasoning until very smooth. Remove and beat the cream into the mixture over a bowl of ice.

2 Pass through a drum sieve to remove all the fine sinews. Add the chopped tarragon and re-check the seasoning. Keep chilled.

3 Remove the legs from the chicken and bone out the thigh and drumstick. Season and fill the cavity with the mousse. Fold the thigh skin over the mousse and re-shape.

4 Roast in the oven on 160°C for approx 20 mins.

5 Soften the butter with the remaining tarragon and place between the skin and flesh of the chicken crown. Roast in the oven on 170°C for approx 20 mins. Remove and allow to rest.

### Grand Veneur sauce

| INGREDIENTS | 4 PORTIONS |
|---|---|
| Chicken stock | ½l |
| Veal stock | ½l |
| Crushed peppercorns | 10 |
| Red wine vinegar | 250ml |
| Red currant jelly | 1Dsp |
| Red wine | 500ml |
| Double cream | 100ml |
| Diced smoked bacon | 75g |
| Chopped shallots | 2 |
| Butter | 50g |

## Method of work

1 Sweat the chopped shallots in the butter along with the bacon and add the crushed peppercorns, vinegar and red wine and reduce by a half.

2 Add the stocks and further reduce until you have a coating consistency.

3 Pass through muslin and finish with the cream.

4 Taste and check seasoning for the balance of sweetness of the red currant jelly and vinegar.

### Parmentier of root vegetables

| INGREDIENTS | 4 PORTIONS |
|---|---|
| Carrots peeled and cut into 1.5cm cubes | |
| Swede peeled and cut into 1.5cm cubes | |
| Baby onions | 12 |
| White chestnuts | 12 |
| Olive oil | 50ml |
| Butter | 100g |
| Chicken stock | 500ml |
| Honey | 50g |
| Chopped parsley | |
| Good-quality salt and white pepper | |

## Method of work

1 Add the carrots and swede to the hot olive oil and butter, sauté and slightly colour the seasoned vegetables.

2 Place in the oven and add the chicken stock. Cook until the stock has evaporated leaving the vegetables nicely cooked and glazed.

3 Add the chopped parsley.

4 Braise the onions in the remaining stock and caramelise with the remaining butter and honey until golden brown. Repeat for the chestnuts.

### To serve

Serve a piece of the leg and half a breast for each person. Celeriac and mustard mash go well with this dish.

# Pulses

## THE CLASSIFICATION OF PULSES

Peas, beans and lentils are collectively known as pulses. There are many varieties with a wide range of flavours and textures. They originate from the legume family, which are pods full of seeds. Generally speaking the seeds are removed and dried and are then called pulses. With approximately 13,000 species, the legume family is the second largest in the plant kingdom.

All pulses are formed in two halves encased in an outer shell or skin; they can however be bought separately e.g. yellow split peas. The advantage of using pulses in the modern day professional kitchen is that they add volume to dishes, combine well with other ingredients and are relatively cheap to use which increases the potential profit margin.

Pulses work well in soups and stews and are an important source of fibre, protein, vitamin B and iron for vegetarians. Dried pulses store well for long periods if kept in dry conditions, in an airtight container and away from the light. It is best to eat them as soon as possible, as they toughen on storage, especially if they are over 1 year old, and will take longer to cook. Split pulses take less time to cook as they are more exposed to the cooking medium, however they do not retain their shape as well and can turn to mush if left unattended to over-cook.

**VIDEO CLIP**
The different pulses available

## ORIGINS OF PULSES

Pulses have been used as food for thousands of years: the lentil was probably one of the first plants that early humans harvested.

Most pulses prefer warm climates to grow but there are a few species which can grow in lower temperatures. They can be eaten fresh or dried and come in a number of varieties with a range of colours, flavours and textures.

**TYPES OF PULSE**

| PEAS | BEANS | | LENTILS |
|------|-------|---|---------|
| ■ Whole green | ■ Lima | ■ Black | ■ Cream/beige |
| ■ Split green | ■ Aduki | ■ Red kidney | ■ Red |
| ■ Split yellow | ■ Haricot | ■ Pinto | ■ Yellow |
| ■ Chickpeas | ■ Flageolet | ■ Cannellini | ■ Puy |
| ■ Marrowfat | ■ Broad | ■ Soya | |
| | ■ Black-eyed | ■ Mung | |

 **CHEF'S TIP**

Because pulses can be quite bland, add a bouquet garni, studded onion, fresh herbs or spices when beginning the cooking process.

# PREPARATION

Pulses need to be thoroughly washed several times if possible to remove dust, dirt and grit. Allow approximately 55g dried weight per portion – once soaked and cooked they will at least double in weight.

Most dried pulses need soaking for a minimum of 8 hours before they can be cooked: the exceptions are all lentils, and green and yellow split peas.

Soaking times usually take 12 hours but it is generally most convenient to soak pulses overnight. Always discard the soaking water, then rinse well and cook in fresh water without any salt, which causes the skins to toughen and makes for longer cooking. Regularly skim the top of the cooking liquid to remove any scum which is naturally produced. Vegetables, herbs, spices and aromatics can be added to the pulses once cooked and either served with the dish or removed and discarded. Canned pulses are already cooked and need to be drained, rinsed and then used as required.

# STORAGE

Pulses are now readily available and are of very high quality. Try to purchase them from a supplier who has a good turnover as pulses deteriorate after 1 year. Pulses should have a good colour and not be wrinkled as this is a sign of age. Keep in a cool, dark, dry well-ventilated area in sealed containers. Keep a date stamp showing when purchased on the containers so good rotation can be introduced.

Once cooked, keep pulses well covered in the refrigerator for up to 3 days.

## Lentils

Lentils originated from the Eastern Mediterranean but are now used extensively in the Middle East and India. They are available whole or split.

Varying in size and colour, red lentils are tasteless, cream/beige have a slightly stronger flavour: Puy lentils have a very distinctive flavour and are excellent when cooked as they hold their shape well.

Red and yellow lentils cook down well, can be puréed and are used a great deal in Indian cooking to create dishes such as tarka dhal, which is the cooked lentil garnished with a 'tarka' of fried garlic and spiced oil.

# Beans

■ *Aduki beans* are small, round, dark red and rich in protein. They are used extensively in the Far East, especially in Japan, and are often used to make flour.

■ *Black-eyed beans* are cream coloured with a black strip which is where they were joined in the pod. They work well in rice dishes, stews and salads.

■ *Black beans* have a shiny black shell and are pure white inside. They are used extensively in Latin America.

■ *Borlotti beans* are Italian beans with a mild flavour. They are used in rice dishes, stews and soups.

■ *Broad beans* are a larger cream-coloured bean which was once used extensively in Europe. Beans in general and broad beans in particular are thought to help in the body's fight against cancer.

■ *Cannellini beans* are similar to haricot beans and are widely used in Italian cookery.

■ *Flageolet beans* are pale green in colour and have a subtle flavour. They are used extensively in Italian and French cookery.

■ *Haricot beans* are possibly the best known of all and are commonly used in tinned baked beans.

■ *Lima beans* are white and small with a sweet flavour, they originate from America.

■ *Mung beans* originated from Asia and are one of the most widely used pulses; the seeds are used as a vegetable and are also used as a bean sprout.

■ *Pinto beans* are very similar to borlotti beans, once cooked they turn pink in colour.

■ *Red kidney beans* are normally dark red-brown, this kidney-shaped bean holds its shape and colour in cooking and is most famous in the dish chilli con carne.

■ *Soya beans* are full of protein making them ideal for vegetarians. Fairly bland in taste, they need a dish with plenty of distinctive flavours. They can be puréed and added to soups and casseroles. They are most commonly found in soya-based products including TVP (textured vegetable protien).

# Peas

Chickpeas have a nutty flavour and are available tinned or dried. Chickpeas are ideal for hot and cold dishes and make up the main part of the dish hummus, which is a Greek dip served with pitta bread and olives.

Whole peas are normally eaten fresh, frozen or tinned but are also available dried.

Split green/yellow peas are great in sauces or stews as they break slightly and give the dish a little extra volume.

Marrowfat peas have a sweet flavour, with a tough skin and floury texture once cooked: best known in the dish mushy peas.

## SOAKING AND COOKING TIMES

| PULSE | SOAKING TIME | COOKING TIME (APPROX) |
|---|---|---|
| Aduki beans | 8–12 hours | 45 minutes |
| Black-eyed beans | 8–12 hours | 45 minutes |
| Black beans | 8–12 hours | 1 hour |
| Borlotti beans | 8–12 hours | 50 minutes |
| Broad beans | 8–12 hours | 1½ hours |
| Cannellini beans | 8–12 hours | 50 minutes |
| Flageolets | 8–12 hours | 50 minutes |
| Haricot beans | 8–12 hours | 1 hour |
| Lima beans | 8–12 hours | 1½ hours |
| Mung beans | 8–12 hours | 40 minutes |
| Pinto beans | 8–12 hours | 1 hour 20 minutes |
| Red kidney beans | 8–12 hours | 50 minutes |
| Soya beans | 8–12 hours | 2½ hours |
| Chickpeas | 8–12 hours | 75 minutes |
| Whole green peas | 8–12 hours | 75 minutes |
| Split peas | Steeped in boiling water for 30 minutes | 40 minutes |
| Whole lentils | Steeped in boiling water for 30 minutes | 40 minutes |
| Split lentils | Steeped in boiling water for 30 minutes | 25 minutes |

These times are all approximate and will vary depending on the age and quality of the pulses being used. The first 10 minutes of cooking (except split peas and lentils) should be continuous boiling to kill the toxins present in most beans. The exception to the rule is soya bean which should be boiled for 1 hour to kill the toxins. Soya and red kidney beans contain the most toxins.

# RECIPES

## Chickpea stew with red onion and chilli peppers

*Cook out with the addition of the tomato concassé and the vegetable stock*

| INGREDIENTS | 4 PORTIONS | 10 PORTIONS |
| --- | --- | --- |
| Tinned chickpeas | 400g | 1kg |
| Diced red onion | 100g | 250g |
| Finely chopped red chilli peppers | 2 | 5 |
| Chopped garlic | 2 cloves | 4 cloves |
| Tomato concassé | 300g | 750g |
| Spinach leaves | 100g | 250g |
| Vegetable stock | 150ml | 375ml |
| Butter | 50g | 125g |
| Diced courgettes | 100g | 250g |
| Diced carrots | 100g | 250g |
| Good-quality salt and white pepper | To taste | To taste |

## Method of work

1  Open the tinned chickpeas and drain in a colander. Wash well under clean water and leave to drain.

2  In a saucepan, sweat the prepared onion, garlic and red chilli peppers in butter for 3 minutes without letting them colour.

3  Add the diced carrot and sweat for a further 3 minutes.

4  Add the tinned chickpeas and diced courgettes and sweat for a further 3 minutes.

5  Put the tomato concassé and the vegetable stock into the saucepan to combine all the ingredients. Simmer for 25 minutes.

6  Wash, pick over and cut the spinach into a chiffonade, adding this to the stew.

7  Thicken slightly if required with some beurre manie (equal quantities of four and butter mixed together to a paste) by dropping tiny pieces into the stew, stirring and cooking out.

8  Correct the seasoning and serve as required.

### CHEF'S TIP

Tinned chickpeas require draining and rinsing well only. If using dried chickpeas, soak overnight and boil separately until tender, refresh in cold water and then continue the recipe as shown.

# Black bean purée with grilled aubergine and yellow pepper

**VIDEO CLIP**
Making a purée of pulses

*Quadrille the sliced aubergine*

### CHEF'S TIP

The Parmesan crisps can be made well in advance but must be kept in an airtight plastic container in a dry environment as they can go soft very quickly.

| INGREDIENTS | 4 PORTIONS | 10 PORTIONS |
|---|---|---|
| Black beans | 300g | 750g |
| Vegetable stock | 100ml | 250ml |
| Diced onion | 80g | 200g |
| Butter | 50g | 125g |
| Chopped garlic | 2 cloves | 5 cloves |
| Yellow pepper (roasted, peeled and deseeded) | 1 each | 3 each |
| Aubergines cut into thick slices | 8 slices | 20 slices |
| Grated Parmesan cheese | 100g | 250g |
| Good-quality salt and white pepper | To taste | To taste |
| Fresh chervil | Sprigs | Sprigs |

## Method of work

1  Soak the black beans for a minimum of 8 hours.

2  Drain and wash well.

3  Place in a saucepan of cold water and bring to the boil, cooking until tender.

4  Preheat an oven to 180°C.

5  Sweat the onions in butter without colour and then add the beans.

6  Cover with the stock and place in the oven to braise until the beans begin to fall apart.

7  Drain any excess liquid and purée the beans in a food processor, season well and retain the mixture to keep warm for serving.

8  Brush the sliced aubergines with olive oil and grill on a chargrill to obtain a quadrille (criss-cross) effect from the bars of the grill.

9  Sprinkle the Parmesan cheese onto a silicone baking mat into a long triangle shape. Bake in a preheated oven at 160°C until bubbling occurs.

10  Remove from the oven and trim the edges into a neat triangle shape, returning to the oven to soften and quickly removing again to manipulate the Parmesan biscuit around a wooden rolling pin.

11  Arrange the aubergines and peppers on the serving plate, setting a quenelle of the black bean purée on top and finishing with the Parmesan crisp and freshly picked chervil.

# Flageolet bean salsa with garlic bruschetta

| INGREDIENTS | 4 PORTIONS | 10 PORTIONS |
|---|---|---|
| Tinned flageolet beans | 300g | 750g |
| Finely chopped shallots | 4 | 10 |
| Tomato concassé | 200g | 500g |
| Olive oil | 4tbsp | 10tbsp |
| Chopped garlic | 2 cloves | 5 cloves |
| Shredded flat leaf parsley | 4tbsp | 10tbsp |
| Chopped red chilli peppers | 1 | 2 |
| Mango in 1cm dice | 4tbsp | 10tbsp |
| Bruschetta bread | 4 × 2cm thick slices | 10 × 2cm thick slices |
| Garlic oil | 4tbsp | 10tbsp |
| Natural yoghurt | 4tbsp | 10tbsp |
| Parsley oil | 2tbsp | 5tbsp |
| Good-quality salt and white pepper | To taste | To taste |

### CHEF'S TIP

The parsley oil used in this recipe is simply a good-quality olive oil blended together with some blanched flat leaf parsley. This can be made well in advance and has a good shelf life if kept in a plastic container and refrigerated. The garlic oil uses a similar process.

### CHEF'S TIP

The falafels can be served with a spicy tomato salsa or the flageolet bean salsa too. Traditionally served as meze (appetisers) they can also be accompanied by a tomato and cucumber salad and tahini (a sesame and garlic sauce).

## Method of work

1. Heat a saucepan with some olive oil and add the garlic, shallots, chillies and beans. Sweat for 5 minutes without letting them colour.

2. Add the tomato concassé, shredded parsley and diced mango, remove from the heat, season well and allow to cool.

3. Drizzle the garlic oil over the sliced bruschetta and grill under a salamander until golden in colour.

4. Decorate the yoghurt onto the service plate with the parsley oil dripped to create an abstract presentation.

5. Set the bruschetta slices (two per portion) in the centre of the plate and spoon the salsa on top.

# Falafel with a mint and lime dip

| INGREDIENTS | 4 PORTIONS | 10 PORTIONS |
|---|---|---|
| Tinned chickpeas | 400g | 1kg |
| Fresh white breadcrumbs | 180g | 400g |
| Thai green curry paste | 2tbsp | 5tbsp |
| Chopped coriander | 3tbsp | 6tbsp |
| Soy sauce | 2tbsp | 5tbsp |
| Sesame seeds | 4tbsp | 10tbsp |
| Lime juice and zest | 2 limes | 5 limes |
| Chopped fresh mint | 3tbsp | 6tbsp |
| Greek yoghurt | 200ml | 500ml |
| Good-quality salt and white pepper | To taste | To taste |

*After dividing and rolling into small balls, coat with the sesame seeds*

## Method of work

1 Place the drained and washed chickpeas into a food blender with the breadcrumbs, curry paste, fresh coriander and soy sauce. Blend until a coarse paste is formed.

2 Season to taste with salt and pepper and blend for a few seconds further.

3 Divide the mix equally (3 balls to a portion).

4 Roll the balls in the sesame seeds and place onto a tray. Cover with plastic film and chill for 30 minutes in a refrigerator.

5 Deep fry at 170°C until golden in colour and then drain well on kitchen paper.

6 Serve with the dip made from the yoghurt, lime juice and grated zest and chopped mint mixed together.

# Chicken and chickpea patties with red pepper dressing

*Form the patties using a stainless steel ring mould to help create the shape*

| INGREDIENTS | 4 PORTIONS | 10 PORTIONS |
|---|---|---|
| Skinless, boneless chicken breasts | 200g | 500g |
| Dried chickpeas | 200g | 500g |
| Finely chopped green chilli | 2 | 5 |
| Fresh coriander | 2tbsp | 4tbsp |
| Fresh mint | 2tbsp | 4tbsp |
| Chopped shallots | 2 | 5 |
| Grated ginger | 1tbsp | 2½tbsp |
| Garlic | 2 cloves | 5 cloves |
| Red pepper cut into brunoise | ½ pepper | 1 pepper |
| White wine vinegar | 80ml | 200ml |
| Caster sugar | 10g | 20g |
| Curly endive | 50g | 125g |
| Wild cress | To garnish | To garnish |
| Good-quality salt and white pepper | To taste | To taste |

## Method of work

1 Soak the chickpeas for a minimum of eight hours and then drain and wash well.

2 Place the chickpeas, chicken, chillies, coriander, mint, shallots, ginger, seasoning and chopped garlic into a food blender or through a mincing machine (using a fine blade).

3 Divide the mix up into equal sized pieces, enough for one pattie per portion.

4 Heat the vinegar and sugar in a saucepan and add the red peppers. Simmer for 1 minute and then allow to cool naturally so that the pepper releases its flavour and juices over time.

5 Heat a shallow frying pan with a little oil.

6 Shallow fry the patties on both sides until golden and cooked through.

7 Arrange on the plate, dress the cress and endive and arrange on the plate next to the patties. Spoon the dressing around the plate as required.

 **CHEF'S TIP**

The patties are best made at least 1 hour before cooking to allow the flavours to develop. Keep the mixture in an airtight plastic container in a refrigerator.

# Black-eyed pea and red lentil curry

*Add the pulses to the onion and spices*

| INGREDIENTS | 4 PORTIONS | 10 PORTIONS |
| --- | --- | --- |
| Black-eyed beans (peas) | 200g | 450g |
| Red lentils | 200g | 450g |
| Finely chopped onions | 150g | 375g |
| Garam masala | 2tbsp | 5tbsp |
| Turmeric | 2tbsp | 5tbsp |
| Ground coriander | 2tbsp | 5tbsp |
| Ground cumin | 2tbsp | 5tbsp |
| Chilli powder | To taste | To taste |
| Vegetable stock | 400ml | 1 litre |
| Coconut milk | 100ml | 250ml |
| Chopped fresh coriander | 1/8 bunch | ¼ bunch |
| Good-quality salt and white pepper | To taste | To taste |

## Method of work

1 Soak the black-eyed peas and lentils separately for a minimum of 8 hours.
2 Place the peas and lentils into separate pans of cold water and bring to the boil, cook until just tender then drain.
3 Heat a little oil in a saucepan and sweat the finely chopped onions and spices in the hot oil for 4 minutes with colour. Add the pulses and continue to cook for a further 2 minutes.
4 Add the stock, bring to the boil and simmer for 10 minutes.
5 Pour in the coconut milk and season the curry well. Check the consistency and finish with chopped coriander.

# Cassoulet

| INGREDIENTS | 4 PORTIONS | 10 PORTIONS |
| --- | --- | --- |
| Haricot beans | 200g | 500g |
| Diced carrot | 50g | 125g |
| Diced onion | 50g | 125g |
| White chicken stock | 300ml | 750ml |
| Tomato concassé | 100g | 250g |
| Diced raw chicken | 100g | 250g |
| Toulouse sausage cut into 1cm thick slices | 100g | 250g |
| Diced shoulder of pork | 100g | 250g |
| Tomato purée | 2tbsp | 5tbsp |
| Bouquet garni | 1 small | 1 small |
| Butter | 100g | 250g |
| Good-quality salt and white pepper | To taste | To taste |

**CHEF'S TIP**

This **cassoulet** is a modern variation on the classical dish which can use duck, goose and offal according to the regional adaptation to give its distinct flavour. It should also be finished with a crust of fine breadcrumbs and gratinated under a salamander. Never use smoked sausages, smoked meat or mutton.

## Method of work

1 Soak the haricot beans for a minimum of 8 hours.

2 Drain and wash well.

3 Boil the beans in plenty of water for 10 minutes then simmer until just cooked and refresh in cold running water.

4 Sweat the chopped onion, carrot and bouquet garni in a saucepan with butter for 4 minutes without colour.

5 Add the diced chicken, pork, tomato concassé and tomato purée and continue cooking for 4 minutes.

6 Add the stock and beans. Bring to the boil and simmer for 30 minutes.

7 Fry the sausage in a separate pan quickly on both sides and add to the cassoulet of beans.

8 Cover the pan and simmer for a further 30 minutes.

9 Check the seasoning and serve.

# Stuffed plum tomato with braised split yellow peas

| INGREDIENTS | 4 PORTIONS | 10 PORTIONS |
|---|---|---|
| Plum tomatoes | 8 each | 20 each |
| Chopped garlic | 2 cloves | 5 cloves |
| Yellow split peas soaked for 8 hours | 200g | 500g |
| Carrot, cut into brunoise | 4tbsp | 10tbsp |
| Onion, cut into brunoise | 4tbsp | 10tbsp |
| Leek, cut into brunoise | 4tbsp | 10tbsp |
| Celery, cut into brunoise | 4tbsp | 10tbsp |
| Butter | 100g | 250g |
| Vegetable stock | 400ml | 1 litre |
| Chopped fresh chervil | 3tbsp | 6tbsp |
| Good-quality salt and white pepper | To taste | To taste |

## Method of work

1 Preheat an oven to 180°C.

2 Wash and remove the eyes of the tomatoes. Cut a third of the top away and carefully remove the seeds with a small spoon.

3 Brush the tomatoes with some melted butter mixed with garlic, season and then chill in a refrigerator.

4 Drain and refresh the peas, place into cold water in a saucepan and bring to the boil, simmering for 10 minutes. Drain well in a colander.

5 Heat some oil in a pan and sweat the brunoise of vegetables for 5 minutes without letting them colour. Add the peas, stock and season.

6 Simmer until tender and most of the liquid has evaporated. Remove from the heat and adjust the seasoning.

7 Spoon the mixture into the tomatoes and bake until just tender, approximately 20 minutes.

8 Present with the fresh chervil.

# Thai-scented crushed broad beans

| INGREDIENTS | 4 PORTIONS | 10 PORTIONS |
|---|---|---|
| Broad beans soaked for 8 hours | 400g | 1kg |
| Lemongrass | 1 stick | 2 sticks |
| Galangal | 25g | 40g |
| Red chilli pepper (bird's eye) | 1 | 2 |
| Fresh coriander | 3tbsp | 6tbsp |
| Garlic | 4 cloves | 10 cloves |
| Coconut milk | 100ml | 250ml |
| Dried breadcrumbs | 100g | 250g |
| Natural yoghurt | 4tbsp | 10tbsp |
| Curry oil (curry spices warmed in oil for 10 minutes and passed through muslin cloth) | 2tbsp | 5tbsp |
| Fresh flat leaf parsley | 5tbsp | 10tbsp |
| Vegetable stock | 400ml | 1 litre |
| Good-quality salt and white pepper | To taste | To taste |

## Method of work

1. Drain, wash and then skin the broad beans.
2. Place the beans into a saucepan with the vegetable stock, broken lemongrass, chopped galangal, chilli pepper and chopped garlic. Season and then stew for 1 hour.
3. Drain any excess liquid from the stew and then place the ingredients into a food processor and blend until quite coarse in texture. Correct the seasoning.
4. Divide the mix equally (3 pieces to a portion) and then roll in the dried breadcrumbs.
5. Deep fry until golden at 180°C.
6. Serve with the curry oil, natural yoghurt and picked flat leaf parsley.

# Braised lemon rice with borlotti beans

| INGREDIENTS | 4 PORTIONS | 10 PORTIONS |
|---|---|---|
| Long grain rice | 200g | 500g |
| Lemon juice and zest | 2 lemons | 4½ lemons |
| Borlotti beans | 200g | 500g |
| Finely chopped onion | 75g | 150g |
| Finely chopped garlic | ½ clove | 2 cloves |
| Shredded fresh basil | 3tbsp | 5tbsp |
| Vegetable stock | 400ml | 1 litre |
| White wine | 50ml | 125ml |
| Good-quality salt and white pepper | To taste | To taste |

*Cooking the borlotti beans*

## Method of work

1 Wash the long grain rice and set into a deep steaming tray. Add the grated lemon zest, juice and a few slices of lemon on top.
2 Pour over a little hot stock, seasoning and place in the steamer to cook.
3 Heat a little oil in a saucepan and add the onion and garlic to sweat for 3 minutes, add the borlotti beans and the white wine and allow the liquid to reduce and cook the beans.
4 Add the shredded fresh basil at the end.
5 When the rice is cooked, separate grains with a fork.
6 Combine the rice with the beans and serve.

| 🄻 CHEF'S TIP | |
|---|---|
| Wild rice added to this dish will give a good colour contrast and a nuttier flavour. The borlotti beans complement the rice because of the size and their bittersweet flavour. | |

# Mushy peas

| 🄻 CHEF'S TIP |
|---|
| Do not use too much salt when boiling as it can toughen the skin of the peas and increase the cooking time. Pulses create a natural scum when boiling so always skim during cooking. |

| INGREDIENTS | 4 PORTIONS | 10 PORTIONS |
|---|---|---|
| Marrowfat peas soaked for 8 hours | 220g | 550g |
| Butter | 40g | 100g |
| Good-quality salt and white pepper | To taste | To taste |

## Method of work

1 Drain and wash the peas well.
2 Place the peas into a saucepan of cold water so they are just covered and then bring to the boil.
3 Add some salt and allow the peas to simmer until cooked. Skim regularly to remove any scum that forms on the surface.
4 The peas will eventually begin to break up.
5 Once cooked remove from the heat, add the butter and season well.

# Assessment of knowledge and understanding

You have now learned about the use of the different types of pulse and how to produce a variety of pulse dishes utilising an array of commodities and cooking techniques.

To test your level of knowledge and understanding, answer the following short questions. These will help to prepare you for your summative (final) assessment.

1 Identify three different types of beans.

i) _____ ii) _____

iii) _____

2 Identify three different types of peas.

i) _____ ii) _____

iii) _____

3 Explain the procedure for storing cooked pulses when not required immediately for service.

_____

_____

4 Explain the reason why mature broad beans should be skinned before use.

_____

_____

5 State the reason why pulses other than split peas require boiling for a minimum of 10 minutes.

_____

_____

6 Explain the reason for washing pulses before cooking them.

_____

_____

# CHEF'S PROFILE

**Name: STEVE LOVE**

**Position:** Chef Patron of The College Arms

## Current job role and main responsibilities:

Owner and head chef of a property that runs 2 restaurants, one for 60 and one for 14, and accommodation of 4 rooms. There are 2 kitchens on site so the job entails the day to day management of both kitchens.

## When did you realise that you wanted to pursue a career in the catering and hospitality industry?

When I was 14 I did a two week work placement in a hotel in Stratford upon Avon. I started in the kitchens and was meant to move on after a week but didn't fancy housekeeping (which is where I was meant to be next) so I asked to stay in the kitchens and really enjoyed it there. All the hours in the job since, I can now blame Terry the Head Chef at The Falcon for.

## Training:

Stratford upon Avon College: 7061 707-1 City and Guilds
Full time B/Tec Certificate in Food and Beverage operations
Part time 706/2 – 3 year apprenticeship at The Welcombe Hotel, Stratford upon Avon
Birmingham College of Food – 706/3

## What do you find rewarding about your job?

The fact that every day is different.

## What advice would you give to students just beginning their career?

Keep you eyes open and try and learn as much as possible. Everyone has something to teach you when you are first starting out. I have always had a note book in my back pocket to write down ideas or recipes.

## Who is your mentor or main inspiration?

My mentor for the last 10 years has been Michel Roux. Since winning the Roux Scholarship in 1997 he has always been there for me, and I always take his advice on board.

## Secrets of a successful chef?:

Complete dedication to the job. The hours are long, the work is hard and you will have no social life, possibly ever. To get to the top and to be the best you have to work harder and be better than every one else. But the rewards are fantastic and when you get to the top the ladies love you so it is all worth it!

## A brief personal profile:

From a work prospective, I have won over 40 medals cooking in competitions and have represented the country on at least 3 occasions cooking internationally.
I won the Roux Scholarship in 1997 and won National Chef of the Year for 2004–2006

## Can you give one essential kitchen tip or technique that you use as a chef:

Season well and taste everything as you are cooking and especially before you serve. It's not just about making the food look nice, it has to taste as good as it looks and so many chefs forget that.

# Braised lentils

| INGREDIENTS | |
|---|---|
| Du Puy lentils | 150g |
| Chicken stock | 300ml |
| Onion (chopped ) | 1 |
| Garlic (crushed) | 2 cloves |
| Pancetta cut into small stripes about 0.5cm wide (or smoked streaky bacon) | 70g |
| Bouquet garni | 1 |
| Olive oil | |
| Butter | 20g |

## Method of work

1  In a suitable size pan heat the oil and butter until frothing. Sweat down the onion and garlic.
2  Add the pancetta.
3  When all the ingredients are soft add the lentils.
4  Mix together and then add the stock and bouquet garni.
5  Put a lid on the pan and cook slowly in a preheated oven on 120°C for 40 minutes or until soft but the lentils are not split.
6  Check occasionally on the lentils, if they are looking dry add a touch of water.
7  Adjust seasoning by adding salt and pepper to taste.
8  Serve now, or cool down on a flat tray and reheat when needed.

# Vegetable protein

## INTRODUCTION

### Soya products

The soya bean has been part of the diet of the Chinese for over 4000 years, and part of the Western diet for 50 years. It is believed that the low rates of colon and breast cancer in China and Japan are attributable to the consumption of soya products.

Soya is the most nutritious of the leguminous seeds. High in protein and cholesterol-free, it contains all eight of the essential amino acids that cannot be made in the body. It is exceptionally versatile and is processed into many products:

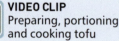
**VIDEO CLIP**
Preparing, portioning and cooking tofu

*Silken and firm tofu*

- *Tofu* The beans are boiled mashed and sieved to make soya milk, which is processed in a similar way to soft cheese. It is pressed and made into several derivatives. Tofu should be kept in a refrigerator for up to one week after purchase. The water should be changed daily and the tofu washed prior to preparation. Tofu does not freeze well as the freezing process changes the texture.

  *Silken tofu* is a good alternative to cream in a vegan diet; it has the same qualities as cream and can be used as a fat-free method of making cream soups, sauces, and desserts.

  *Firm tofu* is the fully pressed version of tofu. It is sold in blocks that can be sliced or diced and used in almost any vegetarian dish. It is quite bland in flavour and benefits from being marinated and sautéed in flavoured oils.

- *Tempeh* Fermented soya beans are cooked and pressed to make tempeh. It is similar to tofu but has a firmer texture and a slightly nutty flavour. Tempeh can be bought chilled and stored for 7 days or frozen and stored up to the use by date.

- *TVP (textured vegetable protein)* Made from processed soya beans, TVP is a dry product that needs rehydrating in hot stock or water. TVP is a meat replacement that can be used in stews or minced meat dishes. Keep in the dry stores in an airtight container with the use by date on display.

### Seitan

Seitan is a wheat-based protein which is made with flour that has a high ratio of gluten, by kneading the flour under several changes of water and then boiling the resultant dough. Seitan lacks flavour and benefits from marinating. As it is precooked, all it needs is to be warmed through, so it can be added at the end of the cookery process. Store in the refrigerator for up to 7 days.

**VIDEO CLIP**
Preparing, portioning and cooking quorn products

## Mycoprotein (Quorn™)

Quorn is made by growing, harvesting and fermenting fungus under controlled conditions. The product is then bound with albumen, textured, flavoured and shaped or sliced to resemble meat. Storage is as per packaging instructions. Quorn can be used as either meat substitute or as one of the many convenience products available under the quorn brand name.

Vegetable proteins are valuable sources of protein for all vegetarians.

*Quorn as mince and diced*

# RECIPES

## TVP moussaka

*Arrange the layers*

| INGREDIENTS | 4 PORTIONS | 10 PORTIONS |
|---|---|---|
| TVP mince (soaked) | 400g | 1kg |
| Aubergines | 600g | 1.5kg |
| Olive oil | 80ml | 200ml |
| Peeled chopped plum tomatoes | 4 | 10 |
| Sliced onions | 150g | 425g |
| Tomato purée | 40g | 100g |
| Chopped parsley | 20g | 50g |
| White wine | 80ml | 200ml |
| Sauce Mornay (see p. 114) | 500ml | 1.25 litres |
| Good-quality salt and mill pepper | To taste | To taste |
| Toasted breadcrumbs | 40g | 100g |

### Method of work

1 Slice the aubergines, sprinkle them with salt in a colander and leave for 1 hour.

2 Wash in several changes of fresh water and allow to dry on a clean cloth.

3 Fry the aubergines until golden brown and drain on dish paper.

4 Fry the TVP and onions in a little oil until brown.

5 Add the remainder of the ingredients, bring to the boil and simmer for 30 minutes. Correct the seasoning.

6 Arrange alternating layers of TVP and aubergines, finishing with a layer of aubergines. Pour on the sauce, sprinkle with the breadcrumbs and bake in the oven at 180°C for 30–35 minutes until the surface is golden brown.

7 Serve hot with green salad.

**CHEF'S TIP**

Salting the aubergines removes a lot of moisture and bitterness. They will absorb less oil and so be less soggy when cooked.

# Stir fried tofu with egg noodles

| INGREDIENTS | 4 PORTIONS | 10 PORTIONS |
|---|---|---|
| Egg noodles | 200g | 500g |
| Firm tofu | 300g | 750g |
| Light soy sauce | 60ml | 150ml |
| Sherry | 40ml | 100ml |
| Sliced red pepper | 1 | 2–3 |
| Sliced red onion | 1 | 2–3 |
| Grated ginger | 40g | 100g |
| Sliced red chilli | 1 | 2–3 |
| Vegetable stock (see p. 110) | 200ml | 500ml |
| Honey | 40g | 100g |
| Cornflour | 15g | 35g |
| Oil | 20ml | 50ml |
| Good-quality salt and pepper | To taste | To taste |

Wash the tofu in clean water

## Method of work

1 Wash the tofu in clean cold water.

2 Dice into 1cm cubes and marinate in the soy sauce and sherry for 2–3 hours.

3 Place the noodles in a dish of seasoned boiling water and allow to stand for 5–6 minutes until regenerated and cooked.

4 Stir fry the onions and peppers for 1 minute. Add the chilli and garlic and continue to cook for 1 minute. Add the stock and bring to the boil.

5 Drain the tofu and stir fry until golden brown.

6 Mix the honey and cornflour with the marinade and add to the stock to thicken (use more or less cornflour as required).

7 Add the tofu to the sauce and serve with the egg noodles.

# Quorn shepherd's pie

| INGREDIENTS | 4 PORTIONS | 10 PORTIONS |
|---|---|---|
| Minced quorn | 500g | 1.25kg |
| Diced onions | 100g | 250g |
| Oil | 40ml | 100ml |
| Tomato concassé | 200g | 500 |
| Vegetable stock to moisten | | |
| Duchesse potatoes (see p. 420) | 500g | 1.25kg |
| Good-quality salt and white pepper | To taste | To taste |

*Wash the tofu in clean water*

## Method of work

1  Cook the onions in the pan until browned.
2  Add the tomato concassé, moisten with a little stock and allow to simmer for 10 minutes.
3  Add the quorn and bring to the boil; correct the seasoning.
4  Place in either individual bowls or earthenware dishes.
5  Pipe the potato on top and bake until golden brown.

> **CHEF'S TIP**
>
> Use a floury potato such as Desiree or Maris Piper to achieve a good crust with the duchesse potato.

# Cajun tofu

*Carve the tofu*

| INGREDIENTS | 4 PORTIONS | 10 PORTIONS |
|---|---|---|
| Tofu blocks | 4 × 125g | 10 × 125g |
| Blackened Cajun spices | 10g | 25g |
| Diced onions | 80g | 200g |
| Chopped red chillies | 1 | 2–3 |
| Crushed garlic | I clove | 2–3 cloves |
| Plum tomato concassé | 500g | 2.5kg |
| Vegetable stock (see p. 110) | 100ml | 250ml |
| Oil | 100ml | 250ml |
| Good-quality salt and pepper | To taste | To taste |
| Vinegar | 20ml | 50ml |
| Sugar | 20g | 100g |

> **CHEF'S TIP**
>
> Avoid frying the tofu with the seasoning as it has a tendency to char and become rather bitter.

## Method of work

1  Drain and wash the tofu, brush with oil and season with blackened Cajun seasoning. Allow the tofu to marinate in the spices for 1 hour.
2  Heat half the oil in a saucepan, add the onions, garlic and chillies a sweat until tender.
3  Add the vinegar and sugar allow to reduce to form a gastrique.
4  Add the tomato concassé and stock and allow to simmer very gently until the sauce has a thick consistency.
5  Bake the tofu in a hot oven until a core temperature of 75°C is achieved.
6  Carve the tofu and serve with sauce, garnished with some chopped parsley.

# Spicy tempeh wrap

| INGREDIENTS | 4 PORTIONS | 10 PORTIONS |
|---|---|---|
| Flour tortillas | 4 | 10 |
| Lettuce | 1 | 2 |
| Sliced tomatoes | 2 | 5 |
| Tempeh | 400g | 1kg |
| Tahini | 20g | 50g |
| Oil | 50ml | 125ml |
| Lemon juice | 20ml | 50ml |
| Parsley, minced | 2tbsp | 4tbsp |
| Clove garlic, minced | 2 | 5 |
| Chopped onion | 1tsp | 1tbsp |
| Onion, chopped | 80g | 200g |
| Grated carrot | 80g | 200g |

*Roll the wrap*

## Method of work

1 Cut the tempeh in large cubes and steam for about 5 minutes.

2 Cool the tempeh and crumble in a bowl. Add the remaining ingredients and mix well with a blender.

3 Make a wrap using the tempeh sandwich filler, lettuce and tomato.

# Quorn chilli

| INGREDIENTS | 4 PORTIONS | 10 PORTIONS |
|---|---|---|
| Quorn mince | 600g | 1.5kg |
| Onions | 80g | 200g |
| Chillies | 2 | 5 |
| Garlic cloves | 2 | 5 |
| Canned tomatoes | 400g | 1kg |
| Canned red kidney beans | 200g | 500g |
| Vegetable stock (approximately) | 200ml | 500ml |
| Sugar | ½tsp | 2tsp |
| Good-quality salt and black pepper | To taste | To taste |
| Oil | 40ml | 100ml |

## Method of work

1 Crush the garlic, chop the onion and chillies, and fry with the quorn until well sweated.
2 Add the sugar, tomatoes and enough stock to moisten.
3 Bring to the boil and simmer very gently for 30 minutes. Add more stock when necessary.
4 Add the kidney beans and simmer for a further 10 minutes.
5 Serve with plain boiled rice and flour tortillas.

*Fry the quorn, chillies, garlic and onions*

# Sweet and sour quorn

| INGREDIENTS | 4 PORTIONS | 10 PORTIONS |
|---|---|---|
| Diced quorn | 400g | 1kg |
| Sliced green pepper | 1 | 2–3 |
| Sliced onion | 100g | 250g |
| Canned pineapple | 200g can | 500g can |
| *The batter* | | |
| Water | | |
| Plain flour | 120g | 300g |
| Cornflour | 30g | 75g |
| Baking powder | 1tsp | 2½tsp |
| Good-quality salt and pepper | To taste | To taste |
| *The sauce* | | |
| Brown sugar | 120g | 300g |
| Rice vinegar | 120ml | 300ml |
| Crushed garlic | 1 clove | 2–3 cloves |
| Grated root ginger | 40g | 100g |
| Tomato ketchup | 80ml | 200ml |
| Juice from the canned pineapple | 80ml | 200ml |
| Oil for frying | | |

## Method of work

1 Make the batter by sieving the flour, cornflour, salt and baking powder together and mixing with enough cold water to form a batter. Add a teaspoon of oil per 4 portions.
2 Cook the quorn by dipping into the batter and deep frying until golden brown and cooked. Drain onto absorbent paper and keep hot for service.
3 Stir fry the onions, diced pineapples and peppers, remove from the wok and put to one side.
4 Mix all the sauce ingredients together and bring to the boil, stir continuously until the sauce thickens and becomes clear.
5 Just prior to service, combine the quorn, vegetables and sauce together and serve immediately.

# Courgette and seitan fritters with chilli marmalade

| INGREDIENTS | 4 PORTIONS | 10 PORTIONS |
|---|---|---|
| Shredded seitan | 200g | 500g |
| Grated courgette | 300g | 750g |
| Grated Parmesan | 40g | 100g |
| Plain flour | 50–60g | 125–150g |
| Eggs | 2 | 5 |
| Oil for frying | | |
| Good-quality salt and mill pepper | To taste | To taste |
| *Chilli marmalade* | | |
| Olive oil | 80ml | 200ml |
| Finely diced onions | 400g | 1kg |
| Chopped garlic | 40g | 100g |
| Hot chillies | 2 | 5 |
| Muscavado sugar | 30g | 75g |

## Method of work for the marmalade

1  Sweat the onions and garlic in the oil for 10–15 minutes, stirring frequently.
2  Add the onions to a food processor along with the sugar and chopped, deseeded chilli.
3  Liquidise to a paste.
4  Return to the pan and stir over a low heat until the liquid has evaporated and the marmalade is thick.

## Method of work for the fritters

1  Grate and season the courgettes with salt and leave in a colander for 10 minutes to allow excess water to be released. Squeeze out the remaining water.
2  Mix the courgettes, seitan, cheese, flour and eggs to make a light paste.
3  Divide the mix and shallow fry the fritters for 3–4 minutes on each side until golden brown and cooked through
4  Serve with a tablespoon of the marmalade and a seasonal salad.

### CHEF'S TIP

The main vegetable can be varied, but remember to use a vegetable that cooks quickly such as sweetcorn.

Sweat the onions

Liquidise the mixture

Mix the ingredients

# Assessment of knowledge and understanding

You have now learned about the preparation and cookery of vegetable protein.

To test your level of knowledge and understanding, answer the following short questions. These will help to prepare you for your summative (final) assessment.

1 List three different types of vegetable protein.

i) _____  ii) _____

iii)_____

2 Give two reasons why the weighing and measuring of ingredients is so important.

i) _____  ii) _____

3 Describe a suitable marinade for vegetable proteins.

_____

_____

4 State the correct temperature for holding a food for hot for service.

_____

_____

# Research Task

Complete the following chart describing how to use, clean and maintain the following items of equipment and the safety considerations associated with them.

|  | CLEANING | STERILISING | STORING | SAFETY PROCEDURES |
| --- | --- | --- | --- | --- |
| Wok |  |  |  |  |
| Serrated-edge knife |  |  |  |  |
| Food processor |  |  |  |  |

# 14

# Bakery products

## LEARNING OBJECTIVES

The aim of this unit is to enable the candidate to develop skills and implement knowledge in the bakery principles of producing a range of bakery products. This will also include information on materials, ingredients and equipment.

At the end of this chapter you will be able to:

■ Identify each type of paste and dough and finished bread product
■ Understand the use of relative ingredients in bakery and in the preparation of pastes
■ State the quality points of various dough and paste products
■ Prepare, bake and present each type of dough and paste product
■ Identify the storage procedures of dough products and health issues of raw ingredients
■ Identify the correct tools and equipment
■ Be competent at preparing and cooking a range of bakery products

# Breads and dough

To make good bread it is important to know the functions of the basic components (flour, salt, water, sugar and yeast), how they can be controlled and the appropriate methods of making the dough for different types of bread products.

The most important components of bread making will now be discussed.

## THE USE OF LIQUIDS IN BREAD MAKING

### Water

Water is essential in bread making to hydrate the insoluble wheat proteins that form gluten. It will also dissolve salt, sugar and other soluble proteins to help form an elastic and soft dough. Water has a noticeable effect on the speed of fermentation – soft-textured dough ferments quicker than a hard and tight dough. The water content will vary according to the absorption rate of different flours. Water is the second most important ingredient in breadmaking after flour and it will also create the humid environment necessary for the development of bread during fermentation.

**CHEF'S TIP**

Insoluble wheat proteins are those that are incapable of being dissolved in a liquid such as water. However, the water softens them to help develop the gluten strands needed in the production of bread.

### Milk

Like water, milk contributes by adding moisture to dough. Its fat content makes it an important agent in helping to achieve a soft texture to the finished product. It also plays a minor role in colouring the product during the baking process and this is primarily due to its sugar content. Whole or skimmed milk powder is the form of milk most widely used in baking. Lactic acid in fresh milk can break down the gluten content over time and can create a sour taste in the finished product.

## THE ROLE OF OTHER INGREDIENTS IN BREAD MAKING

### Salt

Good bread needs salt to offset blandness and bring out the flavours present. It is also necessary because it helps to stabilise the gluten, retain moisture and control the fermenting yeast which affects the final crumb texture and crust colour. Salt can benefit the production of dough and bread significantly by slowing down the action of yeast and helping to retain moisture in the dough.

Obviously the salt content will help improve the flavour of all fermented products, and its inclusion also has an influence on the storage life of bread

*Sea salt flakes, granulated table salt and rock salt*

because it helps to delay the drying-out process. When the salt content is added to the dough can also influence the crumb colour. Salt added at the end of the kneading process will achieve a whitening of the crumb after baking.

Yeast activity is retarded by too much salt being added and excessive amounts will stop fermentation completely. With the yeast activity slowed down, there is a corresponding tightening of the gluten, resulting in a smaller volume and heavy dough.

# THE USE OF FLOUR IN BAKERY

*White strong flour, brown flour and wholemeal flour, wheat grain, malted wheat grain and stoneground flour*

There are two basic types of flour for bread making; wholemeal and strong white flour. Wholemeal flour contains whole wheat grain with nothing added or taken away during processing. Strong white flour has a higher protein content and therefore more gluten than soft flour. Wholemeal flours tend to have a greater water absorption rate than white flours so the dough can be stickier when processing. Extra enzymes found in the bran coating will help to speed up the dough ripening, so the dough temperature for wholemeal bread should be made a little cooler to slow down fermentation. Because the physical and chemical changes in the dough are more rapid, wholemeal dough needs a shorter fermentation time.

When selecting flour to use for breadmaking you should always choose the best quality possible. It is important to be aware of its chemical and physical composition and also to bear in mind other criteria.

1 Colour – to form a clear idea of the colour of the flour it is best to press a small quantity under a sheet of glass. This can be done with more than one flour at a time. This method not only facilitates a comparison of the whiteness of different flours but also allows for an inspection of impurities. The flour should have a regular consistency and not contain any specs of dust, dirt or infestations.

2 Texture – the texture and size of the grains play an important role in kneading and also determine the speed at which the dough rises. The finer the grain the longer the fermentation process can take.

3 Rising ability and elasticity – several factors determine the rising ability and elasticity of flour. The greatest is the quantity of protein available in flour. The higher the amount of protein content the more water will be absorbed, which also means a greater elasticity, strength and ability of the flour to expand.

4 Moisture content – the moisture content of flour must not exceed 16 per cent or the flour will have a shorter shelf life and lower yield. Generally moisture content of flour is about 12 per cent.

5 Absorption ability – this is a measure of the amount of water that can be absorbed by a given quantity of flour. In bread making, it is usually preferable to have flour that can absorb a large amount of water.

Over 25 different varieties of wheat are grown in the United Kingdom. Local millers will carefully select from these, and a small amount of imported wheat, those varieties with the characteristics to produce specific flour. By blending wheat and extracting flours at different stages in the milling process, a mill will typically produce as many as 60 different flours. However, in Britain, whatever the baking characteristics of flour, most fall into one of the following main categories:

- *Wholemeal* – 100 per cent extraction, made from the wholewheat grain with nothing added or taken away.
- *Brown* – usually contains about 85 per cent of the original grain. Some bran and germ have been removed.
- *White* – usually 75 per cent of the wheat grain. Most of the bran and the wheat germ have been removed before milling.
- *Wheat germ* – white or brown flour with at least 10 per cent added wheat germ.
- *Malted wheatgrain* – brown or wholemeal flour with added malted grains.
- *Stoneground* – wholemeal flour ground in the traditional way, between two rotating stones.

## Gluten

Gluten, which is found in flour, traps the gas generated by the fermentation process and holds it in the dough structure. When coagulated in baking it becomes the framework of the loaf and stops it collapsing. There are five wheat proteins: albumin, globulin, proteose, gliadin and glutenin. The first three, which account for 1–2 per cent of the flour, are water soluble and provide the necessary nitrogenous yeast food during fermentation. The last two, which are not water soluble, together form gluten. Gliadin gives dough elasticity, glutenin gives stability.

Gluten is conditioned by many factors including the amount of yeast and how active it is, the amount of salt and water there is in the dough, fermentation time, dough temperature, acidity of the dough and manipulation or kneading.

The approximate protein value in various flours can differ depending on the manufacturer's specifications, but as a general rule they follow the pattern listed in the table.

| FLOUR | PERCENTAGE OF GLUTEN |
|---|---|
| Strong white flour | 12–17 |
| Medium flour | 11 |
| Soft flour | 8–9 |
| Cake flour | 7 |
| Type 55 (blended) | 9–10 |
| Wholemeal flour | 11–15 |

Given good materials in the correct balance, nothing contributes more to successful bread making than kneading, mixing, fermentation and knocking back. Proper mixing gives the gluten the ability to absorb the maximum amount of water and become thoroughly hydrated.

# THE FUNCTION OF YEAST

Yeast is a living organism capable of feeding and reproducing itself when placed in suitable surroundings. It is from the fungi family of plants which changes sugar into carbon dioxide, alcohol and other by-products. The gas is caught up in the gluten network which aerates the dough. Existing as a single cell it is invisible to the naked eye but easily discernible under a microscope.

The second function of yeast, equally vital to producing good-quality bread, is to assist in the ripening or mellowing of the gluten in the dough, so that when the item is baked, the gluten is in a condition which gives evenness to the expanding dough.

For fermentation to occur, yeast needs a source of glucose (a simple sugar). Simple sugars and carbohydrates are converted to glucose by enzymes found naturally in the flour.

*Block yeast, dried yeast and fermenting yeast*

**VIDEO CLIP**
Using different types of yeast

### YEAST ACTIVITY TEMPERATURES

| 1–4°C (34–40°F) | Yeast remains dormant |
|---|---|
| 10°C (50°F) | Yeast cells slowly begin activity |
| 16–21°C (60–70°F) | Yeast cells become more active |
| 21–27°C (70–80°F) | Optimum fermentation range |
| 50°C (120°F) | Reduction in yeast activity |
| 60°C (140°F) | Yeast is killed |

**CHEF'S TIP**

To convert a recipe using fresh yeast to dry yeast, use half of the stated amount of dried yeast.

Fresh yeast must be in good condition to work efficiently. It should be cool to the touch and a creamy colour. Small quantities can be kept pressed into a stone jar at 4°C. If it is dark, soft and has an unpleasant smell then it should not be used. It should never be mixed with dry salt or sugar or dispersed in a strong solution of either, which will kill the yeast.

## The Effect of Temperature on Fermented Dough

It is important to maintain the ideal dough temperature to control the speed of fermentation. Fermentation will begin as soon as the ingredients have been mixed together and kneaded, indeed even the kneading process can increase the temperature of dough. The best temperature for fermentation of dough is between 25–29°C. Above 32°C, the fermentation process becomes more rapid but the dough structure will get progressively weaker, so care must be taken to slow this process down. Under 24°C the fermentation process will be much slower. This is not necessarily bad because gradually the dough will develop greater flavour and a better overall structure to the texture. Without understanding this, it is easy to be tempted to ferment yeast at too high a temperature. This can cause the skinning of the dough and the encouragement of other undesirable characteristics such as lack of flavour in the finished product.

## Enriching Ingredients

Bread is sometimes enriched with fat, milk, eggs or spices to increase the food value, add to the flavour, produce a softer crumb and retard staling. Salt may have to be reduced when using salted butter or margarine, which contains approximately 2 per cent salt. Fermentation is slower in enriched dough, so the dough should be kept a little softer.

Sugar is another ingredient that requires careful usage in the presence of yeast. It should be used sparingly and should never come into direct contact with yeast because the yeast will be broken down chemically and become inactive.

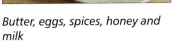

*Butter, eggs, spices, honey and milk*

# BREAD MAKING METHODS

## Bulk Fermented Dough (Straight Dough)

This is the process bakers use to make bread. Flour and salt are blended together with water and yeast. These are mixed to a smooth, clear dough.

The dough is then covered to prevent it drying out and a skin forming; it is given a 'bulk fermentation time' (BFT), when all the ingredients mix together and ferment. The dough is knocked back (de-gassed) after the BFT and kneaded to encourage continued yeast activity, develop the gluten in the flour and promote an even dough temperature.

The dough is rested for a few minutes, covered as always, and is then scaled off to produce various breads. The total BFT can vary from 1 to 12 hours depending on the recipe, so it is best to follow the recipe given.

**VIDEO CLIP**
A commercial bakery producing various fermented products

## Ferment and Dough

This process is intended for heavily enriched dough to allow yeast to become accustomed to high levels of fat and sugar, which slow yeast activity.

In the first stage the ferment (yeast) is blended to a thin batter and fermented with about 20 per cent of the recipe's flour and all of the water. Fermentation time depends on the yeast content, but it is ready when it drops back (the ferment rises so much that it cannot support its own bulk and drops back).

It is best fermented in a prover or similar atmosphere and needs to be sufficiently warm after dropping back to maintain the correct dough temperature.

The ferment is then blended with the remaining flour, salt, fat and milk powder to form a dough. It is then bulk fermented for about the same time as the ferment and then scaled off. This method is sometimes known as a 'flying ferment'.

## Baking

All fermented goods require a hot oven 200–235°C. Goods rich in sugar and fat require a lower temperature. Foods lean in sugar and fat require the higher temperature. For best baking conditions some steam should be present in the oven. A full oven should produce sufficient steam (generated by the goods themselves) otherwise moisture needs to be injected into the oven area. This is to create a slightly humid atmosphere and prevent the skin of the goods setting until they have had a chance to expand. The steam will also help to create a moist eating product.

## Faults Found in Bread

### Under-ripeness

1 High crust colour.

2 Small volume of buns and rolls.

3 Poor shapes split at the sides or top.

4 Tough, close-textured crumb.

Under-ripeness is caused by insufficient fermentation, and may be due to:

■ Insufficient yeast.

■ Too cool a dough temperature.

■ Too much sugar, salt, spice, fat or enriching ingredients.

■ Yeast coming into contact with salt at the mixing stage.

■ Insufficient BFT.

■ Insufficient final prove.

### Over-ripeness

1 Anaemic colour crust.

2 Flat shape, no stability.

3 Loose, woolly crumb.

Over-ripeness is caused by too much fermentation and may be due to:

■ Excessive amount of yeast.

■ Too high a dough temperature.

■ Omission of salt or sugar.

■ Too prolonged dough time. (Final prove)

■ Too prolonged BFT.

> **CHEF'S TIP**
>
> To check if a loaf is correctly baked turn it out and tap the bottom of the bread. It should sound hollow if it is baked properly.

Under-ripe and over-ripe bread rolls

# TERMS USED IN BAKERY

- *Kneading or working the dough.* After the ingredients have been mixed together it requires 'kneading' or 'working'. This is to essentially stretch the dough to develop the gluten structure. Hand kneading should be gentle but thorough in technique.

- *Ferment.* The term 'levain' is also used here and means a mixture of ingredients (usually flour, water and yeast) that is left in a plastic container with a lid and left at room temperature for at least six hours. Added to bread dough this can increase flavour and lightens the finished bread texture.

- *BFT (bulk fermentation time).* This term is used to explain the amount of time required for the first prove of the dough to create the fermentation of the dough.

- **Knocking back.** This is the gentle kneading of the dough after the first prove.

- *Resting the dough.* The dough should be covered with a clean tea towel or plastic sheet for a short period of time. This relaxes the gluten and makes it easier to manipulate into shapes.

- *Scaling.* Pieces of dough are weighed on a scale to help establish portion control and size. Some establishments use a 'dough divider' for this process for the quick dividing of a large piece of dough into small rolls.

- *Shaping.* In France this is known as *la tourne* which means to form elongated loaves. In the strictest sense of the term it means to create the final shape of the bread.

*The dough having the first prove in the prover*

*The dough being gently kneaded after proving*

*Moulding the dough by hand into rolls*

*Proving the moulded dough*

- *Final **prove***. The final fermentation process of the finished and shaped dough to increase the volume. This improves the resulting texture of the bread.

- *Baking*. The dough is now ready for baking. Care must be taken in identifying the correct oven temperature.

- *Steam injecting*. Steam can be introduced into the oven chamber by adding a pan of water into the oven with the dough in the first five to ten minutes to help create a 'hard crust' to bread.

- *Crumb*. This refers to the texture of the baked bread on the inside of the product. An open texture means that large irregular holes (such as ciabatta bread) are produced. A closed texture means that a uniformity of smaller pockets is present (such as Swiss buns or white sandwich bread).

- *Scoring or marking*. Some breads require a scored finish to help identify them or to create an additional finish. This is where a loaf or roll can be slashed with a sharp implement such as a small knife or razor. The cuts are shallow.

- *The Maillard reaction*. When the oven temperature reaches up to between 150–260°C, the moisture on the surface of the dough combines with the broken down starch and proteins within the flour. It forms a crisp golden brown crust with complex 'burnt' caramel flavours. This chemical reaction is known as the Maillard reaction after the scientist who first observed it.

- *Cooling*. The bread is removed from the oven and allowed to cool on large wire racks. These cooling racks allow maximum air circulation which aids the evaporation of any excess moisture.

- *Storing*. The successful storage of yeast breads and products is very important in maintaining the quality of the finished item. Usually bread should be consumed within the day of its production. However, to store bread for a longer period of time it should be completely wrapped in plastic and placed in a refrigerator or an airtight container. Alternatively a freezer can be used to increase the storage time.

> **CHEF'S TIP**
>
> When shaping the dough handle it as little as possible. Over-handling develops the gluten further, making the dough harder to shape.

Bread rolls going into a deck oven

Pan of water used to create steam in the oven chamber

Open-textured bread

Closed-textured bread

Cutting the dough using a sharp modelling knife

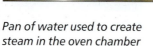
The caramel colour of the surface of bread

Bread placed onto wire cooling racks

Plastic-wrapped and labelled bread

# SPECIALIST BAKING EQUIPMENT

The preparation of equipment when baking bread and dough products is very important. For example, having the oven preheated to the correct temperature is essential so that the product commences cooking as soon as it is placed into the oven. Failure to do this may have a damaging effect on the finished product.

*Weighing scales*  It is of the utmost importance that all ingredients are weighed and measured accurately. One set of measurement should be used (e.g. grams and kilograms). Ensure that scales have been calibrated so that they measure weight correctly.

*Wire cooling rack*  When hot-baked fermented items such as bread, buns and rolls are taken from the oven, it is essential to place them directly onto cooling racks so that the cool air can circulate around each product.

*Electric mixer with dough hook and beater attachment*  The dough hook is used for yeast dough to stimulate the kneading process. It is used to thoroughly mix ingredients and to encourage the development of gluten.

*Rolling pin*  Wooden rolling pins should be stored correctly after cleaning to prevent the wood from distorting. However, polyethylene rolling pins are widely available, keep their shape better and are easier to sanitise.

*Baking sheets*  Some baking sheets are non-stick and some are aluminium-based. The sheets should always be kept clean and dry, ready for use.

*Silicone baking mat*  These mats offer excellent, non-stick baking surfaces. They are reusable, flexible sheets that can withstand extreme temperatures.

*Silicone paper*  This is baking parchment that has been treated with silicone to prevent foods from sticking to it. It will not burn in a hot oven and can be used to protect food when baking and to create piping cones.

*Metal pastry scraper*  Sometimes referred to as a 'bench scraper'. It is used to cut and scale pieces of dough and to clean work surfaces by scraping it against a table to loosen pieces of dough or flour.

# RECIPES

## Basic white bread

*Cut the dough into two equal pieces and shape each piece into balls (boules)*

 **VIDEO CLIP**
Basic bread dough

| INGREDIENTS | 1 LOAF OR 18 BREAD ROLLS | 2 LOAVES OR 40 BREAD ROLLS |
|---|---|---|
| Fresh yeast | 10g | 20g |
| Water at approximately 22–24°C | 350g | 700g |
| Strong white flour | 500g | 1kg |
| Good-quality salt | 7g | 18g |

## Method of work

1 Preheat the oven to 220°C.

2 In a bowl, mix together the water and the fresh yeast. Ensure that the yeast has completely dissolved in the water.

3 Combine the flour and salt and add to the yeast liquid. Mix well.

4 Create a soft, slightly sticky dough, resisting the temptation to add more flour.

5 Scrape any excess ingredients and dough off the sides of the bowl and knead together. Leave the dough to rest for about 10 minutes.

6 Place the dough into a stainless steel bowl and place in a prover or warm place for the bulk fermentation. The BFT should be approximately 30 minutes.

7 Carefully knock back the dough and knead lightly by folding the dough over itself. Leave to rest for a further 10 minutes.

8 Lightly oil a deep 19 x 12cm loaf tin. Cut the dough into two equal pieces and shape each piece into balls (*boules*). Place them side-by-side into the loaf tin. Alternatively, scale off the dough at 45g each to shape into smaller balls for bread rolls.

9 Set onto a baking tray and place into a prover to double in size.

10 Dust some flour onto the top of the loaf or each bread roll and place into the preheated oven. After 15 minutes reduce the heat of the oven to 190°C and bake for a further 25 minutes for the loaf or a further 15 minutes for the bread rolls.

11 Remove from the oven when baked and leave to cool on a wire rack, taking care to remove the bread loaf from the hot tin beforehand.

# Basic wholemeal bread

*Scale off the dough at 45g each to shape into smaller balls for bread rolls*

| INGREDIENTS | 1 LOAF OR 18 BREAD ROLLS | 2 LOAVES OR 40 BREAD ROLLS |
|---|---|---|
| Fresh yeast | 10g | 20g |
| Water at approximately 22–24°C | 350g | 700g |
| Strong wholemeal flour | 500g | 1kg |
| Good-quality salt | 7g | 18g |

## Method of work

1   Preheat the oven to 220°C.

2   In a bowl, mix together the water and the fresh yeast.

3   Ensure that the yeast has completely dissolved in the water.

4   Combine the wholemeal flour and salt and add to the yeast liquid. Mix well.

5   Create a soft, slightly sticky dough, resisting the temptation to add more flour.

6   Scrape any excess ingredients and dough off the sides of the bowl and knead together. Leave the dough to rest for about 10 minutes.

7   Place the dough into a stainless steel bowl and place in a prover or warm place for the bulk fermentation. The BFT should be approximately 25 minutes.

8   Carefully knock back the dough and knead lightly by folding the dough over itself. At this stage it is important not to overwork the dough. Leave to rest for a further 10 minutes.

9   Lightly oil a deep 19 x 12cm loaf tin. Cut the dough into two equal pieces and shapes each piece into balls (*boules*). Place them side-by-side into the loaf tin. Alternatively, scale off the dough at 45g each to shape into smaller balls for bread rolls.

10   Set onto a baking tray and place into a prover to double in size.

11   Sieve some wholewheat flour and sprinkle the cracked wheat pieces retained in the sieve onto the top of the loaf or each bread roll and place into the preheated oven.

12   After 15 minutes reduce the heat of the oven to 190°C and bake for a further 25 minutes for the loaf or a further 15 minutes for the bread rolls.

13   Remove from the oven when baked and leave to cool on a wire rack, taking care to remove the bread loaf from the hot tin beforehand.

### CHEF'S TIP

For a lighter-textured dough replace 200g of the wholemeal flour with strong white flour.

# Country bread *Pain de campagne*

*Manipulate the bourles into baton shapes*

| INGREDIENTS | 3 LOAVES OR 20 BREAD ROLLS | 6 LOAVES OR 40 BREAD ROLLS |
|---|---|---|
| *Fermented dough starter* | | |
| **Strong white flour** | 100g | 200g |
| **Water at 20°C** | 60g | 120g |
| **Fresh yeast** | 5g | 10g |
| *Dough* | | |
| **Strong white flour** | 500g | 1kg |
| **Water at 10°C** | 350g | 700g |
| **Fresh yeast** | 12g | 25g |
| **Good-quality salt** | 15g | 25g |

## Method of work

1  Preheat the oven to 250°C.

2  To make the fermented dough starter, mix the flour and water together with the yeast and gently knead for 10 minutes.

3  Place the ferment into a bowl and cover it with a clean cloth or lid. Rest at room temperature for at least 3 hours.

4  Knock back the ferment, replace in a bowl and repeat the fermentation process for a further 3 hours.

5  To make the country bread; using a stainless steel bowl, mix together the water and the fresh yeast. Ensure that the yeast has completely dissolved in the water.

6  Combine the flour and salt and add to the yeast liquid. Mix well.

7  Create a soft, slightly sticky dough, resisting the temptation to add more flour. Add the ferment starter dough and mix well.

8  Scrape any excess ingredients and dough off the sides of the bowl and knead together. Leave the dough to rest for about 10 minutes.

9  Place the dough into a bowl and place in a prover or warm place for the bulk fermentation. The BFT should be approximately 60 minutes.

10  Carefully knock back the dough and knead lightly by folding the dough over itself. Leave to rest for a further 10 minutes.

11  Cut the dough into three equal pieces and shape each piece into balls (*boules*). Let the dough rest for 2 minutes before manipulating further into baton shapes. Place onto a baking tray on top of a clean tea cloth, separate with a fold in the cloth to prevent from sticking to each other. Alternatively, scale off the dough at 45g each to shape into smaller balls for bread rolls.

12  Place into a prover to double in size.

13  Dust some flour onto a baking tray and carefully transfer the proved loaves onto the tray. Dust the top of the loaf or each bread roll with flour and make some incisions to the surface of the bread for decoration.

14  Place into the preheated oven with a small tray of water to help inject steam into the oven chamber.

15  Bake the rolls for approximately 10–15 minutes and the loaves for 25–30 minutes.

16  Remove from the oven when baked and leave to cool on a wire rack, taking care to remove the bread loaf from the hot tin beforehand.

## CHEF'S TIP

Hold the blade of the sharp knife flat against the surface of the bread at a 30° angle. Ensure that cuts are not too deep.

# Tarragon bread

*Take some fine tarragon leaves and brush onto the tops of each roll with a little water*

| INGREDIENTS | 15 BREAD ROLLS | 30 BREAD ROLLS |
|---|---|---|
| Strong white flour | 450g | 900g |
| Good-quality salt | 10g | 15g |
| Fresh yeast | 15g | 25g |
| Water at 16°C | 250g | 500g |
| Fresh tarragon | 4 large sprigs | 8 large sprigs |
| Cracked black pepper | To taste | To taste |
| Rock salt | To taste | To taste |

## Method of work

1 Preheat the oven to 240°C.

2 In a bowl, mix together the water and the fresh yeast. Ensure that the yeast has completely dissolved in the water.

3 Combine the flour and salt and add to the yeast liquid. Mix well.

4 Create a soft, slightly sticky dough, resisting the temptation to add more flour.

5 Scrape any excess ingredients and dough off the sides of the bowl and knead together. Leave the dough to rest for about 10 minutes.

6 Place the dough into a stainless steel bowl and place in a prover or warm place for the bulk fermentation. The BFT should be approximately 30 minutes.

7 Carefully knock back the dough and knead lightly by folding the dough over itself, this time adding the chopped fresh tarragon and ground black pepper to taste. Leave to rest for a further 10 minutes.

8 Scale off the dough at 45g each to shape into smaller balls for bread rolls. Take some fine tarragon leaves and brush onto the tops of each roll with a little water.

9 Set onto a baking tray and sprinkle a little cracked black pepper and rock salt on top and place into a prover to double in size.

10 Place into the preheated oven. After 15 minutes reduce the heat of the oven to 190°C and bake for a further 10 minutes.

11 Remove from the oven when baked and leave to cool on a wire rack.

### CHEF'S TIP

Spray a little clean, cold water onto your work surface to allow the dough to stick slightly to the work surface, which will help with better shaping.

# Pitta bread

| INGREDIENTS | 8 INDIVIDUAL BREADS | 16 INDIVIDUAL BREADS |
|---|---|---|
| *Ferment Starter* | | |
| Fresh yeast | 4g | 8g |
| Water at 24°C | 125g | 250g |
| Strong white flour | 100g | 200g |
| *Dough* | | |
| Water at 22°C | 180g | 350g |
| Soft white flour | 200g | 400g |
| Strong white flour | 250g | 500g |
| Caster sugar | 25g | 40g |
| Good-quality salt | 5g | 10g |

**CHEF'S TIP**

Ensure that the oven is at the correct temperature for this recipe. It should be very hot! Also that the baking sheet has had plenty of time to reach the required temperature prior to baking.

## Method of work

1  Preheat the oven to 250°C.

2  Create a ferment by mixing together the yeast and the water in a bowl and adding the flour. Mix to a smooth batter.

3  Cover and leave in a warm place to ferment for approximately 1½ hours.

4  To make the dough mix the second water content with the ferment and then add all of the remaining ingredients. Mix to a soft and sticky dough, cover and rest for 10 minutes.

5  Knead the dough and then leave it rest for 30 minutes. Repeat this process one further time.

6  Place a clean baking tray into the oven to heat up. On a lightly floured surface scale off the dough at 100g each. Shape each piece into a ball and leave to rest, covered with a clean cloth for about 15 minutes.

7  Roll out each ball into an oblong about 5–6mm thick.

8  Carefully pick up the individual pitta dough pieces and place onto the hot baking sheet. Bake for 5 minutes without too much colour. Remove from the oven and repeat the process until every piece has been baked.

9  Leave to cool on a wire rack before using.

# Pizza dough

| INGREDIENTS | MAKES 450G | MAKES 900G |
|---|---|---|
| Water at 22°C | 150g | 300g |
| Fresh yeast | 4g | 10g |
| Caster sugar | 5g | 10g |
| Olive oil | 25g (plus a little extra for kneading) | 60g (plus a little extra for kneading) |
| 00 grade flour | 160g | 320g |
| Strong white flour | 110g | 220g |
| Good-quality salt | 5g | 10g |

*Brush the dough with olive oil and dust lightly with sea salt*

## Method of work

1 Mix yeast and the water and then add the sugar and the olive oil.

2 Sieve the flours together and add the salt. Add the yeast liquid and mix together into a soft mass. Scrape any excess ingredients and dough off the sides of the bowl and knead together. Leave the dough to rest for about 10 minutes.

3 Lightly knead the dough and leave to prove at room temperature with a clean cloth covering it for about 1 hour.

4 Divide the dough into 200g balls and roll out each piece into a thin circle. Cover with a cloth and leave to rest for 10 minutes.

5 Preheat the oven to 220°C and lightly brush a baking tray with olive oil. Sprinkle with some polenta.

6 Roll the discs of dough thinner and carefully place each disc onto the prepared baking tray. Brush the dough with olive oil and dust lightly with sea salt.

7 At this stage you can begin to add any type of topping required.

8 Place in the oven for approximately 12–15 minutes depending on how much topping you use. The edges of the pizza should be just crisp to the touch when finished.

### CHEF'S TIP

Different types of pizza topping can be added to the basic tomato base:
- Calzone – mozzarella, prosciutto cotto (or salami), ricotta, olive oil, grated Parmesan or pecorino cheese. The unique aspect of calzone is that it is a folded pizza.
- Napoletana – tomato concassé, garlic, oregano, drizzle of olive oil.
- Quattro Stagioni – ham, mushrooms, artichoke hearts and olives.

# Soda bread

### CHEF'S TIP

This recipe does not keep very well and should be used and eaten on the same day to maintain a good quality product. Soda bread tends to go stale very quickly.

| INGREDIENTS | 1 LOAF OR 18 ROLLS | 2 LOAVES OR 40 ROLLS |
|---|---|---|
| Soft wholemeal flour | 150g | 350g |
| Soft white flour | 180g | 400g |
| Good-quality salt | 4g | 10g |
| Bicarbonate of soda | 4g | 10g |
| Baking powder | 5g | 15g |
| Buttermilk | 290g | 600g |

## Method of work

1 Preheat the oven to 200°C.

2 Sieve all the dry ingredients together and create a well in the centre of the bowl.

3 Pour in the buttermilk and mix lightly to form a soft and sticky dough. Rest for 5 minutes covered by a clean cloth.

4 Knead lightly and rest again.

5 Scale the dough off at 200g and shape each piece into a ball. Rest once more for 5 minutes.

6 Flatten each ball slightly and cut a cross on top without cutting all of the way through the dough. Rest the dough for 20 minutes before baking in the oven for approximately 25 minutes.

7 Remove from the oven when baked and leave to cool on a wire rack.

# Naan bread

*Place the bread carefully into the wok and cook on one side until it has browned slightly*

| INGREDIENTS | 4 BREADS | 8 BREADS |
| --- | --- | --- |
| Water at 22°C | 150g | 300g |
| Fresh yeast | 5g | 10g |
| Soft white flour | 250g | 500g |
| Plain yoghurt | 50g | 100g |
| Good-quality salt | 3g | 6g |
| Baking powder | ½tsp | 1tsp |
| Sunflower oil | | |
| Chopped fresh coriander (optional) | | |

## Method of work

1  Mix the water and the yeast together and add half of the flour. Mix well and cover the bowl and leave to ferment in a prover for 30 minutes.

2  Stir in the yoghurt, remaining flour, salt and baking powder. Mix well to a dough and finally brush some of the sunflower oil over the dough to help prevent skinning. Cover and leave to rest for 15 minutes.

3  Repeat the process of light kneading and resting once more.

4  Divide the dough into equal pieces and knead each piece lightly on an oiled surface. Dust with flour and leave to rest for 5 minutes.

5  Heat a wok over a moderate heat.

6  Taking one piece of dough at a time, roll out into a pear shape using a little more flour if necessary. You should aim to pin the dough out to 3mm thick.

7  When the wok is very hot, brush the surface of the naan bread with some sunflower oil and sprinkle with the coriander if desired. Place a lid on the wok and pin out the next piece of dough, leaving the first to rest briefly.

8  The naan is ready to cook when there is further evidence of fermentation beginning to start: small pockets of air should be forming just underneath the surface of the bread.

9  Place the bread carefully into the wok and cook on one side until it has slightly browned. Flip it over and apply the same cooking process for a further minute.

10  When the naan is cooked on both sides carefully remove from the wok. Keep the naan breads wrapped in a clean cloth in a warm oven, these should be served to the customer within 3–4 minutes of cooking.

# Basic bun dough

*Place into a prover to double in size*

| INGREDIENTS | 14 INDIVIDUAL BUNS | 30 INDIVIDUAL BUNS |
|---|---|---|
| Strong white flour | 475g | 950g |
| Good-quality salt | 5g | 10g |
| Caster sugar | 65g | 130g |
| Milk powder | 10g | 20g |
| Butter | 40g | 80g |
| Whole egg | ½ beaten egg | 1 egg |
| Fresh yeast | 25g | 50g |
| Water | 180ml | 360ml |

## Method of work

1 Preheat the oven to 220°C.
2 In a bowl, mix together the water and the fresh yeast. Ensure that the yeast has completely dissolved in the water.
3 Combine the sieved flour, sugar and salt and rub in the butter.
4 Add the yeast liquid and the beaten egg. Mix well. If using a mechanical mixing machine, use the dough hook and set on second speed for 5 minutes.
5 Create a soft dough resisting the temptation to add more flour.
6 Scrape any excess ingredients and dough off the sides of the bowl and knead together. Leave the dough to rest for about 10 minutes.
7 Place the dough into a stainless steel bowl and place in a prover or warm place for the bulk fermentation. The BFT should be approximately 45 minutes.
8 Carefully knock back the dough and knead lightly by folding the dough over itself. Leave to rest for a further 10 minutes.
9 Scale off the bun dough into 45g balls and leave to rest under a sheet of plastic to prevent from skinning. Mould each bun dough ball into small, neat round buns and place onto a baking sheet.
10 Set onto a baking tray and place into a prover to double in size.
11 Place into the preheated oven. After 15 minutes reduce the heat of the oven to 190°C and bake for a further 20 minutes.
12 Remove from the oven when baked and leave to cool on a wire rack.

**CHEF'S TIP**

Some buns will need to be glazed immediately after they are removed from the oven, but traditionally Devonshire splits (see p. 488) do not need to be. Ensure they are cooled quickly on a wire rack to prevent the bases from becoming moist and eventually soggy.

# Bun glaze

Some bun recipes demand to be glazed immediately after they are removed from the oven. A milk and sugar glaze is normally used, or another syrup.

- 500g sugar
- 500g water
- 2 leaves gelatine

Bring the sugar and water to the boil and soften the gelatine in cold water. Add the gelatine to the sugar solution and pass through a chinois.

# Bun varieties

*Devonshire splits*

## Devonshire Splits

Mould into balls, prove to double size. Bake at 232°C. Cool on a wire rack. Cut a slit three-quarters through the top at an angle. Pipe in a bulb of strawberry or raspberry jam. Follow with a bulb of whipped fresh cream. Dust with icing sugar.

*Swiss buns*

## Swiss Buns

Scale and mould the pieces into balls. Rest for 10 minutes. Elongate the pieces to form fingers. Place on a baking tray, prove, and bake at 232°C for about 12 minutes. Cool and dip into fondant or water icing which may be flavoured or coloured.

*Currant buns*

## Currant Buns

Carefully mix 75–100g currants into the bun dough recipe so that no bruising occurs and proceed for Devonshire splits. When baked glaze immediately.

*Teacakes*

## Small Tea Cakes

Scale and mould as for currant buns. Allow 15 minutes recovery and then pin out to 6 mm thick to an oval or round shape. Set onto a silicone baking tray and lightly dock each one. Bake at 226°C.

**VIDEO CLIP**
Preparing Chelsea buns

## Chelsea Buns

Roll out basic dough to cover an area of 38 cm × 60 cm. Mix 75g brown sugar and 5g mixed spice together, spread this mixture over the dough and sprinkle over with currants. Roll up Swiss roll fashion. Brush the surface with melted butter. Cut into equal slices. Place flat side down onto a square, high-sided baking tray with the pieces almost touching. Prove and bake at 226°C for 15 minutes. When baked brush with a syrup and dust with caster or nibbed sugar.

## Bath Buns

Mix dried fruit and sugar nibs into the basic dough with a little beaten egg. Divide into the appropriate number of buns on a baking sheet lined with a silicone mat, in a rough shape. Prove and sprinkle the tops with nibbed sugar. Bake at 226°C for about 15 minutes. Glaze and then cool.

*Hot cross buns*

# Hot Cross Buns

Add 50–75g currants or sultanas and 5g bun spice to the basic recipe. Place crosses on top of each fruited and spiced bun after the proof. Pipe a thin paste using a plain number 3 tube. Spice may be added in liquid form or as ground spice.

### *Bun cross paste*

- 500g soft flour
- 110g shortening
- 55g milk powder
- 550g water
- 4g baking powder
- 4g salt

Mix all ingredients together to form a smooth paste.

# Belgian Bun, also known as Vienna Bun

Proceed as for Chelsea buns but replace the mixed spice with either cinnamon or ginger. Prove and bake as for Chelsea buns, glaze with white fondant and decorate with a glacé cherry.

*Belgian buns*

# Doughnuts *Boules de Berlin*

| INGREDIENTS | 14 INDIVIDUAL BUNS | 30 INDIVIDUAL BUNS |
|---|---|---|
| Strong white flour | 475g | 950g |
| Good-quality salt | 5g | 10g |
| Caster sugar | 65g | 130g |
| Milk powder | 10g | 20g |
| Butter | 40g | 80g |
| Whole egg | ½ beaten egg | 1 egg |
| Fresh yeast | 25g | 50g |
| Water | 180ml | 360ml |

### CHEF'S TIP

The use of silicone mats on which to bake buns is recommended where there is fruit and sugar which may make the buns stick to the tray and eventually burn.

## Method of work

1 Preheat the oven to 220°C if required, or preheat a deep fat fryer to 185°C.
2 In a bowl, mix together the water and the fresh yeast. Ensure that the yeast has completely dissolved in the water.

*Pipe a little jam into each hole*

3  Combine the sieved flour, sugar and salt and rub in the butter.

4  Add the yeast liquid and the beaten egg. Mix well. If using a mechanical mixing machine, use the dough hook and set on second speed for 5 minutes.

5  Create a soft dough, resisting the temptation to add more flour.

6  Scrape any excess ingredients and dough off the sides of the bowl and knead together. Leave the dough to rest for about 10 minutes.

7  Place the dough into a stainless steel bowl and place in a prover or warm place for the bulk fermentation. The BFT should be approximately 45 minutes.

8  Carefully knock back the dough and knead lightly by folding the dough over itself. Leave to rest for a further 10 minutes.

9  Scale off the bun dough into 45g balls and leave to rest under a sheet of plastic to prevent from skinning. Mould each bun dough ball into small, neat round buns and place onto a baking sheet.

10  If deep frying doughnuts the fat should be clean. When cooking they will need to be turned over as the doughnuts will float.

11  If adding jam to the centre of the doughnuts, one method is to mould the raw dough into balls and press a floured thumb into each. Pipe a little jam into each hole and mould carefully to seal the hole. Prove on an oiled tray and deep fry, drain and finish with a little cinnamon sugar.

## Varieties of doughnut

*Ring doughnut*

***Rings***  Roll out the dough to 12mm thick and cut out rings using two cutters of different dimensions to create a ring. Deep fry and drain before rolling in cinnamon sugar.

*Finger doughnut*

***Fingers***  After moulding to a ball, rest for 10 minutes. Roll out to the form of a finger shape. Cook by deep frying, drain and cool. Split down the centre and pipe a small amount of jam and then fill with cream. Dust with icing sugar. Alternatively, after draining on clean kitchen paper, roll the fingers in cinnamon sugar.

*Apple doughnut*

***Apple doughnuts***  Mould into a ball, rest for 10 minutes and then pin out to a flat circle. Brush half with water and place apple filling in the centre of the other half. Bring to two halves together and secure around the edges to stop the filling from escaping. Prove and deep fry, drain and finish with cinnamon sugar. Alternatively, use the same method to add the apple filling as for jam doughnuts.

## Assessment of knowledge and understanding

You have now learned about the use of the different types of fermented dough and how to produce some bread varieties utilising an array of commodities.

To test your level of knowledge and understanding, answer the following short questions. These will help to prepare you for your summative (final) assessment.

1 Explain the importance of selecting the correct type, quality, quantity of ingredients when meeting dish requirements.

_____

_____

2 State the quality points to look for when producing basic white bread dough.

_____

_____

3 State two reasons you would need to use a thermometer in the production of bread.

i) _____

ii) _____

4 Briefly describe the fermentation process.

_____

_____

5 State how a bread roll is tested in order to see if it is correctly baked.

_____

_____

## Research Task

Complete the following chart describing how to use, clean and maintain the following items of equipment and the safety considerations associated with them.

|  | CLEANING | STERILISING | STORING | SAFETY PROCEDURES |
|---|---|---|---|---|
| Nylon piping bags |  |  |  |  |
| Pastry cutters |  |  |  |  |
| Baker's deck oven |  |  |  |  |

# CHEF'S PROFILE

**Name:** **Paul Wayne Gregory**

**Position:** Creative Director

**Establishment:** Paul Wayne Gregory Ltd – Bespoke Chocolate Artistry

**Current job role and main responsibilities:** Managing and developing company production procedures; research into new ingredients, recipes and methods and ensuring quality control.

**When did you realise that you wanted to pursue a career in the catering and hospitality industry?** I have been in the catering industry all of my working career (18 years) but I did not really fall in love with my work until I started working in the pastry section. It was here that I found my true passion and realised I did not want to do anything else. The long 14-hour days didn't seem long enough, whereas before I couldn't wait to leave.

**Training:** In my late teens, I got job in a major supermarket working in the bakery section. I then went onto train at Westminster College and studied 706 – 1 & 2 courses before working in a number of catering establishments. Years later I then returned to study the City and Guilds 711 part 1 & 2 and 2 years later I studied NVQ level 4. Once I'd finished all my training I decided to work in France, Spain, Ireland and the USA, with short periods of training in Belgium. I think most of my skills and development came whilst I was working as head of a pastry section. I was able to my increase my level of understanding and test how each ingredient affects a recipe. Most of all meeting the two masters I worked with in France and Spain changed me for life. Working with a true master of the art is an experience everyone should embark on if you wish to be good yourself. It sets standards in your mind which you aim to achieve and work towards.

**Experience:**

1   Oriol Balaguer in Barcelona, Spain.
2   Jean Valentine in Paris, France.
3   Searcy's in London, UK.
4   Peacock Ally Dublin, Ireland.

**What do you find rewarding about your job?** I have found working for myself to be the most rewarding job that I have ever had. For the very first time in my career, I can be free doing the thing that I love the most, work! Of course, I am still developing and learning but the fact that people love what I produce is all the reward I could ever ask for.

**What do you find the most challenging about the job?** Balancing a life outside of work has to be the number one challenge! Running your own business demands your commitment 24 hours a day, 365 days a year when you first start. There is never enough time to do every thing in the work place and with a small budget to start with, everything has to be done by YOU! Experimenting is the greatest enjoyment but detrimental if you have no balance of reality! So you need to be in touch with what people are really looking for, as everyone has a different palate.

**What advice would you give to students just beginning their career?** Be honest and ask yourself, is this really what I want to do? And if so, do you have enough determination to devote at least seven years of your life to becoming the best you can be. It is possible to be a great chef but that only comes with time, commitment, and sacrifice.

**Who is your mentor or main inspiration?** It sounds silly but me; I am know what I am capable of doing and achieving, and so far I have only scratched the surface with my own company. Before I wanted to be like this person or that person but they were all main kitchen chefs. I am a pâtisserie chef, why would I want to be like them now? So now I look towards Europe for inspiration in all the great pastry chefs I meet while working and training.

**Secrets of a successful chef:** Focus, determination, a quick learner, observant, someone who loves working hard, has stamina and creativity.

**Can you give one essential kitchen tip or technique that you use as a chef?** Not all your answers can be found from one chef in one kitchen: travel and read!

# Brown Bread

| INGREDIENTS | |
|---|---|
| Whole-wheat flour | 650g |
| Strong flour T45 | 350g |
| Salt | 30g |
| Yeast | 50g |
| Water (adjust where needed) | 550g |

## Method of work

1 Place both flours and salt into a mixing bowl.

2 Place bowl on machine with a dough hook and start machine at minimal speed.

3 Mix the yeast with a little of the warm water and add to the mix.

4 Slowly add the water warm water retain around 100g as different flours from different countries will require more or less water. Adjust the water were necessary.

5 Place the machine on medium speed for 10 mins.

6 Remove the dough from the mixing bowl and place in a clean dry bowl and place into the prover, allow dough to rise till double in size (around 1 hour).

7 Remove bowl from prover and dough from bowl on to a clean dry work surface. Kneed the dough into a ball and allow to rest for 2 mins.

8 Proportion the dough into the required size, place on trays or into moulds and place the tray's back into the prover. Allow the dough to double in size (around 40 mins)

9 Remove tray from prover and place into a hot oven 200ºC, add stream and cook for 8–15 mins depending on size of moulds.

10 The bread should be golden brown on top and sound hollow when tapped at the bottom.

11 Remove tray from oven and place bread on a cooling rack to cool.

# Pastes, tarts and pies

## INTRODUCTION

The pastry department has an important role in the overall operation of a professional kitchen. This specialist area uses techniques that are very different from that of the main kitchen: the correct use of commodities must be understood, from accurate weighing, employing correct mixing methods and baking at the right temperature to utilising fine presentation and decoration skills. This chapter often refers to pastes and dough as separate items. Dough is a product that is produced using fermentation or chemical aeration as a way of introducing expansion or lightness in a product. Owing to the high fat content generally found in pastes and because they have a dense texture they will not rise due to the use of yeast or baking powders, and techniques such as lamination are employed to achieve this.

Among the pastes that are explained in this chapter are shortcrust (pâte brisée) and sweet paste (pâte sucrée). These are fine, short, crisp and crumbly textured pastes which are used to contain or form a base for fillings, various custards and fruits. Puff paste (pâte feuilletée) has a complex texture of alternate fine layers of paste and fat. During the baking process the paste rises up to form thin, buttery flakes of paste. Choux paste (pâte à choux) is a heavily moisturised airy paste which puffs up in the oven to form a crisp outer shell and that is hollow inside. It can be piped into different shapes and is usually filled with creams, mousses and custards. Suet paste (pâte à grasse de boeuf) is normally required to produce sweet puddings that can be steamed or baked and is a soft paste using beef or vegetable suet. Although the confections made from this paste can be classed under hot desserts, the paste can also be rolled out to line pudding moulds to contain fillings such as steak and kidney. Therefore it is classified as a paste.

**VIDEO CLIP**
A pâtisserie in Central London

## SHORT PASTES

There is a specific family of tart and pie pastes, each one having its own method of preparation and uses. Three specific pastes will be explained in this chapter.

1 Shortcrust pastry – la pâte brisée
2 Lining paste – la pâte à foncer
3 Sweet paste – la pâte sucrée

These pastes all come under the collective heading of 'Les pâtes friable', because all of them are short, crisp and friable (crumbly).

Two main methods used to obtain this characteristic crispness:

1 **Rubbing-in** *(sablage)* – the aim of this method is to rub the fat and flour together to prevent the gluten strands from becoming activated, which would result in a tough paste with a hard crust.

2 **Creaming** – in this method the butter is aerated with the sugar before the liquid ingredients are combined and worked to a smooth cream. This mixture contains a large amount of fat, so it tends not to work the flour too much because the flour is added at the last stage.

It is important to remember that if the liquid ingredients used in a paste are composed of fats (for example eggs, instead of water) there is less chance of the gluten within flour being activated, resulting in a flakier and light-textured crust.

## USES OF SHORT PASTES

■ *La pâte brisée* savoury crisp items – quiche, tartlets, **barquettes**, canapés.

■ *La pâte à foncer* sweet pies and tarts with a wet filling – apple, blackberry.

■ *La pâte sucrée* sweet tartlettes, barquettes, flans, pies.

**CHEF'S TIP**

Possible reasons for faults in short pastes:

■ Soggy – too much water, too cool an oven or under-baked.

■ Shrunken – over-handling, stretched during handling or paste not rested sufficiently.

■ Blistered – too dry mixture, fat not incorporated correctly.

■ Hard – too little fat used, over-handling or over-baked.

■ Soft – too much fat used in the recipe or too little water.

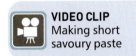

**VIDEO CLIP**
Making short savoury paste

# BASIC RECIPES FOR SHORT PASTES

## Shortcrust pastry *Pâte brisée*

| INGREDIENTS | MAKES APPROXIMATELY 400G |
|---|---|
| Butter | 160g |
| Salt | 5g |
| Soft flour | 250g |
| Egg | 1 |
| Cold milk or water | 1tbsp |

### Method of work

1. Sieve the flour onto a clean work surface or into a stainless steel bowl.
2. Cut the butter (at room temperature) into small pieces and rub into the flour with the salt.
3. When the butter has been successfully rubbed into the flour, incorporate the cold liquid and the whole egg.
4. Gently amalgamate the ingredients together, forming a light dough. Do not overwork this paste.
5. Wrap well in polythene or silicone paper and place in a refrigerator for 30 minutes before using.

**CHEF'S TIP**

This paste will keep well for several days in a refrigerator or for several weeks in a freezer wrapped well in plastic film.

Cut the butter (at room temperature) into small pieces

Rub into the flour with the salt

Gently amalgamate the ingredients together, forming a light dough

# Lining paste *Pâte à foncer*

| INGREDIENTS | MAKES APPROXIMATELY 500G |
|---|---|
| Soft flour | 250g |
| Softened butter | 125g |
| Whole egg | 60g |
| Cold water | 40ml |
| Salt | 5g |
| Caster sugar | 20g |

## Method of work

1 Place the flour onto a clean work surface or into a stainless steel bowl.

2 Cut the butter (at room temperature) into small pieces and rub into the flour with the sugar and the salt.

3 When the butter has been successfully rubbed into the flour, incorporate the cold water and the whole egg.

4 Gently amalgamate the ingredients together, forming a light dough. Do not overwork this paste.

5 Wrap well in polythene or silicone paper and place in a refrigerator for 45 minutes before using.

Rub the butter into the flour with the sugar and the salt

Incorporate the cold water and the whole egg

Wrap well in polythene or silicone paper

# Sweet pastry *Pâte sucrée*

**VIDEO CLIP**
Making sweet paste

| INGREDIENTS | MAKES APPROXIMATELY 530G |
|---|---|
| Soft flour | 250g |
| Butter | 100g |
| Caster sugar | 80g |
| Salt | 5g |
| Whole egg | 100g |
| Vanilla extract | Optional |

## Method of work

1 Place the flour onto a clean work surface or into a stainless steel bowl. Make a well in the centre.

2 Cut the butter (at room temperature) into small pieces and place in the centre of the well with the salt and sugar.

3 Work the butter and sugar with your fingertips until completely creamed together and pale in colour.

4 Slowly incorporate the whole egg, mixing well until the mixture is completely smooth and creamy. At this stage you can add a few drops of vanilla extract to help flavour the paste.

5 Gradually draw the flour into the creamed butter and when all ingredients are thoroughly mixed, lightly work the paste to a smooth texture. Do not overwork the paste at this point.

6 Wrap well in polythene or silicone paper and place in a refrigerator for 60 minutes before using.

**CHEF'S TIP**

This pastry can be quite fragile when baked, so care must be taken when filling and decorating. The raw paste keeps well for a few days in a refrigerator.

**Step-by-step: Preparing sweet pastry**

**STEP 1** Place the flour onto a clean work surface. Make a well in the centre

**STEP 2** Cut the butter (at room temperature) into small pieces and place in the centre of the well with the salt and sugar

**STEP 3** Work the butter and sugar with your fingertips until completely creamed together and pale in colour

**STEP 4** Slowly incorporate the whole egg, mixing well until the mixture is completely smooth and creamy. Add a few drops of vanilla extract to help flavour the paste

**STEP 5** Gradually draw the flour into the creamed butter

**STEP 6** Lightly work the paste to a smooth texture, taking care not to overwork the paste at this point

# Notes on Lining Flans

Roll out the paste evenly, and approximately 3cm larger than the ring to be lined. Brush any excess flour from the paste. The ring can be brushed with melted clarified butter and the tray should be clean.

## Step-by-step: Lining a flan ring with pastry

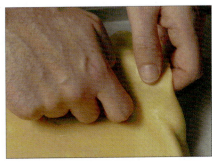

**STEP 1** Roll the paste up on the rolling pin and lay it out over the flan ring

**STEP 2** Using the crooked finger of your right hand gently push the paste into the sides of the flan ring

**STEP 3** Using the rolling pin cut away the excess by rolling it off

**STEP 4** Carefully thumb the paste in the flan ring, so producing an edge all the way around the top. Pinch in from the outside and push in from the inside to produce a decorative edge. Pastry nippers may be used instead

**STEP 6** To bake blind (cuire à blanc): line the flan, cover the inside with a layer of plastic film and fill with baking beans. Allow to rest if necessary and bake at the specified oven temperature

# PUFF PASTRY *Pâte à feuilletée*

## QUALITY SPECIFICATION

Puff paste has a specific structure consisting of numerous alternating layers of *détrempe* (the basic paste) and *beurrage* (the butter or fat used). This structure is obtained by rolling and folding the layers over each other in succession.

- Puff paste should have a firm consistency.

- The basic paste must not become elastic. It is therefore important not to overwork the ingredients while assembling the dough.

- Successful puff paste requires considerable attention to detail when making the basic paste and folding in the butter.

- The different types of puff paste are all prepared in three stages: basic paste, fat (folding in the butter or shortening) and the turning (rolling out the dough). The only exception is the quick puff paste method, in which the butter is mixed in with the basic paste using a slow speed on a mixing machine.

## HOW PUFF PASTRY RISES

Allow the paste to rest for the indicated time. When baking, the heat of the oven melts the butter into the leaves of the basic paste and creates steam from the moisture of the butter. This steam, plus the moisture contained in the basic paste, is released, forcing the leaves to rise one by one. At the same time the starch in the flour will coagulate, strengthening the leaves and helping each to stand separately.

## THREE BASIC METHODS FOR PUFF PASTRY

1 *French method*. It is essential to work on marble to keep the paste cold, using the 'envelope' method to create layers. Fold and give three 'book' turns, resting approximately 30 minutes between each turn.

2 *English method*. Roll the basic paste to an oblong and place the fat on one-third of it. Fold over and give six single turns, resting for at least 30 minutes between each turn.

3 *Scottish method*. The fat is incorporated to the basic paste in pieces. This is a fast method.

## USES OF PUFF PASTRY

- Vol-au-vents
- Fleurons and various savoury decorations
- Bande aux fruits
- Eccles cakes and Banbury buns
- Chaussons aux pommes
- Tart shells for assorted large and individual tarts
- Sausage rolls
- Allumettes.
- Pithiviers
- Mille feuille
- Palmiers
- Cream horns

## CHEF'S TIP

Possible reasons for faults in puff paste:
- Hard – too much water used in the recipe, over-handled or flour insufficiently brushed away during the folding process.
- Shrunken – insufficient resting between turns or over-stretching.
- Soggy – under-baked or oven too cold.
- Uneven rise – uneven distribution of fat, uneven folding and turning, sides and corners not straight or insufficient resting.
- Release of fat during baking – oven too cold, uneven folding and rolling, or paste (détrempe) too soft.

# Puff pastry recipe with pastry margarine *Pâte feuilletée*

| INGREDIENTS | MAKES APPROXIMATELY 530G |
|---|---|
| Strong flour | 1kg |
| Butter | 250g |
| Lemon juice | 1tbsp |
| Salt | 30g |
| Cold water | 500ml (approx) |
| Pastry margarine or butter | 750g |

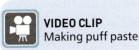

**VIDEO CLIP**
Making puff paste

## Method of work

1 Sift the flour into a bowl.

2 Combine the salt, lemon juice and water.

3 Rub the butter into the flour.

4 Mix in the liquid to form a firm but elastic paste, depending on the flour used and the product to be made.

5 On a lightly floured marble top roll out the paste to form a rectangle twice as long as broad and about 20mm thick. (Alternatively a large envelope can be produced using the French method of preparation.)

6 Take a square of pastry margarine (also 20mm thick) which will fit neatly on to one end of the rolled out paste.

7 Fold the paste back over the fat to enclose it. Seal the edges well.

8 Roll out the paste to between 15–20 mm thick, it must be four times as long as it is broad and a precise rectangle.

9 Give one book turn (double turn). Cover the paste with a sheet of plastic. Rest in a refrigerator for 20 minutes.

10 Repeat this three more times before it is ready to use.

**Step-by-step: Rolling puff pastry with pastry margerine**

**STEP 1** On a lightly floured marble top roll out the paste to form a rectangle

**STEP 2** Take a square of pastry margarine which will fit neatly on to one end of the rolled-out paste

**STEP 3** Roll out the paste to between 15–20mm thick. It must be four times as long as it is broad and a precise rectangle

## STORAGE AND ROLLING OUT

If well wrapped in plastic, puff pastry can be stored for 3–4 days in a refrigerator at 5°C. It is also possible to freeze puff pastry, well wrapped in plastic. Once frozen, the paste should be given 24 hours to defrost before use. Regardless of storage location, the paste should rest, in a cold area after the fourth turn. Wait for the pastry to reach room temperature before attempting to roll it out. If the paste is too cold when it is rolled out, it may tear and cause butter to run onto the baking sheet in the oven during baking.

## CHOUX PASTE

The origin of choux paste dates back to the sixteenth century.

We can attribute the invention to an Italian pastry chef named Popelini. It was not until the eighteenth century that this paste was perfected. In 1760 it was changed with a basic addition of eggs to create the blown and toasted choux paste.

It was Antonin Carême (1784–1837), the famous French chef, who took choux paste and created numerous classical gâteaux and cakes which we now know as French classical pastries.

## THE TECHNIQUE OF PRODUCING CHOUX PASTE

During the first part of the production the chef is looking to cook out the mix of water, fat, flour, sugar and salt. This will change the structure of the starch found in flour to a thick paste.

The second phase is the 're-moisturisation' of the paste with the addition of eggs in order to obtain a paste of piping consistency. During baking the moisture will play an important role in developing steam and providing the raising agent for the paste.

Whilst baking the choux paste, the heat from the oven will convert the moisture from the paste into steam. The eggs and starch found within the paste begin to coagulate, forming an outside layer which will retain the steam inside. The steam will try to escape and in doing so will push and bring about the inflation of the paste which continues to coagulate and will become solid when the paste has cooked. All of this contributes to the choux paste's final appearance.

# Choux paste *Pâte à choux*

| INGREDIENTS | 20 ÉCLAIRS OR 40 PROFITEROLES |
|---|---|
| Water | 150ml |
| Butter | 60g |
| Strong white flour | 90g |
| Sugar | 5g |
| Salt | 5g |
| Whole eggs | 3 |

## Method of work

1 Place the water and fat into a saucepan and bring to the boil.
2 Take off the heat and stir in the sieved flour.
3 Return to the heat and cook out, continuously stirring until it leaves the sides of the pan clean.
4 Allow to partly cool until it can be touched by the fingers and feel warm to the touch.
5 Beat in the eggs a little at a time, making sure that they are well incorporated to produce a 'dropping' consistency.

**STEP 1** Take off the heat and stir in the sieved flour

**STEP 2** Return to the heat and cook out, continuously stirring until it leaves the sides of the pan clean

**STEP 3** Ensure that the eggs are well incorporated to produce a 'dropping' consistency

# USES OF CHOUX PASTE

■ Cream buns
■ Profiteroles
■ Choux paste fritters (beignets)
■ Éclairs.

# SUET PASTE

Suet paste can be cooked by boiling, steaming or baking. It is used for plain puddings that are made of fruits such as apples, gooseberries, blackberries and for dumplings. If correctly produced, it will form a light and soft cooked paste, and the suet will not be evident.

The suet must not be melted before it is used but cut or minced as fine as possible and mixed cold with the flour. If using the suet paste for making dumplings to serve with a stew or boiled mutton, the dough must be rolled out thick, and cut out using pastry cutters to the size required.

A survey of period cookbooks confirms that this particular paste was used to create roly-poly and the spotted dick pudding popular in Victorian times. It was most often served up as a sweet dish, but savoury recipes exist as well. It was also referred to in novels by Charles Dickens and Beatrix Potter. The first printed evidence of the phrase 'spotted dick', as it relates to food, is attributed to Alexis Soyer, the chef of London's illustrious Reform Club, 1849.

> ### CHEF'S TIP
>
> Possible reasons for faults in suet paste:
>
> - Heavy and soggy – too low cooking temperature, leakage in the cartouche or silicone wrapping or too much liquid added.
> - Hard texture – over-handling or over-cooking.

## Suet paste  *Pâte à grasse de boeuf*

> ### CHEF'S TIP
>
> Vegetable suet can replace the beef variety if vegetarian products are to be made using this paste.

| INGREDIENTS | MAKES APPROXIMATELY 500G |
|---|---|
| Soft flour | 250g |
| Baking powder | 5g |
| Beef suet | 150g |
| Good-quality salt | 3g |
| Cold water | 125ml |
| Caster sugar (optional) | 25g |

## Method of work

1  Sift together the flour, baking powder and salt into a stainless steel bowl. Add the suet and mix in lightly.

2  If using sugar as part of the recipe add to the water to dissolve. Make a well in the centre of the flour mixture and add the sugar solution.

3  Mix lightly together to form a firm paste. Rest for 5 minutes in the bowl covered with plastic film before using.

**STEP 1**  Add the suet and lightly mix in

**STEP 2**  Mix lightly together to form a firm paste

**STEP 3**  Rest for 5 minutes in the bowl covered with plastic film before using

# FLOUR

One of the most important factors that influences our choice of flour is the gluten content. Gluten is protein that is present in flour. It provides baked products with strength and structure. Most of the flour used is wheat flour although there is a vast array of different types available to use.

*Strong flour* is sometimes referred to as bread flour. It has a high gluten content which is developed when moisture is added and it is manipulated into a dough or paste. It is mostly used to produce yeast fermented dough such as bread, buns and croissants, and also for choux paste and puff paste.

*Soft flour* sometimes referred to as cake flour. It contains a low gluten content and is more suited to the production of cakes, sponges and short pastes.

*Medium flour* generally known as all-purpose flour. It has slightly higher gluten content than soft. It can be used to produce batters for deep frying where crispness is required for fritters and also be used to create some specialised pastes and biscuits.

*Wholemeal flour* is made from the whole wheat grain which includes the bran layers and the germ. Generally it is used for bread making, but if the milling process has refined the flour to smaller particles it can be used as a healthier option to white flours when producing some pastes. This is due to its high fibre content. Normally this type of flour has a shorter shelf life due to the germ still being present in the flour. For further information on flours refer to Chapter 19.

# FATS AND OILS

When choosing an appropriate fat to be used for a specific baked product, the plasticity of the fat will be a major determining factor. This refers to the ability of the fat to maintain its shape at room temperature but still have the ability to be manipulated. The melting point of the fat ultimately determines its plasticity. Butter is plastic at a cool room temperature but when refrigerated it is too firm. Vegetable shortening is plastic at both sets of temperatures and is therefore easier to work with than butter. However, the greater plasticity of fat, the less desirable it may be to eat because it will have a higher melting point than human body temperature, which means it will not melt in the mouth.

- *Butter* has excellent creamy qualities and the best flavour of all fats. Although it must be used at cool temperatures to maintain its plasticity, unsalted butter is often preferred due to its creamier texture and flavour. It will normally have a fat content of up to 86 per cent.

- *Margarine is* manufactured from various oils and has a similar plasticity and colour to butter. It still contains a similar fat content to butter and is therefore excellent for creaming and using in pastes.

- *Pastry margarine* has a firm texture and high melting point; it is used in the production of puff paste. It lacks colour and flavour and therefore has reduced eating qualities.

- *Lard* has very good shortening qualities in pastes such as short savoury. It is a solid fat that is rendered from pork and has a high melting point with no colour.

- *Oils* are perceived to be healthier due to their higher levels of unsaturated fats. They have no creaming ability so they are not a viable alternative to butter when making short pastes; however, they can be used for dough items and strudel paste.

- *Suet* is a hard fat and does not have creaming properties. Traditionally it is used for the production of suet paste and puddings. It should be stored in a refrigerator and in an airtight container.

Solid fats absorb flavours and odours and need to be stored in the refrigerator away from strong-smelling ingredients; they can also be frozen for several weeks if required. Oils can go rancid more quickly and should always be stored in airtight bottles or containers. If stored in a refrigerator some oils may begin to solidify, so they will need to be brought back to room temperature before using.

# SUGAR

Sugar plays a very important role in bakery. Besides acting as a sweetener, it provides tenderness to baked products, caramelises giving colour, absorbs moisture from the atmosphere to maintain shelf life and moisture in baked produce, aids the aeration process during the creaming of fats and used skilfully it can fashion many different finishes to create confections.

- *Cube sugar* is generally regarded as the most pure form of refined white sugars and is traditionally used for boiled sugar items and to make caramel.

- *Granulated sugar* is a coarse-grained sugar and is used as a sweetener and for dissolving in liquid solutions to make jams, compôtes and stewed fruit products. It can also be used to boil and create caramelised finishes to baked items, such as profiteroles dipped in caramel.

- *Caster sugar* is a fine-grained sugar and is the most widely used sugar in the kitchen. It is used in the production of pastes and aids the creaming process very well.

- *Icing sugar* otherwise known as confectioner's sugar, it is a fine powdered sugar used mainly for the production of icings and glazing.

■ *Liquid glucose* sometimes referred to as corn syrup because it is made from corn starch. This is an important addition to the sugar range because it prolongs shelf life in many baked products and also helps to prevent caramel from returning to its granular form.

■ *Honey* is classified as a natural sugar that has its own distinguished flavour and can be used in certain recipes as a substitute for sugar.

■ *Brown sugar* is generally a granulated sugar that is slightly less refined than white. It contains traces of molasses and often tends to have an acidic flavour. It adds colour, sweetness and flavour to baked goods.

# EGGS

Eggs perform a number of functions such as introducing richness, colour, increased structure and moisture to a product. The pastry kitchen will use large quantities of eggs so it is important to maintain a good stock rotation system.

■ *Fresh* eggs should be refrigerated before use, although some recipes call for eggs to be used at room temperature. It is important that they are as fresh as possible. They are graded according to size: 1 is the largest and 7 the smallest. A standard size is grade 3 and a general rule is that each egg weighs approximately 60 grams.

■ *Frozen* available in 1 kilogram tetrapacks of either yolks, whites and mixed whole eggs. Once defrosted and opened they should be treated exactly the same as fresh egg.

■ *Dried* usually this format is dried albumen and is used to make meringue products and icings. Store in an airtight container and in a cool, dry store room.

# NUTS

Nuts contribute flavour, texture and decorative appeal. They contain proteins, fibre, vitamins and minerals and eaten in moderation can be a healthy addition to any diet, except of course for those with nut allergies. This is why every product that contains nuts in some form *must* be declared on menus or package labels. Nuts contain natural oils that impart flavour; however, because of their fat content, they can go rancid quickly and they must be stored in an airtight container in a cool area. Nuts can be frozen successfully and this will prolong their shelf life.

Nuts can generally be purchased whole, halved, chopped or ground. Chestnuts must always be cooked before using and can be used whole, glacéed (cooked in a sugar syrup) or puréed. It is important to understand products derived from nuts so you can be aware of potential nut cross-contamination in the kitchen. Almond paste and marzipan are made from almonds and sugar; they have a paste-like consistency and are used in many cake, torten and tart recipes or used in petit fours. Praline and praline paste consists of caramelised hazelnuts, this product is used mainly as a flavouring or as a decorative item. Gianduja is a similar product to praline but with the addition of milk chocolate and is finely ground to a smooth paste. It is used to flavour desserts and is also used in confectionery. Coconut products such as milk, cream and desiccated nut are used as flavouring or to add texture.

The flavour of most nuts can be enhanced by lightly roasting or toasting. Although this procedure is quite simple, care must be taken because the fat content in nuts can cause them to burn easily. The nuts should be placed onto a baking sheet and placed into a preheated oven at 170°C. The roasting process should only take approximately 10 minutes and should be checked every 3 minutes or so. There should be a light golden colouration to the nuts before they are ready to be removed from the oven and left to cool to room temperature.

# STORAGE CONCERNS FOR BAKERY ITEMS

Maintaining the quality of ingredients in the pastry kitchen is a concern for all chefs. Many of the commodities used are very prone to contamination and great care needs to be taken to ensure hygienic storage and refrigeration measures are maintained.

- Dairy products and eggs should be stored in air-circulated refrigeration units and kept in clean, covered plastic containers.

- Separate diary and egg products from other ingredients to avoid cross-contamination. A separate refrigerator is best practice if possible.

- Dry commodities need to be stored in clean, sealed plastic containers on clean shelving in a separate storage room. The room needs to be maintained at a constant cool temperature and should have a dry atmosphere.

- Stock rotation should be employed so that all ingredients are used up and then replenished by a new batch of ingredients. The empty container should be cleaned before replenishing.

- It is not recommended to store baked products for long periods of time in a refrigerator because of starch breakdown and loss of flavour.

- To store baked items for short periods in a refrigerator it is essential that they are wrapped in plastic film or placed into airtight plastic containers. Items that contain large amounts of sugar will take longer to become stale.

- Storing baked products in a freezer is an alternative method that works well. However, the baked item should be completely cool before wrapping tight in plastic and then aluminium foil. Label and date the item before freezing.

- Good practice is to blast freeze any item for 30 minutes before placing into a holding freezer. This process helps to maintain moisture content in the product and helps to eliminate potential freezer burn.

# THE USE OF CONVENIENCE PASTES

The use of convenience pastes helps to ease the production of complex pastes such as puff paste and filo paste. The products mean that the utilisation of human resources, time, cost and standardisation of the product is the principal factor for many kitchens. Today's popular use of filo paste is greatly attributed to its success as an easy to use, convenient paste rather than having to spend time making it from fresh.

Most pastes can be purchased as a convenience product in either a frozen or fresh variety. If using frozen paste it is important that the paste is correctly defrosted in a refrigerator in the original packaging it was first purchased (provided that it is hygienic and unperforated). Otherwise the texture of the paste may be altered significantly enough to render it unusable. The paste should then be used and correctly stored following the same guidelines as fresh paste; wrapped in plastic film, refrigerated and labelled accurately. Care should be taken when storing as the paste will become discoloured with a greyish hue if not correctly wrapped.

## SPECIALIST BAKING EQUIPMENT

*Bain marie* A French term for a hot water bath. it is used as a double-boiler with a bowl placed over a pan of simmering water to create light sabayons. It can also be used as a technique to ensure gentle, even baking for custard-based desserts such as crème caramel or cheesecakes.

*Bench and bowl scrapers* The bench scraper, sometimes known as a dough scraper, is a small metal rectangular blade attached to a handle. It is used to cut and scale pieces of dough and to clean work surfaces by scraping it against a table top to loosen pieces of paste and dough. A bowl scraper is plastic, flexible and used to scrape around the inside of mixing bowls to use every last piece of the prepared mixture.

*Disposable piping bag* This is a cone-shaped plastic bag used to pipe various preparations with ease and especially hygienically. Use the bag only once fitted with a nylon piping tube.

*Sieve* A sieve can be a small tool the size of a tea strainer to finish off desserts with a fine dusting of cocoa powder or it can be a large, drum-shaped utensil used to sift flours, ground almonds and icing sugar.

*False-bottomed tart tins* These tins are usually fluted and are excellent for producing fine short paste tart cases. This is because the base is removable making it easy to de-mould the lined, blind baked pastry case.

*Offset palette knife* This is a wide, paddle-style knife usually without a sharp blade. There should be a slight bend to the handle to make it easier to use. They are purchased in varying sizes.

*Grater* Usually made of metal with sharp holes of varying grades. Fruits such as oranges and lemons are rubbed alongside the holes to remove and finely shred the zests. It can also be used to shred chocolate, cheese and vegetables.

*Pastry brush* Indispensable in the pastry kitchen, is used to apply glazes to tarts and desserts, eggwashes and butter to various products. It should always be kept very clean as it can be a major cross-contaminator.

# RECIPES

## Stilton, asparagus and leek tart

| INGREDIENTS | 4 PORTIONS | 10 PORTIONS |
|---|---|---|
| Short paste (see p. 496) | 200g | 500g |
| Stilton cheese | 100g | 250g |
| Chopped fresh mixed herbs (basil, chives, parsley) | 2tbsp | 5tbsp |
| Washed leek | 1 | 2 |
| Fresh asparagus | 8 stalks | 20 stalks |
| Whole egg | 1 | 3 |
| Single cream | 150ml | 400ml |
| Ground black pepper and good-quality salt | To season | To season |

### Method of work

1  Roll out the short paste thinly and line the tartlet tins. Chill for 15 minutes in a refrigerator.

2  Preheat the oven to 200°C and bake the cases blind for approximately 10 minutes. Reduce the oven temperature to 190°C.

3  Wash, peel and trim the asparagus before blanching in boiling salted water and refreshing in iced water. Drain and leave to one side on kitchen paper.

4  Wash, slice and dry the leeks. Quickly sweat them off in a little butter to begin the cooking process. Leave aside to cool.

5  Place the Stilton, herbs, asparagus and leeks in a bowl and mix until they are well blended. Add the egg, cream and pepper and mix again.

6  Divide the mixture evenly into the pastry cases and return to the oven for 10–15 minutes until the filling has just set.

7  Serve warm or cold.

*Divide the mixture evenly into the pastry cases*

**HEALTH & SAFETY**

Adaptations to this recipe include substituting the soft white flour in the pastry for sieved wholemeal flour and using a low fat soft cheese to replace the Stilton.

# Dutch apple tart *Appel taart*

*Layer the lattice over the top*

| INGREDIENTS | 8 PORTIONS (1 × 20CM TART) | 16 PORTIONS (2 × 20CM TARTS) |
|---|---|---|
| Lining paste (see p. 497) | 175g | 350g |
| **Filling** | | |
| Cooking apples such as Bramley, peeled and cored | 1kg | 2kg |
| Demerara sugar | 250g | 400g |
| Sultanas | 100g | 200g |
| Powdered cinnamon | 2tsp | 5tsp |
| Zest of lemon | 1 lemon | 2 lemons |
| Icing sugar | 70g | 140g |
| Crème chantilly to serve | 200g | 400g |

## Method of work

1 Preheat the oven to 220°C.
2 Prepare and rest the lining paste.
3 Line a flan ring with the paste leaving the remaining paste rolled out and cut into strips to create a lattice for the top of the tart.
4 Slice the apples and mix with the sugar, sultanas, cinnamon and grated lemon zest. Place this filling into the lined pastry case and layer the lattice over the top.
5 Eggwash the lattice and bake for 15 minutes, reduce the temperature of the oven to 180°C and complete the baking process for a further 25 minutes.
6 Remove from the oven and dust with icing sugar.
7 Serve warm with the crème chantilly.

# Norfolk treacle tart

| INGREDIENTS | 4 PORTIONS | 10 PORTIONS |
|---|---|---|
| Sweet paste (see p. 498) | 200g | 500g |
| **Treacle filling** | | |
| Golden syrup | 300g | 640g |
| Unsalted butter | 50g | 125g |
| Double cream | 100ml | 275ml |
| Fresh eggs | 2 | 4 |
| Lemon juice and zest | ½ lemon | 1 lemon |
| Breadcrumbs | 80g | 200g |

## Method of work

1. Preheat the oven to 200°C.
2. Gently heat the golden syrup in a saucepan until melting point. Remove from the heat and stir in the butter.
3. Beat in the eggs, cream, lemon zest and juice. Reserve on one side.
4. Line a large tart ring or individual rings as required with the sweet paste and then pour the filling into the pastry case.
5. Create a lattice of pastry on the top of each tart and brush with eggwash.
6. Bake for approximately 30 minutes.
7. Leave to cool and rest for 10 minutes before cutting.
8. Serve slightly warm.

*Create a lattice of pastry on the top of each tart and brush with eggwash*

# Fresh fruit tart

| INGREDIENTS | 4 PORTIONS | 10 PORTIONS |
|---|---|---|
| **Sweet paste** (see p. 498) | 200g | 500g |
| **Crème pâtissière filling** | | |
| **Fresh milk** | 250g | 450g |
| **Caster sugar** | 60g | 120g |
| **Good-quality salt** | 2g | 3g |
| **Cornflour** | 20g | 40g |
| **Custard powder** | 5g | 10g |
| **Egg yolks** | 2 | 4 |
| **Whole eggs** | ½ | 1 |
| **Vanilla extract** | 5g | 10g |
| **Unsalted butter** | 20g | 30g |
| **Fruit decoration** | | |
| **As required** (but can include strawberries, kiwi, star fruit, fresh cherries, peaches, raspberries and banana) | Approximately 75g per portion | Approximately 75g per portion |
| **Apricot glaze** | | |
| **Apricot jam** | 75g | 150g |
| **Water** | 20–30g | 30–50g |
| **Kirsch** (optional) | 5g | 15g |

(see p. 498)

### CHEF'S TIP

Once this tart has been prepared and presented it should be served as quickly as possible. If refrigerated, the pastry will begin to absorb the moisture from the filling and the fruit and eventually begin to collapse.

## Method of work

1. Preheat the oven to 200°C.
2. Carefully line the sweet paste into the tart ring, leaving the paste to slightly overhang the edges.
3. Place a cartouche of baking beans on top and bake blind for 20 minutes.
4. Remove the pastry case from the oven and remove the baking beans.

5   Brush the inside of the pastry case with eggwash.

6   Return to the oven for approximately 5 minutes.

7   Remove from the oven. Leave to cool and rest for 5 minutes before trimming the edges with a serrated knife.

8   Cool to room temperature.

### Crème pâtissier method

1   Reserve 50g of milk to one side and bring the remaining milk to the boil in a saucepan.

2   In a separate bowl mix together the sugar, cornflour, custard powder, salt, 50g milk and vanilla. Add the eggs to this preparation and mix well.

3   Add some of the hot milk to the egg mixture, constantly stirring.

4   Pour the warm egg preparation into the remaining milk, whisking continuously.

5   Return the saucepan to a low heat and continue to cook whilst stirring all the time, taking care not to burn the bottom.

6   When the crème has thickened and the flavour of raw starch has been cooked out, remove from the heat.

7   Beat in the diced butter and then pour the crème onto a baking sheet lined with plastic film, cover the top with another layer of plastic film and cool.

**VIDEO CLIP**
Blind baking and finishing a fresh fruit tart

### To assemble the tart

1   Pipe the crème pâtissier into the pastry case to approximately halfway up.

2   Prepare the fresh fruits by washing, drying and removing any pips and seeds.

3   Arrange the fruit in a decorative manner.

4   Place the apricot jam and water together in a saucepan and bring to the boil, stirring constantly. Add the Kirsch for flavour if required.

5   Pass the glaze through a sieve and bring back to the boil. Carefully brush the glaze carefully onto the fruit immediately.

*Brush the inside of the pastry case with eggwash*

*Trim the edges with a serrated knife*

*Pipe the crème pâtissier into the pastry case to approximately halfway up*

# Orange and lime tart

| INGREDIENTS | 8 PORTIONS (1 × 30CM TART RING) | 16 PORTIONS (2 × 30CM TART RINGS) |
|---|---|---|
| Sweet paste | 250g | 500g |
| Oranges | 3 | 7 |
| Limes | 2 | 3 |
| Eggs | 9 | 18 |
| Caster sugar | 380g | 700g |
| Double cream | 300ml | 600ml |
| Softened gelatine leaves | 2 | 4 |

*When the lime zest glaze has cooled carefully pour and spread it on top of the tart and allow to set*

## Method of work

1 Preheat the oven to 200°C.

2 Butter a flan ring and carefully line the sweet pastry inside. Leave to rest for 15 minutes in a refrigerator.

3 Blind bake in the preheated oven for approximately 20 minutes.

4 Wash and finely grate the zest of the oranges and limes retaining one lime to use for a coarser zest. Extract the juice and mix together.

5 Break the eggs into a bowl and lightly beat in the sugar. Add the cream and lemon, mix and remove any froth on top of this preparation. Place in a refrigerator before use.

6 Lower the oven temperature to 150°C.

7 Pour the filling into the pastry case and bake for approximately 30 minutes or until the lemon filling has just set.

8 When cooked carefully remove the flan ring.

9 Leave to cool down at room temperature for at least 1 hour.

10 Blanch the remaining lime zest in boiling water for 1 minute and refresh. Place the zest into a warmed stock syrup solution (see chef's tip) and place 2 softened leaves of gelatine into it to dissolve.

11 When the lime zest glaze has cooled carefully pour and spread it on top of the tart and set.

12 Portion the tart and serve.

### CHEF'S TIP

To make the stock syrup take 100g water and 100g sugar and bring to the boil, simmer for 3 minutes before adding the softened gelatine leaves and the blanched lime zest. Double this recipe if 16 portions are required.

# Tart Tatin

| INGREDIENTS | 4 PORTIONS | 8 PORTIONS |
|---|---|---|
| Dessert apples such as Braeburn | 6 medium-sized | 12 medium-sized |
| Lemon juice | ½ lemon | 1 lemon |
| Unsalted butter | 120g | 240g |
| Granulated sugar | 200g | 400g |
| Puff pastry or trimmings (see p. 501) | 250g | 500g |
| Flour for dusting | 25g | 50g |

*Cover the bottom of the pan with sugar and arrange the apples, rounded side down, on the bottom of the pan*

## Method of work

1 Preheat the oven to 220°C.
2 Peel, core and halve the apples, sprinkle with lemon juice and reserve to one side.
3 Evenly grease the base of the pan or mould with butter.
4 Cover the bottom of the pan with sugar and arrange the apples, rounded side down, on the bottom of the pan.
5 On a lightly floured surface, roll out the puff pastry.
6 Lay the pastry over the apples, allowing an overlap of 2cm.
7 Tuck in the pastry at the edge of the pan and trim off the excess with a knife.
8 Leave to rest in a cool place for about 20 minutes.
9 Set the pan over a fierce heat for 10–15 minutes, until the butter and sugar are bubbling.
10 Bake in the preheated oven for 20 minutes.
11 Serve turned out onto a plate accompanied with a caramel ice cream if desired.

# Apple and raspberry pie

*Carefully position the lid on the top*

> **CHEF'S TIP**
>
> If the paste cracks or splits as it is being rolled out or placed into the tart ring simply patch the split with small scraps of pastry. Moisten the edges with water to glue them into place and smooth gently with your finger but do not stretch the paste.

| INGREDIENTS | 8 PORTIONS (1 × 20CM TART) | 16 PORTIONS (2 × 30CM TART RINGS) |
| --- | --- | --- |
| Lining paste (see p. 497) | 175g | 350g |
| Filling | | |
| Cooking apples such as Bramley, peeled and cored | 1kg | 2kg |
| Caster sugar | 250g | 400g |
| Raspberries (fresh or frozen) | 200g | 450g |
| Zest of lemon | ½ lemon | 1 lemon |
| Icing sugar | 70g | 140g |
| Crème chantilly to serve | 200g | 400g |

## Method of work

1 Preheat the oven to 220°C.
2 Prepare and rest the lining paste.
3 Line a flan ring with the paste leaving the remaining paste rolled out slightly larger to create a lid for the top of the pie.
4 Slice the apples and mix with the sugar, washed raspberries and grated lemon zest. Place this filling into the lined pastry case and carefully roll up the pastry lid onto a rolling pin, brush the edges of the lined pie with water and carefully position the lid on the top.
5 Eggwash the top and sprinkle with a little caster sugar.
6 Bake for 15 minutes, reduce the temperature of the oven to 180°C and complete the baking process for a further 20 minutes.
7 Remove from the oven and cool slightly on a wire cooling rack.
8 Serve warm with the crème chantilly or vanilla ice cream.

# Gâteau Pithivier

| INGREDIENTS | 8 PORTIONS | 16 PORTIONS |
|---|---|---|
| Puff pastry (see p. 501) | 500g | 1kg |
| Almond essence or dark rum | To taste | To taste |
| Unsalted butter | 125g | 250g |
| Tant pour tant (equal quantities of icing sugar and ground almonds) | 250g | 500g |
| Soft white flour | 25g | 50g |
| Fresh eggs | 2 | 4 |
| Egg yolk lightly beaten with a little milk for eggwash | 1 | 2 |
| Icing sugar, for dusting | 30g | 60g |

## Method of work

1  Work the butter with a beater until very soft.
2  Gradually add the tant pour tant and the flour.
3  Slowly add the eggs, beating between each addition.
4  The mixture should be light. Stir in the almond flavour or dark rum according to your taste.
5  Cut the puff paste into two parts, one slightly larger than the other.
6  Roll out the smaller piece of dough until you have a circle of about 28cm in diameter.
7  Place on a baking sheet lined with silicone paper and use the larger piece of dough to roll out the top. Make it slightly bigger and 1mm thicker.
8  Pipe the almond preparation into the centre of the pastry base, and then spread it with a palette knife to within 3–4cm of the edge.
9  Glaze the exposed edge with eggwash.
10  Place the second circle on top and press the edges of the two circles firmly together so that they are well sealed. Chill for 30 minutes.
11  Press down a 24cm flan ring over the Pithivier and with a sharp knife, trim the overhanging dough into a scalloped shape border. Glaze with eggwash and rest in a refrigerator for 20 minutes.
12  Mark the traditional Pithivier rosette on top with a sharp knife.

### To cook

1  Preheat the oven to 240°C. Bake the Pithivier for 10 minutes, then lower the oven temperature to 220°C. Cook for a further 25 minutes.
2  Sprinkle the Pithivier with the icing sugar and bake for a final 5 minutes to give a sugar glaze.
3  Serve warm with crème chantilly or sauce Anglaise.

Place the second circle on top and press the edges of the two circles firmly together so that they are well sealed. Chill for 30 minutes

Glaze with eggwash and rest in a refrigerator for 20 minutes

Mark the traditional Pithivier rosette on top with a sharp knife

# Coffee and chocolate éclairs *Éclairs au café et chocolat*

| INGREDIENTS | 20 ÉCLAIRS |
|---|---|
| **Choux paste** (see p. 503) | 250g |
| **Fondant** | 300g |
| **Stock syrup** | 90g |
| **Alcohol of choice** (Kirsch, Grand Marnier, Tia Maria) | 20g |
| **Crème pâtissier** | 200g |
| **Dark chocolate** (melted) | 75g |
| **Diluted strong coffee** | 25ml |
| **Assorted confectionery colourings** (optional) | As required |

## Method of work

1 Preheat an oven to 220°C.

2 Place the prepared choux paste into a piping bag and using a 1cm plain tube pipe out 10cm lengths on a silicone baking mat or a lightly buttered and floured baking sheet.

3 Brush the choux with eggwash and bake in the preheated oven for approximately 30 minutes until crisp and light brown in colour.

4 Place on a wire rack and allow to cool down.

5 Take the crème pâtissier and divide it into enough separate bowls to create as many different flavours as required.

6 Flavour the crème pâtissier by adding either melted chocolate, coffee or flavoured alcohols.

7 Pierce the end of each éclair with a knife. Place the flavoured crème pâtissier into different piping bags with a small plain tube and fully fill each éclair.

8 Prepare the fondant by warming in a double boiler to a temperature no higher than 36°C. Add a little stock syrup to create the correct dipping consistency and flavour/colour the fondant as required.

9 Carefully dip the tops of the éclairs into the correct coloured and flavoured fondant and remove the surplus.

10 Spin some melted chocolate over each or set a small motif on top of each éclair before they set. Serve for afternoon tea.

### CHEF'S TIP

To ensure that each éclair is piped to the same size, mark two tramlines down the baking sheet as a guide for the correct size and portion control.

*Pipe out 10cm lengths on a silicone baking mat or a lightly buttered and floured baking sheet*

*Fully fill each éclair crème pâtissier using a piping bag with a small plain tube*

*Carefully dip the tops of the éclairs into the correct coloured and flavoured fondant and remove the surplus*

# Steamed fruit and jam roll

| INGREDIENTS | 4 PORTIONS | 8 PORTIONS |
|---|---|---|
| Suet paste (see p. 504) | 200g | 425g |
| Raspberry or strawberry jam | 125g | 270g |
| Fresh or frozen raspberries or strawberries | 200g | 400g |
| Fresh custard sauce | 200g | 500g |

## Method of work

1 Set the steamer to 118°C.

2 Roll out the suet paste, using a little flour to dust, to a rectangle shape (3cm × 16cm).

3 Warm the jam in a saucepan and then spread over the suet paste leaving 1cm clear on each edge.

4 Slice the wash strawberries and liberally cover the jam surface of the paste (raspberries will not require cutting).

5 Fold over the two short sides by 1cm and then begin to roll the paste from the top downwards.

6 Moisten the bottom edge with milk or water to help secure a seal.

7 Wrap in buttered silicone paper and wrap again in tin foil or a pudding cloth. Tie both ends.

8 Place in the steamer to cook for 1½ hours.

9 Carefully turn out of the silicone when cooked and serve accompanied with the custard sauce.

*Slice the washed raspberries and liberally cover the jam surface of the paste*

You have now learned about the use of the different types of pastes and how to produce a variety of pastry products utilising a range of commodities and preparation techniques.

## Assessment of knowledge and understanding

To test your level of knowledge and understanding, answer the following short questions. These will help to prepare you for your summative (final) assessment.

1  Explain the difference between and oil and a fat.

_____

_____

2  State the reason why weighing and measuring is so important to pastry production.

_____

_____

3  In which paste can icing sugar be used instead of caster sugar?

_____

_____

4  Name the preparation method used for pâte sucrée.

_____

_____

5  Identify the difference between a profiterole and an éclair.

_____

_____

6  Describe the storage procedure for storing raw puff paste.

_____

_____

7  State the reason wholemeal flour is perceived as healthier that white flour.

_____

_____

# CHEF'S PROFILE

**Name: JULIE SHARP**

**Position:** Pastry Chef Lecturer

**Establishment:** New College Stamford

**Current job role and main responsibilities:** Pastry chef lecturer teaching NVQ 1, 2, 3. ABC certificate level 2 and level 3 diploma.

### When did you realise that you wanted to pursue a career in the catering and hospitality industry?

I was interested in cooking from an early age; I would always help my mother bake cakes on a Saturday morning. I loved experimenting with food even then and subjected my family to some weird and wonderful creations that they ate without complaint.

When I left school it seemed like a very natural progression to pursue a career in catering, even then I knew I wanted to specialise in pâtisserie.

**Training:** Southfields College Leicester 2 years 705 / 706–2

Ecole Lenotre Paris I month: petit fours, plated desserts, pâtisserie

706/3 Slough University with Professor Huber

Intermediate and advanced sugar course: Edwald Notter

Bellouet Paris: croissant, Danish and tarts

Certificate in Education 2006

**Experience:** I started my career in small country house hotels and then moved into London and five-star hotels: Landmark Hotel (Marylebone); Mandarin Oriental Hyde Park; Claridges.

Overseas: Lyford Key Club, Bahamas (Private members club); Château Lake Louise, Alberta, Canada; Hôtel Sofitel Melbourne Australia.

### What do you find rewarding about your job?

I get immense satisfaction from seeing the finished product, especially the plated desserts in large banquets when you get to see rows and rows of your desserts all looking identical.

I find the teamwork element of working in kitchens very rewarding. Your colleagues become your extended family and seeing their progression and growth makes the job seem even more worthwhile.

### What do you find the most challenging about the job?

The pastry section is a very diverse and creative area catering for most sections of the hotel. The source of most satisfaction is the challenge of creating new dishes and seeing the finished products being received in a complimentary way.

### What advice would you give to students just beginning their career?

Do not be afraid to ask questions. The more you ask the more you will understand what is expected of you and the fewer mistakes you will make.

### Who is your mentor or main inspiration?

Professor Huber had a huge influence in my pastry career, his depth of knowledge on the subject and his enthusiasm for it is very infectious.

### Secrets of a successful chef:
Enthusiasm, dedication, willingness to learn, ability to be a team-player and good communicator.

### A brief personal profile:
Member of the Academy Culinary Arts.

Pastry chef of the year 2004 (Craft Guild of Chefs).

My interests revolve around anything to do with pastry. It is more of a vocation than a job. It is a way of life.

### Can you give one essential kitchen tip or technique that you use as a chef?

Use all of your senses while cooking.

# Baked apple cheesecake with butterscotch sauce

*Cheesecake mix*

| INGREDIENTS | 4 PORTIONS |
|---|---|
| Cream cheese | 360g |
| Sugar | 90g |
| Lemon juice and zest | ½ |
| Egg yolks | 2 |
| Double cream | 75g |
| Eggs | 80g |
| Apples | 150g |

## Method of work

1   Cream the sugar and cream cheese together.
2   Mix in the eggs and egg yolk.
3   Stir in the lemon zest and juice.
4   Stir in the cream.
5   Dice the apples up and sauté off in some butter.
6   Place in the bottom of a pre-baked tart shell and pour the cheesecake mix over the top.
7   Bake at 120°C until the mix has set.

*Butterscotch sauce*

| INGREDIENTS | 4 PORTIONS |
|---|---|
| Sugar | 125g |
| Glucose | 50g |
| Cream | 375g |

## Method of work

1   Make a direct caramel with the sugar and then add in the glucose and allow to dissolve.
2   Add in the cream.
3   Be careful, as this mix will spit if too much cream is added at once.
4   Cook out.

*Streusel topping*

| INGREDIENTS | 4 PORTIONS |
|---|---|
| Icing sugar | 240g |
| Ground almonds | 240g |
| Butter | 480g |
| Flour | 640g |
| Baking powder | 8g |
| Lemon zest | 3 |
| Pinch of salt | |

## Method of work

1   Rub all the ingredients in together.
2   Then leave to set.
3   Then press through a coarse sieve.
4   Grate onto a baking tray and cook at 200°C until golden brown.

*Clotted cream ice cream*

| INGREDIENTS | 4 PORTIONS |
|---|---|
| Milk | 250g |
| Clotted Cream | 250g |
| Sugar | 125g |
| Egg yolks | 70g |
| Vanilla | |

## Method of work

1   Bring the milk to the boil in a thick-bottomed pan.
2   Whisk the egg yolks and sugar together them pour the boiling milk on to them.
3   Return to the pan and heat gently, stirring continuously until it coats the back of the spoon.
4   Add in the clotted cream and pass through a fine sieve and leave to cool, then churn.

*Apple crisps to garnish the cheesecake*

1   Slice the apples on a mandolin.
2   Place directly into stock syrup.
3   Allow to soak and then place onto a silicone baking mat and dry out under the hot plate lights.

# 15

# Desserts and puddings

UNIT 213

1. Prepare hot and cold desserts and puddings
2. Cook and finish hot and cold desserts and puddings

## LEARNING OBJECTIVES

The aim of this unit is to enable the candidate to develop skills and implement knowledge in the principles of producing a range of hot and cold desserts and puddings as well as cakes, biscuits and sponges. This will also include the understanding of materials, ingredients and equipment.

At the end of this chapter you will be able to:

- Identify each type of dessert and pudding including cakes, biscuits and sponges
- Understand the use of relative ingredients in the production of a variety of desserts
- State the quality points of various dessert dishes
- Understand the different techniques required to prepare and cook each type of dessert and cake
- Identify the storage techniques and procedures of desserts
- Identify the correct tools and equipment used
- Identify the modern and classical presentation skills required for a range of hot and cold desserts as well as cakes, gateaux, biscuits and sponges

# Desserts

## INTRODUCTION TO DESSERTS

Although honey was the first naturally sweet substance recorded, sugar was first thought to have been discovered in India at around 1200 BC. Sugar cane, which is a giant grass, is native to India. According to legend, the ancestors of Buddha came from the land of sugar, or Gur, a name then given to Bengal. The export of sugar cane began to spread through the Middle East, from India towards Europe. In a syrup form, it was considered as the most expensive spice commodity and was used in medicine by the Egyptians even before the Greeks and Romans. Until modern times, sugar was an expensive medicine to Europeans, or a luxury reserved for the rich and powerful.

With the cultivation of fruits, nuts and spices such as cinnamon cooks began to experiment with sweet confections which were often used to help portray great wealth during a banquet. Initially sweets, vegetables, meat and fish dishes were served all together on one table.

**VIDEO CLIP**
A pastry kitchen in a five starred hotel

In the seventeenth century, desserts had become one of the main spectacles of a dinner and ornate designs were presented to allow the chef to demonstrate their skills. The 'king of chefs', Antonin Carême was born into a poor family in 1784. He attained an apprenticeship in a pâtissèrie and eventually worked for Talleyrand, George IV, Tsar Alexander I and the Baron de Rothschild. Throughout his career he dedicated his skills to the art of the pâtissier and generally changed the way menus and food were served. By the time of Carême, desserts were large, elaborate set pieces, often fashioned in great detail. Although Carême took this art form on to greater heights the formation of the dessert as essentially the last course of a meal was born. Nowadays it is usually the dessert course that most people first remember from their dining experience! The word is founded from *desservir* which means 'to remove that which has been served'. Also at the end of the eighteenth century ice creams were being introduced and were usually served frozen into various forms using copper moulds.

In modern times the dessert has become far less elaborate and today's chef has to comprehend and take advantage of many new flavours and ideas. The introduction of a new, healthier lifestyle means that chefs have to produce lighter and sometimes more diet-conscious sweets, confections and desserts.

The specialised nature of the pastry section often means that it tends to operate separately from the main kitchen. The techniques used are very different from those of the main kitchen and they must be understood comprehensively and followed exactly to produce satisfactory results.

# THE CAREFUL READING OF A RECIPE

Reading a recipe carefully is the first skill of a successful pastry chef. Although this sounds tedious, many chefs tend to scan the recipe too quickly and do not pick up on special points or ingredients. If read without thought the recipe will not turn out as required. Dessert recipes are specific in the exact amounts of ingredients and of the techniques employed to utilise them.

Another reason to read each recipe carefully is so that the chef can identify the technique and methods used to produce the dessert and how long it will take. Also, it allows the chef to envisage what each stage will be and ultimately what the final presentation will look like.

Some recipes may need to be calculated to yield a greater portion size. In order to increase the yield of a dessert it is not necessarily the case that you should multiply the ingredients because the recipe may eventually become unbalanced. The first step is to identify the percentage value for each ingredient: when the measurement of the ingredient is increased it maintains the percentage ratio of the original dessert recipe.

A system of increasing the correct portion yield from a base recipe that involves percentages to express the formula used has been developed. This approach identifies the exact increase for each ingredient to meet the portion yield without throwing the recipe out of balance.

The example below illustrates how to use the formula effectively.

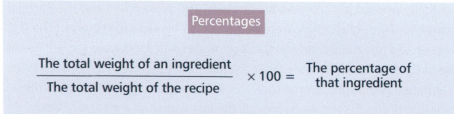

Percentages

$$\frac{\text{The total weight of an ingredient}}{\text{The total weight of the recipe}} \times 100 = \text{The percentage of that ingredient}$$

Note: It may be necessary to round measurements for specific ingredients to help simplify the act of measuring

Using this formula to identify each ingredient in terms of percentage rather than metric weight will ensure that calculations are more accurate when increasing or decreasing a recipe.

# STORAGE CONCERNS FOR INGREDIENTS ASSOCIATED WITH DESSERTS

Maintaining the quality of ingredients for desserts is a concern for all chefs. The commodities used are prone to rapid disintegration, especially fresh fruits and dairy products. Great care needs to be taken to ensure hygienic storage and refrigeration measures are maintained.

■ Dairy products and eggs should be stored in air-circulated refrigeration units and kept in clean, covered plastic containers.

■ Separate dairy and egg products from other ingredients to avoid cross-contamination. A separate refrigerator is best practice if possible.

■ Fruit should be removed from the boxes and trays they were used to journey in as these can be contaminated. The fruit should be stored in clean, plastic trays in refrigerated conditions. Any bruised or damaged fruit should be removed. Bananas should not be stored in a refrigerator because the skin will discolour quickly.

■ Dry commodities need to be stored in clean, sealed plastic containers on clean shelving in a separate storage room. The room needs to be maintained at a constant cool temperature and should have a dry atmosphere.

■ Stock rotation should be employed so that all ingredients are used up and then replenished by a new batch of ingredients. The empty container should be cleaned before replenishing.

■ It is not recommended to store desserts for long periods of time in a refrigerator because of starch break-down and loss of colour and flavour.

■ To store desserts for short periods in a refrigerator it is essential that they are covered in plastic film or placed into airtight plastic containers. Items that contain large amounts of sugar will attract moisture which may deteriorate the dessert quicker.

■ Storing prepared desserts in a freezer is an alternative method that works exceptionally well. However, the dessert should have completely cooled to 5°c or below before placing into plastic boxes. Label and date the item before freezing.

**HEALTH & SAFETY**

It is good practice to blast freeze any item for 30 minutes before placing into a holding freezer. This process helps to maintain moisture content in the product and helps to eliminate potential freezer burn.

# SPECIALIST DESSERT EQUIPMENT

### Grater
A rectangular strip or metal box with sharp holes of varying sizes. This is used to grate the zest of citrus fruits such as lemons and oranges. It can also be used to grate chocolate for decorative purposes.

*Grater*

*Stainless steel moulds*

### Stainless steel moulds
These come in different shapes and sizes and are used to mould mousses, bavarois, crèmes and sponges. Care must be taken when storing large quantities of moulds as they can be quite heavy and will easily bend out of shape. A cheaper alternative to purchasing expensive stainless steel round moulds is to purchase plastic piping from a local DIY store and cut the mould to size.

IMAGES COURTESY OF RUSSUMS.CO.UK

### Ramekin dishes

A ramekin is a small baking dish usually made of ceramic or heat-resistant glass to bake soufflés, cakes and custards. These come in varying sizes.

Ramekin dishes

### Plastic sauce bottles

These are used to pipe sauces onto plates to create intricate designs for the presentation of desserts. They can be warmed up to maintain a hot sauce such as crème Anglaise or used for cold fruit coulis.

Plastic sauce bottles

### Ice cream machine

This is a specialist machine which should always be sterilised before and after use. A good machine will produce a litre of ice cream within a matter of minutes. It has a churning mechanism within a freezing unit so that the mixture can be constantly churned as it sets and eventually freezes. This action will help reduce coarse ice crystals forming within the mixture.

Ice cream machine

### Sugar thermometers

Used to measure temperatures accurately for cooking jams, preserves and sugar. They should be cleaned and sterilised after every use. Care should be taken not to plunge the thermometer into cold water after having measured very high sugar temperatures as this may cause a breakage. digital thermometers are just as effective.

Sugar thermometers

### Copper sugar boiler

These pans are used solely for the cooking of sugar-based confections and syrups. Copper has a good transference of heat but they should be kept scrupulously clean and free of oils and fats. Cleaning with hot water and a mild detergent, followed by a second clean of vinegar and salt and then a rinse with cold water, will obtain the best results.

Copper sugar boiler

### Dariole moulds

These can be purchased in aluminium or stainless steel and are used primarily for the cooking of puddings and pudding soufflés.

Dariole moulds

# MILK AND MILK-BASED PRODUCTS FOR DESSERTS

## Milk

Milk has been an important source of food for thousands of years and is highly regarded for its versatility. Milk contains fat, protein, carbohydrates in the form of natural milk sugar (lactose), calcium, phosphorus, sodium and potassium. Vitamins A, C, D and the B vitamins riboflavin, thiamine and B12 are also present.

The milk that is generally used in the pastry kitchen is obtained from four main sources: cow, goat, soya and ewe's milk. Primarily milk is used as a moisturising agent as it is 87 per cent water. It is also used as an enriching agent depending on the amount used and whether it is full cream, half cream (semi-skimmed) or skimmed.

# Pasteurised Milk

Much of fresh cow's milk is pasteurised to destroy pathogenic bacteria found in fresh milk. There are two ways of pasteurising milk:

1 Heat the milk to a temperature of 145°F and maintain this temperature for 30 seconds and then cool it rapidly.
2 Heat the milk to 162°F for 15 seconds and cool it rapidly.

This general purpose milk contains about 4 per cent fat and keeps for four to five days in a refrigerator.

# Homogenised Milk

This is treated so that the cream content is dispersed throughout the milk. It has the same fat content as pasteurised milk and can be used in all recipes requiring milk.

# Semi-skimmed Milk

With a fat content of 1.5–1.8 per cent, this tastes less rich than full cream milk, but is fine to use for most recipes.

# Skimmed Milk

This milk has a fat content of no more than 0.3 per cent which makes it ideal for anyone wishing to cut down on their fat intake. Since most of the fat has been removed, many of the natural soluble vitamins will also be lost, although the other nutrient values will still remain. The milk looks thinner and is less fatty tasting.

# Channel Islands and Jersey Milk

This is produced from Jersey and Guernsey cows, is normally quite yellow in colour as it has a high fat content of about 4–8 per cent.

# Buttermilk

A liquid by-product of butter making, buttermilk is a thin and unstable liquid which is left after the fat from the cream has coagulated to form butter.

# UHT Milk

Ultra-heat-treated or long-life milk can be kept for several months without refrigeration but once it has been opened it should be treated as normal fresh milk. The fat is evenly distributed during this process and it is therefore a stable milk to cook with.

# Soya Milk

Soya milk retains most of the high nutritional value of the soya bean. It can be used in cooking although it can curdle if mixed with certain hot liquids. Soya milk is an acceptable alternative to milk in the diet of those who are lactose intolerant.

## The Contamination of Milk Products

In general milk keeps less well than for other foods. Contamination can occur with the use of unclean equipment and unhygienic procedures at the initial stage in the dairy or during transit and in the course of improper storage. Fresh milk should be purchased daily and stored:

- In the container in which it is delivered.
- In a refrigerator at below 5°C.
- Away from strong odours such as onion and fish.

# CREAM AND YOGHURT

Cream is derived from milk and is essentially the butterfat content that is separated from the milk. It will pass through the same pasteurisation or sterilisation process as milk and should be treated, transported and stored in the same manner as fresh milk.

## Single Cream

This has a low fat content of 18 per cent which makes it unsuitable for **whipping**. However, it can be used to enrich soups, sauces or for serving as an accompaniment for desserts or coffee. It is also available in UHT form.

## Whipping Cream

Because of its fat content of 35 per cent, whipping cream is ideal for aeration with a wire balloon whisk. Once aerated it can be used to as a decoration medium or folded into bavarois or mousse preparations to lighten the texture. This cream is also suitable for serving in the same way as single cream and is also available in UHT form.

## Double Cream

The fat content of double cream is 48 per cent, which will add richness of texture and flavour to a wide range of dishes. Although it can be aerated, care should be taken not to over-whip the cream so that it becomes grainy and starts to separated. This can happen quite quickly due to the greater fat content.

## Clotted Cream

This is the richest of all creams and has a yellow shade of colour which denotes the high fat content. It contains 55 per cent fat and is very thick in texture. This cream is traditionally manufactured from the English counties of Devon, Cornwall and Somerset. Generally it is used as an accompaniment for desserts and especially with the afternoon tea service of warm scones and fruit preserve.

## Crème Fraîche

This cream is treated with a bacterial culture to create a slightly acidic flavour. It has a similar consistency to that of double cream although it has a 35 per cent fat content.

## Soured Cream

This is a commercially prepared cream which has a similar fat content to single cream. It is made from homogenised cream with a bacterial culture added to create a slightly sour flavour. This can be used to enrich soups and sauces or used as an accompaniment to many dishes.

## Yoghurt

This product has had two active bacteria added to create the thick textured and acidic flavour we associate with yoghurts today. The nutritional qualities of yoghurt vary greatly according to whether it has been produced with whole or skimmed milk and whether it has had cream, sugar or fruit added to it. There may be preservatives or starches added so it is always best to check the labelling on the packaging before purchase. The storage of yoghurt is the same as for fresh milk and cream.

# INTRODUCTION TO HOT DESSERTS

Hot desserts play an important part in the construction of a dessert menu, varying the choice of desserts available. Also, rather obviously, they give a change of temperature to the normal cold dessert that is pleasant, especially during the autumn/winter months. With this temperature change a change in the texture of the dessert appears. The balance of hot desserts to cold desserts on a menu is important and the time of year should influence how many hot desserts should be present. Chefs now use combinations of hot elements and cold elements to produce one dessert (e.g. hot apple pie served with vanilla ice cream) and this has been taken further with the development of warm desserts such as chocolate tart.

## DERIVATIVES OF SOME CLASSICAL 'ENTREMENTS CHAUDS'

| BEIGNETS | BEIGNETS SOUFFLÉ, BEIGNETS DE POMMES |
|---|---|
| Charlottes | Apple charlotte, timbale d'Aremberg |
| Croquettes | Croquette de fruits, croquette de riz |
| Croutes | Croute aux fruits, croute joinville |
| Crêpes | Crêpe Normande, crêpe Suzette |
| Dumplings | Apple dumplings |
| Fruit desserts | Abricots Condé, bananes Bourdaloue |
| Omelettes | Omelette à la confiture, omelette mousseline |
| Pannequets | Pannequets à la confiture, pannequets à la Lyonnaise |
| Fruit pies and tarts | Apple pie (tarte aux pommes) |
| Puddings | Cabinet pudding, queen's pudding |
| Soufflés | Soufflé au chocolat, soufflé au Grand Marnier |
| Strüdel | Apfelstrüdel, kirschenstrüdel |
| Various hot desserts | Clafoutis, kesari bhata (sweet rice Indian style) |

# RECIPES

## Sticky toffee pudding

| INGREDIENTS | 4 PORTIONS | 10 PORTIONS |
|---|---|---|
| Stoned and sliced dates | 175g | 440g |
| Bicarbonate of soda | 1tsp | 2tsp |
| Water | 300ml | 700ml |
| Unsalted butter | 50g | 125g |
| Caster sugar | 175g | 440g |
| Whole eggs | 2 | 5 |
| Self-raising flour | 175g | 440g |
| Vanilla extract | 1tsp | 2tsp |

Butter individual pudding
moulds with some clarified
butter

## Method of work

1 Preheat the oven to 180°C and butter individual pudding moulds with some clarified butter.

2 Bring the water to the boil and add the dates. Boil the dates for 5 minutes before adding the bicarbonate of soda.

3 Cream the butter and the caster sugar together until light. Beat the whole eggs and slowly add to the creamed butter and sugar.

4 Drain the dates and mix into the egg and butter preparation, combining the flour and the vanilla into the preparation at the last moment and folding in gently.

5 Pour the mixture into the prepared pudding moulds, place into a bain marie and bake in the oven for approximately 30–40 minutes. Each pudding should be slightly firm and have a spring to the texture when touched.

6 Serve with a combination of vanilla ice cream (p. 553) and butterscotch sauce (p. 544). Garnish with a sprig of icing-sugar-dusted fresh mint and a caramelised date if desired.

### CHEF'S TIP

Although they can be slightly expensive, Medjool dates from Egypt are best suited for this recipe because they are large and have a sweet, dense flesh.

### HEALTH & SAFETY

The addition of dried apricots to this recipe will increase the fibre content and change the colour and the flavour combination.

# Pear fritters with apricot sauce and almond ice cream

*Prepare the pears by cutting into five equal wedges*

| INGREDIENTS | 4 PORTIONS | 10 PORTIONS |
|---|---|---|
| **Fritters** | | |
| Sweet cider | 300g | 750g |
| Soft white flour | 100g | 250g |
| Caster sugar | 25g | 60g |
| Williams pears, peeled and cored | 4 | 10 |
| Apricot sauce | 350ml | 1 litre |
| Almond ice cream (see p. 553) | 4 quenelles | 10 quenelles |
| Icing sugar | 50g | 120g |
| Fresh mint garnish | 4 pluches | 10 pluches |

## Method of work

1 Preheat the deep fat fryer to 180°C.

2 Mix the cider, flour and sugar together and leave to rest for approximately half an hour at room temperature. Ensure that there are no lumps of raw flour in the mixture.

3 Prepare the pears by cutting them into five equal wedges, and lightly flour each piece.

4 Dip each piece into the batter and transfer into the deep fat fryer. Fry for about 4 minutes until a pale golden colour has been obtained. The fritters will rise to the surface when they are cooked.

5 Carefully remove and drain the fritters, placing them onto absorbent kitchen paper and keeping them warm for service.

6 Cook the remaining fruit in batches following the same procedure.

7 To serve, place five wedges of the pear fritters onto a plate and pour the apricot sauce next to them and add a quenelle of almond ice cream for each portion. Decorate with the mint and a dusting of icing sugar.

### CHEF'S TIP

Bananas, apricots, apples, pineapples and peaches can be deep fried and served in the same way. A combination of fruit sauces or coulis can be served to complement the dish.

### HEALTH & SAFETY

Carefully dip the fritters into the deep fat fryer before letting go at the last moment. This method will prevent the hot fat from splashing up and potentially burning.

# Bread and butter pudding

| INGREDIENTS | 4 PORTIONS | 10 PORTIONS |
|---|---|---|
| Medium-sliced white bread | 10 slices | 25 slices |
| Unsalted butter | 50g | 125g |
| Egg yolks | 6 | 14 |
| Whole egg | 1 | 3 |
| Caster sugar | 130g | 260g |
| Vanilla pod or extract | 1 | 3 |
| Fresh milk | 250ml | 600ml |
| Double cream | 250ml | 600ml |
| Sultanas | 25g | 60g |
| Raisins | 25g | 60g |
| Icing sugar for glazing | 60g | 150g |

## Method of work

1 Preheat the oven to 180°C.

2 Remove the crusts from the bread and melt the unsalted butter. Brush the butter onto each slice of bread. Use any remaining butter to lightly grease the sides of the baking dish used to bake the pudding in.

3 Split the vanilla pod in half and add to the milk and cream combination, slowly bring to the boil.

4 Whisk the egg yolks, whole egg and caster sugar together in a bowl.

5 Pour the boiled milk and cream onto the egg preparation and stir well to form a basic custard.

6 Arrange the bread in layers in the baking dish sprinkling the sultanas and raisins between each layer. Finish with a final layer of bread.

7 Pour the custard mixture over the bread through a chinois to strain the vanilla pod. Leave the custard to soak into the bread for approximately 20 minutes.

8 Place the dish into a bain marie and bake in the preheated oven for approximately 25 minutes or until the pudding begins to set.

9 Remove from the oven, dredge the top with icing sugar and glaze under a hot salamander or coat with a hot apricot glaze. Serve immediately.

*Pour the custard mixture over the bread through a chinois to strain the vanilla pod.*

 **CHEF'S TIP**

To add flavour to the sultanas and raisins, macerate in dark rum or brandy for 12 hours prior to using.

# Chocolate brownie with a vanilla ice cream and dark chocolate sauce

*Pour the preparation into each lined mould and bake in the preheated oven for approximately 25 minutes*

### CHEF'S TIP

If the white chocolate pistoles are not available you can chop up white chocolate into 1cm chunks instead. It is important that you try to use a chocolate that has a minimum of 70 per cent cocoa content as this will have a stronger, almost bitter flavour that will balance with the high sugar content in this dessert.

| INGREDIENTS | 4 PORTIONS | 10 PORTIONS |
|---|---|---|
| Caster sugar | 300g | 750g |
| Whole eggs | 4 | 10 |
| Unsalted butter | 220g | 550g |
| Cocoa powder | 75g | 190g |
| Soft plain flour | 75g | 190g |
| Dark chocolate (70%) | 220g | 550g |
| Pecan nuts | 75g | 190g |
| White chocolate pistoles (optional) | 100g | 250g |
| Vanilla ice cream (see p. 553) | 4 quenelles | 10 quenelles |
| Crème Anglaise (see p. 541) | 300ml | 700ml |
| Dark chocolate | 80g | 200g |
| Icing sugar for glazing | 50g | 100g |

## Method of work

1 Preheat the oven to 180°C, lightly butter individual stainless steel rings and line with silicone paper. Set on a silicone baking sheet ready for use.

2 Ensure that the ice cream has been made in advance. Warm the crème Anglaise in a bain marie and add the chopped dark chocolate. Whisk in the chocolate to melt into the sauce and keep warm for service ensuring that the sauce temperature reaches no more than 78°C.

3 Make the individual chocolate tuiles to a shape and size that fits to the dessert.

4 Using a whisk beat together the caster sugar and eggs to create a light aerated foam.

5 Melt the butter and the chocolate together either in a microwave or over a pan of hot water. Do not overheat the chocolate because it can burn easily.

6 Sieve together the flour and cocoa powder and combine with the egg preparation. Add the melted chocolate and butter mixture and carefully mix together.

7 Chop the pecan nuts and add together with the white chocolate pistoles if required.

8 Pour the preparation into each lined mould and bake in the preheated oven for approximately 25 minutes or until the brownies are just baked and set.

9 Remove from the oven and carefully remove the rings. Leave to cool for a couple of minutes (these are best served warm rather than hot).

10 Place the brownie onto a plate and place a quenelle of the ice cream on top. Dust the top with icing sugar and warm the chocolate sauce to serve around the brownie. Serve immediately.

# Steamed lemon sponge pudding with lemon curd ice cream

| INGREDIENTS | 4 PORTIONS | 10 PORTIONS |
|---|---|---|
| Finely grated lemon zest and juice | 1 lemon | 3 lemons |
| Unsalted butter | 100g | 250g |
| Caster sugar | 125g | 300g |
| Whole eggs | 2 | 5 |
| Egg yolk | 1 | 3 |
| Self-raising flour | 200g | 500g |
| Fresh milk | 1–2 drops if needed | 4–5 drops if needed |
| Lemon curd ice cream (see p. 554) | 4 quenelles | 10 quenelles |
| Vanilla sauce Anglaise (see p. 541) | 400ml | 900ml |

## CHEF'S TIP

Alternative flavour combinations can be used for this recipe such as orange marmalade, chocolate, rhubarb or apricot. If making larger-sized puddings the steaming time will need to be increased to approximately 1 hour and 25 minutes.

## Method of work

1   Preheat the steamer to 118°C and lightly grease and flour each individual pudding mould. Cut small discs of silicone paper the circumference of the top of each pudding mould and brush one side with some melted butter.

2   Beat the unsalted butter and sugar together until the mixture is light in colour and has a fluffy texture. Add the lemon zest. This stage is important to help ensure a successful preparation to combine the eggs.

3   Beat in one egg at a time, ensure that each egg has been completely mixed into the butter preparation before adding another.

4   Add the flour and mix carefully, also adding the lemon juice at this point.

5   Check the consistency of the mixture. If the mixture is slightly heavy mix in a few drops of milk to ensure the correct 'dropping' consistency is obtained.

6   Spoon or pipe the mixture into the moulds up to three-quarters' full. Cover the moulds with the buttered silicone paper discs.

7   Place onto a tray and steam for approximately 45 minutes.

8   Remove from the steamer and de-mould each pudding.

9   Place the pudding onto a plate and place a quenelle of the ice cream to the side. Serve immediately with the warm sauce Anglaise around the pudding.

Beat the unsalted butter and sugar together until the mixture is a pale colour and has a fluffy texture

Beat in one egg at a time

Add the flour and mix carefully

# Vanilla pudding soufflé

| INGREDIENTS | 4 PORTIONS | 10 PORTIONS |
|---|---|---|
| Unsalted butter | 50g | 120g |
| Caster sugar | 50g | 120g |
| Soft white flour | 50g | 120g |
| Fresh milk | 190ml | 400ml |
| Vanilla pod | 1 | 2 |
| Egg yolks | 2 | 5 |
| Egg whites | 2 | 5 |
| Vanilla sauce Anglaise  (see p. 541) | 400ml | 900ml |

## CHEF'S TIP

Derivatives for this basic recipe are:
- Pudding soufflé Saxon: mix the vanilla pudding recipe with grated zest of lemon and finish as the vanilla recipe.
- Pudding soufflé Rothschild: vanilla pudding recipe mixed with candied fruits and square-cut lady finger biscuits soaked in Curacao and served with a Kirsch-flavoured apricot sauce.
- Pudding soufflé Suchard: substitute cocoa powder for some of the flour and addition of some melted chocolate to the panada. Serve with a chocolate sauce.

## Method of work

1 Preheat the oven to 150°C and lightly butter and sugar each individual dariole mould.
2 Cream together the butter and sugar and slowly combine the flour into the mixture. This is sometimes referred to as a panada.
3 Split the vanilla pod and place into a saucepan with the milk, bring to the boil.
4 Add the boiled milk to the panada and return to the stove. Cook out the mixture, stirring all the time until the mixture leaves the sides of the saucepan.
5 Remove the vanilla pod, wash and dry it then cut fine julienne strips with a sharp knife. Dust each pod with icing sugar and place onto a silicone baking mat. Place into the oven to further dry out each strip of vanilla to a crisp. This should take approximately 20 minutes.
6 After the panada has cooled, gradually add the egg yolks.
7 Whisk the egg whites to a peak with a pinch of salt and sugar to help stabilise the aeration.
8 Carefully fold in the egg whites one-third at a time.
9 Deposit the mixture into the prepared dariole moulds, place into a bain marie and bake in the preheated oven for approximately 30 minutes.
10 Remove from the oven when cooked and de-mould each pudding to serve.
11 Place the pudding onto a plate with two dried vanilla strands behind the pudding and serve immediately the warm sauce Anglaise around it.

Lightly butter and sugar each individual dariole mould

Cream together the butter and sugar and slowly combine the flour into the mixture

After the panada has cooled, gradually add the egg yolks

# Crêpe Parisienne with strawberry compôte

*Crêpes Parisienne avec compôte de fraises*

| INGREDIENTS | 4 PORTIONS | 10 PORTIONS |
|---|---|---|
| *Strawberry compôte* | | |
| Fresh strawberries | 450g | 1kg |
| Caster sugar | 150g | 350g |
| Lemon juice | ¼ lemon | ½ lemon |
| Water | 75ml | 150ml |
| *Crêpes* | | |
| Soft white flour | 120g | 250g |
| Caster sugar | 10g | 30g |
| Good-quality salt | 3g | 5g |
| Whole eggs | 2 | 4 |
| Fresh full fat milk | 400ml | 700ml |
| Melted butter | 30g | 60g |
| Brandy | 25ml | 50ml |
| Vanilla macaroons | 10 small | 25 small |

## CHEF'S TIP

Use a good crêpe pan with a heavy base to help ensure even cooking of the crêpe. If it is a new pan then you will need to 'season' it before using by washing and drying it first before placing onto a low heat for about five minutes. Wipe some vegetable oil into the pan using a kitchen cloth and let it cool down before wiping out the oil with a clean cloth. Now you can reheat the pan and use as required.

## Method of work

1   To prepare the crêpes, combine the flour, salt and sugar and slowly beat in the eggs. Stir in one-third of the milk and beat to a smooth paste. Add the rest of the milk and melted butter and leave to rest in a refrigerator for one hour before using. Stir the batter, adding the brandy at the same time, and pass through a chinois. Add a little sunflower oil to a crêpe pan and heat. Chop the vanilla macaroons into small pieces and ladle a little of the batter into the crêpe pan, sprinkle over with some of the small pieces of macaroons. Cook for approximately 1½ minutes on each side with a little colour. Place each cooked crêpe in between small sheets of silicone paper to retain the soft texture and keep warm until needed.

2   To prepare the strawberry compôte, wash and hull the strawberries, cutting any large ones to maintain a uniform size of fruit. Add the strawberries to a saucepan with all of the other ingredients. Begin to cook slowly until the strawberries are cooked but still hold their shape. Reserve to one side to keep warm.

3   Using two crêpes per portion spoon some of the strawberry compôte into the middle of each and gently roll into a cigar shape or into a cornet shape. Serve immediately by dusting each crêpe with icing sugar and place into the centre of a plate with any remaining liquor from the compôte. You can also add a serving of vanilla ice cream or crème chantilly to accompany.

# Apple Charlotte *Charlotte aux pommes*

| INGREDIENTS | 4 PORTIONS | 10 PORTIONS |
|---|---|---|
| Dessert apples | 960g | 2.4kg |
| Sliced white bread, slightly stale | 450g | 1.1kg |
| Caster sugar | 180g | 350g |
| Melted butter | 240g | 500g |
| Grated lemon zest | 1 lemon | 2 lemons |
| Whole clove | 1 | 2 |
| Sauce Anglaise to accompany (see p. 541) | 300ml | 700ml |

## Method of work

1 Preheat an oven to 220°C.

2 Wash, peel and core the apples. Cut into fairly thick slices and place into a saucepan with the sugar, one-quarter of the butter, the finely grated zest of lemon and the clove.

3 Do not add any water, gently stew the apples until they are just cooked and still maintain their shape.

4 Take the slices of bread and remove the crusts. Cut out discs (one to fit the top and bottom of the pudding mould). Cut the remaining bread slices into strips up to 25mm wide.

5 Melt the remaining butter, brush one side of a disc and place into the bottom of a pudding mould. Brush the strips in the same way and place them vertically around the sides of the mould, overlapping without leaving any gaps. Press gently to the sides.

6 Remove the clove from the apple preparation and fill the centre of the mould with the cooked apple.

7 Cover with a disc of bread on top and press down firmly. Place into the preheated oven to bake for approximately 30 minutes, until the bread lining is golden coloured and crisp.

8 Allow to cool slightly before turning out onto a plate and serving with a warm sauce Anglaise.

*Cut into fairly thick slices and place into a saucepan with the sugar, one quarter of the butter, the finely grated zest of the lemon and the clove*

**CHEF'S TIP**

Using dessert apples such as Braeburn will produce a more stable cooked apple than using traditional cooking apples. If the apples used are full of water and the apple preparation is slightly thin, it may be stiffened by adding breadcrumbs to the mixture.

**CHEF'S TIP**

Use wholemeal bread instead of white to increase the fibre content of this dessert.

# Vanilla rice pudding with warm lemon and almond madeleines

*Simmer gently, stirring frequently until the rice is cooked and the liquid has thickened*

### CHEF'S TIP

When cooking the rice pudding it is important to stir frequently to prevent the bottom of the pan from burning. If this happens the burnt 'flavour' will quickly pass through the whole pudding and it will then have to be discarded.

| INGREDIENTS | 4 PORTIONS | 10 PORTIONS |
|---|---|---|
| *Rice pudding* | | |
| Fresh full fat milk | 500ml | 1.25 litres |
| Caster sugar | 60g | 150g |
| Vanilla pod | 1 | 2 |
| Short grain pudding rice | 50g | 125g |
| Salted butter | 25g | 60g |
| Double cream | 50ml | 125ml |
| Egg yolk (optional) | 1 | 2 |
| *Madeleines* | | |
| Unsalted butter | 40g | 75g |
| Whole eggs | 1 | 3 |
| Caster sugar | 40g | 75g |
| Ground almonds | 20g | 40g |
| White soft flour | 40g | 75g |
| Grated zest of lemon | ½ lemon | 1 lemon |
| Icing sugar | 25g | 50g |
| *Rhubarb compôte* | | |
| Fresh rhubarb | 450g | 1kg |
| Caster sugar | 150g | 350g |
| Orange zest | ¼ orange | ½ orange |

## Method of work

1 Preheat an oven to 190°C.

2 For the madeleines, melt the butter in a pan and slowly cook it until a light nut-brown colour has been achieved (do not let the butter burn). Leave the butter to cool for a few minutes and then carefully drain off the fat leaving the residue behind.

3 Whisk the eggs and sugar together using an electric mixing machine. Aerate to soft peaks. Combine the flour, lemon zest and ground almonds together before gradually folding into the egg mixture. Carefully add the melted butter to the mixture and leave to stand for an hour.

4 Lightly grease and flour a madeleine tin (enough for two madeleines per portion) and spoon the mixture into the prepared tin.

5 Bake for approximately 9 minutes until the tops are springy to the touch. Keep in the tins for a couple of minutes to cool slightly and then remove onto a wire rack, dust with icing sugar and reserve warm for service.

6 For the rhubarb compôte, wash, trim and slice the rhubarb. Place all the compôte ingredients together into a saucepan and slowly stew until the rhubarb has cooked through. Remove from the heat and reserve to one side, keeping warm for service.

7 For the vanilla rice pudding, wash the rice in salted water and drain. Bring the milk to the boil and then add the rice, sugar and split vanilla pod.

8 Simmer gently, stirring frequently until the rice is cooked and the liquid has thickened.

9 Remove the vanilla pod (this can be washed and retained to create dried vanilla strands for decoration). Stir in the butter and cream to correct the consistency.

10 Serve warm with two madeleines to accompany the pudding. The warm rhubarb compôte is presented with the rice pudding or can also be served in a separate dish.

# Crème Anglaise

| INGREDIENTS | 4 PORTIONS | 10 PORTIONS |
|---|---|---|
| Full fat fresh milk | 500ml | 1250ml |
| Egg yolks | 6 | 15 |
| Caster sugar | 75g | 150g |
| Vanilla pod | 1 | 2 |

## Method of work

1 Place the milk into a heavy-bottomed saucepan with one tablespoon of the sugar (this will help to prevent the milk from boiling over).

2 Split the vanilla pod in half lengthways and scrape the seeds from within the pod into the milk. Add the vanilla pod too. Slowly bring the milk to the boil.

3 Meanwhile, using a whisk, beat the egg yolks and caster sugar together in a large bowl until pale in colour.

4 At boiling point, remove from the heat and carefully pour it onto the egg yolk mixture, stirring constantly.

5 Return this mixture to the saucepan and cook on a low heat, stirring continuously with a wooden spoon until the sauce thickens enough to coat the back of the spoon. Draw a finger down the back of the spoon to see if an impression has been formed.

6 Alternatively, use a thermometer and ensure that the sauce has been cooked to 85°C.

7 Remove the saucepan from the heat and strain through a chinois into a chilled bowl to prevent the sauce from cooking further and thus overcooking the eggs. Chill until required or serve warm as a custard sauce to accompany hot puddings and tarts.

At boiling point, remove the milk from the heat and carefully pour it onto the egg yolk mixture

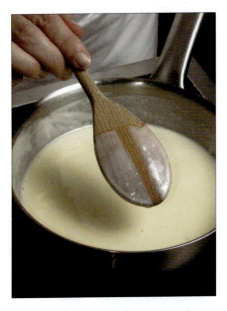

Draw a finger down the back of the spoon to see if an impression has been formed

# Stock syrup

| INGREDIENTS | 750ML | 1½ LITRES |
|---|---|---|
| Granulated sugar | 500g | 1kg |
| Water | 500g | 1kg |
| Liquid glucose | 50g | 100g |

### HEALTH & SAFETY

The use of liquid glucose will help to prolong the shelf life of the stock syrup because it helps to prohibit re-crystallisation of the sugar. The use of honey can help to prevent re-crystallisation but it will also add flavour and colour to the stock syrup.

## Method of work

1 Place the sugar and water into a heavy-based saucepan and heat slowly until the sugar has dissolved.

2 Bring the liquid to the boil and add the glucose at boiling point. Boil for a further 4 minutes and remove from the heat.

3 Cool the liquid and pour into a sterilised plastic container with a tight-fitting lid. This syrup will keep for up to 3 weeks in a refrigerator.

### CHEF'S TIP

It is easier to make plain stock syrup for use in the kitchen as this recipe can always have flavours such as lemon, cinnamon and orange added as you require. For a less dense stock syrup, decrease the sugar content by half. This can be used for moistening fresh fruit salads and poaching soft fruits such as strawberries, raspberries and blackberries.

# Raspberry coulis *Coulis de framboise*

| INGREDIENTS | 750ML | 1½ LITRES |
|---|---|---|
| Fresh raspberries | 800g | 1.7kg |
| Stock syrup (see above) | 200ml | 425ml |
| Lemon juice | 1 lemon | 2 lemons |

## Method of work

1 Carefully wash the raspberries and place into a food blender with the strained lemon juice and the stock syrup.

2 Purée the fruit mixture for approximately a minute until a smooth purée has been obtained.

3 Pass the purée through a fine chinois or muslin cloth and correct the consistency by adding more stock syrup or puréed raspberries.

4 The coulis is now ready for use and will keep for up to 3–4 days in a refrigerator. Alternatively it can easily be frozen.

### CHEF'S TIP

You can replace the use of stock syrup for pure apple juice to create a healthy alternative to using refined sugar. However, this will have an effect on the overall flavour combination of the coulis. Using this uncooked recipe will maintain the qualities and basic vitamin content of the fresh fruit used.

### CHEF'S TIP

Many other fruits can be used in this way, depending on the desired flavour. It is best not to mix different fruits together and sometimes the lemon juice can be omitted if the fruit has a particularly strong acid content, for example kiwi fruit.

*Purée the fruit mixture for approximately a minute*

# Crème pâtissière

*Cook out the crème until it thickens and it has lost its raw flour taste*

| INGREDIENTS | 750G | 1.5KG |
|---|---|---|
| Fresh full fat milk | 500ml | 1225ml |
| Egg yolks | 6 | 14 |
| Caster sugar | 120g | 240g |
| Strong flour | 30g | 90g |
| Custard powder | 10g | 30g |
| Vanilla extract or pod | To taste | To taste |

## Method of work

1 Place the egg yolks and two-thirds of the sugar into a bowl and beat using a whisk until the mixture is pale in colour.

2 Sieve the flour and custard powder together and add to the egg yolk mixture.

3 Combine the milk and the remaining sugar with the vanilla extract and slowly bring to the boil.

4 Carefully pour the hot milk onto the egg yolk preparation and stir in well. Return to the pan and cook over a gentle heat, stirring continuously.

5 Cook out the crème until it thickens and it has lost its raw flour taste. Pour it into a chilled bowl or tray and dust the top with icing sugar to prevent it from forming a skin on the top. As it cools, cover with plastic film.

6 Store in a refrigerator for further use. If correctly stored it will keep for up to 4 days.

### CHEF'S TIP

Classical derivatives of crème pâtissiere are:
- *Crème chiboust* – with the addition of Italienne meringue.
- *Crème mousseline* – with the addition of unsalted butter at room temperature.
- *Crème diplomat* – with the addition of fresh whipped cream.

# Crème chantilly

*A dropping or piping consistency should be obtained*

| INGREDIENTS | 500G | 1KG |
|---|---|---|
| Chilled whipping cream with a 35% fat content | 500ml | 1 litre |
| Icing sugar | 50g | 100g |
| Vanilla extract | To taste | To taste |
| Kirsch (optional) | To taste | To taste |

## Method of work

1 Ensure that the whipping cream, mixing bowl and whisk is well chilled (it is advisable to place the equipment in a refrigerator 30 minutes before use to help stabilise the aeration procedure).

2 Place the cream, sugar and flavourings into the bowl and slowly aerate until a dropping or piping consistency has been obtained.

3 Use the crème chantilly as soon as it is made; however, it can be kept in an airtight container in a refrigerator for up to 12 hours.

### CHEF'S TIP

Crème chantilly is used predominantly as an accompaniment to meringues, bavarois, ice creams and various desserts. Although the name is derived from the château of Chantilly, where the reputation of the fine cuisine of Chef Vatel in the seventeenth century enjoyed adulation, none of the preparations named after it were actually created there.

# Dark chocolate sauce

| INGREDIENTS | 600G | 1.2KG |
|---|---|---|
| Fresh full fat milk | 250g | 500g |
| Dark chocolate (50% minimum cocoa) | 300g | 600g |
| Whipping cream | 125g | 250g |
| Unsalted butter | 30g | 60g |
| Icing sugar | 50g | 100g |

## Method of work

1 Chop the chocolate into small pieces and place into a heavy-bottomed saucepan with the milk and the cream.
2 Slowly bring the liquid to the boil, stirring occasionally to prevent burning.
3 Remove from the heat and stir in the icing sugar and the butter. Pass through a fine sieve into a bowl and cool immediately.

*Remove from the heat and stir in the icing sugar and the butter*

> **CHEF'S TIP**
>
> Cool the chocolate sauce down to 4°C within one hour of production. Place it into an airtight plastic container and refrigerate. This sauce will keep for up to 3 days if correctly stored. To help maintain its liquid consistency during storage a little (up to 50g) glucose can be added to the milk before boiling.

# Butterscotch sauce

| INGREDIENTS | 600G | 1.2KG |
|---|---|---|
| Unsalted butter | 100g | 200g |
| Caster sugar | 125g | 250g |
| Demerara sugar | 125g | 250g |
| Golden syrup | 100g | 200g |
| Double cream | 400ml | 1 litre |

## Method of work

1 Melt the butter in a heavy-bottomed saucepan.
2 Add the caster sugar, demerara sugar and golden syrup and slowly bring to the boil. Stir occasionally.
3 Simmer the sugar solution until an amber colour has been obtained, this should take approximately 4 to 5 minutes.
4 Remove from the heat and very carefully add the double cream.
5 Stir well and place back onto a medium flame to bring back to the boil.
6 Simmer for 3 minutes then pass through a fine sieve into a bowl and cool immediately.

*Remove from the heat and very carefully add the double cream*

> **CHEF'S TIP**
>
> This butterscotch sauce can be used for the sticky toffee pudding recipe. It can also be used hot or cold as a sauce to accompany many desserts and ice creams. To check the consistency simply add a little more cream if too thick or heat the sauce and reduce a little if it is too thin.

> **HEALTH & SAFETY**
>
> When adding the double cream to the boiling sugar great care must be taken. Remove the pan from the heat and add a small stream of cream to start with as the molten sugar will bubble. Stir the rest in with a wooden spoon as this will help to arrest the temperature of the sugar.

# Garnishes and decorations: fruit crisps

*Slice the fruit very thinly on a mandoline and sprinkle it with lemon juice as quickly as possible*

| INGREDIENTS | 20–30 CRISPS |
|---|---|
| Stock syrup | 200ml |
| Fruit of choice – apples, strawberries, peeled pineapple, pears, oranges, lemons or mangoes | |
| Lemon juice | ½ lemon |

## Method of work

1  Preheat the oven to below 100°C.
2  Carefully select the chosen fruit and ensure there are no blemishes or bruising to the flesh. With the exception of mango and pineapple, there is no need to peel the fruit.
3  Slice the fruit very thinly on a mandoline and sprinkle lemon juice over it as quickly as possible.
4  Place the fruit slices to soak in a shallow tray of the stock syrup for approximately ½ a minute before shaking off the excess syrup and carefully placing the slices onto a baking sheet lined with a silicone baking mat.
5  Place into the oven with the door left slightly open.
6  Always check the fruit slices and turn each one over after approximately 1 hour. Leave in the oven for a further hour. The slices are ready when they begin to feel firm, they will become completely crisp once the fruit has cooled.
7  Place in an airtight container for storage. These fruit slices can last for up to one week if they have been properly dried out.

# Garnishes and decorations: bubble sugar

| INGREDIENTS | 1 SHEET CUT INTO VARIOUS SHAPES |
|---|---|
| Isomalt | 200g |
| Red powder food colour | Pinch |

## Method of work

1  Lay a silicone baking mat onto a baking sheet and preheat the oven to 220°C.
2  Place the isomalt into a plastic cup with a tight-fitting lid and add the powdered colour. Shake well to disperse the colour throughout the isomalt.
3  Sprinkle the isomalt over the silicone baking mat and place another silicone mat on top. Place in the oven to melt the Isomalt crystals.
4  Peel back the top silicone mat to check that the isomalt has melted (it should have melted and bubbled after nearly 10 minutes in the hot oven). Remove from the oven and leave to set. Whilst the bubble sugar is still plastic, cut off small pieces and leave to harden in a cool, dry place.
5  Place in an airtight container for storage and place in a cold, dry area and use as required.

# Garnishes and decorations: preserved vanilla sticks

| INGREDIENTS | 20–30 CRISPS |
|---|---|
| Stock syrup | 200ml |
| Used vanilla pods – cut into thin julienne | 20–30 julienne sticks |

## Method of work

1. Preheat the oven to below 100°C.
2. Carefully clean, dry and cut the vanilla pods into very thin julienne sticks.
3. Place the vanilla sticks to soak in a shallow tray of the stock syrup for approximately 30 seconds before shaking off the excess syrup and carefully placing the slices onto a baking sheet lined with a silicone baking mat.
4. Place in the oven with the door left slightly open.
5. Always check the vanilla sticks and turn each one over after approximately 20 minutes. Leave in the oven for a further hour. The vanilla sticks are ready when they begin to feel firm, they will become completely crisp once they have cooled.
6. Place in an airtight container for storage. These vanilla sticks can last for up to one week if they have been properly dried out.

Place the vanilla sticks in a shallow tray of the stock syrup to soak for approximately 30 seconds

### CHEF'S TIP

This is a great way to use vanilla pods once you have previously used them to flavour a preparation, sauce or dessert. An alternative use for used vanilla pods is to put them in a jar of caster sugar so that the still fragrant pod will transfer the vanilla scent to the sugar – thus creating vanilla sugar.

# Garnishes and decorations: chocolate shavings

| INGREDIENTS | |
|---|---|
| Dark, milk or white chocolate couverture in block form | 5kg block |

## Method of work

1. Two persons are required to create these simple shavings.
2. The first person firmly holds the chocolate block in place, keeping it steady all the time.
3. The second person holds a flexible knife and scrapes the side of the chocolate block back and forth to produce fine shavings of chocolate.
4. Place in an airtight container for storage and place in a freezer or a cold dry place and use as required.

The second person holds a flexible knife and scrapes the side of the chocolate block back and forth

### CHEF'S TIP

Great care should be taken when using this technique. Sometimes it is safer to hold the block of chocolate with thick cloth to obtain a stronger grip and protect the hands.

# Garnishes and decorations: chocolate acetate motifs

| INGREDIENTS | 1 SHEET CUT INTO VARIOUS SHAPES |
|---|---|
| Dark, milk or white chocolate couverture | 300g |
| Acetate sheet with a transfer design | 1 |

## Method of work

1 Place the chopped couverture chocolate into a clean, dry plastic bowl and place into a microwave oven.

2 On the highest setting, heat the chocolate for 10 seconds only, remove from the microwave oven and stir with a clean plastic spoon.

3 Place back into the microwave and repeat this process until the chocolate begins to melt (never heat for more than 10 seconds otherwise the chocolate will overheat and can burn very easily).

4 When the majority of the chocolate is melted but there are still a few pieces left unmelted, continue stirring without heating in the microwave until the residual heat melts the remaining pieces.

5 Lay the acetate transfer side up and carefully spread the melted chocolate over it. Keep the chocolate quite thin and leave to cool down.

6 As the chocolate begins to set; using a sharp knife cut squares without cutting through the acetate and then leave to set.

7 Carefully remove each set chocolate square. The acetate design should now have transferred onto the chocolate.

8 Place in an airtight container for storage and use as required.

### CHEF'S TIP

Using a microwave oven to melt chocolate is a quick way of ensuring that 'tempering' occurs without having to resort to alternative methods. Always ensure that the temperature of the chocolate does not exceed 37°C and that the remaining pieces of chocolate melt slowly before using.

Lay the acetate transfer side up and carefully spread the melted chocolate over it

As the chocolate begins to set, using a sharp knife, cut squares without cutting through the acetate, then leave to set

Carefully remove each set chocolate square. The acetate design should now have transferred onto the chocolate

# Garnishes and decorations: caramel and almond swirls

*Carefully remove from the work surface*

| INGREDIENTS | 20 |
|---|---|
| Granulated sugar | 250g |
| Water | 100g |
| Liquid glucose | 50g |
| Flaked almonds | 100g |
| Vegetable oil | 50ml |

## Method of work

1   Lay a silicone baking mat onto a marble slab or stainless steel work surface. Alternatively, if a silicone baking mat is not available, wipe the vegetable oil onto a clean marble surface.

2   Place the sugar and the water into a heavy-based clean saucepan and leave to soak for five minutes.

3   Place the pan onto a medium heat and bring the sugar to the boil. Add the liquid glucose after the sugar has been boiling for 1 minute.

4   Meanwhile, place the flaked almonds onto a baking sheet and toast under a hot salamander until golden in colour. Reserve to one side to cool down.

5   Continue to boil the sugar until a light caramel colour has been achieved. Keep cleaning the inside of the saucepan walls with clean, cold water using a clean pastry brush. This will help to prevent sugar crystals from forming.

6   Remove the saucepan from the heat and arrest the cooking by plunging the pan into cold water for 10 seconds. Let the caramel stand for 2 minutes before using.

7   Sprinkle the flaked almonds over the prepared marble or silicone baking mat.

8   Dip a dessert spoon into the caramel and let a steady, thin stream of hot caramel fall from the spoon. Using this technique draw individual spirals of the streaming caramel onto the flaked almonds and leave to set. Carefully remove from the work surface as the caramel and almond swirls will be quite delicate.

9   Place in an airtight container for storage in a cold, dry area and use as required.

# INTRODUCTION TO COLD DESSERTS

In the majority of dessert menus and sweet trolleys cold desserts play a very significant role. We should not undermine the stature of hot desserts, tarts and various yeast-based desserts that have an important part to play in the constitution of a dessert menu. However, especially in the advent of modern cuisine, cold desserts are more popular with customers and often dominate most of today's dessert menus.

## Advantages of Using Cold Desserts

There are many advantages in the use of cold desserts, which will effect the chef's decision when planning a menu.

1 Colour – A variety of colours can be used to create a decorative dessert. For instance the utilisation of the natural colour of fresh fruit without cooking, which can break down the fruit and lose the colour.

2 A large variety of different desserts – There is a huge range of different cold desserts to choose from and from different ethnic cultures and social and religious festivals. Therefore the chef is easily able to create a balanced menu.

3 Ease of storage – Most cold desserts are easily stored for two days either in the refrigerator at below 5°C or frozen at below −18°C for longer periods.

4 Ease of service – They can be served quickly, efficiently and decoratively with the use of refrigeration and a good mise-en-place system.

5 Use of seasons – An effective use of seasonal dishes can inspire any menu and can be cost-effective, especially if the ingredients have been purchased locally.

6 Creativity – A good pastry chef is able to use a cold dessert as a decorative medium to create a different way of presenting classical and modern cold desserts. It also gives the chef a chance to create different desserts using alternative flavours, texture and colour combinations to tempt customers.

# CLASSICAL DERIVATIVES OF COLD DESSERTS

The list below is a breakdown of different types of cold desserts:

| | | |
|---|---|---|
| 1 | Ices | Sorbets, coupes, sundaes, biscuit glacé |
| 2 | Fruit Desserts | Compotes, coupes, macédoine de fruit |
| 3 | Rice dishes | Riz a l'Impératrice, Condé |
| 4 | Crèmes | Brulee, caramel, régence |
| 5 | Creams | Vanilla bavarois, blancmange |
| 6 | Jellies | Gelée citron, gelée aux liqueurs |
| 7 | Charlottes | Russe, royale |
| 8 | Mousses | Mousse au chocolat |
| 9 | Soufflés | Soufflé froid au citron, soufflé glacé au fraise |
| 10 | Trifles | Sherry, ratafia, strawberry, tipsy cake |
| 11 | Timbales | Bananes suédoise, palermitaine |
| 12 | Miscellaneous | Oeufs à la neige, iles flottante |

# RECIPES

## Crème caramel with caramelized sultanas and mandarins

*Pour a small amount of the caramel into the bottom of individual moulds*

| INGREDIENTS | 4 INDIVIDUAL | 10 INDIVIDUAL |
|---|---|---|
| *Crème caramel* | | |
| Whole eggs | 4 | 8 |
| Caster sugar | 50g | 100g |
| Fresh full fat milk | 500ml | 1 litre |
| Vanilla extract | To taste | To taste |
| Grated nutmeg | To taste | To taste |
| Granulated sugar | 300g | 600g |
| Water | 75g | 150g |
| Sultanas | 50g | 100g |
| Mandarin oranges | 20 segments | 50 segments |
| *To decorate* | | |
| Caramel and almond swirls (page 548) | 4 | 10 |

## Method of work

1 Preheat the oven to 160°C.

2 To prepare the crème caramel, place the milk, vanilla and nutmeg into a saucepan and warm the milk. Mix the eggs and caster sugar together and add the warmed milk. Pass through a fine sieve into a measuring jug and set aside.

3 Place the granulated sugar into a scrupulously clean saucepan and add the water. Leave to soak for a few minutes before bringing to the boil and cooking to a light, amber caramel. Immediately arrest the cooking process by plunging the pan into a bowl of cold water for 10 seconds. Pour a small amount of the caramel into the bottom of individual moulds.

4 With the remaining caramel add a small amount of water to thin the caramel and bring back to the boil. Remove from the heat and add the sultanas and mandarins. Leave to cool and to let the fruit macerate in the caramel solution.

5 Pour the crème mixture on top of the set caramel in the moulds, place into a bain marie and bake in the preheated oven for approximately 40 minutes or until the crème caramels have set. Remove from the oven and bain marie and cool as quickly as possible. Leave in a refrigerator to chill.

6 To present, turn out the crème caramel onto the service plate and spoon around the macerated sultanas in the caramel juice with five mandarin segments per portion. Place the caramel and almond swirl decoration over the crème caramel and serve.

### CHEF'S TIP

It is important not to overcook the crème caramels otherwise small air pockets will set in the crème and create a scrambled texture to the finished dessert.

### CHEF'S TIP

Traditionally, crème caramels are served on their own without any accompaniments. However, on this occasion the matching of the fruits macerated in the remaining caramel adds colour, flavour, texture and balance to the dessert.

**VIDEO CLIP**
Making crème caramel

# Petit pot of chocolate with a banana smoothie

*As the sugars begin to caramelise add the sliced banana and turn over carefully to ensure even cooking and colour*

| INGREDIENTS | 4 INDIVIDUAL | 10 INDIVIDUAL |
|---|---|---|
| *Petit pots of chocolate* | | |
| **Dark chocolate couverture** (minimum 55% cocoa) | 70g | 140g |
| **Fresh full fat milk** | 225ml | 450ml |
| **Double cream** (48% fat) | 200ml | 400ml |
| **Caster sugar** | 80g | 200g |
| **Whole eggs** | 1 | 2 |
| **Egg yolks** | 5 | 10 |
| **Vanilla** | 1 pod | 2 pods |
| *Banana smoothie* | | |
| **Banana sorbet** (page 555) | 3 scoops | 7 scoops |
| **Whipping cream** (35% fat) | 40g | 80g |
| **Fresh milk** | 100g | 200g |
| **Ice cubes** | 3 cubes | 6 cubes |
| *Flambéed bananas* | | |
| **Fresh ripe bananas** | 3 bananas | 8 bananas |
| **Demerara sugar** | 25g | 50g |
| **Caster sugar** | 25g | 50g |
| **Dark rum** | 25ml | 50ml |
| *To decorate* | | |
| **Crème Chantilly** | 4 quenelles | 10 quenelles |
| **Cocoa powder** | To dust | To dust |
| **Julienne vanilla sticks** | 4 | 10 |
| **Fresh mint** | 4 pluches | 10 pluches |
| **Clear bubble sugar** | 4 pieces | 10 pieces |

### CHEF'S TIP

The petit pot of chocolate is a classical dessert that is a set cream. It is partly derived from the crème brûlée but is not finished with caramelised sugar. To prevent the bain marie water from boiling and therefore overcooking the chocolate pots, a sheet of card can be placed to cover the bottom of the bain marie and the pots placed on top with the water. The card will suppress the water temperature and prevent it from boiling whilst in the oven.

## Method of work

1 Preheat the oven to 165°C.
2 To make the chocolate pots, place the chopped chocolate, milk, cream and sugar into a saucepan. Split the vanilla pod in half and scrape the seeds out into the milk, bring slowly to the boil. Ensure that the chocolate has completely melted. Beat together the egg yolks and whole eggs and carefully pour the hot liquid onto them, mixing continuously. Do not over whisk as this creates too much froth (aeration). Pass the mixture through a fine chinois into the dishes and place into a bain marie. Bake for approximately 25 minutes or until each pot of chocolate sets. Chill as quickly as possible and reserve in a refrigerator.
3 To prepare the banana flambé, slice the bananas to approximately 5mm thick. Heat a pan over a medium flame and add the two sugars. As they begin to caramelise add the sliced banana and turn over carefully to ensure even cooking and colour. Finally add the dark rum and flambé to cook out the alcohol content. Transfer the banana to a clean bowl and reserve at room temperature.
4 To make the smoothie, place the banana sorbet, cream, milk and ice cubes into a blender and blend to a thick texture. Pour into chilled shot glasses and reserve in a refrigerator.
5 To present, place a quenelle of crème Chantilly on top of the chocolate pot and lightly dust with cocoa powder and finish with a pluche of fresh mint. Set onto a serving plate and place the shot glass of banana smoothie next to it with a vanilla stick garnish and bubble sugar. Finally spoon some banana flambé onto a presentation spoon and serve.

# Lemon crème brûlée with biscotti

| INGREDIENTS | 4 INDIVIDUAL | 10 INDIVIDUAL |
|---|---|---|
| *Crème brûlée* | | |
| Double cream (48% fat) | 500ml | 1 litre |
| Caster sugar | 80g | 150g |
| Egg yolks | 140g | 280g |
| Lemon zest | 1 lemon | 4 lemons |
| *Biscotti* | | |
| Butter | 60g | 125g |
| Caster sugar | 100g | 225g |
| Whole eggs | 1 | 2 |
| Aniseed | To taste | To taste |
| Lemon zest | ¼ lemon | ½ lemon |
| Soft white flour | 425g | 850g |
| Good quality salt | 3g | 6g |
| Baking powder | 4g | 8g |
| Flaked almonds | 50g | 90g |
| *To decorate* | | |
| Demerara sugar | 50g | 120g |
| Icing sugar for dusting | 40g | 80g |

### CHEF'S TIP

Demerara sugar is untreated cane sugar and its melting point is lower than caster sugar, so it will caramelise more easily. The salamander will need to be preheated to create a very strong heat to caramelise the sugar very quickly. If the heat is not hot enough it will slowly cook the top of the crème brûlée. Sometimes the use of a dessert blowtorch can give a better result.

## Method of work

1   Preheat the oven to 150°C.

2   To prepare the crème brûlée, wash the lemons well and finely grate the zest into a saucepan with the double cream. Slowly bring to the boil. Meanwhile combine the egg yolks and the caster sugar and beat with a whisk to a pale colour. Pour the boiled cream onto the egg yolk mixture and combine all the ingredients before carefully pouring into individual ramekin dishes.

3   Line a deep baking tray with double kitchen paper and place the ramekins on top. Pour in enough hot water to reach three-quarters up the side of the dishes. Place this bain marie into the oven and cook for approximately 30 minutes or until the crème brûlées have just set.

4   Remove each ramekin dish from the bain marie and cool to room temperature before chilling in a refrigerator for at least 2 hours.

5   For the biscotti, preheat the oven to 180°C. Cream together the butter and sugar until this mixture is light and fluffy. Sieve the flour, baking powder and salt together before slowly adding the eggs to the creamed butter. Finely grate the lemon and add to the mixture with the aniseed. Fold in the sieved ingredients and combine the almonds. Leave the paste to rest for five minutes. Mould into log shapes and place onto a baking sheet lined with silicone paper and baking for 20 minutes.

6   Remove from the oven to cool for a few minutes before slicing the biscotti into pieces 5mm thick whilst still warm. Place the slices facedown onto the baking sheet and place back into the oven to bake for an additional 8 minutes, flip over the biscotti and repeat the process until a golden colour has been achieved.

7   Cool on a wire rack and store in an airtight container.

8   To present, preheat a salamander and sprinkle the demerara sugar on top of each crème brûlée. Caramelise under the hot salamander ensuring an even heat distribution to create a complete caramelised sugar crust. Leave to cool down and set. Place the crème brûlée onto a dessert plate with two biscotti slices next to it. Serve immediately.

# Vanilla ice cream *Crème glacée à la vanille*

| INGREDIENTS | 4 PORTIONS | 10 PORTIONS |
|---|---|---|
| Double cream (48% fat) | 200ml | 400ml |
| Full fat fresh milk | 300ml | 600ml |
| Egg yolks | 6 | 12 |
| Caster sugar | 100g | 200g |
| Milk powder | 25g | 50g |
| Vanilla | 1 pod | 2 pods |

## Method of work

1. Using a whisk, beat together the egg yolks, caster sugar and the milk powder until a pale colour has been obtained.
2. Place the milk and cream in a heavy-bottomed saucepan, split the vanilla pod and scrape the seeds into the milk. Add the vanilla pod, bring to the liquid to the boil and simmer for approximately three minutes to help infuse the flavour.
3. Pour the milk onto the egg mixture whisking continuously and return the mixture to the saucepan on a medium heat.
4. Constantly stir the crème with a wooden spoon until it begins to coat the back of the spoon.
5. Pass immediately through a fine sieve into a chilled bowl and continue stirring for another five minutes to release the residual heat from the crème.
6. Place the crème to mature in a refrigerator (stored away from strong-smelling ingredients) for 2 hours before pouring into an ice cream machine and churning to produce the ice cream.
7. Place sterilised container into the freezer for an hour before churning the crème and use this as the container to immediately decant the ice cream into. This will help to prevent the ice cream from melting when removed from the machine.
8. Store the ice cream in an airtight container at –18°C or below.

Alternative flavours can be added to the ice cream.

| FLAVOUR | METHOD OF WORK |
|---|---|
| Almond ice cream | Add 50g of lightly roasted flaked almonds and some almond flavour per 4 portions to the milk/cream when simmering. Finish with 20ml of Amaretto |
| Cinnamon ice cream | Add 1 broken up cinnamon stick per 4 portions to the milk/cream when boiling, simmering and cooking out |
| Coffee ice cream | Add 30g per 4 portions of instant coffee to the milk/cream during simmering |
| Chocolate ice cream | Add 60g of dark chocolate (minimum of 60% cocoa) per portion, broken into small pieces, to the milk/cream during simmering. Ensure the chocolate has completely melted |

| FLAVOUR | METHOD OF WORK |
|---|---|
| Earl Grey tea ice cream | Add 25g per 4 portions of loose Earl Grey tea to the milk/cream during simmering |
| Lavender ice cream | Add 6g of fresh, washed lavender flowers or seeds per 4 portions to the sugar and grind together with a pestle and mortar |
| Lemon curd ice cream | Add 100g of lemon curd to the vanilla ice cream recipe. Replace the vanilla content with the grated zest of 1 lemon |
| Orange ice cream | Add the finely grated zest of 3 oranges per 4 portions to the simmering milk/cream |
| Praline ice cream | Add 50g per 4 portions of praline paste to the simmering milk/cream |
| Pistachio ice cream | Add 50g per 4 portions of pistachio paste to the simmering milk/cream |
| Saffron ice cream | Add a good pinch of saffron strands to the simmering milk/cream |

# Strawberry ice cream *Crème glacée aux fraises*

| INGREDIENTS | 4 PORTIONS | 10 PORTIONS |
|---|---|---|
| **Strawberry purée** | 375g | 750g |
| **Icing sugar** | 75g | 150g |
| **Double cream** (48% fat) | 275g | 550g |
| **Liquid glucose** | 25g | 50g |
| **Lemon juice** | ¼ lemon | ½ lemon |

## Method of work

1  Place the cream, icing sugar and liquid glucose into a heavy-bottomed saucepan and bring to the boil.

2  Meanwhile either wash, hull and purée the required amount of fresh strawberries or alternatively use a good-quality fruit purée. Add the lemon juice to the purée.

3  When the cream has boiled, cool for five minutes before combining with the strawberry purée. Pass through a chinois and pour into the ice cream machine and churn.

4  Place a sterilised container into the freezer for an hour before churning the crème and use this as the container into which to immediately decant the ice cream. This will help to prevent the ice cream from melting when removed from the machine.

5  Store the ice cream in an airtight container at −18°C or below.

 **CHEF'S TIP**

Always ensure that the fruit is perfectly ripe to obtain the best flavour and colour to the ice cream. The use of lemon juice in this recipe will enhance the fruit flavour and the acid present will help to maintain the colour. Strawberries contain high quantities of vitamin C when at the peak of their season.

Alternative flavours can be added to this recipe.

| FLAVOUR | METHOD OF WORK |
|---|---|
| Apricot ice cream | Replace the quantity of fruit purée with apricot purée. |
| Banana ice cream | Replace the quantity of fruit purée with a banana purée. Finish with 20ml of dark rum. |
| Mango ice cream | Replace the quantity of fruit purée with a mango purée. |
| Passion fruit ice cream | Replace the quantity of fruit purée with fresh passion fruit with the seeds removed. |
| Peach ice cream | Replace the quantity of fruit purée with a peach purée. Finish with 20ml of peach schnapps. |
| Raspberry ice cream | Replace the quantity of fruit purée with a raspberry purée. |

# Banana sorbet

| INGREDIENTS | 4 PORTIONS | 10 PORTIONS |
|---|---|---|
| Banana purée | 375g | 750g |
| Sorbet syrup (see chef's tip below left) | 150ml | 300ml |
| Fresh milk | 100ml | 200ml |
| Lemon juice | ¼ lemon | ½ lemon |

## Method of work

1 Place the sorbet syrup and fresh milk into a saucepan and bring to the boil.
2 Meanwhile peel and slice the ripest possible bananas, removing any bruises or discolouration, and purée in a food processor with the lemon juice.
3 When the milk and stock syrup has boiled, remove from the heat and stir in the banana purée. Cool for five minutes before blending once again in the food processor. Pass through a chinois and chill in a refrigerator.
4 Pour the mixture into the ice cream machine and churn to freeze. The sorbet should have a firm consistency.
5 Place a sterilised container into the freezer for an hour before churning the crème and use this as the container to immediately decant the sorbet into. This will help to prevent the sorbet from melting when removed from the machine.
6 Store the sorbet in an airtight container at −18°C or below.

Alternative flavours can be added to the above recipe as follows:

| FLAVOUR | METHOD OF WORK |
|---|---|
| Apricot sorbet | Replace the quantity of fruit purée with apricot purée. Replace the milk content with sorbet syrup. |
| Mango sorbet | Replace the quantity of fruit purée with a mango purée. Also replace the milk content with sorbet syrup. |

### CHEF'S TIP

The use of the right density of sorbet syrup is very important to help the sorbet freeze to the correct consistency. The recipe given here should be used for all further sorbet recipes.

750g granulated sugar
650ml water
70g glucose syrup

Bring all the ingredients to the boil in a saucepan and simmer for 3 minutes. Strain through a chinois and use only when completely cold. This syrup should keep in an airtight container in a refrigerator for up to 2 weeks.

| FLAVOUR | METHOD OF WORK |
|---|---|
| Melon sorbet | Replace the quantity of fruit purée with fresh melon flesh with the seeds removed. Replace the milk content with sorbet syrup. |
| Strawberry sorbet | Replace the quantity of fruit purée with a strawberry purée. Replace the milk content with sorbet syrup. |
| Raspberry sorbet | Replace the quantity of fruit purée with a raspberry purée. Replace the milk content with sorbet syrup. |

# Caramel mousse

| INGREDIENTS | 4 PORTIONS | 10 PORTIONS |
|---|---|---|
| Granulated sugar | 125g | 250g |
| Liquid glucose | 25g | 50g |
| Water | 50g | 100g |
| Double cream (48% fat) | 125g | 250g |
| Water | 50g | 100g |
| Egg yolks | 2 | 5 |
| Caster sugar | 25g | 50g |
| Gelatine leaves | 3 leaves | 6 leaves |
| Whipping cream (35% fat) | 300g | 630g |
| *Glaze* | | |
| Caster sugar | 80g | 175g |
| Liquid glucose | 45g | 90g |
| Clarified butter | 25g | 50g |
| Apricot jam | 125g | 250g |
| Gelatine leaves | 2 leaves | 4½ leaves |
| *Finishing and decoration* | | |
| Vanilla sponge sheet (p. 573) | 4 small discs | 10 small discs |
| Crème chantilly | 150g | 300g |
| White chocolate motif | 4 | 10 |

## Method of work

1 Place the granulated sugar and water into a heavy-bottomed pan and bring to the boil. Add the liquid glucose and boil to an amber, caramel colour.

2 Remove the pan from the heat and leave to settle for 2 minutes before adding the second amount of water and then the double cream very carefully. Place back on the heat and bring to the boil, stirring constantly to melt the caramel into the cream.

3 Blend together the egg yolks and the caster sugar, beat with a whisk until a pale colour has been achieved. Soften the gelatine leaves in cold water.

4   Add the boiled caramel cream to the egg yolks and mix well before returning to the pan and placing over a medium heat. Stirring constantly with a wooden spoon, cook the caramel cream until it begins to coat the back of the spoon.

5   Remove from the heat and add the softened gelatine. Continue stirring for a few more moments before passing the liquid through a sieve into a chilled bowl. Continue to cool down the liquid and then place into a refrigerator to half set.

6   Aerate the whipping cream to form soft peaks.

7   Set the disc of sponge in the base of individual moulds ensuring that the disc is at least 10mm smaller than the mould.

8   When the caramel cream is half set, carefully fold in the whipped cream and then transfer the mousse into each mould. Place in a refrigerator to set.

9   To make the glaze, soften the gelatine leaves in cold water and place the sugar and the glucose together in a heavy-bottomed saucepan. Slowly heat the glucose and sugar over a medium heat to create a dry caramel. When the correct amber-caramel colour has been achieved, add the melted clarified butter and apricot jam. Mix these ingredients together well and finally add the gelatine leaves. Pass through a chinois into a bowl to cool down.

10   When the glaze has cooled and the mousse is set, spread a little of the caramel glaze on top of each mousse using a small palette knife. Sometimes it is easier to warm the mousse ring carefully to release the mousse from the mould and push the mould up by 2mm and hold it in place with a plastic scraper before then applying the glaze. Using this method will give a level finish to the top of the mousse.

11   Place into a refrigerator to set for 1 hour.

12   To serve, remove the mould and place a small quenelle of crème chantilly on top with the chocolate motif for decoration. An apricot coulis could accompany this dessert.

## Step-by-step: Preparing a caramel mousse base

**STEP 1** Add the liquid glucose to the boiling sugar and cook to an amber caramel colour

**STEP 2** Remove the pan from the heat before adding the second amount of water, and then the double cream, very carefully

**STEP 3** Soften the gelatine leaves in cold water

### CHEF'S TIP

Whipped cream is a delicate and unstable foam. When aerating whipping cream ensure that the bowl being used is chilled and so is the cream. This will help to ensure aeration. If the cream becomes over-whipped when combining the cream with the caramel cream preparation the mousse will split and the texture will be heavy and grainy.

# Chocolate mousse

Chocolate shavings (see p. 546)

| INGREDIENTS | 4 PORTIONS | 10 PORTIONS |
|---|---|---|
| Dark chocolate (60% minimum cocoa) | 120g | 260g |
| Unsalted butter | 20g | 50g |
| Egg yolks | 4 | 10 |
| Egg whites | 4 | 10 |
| Caster sugar | 75g | 170g |
| To decorate | | |
| Chocolate motif | 4 | 10 |
| Chocolate shavings (see p. 546) | 50g | 75g |
| Crème chantilly (optional) | 150g | 400g |
| Icing sugar for dusting | 50g | 75g |

## CHEF'S TIP

There are many additions that can be made to enhance this basic recipe.

- Chocolate and orange – add finely grated zest of 1 orange to the chocolate and 25ml of Grand Marnier to the egg yolks for 4 portions.
- Chocolate and brandy – add 25ml brandy to the egg yolks for 4 portions.
- Chocolate and whisky – add 25ml whisky to the egg yolks for 4 portions.
- Chocolate and praline – add 25g praline paste to the melted chocolate for 4 portions.

## Method of work

1. Chop the chocolate up into small pieces and place into a glass bowl with the unsalted butter. Cover the bowl tightly with plastic film and melt in a bain marie of hot water or use a microwave oven and melt in ten second bursts.

2. Aerate the egg whites with one-quarter of the caster sugar to soft peaks.

3. Beat the egg yolks with the three-quarters of the caster sugar until they are pale in colour. Combine the melted chocolate to the egg yolks and mix well.

4. Lightly fold in the whipped egg whites to the chocolate mixture and place into a piping bag with a plain tube.

5. Pipe the chocolate mousse into a cappuccino cup or alternatively into a serving glass and refrigerate until required.

6. To serve, arrange some chocolate shavings on top of each mousse, place the chocolate motif and dust with a little icing sugar for effect. Crème chantilly can also be used for decoration.

# Summer fruit pudding

| INGREDIENTS | 4 PORTIONS | 10 PORTIONS |
|---|---|---|
| Strawberries | 100g | 250g |
| Raspberries | 100g | 250g |
| Redcurrants | 100g | 250g |
| Blackcurrants | 50g | 150g |
| Blackberries | 100g | 250g |
| Caster sugar | 150g | 350g |
| Sliced white bread | 240g | 600g |
| *To decorate* | | |
| Fresh mint | 4 pluches | 10 pluches |
| Crème chantilly | 150g | 400g |
| Icing sugar for dusting | 50g | 75g |

## Method of work

1 Ensure all the fruits are ripe and carefully wash and hull where necessary.

2 Place all the fruits and sugar together into a large saucepan and slowly stew over a medium heat. Continue cooking whilst retaining the shape of the fruit. Overcooking will result in the fruit turning into a purée.

3 Remove from the heat and leave to cool down.

4 Using individual pudding moulds cut the crusts of the bread and trim slices to fit around the sides of the moulds and discs for the top and bottom. Line the bottom of the mould by dipping one side of the bread disc into the fruit stew and placing it downside in the bottom of the mould.

5 Repeat this process to line the sides of the mould before filling the mould with the cooked fruit. Cover with one further disc of bread and press down firmly.

6 Place a sheet of plastic film over the top of the moulded pudding and place a flat baking sheet on top, weighed down to compress the pudding to help set it. Place in a refrigerator for a minimum of 12 hours to set and for the bread to soak the juices of the fruit and change colour.

7 De-mould the summer pudding and place onto a dessert plate accompanied by a quenelle of crème chantilly and fresh mint.

### CHEF'S TIP

If there is some stewed fruit remaining after making the summer puddings, it can be puréed and mixed with a little stock syrup to create an accompanying sauce to serve alongside the pudding.

# Strawberry bavarois *Bavarois aux fraises*

| INGREDIENTS | 4 PORTIONS | 10 PORTIONS |
|---|---|---|
| Fresh strawberries | 200g | 550g |
| Egg yolks | 2 | 5 |
| Gelatine leaves | 3 leaves | 6 leaves |
| Fresh full fat milk | 180ml | 400ml |
| Caster sugar | 50g | 120g |
| Whipping cream (35%) | 250ml | 600ml |
| *To decorate* | | |
| Vanilla sponge discs | 4 | 10 |
| Fresh mint | 4 pluches | 10 pluches |
| Fresh strawberries | 2 | 5 |
| Strawberry coulis | 200ml | 600ml |
| Crème chantilly | 150g | 400g |
| Icing sugar for dusting | 50g | 75g |

## Method of work

1 Soak the leaf gelatine in cold water.

2 Beat the egg yolks and caster sugar until pale in colour.

3 Meanwhile, bring the milk to the boil in a saucepan. Pour onto the egg yolk mixture and combine.

4 Pour back into the saucepan and place on a medium heat. Stirring constantly with a spoon, cook out the crème until the sauce coats the back of the spoon. Remove from the heat, add the softened gelatine and dissolve in the crème. Pass through a fine sieve into a chilled bowl.

5 Wash, hull and place the strawberries into a food processor and blend into a purée. Add this purée to the base preparation and place into a refrigerator to chill and half set.

6 Aerate the whipping cream and carefully fold into the base preparation.

7 Place the discs of vanilla sponge in the bottom of each individual mould. Equally divide the Bavarois preparation between the moulds and set in a refrigerator for 1 hour.

8 To serve, de-mould the strawberry bavarois and place onto a dessert plate accompanied by a quenelle of crème chantilly, half a strawberry and fresh mint dusted with icing sugar. Serve with the strawberry coulis.

*Add this purée to the base preparation and place into a refrigerator to chill and half set*

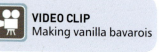

### CHEF'S TIP

When cooking out the egg yolks and milk it is important not to let this mixture boil. Overheating will allow the egg protein to scramble.

**VIDEO CLIP**
Making vanilla bavarois

# Vanilla meringue nests with ice cream  *Vacherin glacé*

| INGREDIENTS | 4 PORTIONS | 10 PORTIONS |
|---|---|---|
| Egg whites | 6 | 12 |
| Caster sugar | 230g | 460g |
| Vanilla extract or pods | 1 pod | 2 pods |
| *To decorate* | | |
| Preserved vanilla sticks (see p. 546) | 8 sticks | 20 sticks |
| Vanilla ice cream (see p. 553) | 4 scoops | 10 scoops |
| Strawberry coulis | 150ml | 400ml |
| Mango coulis | 100ml | 200ml |
| Fresh mint | 4 pluches | 10 pluches |
| Icing sugar for dusting | 50g | 100g |

### CHEF'S TIP

To test if the meringue is at the correct consistency to pipe, place a fingertip into the meringue and pull it out. If the meringue creates a stiff, long, spiked 'fingernail' then it is ready to be piped.

### HEALTH & SAFETY

Salmonella is a bacteria most commonly associated with eggs. Precautions should be taken when using fresh eggs such as ensuring that the shell is clean. Salmonella is destroyed at 71°C but egg whites coagulate at between 61–65°C. The addition of other ingredients to meringue such as sugar forces the temperature for coagulation higher so that the meringue will coagulate at a similar temperature to destroying bacteria.

## Method of work

1  Preheat the oven to 120°C.

2  Place the egg whites into a large bowl and using a balloon whisk create a foam that begins to soft peak. Now begin to gradually add the sugar and the vanilla (if using vanilla pods scrape the seeds out and mix with the sugar first).

3  Continue whisking until egg whites have all the sugar incorporated and they show signs of stiffening and holding their own peaks. Other points to look for are that the meringue should be glossy and smooth.

4  Placing the meringue into a piping bag with a star tube, pipe a small individual disc approximately 60mm in diameter onto a silicone baking mat on a double baking sheet. On the edges of the disc pipe a circle to create a collar. Pipe one more circle on the crown to raise the height of the collar without it collapsing. If desired sprinkle with a few poppy seeds.

5  With any remaining meringue, transfer to another piping bag with a small plain tube and pipe straight tubes up to 16cm long onto a baking sheet lined with silicone paper. Sprinkle the ends with poppy seeds.

6  Place the baking sheets into the oven and then turn off. Leave the oven door slightly open and let the meringue shells dry for at least 8 hours and the meringue straws for about 2 hours.

7  When dried out, leave to cool on a wire rack for a further hour before serving. The centre of the meringue should not be soft and uncooked.

8  To serve, place the meringue nest in the centre of the plate and position the ice cream of your choice inside it. Decorate with the meringue straws, preserved vanilla sticks and fresh mint pluches. Finish with the two fruit coulis presented on the plate.

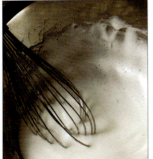

*1. Place the egg whites into a large bowl and using a balloon whisk create a foam that begins to soft peak*

*2. Gradually add the sugar and the vanilla*

*3. Continue whisking until the egg whites have all of the sugar incorporated and show signs of stiffening and holding their own peaks*

# Floating islands with passion fruit

*Make 3 quenelles of meringue per portion and place into the simmering milk to poach for two minutes*

| INGREDIENTS | 4 PORTIONS | 10 PORTIONS |
|---|---|---|
| Egg whites | 6 | 12 |
| Caster sugar | 230g | 460g |
| Vanilla Extract | | |
| *Poaching the meringue* | | |
| Fresh full fat milk | 1 litre | 2 litres |
| Vanilla pod | 1 pod | 2 pods |
| *Vanilla cream* | | |
| Poaching milk | As used | As used |
| Egg yolks | 5 | 10 |
| Caster sugar | 75g | 150g |
| *Passion fruit dressing* | | |
| Fresh passion fruit | 8 passion fruit | 20 passion fruit |
| Stock syrup (see p. 542) | 75ml | 140ml |
| To decorate | | |
| Caramel and almond swirls (see p. 548) | 4 small discs | 10 small discs |

## Method of work

1 Split the vanilla pods lengthways and place into a large shallow pan with the fresh milk. Bring to the boil and reduce to a simmering point.

2 Using an electric mixing machine with a whisk attachment beat the egg whites to soft peaks before slowly raining in the caster sugar and adding the vanilla extract. Beat until a firm stiff meringue has been achieved.

3 Make 3 quenelles of meringue per portion and place into the simmering milk to poach for two minutes. Turn the quenelles over and poach for a further two minutes.

4 Removed with a slotted spoon and leave to drain on a small tray with kitchen paper. Continue to poach the meringue until you have the required set portions.

5 Cool the quenelles and refrigerate until service.

6 Pass the milk through a chinois. At this point the milk should have been reduced by half and there should be approximately 500ml remaining.

7 Whisk the egg yolks with the caster sugar to begin preparing the vanilla sauce. Add the remaining poaching milk and continuously stir over a medium heat until it begins to coat the back of a spoon.

8 Remove from the heat and continue stirring to dissipate the residual heat. Cool down before placing into the refrigerator to chill.

9 To make the passion fruit dressing, remove the flesh from inside the passion fruit and mix together with the stock syrup. Discard the passion fruit shells and reserve the dressing for service.

10 To serve, place some of the vanilla cream into dessert bowls and position the poached meringues to float on top. Drizzle the passion fruit dressing over the meringues and finish with a caramel and almond swirl.

**CHEF'S TIP**

When poaching the meringue it is important not to let the milk boil. The excessive heat will cause the meringue to 'soufflé' and eventually when cooling down it will drop and begin to weep excess moisture.

**CHEF'S TIP**

The poached meringue should always be turned over and should be firm to the touch when testing for cooking. This dessert can also be served warm during the winter months with hot caramel spooned over the meringue just before service.

# Saint Clement's cheesecake

*Mix in the melted gelatine and then the softly whipped cream*

| INGREDIENTS | 1 × 23CM RING | 2 × 23CM RINGS |
|---|---|---|
| Egg whites | 125g | 250g |
| Caster sugar | 125g | 250g |
| Gelatine leaves | 4 leaves | 9 leaves |
| Cream cheese | 125g | 250g |
| Cointreau | 30g | 60g |
| Whipping cream | 30g | 60g |
| Lemon zest and juice | 1 lemon | 2 lemons |
| Orange zest and juice | 1 orange | 2 oranges |
| Whipped cream in soft peaks | 360ml | 750ml |
| Mandarin oranges | 3 | 6 |
| *Finished dessert* | | |
| Vanilla sponge disc (20cm in diameter) | 1 | 2 |
| White chocolate shavings | 50g | 75g |
| Crème chantilly (optional) | 150g | 400g |
| Icing sugar for dusting | 50g | 75g |

## Method of work

1 Place a thin disc of vanilla sponge in the bottom of a torten ring.
2 Segment the mandarin oranges and position on top of the sponge disc.
3 Soften the gelatine leaves in cold water.
4 Aerate the egg whites with one-quarter of the caster sugar to soft peaks. Gradually fold in the remaining caster sugar and set aside.
5 Place half the Cointreau in a pan with the softened gelatine and warm over a medium heat to melt.
6 Combine the cream cheese, whipping cream and the remaining Cointreau in a bowl before slowly mixing in the finely grated zests and juice of the lemon and orange.
7 Mix in the melted gelatine and then the softly whipped cream.
8 Lightly fold in the meringue mixture to the cheese preparation and carefully pour the mixture into the prepared torten ring.
9 Place in the refrigerator to set for approximately 1 hour.
10 To serve, remove from the torten ring by carefully warming the outside of the ring with a clean cloth soaked in hot water or using a gas torch. Spread some crème chantilly on top of the cheesecake, arrange some chocolate shavings on top and dust with a little icing sugar for effect.

**CHEF'S TIP**

Always wash the gelatine sheets carefully in clean water after soaking to soften them, to eliminate any unsavoury taste. Then squeeze out the excess water, melt and use as directed in the recipe.

**CHEF'S TIP**

Replace the sponge base with a recipe of 50 per cent wholemeal biscuit and 50 per cent lightly grilled oats mixed with some melted butter and pack in the bottom of the mould to use as a replacement base. This will increase the fibre content of the dessert.

## Assessment of knowledge and understanding

You have now learned about the use of different desserts and how to produce a variety of products utilising an assortment of commodities and preparation techniques.

To test your level of knowledge and understanding, answer the following short questions. These will help to prepare you for your summative (final) assessment.

1  State two processes in the pastry kitchen which are most likely to kill food poisoning bacteria.

i) _____

ii) _____

2  Explain the reasons for sterilising the ice cream machine before and after use.

_____

_____

3  Describe how hot desserts can be modified to take account of healthy eating trends.

_____

_____

4  Name three desserts that can be produced from eggs, milk, cream and sugar.

i) _____   ii) _____

iii) _____

5  State the reason that diary products are pasteurised when making an ice cream.

_____

_____

## Research Task

Complete the following chart describing how to use, clean and maintain the following items of equipment and the safety considerations associated with them.

|  | CLEANING | STERILISING | STORING | SAFETY PROCEDURES |
|---|---|---|---|---|
| Silicone baking mats |  |  |  |  |
| Nylon piping bags |  |  |  |  |
| Ice cream machine |  |  |  |  |

# CHEF'S PROFILE

**Name: MATT OWENS**

**Position:** Executive Pastry Chef at Circadia producing and developing desserts for the All Leisure Division which services such events as "Ryder Cup Grand National, Paris Air Show" and dinners at National History Musieum, Tower London, Albert Hall all on corporate level or above.

### When did you realise that you wanted to pursue a career in the catering and hospitality industry?

My father was a window cleaner for London restaurants. Watching the chefs cooking sparked the drive. I joined cubs and scouts and won competition cooking, so from the age of around 9 years old I was keen to cook.

**Training:** My college training was the 3 year professional chefs' diploma at Westminster College, Vincent Square. I then returned to take 706/3 Advanced Pastry. I started working in local restaurants in the evenings and during the day I went to college.

**Experience:** My first hotel was the Sheraton Heathrow from there I have worked at Selsdon Park Hotel in Surrey, Sopwell House Hotel in St Albans, Millennium Gloucester Hotel in London, Four Seasons Hotel in Park Lane, Waldorf Hotel in Park Lane to now for Compass All Leisure at Circadia.

### What do you find rewarding about your job?

As schools and college liaison officer for The Craft Guild of Chefs I get the opportunity to meet the future chefs early in their career. It is always a pleasure to meet them in the industry after seeing them at college and share their success with them.

### What do you find the most challenging about the job?

The role I have now is very demanding as it involves always meeting the customers' needs, which can be very varied. It involves constant research and product awareness to keep up with the market trends.

### What advice would you give to students just beginning their career?

Never stop wanting to learn. Attend as many events as you can and try to be involved with organisations. Look around shops, talk to people, make the effort to find out about techniques and products.

### Who is your mentor or main inspiration?

I have always thought that Raymond Blanc is someone to look up to. He has a massive passion for excellence and attention to detail. Something we could all concentrate a little more on at times.

**Secrets of a successful chef:** The more you put in to the industry the more you will achieve and be recognised for. You must have passion to succeed and be successful.

### Can you give one essential kitchen tip or technique that you use as a chef?

Always listen and ask if not sure. Stay keen and take pride in what you do.

# Modern trifle

## INGREDIENTS

| Dark chocolate | 90g |
|---|---|
| White chocolate | 90g |
| *For collars and garnish* | |
| Sponge disks to fit choc moulds lightly soaked with kirsch, sandwich with deseeded raspberry jam | 8 |
| Strawberries hulled and quartered | 60g |
| Raspberries | 35g |
| Blackberries | 30g |
| *Jelly* | |
| Champagne | 200ml |
| Water | 200ml |
| Sugar | 120g |
| Leaves soaked gelatine | 3 |
| *Rhubarb Ice Cream* | |
| Rhubarb purée | 500g |
| Caster sugar | 160g |
| Water | 250ml |
| Whipping cream | 500ml |
| *Syllabub* | |
| Sweet sherry | 150ml |
| Caster sugar | 50g |
| Zest and juice from lemons | 2 |
| Tablespoon brandy | 3 |
| Double cream | 300ml |
| Vanilla pod | ½ |
| *Tuille Biscuit* | |
| Icing sugar | 15g |
| Egg white | 15g |
| Melted butter | 15g |
| Soft flour | 15g |
| *Bubble Sugar* | |
| Granulated sugar | 100g |
| Liquid glucose | 25g |
| Lemon juice | 5ml |
| *Macaroon* | |
| Icing sugar | 55g |
| Ground almond | 30g |
| Egg white | 1 |
| Flavouring, i.e. raspberry or vanilla | optional |

## Method of work

1 Temper the chocolate
2 Spread on acetate sheets and set in mousse collar

### Jelly

1 Boil champagne water sugar
2 Add soaked gelatine
3 Allow to cool

### Rhubarb ice cream

1 Simmer all ingredients
2 Pour into machine and churn

### Syllabub

1 Boil sherry, allow to cool
2 Add zest and juice from the lemon stand for 4 hours
3 Strain and then add half whipped cream
4 Add sugar and vanilla whip to piping consistency

### Tuille biscuit

1 Blend all ingredients till smooth
2 Chill one hour
3 Pipe mixture in spiral – bake 190ºC for 6–8 minutes
4 Place over cup allow to cool

### Bubble sugar

1 Boil to 150ºC pour on parchment paper and lift carefully
2 Allow to cool

### Macaroon

1 Whisk whites and sugar
2 Fold in almonds
3 Pipe allow to stand for 1 hour
4 Bake 170ºC–180ºC  for 8–10 minutes

### Assembly

1 Place sandwich sponge in bottom of chocolate coilers.
2 Divide berries between 4 moulds, pour on jelly to cover.
3 Set in fridge
4 Place macaroon on jelly (you may soak with sherry etc)
5 Pipe syllabub to fill moulds
6 Ball ice cream garnish as picture

# Cakes, biscuits and sponges

## INTRODUCTION

Cakes are synonymous with many celebrations across the world. Birthdays, anniversaries, engagements, weddings and religious festivals are just some examples. The cake varieties are endless and can be in the form of light, aerated sponges to heavy and rich confections. These cakes and sponges can be prepared in a variety of ways, however the actual basic mixing methods are few and once mastered the chef has the versatility to create limitless types of cakes and sponges.

This chapter discusses the different types of cakes, biscuits and sponges. It is important to be aware of the categorisation of these confections for the purpose of production.

**VIDEO CLIP**
A cake decorating competition in a salon culinaire

| CAKE | SPONGE | BISCUIT |
|------|--------|---------|
| Cup cakes | Genoese | Viennese biscuits |
| Scones | Swiss roll | Cookies |
| Wedding cakes | Chocolate | Macaroons |
| Dundee | Victoria | Langue du chat |
| Madeira | Plain sponge | Biscuit à la cuillere |
| Financiers | Othellos | |
| Madeleines | | |

## THE ROLE OF AFTERNOON TEA CAKES AND PASTRIES

Afternoon tea or high tea differs from country to country and from establishment to establishment. In this country, however, it is generally accepted that afternoon tea service commences at 4.00 p.m. and will usually offer a range of different types of teas (Darjeeling and Assam for instance), a good selection of sandwiches and assorted small cakes and pastries. In England, and particularly Devon and Cornwall, the highlight of afternoon tea is the service of warm scones, fruit preserves and clotted cream. This traditional regional delight will now be found in one form or another on most afternoon tea menus.

Initially afternoon tea was introduced by the upper classes as a way of filling in the gap between luncheon and dinner. Now, however, it is a chance for most high-class establishments to show the skills of their chefs and most importantly the skills of the pastry chef. The idea is to produce small, light and well-presented cakes and pastries that will create a positive lasting memory on the palette of the customer.

It is imperative that each pastry or cake is not too complicated in production and that there should be a good variety of flavours and textures within the menu. Also, of course, freshness, appearance and attention to detail (e.g. pâte sucrée should be light, crisp and thin) should be closely monitored.

*Afternoon tea at the Ritz Hotel*

# CAKE PREPARATION METHODS

To help determine the method of preparation required for each recipe, cakes and sponges can fall broadly into two separate categories – cakes high in fat and cakes low in fat.

Cakes that have a high quantity of fat rely on fats to keep the gluten development minimal in order to produce a tender product. These types of cakes have a longer shelf life because of the high fat content, which slows down the staling process. They also tend to be richer and have higher moisture content. The basic preparation methods employed are shown in the table.

| | SUGAR BATTER METHOD (SOMETIMES KNOWN AS CREAMING) | FLOUR BATTER METHOD (SOMETIMES KNOWN AS THE TWO-STAGE METHOD) | ONE STAGE METHOD |
|---|---|---|---|
| 1 | Cream together the fat and sugar until light and fluffy. | Whisk the sugar and egg content to form an aeration. | Blend all the dry ingredients together. |
| 2 | Carefully add the egg content, one at a time. | Cream the fat with an equal proportion of flour. | Combine all liquid ingredients together. |
| 3 | Add the flour and other dry ingredients, alternating with wet ingredients if there are any to add. | Carefully combine the aerated egg into the creamed fat in four stages. | Carefully incorporate the wet ingredients to the dry ingredients. |
| 4 | Combine any fruits, nuts or other ingredients. Ensure even distribution of all ingredients. | Combine the remaining flour, other dry ingredients and any fruits or nuts. | Mix any other ingredients such as fruit to the batter. |

Cakes that are low in fat require alternative ingredients to help tenderise the texture. These types of cake tend to have a high sugar content to assist this process. Usually the method employed is to aerate the egg content with the sugar to produce light, airy foams. This will produce a cake/sponge that is drier but flexible and does not crumble as easily as those cakes high in fat. These cakes are used to produce gâteaux and torten and can be used in desserts such as Charlottes. The basic preparation methods employed are usually:

| | GENOESE METHOD (SOMETIMES KNOWN AS A WHOLE EGG FOAM) | SEPARATED EGG METHOD | AERATED EGG WHITE METHOD |
|---|---|---|---|
| 1 | Whole eggs and warmed sugar are whisked to a foam. | Egg yolks and a percentage of the sugar are beaten. | Dry ingredients with a percentage of the sugar are combined. |
| 2 | Sieved dry ingredients are carefully folded in. | Egg whites and the remaining sugar are aerated. | Egg yolks and other liquids and flavours are added. |
| 3 | Melted butter can be added at the end. | Egg whites are folded into the yolk mixture alternately with the dry ingredients. | Egg whites are aerated with remaining sugar and folded into the batter. |

# SPONGES

Air becomes incorporated in the form of bubbles when eggs are beaten or whisked. The protein albumen, which is present in the white of an egg, has the ability to trap air. In sponge making the eggs are whisked with the sugar until light and thick, and the flour is then folded in carefully which helps to strengthen the structure of the albumen.

To aid this process all utensils and mixing bowls should be perfectly clean and free from any fat. The presence of fat will break down the initial structure of albumen trying to 'envelope' the air during mechanical aeration. In order to achieve the maximum aeration of the eggs, best results are achieved by whisking the eggs and sugar over a bain marie of hot water. The temperature should be around 32°C and not too hot as this would cook the eggs. Alternatively the sugar can be placed onto a baking sheet and warmed in an oven prior to whisking with the eggs.

Whisk until the mixture becomes thick and light. It should be thick enough to leave the mark of the whisk for a few seconds after it has been removed, otherwise known as the 'ribbon stage'.

For best results always bake at between 182–204°C.

# BAKING

The aim when baking cakes and sponges is to cook them as quickly as possible without imparting too much colour to the crust. Various factors will affect the baking of cakes and adjustments will need to be made to the overall baking temperature to compensate for this.

## Richness of the Recipe

The higher content of sugar within a recipe means that over-cooking and too high a temperature will caramelise the colour of the cake or sponge quickly before it is thoroughly baked. The oven temperature must be cool to medium to prevent this occurrence.

## Size of the Cake/Sponge

The smaller the size of the cake or sponge to be baked the quicker it will cook. Larger cakes will require a lower temperature because they will remain in the oven for a longer period of time.

## Shape of the Cake/Sponge

An appreciation of the shape of the cake or sponge to be baked is important. This is because a large quantity of Genoese sponge can be baked rapidly in large, thin sheets as opposed to 20cm cake rings. This is because of the depth of the mixture to be baked. The bigger depth should have a cooler oven temperature to facilitate the correct cooking of the item.

## Humidity

The oven chamber should create a humid environment in order to achieve a level top to a cake and to help with consistent and thorough baking. Sometimes a pan of boiled water added to the oven chamber will help create a humid atmosphere.

## Addition of Other Ingredients

Certain additions such as honey, glucose or inverted sugars can increase the overall colour of the finished cake because these are sugar-based ingredients. The baking temperature therefore needs to be lowered. A large amount of preserved or dried fruit will increase the heaviness of a cake and the temperature of the oven needs to be reduced, so too will decorative items such as sugar and almonds to be sprinkled on the top of a cake.

---

**CHEF'S TIP**

How to tell when a cake is baked? There are three basic ways of revealing when a cake is correctly cooked.

- The cake contracts from the side of the baking tin.
- The cake springs back when it is gently pressed with a finger.
- A skewer or small knife is inserted gently into the centre of the cake and is removed to reveal an implement free of crumbs and clean of the mixture.

# BASIC FAULTS IN CAKE PRODUCTION

*Cake sinking in the middle:*

- ■ Undercooked.

- ■ Knocked heavily prior to being cooked in the oven.

- ■ Too much liquid added to the recipe.

- ■ Too much baking powder used.

- ■ Too much sugar used (coupled with a dark crust colour).

*Fruit sinking in cakes:*

- ■ Too much sugar used.

- ■ Fruit was too large and still wet.

- ■ Baking temperature too low.

- ■ Too much baking powder used.

- ■ Cake mixture is too light to hold the fruit.

*Small volume and heavy texture of finished cake:*

- ■ Insufficient aeration caused by either a lack of baking powder or lack of aeration in the egg content.

- ■ Lack of sugar used in the recipe.

*Peaked top to the cake:*

- ■ Over-mixed cake mixture.

- ■ Flour used was too strong.

- ■ Oven is too hot and dry.

Please note that some cake recipes require a peaked top as part of their overall presentation: it is not necessarily a fault.

# STORAGE CONCERNS FOR CAKES, SPONGES AND BISCUITS

Maintaining the quality of cakes, sponges and biscuits during storage is a significant issue. Staling and moisture absorption are aspects that need to be considered. Staling refers to a loss of moisture from baked products such as cakes, biscuits, sponges and yeast goods which results in a dry, hard and firmer-textured product. Sometimes this is associated with lack of flavour or even rancid taste.

Moisture absorption occurs when moisture from the atmosphere is absorbed into the baked product. The outside crust will become soft in certain baked products such as heavy cakes and yeast goods. Below are a number of steps that need to be taken to help ensure the correct storage procedures are maintained to guarantee a longer shelf life of baked products such as cakes, sponges and biscuits.

■ Dry commodities need to be stored in clean, sealed plastic containers on clean shelving in a separate storage room. The room needs to be maintained at a constant cool temperature and should have a dry atmosphere.

■ Stock rotation should be employed so that all ingredients are used up and then replenished by a new batch of ingredients. The empty container should be cleaned before replenishing.

■ It is not recommended to store baked items for long periods of time in a refrigerator because of starch breakdown and eventual loss of colour and flavour.

■ To store baked products for short periods in a refrigerator it is essential that they are covered in plastic film or placed into airtight plastic containers. Items that contain large amounts of sugar will attract moisture which may have an adverse effect on flavour and texture.

■ Storing baked products in a freezer is a method that works exceptionally well. The baked product should be completely cooled before wrapping it airtight in plastic wrapping and then in aluminium foil. Place this into a plastic bag, sucking out as much air from the packaging as possible. Label and date the item before freezing. Good practice is to blast freeze any item for 30 minutes before placing into a holding freezer. This process helps to maintain moisture content in the product and helps to eliminate potential freezer burn.

# SPECIALIST BAKING EQUIPMENT

| PICTURE | DESCRIPTION |
|---|---|
|  | An electric mixer is an invaluable piece of equipment used in the bakery or pastry kitchens. Most mixers are planetary mixers and can be either tabletop or the larger floor-standing versions. The one feature that all these mixers have is that the mixing bowl remains fixed in one position whilst the mixing tool fits into an attachment arm that rotates 360° to reach all the areas inside the mixing bowl. Attachments can be whisks, beaters and dough hooks with different speeds able to be implemented to mix diverse preparations. |
| | Stainless steel cake rings have no top or bottom. They come in various sizes and can be used to bake in or to mould up layers of sponge bases with fillings that need to set into a specific shape. Some of these rings are expandable to create differing size requirements. |
| | Muffin tins and individual cake tins come in varying sizes according to their traditional shape. The tins require careful cleaning and drying without scratching the moulded impressions. |
| | Silicone baking moulds with non-stick, flexible surfaces have revolutionised baking for the chef. They withstand very hot temperatures and are moulded into separate shapes. They require no greasing or flouring and only need to be wiped clean with a damp cloth. |
|  | A springform baking tin is a round tin with a removable base. It usually has high sides for baking all types of sponges and cakes and the sides of the tin can be detached for ease of removing baked products. |

# RECIPES

## Genoese sponge *Génoise*

| INGREDIENTS | 1 × 20CM DEEP-SIDED TIN | 2 × 20CM DEEP-SIDED TINS |
|---|---|---|
| Medium whole eggs | 4 | 8 |
| Warmed caster sugar | 120g | 240g |
| Sieved soft flour | 120g | 240g |
| Melted butter | 25g | 50g |
| Vanilla extract (optional) | | |

**VIDEO CLIP**
Making a Genoese sponge

**CHEF'S TIP**

Caster sugar is standard for Genoese. It helps to warm the sugar through, either in the oven or in the microwave when using small quantities. About 40°C is an adequate temperature. Too much sugar added to the mixture will result in a tougher texture and darker sponge colour.

## Method of work

1 Preheat the oven to 180°C.

2 Whisk the sugar and eggs together, first to dissolve the sugar and then to form a stiff, light sabayon.

3 After whisking the foam should be at the classic 'ribbon' stage. Rain the flour into the egg/sugar foam and incorporate the flour by hand.

4 When the flour is almost completely folded in, pour in the butter (this must not be hot). Scoop the Genoese mixture into the prepared tins (greased with butter and floured or lined with silicone paper) to about three-quarters full.

5 Place in the oven and bake for about 30 minutes. The time may vary by a few minutes either way according to the quantity, the tin thickness and the oven.

6 There are two tests to check whether the sponge is baked. First, press the surface in the centre and it should spring back. Second, the sponge should start to shrink from the edges.

7 Turn out onto either a cooling wire rack or silicone paper sprinkled with a little semolina.

*Rain the flour into the egg/sugar foam*

*Incorporate the flour by hand*

*When the flour is almost completely folded in, pour in the butter*

# Sponge fingers (separated egg sponge method)

*Biscuit à la cuillère*

| INGREDIENTS | 400G | 800G |
|---|---|---|
| Fresh whole eggs | 4 | 8 |
| Caster sugar | 110g | 220g |
| Sieved soft flour | 100g | 200g |
| Vanilla extract | | |
| Icing sugar | 50g | 100g |

## Method of work

1 Preheat the oven to 220°C.

2 Carefully separate the egg yolks from the whites and place into separate mixing bowls.

3 Beat the egg yolks with two-thirds of the caster sugar to a soft ribbon consistency.

4 Aerate the egg whites until soft peaks have been developed adding the remaining sugar and continuing to beat until the egg whites have held the sugar and the peaks have become firmer.

5 Fold one-third of the egg whites into the egg yolks using a spatula.

6 **Fold in** the remaining egg whites and carefully fold them into the mixture.

7 Before the egg whites and yolks have been completely combined, rain the flour into the egg/sugar foam and incorporate the flour until the mixture has become smooth.

8 Using a piping bag with a 15mm plain tube, pipe the mixture as quickly as possible onto a baking sheet lined with silicone paper or a silicone baking mat. Pipe 10cm long fingers for each biscuit.

9 Lightly dust them with icing sugar, leave to rest for 3 minutes and then dust with icing sugar again.

10 Place in the oven and bake for about 8 minutes. The time may vary by 2 minutes either way according to the quantity and the oven.

11 Lift the biscuits off the baking sheet onto a cooling wire rack.

*Using a piping bag with a 15mm plain tube, pipe the mixture onto a baking sheet lined with silicone paper or a silicone baking mat as quickly as possible*

### CHEF'S TIP

Many chefs turn out the baked sponge onto silicone paper sprinkled with sugar. This increases the overall sweetness of the sponge as the sugar clings to it when cooling down. Using semolina is better because it has no sweetness or flavour value and will easily brush off the cooled sponge.

# Chocolate Genoese *Génoise au chocolat*

| INGREDIENTS | 1 × 20CM DEEP-SIDED TIN | 2 × 20CM DEEP-SIDED TINS |
|---|---|---|
| Medium whole eggs | 4 | 8 |
| Warmed caster sugar | 120g | 240g |
| Sieved soft flour | 85g | 165g |
| Cocoa powder | 35g | 75g |
| Melted butter | 25g | 50g |

## CHEF'S TIP

This recipe can also be used as a basis for various gâteaux and desserts. Simply spread the mixture onto prepared baking sheets and bake for 6 minutes and cool in the same way as for Genoese. Cut out into required shapes as appropriate. Wrap individually in plastic film and store in a refrigerator for a day prior to use.

## Method of work

1 Preheat the oven to 180°C.

2 Whisk the sugar and eggs together, first to dissolve the sugar and then to form a stiff, creamy sabayon.

3 After whisking the foam should be at the classic 'ribbon' stage.

4 Sieve the cocoa powder and flour together and carefully rain into the egg/sugar foam and incorporate the flour/cocoa by hand.

5 When the flour/cocoa is almost completely folded in, pour in the butter (this must not be hot). Scoop the Genoese mixture into the prepared tins (greased with butter and floured or lined with silicone paper) to about three-quarters full.

6 Place in the oven and bake for about 30 minutes. The time may vary by five minutes either way according to the quantity, the tin thickness and the oven.

7 There are two tests to check whether the sponge is baked. First, press the surface in the centre and it should spring back. Second, the sponge should start to shrink from the edges.

8 Turn out onto either a cooling wire rack or silicone paper sprinkled with a little semolina.

*To check whether the sponge is baked, first, press the surface in the centre and it should spring back*

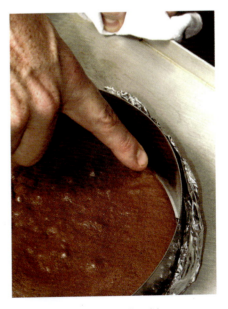

*Secondly, the sponge should start to shrink from the edges of the tin when it is cooked*

# Swiss roll *Biscuit roulade*

| INGREDIENTS | 400G | 800G |
|---|---|---|
| Fresh whole eggs | 4 | 8 |
| Caster sugar | 110g | 220g |
| Sieved soft flour | 80g | 160g |
| Potato flour | 40g | 80g |

### CHEF'S TIP

A chocolate version can be produced by substituting 25g of the potato flour for cocoa powder.

## Method of work

1 Preheat the oven to 200°C.

2 Carefully separate the egg yolks from the whites and place into separate mixing bowls.

3 Beat the egg yolks with two-thirds of the caster sugar to a soft ribbon consistency.

4 Aerate the egg whites until soft peaks have been developed adding the remaining sugar and continuing to beat until the egg whites have held the sugar and the peaks have become firmer.

5 Fold one-third of the egg whites into the egg yolks using a spatula.

6 Add the remaining egg whites and carefully fold them into the mixture.

7 Before the egg whites and yolks have been completely combined, sieve the potato starch and flour together and carefully incorporate into the egg/sugar foam until the mixture has become smooth.

8 Spread the mixture onto a silicone paper lined baking sheet.

9 Place in the oven and bake for about 8 minutes. The time may vary by 2 minutes either way according to the quantity and the oven.

10 Carefully remove the sponge from the baking sheet and place onto silicone paper, lightly sprinkled with semolina. Carefully peel off the silicone paper, gently roll up and allow to cool.

11 After cooling unroll and fill with the required filling such as jam or crème chantilly, trim the edges and roll up, shaping back into a Swiss roll.

Carefully incorporate the flour into the egg/sugar foam until the mixture has become smooth

Spread the mixture onto a silicone paper-lined baking sheet

Peel off the silicone paper, gently roll up and allow to cool

# Cat's tongue biscuits *Langue du chat*

| INGREDIENTS | 75 4CM BISCUITS | 150 4CM BISCUITS |
|---|---|---|
| Softened butter | 60g | 120g |
| Caster sugar | 60g | 120g |
| Egg whites | 45g | 90g |
| Soft flour | 65g | 125g |
| Vanilla extract | 2g | 5g |

## Method of work

1 Preheat the oven to 220°C.
2 Beat together the softened butter and the caster sugar until light in colour and fluffy in texture.
3 Gradually incorporate the egg whites to soften the mixture and then add the vanilla and the flour. Beat to a paste consistency.
4 Place the mixture into a piping bag with a 6mm plain tube. Pipe the mixture into 4cm fingers onto a lightly greased baking sheet. Allow sufficient space between each piped finger as the mixture will spread initially when baking.
5 Place in the oven and bake until the edges of each biscuit have a light golden colour.
6 Carefully remove the langues du chat from the baking sheet whilst still hot and place onto a wire cooling rack.
7 After cooling, store in an airtight container prior to using.

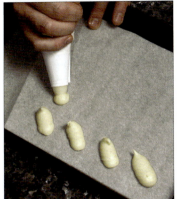

Pipe the mixture in 4cm fingers onto a lightly greased baking sheet

### CHEF'S TIP

These biscuits are used for decoration for various gâteaux, desserts, cakes and torten. They can accompany ice cream dishes, sweet dessert wines or they can be made into petit fours:

- Marquis – sandwich two langues du chat with praline-flavoured ganache. Dip each end in chocolate and pipe the word Marquis in chocolate on top of the biscuit.
- Copeaux – Pipe the langues up to 8cm in length. When baked, immediately curl around a dowel to create a curl.

# Raspberry Financier *Financier framboise*

| INGREDIENTS | 16 INDIVIDUAL | 35 INDIVIDUAL |
|---|---|---|
| Icing sugar | 165g | 330g |
| Ground almonds | 60g | 120g |
| Soft flour | 65g | 125g |
| Baking powder | 3g | 5g |
| Glucose or trimolene | 15g | 30g |
| Egg whites | 160g | 340g |
| Brown butter | 90g | 180g |
| Vanilla extract | 2g | 4g |
| Raspberry liqueur | 15g | 30g |
| Raspberries | 16 | 35 |

Pipe the mixture into individual Financier moulds

## Method of work

1 Preheat the oven to 220°C.

2 Combine the icing sugar, flour, baking powder, ground almonds and vanilla in a mixing bowl and slowly add the glucose (or trimolene).

3 To create a brown butter, heat the butter in a pan and slowly cook until a nut brown colour is achieved. Remove from the heat and allow the butter to settle before pouring off the butter, leaving the sediment and residue in the pan.

4 Add the brown butter, raspberry liqueur and egg whites to the dry mixture. Mix well until the ingredients have been blended to a smooth paste.

5 Place the mixture into a piping bag with a 10mm plain tube. Pipe the mixture into individual Financier moulds (the flexi-pan silicone moulds are best to use on this occasion). Place a raspberry in the centre of each financier.

6 Place in the oven and bake for approximately 8 minutes.

7 Carefully remove the Financiers from their moulds whilst still hot and place onto a wire cooling rack.

8 After cooling, store in an airtight container prior to using.

# Lemon loaf cake *Gâteau au citron*

Line a loaf tin with double thickness of silicone paper and distribute the mixture into the tin

| INGREDIENTS | 1 LARGE LOAF TIN | 2 LARGE LOAF TINS |
|---|---|---|
| Whole eggs | 125g | 250g |
| Caster sugar | 175g | 350g |
| Salt | 3g | 5g |
| Double cream | 75g | 150g |
| Soft flour | 135g | 270g |
| Baking powder | 3g | 5g |
| Finely grated lemon zest | 2 lemons | 3 lemons |
| Melted, clarified butter | 50g | 100g |
| Apricot glaze (see p. 588) | 50g | 100g |
| Lemon water icing (see p. 587) | 40g | 80g |

## Method of work

1　Preheat the oven to 180°C.
2　Mix together the eggs, caster sugar, salt and double cream. Ensure that all the ingredients have been thoroughly mixed.
3　Add the sieved baking powder and flour, and the lemon zest with the clarified butter at the end. Beat all the ingredients together until a smooth paste has been obtained.
4　Line a loaf tin with double thickness silicone paper and distribute the mixture into the tin, evening it out with a scraper.
5　Place in the oven and bake for approximately 50 minutes, checking every so often to ensure even cooking and that the crust is not colouring too quickly.
6　When baked, remove the cakes from their moulds whilst still hot and place onto a wire cooling rack.
7　Brush immediately with hot apricot glaze and then with the lemon water icing.
8　After cooling, store in an airtight container prior to using.

# Banana bread

| INGREDIENTS | 2 MEDIUM LOAF TIN | 4 MEDIUM LOAF TINS |
|---|---|---|
| Unsalted butter | 140g | 280g |
| Icing sugar | 220g | 440g |
| Salt | 2g | 4g |
| Eggs | 2 | 4 |
| Walnuts | 50g | 100g |
| Banana purée | 300g | 600g |
| Raisins | 100g | 200g |
| Soft flour | 280g | 560g |
| Baking powder | 10g | 20g |
| Nutmeg | 2g | 4g |
| Apricot glaze (see p. 588) | 50g | 100g |

## Method of work

1　Preheat the oven to 170°C.
2　Beat together the butter, icing sugar and the salt. Ensure that all three ingredients have been thoroughly beaten so that they are light and fluffy.
3　Add the eggs one at a time, and mix into the creamed butter.
4　Add the sieved baking powder and flour, then the banana purée with the nuts, raisins and nutmeg. Beat all the ingredients together until a smooth paste has been obtained.
5　Line a loaf tin with double thickness silicone paper and distribute the mixture into the loaf tins.
6　Place in the oven and bake for approximately 60 minutes, checking every so often to ensure even cooking and that the crust is not colouring too quickly.
7　When baked, remove the cakes from their moulds whilst still hot and place onto a wire cooling rack.
8　Brush immediately with hot apricot glaze and then sprinkle the top with some blanched walnuts.
9　After cooling, store in an airtight container prior to using.

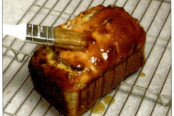

*Brush immediately with hot apricot glaze and then sprinkle the top with some blanched walnuts*

# Coffee gâteau *Gâteau mocha*

| INGREDIENTS FOR THE GÂTEAU | 1 × 12 PORTION CAKE | 2 × 12 PORTION CAKES |
|---|---|---|
| Vanilla Genoese sponge (see p. 573) | 1 × 20cm | 2 × 20cm |
| Coffee buttercream (see p. 587) | 450g | 900g |
| Toasted nib almonds | 200g | 400g |
| Coffee-flavoured stock syrup (see p. 542) | 200ml | 400ml |
| Melted dark chocolate | 75g | 150g |
| Chocolate coffee beans | 12 beans | 24 beans |
| Cake card | 1 × 20cm | 1 × 20cm |

## CHEF'S TIP

There are many different types of buttercream-based gâteau that can be produced for afternoon tea service or for a simple buffet:

*Gâteau Nelusko* cut a chocolate Genoese into three layers. Sandwich with praline buttercream and coat the sides too. Mask the side with grated chocolate. Mask the top with chocolate fondant and decorate with rosettes of chocolate buttercream. On top of the rosettes pipe chocolate run-outs. Lightly sprinkle some chopped pistachio nuts on each portion.

*Gâteau Mexicain* cut a vanilla Genoese into layers, macerate with rum-flavoured syrup. Layer with coffee buttercream between the bottom two layers and on the next layer with chocolate buttercream. Mask the sides with roasted chopped or flaked almonds. Glaze the top with hot apricot glaze, then glaze with coffee fondant and marble it with chocolate. Finish with a few rosettes of buttercream.

## Method of work

1. Carefully slice the sponge into three equal discs. Brush each disc well with the coffee-flavoured stock syrup.

2. Place the top sponge disc onto the cake card and spread with some of the coffee-flavoured buttercream. Place another disc on top and repeat the process, position the final disc on top.

3. Coat the top and the sides of the cake evenly and smoothly with the buttercream.

4. Using a comb scraper, run the scraper around the side of the cake to create even grooves in a decorative effect.

5. Carefully cover the bottom of the sides of the cake with the toasted nib almonds, 1cm high.

6. Using the melted dark chocolate in a small silicone paper piping bag, create small chocolate motifs onto silicone paper or an acetate sheet. Leave to set in a cool place for a few minutes.

7. Using a 6mm star piping tube, pipe rosettes of the remaining buttercream to display the portion control of each cake (12 rosettes per cake). Carefully arrange a chocolate motif on each rosette with a coffee bean.

8. With the remaining chocolate pipe the word *Mocha* on the centre of the gâteau and place onto a suitable display dish for service.

Brush each disc well with the coffee-flavoured stock syrup

Run the scraper around the side of the cake to create even grooves in a decorative effect

Pipe small chocolate motifs onto silicone paper or an acetate sheet

# Chantilly gâteau *Gâteau Chantilly*

| INGREDIENTS | 1 × 12 PORTION CAKE | 2 × 12 PORTION CAKES |
|---|---|---|
| Vanilla Genoese sponge (see p. 573) | 1 × 20cm sponge | 2 × 20cm sponges |
| Chantilly cream (see p. 543) | 450g | 900g |
| Langue du chat biscuits | 25 | 50 |
| Kirsch-flavoured stock syrup (see p. 542) | 200ml | 400ml |
| Langue du chat discs | 12 | 24 |
| Cake card | 1 × 20cm | 2 × 20cm |

## Method of work

1   Carefully slice the sponge into three equal discs. Brush each disc well with the Kirsch-flavoured stock syrup.

2   Place the top sponge disc onto the cake card and spread with some of the chantilly cream. Place another disc on top and repeat the process, position the final disc on top.

3   Coat the top and the sides of the cake evenly and smoothly with the chantilly cream.

4   Using a comb scraper, run the scraper around the side of the cake to create even grooves in a decorative effect.

5   Trim the bottoms and sides of each langue du chat biscuit and arrange neatly around the sides of the gâteau so that they reach half way up the side.

6   Using a 6mm star piping tube, pipe rosettes of the remaining chantilly cream to display the portion control of each cake (12 rosettes per cake). Carefully arrange a langue du chat disc on each rosette.

7   Place onto a suitable display dish for service.

*Carefully slice the sponge into three equal discs. Brush each disc well with the Kirsch-flavoured stock syrup*

*Trim the bottoms and sides of each langue du chat biscuit and arrange neatly around the sides of the gâteau so that they reach halfway up the side*

# Scones

| INGREDIENTS | 15 5CM SCONES | 25 5CM SCONES |
|---|---|---|
| Medium flour | 225g | 450g |
| Baking powder | 15g | 30g |
| Caster sugar | 40g | 65g |
| Butter | 50g | 100g |
| Salt | 2g | 4g |
| Milk powder | 5g | 10g |
| Fresh full fat milk | 150ml | 275ml |

## Method of work

1   Preheat the oven to 200°C.
2   Sieve the flour, milk powder, salt and sugar together.
3   Rub the butter into the dry ingredients until an even consistency resembling ground almonds has been obtained.
4   Make a well in the centre of the mixture and add the milk.
5   Carefully mix lightly to a clear paste.
6   Leave the scone paste to rest for ten minutes in a bowl covered with plastic film.
7   Now roll the paste out to approximately 15mm thick and cut out with a plain 5cm round pastry cutter. Place onto a baking sheet lined with a silicone baking mat or a lightly greased baking sheet.
8   Place the scones into a refrigerator to rest for a further ten minutes, covered with plastic film.
9   Remove the plastic film and carefully brush each scone with eggwash.
10  Bake in the oven for approximately 15 minutes or until they are well-risen with a golden colour.
11  Remove the scones from the baking sheet onto a wire cooling rack.
12  Serve the scones warm with butter, strawberry jam and clotted cream.

### CHEF'S TIP

Varieties of scones include:
*Fruit scone* add 90g of sultanas per 225g of flour and add the fruit at the same time the liquid is added to prevent the fruit from breaking up.
*Oatmeal scones* replace half the flour with oatmeal.
*Coconut scones* add 25g desiccated coconut to the flour. After eggwashing the top of the scone, dip half of the scone into desiccated coconut for decoration before baking.

# Victorian fruit cake

*Place the mixture into the prepared baking tin*

**VIDEO CLIP**
Making fruit cake

| INGREDIENTS | 1 × 20CM DEEP ROUND CAKE | 2 × 20CM DEEP ROUND CAKE |
|---|---|---|
| Butter | 225g | 450g |
| Soft brown sugar | 225g | 450g |
| Whole eggs | 4 | 8 |
| Soft flour | 210g | 420g |
| Baking powder | 15g | 30g |
| Raisins | 225g | 450g |
| Sultanas | 225g | 450g |
| Glacé cherries | 100g | 200g |
| Mixed spice | 5g | 10g |
| Brandy (optional) | 10ml | 20ml |
| Orange zest and juice | 1 orange | 2 oranges |

## Method of work

1 Preheat the oven to 150°C.
2 Lightly grease and line a 20cm deep round cake tin with double silicone paper.
3 Place all the raisins and sultanas together and wash in clean, cold water. Drain and add the glacé cherries, brandy and orange zest and juice. Leave this to soak for 2 hours.
4 Beat together the butter and the soft brown sugar until light and slowly add the eggs, one at a time, clearing the mixture before adding further eggs.
5 Sieve the flour, baking powder and the mixed spice together and incorporate into the sugar batter.
6 Combine all the fruit and juices into the mixture and mix together carefully, taking care not to break the fruit.
7 Place the mixture into the prepared baking tin, level the top with a scraper and place in the oven to bake for approximately 2 hours.
8 Halfway through the baking process it is advisable to place a sheet of silicone paper on top of the cake to prevent over-colouring.
9 When cooked the cake should be firm to the touch, and a skewer or knife inserted into the centre should come out clean.
10 Remove from the oven to cool down still in its tin for 30 minutes, then turn out and cool completely on a wire cooling rack.
11 When cooled, brush the top of the cake with an apricot glaze and either decorate with marzipan or glacé fruits or serve it as it is.

# ASSEMBLING AND DECORATING GÂTEAUX

The difference between gâteaux and torten is very fine and, in some cases, it is impossible to tell one from the other. Each term means a large decorated cake. The name 'gâteau' is the French term and the word 'torte' is German. The definition that a torte should be divided into portions within the decoration is the accepted British interpretation, but if classical cakes such as Sacher torte are being sold as a whole it is best to retain the descriptive name of the torte.

Except for specialities, the make-up of most gâteaux is similar to torten. It usually consists of an enriched sponge or Genoese, sandwiched with buttercream, fresh cream, ganache, curd, jam, with or without fruit, liqueur, chocolate, nuts, etc. Buttercream, fresh cream or fondant can be then used to cover the sponge and suitably decorated. Gâteaux may be named according to the type of flavours and mixings used.

**Step-by-step: Procedure for assembling a gâteau**

**Step 1** Trim the edges of the sponge as required

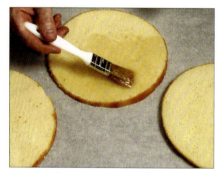

**Step 2** Unless specifically specified the sponge should always be cut into three equal layers and if the sponge used is fairly dry, such as a Genoese, then each layer should be brushed with a flavoured stock syrup appropriate to the main flavour of the gâteau

**Step 3** Apply the filling using a piping bag to help achieve a uniform layer

**Step 4** Continue by placing the second sponge disc on top and repeating the process until the third and final layer is placed on top (note that the top sponge layer is usually the bottom of the initial sponge because the shape is more defined)

**Step 5** Finish the top of the gâteau with a clean palette knife. The gâteau is now ready for decorating

 **VIDEO CLIP** Layering and decorating a fresh cream gâteau

# ICINGS, CREAMS, GLAZES AND COVERINGS

There are a variety of icings, creams, glazes and coverings that the chef can use to coat and decorate any gâteau or cake. They have numerous advantages in their use because they contribute flavour, colour and texture to the finish. However, they will also improve the appearance greatly by the way they are carefully applied and the gâteau or cake will have its storage life improved because the coating will form a protective sheet around the sponge.

There are six distinct types of coatings, shown in the table.

| ICINGS | CREAMS | BUTTERCREAMS | GLAZES | PASTES | FUDGE ICINGS |
|---|---|---|---|---|---|
| Fondant | Chantilly | Basic | Gelatine-based | Marzipan | Caramel |
| Royal | Whipped cream | French | Pectin-based | Cover | White |
| Water icing | | Italian | Jam-based | | Chocolate |
| | | | Chocolate | | |

# RECIPES

## Fondant icing

| INGREDIENTS | 250G | 500G |
|---|---|---|
| Pre-prepared fondant | 250g | 500g |
| Clear, unflavoured stock syrup (see p. 542) | 50g | 75g |
| Colour (optional) | To taste | To taste |
| Alcohol or flavouring (optional) | To taste | To taste |

### Method of work

1 Heat the fondant over a warm bain marie, stirring constantly to thin down and slightly melt the icing. Do not heat it over 38°C, otherwise the glossy sheen of the fondant will be lost.

2 If the fondant is too thick for use, slowly add a few drops of the stock syrup and stir in. Continue this procedure until the correct consistency is achieved.

3 Add the flavouring and colouring at this stage if required.

4 Apply the warm fondant by pouring it over the item or by dipping items into it.

**CHEF'S TIP**

To help the fondant maintain its shine when it has been applied to a particular item such as pastry or a gâteau, a fine layer of apricot jam can be brushed onto the surface before applying the fondant.

**HEALTH & SAFETY**

Fondant should always be stored in an airtight container prior to use to prevent it from drying.

# Royal icing

## Royal icing

| INGREDIENTS | 500G | 1KG |
|---|---|---|
| Icing sugar | 500g | 1kg |
| Cream of tartar | ½g | 1g |
| Fresh egg whites | 60g | 125g |

### Method of work

1  Place the icing sugar into a clean bowl.
2  Add the cream of tartar and slowly beat in the egg whites, a little at a time, until a smooth paste is produced.
3  Keep any unused royal icing covered with a clean, damp cloth or plastic film at all times to prevent the icing from hardening.

### CHEF'S TIP

The cream of tartar is added to help maintain the 'whiteness' of the royal icing. A few drops of lemon juice can be also added and this addition will also help the royal icing to harden. The addition of a little glycerine will help to maintain a softness to the icing after it has hardened.

# Basic buttercream

| INGREDIENTS | 250G | 500G |
|---|---|---|
| Unsalted butter | 70g | 125g |
| Shortening | 45g | 70g |
| Icing sugar | 125g | 250g |
| Lemon juice | 1g | 2g |
| Vanilla extract | 2g | 4g |
| Warm water | 15g | 30g |

### Method of work

1  Using a machine with a beater/paddle attachment, cream together the butter, shortening and sugar.
2  Add the lemon juice and vanilla and continue beating the mixture until it is light and fluffy in texture.
3  Finally, slowly add the warm water whilst beating. This will develop a slightly softer texture.

### CHEF'S TIP

Egg whites may be added instead of the water to give a slightly lighter texture to the buttercream, egg yolks can be added to give a somewhat richer buttercream.

# Water icing

| INGREDIENTS | 500G | 1KG |
|---|---|---|
| Icing sugar | 500g | 1kg |
| Hot water | 90ml | 180ml |
| Glucose | 25g | 50g |
| Vanilla extract, lemon juice or alcohol to flavour | To taste | To taste |

## Method of work

1 Place the icing sugar into a clean bowl.
2 Add the hot water, glucose and flavouring and mix to a smooth consistency.
3 To use, make sure the temperature of the icing is at 38°C. Apply to the product to be glazed.

# French buttercream

| INGREDIENTS | 250G | 500G |
|---|---|---|
| Caster sugar | 125g | 250g |
| Water | 40g | 60ml |
| Egg yolks | 45g | 90g |
| Softened, unsalted butter | 150g | 300g |
| Vanilla extract | 2g | 4g |

## Method of work

1 Combine the sugar and the water in a clean, heavy-based saucepan (preferably copper). Let the sugar dissolve for a few minutes before bringing to the boil.
2 Continue to boil whilst constantly monitoring the temperature using a sugar thermometer. The sugar solution should eventually reach 115°C before removing it from the heat.
3 Whilst the sugar is boiling, using a mixing machine with a whisk attachment, beat the egg yolks at a fast speed for two minutes.
4 After the sugar has reached the correct temperature, slowly pour a thread of the hot liquid into the egg yolks whilst whipping the yolks on a medium speed.
5 Continue to add all of the sugar solution and continue to whip the yolks until the mixture is completely cooled and the yolks are pale and thickened.
6 Whisk in the butter, a little at a time on the machine. Finally beat in the vanilla. If the buttercream is too soft, place it in a refrigerator to firm it up.

### 🔥 HEALTH & SAFETY

Buttercream can be stored covered in a refrigerator for several days. However, it should always be used at room temperature so that the correct consistency is obtained.

Before using, remove the buttercream from the refrigerator at least 1 hour ahead of the time and wait until it reaches room temperature. If it needs to be warmed quickly, beat the buttercream over a bowl of warm water to prevent curdling.

# Fruit gelatine-based glaze

| INGREDIENTS | 300G | 600G |
|---|---|---|
| Gelatine leaves | 4 leaves | 8 leaves |
| Caster sugar | 90g | 180g |
| Water | 60g | 120g |
| Glucose | 30g | 60g |
| Fruit purée | 150g | 300g |

## CHEF'S TIP

Nearly all types of fruit purée can be used for this recipe. Pineapple and kiwi fruit are the exceptions because of their ability to break down the structure of gelatine as they produce an enzyme that does this.

## Method of work

1 Soften the gelatine leaves in cold water.
2 Place the sugar, water and glucose into a saucepan and heat until the sugar has dissolved. Remove from the heat and stir in the softened gelatine.
3 Add the fruit purée and mix well.
4 Strain the mixture through a chinois or fine strainer.
5 Pour over the top of a cake or dessert and quickly spread to the edges with a palette knife. One 300g batch will make enough for a large 20cm cake.

# Chocolate glaze

| INGREDIENTS | 600G | 1.2KG |
|---|---|---|
| Fresh milk | 100g | 210g |
| Double cream | 75g | 150g |
| Caster sugar | 50g | 100g |
| Water | 50g | 100g |
| Glucose | 50g | 100g |
| Chopped dark chocolate | 375g | 750g |

## Method of work

1 Place the sugar, milk, cream, water and glucose into a saucepan and heat until the sugar has dissolved. Bring to the boil and remove from the heat.
2 Add the dark chocolate and mix well.
3 Strain the mixture through a chinois or fine strainer.
4 Pour over the top of a cake or dessert and quickly spread to the edges with a palette knife. 1.2kg is enough to coat 4 × 20cm cakes.

# Caramel fudge icing

| INGREDIENTS | 500G | 1KG |
|---|---|---|
| Demerara sugar | 450g | 750g |
| Double cream | 180g | 360g |
| Unsalted butter | 100g | 200g |
| Salt | 1g | 2g |
| Vanilla extract | 3g | 5g |

## Method of work

1  Combine the demerara sugar and cream in a saucepan. Bring to the boil and continue cooking until a temperature of 115°C has been reached.

2  Pour the mixture into a bowl of a mixing machine and let it cool down by mixing slowly with the beater/paddle attachment.

3  Slowly add the butter and salt and continue to mix at a slow speed until cool.

4  Add the vanilla and beat the icing until it is smooth and creamy in texture.

5  If necessary the consistency can be further adjusted with hot water.

## Assessment of knowledge and understanding

You have now learned about the use of different sponges, cakes and scones and how to produce a variety of products using an array of commodities and preparation techniques.

To test your level of knowledge and understanding, answer the following short questions. These will help to prepare you for your summative (final) assessment.

1 Explain two ways of telling that butter is rancid.
  i) _____
  ii) _____

2 Explain how the creaming method differs from the whisking method.
  _____
  _____

3 Explain why the presence of grease can destroy the aeration process of a Genoese sponge.
  _____
  _____

4 Give examples of cakes or sponges that use the following preparation techniques:
  (a) Creaming _____
  (b) Addition of melted butter _____
  (c) Folding _____
  (d) Aeration _____
  (e) Separation of eggs. _____

5 When baking cakes, identify what may happen if they are moved or knocked while in the oven.
  _____
  _____

6 State what will happen to the finished cake with the following deficiencies:
  (a) too much baking powder _____
  (b) too much sugar _____
  (c) too much liquid. _____

# 16

# Healthier foods and special diets

## LEARNING OBJECTIVES

The aim of this unit is to enable the candidate to develop skills and implement knowledge in the preparation and cookery principles of healthy dishes and eating. This will also include materials, ingredients and equipment.

At the end of this chapter you will be able to:

- Identify each variety of healthy eating dish and techniques
- Understand the use of relative ingredients in the cookery of healthier dishes
- State the quality points of various commodities and dishes
- Prepare and cook each variety of healthier dish
- dentify the storage procedures of healthier ingredients
- Have a concise knowledge of preparing and cooking a range of healthier-derived dishes

# CURRENT GOVERNMENT GUIDELINES FOR HEALTHY EATING

A balanced diet is one made up of a variety of foods in the correct proportions.

This ensures your body obtains enough of what is required and is in no way deficient in proteins and vitamins. In fact, recommendations on diet are now laid out not just to prevent deficiency, but to actively promote optimal health.

**VIDEO CLIP**
How to make food healthier during cooking

Nutritional requirements vary depending on a person's age, sex and overall level of fitness, and with this in mind the Department of Health have set guidelines accordingly. Most of us recognise the term RDA (Recommended Daily Allowance). RDAs have been revised and are now set as DRVs (Dietary Reference Values), which are tailored to certain population groups. However, between the ages of 19 and 50 your requirements do not vary a great deal.

For the average adult, it is recommended that approximately half of our energy should be provided by carbohydrates, 35 per cent from fats and 15 per cent from protein. For most, putting this into practice will mean making sure that they eat a variety of different foods, with emphasis on foods rich in starch and fibre and smaller proportions of fats and sugars. Also, actively trying to eat more fruit and vegetables is always important as they contain many of the wide range of vitamins and minerals the body needs. The government gives recommendations for suitable carbohydrates, fats and proteins that they believe contribute towards a healthy and balanced diet and further detail the benefits that these products provide as follows.

## Carbohydrates

**VIDEO CLIP**
Adding health foods to dishes

Starchy foods should make up about a third of the food we eat. With the introduction of diets such as low carbohydrate regimes, people generally now seem to be eating less of these and often mistake starchy foods as being fattening, but they actually contain less than half the calories of fat unless the food item has fats added for cooking or serving.

Starchy foods are rich in insoluble fibre and contain valuable nutrients which form part of a healthy diet. Examples of healthy carbohydrates are all varieties of bread. Potatoes, plantain, yam, sweet potato, wholegrain breakfast cereals, cous cous, bulgur wheat are also good examples.

## Fats

It is important to have some fat in our diet because fat helps the body absorb some vitamins; it is a good source of energy and a source of the essential fatty acids that the body cannot make itself.

Eating fatty foods increases energy levels which mean enhanced changes of increasing weight. To maintain a healthy and a suitable weight fatty foods should only occasionally be eaten and lower fat alternatives should be used wherever possible. A further recommendation is to increase the intake of omega 3 fatty acids, which are found in foods such as oily fish.

Too much *saturated fat* can increase the amount of cholesterol in the blood, which increases the chance of developing heart disease. Examples of products high in these are meat products such as meat pies, sausages, hard cheese, butter and lard, pastry, cakes and biscuits.

The effect of *trans fats* to our health imitates that of saturated fats, with some evidence suggesting that they may actually even be worse. This type of fat is usually found in products such as biscuits and cakes, fast food and pastry.

*Unsaturated fats* can be a healthy choice as they can actually reduce cholesterol levels and provide us with the essential fatty acids that the body needs. They include the unsaturated fats found in oily fish, which may further help to prevent heart disease. Products such as oily fish, avocados, nuts and seeds, sunflower oil/spread, rapeseed oil/spread, olive oil/spread and vegetable oils all contain unsaturated fats.

## Protein

Protein is contained within most of the main food groups and includes eggs, fish, meats, milk and dairy. Following the recommendations for a healthy intake of fats, these products should be consumed daily, but in small amounts and via a healthier lower-fat alternative. When using foods that contain protein in dishes as part of a healthy diet, we must consider issues such as seasoning and sauces which can transform a food that contains many benefits into an unhealthy option.

### DAILY CALORIE GUIDELINES COVERING ALL AGE GROUPS

| AGE IN YEARS | MALE KCALS | FEMALE KCALS |
|---|---|---|
| 1–3 | 1230 | 1165 |
| 4–6 | 1715 | 1545 |
| 7–10 | 1970 | 1740 |
| 11–14 | 2220 | 1845 |
| 15–18 | 2755 | 2110 |
| 19–49 | 2550 | 1940 |
| 50–59 | 2550 | 1900 |
| 60–64 | 2380 | 1900 |
| 65–74 | 2330 | 1900 |

**CHART OF RECOMMENDED DAILY AMOUNTS**

| FOOD GROUP | DAILY PORTIONS | WHAT IS ONE PORTION? |
|---|---|---|
| Bread, cereal, rice, pasta and potatoes | 5–14 portions | 1 slice wholemeal bread<br>1 small egg-sized potato<br>3tbsp breakfast cereal<br>2 heaped tbsp cooked pasta or rice |
| Vegetables | 2–3 as part of the minimum 5 a day | 1 medium-sized mixed salad<br>3–4 tbsp cooked vegetables<br>150ml vegetable juice |
| Fruit | 2–3 as part of the minimum 5 a day | 1 medium fresh fruit e.g. orange, apple<br>2 satsumas or kiwi fruit<br>7 strawberries<br>150ml fruit juice |
| Milk, yoghurt and cheese, dairy | 2–3 portions | 200ml semi-skimmed milk<br>150g low fat yoghurt<br>125g cottage cheese<br>20–30g cheese |
| Meat, poultry, fish, pulses, nuts, seeds and eggs | 2–3 portions | 85–100g cooked poultry, fish or lean red meat<br>3–4tbsp cooked dried beans<br>2tbsp peanut butter<br>3tbsp nuts or seeds |

# DIETS, FOOD TRENDS, HEALTHY EATING AND INTOLERANCES

Most diets will follow a set format, creating a balance between the main food groups. However, due to people's concerns regarding weight loss, certain diets will focus only on selective food groups rather than encompassing all of them, therefore usually creating dramatic results but only in the short term. This can prove challenging for any chef who is asked to provide a specific dish that needs to be created by following rules specific to the customer's diet. More importantly, in order to create such dishes, key ingredients, flavours and textures often have to be sacrificed and therefore the overall quality of the dish can be compromised.

A healthy diet is one which is balanced and takes into consideration all the main food groups, balancing these with quality ingredients, variation and all in moderate proportions as referred to in the nutritional tables in this chapter. Along with regular exercise and a sensible lifestyle, keeping fit and healthy is quite simply down to common sense and taking the time to cater for these factors on a daily basis, therefore making it part of your lifestyle as a whole.

# ADDITIONAL INFORMATION FOR ALLERGIES AND SPECIAL DIETS (RELIGION, HEALTH ETC.)

## Allergies and Intolerances

Food intolerance and food allergy are both types of food sensitivity.

For a *food allergy*, the immune system reacts to a particular food, believing it is not safe, and in severe circumstances this can cause a life-threatening reaction. Theoretically any food can cause an allergy, there are actually only eight main foods, named by the Food Standards Agency, that are held responsible for approximately 90 per cent of allergic reactions to food in the UK. These are: milk, eggs, peanuts (groundnuts), nuts (including Brazil nuts, hazelnuts, almonds and walnuts), fish, shellfish (including mussels, crab and shrimps), soya and wheat.

In the case of *food intolerances*, this does not involve the immune system and is generally not life-threatening. However, eating food to which someone is intolerant can make people ill or may affect their long-term health.

The substance in food that causes an allergic reaction in certain people is called an allergen. Allergens are normally proteins, and there is usually more than one kind of allergen in each food substance.

Most allergic reactions to food are mild, but sometimes they can be very serious. If someone has a food allergy they can react to just a tiny amount of the food they are sensitive to.

With strict food labelling guidelines now in place, it is much easier to identify ingredients contained in the products that you are purchasing and to find suitable alternatives for allergy or intolerance sufferers.

## Milk Allergy and Intolerance

Milk is one of the most regularly experienced food allergies and intolerances, usually occurring in young children. Cow's milk is the most common cause. Sheep's milk and goat's milk cannot be used as substitutes for allergies or in the case of lactose intolerance as they have a very similar protein structure to that of cow's milk.

Soya milk is now commonly used as a substitute, but it is recommended that the person with an allergy consults medical advice before trying any alternatives as these may also contain vitamins or proteins that could affect the health.

## Eggs

As with milk, the basis of eggs causing allergic reactions is the protein: in this case the three proteins that are present in the egg white – ovomucoid, ovalbumin and conalbumin. In a few cases, egg allergy can cause anaphylaxis. The cooking of eggs can destroy some of these allergens but not all, which means that if some people are allergic to certain proteins but not others, they will only react to raw eggs.

## Peanuts and Nuts

Peanuts, hazelnuts, pecans, walnuts, almonds, Brazil nuts and cashew nuts are most likely to cause allergic reactions.

Those who suffer with nut allergies must carefully consider all foods that they consume, as a large number of foods are made using nut oils or will have been produced in a factory where nuts have been or are present and could possibly contaminate other foods.

Peanuts can cause the most severe of allergic reactions and anaphylaxis, and is highly transferable to sufferers. For example, just the smell of peanuts can cause a reaction.

All of these nuts, on rare occasions, are capable of causing anaphylaxis in people who are allergic.

## Fish and Shellfish

Those that are allergic to fish or shellfish will usually experience an allergy to all types as they contain very similar allergens and can often cause severe reactions, including anaphylaxis. In the case of shellfish, even the vapours when cooking can cause a reaction.

## Soya

This product is commonly used as a substitute for other allergen products or to cater for those with religious or special dietary requirements, i.e. vegans. Soya very rarely causes severe reactions, but it should be noted that many products including bakery goods, sweets, drinks, breakfast cereals, ice cream, margarine, pasta and processed meats can contain soya.

## Wheat

The main allergen in wheat is the protein called gliadin, which is found in gluten and because of this it is common for those that suffer with a wheat allergy to be recommended that they eat a gluten-free diet. Wheat allergy and coeliac disease are completely different conditions, so foods that are labelled as being 'gluten-free' may not necessarily be suitable for those who suffer with a wheat allergy.

# SPECIAL DIETARY REQUIREMENTS

Often there are medical, religious or ethical reasons for people choosing a particular special diet, which will dictate the foods that they can and cannot eat. A few examples of special diets are given below.

## Kosher Food – Religious

Within Jewish law certain foods are prohibited. Animals that can be eaten must have cloven hooves and chew their cud like cows and goats, but animals such as pigs and horses are excluded. Fish that have fins or scales are permitted, but catfish and shellfish are not.

Land animals have to be sacrificed before being eaten and the laws of kashrut dictate how they must be killed and prepared according to strict procedures. There are no rules to follow in the killing or preparing of fish. In order to be confirmed as kosher meat, they must be slaughtered with one stroke of a sharp, clean knife across the throat, which is supposedly painless, and this cut is performed only by a Jewish butcher, or *shohet*, under the supervision of a rabbi. After slaughtering the animal the blood must be drained from the meat, which is usually done by soaking and salting and then the body must be inspected closely for any deformities or illnesses, which if found would render it non-kosher. Animals which have died a natural death may not be eaten.

## Islamic Food – Religious

Within the Islamic religion certain foods are prohibited. Examples include pork and its by-products (such as gelatine), blood and the flesh of animals that have died without being ritually slaughtered and fully bled.

Some Muslims will not eat the animal's meat if they are uncertain as to how an animal has been slaughtered as they place particular importance on the animal having been slaughtered in a humane fashion, with the remembrance of God and gratefulness for this sacrifice of the animal's life. If this cannot be ascertained, then the meat will not be considered Halaal, and is rendered inedible. Islam also places importance on the animal having been bled properly, as otherwise it would not be considered healthy to eat.

## Vegetarianism

Vegetarians will not eat any form of meat, whether this is meat, game, poultry, fish or shellfish, although some forms of vegetarianism may consume the latter two. They do, however, consume the by-products from animals, such as milk, eggs and other dairy products.

Generally, vegetarians do not agree with the killing of animals for human consumption, believing this to be cruel and distressing to the animal and completely unnecessary, maintaining that the natural produce of 'the soil' i.e. fruit, vegetables, nuts and seeds, and the natural by-produce of animals (which is not seen to distress or harm the animal in any way) can provide all necessary dietary requirements.

Meat, game, poultry, fish and shellfish all form part of the main food group and provide important proteins, vitamins and minerals. A vegetarian's diet must consist of alternative foods that will compensate for the lack of protein and vitamins associated with meat and fish products.

Foods such as eggs and dairy products will contain reasonable amounts of alternative proteins, calcium and vitamins which, in controlled amounts, can contribute towards providing a healthy diet. Furthermore, nuts and seeds, pulses, soya, quorn and tofu or mycoprotein products can also help provide a balanced and healthy diet. It is usually recommended that vegetarians take some form of vitamin and mineral supplements in addition to their diet, so that they are able to replace any that are not present in the foods that they can eat or that are present but in such small amounts they are not beneficial on their own.

## Vegans

Vegans are much stricter than vegetarians and will not eat any form of animal or their by-produce, or even wear items of clothing or accessories such as leather shoes.

As a vegan's diet consists of so few of the main food group and is therefore lacking in essential proteins, calcium, vitamins and minerals, it should be substituted by alternative means, i.e. tablets and supplements. However, with dramatic improvements and advancement in scientific knowledge alternative products are now being created and more readily available that can help contribute towards a healthy balanced diet, i.e. derivatives, genetically engineered foods and chemical substitutes.

## Gluten-Free – Free of Wheat, Barley, Rye

Gluten-free diets will apply to those that have intolerance or an allergy to the proteins found in flour gluten and in some cases, but not necessarily, to those suffering from coeliac disease. Natural alternatives to wheat flour, barley and rye include rice flour, tapioca flour, potato flour, cornflour, cornmeal, soya flour, gram flour and buckwheat flour. There are a number of others but these are the most widely available.

Some coeliacs may be able to tolerate a small quantity of pure oats but others may not, and there is a great deal of uncertainty as to whether oats are suitable or not for those with this condition. The difficulty with oats is obtaining a pure or unrefined product that is completely free from contamination by wheat either in the field or in the milling process.

There are many pre-prepared foods that may unknowingly contain gluten and should therefore be avoided at all costs. These include items such as stock cubes, baking powder, packet suet, mustard powder, ready grated cheese, soy sauce and some processed meats.

When cooking food for a gluten-free diet, you should ensure for example that items are not cooked in fat that has been used to cook products containing gluten otherwise contamination will occur.

# Lactose-Free – Free of Unfermented and Untreated Milk

Lactose is a sugar found within dairy products and therefore appears in a vast number of pre-prepared food products, specifically processed foods.

Alternatives include such items as rice milk, soya milk and the more recently available 'lactose-free' milk, which can also be used in powder form. Cream alternatives are also available.

Food labelling needs to be carefully checked when purchasing or using items, as a higher percentage of commonly used foods will contain lactose in one shape or form, i.e. milk powder in bread products, breaded or battered coatings on foods and butter in pastry products and sauces.

# Diet Trends – Weight Loss or General Health

Diet trends are very common, with people in general being far more aware of healthy eating and conscious of their body weight.

When planning a menu, consideration should be taken so that certain dishes or items will fit the criteria required to match these trends. Diet trends usually vary in levels of certain items contained within foods that should be consumed, such as low salt and/or sugar, high or low protein and high or low carbohydrates, depending on what the individual diet dictates. The easiest way to cater for this is to cover the main food groups as widely as possible within the remit of a menu.

## Assessment of knowledge and understanding

You have now learned about healthy eating and how to produce a variety of healthy dishes utilising an array of commodities and cooking techniques.

To test your level of knowledge and understanding, answer the following short questions. These will help to prepare you for your summative (final) assessment.

1 Name two ways of choosing quality ingredients when writing a menu.
   i) _____ ii) _____

2 Give examples of two alternatives to using sugar in cooking.
   i) _____ ii) _____

3 State an alternative name that can be given to salt when shown on the nutritional labelling of products.
   _____

4 Give two examples of healthier ways of making hot sauces that would have otherwise used cream as a base.
   i) _____ ii) _____

5 Steaming is a healthy cooking method but one where you must ensure necessary safety precautions are taken into consideration. Explain how this cooking method can be carried out in a safe manner.
   _____
   _____

# Glossary of terms

**00 flour** speciality flour used in pasta making as it has a high gluten content

**à la** (French) The style of, such as: à la Francaise (the style of the French)

**à la bourgeoisie** (French) The style of the family (family style)

**à la broche** (French) Cooked on a skewer.

**à la carte** (French) Items on the menu that are priced individually and cooked to order

**à la Florentine** (French) 'In the style of Florence'. Generally refers to dishes served on a bed of spinach and gratinated with sauce Mornay

**à la Française** In a French style

**à la grecque** In the Greek style

**à la minute** (French) Cook food at the last minute

**à la portugaise** In the Portuguese style, cooked with tomatoes, oil and herbs

**à la Provençal** (French) Dishes prepared with garlic and olive oil

**à la Russe** (French) In the Russian style

**à point** (French) food cooked just to the perfect point of doneness, when cooking beefsteaks 'à point' means that a steak is cooked medium

**abats** (French) Offal

**acetic acid** A natural organic acid present in vinegar and citrus juices

**acidulate** To give a dish or liquid a slightly acidic, tart or piquant taste by adding some lemon juice, vinegar, fruit juice. Also, one can acidulate fresh cream by adding lemon juice to get sour cream

**acidulated water** Water to which a mild acid, usually lemon juice or vinegar, has been added to prevent sliced fruits (especially apples and pears) and peeled or cut up vegetables (i.e. artichokes and salsify) from turning dark during preparation

**additives, food** Substances added to food to maintain or improve nutritional quality food quality and freshness or to make food more. Additives are strictly regulated. Manufacturers must prove the additives they add to food are safe

**ageing** A term used to describe the holding of meats at a temperature of 1–4°C for a period of time to break down the tough connective tissues through the action of enzymes, thus increasing tenderness

**agneau** (French) Lamb

**al dente** Italian for 'to the tooth'. It refers to the firm but tender consistency of a perfectly cooked piece of pasta

**albumen** The protein portion of the egg white, comprising about 70 per cent of the egg. Albumen is also found in animal blood, milk, plants and seeds

**aloyau de boeuf** Sirloin of beef

**amandine** (French) Prepared with or garnished with almonds

**ambient temperature** Room temperature

**amuse bouche** This is a pre-starter or mouth pleaser given as an opening for the coming menu

**anaphylaxsis** A severe allergic reaction which can be fatal

**Anglaise** (French) English style

**antioxidants** Substances that inhibit the oxidation of meat, vegetables and fruit. They help prevent food from becoming rancid or discoloured

**appareil** A mixture of different ingredients to be used in a recipe

**aromates** A mixture of herbs and spices to increase or bring out flavours in a dish

**ascorbic acid** Vitamin C

**aspic** Clear savoury jelly

**au blanc** (French) Meaning 'in white'. Foods, usually meats, that are not coloured during cooking

**au bleu** 1. A term for the cooking method for Trout: 'Truite au bleu'. The fish is taken from a fish tank, killed, gutted, trussed and slid into boiling court bouillon. The fish skin is not washed. This gives a characteristic silver blue finish to the finished dish. 2. A steak cooked very rare

**au four** Baked in the oven

**au gratin** (French) Food topped with a sauce and cheese or breadcrumbs, then baked or glazed under a salamander

**au jus** (French) Served with natural juices

**au lait** (French) With milk

**au naturel** (French) Food that are simply cooked with little or no interference in its natural appearance or flavour

**au vin blanc** (French) Cooked with white wine

**bacteria** Micro-organisms that isoning

**baguette** A French bread that is formed into a long, narrow cylindrical loaf. It usually has a crisp brown crust and light, chewy interior

**bain marie** (French) water bath used to cook or store food

**bake** To cook in an enclosed oven

**bard** To wrap meat, poultry or game with bacon or pork fat. The bard will render during cooking and impart succulence and flavour

**barquette** Boat-shaped pastry case or mould

**baste** To pour drippings, fat, or stock over food while cooking

**beard** The common name for the hair-like filaments that shellfish such as oysters and mussels use to attach themselves to rocks. They must be trimmed before the shellfish are prepared

**beat** To introduce air into a mixture using a utensil such as a wooden spoon, fork or whisk, in order to achieve a lighter texture

**beurre fondue** Melted butter

**beurre manié** A raw mixture of one part flour and two parts butter in equal quantities used as a thickening agent

**beurre noir** Black butter (can be served with skate wings and brains)

**beurre noisette** Nut-brown butter served with fish meunière

**blanch** To place foods in boiling water or oil briefly either to partially cook them or to aid in the removal of the skin (i.e. nuts, tomatoes). Blanching also removes the bitterness from citrus zests

**blend** To mix together ingredients, usually of different consistencies, to a smooth and even texture, utilising a utensil such as a wooden spoon or blender

**blind bake** To bake pastry without the filling. Metal weights or dried beans are usually used to keep the pastry from rising

**blinis** Pancake made from buckwheat flour and yeast

**boil rapidly** Food is submerged into boiling liquid over a high heat and the bubbling state is maintained throughout the required cooking period. This method is also used to reduce sauces by boiling off the liquid and reducing it to a concentrated state

**boil** To bring a liquid to boiling temperature and to maintain it throughout the cooking time

**bouchee** A small puff pastry case with high sides and a hollow middle

**bouillon** 1. Any broth made by cooking vegetables, poultry, meat or fish in water. The strained liquid is the bouillon, which can form the base for soups and sauces. 2. A salt paste used as a stock

**bouquet garni** A faggot of herbs and aromatic vegetables, usually parsley, thyme, bay leaf, carrot leek and celery. Tied together and usually dangled into a stockpot on a string. These herb bundles give the stew, soup or stock an aromatic seasoning. The bouquet garni is removed before serving

**braise** A cooking method where food (usually meat) is first browned in oil and then cooked slowly in a liquid (wine, stock or water).

**bresaola** Beef cured in a wine rich brine. It is then air dried and sliced very thinly for service

**brine** A strong solution of water and salt used for pickling or preserving foods

**broil** The American term for browning under the grill

**brunoise** 1mm dice

**buffet** A buffet is a meal where guests serve themselves from a variety of dishes set out on a table or sideboard

**butterfly** To cut food (usually meat or seafood) leaving one side attached and to open it out like the wings of a butterfly

**buttermilk** Milk product that is left after the fat is removed from milk to make butter

**calorie** Unit of heat; 1 calorie = 3.968 I.E.. The heat required raising 1 gram of water 1 degrees centigrade

**canapé** A base of bread, pastry or porcelain onto which savoury food is place as a pre-dinner snack or as a course at the end of a meal prior to dessert

**caramelise** To allow the surface sugars of food to caramelise, giving a characteristic colour and aroma

**Caroline** A savoury mini éclair that can be served hot or cold with a filling on buffets

**carpaccio** Originally, paper-thin slices of raw beef with a creamy sauce, invented at Harry's Bar in Venice. In recent years, the term has come to describe very thinly sliced vegetables, raw or smoked meats, and fish

**carte du jour** Menu of the day

**cartouche** A circle of greaseproof or silicone paper used to prevent dishes from forming a skin or losing moisture

**carving** Term used for slicing or cutting items, usually for customers or in front customers

**casing** A synthetic or natural membrane (usually pig or sheep intestines) use to encase food such as sausages

**casserole** To cook in a covered dish in the oven in liquid such as stock or wine

**cassoulet** A classic French dish the Languedoc region consisting of white beans and various meats (such as sausages, pork and preserved duck or goose)

**caul** Also known as crepinette (lamb) or crepin (pork) it is a thin, fatty membrane that lines the stomach cavity of pigs or sheep. It resembles a lacy net and is used to wrap and protect foods such as pâtés, ballotines etc. The fatty membrane melts during cooking. It should be soaked in slightly salted water before use

**chapelure** Dried fresh breadcrumbs

**charcuterie** (French) cured or smoked meat items

**chaud** (French) Hot

**chaud-froid** A dish that is prepared hot but served cold

**chef** (Fr ) A culinary expert. The chief of the kitchen

**chef de partie** (French) 'Chief of the section' a chef who leads a team of assistants in a section

**chemiser** To line or coat a mould with a substance (either sweet or savoury)

**chiffonade** (French) 'Made from rags'. In cooking it refers to a small chopped pile of thin strips of an ingredient. Usually it is raw, but sometimes sautéed

**chine** Usually refers to the removal of the backbone on a cut of meat such as a rack of pork

**chinois** A metal conical strainer

**clamart** Any dish that either contains peas or pea purée

**clarified butter** Clarified by bringing to the boil until it foams and then skimming the solids from the top or straining through muslin before use

**clarify** To clear a cloudy liquid by removing the sediment

**clouté** An onion studded with cloves and bay leaf

**coagulate** To solidify protein with heat

**coat the spoon** When a substance is rendered thin/thick enough so that when a wooden or metal spoon is inserted into it and taken out, the substance leaves a thin film 'coating the spoon'

**coat** To cover with a thin film of liquid, usually a sauce

**cocotte** A fireproof dish usually made from porcelain

**coddling** Cooking just below the boiling point, for example coddled eggs

**collagen** White connective tissue that gelatinises with long slow cookery

**collop** Small thin slices of meat, poultry, fish but mainly referred to as slices across the tail of lobster

**commis chef de partie** (French) A qualified chef who is an assistant to a chef de partie

**compote** Stewed fruit

**compound salad** A salad with more than one ingredient

**concasse a cuit** A cooked small dice of peeled tomatoes

**concassé** Coarsely chopped, e.g. tomato concassé

**confit** A method of preserving meat (usually goose, duck or pork) whereby it is lightly cured and slowly cooked in its own fat. The cooked meat is then packed into a crockpot and covered with its cooking fat, which acts as a seal and preservative. Confit can be stored in a refrigerated up to 6 months

**consommé** Clear soup

**coquille** (French) Shell

**cordon** A dish that is surrounded by a thin line of sauce

**Cordon Bleu** (French) 'Blue ribbon'. A term used to describe high quality household cookery

**correct** Adjust the seasoning and consistency of a soup or sauce

**coulis** Fine purée of fruit

**court bouillon** A cooking liquor made by cooking mirepoix in water for about 30 minutes then adding wine, lemon juice or vinegar. The broth is allowed to cool before the vegetables are removed

**couverture** A type of chocolate used for the preparation of cakes, confectionery and a variety of desserts; containing at least 35 per cent cocoa butter and a maximum of 50 per cent sugar

**cream** The process where sugar and softened butter are beaten together with a wooden spoon, until the mixture is light, pale and well blended. This process may also be carried out with a hand-held mixer or in a food processor

**Crecy** Any dish that will contain carrots

**crêpe** (French) Pancake

**crimp** To seal the edges or two layers of dough using the fingertips or a fork

**cross-contamination** The transfer of pathogen from contaminated food to uncontaminated food

**croute** A bread or pastry base that is used to hold sweet or savoury items

**croûtons** Shaped bread that is fried or toasted to accompany soups, entrées or as a base for canapés

**crudités** Raw vegetables, served with a dip

**curdle** The state of a liquid or food, such as eggs, to divide into liquid and solids, usually due to the application excess heat or the addition of an acid such as lemon juice

**curing** The preservation of food items using acidic liquids, salt or marinating

**cut in** To incorporate fat into a dry ingredient, such as flour, by using a knife and making cutting movements in order to break the fat down

**cutlet** A cut of lamb or veal from the loin with the rib bone attached

**dariole** Small mould used to cook individual portions of food, e.g. summer pudding

**darne** A cut of round fish on the bone

**daube** A slow-cooked stew, usually of beef in stock with vegetables and herbs. Traditionally cooked in a sealed daubiere

**debone** Remove bones from meat, fish or poultry

**deep fry** The process of cooking food by immersion in hot fat or oil in a deep pan or electric fryer to give a crisp, golden coating

**deglaze** To add liquid such as wine, stock or water to the bottom of a pan to dissolve the caramelised drippings so that they may be added to a sauce, for added flavour

**degrease** Skim the fat from food e.g. stock

**demi glace** A thick, intensely flavoured, glossy brown sauce that is served with meat

**desalting** The removal of salt from foods. Food is soaked in cold water or washed under running water to dissolve the salt. Some foods such as salt cod require long, overnight soaking

**detrempe** A mixture of flour and water for making a dough or a puff paste

**diced** Cut into cubes

**disgorge** To soak meat, poultry, game or offal in cold water to remove impurities

**doria** Food cooked with or garnished with cucumbers

**dorure** Glazing with an egg mixture on raw pastries and dough before baking to produce an attractive coloured finish

**dredging** To coat with dry ingredients such as flour or breadcrumbs

**drizzle** To drip a liquid substance, such as a sauce or dressing, over food

**drying off** The removal of excess moisture from foods during cooking. Not to be confused with drying or reducing. An example of drying off is when potatoes are placed over a low heat after having been drained in order to dry them off before mashing

**dusting** To sprinkle with sugar or flour

**duxelle** Minced mushrooms and shallots cooked until dry

**Ecossaise** (French) Scottish

**eggwash** Beaten egg used to coat food as a glaze or are as a binding agent

**elastin** Yellow connective tissue that doesn't break down during cooking

**eminé** (French) Cut fine, or sliced thin

**emulsify** The blending of two liquids that wouldn't naturally combine into each other without agitation. The classic examples are oil and water, French dressing and mayonnaise

**en croute** Cooked in pastry e.g. Beef Wellington

**en papilotte** (French) cooked in a folded greaseproof bag

**enrober** To completely cover a food item with a liquid

**entrecote** A steak cut from the boned sirloin

**entrée** (French) main course of meat or poultry that is not bake or roasted

**escalope** (French) Refers to a thinly sliced, boneless, round cut of meat that is batted until very thin

**espagnole** Basic brown sauce

**farce** (French) Forcemeat or stuffing

**farci** Stuffed

**flake** To separate segments naturally e.g. cooked fish into slivers

**flambé** Ignite alcohol on a dish e.g. Crepe suzette or Christmas pudding

**fleurons** Crescent-shaped puff pastry used to garnish fish dishes

**flute/fluting** Used in pastry or biscuit making as a decoration. Pies and tarts are fluted around the edge by pinching the pastry between the forefinger and thumb to create v-shaped grooves

**fold in** To gently combine lighter mixtures with heavier ones usually using a metal spoon or spatula in a cutting or slicing 'J' movement whilst slightly lifting the utensil

**forcemeat** Ground meat or meats, mixed with seasonings used for stuffing

**freezer burn** Food that is left uncovered in the freezer desiccates and becomes unusable

**fricassée** A white stew where the meat or poultry is cooked in the sauce

**fritture** Deep fat fryer

**froid** (French) Cold

**fromage** (French) Cheese

**fumé** (French) Smoked

**game** Name given to wild feathered and furred animals hunted in certain seasons

**Garde Manger** (French) The person in charge of cold meat department

**garnish** To decorate. Also referring to the food used to decorate

**gastrique** A reduced mixture of vinegar and sugar used in the preparation of sauces and dishes with a high degree of acidity. For example tomato sauce

**gastronorm** Plastic storage containers used by the catering industry. They come in standard sizes

**glaze** To give a food a shiny appearance by coating it with a sauce or similar substance such as aspic, sweet glazes or boiled apricot jam

**goujons** Goujons are small strips cut from a fillet of flat fish, often panéd or dipped in batter, and then deep fried

**gourmet** (French) Food connoisseur

**grate** To reduce a food to very small particles by rubbing it against a sharp, rough surface, usually a grater or zester

**grease** To cover the inside surface of a dish or pan with a layer of fat, such as butter or margarine or oil using a brush or kitchen paper

**grill** 1. To cook foods with radiated heat 2. A grills are cooking equipment that radiate heat from below e.g. barbecue

**gross brunoise** 1 cm square dice

**hacher** To cut very finely (often with a mincing machine)

**hanging** Hanging meat from a hook at a controlled temperature to facilitate ageing (see *ageing*)

**hors d'oeuvre** Small dishes served as the first course of the meal

**infusion** Liquid derived from steeping herbs, spices, etc.

**jardiniere** Batons of vegetables

**julienne** (French) A cut of meat, poultry, or vegetables, which has the same dimensions a match

**jus** (French) 'Juice'. Usually refers to the natural juice from meat

**jus lie** (French) Thickened gravy

**knead** A rhythmic action in dough making whereby one end of the dough is secured by the heel of one hand and stretched away then pulled back over the top. In bread making, two hands are used

**knocking back** To release pockets of gas in fermented dough before shaping and proving

**lait** (French) Milk

**larding** Larding fat cut into strips inserted into meat with a special needle. Used to add and moisture to meat

**lardons** Bacon that is cut into small dice

**legumes** (French) Dried beans, peas, lentils etc.

**liaison** A binding agent made up of egg yolks and cream, used for enriching soups and sauces

**Lyonnaise** Refers to dishes accompanied by sauted onions

**macedoine** A neat dice of mainly vegetables which measure ½ cm square

**macerate** To soak a fruit in a liqueur or wine. This softens the fruit while releasing its juices and absorbing the macerating liquid's flavours

**marinade** A mixture or wet and/or dry ingredients used to flavour or tenderise food prior to cooking

**marinate** To let food stand in a mixture called a marinade (such as a liquid, dry cure, or a paste) before cooking. Some marinades add flavour. Others that contain acids, enzymes or fruits such as lemon, wine, vinegar, yoghurt or mangos, papaya or kiwi fruits help to tenderise

**melba toast** thin triangular pieces of crisp toast classically served with pâté

**menthe** (French) Mint

**minced** Ground, or chopped, usually refers to meat fish, or poultry

**mirepoix** A mixture of diced aromatic vegetables e.g. carrots, onions, celery and leek

**mise en place** Basic preparation prior to cooking

**monosodium glutamate** A flavour enhancer which is a type of salt

**monte au beurre** Addition of butter to create an emulsion of cooking liquor and butter

**mousse** A sweet or savoury preparation that has a very light consistency

**nape** To cover an item with either a hot or cold sauce

**navarin** A brown stew of mutton or lamb

**noir** (French) Black

**noisette** A cut from a boned loin of lamb

**nouilles** (French) Noodles

**nutrients** The essential parts of food that are vital to health

**oeuf** (French) Egg

**offal** The name given to the edible internal organs of an animal

**open sandwich** A sandwich that has a base only of various varieties of bread

**palatable** Pleasant to the taste and edible

**panache** A selection of vegetables

**panada** A paste of various bases, either bread, flour or potato, used to thicken or bind products

**pané** Passed through seasoned flour, beaten egg and then breadcrumbs

**pané à la Francaise** Passed through seasoned milk and seasoned flour. Used as a coating for fried foods

**pané Anglaise** A coating of flour, eggwash and breadcrumbs

**papillote** (French) Cooked in foil or parchment paper to seal in flavour, then served and cut open at table

**parboiling** To cook by boiling partially for a short period of time

**parfait** (French) 'perfect'. A smooth pâté or iced dessert which can be sliced leaving an even and consistent appearance

**pass** Push liquids or solids through a sieve

**pate** (French) 'Paste'. 1. Pâté refers to either a smooth or coarse product made from meat, poultry, fish, vegetable, offal or game that has been blended and cooked with cream, butter and eggs. 2. Pate is different base pastry products, sweet, short, lining, puff, choux

**pathogen** Micro-organisms that can cause food poisoning

**paupiette** Rolled and/or stuffed fillet of flat fish

**pavé** A square or diamond-shaped piece of meat, poultry or fish but can also refer to pastry or cakes

**paysanne** Vegetables cut into thin slices

**pesto** Rustic Italian dressing made with basil, garlic, olive oil and pine nuts

**petit** (French) Small

**petit pois** (French) Small peas

**pipe** To shape or decorate food using a forcing bag or utensil fitted with a plain or decorated nozzle

**piquante** A dish or sauce that is sharp to the taste

**pluche** Small tips of salad leaves or herbs as a garnish

**poach** To cook food in hot liquid over a gentle heat with the liquid slightly below boiling point

**pressing** To apply pressure to items to help shape or remove excess moisture, e.g. terrines to help them keep an even layering or sweatbreads to remove excess liquid

**prove** To allow yeast dough to rise

**purée** A smooth paste of a particular ingredient or a soup that is passed through a sieve

**quenelle** A poached dumpling, mousseline or cream presented in an oval shape. Classically made of veal or chicken

**ragout** A stew of meat or vegetables

**ramekin** Individual or small ceramic round baking dish

**rasher** Thin slice of bacon

**rechauffer** Reheat food for service

**reduce** To concentrate the flavour of a liquid by boiling away the water content

**refresh** To plunge food into, or run under, cold or iced water after blanching to prevent further cooking

**reticulin** A structural protein resembling elastin

**roast** To cook food in an oven or on a spit over a fire with the aid of fat

**roux** Fat and flour cooked to white, blond and brown colours used to thicken sauces and soups

**rubbing in** The incorporation of fat into flour. Butter is softened and cubed then gently rubbed between the thumb and forefinger, lifting the mixing at the same time, until the fat is fully incorporated and the mixture resembles fine breadcrumbs in appearance

**salad tiède** A salad with the addition of warm or hot ingredients

**salamander** A small contact grill and poker used to brown or gratin foods or a term to describe an overhead grill

**salami** A charcuterie product made of ground pork or beef originating in Italy

**sauté** Cook quickly in shallow fat

**savouries** A small after meal dish or item as an alternative to a dessert or cheese

**savoury sorbet** A flavoured water ice using savoury ingredients such as tomatoes

**scald** To heat a liquid, usually milk, until it is almost boiling at which point very small bubbles begin to form around the age of the pan

**score** To make shallow incisions with a small knife

**seal** Caramelise the outer surface of meat

**sear** To brown the surface of food in fat over a high heat before finishing cooking by another method, in order to add flavour

**season to taste** Usually refers to adding extra salt and pepper

**sec** (French) meaning dry

**shallow fry** To cook in oil or fat that covers the base of a shallow pan

**shred** To tear or cut into food into thin strips

**sift** To pass a dry ingredient, such as flour, through a sieve to ensure it is lump free

**simmer** To maintain the temperature of a liquid at just below boiling

**simple salad** A salad with only one ingredient, e.g. tomato salad

**skim** To remove impurities from the surface of a liquid, such as stock, during or after cooking

**skin (to)** The removal of skin from meat, fish, poultry, fruit, nuts and vegetables

**slice** To cut food, such as bread, meat, fish or vegetables, into flat pieces or varying thickness

**smoking** Hot or cold method of curing and flavouring food using wood, herbs or spices

**soaking** To immerse in a liquid to rehydrate or moisten a product

**sorbet** A smooth frozen ice made with flavoured liquid-based ingredients such as fruit

**sous chef** (French) 'Under chief'. Second to the head chef

**steam** The cooking of food in steam, over rapidly boiling water or other liquid. The food is usually suspended above such liquid by means of a trivet or steaming basket, although in the case of puddings, the basin actually sits in the water

**steep** To soak food in a liquid such as alcohol or syrup until saturated

**stir fry** To fry small pieces of food quickly in a large frying pan or wok, over a high heat, using very little fat and constantly moving the food around the pan throughout cooking, keeping them in contact with the hot wok

**stock** A cooked flavoured liquid that is used as a cooking liquor or base for a sauce

**sweat** To cook gently in a little fat without colour

**table d'hote** Set menu at a set price

**terrine** A dish used to cook and present pâté

**timbale** A small high-sided mould

**tronçon** A cut of flat fish on the bone

**truss** To tie up meat or poultry with string before cooking

**vegan** Someone who will not eat any animal product

**vegetarian** Someone who doesn't eat meat or fish but will eat animal products such as milk, eggs and cheese

**velouté** (French) A sauce made with stock and a blond roux, finished with a liaison of cream and egg yolks

**viande** (French) Meat

**whip** To beat an item, such as cream or egg whites, to incorporate air

**whisk** To beat air into a mixture until soft and aerated

**zester** A hand-held tool with small, sharp-edged holes at the end of it, which cuts orange, lemon or grapefruit peel into fine shreds

# Recipe Index

# General Index